THE ESSENTIAL FRANKFURT SCHOOL READER

THE ESSENTIAL FRANKFURT SCHOOL READER

Edited by
Andrew Arato & Eike Gebhardt
Introduction by
Paul Piccone

CONTINUUM · NEW YORK

1990
The Continuum Publishing Company
370 Lexington Avenue, New York, NY 10017

Printed in the United States of America

Library of Congress Cataloging in Publication Data
Main entry under title:

The Essential Frankfurt school reader.

  Originally published. New York: Urizen Books,
c1978.
  Bibliography: p.
  Includes index.
  1. Mass society—Addresses, essays, lectures.
2. Political science—Addresses, essays, lectures.
3. Economics—Addresses, essays, lectures.
4. Social sciences—Methodology—Addresses, essays,
lectures. I. Arato, Andrew. II. Gebhardt, Eike,
III. Title: Frankfurt school reader.
HM101.E745 1982   300   82-8063
ISBN 0-8264-0194-5   AACR2

Contents

8981

Preface

The critical theory of the Frankfurt School is no longer a stranger to an English-speaking audience. Several volumes of Adorno, Horkheimer and Benjamin have recently been published, not to speak of the already available works of Marcuse, Neumann, Kirchheimer, Lowenthal and Fromm. There is a significant semiofficial biography of the school by Martin Jay as well as a whole range of treatments both sympathetic and hostile in the recent books of Russell Jacoby, William Leiss, Trent Schroyer, Susan Buck-Morss, George Lichtheim, Zoltan Tar, Perry Anderson, Philip Slater and Alasdair MacIntyre, and in the journals *Telos, New German Critique* and *Social Research*.

In this context, the purpose of our anthology is threefold. (1) We want to concentrate on the social theories of the School, usually interpreted from the point of view of the somewhat later sociophilosophical synthesis, impressive but far less flexible, that correctly goes under the name of "critique of domination" and "critique of instrumental reason. (2) We want to correct some widespread misconceptions about the political and intellectual purposes of the School, as well as refute the myth of a single, unified critical theory of society. At least eight authors are, therefore, represented in the volume. (3) We want both to introduce undergraduate students of sociology, political science, philosophy and intellectual history to critical theory, *and* to provide advanced students as well as working scholars with a number of hitherto untranslated or inaccessible texts. Almost no selection from an easily available source is therefore reproduced. These three criteria have served as our guiding principles of selection. For reasons of space, we had to restrict ourselves to the works of the first generation of critical theorists. In any volume subsequent to this Reader, the figure of Habermas would inevitably play a major role.

In light of the essay character of all our selections, we sought to provide the reader with a range of introductory and explanatory materials: (1) A general introduction by Paul Piccone; (2) extensive introductions to each of the three parts of the anthology: "Political Sociology and Critique of Politics" by Andrew Arato; "Esthetic Theory and Cultural Criticism " (first four sections by Arato, last section by Gebhardt); "A Critique of Methodology" by Eike Gebhardt; (3) biographical notes; (4) a bibliography of works of the authors in English by Matthew Smosna; (5) prefatory notes to each selection by Gebhardt and Arato.

It was our primary intention to locate our authors and their works intellectually and politically, and to supply as many of the missing links in their argumentation as possible. That is, we sought to reconstruct *immanently* three major dimensions of the Frankfurt School's theoretical spectrum: political sociology, cultural theory and critical methodology. Above all, we wanted to avoid judging them from a transcendent vantage point. Our conception of immanent critique derives from Adorno. Our interest lies in those internal tensions, differences, oppositions, problems and debates, in a word, in those "antinomies," which drive the self-critique of critical theory forward as a forceful witness to the hope that theory is still capable of addressing itself to radical and liberating needs.

Andrew Arato

Eike Gebhardt

General Introduction

"Critical theory," the umbrella for a whole spectrum of positions associated with the Frankfurt Institute for Social Research, has finally, after long delay, an opportunity to become an integral part of English-speaking culture. Comprised of philosophers, literary critics, sociologists, psychologists, economists and political scientists—of whom Theodor W. Adorno, Walter Benjamin, Erich Fromm, Max Horkheimer, Otto Kirchheimer, Leo Lowenthal, Herbert Marcuse, Franz Neumann and Friedrich Pollock are the major figures—the Frankfurt School came into existence in the mid-1920s as an association of Left intellectuals that formed the privately funded Institute for Social Research.

The concept of "critical theory" derives from the traditions of Kantian critical philosophy and of Marxian critique of ideology. Kant himself defined his late philosophy as critical, and entitled his three greatest works "Critiques"—of pure theoretical reason, of practical reason and of esthetic and teleological judgment. Critique, in the Kantian sense, is an analysis of the conditions of possibility *and* the limits of rational faculties undertaken by reason itself: assuming a self-reflective or "transcendental" posture, reason analyzes and criticizes itself in the process of its world-constituting "legislating activity". For Kant, Newtonian physics and Euclidian geometry constituted the crowning achievements of rational synthesis. He believed that the logical, categorical foundations of these sciences represented the conditions of the possibility of objective experience as such. Basing itself on this interpretation of Kant (there are of course others), one wing of *fin de siècle* Neo-Kantianism sought to broaden the Kantian meaning of critique by making history (cultural and social) the primary theme of transcendental or critical self-reflection. From Dilthey and Rickert to Simmel and Max Weber, the implicit and/or explicit project of philosophy became a "critique of historical reason." To be sure, Kant left to prosterity several key essays on history which examine the limits and possibilities of progress, but, as is evident from his theme, he was deeply swayed by the eighteenth-century way of viewing these problems. The nineteenth century, however, became an age of the highest conceivable degree of historical experience, learning, research and reflection; and any new critical philosophy of history had to interpret the works of Ranke, Taine, Michelet, Burckhardt, Droysen, etc. The Hegelian critique of Kant—short of what the Neo-Kantians saw as Hegel's speculative, "panlogical" excesses—also had to be integrated. So in an age when natural science enjoyed its highest prestige, one group of primarily German (but also French and Italian) thinkers systematically attempted to replace nature by culture, science by history as the focus of philosophical concern, an attitude also typical of the early mentors of the Institute's members: Hans Cornelius, Martin Heidegger and Edmund Husserl, as well as of the single most important Marxian influence on the Institute, Georg Lukács.

The second main source of critical theory was the Marxian tradition of ideology critique. This critique refers not just to the simple discovery of systematically concealed interests behind theories, but also and even primarily to the explosive confrontation of the true and false dimensions of existing theories of reality as exemplified by Marx's mature critique of political economy. In fact, Marx too used the word critique in the titles or subtitles of at least eight finished and unfinished works. The Kantian idea of categorical self-reflection and the demonstration of the limits of the science criticized was surely incorporated in Marx's concept, but so was Hegel's objection that Kant assumed the given "facticity" and "positivity" of existing sciences. Accordingly, Marx's oeuvre intended to be both the criticism of science (of classical political economy) and a new *critical science* (a political-economic crisis theory). The actual methodoiogy of Marx's mature critique thus is more deeply rooted in Hegel's *Phenomenology* and *Philosophy of Right* than in the Kantian tradition.

Given the theoretical sources of critical theoi y and its Marxian political thrust, it is hardly surprising that its reception in the English-speaking world was not what it would have deserved. Still, critical theory has not been a total stranger to the English-speaking world, at least since the late 1930s. Horkheimer and Adorno spent a crucial period of their lives in the U.S., relocating the Institute and the journal *Zeitschrift für Sozialforschung,* whose last volumes were published in English. Neumann and Kirchheimer spent their last years in the U.S., and their reputations as great teachers influenced some American political scientists. Fromm became a leading member of the American Neo-Freudian school, and although he broke with the Institute, he has never given up the characteristic Frankfurt project of the Marx-Freud synthesis. Lowenthal and Marcuse, finally, continue the tradition of Frankfurt critical theory in America into the present day, with the latter playing a key role for the theoretically inclined minority of the New Left of the 1960s. Nor has the influence of critical theory on academia been totally negligible. During their stays in New York and Los Angeles, Adorno and Horkheimer had a conflict-ridden but perhaps not fruitless relationship with American sociologists, as demonstrated by the volume *Mass Culture* (with articles by Adorno and Lowenthal) that was published much later. Better known is the series of empirical and theoretical projects on the study of prejudice and the authoritarian personality which brought Adorno and Horkheimer into working contact with a number of scholars (Bruno Bettelheim, Morris Janowitz et al.) whose intellectual development, however, has since taken different directions. More important were contacts with men like Hans Gerth and Benjamin Nelson who were to convey, in spite of their reservations, something of the content and the spirit of critical theory to future generations of students. In this last respect the work of such collaborators of the Institute as Marcuse, Neumann, Kirchheimer, Gerhard Meyer and K.A. Witt-

fogel probably laid much of the groundwork for the emergence
of an American critical social science. We should certainly interpret the very positive remarks of C. Wright Mills on the
Frankfurt School in this way. Finally, under the impact of the
New Left, what was submerged in the 1950s and early 1960s sur-
faced in the late 1960s and 1970s as a revival of critical theory,
though primarily on the level of the history of ideas. First-rate
books by Martin Jay, Trent Schroyer, Bruce Brown, Russell
Jacoby, Susan Buck-Morss, and William Leiss; translations of
the works of Adorno, Horkheimer and Benjamin; the success of
Marcuse's works; and the emergence of several journals (*Telos,
New German Critique, Theory and Society,* etc.) that are strongly influenced by critical theory have all created an atmosphere
within which the heritage of the Frankfurt School could begin to
be fully appropriated. What is still missing, however, is a large-
scale reconstruction of this heritage in accordance with the needs
of the new political and social situation.

In other words, the older, highly selective and limited,
reception of the Frankfurt School failed to lead to a deep
understanding of its theoretical trajectory; the new reception,
which fully reconstructs the tradition only in the realm of the
history of ideas, has not yet opened the way to new theoretical
departures.

To speak of "critical theory" as a systematically elaborated
account of social reality is possible only at a distance from the
subject that tends to blur all significant differences existing
among the various members of the Frankfurt School. In fact,
close examination reveals that there are at best only critical
theorists confronting a common problematic within more or less
the same cultural tradition. Yet, discussions of "critical theory"
need not become wanderings into "the night in which all cows
are black" if the focus is shifted from the particular theoretical
tenets whose contradictory multiplicity resists systematization to
the odyssey of the problematic itself. Such a trajectory, fully
presented by *The Essential Frankfurt School Reader*, begins
with critical theory's emergence from the first generation of
Hegelian Marxists (Lukás and Korsch), moves through its interpretations of Stalinism, Fascism and the New Deal and its attempts to provide a theory of American society, and closes with

its final inability to come to grips with the new state-regulated, capitalist social formation. This outcome was the result of key theoretical choices made earlier in the effort to revitalize and make historically relevant the Hegelian Marxist tradition without abandoning its general philosophical framework.

Thus, to provide a general evaluation of critical theory that does not violate its very spirit, one must first and foremost grasp the particularity and specificity of its problematic without forcibly reconciling internal contradictions, conflicts and shifts. Simultaneously one must *critically* locate its one-sidedness, from the privileged vantage point of the present, by clarifying the relation between the confused and ambiguous aspects of the theory's formulations and its historical context. Such an account must explain the consciously esoteric thrust of at least the key members of the Institute, their "planned" failure to have a broad lasting impact, and the reasons why a different social analysis can avoid the self-contradictions which a more popular presentation of the original critical theory would have precipitated.

Though the first generation of critical theorists had *literary* as well as philosophical aspirations and generally wrote (Adorno and Benjamin especially) with great elegance, incisiveness and elaborate finesse, American resistance to the easily detected heavy drone of the complicated underlying thought processes endemic to German philosophy appears to have diminished appreciation of their profundity as well as of their intelligence, and an ingrained American habit of reading literally missed the metaphoric intent of many of their paradoxically couched formulations. On the level of language the misreception can perhaps be explained simply (and demonstrated) in terms of syntax. On the level of meaning the difficulty resides with what is spelled out in one cultural tradition and what is left unsaid in another.

Thus, the fact that critical theory has failed to receive, especially in the English-speaking world, anything close to the cultural reception that would appear to be its due, is neither primarily the result of conspiratorial efforts on the part of traditional theorists to ignore its emancipatory content, nor of the administrative apparatus's attempt to repress its revolutionary aspirations. Rather, it is a consequence of some of the more paradoxical features of the theory itself, first its attempt to conceal its Marxian character, and subsequently, in its American phase, its effort to prevent its instrumentalization by those very forces that the theory had sought to oppose. Here I am focusing only on the main contributions of the Institute, the work of Horkheimer, Adorno, and to a lesser extent Marcuse. The choice of a deliberately obscure mode of expression was not merely an unavoidable by-product of either the complexity of the phenomena they chose to investigate or of their theoretical heritage, but was inextricably linked with the problematic character of their attempt to create a theory of emancipation in a context where all organized or organizable opposition had long since capitulated. Within such a predicament, to make the theory conceptually accessible through the reified language of the logic of domination would have meant to expose it to instrumentalization by that same administered society against which it was aimed. Thus, internal complexity and obscurity were to be in themselves guarantees that the process of decoding explosive theoretical contents would shatter the reification resulting from automatic readings and conceptual commodification.

It is precisely this dilemma (which is also that of a large body of modern art) which provides the key to understanding the full trajectory of the Frankfurt School from Horkheimer's takeover of the Institute's directorship in 1931, to its eventual dissipation in the late 1960s. That the attempt to refurbish a critical Marxian theory was made in the face of the disappearance of its potential audience explains the generally unenthusiastic reception of critical theory, both by an academic community deemed by the theory itself to be relatively irrelevant and undergoing increasing cretinization in its phase of technocratic rationalization, and by a broader public sphere, of whose existence critical theory itself constituted a prolonged obituary. In short, the theory ruled out any reception other than the one which it actually received. To further complicate things, this paradoxical state of affairs tended to become ontologized in such a way that the political impotence it presupposed was turned into a theoretical virtue, and all possible alternatives tended increasingly to be ruled out in principle. Ultimately critical theory was forced to justify itself in terms of a future emancipation which was otherwise shown to be unrealizable.

Adorno's final antagonistic confrontation with those very students that he himself had helped to radicalize typifies the unfortunate political corner into which critical theory had managed to paint itself: it tended to help create an explosive audience which it had to subsequently defuse—not just on the basis of intrinsic shortcomings, but on what ultimately were ontological grounds.

Contrary to Left conventional wisdom, according to which the quandaries of critical theory are the result of its having jettisoned fundamental Marxist assumptions, the real problem was the exact opposite: the unwarranted retention of too much traditional Marxist baggage. Initially operating inside a framework that promised a socialist pot of gold at the end of the capitalist rainbow, early critical theorists—particularly Horkheimer up to the late 1930s—could only see Fascism as the infamous last stage of capitalism, and Stalinism, despite all of its internal shortcomings, as a transitory stage to authentic socialism. And even after the theoretical shifts of the early 1940s,[1] and Adorno's official joining of the inner group,[2] their analyses of American society remained caught within this framework— minus the happy ending. Since *Dialectic of Enlightenment* had successfully exploded the earlier myth of historical progress toward a necessarily emancipatory socialism, the future became immensely more problematic. Adorno was no longer able to articulate "concrete social theory," as Lukács had, by relating to a totality (or rather to the totalizing act of an identical subject-object).[3] As early as 1931, Adorno had rightly understood that the collapse of the proletariat's role as the tendential totalizing subject-object of history rendered the concept of totality problematic.[4] Unwilling at that point to radically revise the Marxist philosophy of history, critical theorists had gradually turned to psychoanalysis to explain the collapse of potential proletarian opposition while safeguarding lingering emancipatory promises in the biological dimension.[5]

This explains why Marcuse's *One-Dimensional Man* and Adorno's *Minima Moralia* exist as two antinomic yet complementary theories of American society. Marcuse stubbornly continued theorizing on the macrological level in a fashion apparently ruled out by the collapse of the Lukácsian project, a collapse which had left no suitable collective epistemological foundation immune from the pitfalls of a theory positing the mythological identity of subject and object. For Adorno, on the other hand, social theory was possible only be escaping into esthetics, where micrological analyses of the particular provide aphoristic glimpses of that "false totality" no longer immediately apprehensible through discredited traditional conceptual means. Where Marcuse's *macrological* approach leads him to narrate a story which cannot have a happy ending—which accounts for his subsequent frenzied search in the social periphery for potential revolutionary subjects—Adorno's *micrological* analysis succeeds in salvaging revolutionary subjectivity in social theory as art, but at the price of destroying any possible normative political mediational function.

Nevertheless, their shared reception of psychoanalysis allows both Marcuse's and Adorno's analyses to complement each other within an antinomic framework which, in spite of irresolvable dualism, still aspires to remain dialectical. In attempting to rescue the Marxist philosophy of history from the theoretical ruins of *History and Class Consciousness,* Horkheimer's and Adorno's use of psychoanalysis successfully destroyed the dialectic and eventually resulted in *Dialectic of Enlightenment*, which constitutes the most far-reaching revision of precisely that Marxist philosophy of history that it was meant to preserve. In short, the psychoanalytic turn led to the ontologization of the socio-historical predicaments of American society in transition from entrepreneurial to advanced capitalism (understood as a new state-regulated social formation), with the result that the historicity of this transitional phase was altogether ignored. Thus, when the crisis of one-dimensionality erupted, it became impossible to theoretically grasp the nature of the new developments.

In Adorno especially, the dialectic becomes dehistoricized to cover the whole of Western civilization as the genesis of the domination of the concept. Consequently, critical theory does not even attempt to prefigure the future by elaborating the mediations necessary to bring it about, and becomes purely defensive: it ultimately retreats to defend particularity, autonomy and nonidentity against an allegedly totally administered society where thinking itself appears as a dispensable luxury. To the extent that the politicization of the productive process and the development of the culture industry lead to the colonization of consciousness, thus systematically ruling out any form of internal opposition, the logic of domination unfolds unchecked toward the even more disastrous manifestations of Auschwitz, the Gulag and Hiroshima. The psychoanalytic theory of socialization and the analysis of the "totally administered society" combine to checkmate all the remaining hopes of social emancipation. In the late 1950s, critical theory becomes increasingly hermetic, with its analysis of one-dimensionality becoming the pervasive theme, except for occasional detours through politically impotent esthetic maneuvers. The subject disappears, society becomes all-powerful and intellectuals can only escape into abstruseness and isolation to avoid homogenization, instrumentalization, or in extreme cases, even annihilation.

Paradoxically, what this account ended up losing was precisely that nonidentity which it sought to preserve. Instead, it embalmed and reified it within an increasingly rigid and objectivistic reproduction of the given that has alredy been frozen by the all-pervasiveness of the concept. Although his aphorisms retain their critical edge by escaping into a poetic mode of discourse, when Adorno attempts to defend critical theory against positivist adversaries he lets the orthodox Marxist cat out of the bag: on the macrological level the totality remains an absolutely irreplaceable category, the model of exchange rationality remains the basic principle of modern society and the economic crisis theory looms on the horizon. Large chunks of traditional Marxist doctrine resurface wholly unaffected by the *aqua regia* of critical theory. Legitimated by psychoanalysis, they remain unchallenged even by the overthrow of the Marxist philosophy of history whose rescue had originally required the introduction of the psychoanalytic dimension. Although operating on different levels, Marcuse's *One-Dimensional Man* ultimately spells out what Adorno's *Minima Moralia* merely alludes to. Both approaches eventually converge on a similar pessimistic evaluation of emancipatory prospects.

The theoretical trajectory that is usuall understood as mature "critical theory," fully elaborated during the 1950s and early 1960s as the completion of analyses begun in 1940 and typified by *Dialectic of Enlightenment*, brilliantly captures the Cold War period, the plastic 1950s and in general the post-New Deal American society which was rapidly hegemonizing most of the world. It was unable, however, to foresee or come to grips with what Habermas in *Legitimation Crisis*[6] calls the rationality or planning crisis which looms as the fundamental crisis of the overadministered society. This crisis requires a complete reversal of the logic of one-dimensionality so as to prevent the very system from grinding to a halt through the reams of bureaucratic paperwork.

With the final collapse of any hope for the Marxist model in the 1970s, the changing function of critical theory should not come as a complete surprise. Late capitalism finds itself unable to provide free space for the emancipatory tendencies which it needs to guarantee its own continued world domination in a context characterized by a rapidly decaying "Communist" world and a Third World unable to successfully modernize. What this analysis entails as a precondition for a meaningful relaunching of critical theory and a full understanding of its heritage is a *self-historicization* within a new periodization of twentieth-century capitalism. In short, it means locating the one-dimensionality thesis as the critical awareness of the transitional phase between entrepreneurial and advanced capitalism, while locating traditional Marxism as a critique of entrepreneurial capitalism and searching for a yet to be developed critical perspective to deal with the present.

Already prefigured at the turn of the century when the crisis of entrepreneurial capitalism seemed to have entered into its final phase, but fully institutionalized only after the 1929 crash, the age of one-dimensionality meant the increasing extension of collective capital over every facet of life—even to the point of reconstituting character structure and personality to accord with the new requirements of rationalization.

The first thirty years of this century are marked not only by the blossoming of a variety of Marxist theories, but also by the prefiguration of various successful and unsuccessful institutions of the coming welfare state. After pre-World War I progressive legislation, scientific management, and the integration of earlier forms of opposition (essentially organized labor) have been finally institutionalized during and after the New Deal, such strictures as Prohibition and other overtly represeive projects could be dropped. The new situation no longer required them to generate the new phase of capitalist rationalization. As a matter of fact, they stood in its way. In certain European states, such institutionalization was only possible through authoritarian means; in the U.S. the lack of a powerful opposition was a major factor in making for a peaceful and relatively smooth transition.

Thus, the institutional shift from entrepreneurial capitalism to the New Deal meant a rationalization of capital mediated by the state and a redirection of *extensive* into *intensive* growth.[7] The tendency toward one-dimensionality resulted from a massive attempt to annihilate all specificity and otherness left over from previous social formations so as to create the conditions necessary for this restructuring of capitalism. Taylorization, capital-intensive technology, the culture industry and consumerism combined within a production system that was based on the automobile and military expenditures, and this facilitated the penetration of capitalist relations into all crevices of everyday life. One-dimensionality as the tendential fulfillment of the dialectic of Enlightenment—which Horkheimer and Adorno unjustifiably dehistoricized and projected back onto the whole trajectory of Western civilization from Odysseus to Hitler—assumed the characteristics that Marcuse has so trenchantly described, and eliminated all remaining obstacles. The homogenization and depersonalization associated with this period—i.e., the domination of the concept and of capital's abstract instrumental reason—constitute the historical limit of this transitory rationalizing phase. The full triumph of one-dimensionality corresponded to the exhaustion of the model that generated it.

Ultimately this required a reversal of the logic of one-dimensionality which was greatly facilitated by the system's successful obliteration of all potential and even imagined internal opposition during the Cold War and its aftermath. No longer meaningfully challenged, the system can allow harmless new forms of institutional free space within which spontaneity and negativity thrive, and can thus generate much-needed control mechanisms. In fact, the system's immediate response is to attempt to generate such opposition. This explains the recent phenomenon of counterbureaucratic bureaucracies that tend to reproduce the very problems they are meant to solve. The contradiction remains that, for the planned society, effective negativity must be spontaneous and unplanned, and therefore cannot be bureaucratically plotted out. At best, it can only be encouraged by creating free institutional space within which to develop.

While it is not at all clear whether the growing institutional liberalization will succeed in providing the needed negativity, this new social tendency paves the way for a development and reception of critical theory that has hitherto been unimaginable. Potential assimilation by the administrative apparatus is no longer a major danger when the other side of integration is precisely freedom to formulate even emancipatory projects, and when the latent revolutionary otherness within which the first generation of critical theorists operated has turned out to be a mythical leftover of a never fully transcended Marxist heritage. Within the newly created institutional free space, critical theory can not only renew itself but can also seek the kind of broad popular base previously ruled out in earlier formulations of the theory. An historically accurate reconstruction of critical theory's own trajectory from its inception becomes a precondition for any future renewal. In this respect, *The Essential Frankfurt School Reader* should greatly aid in setting the historical record straight on any number of as yet incompletely investigated topics. The selected texts present critical theory at a relatively open and not yet fully esoteric stage where a pessimistic philosophy of history has not yet swallowed social analysis. The possibility of theoretical renewal, especially in the areas of political and cultural theory, depends on our active assimilation of precisely this stage of the theory, which yields the first approximations toward a new critical sociology and a new philosophy of history with emancipation in mind. We might say that the texts—in their uneasy unity—constitute a prolegomenon to any future critical theory of society.

Paul Piccone

Notes

1. For a detailed discussion of this issue, see Andrew Arato's "Introduction" to Part I, as well as the essays included there.

2. Cf. Martin Jay, *The Dialectical Imagination* (Boston, 1973), pp. 65ff.

3. Georg Lukás, *History and Class Consciousness,* trans. Rodney Livingstone (Cambridge, Mass., 1971), p. 10.

4. Cf. Benjamin Snow, "Introduction to Adorno's 'The Actuality of Philosophy'," *Telos*, XXXI (Spring 1977), pp. 113-119.

5. For a systematic critique of the Frankfurt School's reception of psychoanalysis, see Jessica Benjamin, "The End of Internalization: Adorno's Social Psychology," in *Telos* XXXII (Summer 1977), pp. 42-46.

6. Jürgen Habermas, *Legitimation Crisis,* trans. Thomas McCarthy (Boston, 1975), pp. 61-68.

7. Cf. Mihaly Vajda, "Crisis and the Way Out: The Rise of Fascism in Italy and Germany," In *Telos*, XXI (Summer 1972), pp. 3-26, and Habermas, *Legitimation Crisis* op. cit., pp. 24ff. and pp. 33ff.

Political Sociology and Critique of Politics

Critical Marxism and the Frankfurt School

In introducing the political theory of the Frankfurt School we are forced to begin with a warning: especially in the area of political science or political sociology the older generation of critical theorists from Horkheimer, Marcuse and Pollock to Kirchheimer and Neumann formed a genuine "school" intellectually and institutionally only at one time—during the American period of the *Zeitschrift für Sozialforschung*. Before and after, their positions, though frequently overlapping or contiguous were not subject to the kind of collective critical work that characterizes a school. Our aim in focusing on this period of the Frankfurt School is twofold: (1) we want to depict the political origin and formative context of what is called critical theory *today* (as against the 1930s when it was a code-name for Marxism in general), and (2) we want to present the theory that emerged from the critical evaluation and analysis of this context. We do believe that despite the considerable variety of viewpoints something like a unifiable theory (or theoretical spectrum) did emerge from the efforts of Kirchheimer, Neumann, Pollock and Horkheimer in particular, a political theory best considered under the heading of political sociology rather than political economy. This political sociology (specifically of state organized industrial social formations) was to provide part of *the groundwork* for the later (and better known) social philosophy of Horkheimer, Adorno and Marcuse, *the missing complement* to Adorno's cultural criticism, and *the anticipation* of the much later critique of politics in the works of Jürgen Habermas and Claus Offe.

The crucible of the whole "critical Marxist" or "Western Marxist" or "Hegelian Marxist" enterprise was the failure of the German Revolution (1918-1921) and the success of the Russian Revolution (1917). The determinist, evolutionist, economistic social theory of classical Social Democracy, the first political heir of Marx and Engels, was discredited by the generally conservative and even nationalist behavior of most Social Democratic parties and unions during World War I. The Bolsheviks, who—along with other groups—split off from the Second International during these events, therefore remained unsullied by the compromise and surrender of Social Democracy. But they inherited the mantle of revolutionary orthodoxy not because of their purity, or even because of their superior theoretical and political "line," but because of the unexpected success of radical revolution in Russia. With the exception of a few strategic but not highly theoretical departures the Bolsheviks did not revise the "world view" of 19th century Marxism, and with the partial exception of Lenin's *State and Revolution* did not modify *but* in fact put into practice the authoritarian implications of one side of that world view. On the level of philosophy, anticipating far worse things to come, Lenin himself clearly exacerbated the regressive tendencies of Marxist orthodoxy by moving back toward the 18th century materialism Marx already repudiated.[1] As a result no sophisticated theory was available in 1918-19 to elaborate the implications of the Russian Revolution for the more advanced countries of the West. The Marxism-Leninism that was to be forced upon all European Communist parties during a period of so-called "Bolshevization" was even less relevant to Western Europe than the writings of the few remaining major theorists of Social Democracy (K. Kautsky, O. Bauer, M. Adler et al.) The historical rupture implied by the whole period of the October Revolution, and in particular the experience of council (soviet) government in Russia, Germany, Hungary and Italy, received an adequate theoretical interpretation neither among Western social democrats who refused to recognize the importance of these events, nor among Russian Bolsheviks who in the 1920s, having already reduced the councils to organs of state administration, were already on the way toward turning Marxism into a crude pseudoscientific dogma of legitimation.[2]

The task of the theoretical reconstruction of Marxism was initially possible only at the periphery of some of the Western Communist parties, and even here not for long. The Hungarian Georg Lukács was eventually (after 1930) forced to completely renounce his fundamental 1923 work, *History and Class Consciousness*.[3] The German Karl Korsch was booted out of the German Communist party for his defense of his 1923 work *Marxism and Philosophy*,[4] and the Italian Antonio Gramsci was "protected" from the Communist International only by Mussolini's prison where he wrote the so-called *Prison Notebooks*.[5] As different as these theorists were intellectually and politically, they shared two important influences: they had been intellectually formed outside the Marxist tradition, primarily in contexts dominated by the revival of German Idealism, and they were decisively shaped by the October Revolution and by the various council experiments in which all three had played crucial political roles. The new intellectual cast of mind helped them reconceptualize the political experience; all three theorists drew heavily on the hitherto badly known background of Marxism in German Idealism to work out a theoretical posture adequate to the new historical situation. The new theory was first formulated in terms of a new philosophy, a "philosophy of praxis" (the term is Gramsci's) the central concepts of which (praxis, alienation, hegemony, reification and mediation)[5a] represented Marxian translations of key concepts of Kant, Fichte, Hegel and some of their modern followers. This "philosophy of praxis" represented the first phase of what we would like to call "critical Marxism." In retrospect it is important to stress the lack of success of the "philosophy of praxis" on the level of social theory. Lukács's theory of reification suffered from his acceptance of two rather inconsistent doctrines: of Luxemburg's mechanical theory of inevitable capitalist collapse and of Lenin's voluntarist theory of organization. Korsch, plagued by an exaggerated historicist relativization of the relationship of theory and practice, contributed little to a new social theory. Gramsci, who was the most productive of the three in this area, developed a theory of state, party and modernization more adequate to justify the *de facto* actions of the new Bolshevik state than to comprehend the new historical realities and possibilities of Western Europe. The three major theorists of the first phase of the critical Marxist enterprise did not explicitly give up (with the possible exception of Gramsci) the 19th century theory of the more or less necessary crisis-ridden death agony of the capitalism Marx himself had analyzed. None of them could imagine anything but a socialist society in transition to communism replacing capitalism. Ultimately their most important contribution to a Marxian political sociology can be summed up by the key philosophical claim that the new socialist society, whatever the necessary historical tendencies of the present, could be predicated only on the conscious and self-conscious actions of human subjects who anticipated in their self-organization and intersubjective relations the structure of the future. Hence, confronted by the decline of revolutionary possibilities in the West after 1923, their explanation had to restrict itself to the crisis of revolutionary subjectivity: to the "ideological crisis" of the proletariat (Lukács) or the cultural-political hegemony of the bourgeoisie (Gramsci). It is our thesis that the second phase of critical Marxism, the critical theory of the Frankfurt School, had a chance to surpass its predecessors precisely because of its insights and greater flexibility in two key areas of social theory—political sociology and theory of culture.

How did these insights and this flexibility come about? For the early years of Frankfurt critical theory we must speak of a project that, whatever its political independence and theoretical originality, belongs to the political circle drawn by the first phase of critical Marxism. A detailed comparison of the views of Horkheimer, the founder of critical theory in the 1930s, with those of Lukács et al. would be out of place here. But we should indicate some major points of contact. Horkheimer from the beginning did not accept the crude scientistic epistemology of Social Democratic and Communist orthodoxies, but this should not lead us to postulate an already implicit break with Marxism. Rather the method of historical materialism was used to examine its own genesis and presuppositions in the manner of Lukács and Korsch.[5b] The resulting originality lay in Horkheimer's greater clarity about the transformation of capitalist society, more evident in the 1930s than earlier. The emergence of Frankfurt critical theory itself was accordingly located by Horkheimer in an epoch in which collective, monopoly capital relaces individual competitive capital.[6] Although this claim was already deepened by allusions to key future Frankfurt School themes: the rise of the authoritarian state, the massification of culture and the decline of the individual, Horkheimer's overall Marxist orthodoxy was not yet in doubt. The ultimate object and terrain of the critical enterprise remained political economy, and the primacy of economic determination was insisted on even in contexts where Lukács himself was far more flexible, e.g. in the case of social formations where kinship systems played the major organizing role.[7] Whereas Lukács restricted the "primacy of the economic" to the capitalist social formation, the early Horkheimer, in this sense more orthodox, was able to follow Lukács only when ascribing a functional primacy to politics in the period of transition to socialism, and under socialism itself.[8]

It is true that Horkheimer was never mechanically reductionistic *vis-à-vis* politics and culture. One might say that he gets maximum mileage from Engels's famous letters on historical materialism, concerning the reciprocity of various social spheres and determination by the economy only in the last instance. This is the area where Horkheimer made his first original contributions to Marxist theory, an area that brought him close to the independent contemporary "researches" of Antonio Gramsci. The major historical link between the two men was the necessity to interpret fascism from a Marxian point of view. According to Horkheimer, direct and violent translation of economic domination to political power ("domination" in Gramsci) is only one and not the best source of the stability of a mode of production. To be genuinely effective power must be translated into authority based on (explicit, implicit or introjected) consent that is mediated by cultural institutions (family, school, religion, workplace, etc.). To use Max Weber's language, power must become legitimate domination (for Gramsci, hegemony). The actual dynamics of society, the rate of social change, cannot therefore be derived from the economy alone, but depends rather on the specificity of cultural institutions and even specific effects of these on personality structure. Here, Horkheimer in contradistinction to the major representatives of the first phase of critical Marxism, calls on Freud's theory of internalization for help. He stresses however that the spheres of culture and personality structure do not determine the direction and the ultimate meaning of change *in the last instance*. If the erosion of the bourgeois family and of bourgeois culture (both of which Horkheimer felt protective of under the circumstances) in the "process of rationalization" (Weber) undermines the ideological integration of capitalism, this can only accelerate a verdict that the contradiction of forces and relations of production has already pronounced on the existing system. And if other cultural processes (such as the reification of consciousness) interfere with the formation of revolutionary subjectivity the same verdict is merely retarded.

On this last point Horkheimer rejoins Lukács to a far greater extent than his interpreters realize. What we have here is Lukács's concept of ideological crisis inflated to a general historical category linking consciousness and social change. More specifically, when speaking of his own time Horkheimer uses implicitly the same notion of ideological crisis when he indicates his general allegiance to the proletariat, but his inability to take theoretical guidance from its "empirical consciousness." Lukács, in 1923, was certainly not consistent on this point *but* his best-known (though not theoretically the best) position was identical to what Horkheimer (and as we will see even Adorno) was to adopt, with one crucial difference. Horkheimer in 1937 refused to recognize any existing party as the representative of class consciousness—although in a theoretically Leninist manner he does refer to the possibility of historically true consciousness being the possession of a relatively small group.

On the issue of authority Horkheimer's position was even more clearly Leninist, and here an attitude still sympathetic to the Soviet Union must be assumed. Therefore the magnitude of his shift in political theory in the period of 1937-40 cannot be minimized.[9] According to Horkheimer (1937) not all authority is regressive. Our technical domination of nature is always progressive; only the utilization of its methods *vis-à-vis* other men is dangerous.[10] Even on this last point Horkheimer was rather inconsistent. Just a year earlier[11] criticizing anarchism he indicated that authority which increases production is also progressive. In particular he mentions the hierarchical position of expert and manager in industry *vis-à-vis* labor, as well as the necessarily authoritarian dimension of the central plan of a new, socialist society *and, nota bene*, of the revolutionary party engineering the transition to planned society. Authority is here justified (as in Gramsci) by "historical progress," and if the Soviet Union is not specifically mentioned we can chalk this fact up to Horkheimer's caution in French and later American exile.[12] Only the events between 1937 and 1940 (the trials, the pact, the apparent convergence of many though surely not all Nazi and Soviet institutions and practices, and the dangers of the World War) led to serious theoretical revision in this context. Part I will focus on the political-theoretical position the revision made possible, a many-sided theory of the liberal capitalist social formation, and of its transition to politically interventionist formations.

Liberal Capitalism and the End of Reason

It is well known that with the courageous exception of Walter Benjamin, who had an entirely different attitude to modernity, the members of the Frankfurt School had more than a modicum of theoretical nostalgia for aspects of the earlier, liberal phase of capitalist development. The new was symbolized for them by the politics of fascism and the kitsch world of the *Kulturindustrie*. But on one point they were emphatic: since the earlier phase of capitalism was potentially or even inevitably the source of the later, all programs of return to liberalism would be bankrupt.[13] First of all the liberal capitalist economy led (though not smoothly and without rupture) to the economics of the present. Liberal capitalism was defined by the primacy of market (and private property) relations freed of all political controls inherited from absolutism. The central institutional core of the system was the wage labor-capital relationship, for all the Frankfurt theorists translatable into the nexus of "free labor" and the owner/manager of capital. The purpose of the system is the accumulation of capital which, regulated by the laws of competition, involves all the economic crisis phenomena that Marx had worked out in *Capital*. The capitalist response to competition and crisis is concentration, centralization and rationalization (Weber) in all spheres of life. These processes however imply the passing of liberal capitalism and not only in the economic area.

Most, though not all, Frankfurt theorists believed that the political system most in line with liberal (*laissez faire*) capitalism was itself liberal in form, based on parliamentary representation and protection of individual liberties.[14] They all knew of course that the liberal state was as strong as it had to be to reproduce the free movement of the economic parameters of the system,[15] but they also believed that the period of monopoly capitalism makes plausible or even requires a qualitatively stronger and more active state, one that can directly intervene in the economy and act decisively against the real enemies of the capitalist system, including small-scale capital itself. The point is stressed over and over again by all critical theorists that the new economic and political system of the 1930s represents the capitalist (or state capitalist) response to the unavoidable and disruptive economic consequences of classical, liberal capitalism.[16] We have said that all members of the Frankfurt School agreed that any attempt at return to liberalism is political bankruptcy. Nevertheless, and this has been the source of many a confusion, several members of the circle concentrated on those aspects of liberal capitalist society that they took to be increments in the process of human emancipation, moments that are to be preserved or remembered—for the sake of a liberated future.

From a general sociophilosophical point of view, Max Horkheimer's "End of Reason" (1940), the first article reproduced below, sums up the crucial argument—reviving a point from Marx himself—on the simultaneous birth and de-substantialization of individuality with the destruction of relations of personal bondage that characterized pre-bourgeois European society.[17] The new individuality, because defined by self-preservation, was victimized by a development that integrated individuals into more and more complex, mechanical, reified networks of relations—leaving finally no self to be preserved. But as long as market rationality and parliaments were not replaced by the manipulation of monopolistic competition and the terror of authoritarian states, the remnants of new individuality of the liberal era still embodied essential values of freedom, substantive reason, and striving for happiness. So far nothing new, nothing beyond Marx, the young Marx at least. But Horkheimer went on to stress crucial parameters of individuality late capitalism came to threaten, parameters that Marxist social theory has either neglected or dealt with in a mechanically reductionist fashion. The reduction was not unlike the "reduction" that was to occur in authoritarian states, one of which could legitimate itself by a suitable version of Marxist theory. Horkheimer himself, following Hegel, the Kierkegaard of *Either/Or* (and his own 1936 study), stressed the bourgeois family as the birthplace and one of the last defenses of the last traces of substantial individuality. Not that he did not realize its many repressive and integrative functions. But he also saw another side. The relationships of mother and child and the sexual relationship, before they are functionalized, are the refuge of sensitivity in a society dominated by economic reason, the last intersubjective sources of personal substance in a world where subjectivity is defined in terms of egoistic self-preservation.

None of this goes far beyond the 1936 essay "Authority and the Family" which we have subsumed under the first phase of the critical Marxist project. The claim that bourgeois individuality is definable sociol-psychologically in terms of a family and juridically in terms of property relations was simply adopted from the earlier work. Nevertheless "The End of Reason" (1940) was the harbinger of a new position. The critique of the "abstract negation" of liberal individuality was new with Horkheimer in 1940. The abstract negation of liberalism was understood in terms of a collectivism based on the massified, atomized fragments of the disintegrating family, and especially of the transcendence of private property and its market context through the comprehensive, central plan. The Frankfurt critique of liberal capitalism could confront ideal with reality (within the reality under analysis) and individuality as self-development with individuality as self-preservation (i.e. individualism as a step in human development with individualism as an ideological veil masking the new atomization and functionalization of concrete individuals). The basis of the older critique was therefore a two-dimensional reality, open to what Horkheimer and Adorno called immanent criticism. But as the critical theorists from the "End of Reason" to Marcuse's *One-Dimensional Man* (1963) were to claim, the reality that replaced liberal capitalism, the new society whose aspects were uncritically projected by the developmental theory usually deduced from the Marxian critique of political economy, was "one-dimensional." The new critical theory discovered itself in a historical context where the domination of men over men and (a new Frankfurt theme) over nature was justified or veiled by no traditional or even old bourgeois ideals but only by technical efficiency.[18] If the other side of the commodity or money fetish was the birth of the individual, the other side of the latter's decline was the "technological veil." The total, central plan which represented a new stage of freedom in orthodox Marxism, and even in critical theory of the 1930s, was now presented by Horkheimer as the tool of authoritarian politics, as the new "fetish." Man's control over nature, another classical Marxian desideratum originally uncontested by critical theory, was according to the Horkheimer of 1940 necessarily the stuff of the new ideology. Here we have the beginnings of the "critique of instrumental reason" which Adorno and Horkheimer eventually unfolded as a speculative philosophy of history. One must realize however that the original context of the new critique, the new critical theory—in other words the second phase of the critical Marxist project—was not initially a philosophy of history nor even a merely social-philosophical juxtaposition of liberalism and the authoritarian state. Rather the first version of the critique of instrumental reason implied an immanent critique of politics that attempted the critical analysis of the new fetish of technological rationality, hoping to discover the dynamics of the society that was fetishistically disguised.

The bulk of the essays reproduced in this chapter represent the kind of political sociology that the new departure in critical theory presupposed. Otto Kirchheimer's essay, for example, contrasts favorably the liberal (ideal) form of parliamentary compromise based on individual voices themselves kept in check by the institutions of public opinion with mass democratic political compromise based on pluralistic pressure groups in which the member individual tends to lose the right of legal and political recourse. Here was at least some of the political content of the speculative thesis of the "end of the individual." According to Kirchheimer (in a link typical for Frankfurt theory), pluralist compromise foreshadowed fascist compromise based on strictly enforced deals among groups wholly authoritarian toward their involuntary membership.[19]

If Kirchheimer defended liberal compromise against both forms of pluralism (democratic and fascist), Franz Neumann was to do the same in the area of public law. In this context the two theorists were very close together. Neumann[20] in particular was not afraid of revising the position of both Marx and Weber on the rule of formal laws that characterized the liberal epoch. Indeed formal, rationalized general laws have the functions of obscuring the domination by the bourgeoisie (Marx), and of rendering the economic system calculable (Weber). However they also guarantee a minimum of individual freedom and equality. All substitution of particularized, substantive law for the general and formal meant to Neumann the conversion of judges into policemen. The crucial step in this process of the destruction of justice occurred under fascism once again, but Neumann did not exclude either the Soviet Union, or some of the immanent tendencies of monopoly capitalism from producing similar results.

If the major theorists of the Frankfurt School, Horkheimer, Marcuse and Adorno, were rarely so laudatory as Neumann and Kirchheimer about the achievements of liberalism in the sphere of politics and law, in the context of art especially—but also philosophy—they produced (as we will see in Part II) perfectly analogous arguments. They judged the movement from autonomous though undemocratic "art for art's sake" (the cultivation of high culture as an end in itself) to a mass culture produced and manipulated by culture industries in exactly the same terms as Kirchheimer did the changing structure of political compromise: as the surrender of the last aspects of individual autonomy, as the preparation of key elements of the fascist system.[21] This last point is illustrated in Adorno's "Freudian Theory and the Pattern of Fascist Propaganda" and this essay along with Horkheimer's "Authoritarian State" (both reproduced below) give clear indications of that cultural catastrophe which was the experiential context of most of what we know as Frankfurt critical theory. It is fair to say that the theory was born in an attempt to theoretically account for the authoritarian states, both in relationship to the liberalism they replaced and in relationship to one another, in the context of the experience of fascism.

The Authoritarian State: Old or New Order?
In the mid-1930s the term authoritarian state already appeared in the Frankfurt vocabulary, but exclusively in relationship to German fascism. At the same time the capitalisms of the day were understood as monopoly capitalism, still dominated by the "law of value" even though certain structural changes (shift from ownership to managerial

control) were noted. The German "authoritarian state" was seen as perhaps the most plausible political form of monopoly capitalism.[22] Franz Neumann held this position as late as 1942 in his book *Behemoth*, denying in a debate (with Pollock) the possibility of a new social formation in which the state replaces collective capital, i.e. state-planned capitalism or "state capitalism," of which National Socialist Germany represented only one variant. But by this time Neumann, arguing on the basis of an orthodox Marxist economic theory, did not represent the main tendency of critical theory. It is true that in 1939, in "Die Juden und Europa," Horkheimer himself for a moment approached the orthodoxy of the Dimitrov thesis identified with the Communist International of the Popular Front period: Market capitalism has collapsed; state reform of the old social-economic structure is an illusion. Fascism is "logically" the last stage of capitalist development. The old fetishes of exchange and the anonymity of domination are here replaced by direct political means and "open terroristic" domination. But as Horkheimer well knew, no society can be integrated only by open force alone, and by the "End of Reason" (1940) the last stress was partially replaced by one on the technological veil (technocratic fetish). Here Horkheimer followed Marx's example rather than Marxist dogma, with the technological veil being the analogue of the commodity fetish. And in the somewhat later "Authoritarian State" Horkheimer, now including a critique of the Soviet Union for the first time in his analysis, speaks of three different variants of the authoritarian state, of which German fascism was not even the most streamlined and rationalized. The break with the official Marxisms of the time could not have been more complete.

Between 1940 and 1941 several Frankfurt theorists investigated the characteristics of the new social formation which some of them called "state capitalism," with nearly all of them publishing at least one work on German fascism in particular.[23] The basic questions were these: (1) Can the old liberal capitalism survive or be restored? (2) Is there a possibility of a new state-regulated antagonistic social formation, replacing capitalism but in some respects continuous with it? (3) If so, what are the conditions of possibility of transition and can they be countered? (4) What are the structure and the dynamics of this new social formation? Does it obey some of the "laws" of the old? If not, does it have its own immanent crisis tendencies—economic or otherwise? For the first question the answer was a unanimous although sometimes slightly qualified no. For the second question the answer was yes except for Gurland, Grossmann and Neumann, with the last soon abandoning part of his position.[24] Here we are especially interested in the answer which the main line of critical theory in the 1940s (Horkheimer and Pollock) gave to the question about the very possi-bility of new post-capitalist and yet antagonistic social formations. The position of the 1940s indicating that new "statist" social forma-tions have already emerged (at least tendentially) in three different forms was attained only gradually. We have already reviewed the social-philosophical summary of the shift in Horkheimer's work. Its political-economic meaning, in many respects even more dramatic, is best visible in the theoretical development of Friedrich Pollock. As early as two *Zeitschrift* articles of 1932 and 1933, "Die Gegenwärtige Lage des Kapitalismus und die Aussichten einer planwirtschaftlichen Neuordnung" and "Bemerkungen zur Wirtschaftskrise,"[25] Pollock rejected all attempts to assimilate the current economic crisis ("the Great Depression") to previous crises of the capitalist economy. According to him, new structural elements *within* capitalist develop-ment—increasing centralization and monopolization, state interven-tion (as yet planned and arbitrary) and vast increases in the use of industrial technology—have definitely damaged the self-regulation of the capitalist market system. While this diagnosis indeed led Pollock to argue for the end of liberal capitalism based on the "automatic," "self-regulating" market, the ascendancy of individual enterprise, and parliamentary government,[26] he had no doubt that the short-run replacement would be only a renewed capitalism: merely a new constellation on the ground of the existing system of social relations, i.e. monopoly capitalism. Pollock never considered this solution to be a stable one. That his views were appropriately in flux is shown by a comparison of the two articles in question. On the basis of the capitalist crisis and the survival of planning efforts in the Soviet Union (which Pollock studied in the late 1920s), both articles maintain that economic planning is the already present future ("womb") of indus-trial societies. Neither article—presupposing Lukacs's stress on the subjective factor—considers this result necessary in the purely economic sense.[27] A prolonged period of economic stagnation, for example, is repeatedly considered as a possibility. This was the meaning for Pollock of monopoly capitalism without planning. In 1932 Pollock offered only the long-term alternatives of capitalist planning in the existing social context and revolutionary socialist planning.[28] However in 1933 he outlined a third objective possibility. He now indicated a version of monopoly capitalism regulated or controlled by the state in a new sense altogether: abolishing the freedom of contracts; nationalizing *some* key economic sectors; partially subordinating profitability to growth as the key economic criterion; and guaranteeing the survival of the private, monopolistic sector through fiscal policy, government orders and direct subsidies.[29] Pollock was not yet speaking of the emergence of a new social formation. The changes represented by his third model only involved political economic adaptation to the old social-economic relations of production either by destroying or by constraining the proverbially threatening forces of production or by "stretching" to the limits the existing relations to accommodate the ever-growing productive forces. The connoisseur will appreciate here the surviving bits of orthodox Marxist folklore in the "critical theory" of the 1930s. The "stretching" in question could go so far, according to Pollock, that total capital in the form of the state actually plans the economic process. Overgeneralizing from the extremely recent German experience Pollock tended to consider the authoritarian framework essential for this last solution.[30] Again departing from his position of a year earlier, he now argued that capitalist planning would be supported by the leadership of key monopolies and the state bureaucracy, but only initially by the middle classes. This relative weakness of social base required in Pollock's eyes the authoritarian state. Thus Pollock in 1933, as Marcuse in 1934 and Horkheimer as late as 1939, pronounced the authoritarian state the logically necessary political form of a stabilized monopoly capitalism. Again we should note the partial convergence of Comintern doctrine and the first version of critical theory.

The orthodoxy of the critical theory of the 1930s was not based on a de-emphasis of the "superstructural" spheres of politics and culture which would have been highly irresponsible in the circumstances of Nazi Germany. There were good historical reasons at least until 1936 to consider Nazi Germany fundamentally capitalist. Though he did not seem to resist the reinterpretation of Marxist theory as critical theory or critique of ideology, Pollock was rather insistent on one of the original meanings of "critique": the project of uncovering the roots and possibilities of crisis.[31] Pollock believed in 1933 at least that the authoritarian system emerging in 1933, unlike the planned society of the Soviet Union,[32] still had the original crisis *tendencies* of liberal capitalism. Thus even if the frozen surface of National Socialist Germany with all its horrors differed totally from that of the classical capitalist system, the internal economic dynamic—crucial for the Marxist—remained the same. Pollock was certainly not stupidly optimistic about this state of affairs in the manner of

Comintern orthodoxy. In his eyes one crucial politically dynamic aspect of liberal capitalism was now missing, not just in Germany but in other capitalist societies: the "subjective factor," the potential agent of transformation, the revolutionary proletariat. The 1933 essay is perhaps the first to ground this basic belief, or rather fear, of critical theory; among the causes for the decline of the revolutionary proletariat Pollock names the destruction of the skilled, educated working class by modern, rationalized methods of production as well as new methods of mass manipulation and violent repression.[33] In this respect too, the fascist experience can be considered formative for critical theory.

In the essays of the 1940s reproduced below Pollock and Horkheimer clearly built their analysis of the authoritarian state on the economic theory developed by the former in the 1930s. Yet they broke with this theory in one fundamental respect rich in new implications: the states that solved (or avoided) the final crisis of capitalism were now construed as representatives of a new social formation, "the authoritarian state" or "state capitalism." It is our thesis that because Horkheimer included the Soviet Union among antagonistic and exploitative social formations he opened the possibility of considering state-integrated industrial-social formations as the proper terrain of a *new* Marxist critique. Only in the Soviet Union was the reality of the "primacy of the political" inescapable, but unless the idea of the Soviet Union as a "transitional society" (to socialism, that is) was rejected, no comparison with "antagonistic societies" seemed possible either theoretically or politically. The Frankfurt theory of the 1930s, despite Pollock's affinity to an economic theory that dealt with alternative possibilities and not necessities, was still wedded to the simple alternatives for late industrial societies: "socialism" or "capitalism." In the Soviet Union of 1940 they finally saw a third alternative, one that drove critical theory beyond the facile acceptance of the politically instituted plan as progress. Only the critique of the Soviet Union allowed the critique of the political plan to replace the critique of the system of commodities, the critique of the state to replace the critique of political economy.

If the first version of the theory that confronted the "primacy of politics" in the contexts of the New Deal, the Soviet Union and Nazi Germany anticipated elements of both convergence and totalitarianism theses (hence the often noted analogy to Bruno Rizzi's and James Burnham's contemporary works),[33a] this was so only in terms of its descriptive elements. Horkheimer and his colleagues dealt with the emergence and the possible future of "authoritarian states" in terms colored by an entirely different philosophical posture. As a result their theory can be differentiated by considering question 3 above relating to the genesis of the authoritarian state.

The Emergence of Nazi Germany and Soviet Russia as Authoritarian States

We have already indicated that critical theory saw the prolonged world depression as the objective context for the emergence of National Socialism. As usual there was no disregard of the subjective factor. Already in 1934 Herbert Marcuse systematically investigated the pseudo-Gemeinschaft ideology of the fascist mass movement, while Erich Fromm in the 1930s and 1940s and Adorno between 1940 and 1951 produced important studies on the social psychology of fascism.[34] In this context the Institute's work was more sophisticated than most contemporary analysis of fascism. From the point of view of Marxian-Lukácsian analysis of the socialization of society and the destruction of community, Marcuse was able to show the attraction to broad strata of ideologies of nature, folk, blood and soil, ideologies that attacked urbanization, industrialization and modernization. The promise of National Socialism was to reverse the isolation, anomie and proletarization of the petty bourgeois and prevent the further economic decline of the peasant, in a new national community. But since on the ground of "civil society" with exchange as the social nexus no community was possible, the new ideology could only operate on a terrain of irrationality. The same irrationalism disguised also the contradiction between the promise of neomedieval, artisan socialism and the always present tendency of fascism to reconstruct large-scale capitalism on a new basis. The question that Marcuse did not really ask in 1934 was why irrational motives predominated over rational interests in the active and passive mass bases of National Socialism. The project of the Freud-Marx synthesis which emerged at the peripheries of Marxist politics and the psychoanalytic movement faced this as its most important question.[35] The originators of this project were Wilhelm Reich and the associate of the Frankfurt Institute, Erich Fromm. But from his unpublished researches of the 1940s to the essay reproduced below and the more famous "Elements of Anti-Semitism" in *Dialectic of Enlightenment*, it was Adorno who appropriated the result of the Freud-Marx "synthesis" for the major tendency within critical theory. In relationship to the genesis of the mass psychology of fascism he was able to show how the *projection* of anticapitalism in a direction not dangerous to capital (i.e. the obsolete commercial capitalism associated with the Jews) and the irrational identification with the state, the leader, and the anonymous mass could replace and satisfy the need and desire for concrete, non-mythological community. Fascism for Adorno releases the subjectivity of destroyed subjects in the form of paranoia and irrational, aggressive projection. The manipulation of fascist agitators, effective only *vis-à-vis* anomic and accidental crowds ("masses"), represents the technology of "psychoanalysis in reverse." The last phrase is used by Adorno also in relationship to the mass culture of late capitalist cultural industries. It was his belief that the socio-psychological manipulation of fascism that is based on the utilization of the irrational, is anticipated and prepared by the mass-cultural reduction of the last traces of *ego* into *id*. Thus, socio-psychologically at least, Adorno was able to present fascism as a general problem of late bourgeois society. Here lay the root of his tendency to present the world of the culture industry as completely without hope.

It is in this context especially that the emergence of the Soviet form of the authoritarian state could never be assimilated to the analysis of merely one type of social formation, the "authoritarian state" or "state capitalism". The first Frankfurt theorist to consider the transition to a fully authoritarian state in the Soviet Union was Otto Kirchheimer. In 1933, several years before his association with the Institute, Kirchheimer investigated the consequences of both the excess of utopianism and the excess of party-oriented realpolitik for the popular democratic soviets, or councils. Revising an earlier[35a] and more favorable assessment of Soviet politics, the essay "Marxism, Dictatorship, and the Organization of the Proletariat" criticized both the "primitive democratic dreams" of Lenin's *State and Revolution* and the authoritarian tendencies of Bolshevik organization. The latter in particular, according to Kirchheimer, led to an identification of party with bureaucratic state administration, destroying through the acceptance of bureaucratic forms both intraparty democracy and the earlier dynamic links to the underlying population. For a centralized and centralizing party in control of the bureaucratic state, however, the loss of contact with their mass base could only mean terror. Here was a creative (though only implicit) application of the Marxian analysis of Jacobinism to the Soviet Union, more convincing than Trotsky's uncertain juggling with the slogans of "Thermidor" and "Bonapartism." The main line of critical theory represented by Horkheimer, did not, as we have said, pick up on these key themes in the period of its distant admiration for the Soviet Union, the 1930s. In fact until Marcuse's much later (1957) *Soviet Marxism* no Frankfurt-type analysis of the Soviet Union was attempted. Horkheimer's "Authoritarian State," which we have already introduced as the theoretical watershed in the politics of critical theory precisely in relation to the Soviet Union, was only a partial exception in this context. The essay certainly reveals the deep effect on critical theory of Soviet developments and of the parallel ossification of the working-class movement in the West. But its theoretical claims about Bolshevism were rather well known, though not for that reason false. Horkheimer's analysis of the continuity between bureaucratic working-class organization and "integral statism" only repeated arguments often drawn from Max Weber. On the other hand the assumption of Horkheimer's immanent critique (repeated by Marcuse in 1957) that the admittedly most consistent form of the authoritarian state was because of its working-class ideology the most open to liberating, cataclysmic social change (based on a new council movement) derived from an inadequate analysis of Soviet conditions and of the nature of Soviet Marxism as a pseudoscience of legitimation. Much more convincing was Franz Neumann's suspicion in 1951—rejected by Marcuse in 1957—that the failure of "permanent revolution" in its international context and the failure of democratic revolution internally not only led to the totalitarian politics of the Five-Year Plans *but* converted the holders of political power into a new class. Thus a "preparatory dictatorship" became a permanent one.[36] Unfortunately because of a hidden orthodox Marxist bias that expects dynamic change only from global subjects, the older critical theory could never contribute much to the analysis of the limits of this permanence.

Without the same sharpness of *political* vision as Neumann and Kirchheimer, Horkheimer was nevertheless remarkable for deducing the *theoretical* consequences of the political deformation of an originally Marxist movement. Contrary to all his earlier positions he now understood that the reading of Marx's critique of political economy as a *positive* theory of development from market to planned economy anticipates the collapse of liberal capitalism, but of the "new society" only its authoritarian form. This was the political side of the famous Frankfurt redefinition of Marxism as the critique of ideology. Furthermore, to be more precise, even the *negative* critique of the capitalist market-oriented "anarchy of production" could easily imply the legitimation of the "abstract negation" of the authoritarian central plan. This was the political meaning of another famous Frankfurt theoretical move, from the critique of political economy to the critique of instrumental reason. Horkheimer did not argue that Marxian theory necessarily implied its own theoretical deformation any more than the working-class movement necessarily led to the authoritarian state. Instead he seemed to believe that neither, in their classical form, were sufficiently protected against deformations that anticipated the new system of domination. And as he saw critical theory to be the theoretical corrective, in 1940 (no matter how briefly) he saw council communism as the analogous political corrective. The two found each other in that brief moment when the main theorists of the Frankfurt persuasion included the Soviet Union in their general critique without abandoning all hope in a Marxian politics. The key to the brief duration of this moment lies in the different types of conceptualization that explored the genesis of the third type of the "authoritarian state" or "state capitalism," the type represented by the New Deal and all later neocapitalist social formations.

The Emergence, Structure and Dynamics of Neocapitalism

The specific historical matrix for the emergence of neocapitalism (to use a neutral term for the democratic or manipulated version of "state capitalism") was for all Frankfurt theorists the "Great Depression." Pollock's already mentioned analyses of the 1930s led to some doubt about the possibility of a non-fascist solution to the problem of capitalist planning, even though in economic abstraction he was able to build such a model. By 1940, in American exile, most Frankfurt theorists shifted their emphasis to this possibility. The results were by no means harmonious. Here one can no longer speak of theoretical unity or even a merely two-sided debate concerning the possibility or impossibility of "state capitalism". The arguments of Kirchheimer (a partisan of the concept of monopoly capitalism) on the changing structure of political compromise from liberalism to mass democracy were perfectly analogous to those of Adorno and Horkheimer on the degeneration of high culture in the pseudo-democratic culture industry.[37] This line of argument presupposed a concept of manipulated state capitalism representing a closed and increasingly totalitarian system (as in Marcuse's *One-Dimensional Man*). On the other hand Pollock and Neumann, who clashed on the concept of state capitalism, seem to agree on the possibility of a democratic version of state capitalism (or monopoly capitalism) that would prepare the ground for a society based on genuinely democratic planning. Even though

Herbert Marcuse in 1941, in "Social Implications of Modern Technology" (reproduced below), seems to share the hope of Pollock and Neumann, the essay itself began just that analysis of the "technological veil," of science and technology as ideology, which in his later writings unmasks many totalitarian features of contemporary formal democracies that increasingly replace liberal ideology and the demand for a genuine public opinion by the imperatives of merely technical efficiency. In Marcuse's later work the stability of state capitalist systems is all the more fateful and impenetrable when the technological veil (rather than liberal ideology or direct domination) becomes the principle of social integration. In other words when Marcuse came to abandon all hope in democratic reform he was to draw (against all his inclinations) conclusions implying too much structural stability for late capitalism. The same was more or less true for his 1957 analysis of the Soviet Union, where he was able to juxtapose streamlined, bureaucratic, self-reproducing domination with only the supposedly liberating tendencies of the central plan *and* whatever still survives of Marxist ideology.[37a]

It will easily be seen that in the absence of a single posture and definition, the genesis of a version of state capitalism represented by the New Deal was also conceived differently (as "democratic" or "manipulated"). Those theorists who concentrated on the manipulated, closed, authoritarian features of the system (Horkheimer, Adorno, Kirchheimer and the later Marcuse) focused on the objectively necessary response of capitalism to crisis and the conquest of the subjective factor by the political organizations of pluralist mass democracy and by the culture industry (in a manner analogous to the fascist "psychoanalysis in reverse"). The theorists who insisted on the juridical-legal protection of civil rights and the survival of some residues of popular political participation under late capitalism (Neumann and Pollock) postulated a New Deal type of system as the achievement of the democratic forces (unions, reformist parties etc.) battling against the other historical alternative, fascism. Not surprisingly the results led to at least two types of theories concerning the structure and the dynamics (question 4 above) of the new social formation. The theory postulating the conquest of the subjective factor led to (or perhaps already presupposed) the Adorno-Horkheimer theory of the culture industry and eventually to Marcuse's *One-Dimensional Man*; the theory focusing on the role of democratic mass movements led to Pollock's theory of "State Capitalism" and eventu-

ally to the Offe-Habermas theory of political crisis. Since our concern
in this chapter is the political sociology of the older Frankfurt School
generation we will concentrate especially on Pollock's theory.

Pollock's "State Capitalism" (reproduced below) is indeed open
to the objection (e.g. Neumann's) that the elements of its basic model
were put together from Pollock's studies (1920s) on Soviet planning,
from his work on Keynes, from his particular understanding of the
Marxian crisis theory and from his knowledge of the National Socialist economy.[38] Closer analysis of course shows that the elements of
this combination point to different social structures, and the convergence of the economic structures of the post-liberal capitalist social
formations is true only in carefully limited respects. Nevertheless
Pollock's essay, as well as Horkheimer's essays of 1940, are based on
a powerful insight that validates the effort from the start: the change in
function of political economy, the end of the primacy of the economic
under industrially advanced contemporary social formations and the
necessity of the replacement of political economy as the framework
and object of Marxism as critique. In "State Capitalism" and even
more systematically (though less extensively) in the contemporary
essay "Is National Socialism a New Order?" Pollock investigated the
structure of state capitalism by outlining the parameters of state
regulation of an industrialized economy, of the class structure, and of
the ideological integration (here Marcuse's earlier and Adorno's later
essays were more subtle) and political domination of individuals. He
also did not forget the question about the future-oriented dynamics of
the system. Although Pollock boldly declared economic laws and
economic crisis tendencies to be dead, he did not, especially in "State
Capitalism," postulate a stable society. His most important point in
this context (the others are also worth the attention of the reader) was
the postulate (presumably derived from Soviet experience) of the
political struggle among different elite groups and indirectly the
underlying population over the disposition and priorities of the undemocratic central plan. In other words, Pollock was moving toward a
political crisis theory of state capitalism later revived by such theorists
as Serge Mallet, Claus Offe and Jürgen Habermas.

It is easily documentable that one year later when Pollock wrote
"Is National Socialism a New Order?" the dynamic aspects of his
incipient crisis theory were replaced by a mere appeal to democratic
forces to establish (or to protect) the right kind of state capitalism. A
critical monograph on his work could probably show that having
abandoned the classical Marxian dialectic of labor and consciousness

that leads to the global subject of praxis, the revolutionary working class *without* transforming the locus of critique to *culture* as well as *politics*, Pollock could in principle not discover any systematic possibility of a conscious challenge to state capitalist integration. Hence the most abstract of all possible answers: a moral appeal by the isolated theorist.

Some of the recent work of Habermas (a student and associate of Adorno) throws much-needed light on just this problem complex. The replacement of the critique of political economy by the critique of politics is not without consequences for the structure of critique itself. Classical political economy was not only an expression of the integration of liberal capitalism through the self-regulating market; it was also a key ideology *disguising* class hierarchy through the appearances of equivalent exchange, and *grounding* the formally homologous but independently generated norms of liberty and equality, interpreted in practice as liberty and equality of property owners.[39] The critique of political economy could be therefore both an immanent critique of the democratic norms of civil society in the context of their bourgeois deformation, and a defetishizing critique of the socially necessary illusions of the stability and equilibrium of market-integrated capitalist economy.[39] In the form of "immanent critique" the critique of political economy addresses the potential consciousness of the subjective agents that could transform capitalist society; in the form of defetishization the same critique unfolds the framework of those economic crises that makes this transformation objectively possible. However, the growth of state intervention destroys this solid link between the two types of critique in the works of Marx. State regulation of capitalist economies displaces political-economic controls into a political-administrative sphere, and at the same time places an entirely new burden (given the decline of the normative-ideological functions of the market in the context of state intervention and "imperfect competition") on the sphere of culture. The latter must now provide normatively compelling political-legal legitimations and private personal motivations for the maintenance of the system. Since the political-administrative domain defends itself from public scrutiny precisely by means of the technological veil, a critique of technocratic politics (for Habermas, systems theory) may indeed reveal potential ruptures (e.g. "rationality crisis") of state-capitalist integration. But only a critical analysis of the sphere of culture (where autonomous, self-generated norms may conflict with the ideological requirements of the system) can demonstrate and perhaps promote the possibility of

conscious resistance by those whom the whole critical enterprise
proposes to address. Pollock's critique of the politics of state capitalism clearly omits this last step. But if a critique of politics *alone*
replaces the critique of political economy, the system criticized,
whatever its technical imbalances, will appear petrified—or at most
oscillating between disruption and readjustment. Hence the pessimistic outcome of Pollock's critique of politics.

We must immediately ask whether those of Pollock's colleagues
for whom culture rather than politics became the new object of
critique, for whom the theory of the culture industry became the
theory of late capitalism, were able to move toward a theory of the
cultural crisis of "state capitalism," a crisis theory that would indicate
the new context of actively critical subjectivity. Therefore we must
look ahead for a moment to the theory of the culture industry. But
here, too, the abandonment of the revolutionary proletariat, in the
context of a hidden orthodoxy that possessed no other key to revolutionary emancipation, meant the acceptance of a state's view of the
new social formation. Instead of a framework of crisis, Adorno and
Horkheimer tended to see state capitalist (or late capitalist) culture as
that of inevitable manipulation and control operating on the total
social level and in the personality structure of individuals. The reason
for their profound pessimism is however just the opposite of Pollock's: Hidden orthodoxy instead of the absence of cultural analysis;
instead of linking cultural theory to the political crisis theory of state
capitalist social formations that was available in fact in Pollock's
work, they proceeded in the important book *Dialectic of Enlightenment*—under the political impact of both the fascist experience and
the disastrous fate of the Russian Revolution—to anchor the critique
of the late capitalist culture industry in a destructive, negative hermeneutics (or philosophy of history) of all civilization. Of Pollock's
critique of politics they have incorporated in the end only its pessimistic outcome. When, however, key concepts like reification, the fetish
of technology, the petrifaction of language and the mythological
consequences of the Enlightenment's struggle against myth are extended so as to cover all of history—and the very mode of the self-
humanization of man in the animal world—no locus of liberation can
be available in either past, present or future culture. To be more
precise the locus of liberation then would be necessarily narrowed to
the staunchest, most self-reflective and self-critical forms of criticism
in autonomous art *and* critical philosophy.

In the context of the genesis of Frankfurt cultural critique this pessimistic answer was not preordained. The debate between Walter Benjamin and T.W. Adorno, which we will present and explore in the next part, shows a fluid theoretical context that was frozen only somewhat later when a new philosophy of history (or rather a negative hermeneutics with universal aspirations) swallowed (temporarily) critical theory itself.

The End of Reason

By Max Horkheimer

The essay, first published in Studies in Philosophy and Social Sciences, *Vol. IX (1941), introduces the reader to key social-philosophical concepts of critical theory: the domination of nature, the decline of the individual and the technological veil. At the same time, the political context of these concepts is explored. Horkheimer points to the decline of liberal capitalism and the emergence of state interventionist systems. "The End of Reason" represents an instructive contrast to Horkheimer's earlier, more orthodox Marxist and later, more speculative social-philosophical statements.*

The fundamental concepts of civilization are in a process of rapid decay. The rising generation no longer feels any confidence in them, and fascism has strengthened their suspicions. The question of how far these concepts are at all valid clamors more than ever for answer. The decisive concept among them was that of reason, and philosophy knew of no higher principle. It was supposed to order the relationships among men and to justify all the performances demanded of them. The church fathers and the guiding spirits of the Enlightenment agreed in their praise of reason. Voltaire called it "God's incomprehensible gift to mankind" and "the source of every society, institution, and order."[1] Origen said we should not compare men, even bad men, to animals, in order that we might not dishonor reason.[2] To the ancient world, reason was the masterful principle of creation,[3] to Kant, its triumph was the hidden yet certain trend of world history notwithstanding all retrogression, interludes of darkness, deviations.[4] It is from this ideal of reason that the ideas of freedom, justice and truth derived their justification. They were held to be innate to it, intuited or necessarily conceived by it. The era of reason is the title of honor claimed by the enlightened world.

The philosophy this world produced is essentially rationalistic, but time and again, in following out its own principles, it turns against itself and takes the form of skepticism. The dogmatic or the skeptical nuance, depending on which was given the emphasis, in each case determined the relation of philosophy to social forces, and in the shifting fortunes of the ensuing struggle, the changing significance of rationality itself became manifest. The concept of reason from the very beginning included the concept of critique. Rationalism itself had established the criteria of rigidity, clarity and distinctness as the criteria of rational cognition. Skeptical and empirical doctrines opposed rationalism with these selfsame standards. The left-wing Socratic opposition branded Plato's academy a breeding place of superstition, until the latter moved toward skepticism. Siger of Brabant and Roger Bacon fought the scholastic rationalism of Thomas Aquinas until his own order, after Duns Scotus, gave way to more empirical tendencies. Progressive and reactionary thinkers alike, the materialistic physicians and Gassendi, the Jesuit, protested against Descartes' doctrine of the spiritual nature of man. Kant was told even in Germany that his philosophy boasted without justification of its victory over Hume's skepticism.[5]

Skepticism purged the idea of reason of so much of its content that today scarcely anything is left of it. Reason, in destroying conceptual fetishes, ultimately destroyed itself. Formerly, it was the herald of eternal ideas which were only dimly shadowed in the material world. Later, it was supposed to recognize itself in the order of natural things and to discover the immutable forms of reality in which eternal reason was expressed. Throughout the millenia philosophers believed that they possessed such knowledge. Now they have learned better. None of the categories of rationalism has survived. Modern science looks upon such of them as Mind, Will, Final Cause, Transcendental Creation, Innate Ideas, *res extensa* and *res cogitans* as spooks, despising them even more than Galileo did the cobwebs of scholasticism. Reason itself appears as a ghost that has emerged from linguistic usage. According to most recent logics, the grammar of everyday language is still adapted to an animistic pattern of thought, continuously hypostatizing states and actions as nominatives, so that within this language "life calls," "duty demands" and "the nothing threatens." By this method, reason comes to "make discoveries" and to "exist as one and the same in all men." The name of such reason is held to be a meaningless symbol, an allegorical figure without a function, and all ideas that transcend the given reality are forced to share its disgrace. Since this opinion has pervaded every stratum of our society, it does not suffice to propagate freedom, the dignity of man or even truth. Any attempts along this line only raise the suspicion that the true reasons behind them are either held back or are entirely lacking.

Nevertheless, reason has not been cancelled altogether from the vocabulary of those who are up to date, but has only been reduced to its pragmatic significance much more radically than ever before. Gone are the teachings of rationalistic metaphysics, but the patterns of rationalistic behavior have remained. Locke once wrote, "the word reason in the English language has different significations; sometimes it is taken for true and clear principles; sometimes for clear and fair deductions from those principles; and sometimes for the cause, and particularly the final cause."[6] He appended four degrees of reason: discovering truths, regularly and methodically ordering them, perceiving their connections, and drawing the right conclusion. Apart from the final cause, these functions today still are held to be rational. Reason in this sense is as indispensable in the modern technique of war as it has always been in the conduct of business. Its features can be summarized as the optimum adaptation of means to ends, thinking as an energy-conserving operation. It is a pragmatic instrument oriented to expediency, cold and sober. The belief in cleverness rests on motives much more cogent than metaphysical propositions. When even the dictators of today appeal to reason, they mean that they possess the most tanks. They were rational enough to build them; others should be rational enough to yield to them. Within the range of Fascism, to defy such reason is the cardinal crime.

As close as the bond between reason and efficiency is here revealed to be, in reality so has it always been. The causes of this interconnection lie within the basic structure of society itself. The human being can fulfill his natural wants only through social channels. Use is a social category, and reason follows it up in all phases of competitive society; through reason the individual asserts or adapts himself and gets along in society. It induces the individual to subordinate himself to society whenever he is not powerful enough to pattern society upon his own interests. Among primitives the individual's place in society was determined by instinct; in modern society, it is supposed to be determined by reason, that is to say, by the individual's consciousness of where his advantage lies. Even Greek idealism was to a large extent pragmatic in this sense and identified the good and the advantageous, the beautiful and the useful,[7] putting the welfare of the whole before the welfare of its members. The individual was nothing apart from that whole. The entire humanistic tradition of philosophy tried to bring the two together. Reason, in humanism, aimed at the proper balance between what is good for the individual and what is good for the totality.

The *Polis* was guided by the ideal of harmony between the individual interest and the common good. The medieval towns and the political theorists of the rising national state renewed this ideal. Harmony was supposed to come about through the sphere of law. Whoever desires to live among men has to obey their laws—this is what the secular morality of Western civilization comes down to. Montaigne says in discussing Socrates that as long as we seek refuge in religion we have one guide only, that each must obey the laws of his country.[8] Rationality in the form of such obedience swallows up everything, even the freedom to think. This is the one point on which De Maistre agrees with the French revolution. "Government is a veritable religion: it has its dogmas, its mysteries, its ministers . . . the primary need of man is that his growing reason . . . be lost in the national reason so that it may change his individual existence into another, common, existence, just as a river that flows into the ocean always exists in the mass of water though without a name and without a distinct reality. What is *patriotism?* It is that national reason of which I speak; it is the *abnegation* of the individual."[9] This brand of reason also prevailed in the cults of the French revolution. Mathiez, the apologist for Robespierre, says that the religion of reason had as much intolerance in it as did the old religion. ". . . It admits of no contradiction, it requires oaths, it is made obligatory by prison, exile or the scaffold, and like religion proper it is concretized in sacred signs, in definite and exclusive symbols which are surrounded by a suspicious piety."[10]

The basic unity of the period obliterates differences of opinion. The enthusiasm of the counterrevolution and of the popular leaders not only joined in a common faith in the executioner but also in the conviction that reason may at any time justify renouncing thought, particularly of the poor. De Maistre, a belated absolutist, preaches forswearing reason for reason's sake. The others set up the *Comité de Salut Publique*.

The individual has to do violence to himself and learn that the life of the whole is the necessary precondition of his own. Reason has to master rebellious feelings and instincts, the inhibition of which is supposed to make human cooperation possible. Inhibitions originally imposed from without have to become part and parcel of the individual's own consciousness—this principle already prevailed in the ancient world. What is called progress lay in the social expansion of it. In the Christian era, everyone was to bear the cross voluntarily. For those at the base of the social pyramid, however, the harmony between the universal and the particular interest was merely a postulate. They had no share in that common interest which they were asked to make their own. It was never quite rational to them to renounce their instincts, and as a result they never were quite reached by civilization, but were always made sociable by force. This is what dictatorship always has been based upon. The *beati possidentes*, however, rightly regarded the political and spiritual powers as agencies of their own. They fulfilled for themselves the idea of a rational civilization insofar as their sociability was derived from their knowledge of their individual interests. The latter remain the rational criteria for the harmony between the universal and the particular interest.

The difficulties of rationalistic philosophy originate from the fact that the universality of reason cannot be anything else than the accord among the interests of all individuals alike, whereas in reality society has been split up into groups with conflicting interests. Owing to this contradiction, the appeal to the universality of reason assumes the features of the spurious and the illusory. Reason's claim to be absolute presupposes that a true community exists among men. By denying the reality of universal concepts and pointing to existing reality instead, the empiricists are right as against the rationalists. On the other hand, the rationalists are right as against the empiricists in that, through what is implied in their concept of reason, they uphold the potential solidarity of men as an ideal against the actual state of affairs in which solidarity is asserted with violence and catastrophe. At the close of the liberal era, however, thinking in terms of mere existence, of sober self-preservation, has spread over the whole of society. All men have become empiricists.

The definition of reason in terms of individual self-preservation apparently contradicts Locke's prototypical definition, according to which reason designates the direction of intellectual activity regardless of its external goal. But Locke's definition still holds true. It does not liberate reason from the atomic self-interest of the individual. It rather defines procedures which more readily suit whatever goal self-interest may require. The increasingly formalistic universality of reason, far from signifying an increasing consciousness of universal solidarity, expresses the skeptical separation of thought from its object. Thought becomes what it was designated to be during the Aristotelian beginnings of empirical science, namely, an "organon". As a consequence of Locke and Kant, thought no longer conceives the objects as they really are, but contents itself with ordering and classifying supposedly pure data. The triumph of nominalism goes hand in hand with the triumph of formalism. In limiting itself to seeing objects as a strange multiplicity, as a chaos, reason becomes a kind of adding machine that manipulates analytical judgments. The objects could be regarded as an unqualified mass in philosophy because economic reality had levelled them, rendering all things equivalent to money as the common denominator. In the face of such levelling, the proper being of the object is no longer taken into account. Cognition thus becomes that which registers the objects and proceeds to interpret the quantified expressions of them. The less human beings think of reality in qualitative terms, the more susceptible reality becomes to manipulation. Its objects are neither understood nor respected.

The sheer multiplicity of objects has its counterpart in the so-called pluralism of ends, according to which a gulf exists between the scientific judgments and the realm of values. As a result, the value judgment has nothing to do with reason and science. It is regarded as a matter of subjective preference whether one decides for liberty or obedience, democracy or fascism, enlightenment or authority, mass culture or truth. Freedom of choice, however, has always been the privilege of the small groups which enjoyed a life of abundance. For them it was possible to select among the so-called cultural goods, always provided that these goods were in harmony with their interests of dominion. This was the only pluralism of values that materialized. Wherever the values in question affected the base of European society, they were predetermined. The will to self-preservation of the upper strata of society, though it was rent asunder by competition, unequivocally defined the course of action against slaves, serfs and masses. The perpetuation of privileges was the only rational criterion which determined whether one should fight against or collude with other interests and groups, maintain constitutional government or take the step to authoritarianism. The great historic decisions differed from one another in being farsighted or nearsighted, not in the nature of their ends.

Self-preservation was also at the root of the variety of attributes characterizing individuality. Poise, rank, propriety, gallantry, still are what pragmatism mistakes them to be, habitual forms of the individual's adjustment to the social situation. In the distant past all who behaved at variance with these norms were threatened with loss of class standing. Today, the norms are remnants of those past forms of society in which the individual was lost without them. They still retain the mark of these times, but with the loss of their purpose they have lost their vigor. As the ornaments on useful objects point to past techniques of production, the imperfection of which they retain as adornments, so the now impotent human standards of behavior inherited from feudal ages still bear the hallmark of the violence which the lords of the past had to exercise against themselves for the sake of their own adjustment. In the present state of society these human traits assume the reconciliatory character of the purposeless, but they still adapt themselves very well to prevailing ends. The aristocrat, who left the domestic market to the businessman, attempted instead to conquer the foreign market for him. Aristocrats held their monopoly as warlords for the businessman until the new technology of war brought about the inevitable alteration. They held it even at a time when bourgeois norms, attitudes, and reactions, such as thrift and integrity, already began to share the fate of aristocratic standards of behavior. The latter owed their glory chiefly to the efforts of the middle class to strengthen its position by glorifying its predecessors. This solidarity with past rulers is derived from a common attitude to the rest of society. Power is made to appear as eternal. One's own prestige is enhanced if functionaries of the middle class like Napoleon Bonaparte find their place in the pantheon of history side by side with other great lords and executioners, regardless of whether they were friends or enemies. At home, the well-to-do imitate what they call style; in their offices they abide by the standards of business morality, since their class cannot exist without a discipline of its own; as against internal and external competitors and as against the masses, however, they practice that which actually links them to the historical tradition, namely, integral self-preservation.

This self-preservation may even call for the death of the individual which is to be preserved. Sacrifice can be rational when it becomes necessary to defend the state's power which is alone capable of guaranteeing the existence of those whose sacrifice it demands. The idea of reason, even in its nominalistic and purified form, has always justified sacrifice. During the heroic era, the individual destroyed his life for the interests and symbols of the collectivity that guaranteed it. Property was the institution that conveyed to the individual the idea that something of his existence might remain after death. At the origin of organized society, property endured while generations passed away. The monadic individual survived by bequeathing it. Through the legacy, the individual perpetuated himself even after his death, but he did not contradict the principle of self-preservation if he sacrificed his life .o the state whose laws guaranteed this legacy. Sacrifice thus took its place as a rational institution.

The rationality of sacrifice and self-renunciation, however, was differentiated according to social status: it decreased with decreasing wealth and opportunity, and eventually became compulsory. As against the poor it has always been rational to supplement reason with earthly and heavenly justice. Voltaire admits that reason might triumph for decent people, "but the *canaille* is not made for it."[11] "We have never intended to enlighten shoemakers and servants—this is up to apostles,"[12] he says.

For the masses, the road from one's own interest to that of preserving society was devious and long. In their case, one could not rely upon rational and self-imposed renunciation of instincts or drives. If a Greek slave or a woman had spoken and acted like Socrates she would have been a fool, not a sage. Socrates, by his death, elevated loyalty to the laws of the state above all else. Within the era of conscience that he initiated rationality pertained to those who were socially more or less independent.

The masses turned to religion, but their doing so did not affect the basic rationality of self-preservation. Rationalism has no right to complain about Luther. The latter called reason a beast and a whore only because at his time reason could not of itself cause the individual to suppress his appetites. The religious Reformation trained men to subordinate their lives to more remote ends. Instead of surrendering to the moment they were taught to learn objective reasoning, consistency, and pragmatic behavior. Man was thus not only strengthened in his resistance to fate but was also enabled to free himself now and then from the overpowering mechanism of self-preservation and expediency. Such contemplative pauses, however, could not prevent the interest of the prevailing order from spreading its roots in the hearts of men. Protestantism promoted the spread of that cold rationality which is so characteristic of the modern individual. It was iconoclastic and did away with the false worship of things, but by allying itself with the rising economic system it made men dependent upon the world of things even to a higher degree than before. Where formerly they worked for the sake of salvation, they were now induced to work for work's sake, profit for profit's sake, power for power's sake. The whole world was transformed into a mere "material". If the new spirit served as an anodyne for the people, it was at least one that eased the surgery, foreordained by rationalism, which the industrial system worked on their bodies and minds. There was no other path from the medieval workshop to the assembly line than through the inversion of external compulsion into the compulsion of conscience. It produced the machine-like assiduity and pliable allegiance required by the new rationality. Calvin's theocratic irrationalism eventually revealed itself as the cunning of technocratic reason which had to shape its human material. Misery and the poor laws did not suffice to drive men into the workshops of the early capitalistic era. The new spirit helped to supplement the external pressures with a concern for wife and child to which the moral autonomy of the introverted subject in reality was tantamount. Today, at the end of this process which originated in Renaissance and Reformation, the rational form of self-preservation boils down to an obstinate compliance as such which has, however, become indifferent to any political or religious content. In fascism, the autonomy of the individual has developed into heteronomy.

The totalitarian order marks the leap from the indirect to direct forms of domination, while still maintaining a system of private enterprise. The National Socialists do not stand outside the pattern of economic trends. The gangster theory of National Socialism must be taken even more seriously than it is by those who believe that a normal state of affairs could be restored as soon as the fester has been removed. Government in Germany was not usurped by gangsters who forced an entry from without; rather, social domination led to gangster rule by virtue of its own economic principle. During the era of free industrial economy when none of the many decentralized enterprises was so powerful that it did not need to compact with the others, self-preservation was restricted by standards of *humanitas*. Monopolism has again abolished these restrictions and led social domination back to its true nature which had continued to operate only where the humane form of domination had left some loopholes to inhumanity, in the petty rackets and rings of the big cities. They knew of no other law than the discipline they inevitably had to have in order to plunder their clients. Procurers, condottieri, manorial lords and guilds have always protected and at the same time exploited their clients. Protection is the archetype of domination. After the interlude of liberalism, economic tendencies in Europe progressed toward a new and total protectionism. Only the great combines survived competition. They were strong enough to destroy the separation of powers and the network of guarantees and rights. The monopolies and their government constituted an impenetrable jungle for the masses. The magnitude and diversity of the tasks of the prevailing cliques, the all-embracing character of which still distinguishes them from racketeering, turns into comprehensive planning on the one hand and on the other into an attack on mankind as such. This is the inevitable result of the economic development itself. The same sociological mechanisms apply to the monopoly and to the city racket. The latter had previously shared the spoils with other rackets of the same branch, but the growth of communication and the progressing centralization of the police made it impossible to continue with small bribes and the procurement of new henchmen and guns. The racket was forced to mechanize its business and to undertake the costly task of affiliating it to large political organizations. Such investments are profitable only if the spoils do not have to be divided. In the racket, cartelization asserts itself. The rackets in the cities and in the entire country are driven to unification unless the police succeed in eradicating them in time. A study of such border phenomena as racketeering may offer useful parallels for understanding certain developmental tendencies in modern society. As soon as the concentrated power of large property has reached a certain point, the struggle continues on a broader scale and develops, under the pressure of giant investments necessitated by the progress of technology, into the struggle for world conquest interrupted only by periods of precarious compromise. From this point on, the differences of goals and ideals within the power hierarchy recede before the differences in the degree of docility. The *élites* must see to it, even against their own will, that in the social order everything is rigidly coordinated. Under totalitarian conditions of society, reliability decides upon the allocation of all positions of trust, whether a manager of a provincial factory is to be appointed or the head of a puppet government. Side by side with efficiency, human qualities of a kind again win respect, particularly a resolution to go along with the powerful at any cost. For the trustees are mere delegates. He who is worthy of his task is not to show any traces of that which the self-criticism of reason has destroyed. He must embody the self-preservation of a whole that has become identical with the liquidation of humanity. At the beginning of the history of modern rackets stand the Inquisitioners, at its end the fascist leaders. Their henchmen, living their lives face to face with catastrophe, have to react correctly until they fall victim to the rational principle that none may abide too long.

Present-day contempt of reason does not extend to purposive behavior. The term mind, insofar as it designates an intellectual faculty or an objective principle, appears as a meaningless word unless it refers to a coordination of ends and means. The destruction of rationalistic dogmatism through the self-criticism of reason, carried out by the ever renewed nominalistic tendencies in philosophy, has now been ratified by historical reality. The substance of individuality itself, to which the idea of autonomy was bound, did not survive the process of industrialization. Reason has degenerated because it was the ideological projection of a false universality which now shows the autonomy of the subject to have been an illusion. The collapse of reason and the collapse of individuality are one and the same. "The ego is unsavable,"[13] and self-preservation has lost its "self." For whom can an action still be useful if the biological individual is no longer conscious of itself as an identical unit? Throughout its various stages of life the body possesses only a questionable identity. The unity of individual life has been a social rather than natural one. When the social mechanisms which made for this unity are weakened as they are today, the individual's concern for his self-preservation changes its meaning. What previously served to promote man's development, the joy in knowledge, living through memory and foresight, pleasure in oneself and others, narcissism as well as love, are losing their content. Neither conscience nor egoism is left. The moral law has become inadequate for those who are supposed to obey it, and the authority which it previously invoked has disappeared. Morality had to disappear, since it did not conform with its own principle. It pretended to be independent of empirical individuals, unconditionally universal. But its universal form perpetuated antagonisms among individuals and a tyranny over men and nature. It is vain to hope that in better times men will return to morality. Yet even in fascism it has left its traces within men, and these at least have been freed of spurious positivity. Morality has survived insofar as men are conscious that the reality to which they yield is not the right one. Nietzsche proclaimed the death of morality; modern psychology has devoted itself to exploring it. Psychoanalysis as the adjustment form of modern skepticism triumphed over moral law through its discovery and unmasking of the father in the superego. This psychology, however, was the "owl of Minerva" which took its flight when the shades of dark were already gathering over the whole sphere of private life. The father may still possess a superego, but the child has long unmasked it, together with the ego and the character. Today the child imitates only performances and achievements; he accepts not ideas, but matters of fact.

With the disappearance of independent economic subjects, the subject as such disappears. It is no longer a synthetic unit; it has become senseless for it to preserve itself for some distant future or to plan for its heirs. In the present period the individual has opportunities only on short term. Once secure property has vanished as the goal of acquisition, the intrinsic connection between the experiences of the individual disappears. Concern for property under orderly competition and the rule of law has always been constitutive of the ego. Slaves and paupers had no individuality. The "premise of all my acting in the sensuous world, can only be as part of that sensuous world, if I live amongst other free beings. This determined part of the world . . . is called . . . my *property*."[14] The concept of the ego "must also will a future state to exist, which shall have resulted from the present state, in consequence of the rule which he followed when he resolved upon his act of causality."[15] Property and the orderly functioning of property relations were the referents of the notion of one's own past and future. Today the individual ego has been absorbed by the pseudo-ego of totalitarian planning. Even those who hatch the totalitarian plan, despite and because of the huge mass and capital over which they dispose, have as little autonomy as those they control. The latter are organized in all sorts of groups, and in these the individual is but an element possessing no importance in himself. If he wants to preserve himself he must work as part of a team, ready and skilled in everything, whether in industry, agriculture or sport. In every camp he must defend his physical existence, his working, eating and sleeping place, must give and take cuffs and blows and submit to the toughest discipline. The responsibility of long-term planning for himself and his family has given way to the ability to adjust himself to mechanical tasks of the moment. The individual constricts himself. Without dream or history, he is always watchful and ready, always aiming at some immediate practical goal. His life falls into a sequence of data which fit in advance the questionnaires he has to answer. He takes the spoken word only as a medium of information, orientation, and command. The semantic dissolution of language into a system of signs, as undertaken by modern logistics, transcends the realm of logic. It draws its conclusions from a state of affairs which surrenders language to the rule of monopoly. To be accepted, men must sound like the vocal chords of the radio, film and magazine. For in point of fact, no one seems to make his living by himself, and everyone is suspect in mass society. Everyone needs a permanent alibi. The individual no longer has any future to care for, he has only to be ready to adapt himself, to follow orders, to pull levers, to perform ever different things which are ever the same. The social unit is no longer the family but the atomic individual, and the struggle for life consists in his resolving not to be annihilated at any moment in the world of apparatuses, engines and handles.

Bodily strength is not the chief point, but it is important enough. To a large extent, it is not a natural quality. It is a product of the social division of labor, one that is necessary for production and supplied by whole strata of society to whom no other reason for existence was left except to supply it. Those among the dominated strata who excel in brute force reflect the injustice that the ox which treads out the corn has always been muzzled. Culture was the attempt to tame this element of brute force immanent in the principle of bodily strength. Such taming, however, concealed the fact that physical exertion remained the kernel of work. The counterpart of this concealment was the glorification of bodily strength in ideology, expressed in encomia to every brand of greatness,—intellectual giants as well as muscle men at county fairs, in Wagner's *Gesamtkunstwerk*, in the monster stadium. Today, the ideological veil has been lifted and the principle of bodily strength has been openly propagated in the form of strong-arm methods and purges.

Contemporary individuals, however, need presence of mind even more than muscles; the ready response is what counts, affinity to every kind of machine, technical, athletic, political. Previously, men were mere appendages to the machine, today they are appendages as such. Reflective thought and theory lose their meaning in the struggle for self-preservation. Fifty years ago psychological experience, skillful argumentation, foresight in business were still instruments of progress in society. Prior to the mechanization of the office, even the accountant had to use not only his dexterity but also his intellect. With the total incorporation of the enterprise into the realm of monopoly, rational argumentation loses its force. It now bears the hallmarks of that sales talk in the service of which it was formerly used, and which the victorious monopoly can dispense with. The distrust which peasants and children display for glib persons has always preserved the notion of that injustice which made language the servant of gain. The muteness of men today is largely to be blamed on language which once was only too eloquent against them.

Today, man needs factual knowledge, the automaton ability to react correctly, but he does not need that quiet consideration of diverse possibilities which presupposes the freedom and leisure of choice. The liberty which the market offered to the producers, consumers and their multifold intermediaries, although it may have been abstract and deceptive, had at least permitted a certain range of deliberation. In the monopolistic apparatus none possesses that time and range. Each has to respond quickly, to innervate promptly. Under totalitarian planning, men are dominated by the means of production even more than they were under the market system. Lack of efficiency is a capital offense. The brief period of spare time which still remains to men in their daily lives is now protected against waste. The danger that it will degenerate into otiosity, a state always despised so much by industry, is warded off. Since Descartes, philosophy was one great attempt to place itself as science in the service of the prevailing mode of production, an attempt opposed only by very few thinkers. With the abolition of *otium* and of the ego, no aloof thinking is left. The social atoms, though they may still yearn for liberation, have lost the speculative sense, in the good and bad connotation of that term. The outlook is dark for philosophy. Without *otium* philosophical thought is impossible, cannot be conceived or understood. In such a state of affairs, the argumentative procedure of traditional philosophy appears as helpless and idle talk. At the last minute, phenomenology attempted, paradoxically enough, to elaborate a mode of thinking without disputation, but positivism, in which this philosophy originated, became its heir. It removed thought from philosophy and reduced the latter to the technique of organizing, by reproduction and abridgment, the matters of fact given in the world of sense. In positivism, reason sustains itself through self-liquidation.

With the decline of the ego and its reflective reason, human relationships tend to a point wherein the rule of economy over all personal relationships, the universal control of commodities over the totality of life, turns into a new and naked form of command and obedience. No longer buttressed by small-scale property, the school and the home are losing their educational function of preparing men for life in society. Living and being prepared have become one and the same thing, just as with the military profession. In school, the hierarchy of sport and gymnastics triumphs over the classroom hierarchy which has never been accepted wholeheartedly by children anyhow. The disputed authority of the teacher decreases in favor of an unconditional and anonymous, but ever-present, authority whose demands now have preference. This is the authority of the omnipotent standards of mass society. The qualities which the child needs in this society are imposed upon him by the collectivity of the school class, and the latter is but a segment of the strictly organized society itself. The teacher has the choice of winning the pupil's favor, even by harshness if need be, or of being ridiculed. Compared with the skills which are required of the individual today, the curriculum possesses only a subordinate value. Children learn quickly to know the automobile and radio inside out. They are born with this knowledge, which is not essentially different from knowledge of the most complicated machine, and they can do without science. School physics is obsolete in a twofold sense: it is equally remote from the mathematical consequences of relativity and quantum theory (which have long since passed beyond the limits of representation) and from the practical dexterity which alone matters to the pupil. The teacher cannot mediate between the realm of theory and practice, since the transition from practical observation to theory is no longer recognizable. The highest theory is still a mode of blind technique, as much as repair work is. Both are accomplished by sheer skill, the one in the study, the other in the shop. The difficulties which the theoretical physicist experiences when asked to cross from his mathematical syntheses of different conceptual realms to the world of objects is about the same as the inability of the most skillful mechanic to cross from manipulation of the motor to the principles of its working. Physical knowledge is split into knowledge of handling and knowledge of fields, and this cleavage resulting from the division of labor affects the student's relation to knowledge as such. The exploration of meanings is replaced by an acquaintance with functions. The animistic carryovers of theory are weeded out and this triumph at the same time implies a *sacrificium intellectus*. Technical practice can get along without physics, just as the film star can get along without an apprenticeship and the fascist statesman without learning. Education is no longer a process taking place between individuals, as it was when the father prepared his son to take over his property, and the teacher supported him. Present-day education is directly carried out by society itself and takes place behind the back of the family.

Childhood becomes a historical phenomenon. Christianity inaugurated the idea of childhood in its glorification of the weak, and the bourgeois family sometimes made that idea a reality. During the

Christian era up to the Enlightenment, however, reason operated on the child as an external compulsion to self-preservation which crushed everything that could not defend itself. The sculpture and painting of the middle ages, which did not differentiate between physically and socially inferior beings, revealed the secret of the *ordo* and hierarchy, namely, who could with impunity beat whom. Children who in the Christian world suffered the tortures of Hell were, in the Enlightenment world, rewarded with the Christian heaven. Happiness shall be theirs because they have been chosen as the symbols of innocence. In his adoration of his children, the enlightened businessman of the 19th century could mourn his lost religion without becoming superstitious. Children symbolized the Golden Age as well as the promising future. The rationalistic society gave children legends and fairy tales so that they might mirror hope back to their disillusioned elders. The latter created the idyll of childhood in order to escape between the horns of sober knowledge and ideology, from a dilemma which, in the face of ever threatening social upheavals, they could not resolve. The child ideal reflected the truth within the lie that kept the underlying population in line, the utopia of eternal happiness. This utopia was the place of last resort for the religious ideals of those times in which the bourgeois themselves were still among the underlying.

They can do without this utopia today. In monopolistic society, childhood and adolescence have become mere biological processes. Puberty is no longer a human crisis, for the child is grown up as soon as he can walk, and the grown-up in principle always remains the same. Development has ceased to exist. During the heyday of the family the father represented the authority of society to the child, and puberty was the inevitable conflict between these two. Today, however, the child stands face to face with society at once, and the conflict is decided even before it arises. The world is so possessed by the power of what is and the efforts of adjustment to it, that the adolescent's rebellion, which once fought the father because his practices contradicted his own ideology, can no longer crop up. The process which hardens men by breaking down their individuality—a process consciously and planfully undertaken in the various camps of fascism—takes place tacitly and mechanically in them everywhere under mass culture, and at such an early age that when children come to consciousness everything is settled. Since Freud, the relation between father and son has been reversed. Now, the rapidly changing society which passes its judgment upon the old is represented not by the father but by the child. The child, not the father, stands for reality. The awe which the Hitler youth enjoys from his parents is but the pointed political expression of a universal state of affairs. This new relationship affects even the very first years of life during which father image and superego are supposed to arise. Psychologically, the father is represented not by another individual but replaced by the world of things and by the crowd to which the boy is tied.

The elimination of the conflict between individual and society also affects love. With the passing of the authority of the father the danger of catastrophic conflicts with the family fades away. Yet they had kindled abandon. Today, sex seems to be emancipated and still oppression goes on. Social regimentation of the relations between the sexes had gone far before racial eugenics consummated this process; it was expressed by the standardized normalcy in all spheres of mass culture. Eugenics has its roots in the Enlightenment. Science objectified sex until it could be manipulated. In its inhuman soberness, Kant's definition of marriage as a contract for the mutual possession of the sexual organs indicts inhuman sexual privileges according to the standards of natural law. This definition had, in the 19th century, made its way into the practice of men. In contemporary mass society, the sexes are levelled in that both regard their sex as a thing over which they dispose without illusion. Girls strive to come off as well as they can in the competition with other girls, and, in their eyes, flirtation enhances prestige rather than future pleasure. With Kant, they take sex as a property possessing an exchange value. Wedekind once demanded freedom of prostitution because he thought that women could catch up with male society only through conscious use of their sole monopoly. The modern girl, however, wins her freedom by exploiting the patriarchal taboo which humiliates her by placing her on a pedestal. Sex loses its power over men. It is turned on and off according to the requirements of the situation. Men no longer lose themselves in it, they are neither moved nor blinded by love. Under National Socialism extramarital intercourse is among activities encouraged by the state as socially useful forms of labor. Love is organized by the state. During good times, children are trained as future heirs; during bad times, as prospective breadwinners for their parents; under fascism they are produced under the auspices of the state and delivered to it as a kind of tax, if one can still speak of taxes in a society wherein one group of magnates exploits all the rest of the population. Taxes have an obvious significance under fascism. With property owners, they contribute to accelerating the process of centralization and to beating down weaker competitors. With the masses, their money form becomes transparent and shows forth as toil in the service of power. Part of this toil is the labor of childbirth. Under National Socialism, the girl's refusal of herself to men in uniform is deemed to be as unbecoming as ready surrender formerly was. In Germany, the image of the Virgin Mary had never quite replaced the archaic cult of the woman. Under the surface of Christian civilization memories of matriarchal conditions were never quite extinguished. These vestiges continued to assert themselves in the common antipathy to the old spinster as well as in the German *Lied's* devotion to the deserted mistress, long before National Socialists ostracized prudes and celebrated illegitimate mothers. But the ascetic beatitude of the Christian virgin by far surpassed the pleasure authorized by the National Socialist regime and fed with memories of the buried past. The National Socialist regime rationalizes the mythical past which it pretends to conserve, calling it by name and mobilizing it on behalf of big industry. Where this archaic heritage did not explode the Christian form and assume Teutonic features, it gave to German philosophy and music their specific tone. The mythology in National Socialism is not a mere fake, but the spotlight thrown upon this surviving mythology liquidates it altogether. National Socialism has thus accomplished in a few years what other civilizations took centuries to achieve.

The sexual freedom prescribed by the population policy does not cure the anxiety of the world of sexual taboos but expresses mere scorn of love. Love is the irreconcilable foe of the prevailing rationality, for lovers preserve and protect neither themselves nor the collectivity. They throw themselves away; that is why wrath is heaped upon them. Romeo and Juliet died in conflict with society for that which was heralded by this society. In unreasonably surrendering themselves to one another, they sustained the freedom of the individual as against the dominion of the world of things. Those who "pollute the race" in National Socialist Germany remain loyal to the life and death of these lovers. In the inhuman world of National Socialism, which reserves the name of hero to clever yet beguiled youths who in conceiving, begetting and dying are but victims of a monstrous population policy, the racial crime resurrects what once was called heroism, namely, loyalty without prospect and reason. The sad tryst of those who cannot change their ways is blinded to the rationality which triumphs outside. The daybreak in which the SS men surprise the careless, lights up the monstrosity that reason has become—ingenuity, cleverness and readiness to strike. These lovers have not kept pace with the course of society and therefore cannot hope for its clemency in the streamlined world. Their agony in the concentration camp, which the shrewd adherents of the Third Reich deem right and just because those punished were neither reasonable nor clever, reveals the truth behind fascism's emancipation of sex and behind the concession existence it entails. What is encouraged as wholesome sexuality is an expression of the same fiendish rationality that harries love.

What fascism does to the victims it selects as examples for its unlimited power seems to defy all reason. Its tortures transcend the power to perceive or imagine; when thought attempts to comprehend the deed, it stiffens with horror and is rendered helpless. The new order contradicts reason so fundamentally that reason does not dare to doubt it. Even the consciousness of oppression fades. The more incommensurate become the concentration of power and the helplessness of the individual, the more difficult for him to penetrate the human origin of his misery. The tattered veil of money has been replaced by the veil of technology. The centralization of production which technology has made necessary conceals the voluntary concord among its leaders. More than ever, crises take the guise of natural and inevitable phenomena and tend to destroy entire populations as they ravage continents for reserve supplies. The dimensions of this process are so superhuman that even the imagination which has withstood the mutilation of mass culture hesitates to derive this state of affairs from its social origin.

Injustice has never been more blindly accepted as a visitation of superhuman fate than it is under the spell of fascism today, when everyone talks of revamping society. Hope has been overshadowed by the consciousness of universal doom. Everyone feels that his work perpetuates an infernal machine from which he manages to wheedle enough time to live, time that he proceeds to lose back by attending the machine. Thus he keeps going, expert in handling every situation and in understanding none, scorning death and yet fleeing it. To men in the bourgeois era, individual life was of infinite importance because death meant absolute catastrophe. Hamlet's line, "the rest is silence," in which death is followed by oblivion, indicates the origin of the ego. Fascism shatters this fundamental principle. It strikes down that which is tottering, the individual, by teaching him to fear something worse than death. Fear reaches farther than the identity of his consciousness. The individual must abandon the ego and carry on somehow without it. Under fascism, the objects of organization are being disorganized as subjects. They lose their identical character, and are simultaneously Nazi and anti-Nazi, convinced and skeptical, brave and cowardly, clever and stupid. They have renounced all consistency. This inconsistency into which the ego has been dissolved is the only attitude adequate to a reality which is not defined by so-called plans but by concentration camps. The method of this madness consists in demonstrating to men that they are just as shattered as those in the camps and by this means welding the racial community together. Men have been released from such camps who have taken over the jargon of their jailers and with cold reason and mad consent (the price, as it were, of their survival) tell their story as if it could not have been otherwise than it was, contending that they have not been treated so badly after all. Those who have not yet been jailed behave as if they had already been tortured. They profess everything. The murderers, on the other hand, have adopted the language of the Berlin night club and garment center. The sphere of trade and business remains a reality only in the struggles and transactions among captains of industry and is there removed from the eye of the little man, nay, even of the big man. But the language of market mentality, Jewish slang, the vernacular of salesmen and traders who have long been humiliated, survive on the lips of their suppressors. It is the language of winks, sly hints, complicity in deceit. The Nazis call failure *Pleite*, he who does not watch his step in time is *meshugge*, and an anti-Semitic song says that the Americans have no idea *was sich tut*. The instigators justify their pogrom by saying that once again all was not quite *kosher* with the Jews. Getting through by hook or crook is the secret ideal, and even the SA troopers envy the Jewish brains which they cudgel. They imagine that the Jewish shrewdness they strive to imitate reflects the truth which they have to deny to themselves and to destroy. If this truth has once and for all been discarded and men have decided for integral adjustment, if reason has been purged of all morality regardless of cost, and has triumphed over all else, no one may remain outside and look on. The existence of one solitary "unreasonable" man elucidates the shame of the entire nation. His existence testifies to the relativity of the system of radical self-preservation that has been posited as absolute. If all superstition has been abolished to such a degree that only superstition remains, no stubborn man may wander around and seek happiness anywhere except in unrelenting progress. The hatred of Jews, like the lust to murder the insane, is stimulated by their unintelligible faith in a God who has everywhere deserted them and by the unconditional rigidity of the principle they maintain even unwittingly. Suspicion of madness is the unperishable source of persecution. It originates from distrust of one's own pragmatic reason.

Pain is the means of calling men back from the noumenal world into which all empiricist philosophers and even Kant forbade them to penetrate. It was always the best teacher to bring men to reason. Pain leads the resistant and wayward, the phantast and utopian back to themselves. It reduces them to the body, to part of the body. Pain levels and equalizes everything, man and man, man and animal. It absorbs the entire life of the being whom it racks, reducing him to a husk of pain. Mutilation of the ego, with which the whole of mankind has been afflicted, thus again repeats itself in each case of torture. The practical requirements that enmesh man at every moment, the pragmatic rationality of the industrial era, completely absorb the lives of their victims. Pain is the archetype of labor in a divided society and at the same time its organon. Philosophers and theologians have always exalted it. Their paeans to it reflect the fact that mankind has hitherto known labor only as an effluence of domination. They justify pain because it drives men to reason. Luther translates the 90th psalm as "Teach us to learn we must die in order to become prudent." Kant says that "Pain is the sting of activity,"[16] and Voltaire that "this feeling of pain was indispensable to stimulate us to self-preservation."[17] The Inquisitors once justified their abominable service to their predatory rulers by saying that they were commissioned to save the errant soul or to wash out its sins. Their language already pictures heaven as a kind of Third Reich which the unreliable and scandalous could attain by way of a training camp. If one of these unhappy victims of the Inquisition escaped, requests were issued for his extradition describing him "as one insanely led to reject the salutary medicine offered for his cure, and to spurn the wine and oil which were soothing his wounds."[18] The Inquisition manifested the rage of those who sensed that the inculcation of Christianity had not quite successfully been accomplished, a rage which later, in fascism, led to open repudiation of Christianity. Fascism has reinstated pain on its throne. During the breathing spells of civilization, at least in the civilized mother countries, brute physical pain was inflicted only upon the abjectly poor; to others it loomed on the horizon only as the *ultima ratio* of society. Under fascism, society has invoked this *ultima ratio*. The contradiction between what is requested of man and what can be offered to him has become so striking, the ideology so thin, the discontents in civilization so great that they must be compensated through annihilation of those who do not conform, political enemies, Jews, asocial persons, the insane. The new order of fascism is reason revealing itself as unreason.

What remains of reason in its contemporary decline, however, is not just the perseverance of self-preservation and the persistence of that horror in which it culminates. The age-old definition of reason in terms of self-preservation already implied the curtailment of reason itself. The propositions of idealistic philosophy that reason distinguishes man from the animal (propositions in which the animal is humiliated just as man is in the converse propositions of the materialist doctors) contain the truth that through reason man frees himself of the fetters of nature. This liberation, however, does not entitle man to dominate nature (as the philosophers held) but to comprehend it. Society, governed by the self-preserving rationality of *élites*, has always also preserved the life of the masses, although in a wrong and accidental form. Reason has borne a true relation not only to one's own existence but to living as such; this function of transcending self-preservation is concomitant with self-preservation, with obeying and adapting to objective ends. Reason could recognize and denounce the forms of injustice and thus emancipate itself from them. As the faculty of calling things by their name, reason is more than the alienated life that preserves itself in the destruction of others and of itself. To be sure, reason cannot hope to keep aloof from history and to intuit the true order of things, as ontological ideologies contend. In the inferno to which triumphant reason has reduced the world it loses its illusions, but in doing so it becomes capable of facing this inferno and recognizing it for what it is. Skepticism has done its job. Ideals seem so futile today that they can change as rapidly as agreements and alliances do. Ideology consists more in what men are like than in what they believe—in their mental constrictedness, their complete dependence upon associations. They experience everything only within the conventional framework of concepts. Any object is comprised under the accepted schemata even before it is perceived. This and not the convictions of men constitutes the false consciousness of today. Today the ideological incorporation of men into society takes place through their "biological" pre-formation for the controlled collectivity. Even the unique becomes a function and appendage of the centralized economy. Culture, exalting the unique as the resistive element amid a universal sameness of things is an ingredient rather than an opponent of mass culture; the unique becomes the shingle of monopoly. The essence of Paris and of Austria had become merely a function of that America from which they differed. The self in dissolution becomes recognizable as ideology. It was not only the basis of modern self-preservation but also the veil concealing the forces that destroyed it. What applies to the unique equally applies to the living self. With the dissolution of the self the disproportionate reaches of power become the only obstacle to insight into their obsolescence. Mutilated as men are, in the duration of a brief moment they can become aware that in the world which has been thoroughly rationalized they can dispense with the interests of self-preservation which still set them one against the other. The terror which pushes reason is at the same time the last means of stopping it, so close has truth come. If the atomized and disintegrating men of today have become capable of living without property, without location, without time, they also have abandoned the ego in which all prudence and all stupidity of historical reason as well as its compliance with domination was sustained. The progress of reason that leads to its self-destruction has come to an end; there is nothing left but barbarism or freedom.

Changes in the Structure of Political Compromise

By Otto Kirchheimer

This article, first published in Studies in Philosophy and Social
Sciences *Vol. IX (1941), traces the transition from liberal capitalism
to organized capitalism (monopoly capitalism and National
Socialism) from the viewpoi |t of the crucial institutions of political
compromise. Here we have one of the few political-sociological
attempts from within critical theory to explain the institutional context
of the world-historical transition presupposed, for example, by
Horkheimer's "End of Reason." Kirchheimer indeed gives us
empirical documentation of the generic links between pluralist mass
democracy and the fascist state. Nevertheless, it is a special virtue of
his essay that it does not point to a simple or complete convergence of
all authoritarian states, unlike some contemporary works of critical
theory.*

Modern political theory has established a close relationship between
political compromise and government in a developed industrial society.[1] In this context, compromise means that the foremost political
decisions are reached by agreement among individuals as well as
among social groups. The following remarks will not evaluate this
definition but will try to analyze the conditions and nature of compromises as far as they influenced the European political system under
liberalism, mass democracy, and fascism. To the latter stages correspond three different types of agreement which have characterized

European constitutional history: to liberalism corresponded the complex of working agreements among parliamentary representatives and between them and the government; to mass democracy, the agreements between voluntary associations; and to fascism, the pacts by which the heads of the compulsory estates distribute power and booty.

Compromise Under the Representative System and Under Mass Democracy

In his reflections on the French Revolution, Burke, with characteristic vehemence and pointedness, depicts the shift in the location of power to the plutocratic oligarchies, a development which, according to him, had been initiated by the revolutionary policy of confiscation. The "volatilization of property," of which this representative of the English landed aristocracy accuses the revolutionary legislators, is responsible for the creation of a commonwealth founded on "gaming," in comparison with which, in Burke's opinion, the "known scandals of history amount to comparatively little."[2]

The all-embracing medium of money profoundly conditioned the political institutions of the era. Today we are accustomed to regard money more in its role as one technical means of domination among many. But this purely technical role of money is a phenomenon which did not appear until the monopolistic period. In any case the nineteenth century saw the incontestable application of the sociological thesis that the personal security derived from the possession of money was the most concrete form and expression of confidence in the public order.[3]

Possession of money was just as important for the political weight of an individual within the nation as the degree of creditworthiness is for the nation's position in the international concert. Legal equality of citizens and equality of states before international law were the juristic premise for the working of the free exchange process.[4]

An integral part of the representative system was the conception of an agent who was no longer bound by the estates but who at the same time had not yet become a spokesman tied to definite group interests. The French constitution of 1791, Sect. III, Art. 7, by denying the admissibility of binding instructions given by the electorate to the representatives, marks the final transition from the *mandat impératif* of the estates to the representative system of the nineteenth century.[5] Theories of public law have taken the opportunity to stress the element of freedom contained in the condemnation of the *mandat impératif*, this condemnation being the very basis of the representative system.[6]

In its relatively pure form, the representative system did not prevail in Europe for a particularly long period. Even at the beginning it was alloyed by elements of absolutism and by elements of the still older estate system. Its period of fruition occurred in the second and third quarter of the nineteenth century when it combined with the doctrine of public opinion. Its territorial extension was confined to those states "where there is no honest poverty, where education is diffused and political intelligence common,"[7] that is to say, to the sphere of developing capitalist economy. With the decline of the central position of money as a universal measuring rod and with the effacement of the correlative independence of representation by the monopolizing society, the remnants of the representative system were becoming rapidly submerged. This process characterized the period of mass democracy.

The political system of mass democracy had, as one of its decisive characteristics, the antagonism between public control of government and private control of central banks. The latter had most important public functions. When the central bank legislation of the nineteenth century took shape, there was no doubt as to the political significance of the administration of this type of joint-stock company, "on whose wisdom it depends whether a country shall be solvent or insolvent."[8]

Robert Peel, when he introduced the Bank Charter Act of 1844, described the sphere of influence which the domination of the credit apparatus brings with it, and his words show a tendency to reification typical of the period: "There is no contract, public or private, no engagement internal or individual which is unaffected by it [the bill]. The enterprises of commerce, the profits of trade, the arrangement made in all the domestic arrangements of society, the wages of labor, pecuniary transactions of the highest amount and of the lowest, the payment of the national debt, the provision for the national expenditure, the command which the coin of the smallest denomination has over the necessities of life are all affected by the decision to which we may come."[9] This administration of the central bank, by far the most important office in Great Britain of those "outside the gift of the Crown,"[10] is carried on by officials elected from among the ranks of the banking community. If Brooks Adams appears to have been too pointed in his opinion that the Bank Act of 1844, by yielding the control of the currency to bankers, marked a definite transfer of sovereignty to Lombard Street,[11] it is only because in the nineteenth century there was no serious conflict between Whitehall and Lombard Street. Since throughout the nineteenth century the restricted parliamentary franchise did not permit of any disharmony between the interests of the financial community and those of parliamentary government, the relation between the central bank and the government was equally unproblematic, whether the central bank had statutory independence or whether it was to some extent subject to governmental regulation. This state of affairs was only rarely interrupted; symptomatically, interruption occurred in 1870 when the defeatist interests of the upper middle class, anxious for the rapid termination of the Franco-Prussian war, found themselves faced by the credit requirements of a government presided over by Gambetta and having a policy of resistance *à l'outrance*. But even in this period the respect for the reputation of the *Banque de France*, which was supposed to represent public credit, was very high, as may be seen from the humble restraint of the Paris Commune's delegate to the bank.[12] Even the change in the governorship, effected by Gambetta when he returned to power in 1882, had no real significance.[13]

In the postwar period of mass democracy, it becomes generally recognized that the complete independence of the central bank as a transmission belt for the financial community can be profitably used to hold the government and parliament in check. One of the earliest resolutions of the Council of the League of Nations insists on the independence of central banks from governmental interference.[14] The more the respective countries were dependent on outside loans, the more stringent were the requirements for the noninterference of governments in the central banks, which in their turn were subjected to a system of mixed control exercised by private national and international financial interests. Thus the degree of independence of a small country was basically conditional upon whether it had to deal with a unified creditor pool—as Austria had to do with its creditors, pooled under the auspices of the League of Nations—or whether political competition between prospective creditor nations left the governments with a greater amount of liberty of movement in their foreign policy—as in the case of the Balkan nations. The desires and demands of the home banking community were reinforced by the backing of international banking organizations which, in the persons of financial commissioners and representatives, resided in the respective capitals themselves, and this was one of the decisive factors favoring or obstructing changes in the political balance in those countries.[15] In

Germany the Bank Law of 1924 took most of the powers which the government formerly had exercised and transferred them to the Board of Directors of the *Reichsbank*—and to a much lesser degree to the internationalized *"Generalrat"* and the stockholders.[16] In this new fortified position the presidency of the *Reichsbank* very soon became the cohesive organism about which gathered the big financial and industrial interests. It acted as a channel of communication for them and as their accredited representative in their dealings with the government. In this function, for instance, *Reichsbank* president Schacht was instrumental in barring the cities from further access to the foreign loan market in order to prevent the extension of their successful competition with the privately owned public utilities.[17]

This intervention was also felt in the case of the so-called Hilferding Loans, and it was of primary importance in the German crisis of 1929 which led to the downfall of the last parliamentary government. When MacDonald replaced the second Labour Cabinet with his National Government, it was likewise the administration of the Bank of England that was instrumental in provoking this change by asking for budget cuts known to be unacceptable to most of the labor leaders.[18] The strategic position of the Bank was enhanced by the very fact that, had its demands been refused, the necessary loans would not have been forthcoming.

In many aspects, postwar France represents a special case. In Germany or England, the strategic position of the central banks was only made use of as a last resort. In contrast to this restraint, the *Banque de France* and the parliamentary government represent the two opposite poles around which the whole social and political life of the nation revolved in the twenties. Several factors worked together to create this situation. The extraordinarily large public debt, which was carried over from the war and which was not wiped out by such a thorough inflation as in Germany, was an adverse condition to start with. It was aggravated by the inability to obtain sufficient tax revenue from the defective system of income taxes, which, in itself a symbol of middle-class selfishness, was effectively supplemented by what was probably the lowest level of tax morality known in modern history. These conditions reduced the government to a state of perpetual dependency upon the bankers, whether for bridging a temporary shortage of cash for some weeks or months, or in order to place new loans. Under these conditions the help of the *Banque de France* was indispensable either for rediscounting the treasury bonds taken over by private banking institutions, for conducting a generous nation-wide campaign in favor of new loans through its system of branches, or for procuring a foreign loan. The strategic advantage which the chronic difficulties of the government gave to the private regents of the bank, whose attitude was shared by the government-appointed governor, was invariably used whenever an undesirable government had to be outmaneuvered.

The story repeats itself over and over again in 1924, 1928, 1932, and 1936. The electorate shows tendencies to the left and puts into power some government combination shaped according to this image. But scarcely has the government begun to develop a timid program of social reform when the *crise de confiance*, with all the well-known features of the fall in the value of government bonds and the export of gold and foreign exchange, gets into full swing. The government finds it difficult to obtain even short-term credits, and with the depreciation of its long-term credit, the *deus ex machina*, the new long-term loan or, what is the desire of each successive minister of finance, the conversion of interest rates is out of the question. With a little help from the governor and regents of the bank, who chastise the wrong set and are prepared to oblige the right set of politicians, the untrustworthy government disappears, *la rente* goes up, and all reforms are forgotten.[19] In the twenties this system worked fairly smoothly—apart from the fact that in 1928 the *Banque de France* forced on its own hero, Poincaré,[20] a much too low stabilization level for the franc, and that this later proved a distinct disadvantage. In the thirties, however, this process of "correcting" the popular will ran into difficulties. The *Banque de France* then tried to force its deflationary policy *à outrancé* on successive political combinations. It succeeded only at the third attempt with the accession of Laval to the premiership. From this time on, the revision of the statute of the bank and the synchronization of its administration with the political leadership became the catchword of the formative period of the *Front Populaire*. But significantly enough, when the victorious *Front Populaire* abolished the overlordship of the *Banque de France* and tried, according to the popular slogan, to transform it into the *Banque de la France*, it did not have enough power to stop the flight of the franc. When the French republic was already drawing its last breath, the financial community reserved its *liberum veto* against the government decree-powers by prohibiting close scrutiny of the "éternels mobilisés de l'armée Condé,"[21] i.e., by refusing to put the principle of exchange control into effect. Paradoxically enough, the Enabling Act, given by Parliament to the Chautemps cabinet on June 30, 1937,[22] marks precisely the point at which the private manipulators of the financial apparatus retained their leadership while destroying the political fabric as a whole. This act enables the ministry to take all necessary measures but refuses it the most essential means for their execution. It orders the ministry "to assure the suppression of attempts to undermine public credit, to fight against speculation, to further economic recovery, price control, budget balancing, and, *without control of exchange*, to defend the gold holdings of the Bank of France." France is an extreme case. In no other country was the conflict between political democracy and private command over the sources of credit allowed to develop so far as to lead to the complete breakdown of the whole social organism.

Successive devaluation in different countries, the control of foreign commerce and exchange, and the abandonment of the cherished doctrine of budget equilibrium in favor of deficit spending have done away with the dependence of the government upon the whim of private bankers. To a certain extent the so-called investors' strike in the privately owned section of the economy—that is to say, the increasing difficulties in the profitable employment of capital—has contributed to this turn of events by establishing exceedingly low interest rates for government loans, especially in the United States. At any rate, the political importance of this change is evident. The government which has developed into the largest customer of industry, often buying more than 50 percent of the national output, is today in a strategically much more advantageous position than any other competitor for power. The possibility which always hung in suspense over the heads of previous governments in the pre-crisis period, that the financial interests might exercise their veto to throw the currency system out of gear, now seems remote and perhaps even nonexistent.[23]

But at the same time there is apparently a fairly widespread belief that the new system of government spending and the more or less complete abandonment of the doctrine "that natural forces may produce recovery" is intended to uphold the system of "production of wealth by private activity and enterprise."[24] In other words, the abandonment of the supremacy of money as an automatic regulator of social relationships is not supposed to cause a serious break in the scale of social evaluations prevalent in our society. But to what degree the desires which accompany the changes in the relationship between the government and the financial and industrial community may be fulfilled, modified, or entirely thwarted depends upon the relationship between the various social forces and the form they assume under the changed conditions. The relationship that persisted between the financial community and the government up to the last crisis may illuminate the degree to which political power was exercised in the form of indirect power. The symbols of politics appealed and appeared to us with the entire emotional apparatus which we were accustomed to find on the front page of newspapers. Yet, for the realities of political power, their evaluation and appreciation, we had to turn to the financial page. We were certain that the deterioration we could see there would rapidly spread to the front page until a change in symbols would reestablish a balance between both.

In our day, the balance is definitely shifting in favor of government, marking a world-wide tendency that has been consummated in the authoritarian countries. Fascist authors have been quick to conclude that in these countries all indirect power has been replaced by direct power. If this transition from indirect to direct power has a more than merely technical meaning, it implies that the antagonism between state and society, and with it the compromise structure of the state, has permanently disappeared in civil affairs, and that there is no longer any contradiction between the social content and the political form of a society. In reality, however, the contradictions continued to prevail unabated, and what changed was only the form and structure of the compromise. The general tendency of this change leads away from the liberalistic form of compromise, which was essentially a delimitation of spheres between the individual and the government, to a compromise among conflicting power groups. This tendency may be illustrated by the shifting emphasis in the ideology of compromise.

In the liberalistic period, it was Herbert Spencer who gave an evolutionary superstructure to the doctrine of political compromise.[25] Political compromise was the vital condition of a society which marched toward ever higher forms. John Morley's[26] distinction between legitimate and illegitimate compromise furnished the specifically liberalistic element. The legitimacy of the compromise, he wrote, consists in the right of the outvoted individual or minority to uphold and advocate publicly the principles which the majority has rejected. The essence of the compromise thus lies in the guarantee of dissent which is regarded as the guarantee of a liberal system of government. This characteristically individualistic argument, however, recedes in John Stuart Mill's famous *Considerations on Representative Government*.[27] Here, the compromise becomes a group compromise. Mill declares that the very existence of representative government requires it to maintain a balance between capital and labor and their respective satellites. His idea of compromise betrays a desire to avoid the possibility of one social group gaining predominance over the others. In general, the justification of the idea of compromise varies with the social and political affiliations of its advocates. One of the last forms of the doctrine is to be found in the Austro-Marxian theory of the provisional equilibrium between the social classes.[28]

What was the reality which corresponded to the changing ideology of compromise? In a strictly technical sense the sphere of compromise expanded with the transition from competitive to monopoly capitalism. The growth of huge social units which accompanied the modern industrial process had a dual impact upon organizational developments. While destroying the older personalized form of association, it prepared the way for an intricate framework of working agreements among the monopolies which emerged victorious from the liberal era. The day-to-day compromise which the politically independent representative in liberalistic society concluded with the government and with his colleagues has given way to the compromise between large social and political organizations in the "pluralistic" state. What seems most interesting from a constitutional point of view is the transformation of the liberal rights of the individual—John Morley's guaranteed right of the individual to dissent as premise of the working of the compromise itself—into a set of guarantees for the existence of the accredited social groups, the partners in compromise. This process of absorption of individual rights by monopolistic groups, although noticeable throughout the whole world, was especially apparent under the Weimar Constitution, where the mixture of traditional liberties and status quo guarantees under the misleading title of fundamental rights offered an excellent legal starting point for such developments.[29] Property rights became a protective screen for the process of monopolization, freedom of religion was used to strengthen the existing religious corporation, and freedom of speech and association had to be supplemented by strong protecting organizations in order to obtain recognition. It was the social group, as far as it was recognized by other groups, that got protection, not the individual. A member of a group found the authorities willing to protect him as against his group only in extreme cases or if the degree of social legitimacy of the group was rather problematic. And if one of the traditional rights of the individual was challenged, it could prevail only in the form of a group guarantee.[30] The individual was thus forced into the group, and this fact, in turn, consolidated the status of the group. The functioning of political compromise became increasingly dependent upon the workability of pacts among the predominant associations of capital and labor as well as among the organizations within each of these categories.

Compromise Under National Socialism

With the disappearance of the old compromise structure and its accompanying internal checks in Europe, a new type of government is emerging of which, at first glance, greater independence and power seem the outstanding characteristics. The new type is found in various more or less transitional forms. The automatic integration of the political structure by money in the nineteenth century and the systematic use of the credit apparatus to this end in the period of mass democracy has given way to forms of domination by institutionalized monopolies. These changes have occurred in their most pointed form in Germany.

The German economic system consists of various monopolies in which the competitive elements have only an "oasis" character.[31] The monopolies are of three kinds: the government's labor monopoly, the private monopolies in industry, and the Food Estate. The character of these monopolies must be defined in terms of their relationship to the public authorities and in terms of their inner structure. Whereas the monopoly for industrial and agricultural labor is a public monopoly under joint state and party control, allowing few opportunities for self-expression to individuals, the industrial monopolies and those in the Food Estate are administered by private interests which have been given a public character.[32] As such they form the backbone of a new system of guarantees which has taken over the role of the checks and balances inherent in the social structure under the older compromise system.

The first of these guarantees applies to the privileged groups in general. The abolition of institutional fluctuations produced by the democratic process of elections and the replacement of this process by a "strong government" has dispensed with the need to rely on the pressure potentialities of credit control. Greater security is calculated not only to outweigh the restrictions in the possible choice of investments, especially the inability to diminish risks by investing abroad, but also to counterbalance the diminished degree of personal freedom. There is an increased economic security for the propertied and professional classes as a whole to replace the smaller degree of individual liberty and the arbitrariness which the individual finds in the totalitarian state. For various reasons the democratic government of the Weimar Republic distributed unsystematic favors and, although not having promised to do so, was forced to take over the bulk of losses in the realm of banking and heavy industry. The economic policies of the fascist government, however, have not only reduced these risks almost to nil, but have enabled big industry to make investments which are required by conditions of modern technology, but to which, because of the risks involved, it was formerly unable or unwilling to commit itself. A further guarantee lies in the active encouragement of the process of monopolization and cartelization and the transformation of a private power position that was only tolerated by law into a monopoly that remains private, yet is vested with public power.

This monopolization takes two forms: first, cartelization is extended through the establishment of a complete network of market regulating bodies in every sphere, and second, the number of independent units in a given field is progressively reduced. Both processes are intimately interrelated. The cartel policy of National Socialism shows three stages of development. At the beginning, in 1933, we find a policy of active help granted to private market organizations in two ways, first, by considerably restricting the jurisdiction of the Cartel Tribunal, and second, by making cartelization compulsory and compelling outsiders to attach themselves to existing cartels. Even at this stage we can see a process which is significant for the new relationship between industry and the public authorities. Every increase in organizational power granted to the private industrial and trade associations is accompanied by an increase in the supervisory power of the corresponding government agencies. Whereas "state sovereignty" is used to "give the cartel power it could not obtain on a voluntary basis,"[33] the government builds up its own apparatus which acts as an organ to harmonize the group interests of business with the interests of other recognized social groups. The second stage occurs when the official organization of industrial self-administration, which has replaced the earlier *Reichsverband der deutschen Industrie* and its branches, emerges as an active agent in the process of cartelization. In theory, the system of industrial groups and chambers now formed is specifically excluded from any tasks pertaining to market regulation, although its jurisdiction embraces almost all other fields of industrial policy and organization. But in practice it is inevitable that the cartels, the supervision of which is one of the main tasks of this new organization, soon begin to dominate these official organizations. In the years 1936 and 1937, when attacks were being launched against the price level produced by this thoroughgoing cartelization, and when the office of the Price Commissioner was created, there was a kind of sham battle against this growing identity between the official groups and the private organizations which regulated the market. But in this battle no use was ever made of the coercive machinery of the government, and the Reich Ministry of Economic Affairs contented itself with issuing orders asking for reports and justifications of this identity of personnel and with promulgating general lines of direction.[34] Even this sham battle soon subsided, and in 1939 we reach the third stage in which the cartels, in their role as executive organs of the Reich Boards, are officially recognized as "all-embracing organs of market regulation."[35] As mandatories of the Reich Boards, which, in their turn, are independent legal personalities though subordinate to the Ministry of Economic Affairs, they now to an increasing degree regulate the distribution of both raw material and finished products.[36] Thus the process of cartelization has reached its logical conclusion in the final merger of private power and public organization.[37]

The process of concentration which accompanied thoroughgoing cartelization was accelerated for many reasons. The necessity for maximizing the speed of all deliveries pertaining to armaments required the use of labor-saving devices which, in their turn, depended on substantial investments—a need which became more and more evident with the increasing scarcity of labor. The shortage of raw materials worked against the small firms which had few import and bureaucratic connections of their own, and the expropriation of the Jews led in the same direction. In commerce, and especially in retail trade and handicraft, firms with the largest turnover increased their competitive advantages as they were able to obtain a greater supply of goods for distribution. They were also able better to withstand the reduction of the profit margin, necessitated by the rather rigid control of prices for consumers' goods.

The economic pressure leading to concentration is accompanied by direct legal pressure. This has been used most vigorously against the owners of small shops and workshops. Pressure by powerful competitors who want to increase their sales in order to balance other unfavorable developments in cost factors has been aided and abetted by the government's desire to force marginal shop-owners into the factories. At first there was a process of indirect strangulation by governmentally approved exclusion from discounts, if the small shops did not reach a certain sales figure, and pressure was exercised in the same direction through a closer supervision of smaller plants by the social honor courts. This was soon followed by legislation aimed at a wholesale combing-out.[38] The slow disappearance of the small businessman is speeding up; shops are closed if they are deemed unnecessary for the national economy, the debts, as far as is thought advisable, are paid by official organizations, and the former shop-keepers and businessmen are sent off to the factory.

For industry as such, the direct legal measures furthering concentration are of a double nature. In the first place, the process of compulsory standardization of types carried on from 1938 deprives many producers of their independent status and thrusts them down to the level of specialized departments of larger units by restricting them to the production of parts of the finished product. This was especially the case in the automobile industry. The war has given new force to this development by causing the compulsory closure of the technologically more backward factories. Some of the owners of these have been entirely removed from the field and have become mere rentiers; others have been temporarily degraded to the level of wholesalers in their respective fields, receiving a special "colleague discount" which had to be given to them by the more fortunate members of the industry.[39] Whatever the manifold individual variations in the various industries, it is clear that, in spite of a somewhat contradictory ideology, the mergers that have thus been brought about tend to become permanent and tend permanently to eliminate the units which were closed provisionally.[40]

The stronger the organizations, the greater the degree of liberty they have in administering the regulations that apply to their members. At the bottom, in handicraft, where the head of the organization lives more from his proved devotion to the National Socialist cause than because of the weight of his economically and financially weak organization, the administration's direct interference is comprehensive. The head of the organization simply acts as an executive organ of the state bureaucracy in combing out the weaker members.[41] In the sphere of large-scale business the transformation of positions of private power into public organs of economic "self-administration," though accompanied by the transfer of legal omnipotence to the supervisory ministries and special boards, has increased rather than decreased the power of those who dominate the organizations. Behind the legal screen of the leader principle which requires that the group leaders be appointed by the public authorities, the absolutistic principles governing monopolized business groups continue unabated, especially since the complete demise of the stockholders as a supervisory organ. Even the legal prescriptions have to take this reality into account, and the group leader is required to submit to annual votes of

confidence by his advisory boards. A negative vote would not legally
be followed by his dismissal but, as the official commentator says,
would only necessitate inquiries by higher bodies.[42] But, of course, the
social function of this vote of confidence cannot be obscured by
placing it in the context of the new constitutional phraseology. It
expresses the state of affairs which prevails throughout the organizational setup of German industry. The advisory board is constituted as
an oligarchical body dominating through the same persons both private cartels and official trade organizations. Under the officially
sanctioned leadership of one of the industrial lords, who is *primus
inter pares* so far as the monopolists are concerned and who is leader
so far as the plebeian rest is concerned, the professional bureaucratic
personnel administers the law for the whole group. Consequently, this
personnel has the task of adjusting the various interests within the
group, either as the agency of last resort, or, as is increasingly the
case, as a kind of preliminary sifting organ whose reports provide the
raw material for the official decisions of the Reich Ministry of
Economic Affairs. It represents, so to speak, the group interest as
against the interest of the individual concern. Although this function
served to strengthen the independence of the group bureaucracy as
against individual concerns, this process did not go very far. The
constitutional framework governing the organization of the group
makes the group administration partial to the big interests within its
jurisdiction no less than did its forerunner under the Weimar Republic.
Every big concern has its own specialists who zealously and compe-
tently watch the work of the representative of the group. Significantly
enough, the democratic element, a remnant of earlier estate ideas,[43]
which would have required a vote of confidence from all members,
not only from the advisory board, was already removed from the
statute book by executive order in 1935,[44] and the relations between
leadership and small and medium-sized producer have been adapted to
the German reality. The status of the smaller producers has been
changed from that of active participants into that of objects of propaganda. The war has not altered any part of this organizational structure. On the contrary, the building up of District Economic Boards has
only established these characteristics the more firmly. At the same
time, when the provincial and regional state bureaucracy was given
supervisory power over the distribution of consumers' goods for the
whole population, the presidents of the regional organizations of trade
and industry, of the Chambers of Industry and Commerce, saw themselves raised to the rank of Reich commissioners with the duty of

seeing to it that the tasks of production were carried through.[45] And when the most recent legislation tried to reduce war profits, it likewise to a large extent placed the power to determine what is to be considered appropriate profit in the hands of the groups whose members were the very ones to make the profit.

To a large measure the governing ranks of the Chambers of Industry and of the Economic Groups are the ones that, either directly or by the weight of the advice which their experts set before the state bureaucracy, decide on the chances of making profits from any given means of production. This method of determining the use to which a given means of production will be put has become the rule rather than the exception. Many owners have been totally or partially deprived of the possibility of making use of their machinery. The measures by which these expropriations have been carried through have a dual aspect. In most of the cases covered by the government's authority, quota restrictions and other measures have been actually carried through by the career group officials who have been vested with public authority, the profit of such operations accruing to certain members of the group. In the case of Jewish expropriation the question of indemnity for the damaged person does not arise.[46] In the other cases interference with private property invariably raises the question of indemnity. Under the Weimar Republic the courts that had jurisdiction over expropriation claims gave a very extensive interpretation to the concept of expropriation by public authorities. It was to be expected under fascism that such an interpretation, as well as the insistence on full compensation, would be upheld by the courts in all cases where the physical property was left intact but where its profitable use was excluded in consequence of a governmental authorization or decree. The government therefore decided to throw the traditional procedures overboard. The differences arising from the transformation of the apparatus of production were to be treated as a pure intragroup concern and there was to be no appeal to an outside authority.

So we can see that the tendency already mentioned as characteristic of mass democracy, the absorption of individual rights in group rights, reaches its extreme form. This tendency was already visible in the cartel legislation of 1933, which prevented the Cartel Tribunal from interfering in disputes arising between members and the cartel. The principle of refusing to grant access to regular courts was also soon employed in numerous decrees, especially in those concerning the Food Estate (agriculture). These ruled that the parties have to content themselves with the decision of an intragroup arbitration court or, as far as questions of quotas are concerned, with committees of complaint provided for by their respective organizations.[47] The same state of affairs has prevailed in regard to the compensation granted in the case of compulsory shutdown of plants for the duration of the war. Here, too, the economic groups have sole jurisdiction in deciding whether and what indemnity should be given, and appeal is possible only to the Reich Economic Chamber, the coordinating body of these organizations. The remarkable feature of this legislation is, first, the abandonment of the principle, accepted throughout the liberal era and still acknowledged by the regular courts in Germany, that the individual should not suffer any loss through the acts of expropriation, that he should receive either a full or at least an ''appropriate'' indemnity.[48] If an indemnity is granted, it is granted by equity and not by law, and to say, as does the official language, that the ''vital necessities of the whole region have to be considered before the interests of the individual'' is only another way of justifying the redistribution of property.[49] But even more important than the degree of indemnification granted on account of the loss of professional and economic status is the fact that these rules deny access to the courts and, by so doing, close the iron ring which the new economic constitution of the monopolistic society places around the less favored members of a business or trade group. They are prevented from combining with other social groups or airing before a public forum their grievances against the monopolist dominating the group. The increasing factual subservience to the command of a monopoly-dominated group has now become a legalized subservience.

Industry and agriculture are not the only realms in which the dominant forces of the group have seized the right of decision in intragroup controversies—even where these controversies only thinly veil the life struggle of marginal firms against monopolies. The same process is to be found elsewhere in the German political structure. One might almost determine the status of the different groups in Germany by the degree to which they have attained the *privilegium de non appellando*, to adopt a well-known concept from German constitutional history. That is to say, one might determine their status by the extent to which they have succeeded in depriving the individual member of the group of the possibility of appealing to external bodies against group decisions. This *privilegium de non appellando* exists in its most concentrated form in the army. The army command is made absolute master over every individual in its service by virtue of denying any separation between the personal and the professional status of its members. Business does not need to strive for such a position; it is satisfied to control the social and economic functions of its members. As regards members of the state bureaucracy and of the party and its affiliated organizations, we have to differentiate between the direction of public affairs and the task of controlling the population. In so far as this first function is concerned, no judicial interference is allowed. The ever expanding lists of activities which, by legislative order, are excluded from any judicial examination make the discussion of whether the judiciary may itself decide which acts are to be included in the category of political acts, and therefore to be exempted from examination, a mere theoretical squabble.[50] The judiciary has thus been degraded from the rank of an arbiter of intergroup conflicts to that of an "assistant"[51] of the administration. The judiciary competes with the various administrative services[52] as an organ to enforce discipline in the lower ranks of the bureaucracy, in the party, and among the population at large. The "taylorized" methods adopted especially in the administration of criminal law largely through granting the public prosecutor a dominant position over the procedure, and allowing a quick and "satisfying" disposal of a maximum of cases unhampered by procedural quirks,[53] have torn away the sanctity of the judiciary[54] and have deprived the government of the moral and propagandistic value inherent in the services of the judiciary. It becomes less important as a problem whether the regular judiciary or a service bureaucracy is chosen to carry out these functions, and the field is left open for minor rivalries. However, even here the observed tendency to acquire as far as possible the *privilegium de non appellando* is always noticeable throughout the administrative services of party and state bureaucracy.

Within the constitutional framework of the Weimar Republic, it became the function of the bureaucracy continually to keep under scrutiny the relationship between big business and labor, but also to preserve the status quo of agriculture and small-scale business. The cohesive element which united the bureaucracy was the preservation of its social status against encroachments from the outside and, whenever feasible, the desire to extend its activities. The ideological emphasis on its impartial service to the nation as a whole hid the fact that, as far as the object of its policies was concerned, the unity was more apparent than real. The controversies between the social groups reappeared in somewhat mitigated form, free of propagandistic tinge, in the relationship between the various divisions of the public services. When we try to assess the impact of the changes in the political

power structure on the bureaucracy and on its relationship to the
National Socialist party, we realize that the unity of the bureaucracy
was shaken still more. In part it lost its identity through its steady
permeation by, and association with, the party machine, and in part its
general negative attitude to outside control lost its *raison d'être* in the
new and much less controlled setup.[55] Thus we are confronted with the
strange picture of an intense centralization within each administrative
unit going hand in hand with certain tendencies to departmentaliza-
tion. Each of the highest subleaders jealously guards against a loss of
status by being subjected to anybody's command but the Führer's. As
in older systems, what counts is the individual's proximity to the
supposed fountain of the charisma itself, not the fact of belonging to
the rational council of government. In consequence, "the position of
Ministers of the Reich has undergone a fundamental change. They do
not form a collegium, an organizational unit."[56] The number of
administrative organizations under the direct command of the Führer
and exempt from any other supervision is steadily increasing. And the
interpenetration of party and bureaucracy leads to jurisdictional regulations compared with which the most difficult intricacies of federal
problematics are relatively easy to follow. Thus, for example, we
have such a figure as the Reichsführer SS who, as head of the police, is
administratively incorporated in the Reich Ministry of the Interior
without, however, being subject in his decisions to the approval of the
Reich Minister.[57]

The official constitutional theory likes to regard the relationship
between state and party as one between a technical apparatus and a
political movement, the former following the directions of the latter,
which is supposed to be the immediate expression of national life and
will. The official ideology, therefore, sees the party as an indissoluble
unit. In reality the structure of the National Socialist party and its place
in the political power structure of modern Germany can only be
understood in terms of its dual function. First, the National Socialist
party arose as a mass party and as such is the heir to the other mass
parties which existed during the era of mass democracy. Second, the
party and the state bureaucracy together constitute an organ of mass
domination. It is a competitor of, and later an heir to, the left-wing
mass parties. It not only tries to cater to the economic desires of its
followers but also incorporates in its structure some vision of a new
political order. The fact that its following is a heterogeneous one
makes necessary a constant shift in the ideology, a greater emphasis

on the purely political elements of the new order as against the economic basis, and heavier emphasis on propaganda—lest its following dissolve into its separate social components. When the trade unions and left-wing political parties were destroyed, the new mass organizations of the National Socialist party took over at least some of the social functions of the defunct groups. The numerous individuals who, both before 1933 and to a certain extent afterwards, transferred their loyalty to the National Socialist organization helped to establish this continuity.[58] In the conditions of party pluralism under the Weimar Republic, in order to balance the heterogeneity of its membership, the National Socialist party had not only to adopt a special vehemence in the competition for political power but also to establish the principle of an unquestionable faith in its leadership. Having achieved predominance in the state, but being without a clearly defined social program, the party followed the line of least resistance. It confirmed the titles of business and the army but at the same time hastened to build up a competitive apparatus of its own, gradually reinforcing it with the services of the technically efficient state bureaucracy.

This process changed the structure of the party itself and brought the party's ever present bureaucratic element sharply to the fore. The party proved no support for the independent middle classes in their struggle for survival but, instead, actually hastened their final decline more than any other single factor in modern German history. On the other hand, the capture of the state machinery by the party, the vast extension of this machinery, and its duplication in many cases by a corresponding party bureaucracy, though depriving many of the middle-class elements of their position in the process of production, gave them in compensation economic security and social standing.[59] The fact that, although many of the new functionaries have come from the independent middle classes, this same middle class was crushed as never before with the active help of the new bureaucracy shows how far and fast this new social group has already traveled in its alienation from its earlier basis. Besides demonstrating that the new group was becoming separated from its earlier social interests, this also testifies to its adaptation to the various (often far-flung) new tasks with which it has been entrusted, jointly with, or in addition to, the state bureaucracy. Whereas the party official rises to a position of equality with the government official and even in some cases succeeds in entering the ranks of the business group, the lower party member only holds honorary and onerous office and becomes almost indistinguishable from the ordinary nonparty citizen as a zealously watched object rather than a subject of political power.

The new legislation concerning administrative leadership in the *Landkreise*,[60] which has been given much attention in Germany,[61] must be understood as a rearguard action which, for propagandistic aims, attempts to revive the theoretical conception of the unified party as an independent entity in its relationship to the state bureaucracy. It starts from the principle that leadership over persons (*Menschen-führung*) is exclusively the task of the party. The competent party official is responsible to his party superior for the conduct and attitude of the population. The township president or the mayor, however, is responsible for the orderly execution of all administrative tasks in the framework of legal jurisdiction. Both organs are forbidden to meddle in each other's business. The psychological usefulness of such a regulation is undeniable. It protects the party official against requests from the rank and file of the membership by emphasizing a separation which for all practical purposes does not exist, and after laying down these principles the statute itself has thus to define the different degrees of cooperation between both hierarchies. Though the relation between party and bureaucracy may give rise to ostentatious jurisdictional disputes, it is not in these that we find the deeper-lying conflicts, but within the structure of the party itself. So long as the party has not exclusively become a huge apparatus for mass domination, so long as the desires, fears, and wishes of the atomized masses still filter through the numerous channels of party organizations, like the Labor Front and the National Socialist Welfare Agency, which exercise *Betreuungsfunktionen*, duties of a "guardian of the masses," there are still some deteriorated remnants of the earlier form, the mass party. Even in their bureaucratic form, those elements of the party which are entrusted with the care of the masses represent, in some degree, the unrepresented sections of the community who have no independent voice in the balance of power.

By carefully restricting itself exclusively to the military sphere, the army, from the very beginning, was able to uphold the independence it had reestablished under the Weimar Democracy. Business, trade, and the independent ranks of agriculture became a closed monopoly. Government and party not only accepted its inner power distribution as they found it but actively helped to drive it still more pointedly in the direction of an oligarchic combine. The relationship of these groups to the army and the party hierarchy is in flux; especially the respective weight of the party bureaucracy and the army is subject to sudden shifts, owing to the impact of the war changes, the transitional or permanent character of which is not yet discernible. But one permanent pattern stands out. While sections of the new party and state bureaucracy act as transmission belts for those groups sufficiently vocal in their own right, other parts of the state and party bureaucracy which exercise the *Betreuungsfunktion* represent the unrepresented.[62] The compromise between the more articulate groups and these "guardians of the masses" more often than not resembles the arbitration award of Marshal Balbo who, while permitting a salary reduction asked for by the employers, awarded to the workers of Ferrara the *epitheton ornans* "valiant."[63] One of the chief compromises, if not *the* chief compromise, they concluded in the name of the unrepresented, the "Leipzig Agreement of 1935," was as farcical as the Balbo award. By this agreement the "Self-Administration of German Economy" became formally affiliated with the Labor Front. No practical consequences, however, were ever drawn from this "liaison."[64] But there is compromise, nevertheless, as in every other society which has a high degree of social stratification.

In the compromise structure of National Socialism as it arose after the disappearance of all independent representation of the masses, the old question is brought to the fore: how can the interest of the various partners to the compromise, the monopolies, army, industry, and agriculture as well as the diversified layers of party bureaucracy, be brought to a common denominator? It is apparent that the Führer, or, as we should more appropriately say, the group of persons identified with the Führer, has established an authority which acts as an ultimate arbiter in all cases where the respective monopoly groups are not able to reach a decision by themselves. The leadership is able to decide intergroup differences with relative ease, and these decisions are carried through with a minimum of resistance only because the unfolding program of expansion has given the various groups the possibility of extending their activities (though on a different plane) and of satisfying their desires without too much need of getting in each other's way.[65] The ultimate decision of the Führer group is therefore the more easily accepted the more it takes the form and function of a permanent guarantee of the imperialist order.[66] It is this interdependence between the unquestionable authority of the ruling group and the program of expansion which offers the characteristic phenomenon of the compromise structure of the fascist order, directs its further course, and decides upon its ultimate fate.

To summarize our remarks, we can describe the changes in political compromise as follows. During the liberal period of modern society, political compromise operated among parliamentarians and between them and the government. Every representative acted on his own, promoting certain financial, business, and agricultural interests and changing allegiance from one to another of them according to his own interests and judgment. Thus, through individual agreements the functioning of parliament was constantly kept in harmony with the prevailing economic structure. With the beginnings of "mass democracy" (about 1910-11), the task of keeping political compromise in harmony with the economic structure devolved to a considerable extent upon the central banks. At the same time, the agreements tended to evolve from individual ones into voluntary compacts between the main groups of capital and labor and their subdivisions.

Fascism characterizes the stage at which the individual has completely lost his independence and the ruling groups have become recognized by the state as the sole legal parties to political compromise. Since money, a rather adequate expression of social power during the liberal period, ceased to mediate between economic and political life, another coordinator of public life was sorely needed. There remained only the institution of leadership to arbitrate between the groups. Its power rests on its ability to compensate every group sacrifice with advantages which, however, can ultimately be got only in the international field, that is to say, through imperialist policy.

State Capitalism:
Its Possibilities and Limitations

By Friedrich Pollock

In this essay, first published in Studies in Philosophy and Social Sciences *Vol. IX (1941), Pollock presents us with a carefully worked out economic model of "state capitalism" as a postcapitalist social formation. The essay derives its crucial insights from several contexts: Pollock's own study of Soviet planning, Keynesian theory and the debate about socialist planning in the 1930s. The claim of the end of the "primacy of the economic" and the rejection of political economy as the main context of critical theory are his most dramatic conclusions. Nevertheless, the reader should notice that Pollock is not postulating a stable and impenetrable society in the manner of the later "totalitarianism thesis." Instead, he searches, with some limited success, for the possibility of a political crisis theory.*

Nothing essentially new is intended in this article. Every thought formulated here has found its expression elsewhere. Our aim is to bring widely scattered and often conflicting ideas into a somewhat consistent summary which may form the starting point for a discussion of the workability of state capitalism.

In regard to the method of this study, the following points ought to be emphasized. Whether such a thing as state capitalism exists or can exist is open to serious doubt. It refers here to a model[1] that can be constructed from elements long visible in Europe and, to a certain degree, even in America. Social and economic developments in

Europe since the end of the first world war are interpreted as transitional processes transforming private capitalism into state capitalism. The closest approach to the totalitarian form of the latter has been made in National Socialist Germany. Theoretically the totalitarian form of state capitalism is not the only possible result of the present process of transformation. It is easier, however, to construct a model for it than for the democratic form of state capitalism to which our experience gives us few clues. One of our basic assumptions is that 19th century free trade and free enterprise are on the way out. Their restoration is doomed for similar reasons as was the attempt to restore feudalism in post-Napoleonic France. The totalitarian form of state capitalism is a deadly menace to all values of western civilization. Those who want to maintain these values must fully understand the possibilities and limitations of the aggressor if their resistance is to meet with success. Furthermore, they must be able to show in what way the democratic values can be maintained under the changing conditions. If our assumption of the approaching end of the era of private capitalism is correct, the most gallant fight to restore it can only lead to a waste of energy and eventually serve as a trail-blazer for totalitarianism.

The Concept "State Capitalism"

In the rapidly growing literature on the coming social order, the word "state capitalism" is eschewed by most authors and other words stand in its place. "State organized private-property monopoly capitalism," "managerial society," "administrative capitalism," "bureaucratic collectivism," "totalitarian state economy," "status capitalism," "neo-mercantilism," "economy of force," "state socialism" are a very incomplete set of labels used to identify the same phenomenon. The word state capitalism (so runs the argument) is possibly misleading insofar as it could be understood to denote a society wherein the state is the sole owner of all capital, and this is not necessarily meant by those who use it. Nevertheless, it indicates four items better than do all other suggested terms: that state capitalism is the successor of private capitalism, that the state assumes important functions of the private capitalist, that profit interests still play a significant role, and that it is not socialism. We define "state capitalism" in its two most typical varieties, its totalitarian and its democratic form, as a social order differing on the following points from "private capitalism" from which it stems historically:

(1) The market is deposed from its controlling function to coordi-

nate production and distribution. This function has been taken over by a system of direct controls. Freedom of trade, enterprise and labor are subject to governmental interference of such a degree that they are practically abolished. With the autonomous market the so-called economic laws disappear.

(2) These controls are vested in the state which uses a combination of old and new devices, including a "pseudo-market," for regulating and expanding production and coordinating it with consumption. Full employment of all resources[2] is claimed as the main achievement in the economic field. The state transgresses all the limits drawn for peacetime state activities.

(3) Under a totalitarian form of state capitalism, the state is the power instrument of a new ruling group, which has resulted from the merger of the most powerful vested interests, the top-ranking personnel in industrial and business management, the higher strata of the state bureaucracy (including the military) and the leading figures of the victorious party's bureaucracy. Everybody who does not belong to this group is a mere object of domination.

Under a democratic form of state capitalism, the state has the same controlling functions but is itself controlled by the people. It is based on institutions which prevent the bureaucracy from transforming its administrative position into an instrument of power and thus laying the basis for transshaping the democratic system into a totalitarian one.

The Heritage of the Market System

We start from the assumption that the hour of state capitalism approaches when the market economy becomes an utterly inadequate instrument for utilizing the available resources. The medium-sized private enterprise and free trade, the basis for the gigantic development of men's productive forces in the 19th century, are being gradually destroyed by the offspring of liberalism, private monopolies and government interference. Concentration of economic activity in giant enterprises, with its consequences of rigid prices, self-financing and ever growing concentration, government control of the credit system and foreign trade, quasi-monopoly positions of trade unions with the ensuing rigidity of the labor market, large-scale unemployment of labor and capital and enormous government expenses to care for the unemployed, are as many symptoms for the decline of the market system. They became characteristic in various degrees for all industrialized countries after the first world war.[3]

The materials collected recently by various government agencies demonstrate how far a similar development has gone in the United States. The disturbances of the market mechanism caused by monopoly have been accentuated by a technical revolution in contemporary farming. A shattering dislocation of the world market since the First World War has blocked the channels of export which were instrumental in overcoming market difficulties during the 19th century. The danger involved in this situation has been recognized and great efforts are being made to solve the problem of creating full employment while freeing the American market system from the forces which strangle it. Analogous developments may reach a point where no measures short of a reorganization of the economic system can prevent the complete disintegration of the social structure. Such a reorganization might take place by a long succession of stop-gap measures, many of them contradicting each other, without a preconceived plan, and often very much against the original intentions of their authors. Theoretically it is possible to construct an integrated model of the new organization which might replace the outworn system, with a promise of achieving two goals: to guarantee full employment and to maintain the basic elements of the old social structure.

If the market system is to be replaced by another organizational form, the new system must perform certain functions which are necessarily connected with the division of labor. In broadest terms, these "necessary"[4] functions fall into three groups: coordination of needs and resources; direction of production; and distribution; implying

(1) a way of defining the needs of society in terms of consumers goods, reproduction of plant, machinery and raw materials, and expansion,[5]

(2) allocation of all available resources in such a manner that full employment and "utmost" satisfaction of the recognized needs are attained,

(3) coordination and control of all productive processes in order to obtain best performance, and

(4) distribution of the social product.

The basic weaknesses of the market system in performing the "necessary" functions have been discussed again and again as its waste and inefficiency increasingly overbalanced its earlier achievements. Criticism was voiced mainly against the shortcomings of the price mechanism in directing production, the contradictory performance of the profit motive which obstructs the use of the available resources, and the murderous mechanics of coordinating the dis-equilibrated economy, that is, the business cycles with their cumulative processes of destruction. But while before the First World War the market mechanism was still workable, even if it was always far from performing in practice what it was supposed to do theoretically, the intrusion of monopolies with their rigid prices gradually caused the breakdown of the market system in an ever growing sphere.

A New Set of Rules

State capitalism replaces the methods of the market by a new set of rules based upon a combination of old and new means.

(1) A general plan gives the direction for production, consumption, saving and investment. The introduction of the principle of planning into the economic process means that a plan is to be constructed for achieving on a national scale certain chosen ends with all available resources. It does not necessarily imply that all details are planned in advance or that no freedom of choice at all is given to the consumer. But it contrasts sharply to the market system inasmuch as the final word on what needs shall be satisfied, and how, is not left to the anonymous and unreliable poll of the market, carried through *post festum*, but to a conscious decision on ends and means at least in a broad outline and before production starts. The discussion on planning has come to a point where it seems as if the arguments raised against the technical workability of such a general plan can be refuted.[6] The genuine problem of a planned society does not lie in the economic but in the political sphere, in the principles to be applied in deciding what needs shall have preference, how much time shall be spent for work, how much of the social product shall be consumed and how much used for expansion, etc. Obviously, such decisions cannot be completely arbitrary but are to a wide degree dependent upon the available resources.

(2) Prices are no longer allowed to behave as masters of the economic process but are administered in all important sections of it. This follows from the principle of planning and means that in favor of a planned economy the market is deprived of its main function. It does not mean that prices cannot exist any longer, but that if they do they have thoroughly changed their character. Nothing may seem on the surface to have changed, prices are quoted and goods and services paid for in money; the rise and fall of single prices may be quite common. But the relations between prices and cost of production on the one side and demand and supply on the other, while strictly

interconnected in their totality, become disconnected in those cases
where they tend to interfere with the general plan. What remains of the
market system behaves like its predecessor but its function has
changed from a general manager of the economic process into a
closely controlled tool.[7] In the last decades administered prices have
contributed much toward destroying the market automatism without
creating new devices for taking over its "necessary" functions. They
served to secure monopoly profits at the expense of the non-monopolistic market prices. Under state capitalism they are used as a supplementary device for incorporating production and consumption into
the general plan.

(3) The profit interests of both individuals and groups as well as
all other special interests are to be strictly subordinated to the general
plan or whatever stands in its place. To understand the consequences
of this principle leads far towards understanding totalitarian striking
power. There are two conflicting interpretations of the role of profit
interests in Nazi Germany. The one claims that the profit motive still
plays the same role as before; the other states that the capitalists have
been deprived of their social position and that profit in the old meaning
does not exist any longer. We think that both tend to overlook the
transformation of such a category as "profit" in modern society.
Profit interests may still be very significant in the totalitarian forms of
state capitalistic society. But even the most powerful profit interests
gradually become subordinate to the general "plan." No state capitalistic government can or will dispense with the profit motive, for two
reasons. First, elimination of the profit motive would destroy the
character of the entire system, and second, in many respects the profit
motive remains as an efficient incentive. In every case, however,
where the interest of single groups or individuals conflicts with the
general plan or whatever serves as its substitute, the individual interest
must give way. This is the real meaning of the ideology *Gemeinnutz
geht vor Eigennutz*. The interest of the ruling group as a whole is
decisive, not the individual interests of those who form the group.[8]
The significance of this state capitalist principle can be fully grasped
when it is contrasted with recent experiences in countries where
private capitalism still prevails and where strong group interests
prevent the execution of many urgent tasks necessary for the "common good". This needs no bad will or exceptional greed to explain it.
In a system based upon the self-interest of every person, this principle
can sometimes be expected to come to the fore in a form that contradicts the optimism of its underlying philosophy. If ever the state-

ment was true that "private vices are public benefits," it could only have been under conditions where the typical economic unit was comparatively small and a free market functioned.

State capitalist policy, which opposes liberalism, has understood that there are narrow limits beyond which the pursuit of private interests cannot be reconciled with efficient general planning, and it has drawn the consequences.[9]

(4) In all spheres of state activity (and under state capitalism that means in all spheres of social life as a whole) guesswork and improvisation give place to the principles of scientific management. This rule is in conformity with state capitalism's basic conception of society as an integrated unit comparable to one of the modern giants in steel, chemical or motorcar production. Large-scale production requires not only careful general planning but systematic elaboration of all single processes. Every waste or error in preparing materials and machinery and in drafting the elements of production is multiplied numerous times and may even endanger the productive process as a whole. The same holds true for society as soon as the previous differentiation between private cost (e.g., wages) and social cost (e.g., unemployment) is replaced by a measurement of the single process in terms of its ability to obtain what the planner considers the most desirable social product. But once this principle of "rationalization" has become mandatory for all public activities, it will be applied in spheres which previously were the sanctuary of guesswork, routine and muddling through: military preparedness, the conduct of war, behavior towards public opinion, application of the coercive power of the state, foreign trade and foreign policy, etc.[10]

(5) Performance of the plan enforced by state power so that nothing essential is left to the functioning of laws of the market or other economic "laws."[11] This may be interpreted as a supplementary rule which states the principle of treating all economic problems as in the last analysis political ones. Creation of an economic sphere into which the state should not intrude, essential for the era of private capitalism, is radically repudiated. Replacement of the mechanics of *laissez faire* by governmental command does not imply the end of private initiative and personal responsibility, which might even be put on a broader basis but will be integrated within the framework of the general plan. During the non-monopolistic phase of private capitalism, the capitalist (whether an individual or a group of shareholders represented by its manager) had power over his property within the limits of the market laws. Under state capitalism, this power has been

transferred to the government which is still limited by certain "natural" restrictions but free from the tyranny of an uncontrolled market. The replacement of the economic means by political means as the last guarantee for the reproduction of economic life, changes the character of the whole historic period. It signifies the transition from a predominantly economic to an essentially political era.[12]

Under private capitalism, all social relations are mediated by the market; men meet each other as agents of the exchange process, as buyers or sellers. The source of one's income, the size of one's property are decisive for one's social position. The profit motive keeps the economic mechanism of society moving. Under state capitalism men meet each other as commander or commanded; the extent to which one can command or has to obey depends in the first place upon one's position in the political set-up and only in a secondary way upon the extent of one's property. Labor is appropriated directly instead of by the "roundabout" way of the market. Another aspect of the changed situation under state capitalism is that the profit motive is superseded by the power motive. Obviously, the profit motive is a specific form of the power motive. Under private capitalism, greater profits signify greater power and less dependence upon the commands of others. The difference, however, is not only that the profit motive is a mediated form of the power motive, but that the latter is essentially bound up with the power position of the ruling group while the former pertains to the individual only.

Control of Production

A discussion of the means by which state capitalism could fulfill its program must hew closely to the technical and organizational possibilities available today in all highly industrialized countries. We refer not to any future developments but to the use which could be made here and now of the available resources. If, however, it can be shown that a state capitalist system can carry out more successfully than the market does the "necessary" functions required by the division of labor, it seems reasonable to expect that much greater resources could be made available within a short period. State capitalism must solve the following problems in the sphere of production if a rising social product is to result: create full employment based upon coordination of all productive units; reproduce the existing resources of plant, raw materials, management and labor on a level adequate to technical progress; and expand the existing plant. All these tasks must be embodied in the general plan. Given this plan, the execution hinges upon the solution of merely technical and administrative tasks instead of on the economic task of producing for an unknown and largely unforeseeable market. Production is for a clearly defined use, not "commodity" production in the meaning of a market system.[13] The experiences piled up by modern giant enterprises and associations of enterprises in carrying through enormous plans make total production control technically possible. Specific means of control include modern statistical and accounting methods, regular reporting of all changes in plant and supply, systematic training of workers for future requirements, rationalization of all technical and administrative processes and all the other devices developed in the huge modern enterprises and cartels. In addition to these traditional methods which have superseded the occult entrepreneurial art of guessing correctly what the future market demand will be, the state acquires the additional controlling power implied in complete command over money and credit. The banks are transformed into mere government agencies.[14] Every investment, whether it serves replacement or expansion, is subject to plan, and neither oversaving nor overexpansion, neither an "investment strike" nor *"Fehlinvestitionen"* can create large-scale disturbances. Errors which are bound to occur can be traced with comparative ease owing to the central position of the planning board. While they may amount to sheer waste, their damaging effects may be minimized by charging them off to the economy as a whole instead of to a single enterprise. Besides the banks, many of the organizations developed by business interests (trade associations, cartels, chambers of commerce, etc.) serve as, or are transformed into, government agencies for the control of production. The rigid control of capital, whether in its monetary form or as plant, machinery, commodities, fundamentally transforms the quality of private property in the means of production and its owner, the "capitalist." While a good many of the risks (not all of them) borne by the owner under private capitalism might have been eliminated, only so much profit is left to him as the government sees fit to allow. Regulation of prices, limitation of distributed profits, compulsory investment of surplus profits in government bonds or in ventures which the capitalist would not have chosen voluntarily, and finally drastic taxation—all these measures converge to the same end, namely, to transform the capitalist into a mere rentier whose income is fixed by government decree as long as his investments are successful but who has no claim to withdraw his capital if no "interests" are paid.

The trend toward the situation described in our model has been

widely discussed during recent years. An extreme statement is that of
E. F. M. Durbin: "Property in industrial capital has wholly lost the
social functions supposed to be grounded in it. It has ceased to be the
reward for management, and it has largely ceased to serve as a reward
for personal saving. Property in capital has become the functionless
claim to a share in the product of industry. The institution is worse
than indefensible—it is useless."[15] The same phenomenon is
criticized in the following comment: "Emphasis of management
today is not upon venture, upon chancetaking as capitalism requires,
but is upon price control, market division, avoidance of risk. This may
be good short-range policy. But: if business isn't willing to take
chances, somebody soon is going to ask why it should enjoy profits,
why the management cannot be hired by Government, which is called
on to do all the chancetaking, and might want to direct industry."[16]

This trend toward losing his social function as the private owner
of capital has found its expression in the stockholder's loss of control
over the management. It has culminated so far in the new German
legislation on joint-stock companies in which the stockholders are
deprived by law of any right to interfere with management.

To sum up, under state capitalism the status of the private
capitalist is changed in a threefold way.

(1) The entrepreneurial and the capitalist function, i.e., direction
of production and discretion in the investment of one's capital, are
separated from each other. Management becomes virtually independent of "capital" without necessarily having an important share in
corporate property.

(2) The entrepreneurial and capitalist functions are interfered
with or taken over by the Government.

(3) The capitalist (insofar as he is not accepted as entrepreneur on
the merits of his managerial qualifications) is reduced to a mere
rentier.

Here the question of incentive arises. In private capitalism, the
decisive incentives for the capitalist to maintain, expand and improve
production are the profit interest and the permanent threat of economic
collapse if the efforts should slacken. The non-capitalists are driven to
cooperate efficiently by hunger and their desire for a better life and
security. Under state capitalism, both groups lose essential parts of
their incentive. What new devices will take over their most "necessary" functions? What will prevent stagnation and even regression in
all spheres of state capitalistic society? In relation to the majority of
the population, those who neither own nor command the means of

production, the answer is simple. The whip of unemployment is replaced by political terror, and the promise of material and ideologi| cal rewards continues to incite to the utmost personal effort. The profit motive still plays an important role for capitalists and the managerial bureaucracy, since large compensation is granted for efficient investment and management. Personal initiative is freed from obstructing property interests and systematically encouraged.[17] Within the controlling group, however, the will to political power becomes the center of motivation. Every decision is at bottom oriented to the goal of maintaining and expanding the power of the group as a whole and of each of its members. New industrial empires are being built and old ones expanded with this goal in mind. But we also have here the source of the principle that individual interests must always be subordinated to the common (group) interest. This principle in turn contributes decisively to strengthening governmental control, since only a strong government can integrate conflicting interests while serving the power interests of the whole group.

Control of Distribution

"We have learned how to produce everything in practically unlimited quantities, but we don't know how to distribute the goods." This is the popular formulation to describe the riddle of private capitalism in its latest phase.

Given a general plan and the political power to enforce it, state capitalism finds ample technical means for distributing everything that can be produced with the available resources. The main difficulty of private capitalism is eliminated by the fact that under state capitalism the success of production does not necessarily depend upon finding buyers for the product at profitable prices in an unstable market, but is consciously directed towards satisfying public and private wants which are to a large extent defined in advance. Adjustments which must be made as a result of technical errors in the general plan or unexpected behavior in consumer demand need not lead to losses for the individual producer and even less to economic disaster for him. Losses easily can be pooled by the administration. The means which are available for carrying over the "necessary" distributive function of a competitive market may be conveniently classified into direct allocation (priorities, quota, etc.) and administered prices. The former applies above all to the distribution of goods to producers, the latter refers mainly to the sphere of consumption. There is, however, no sharp dividing line between the fields of application of the two means.[18] Labor is the outstanding example in which a combination of both methods is applied.

In constructing a rough model of the distributive mechanism under state capitalism, we always have to keep in mind that production and producers' consumption are two aspects of the same process. Since under modern conditions producer and consumer are, as a rule, not the same person, distribution serves as a means of integrating them. The production plan is based on a comparatively arbitrary decision as to how much of the social product is to be available for consumption and how much is to be used for expansion.

All major problems of distribution under state capitalism have been discussed thoroughly in the literature on socialist planning published within the last decade.[19] While all writers in favor of a planned society agree that the tyranny of the market must be abolished, differences of opinion exist on the question of where to draw the limits for the use of a pseudo-market. Some writers recommend that the managers of the socialized industry should "behave as if under competitive capitalism." They should "play at competition."[20] A model partly constructed on the results of this discussion may be used to illustrate how distribution works under state capitalism. The distribution of goods to producers starts from the following situation:

(1) Most productive facilities are privately owned but controlled by the government;

(2) Each industry is organized in cartels;

(3) Prices react to changes in supply and demand as well as to changes in the cost structure within the limits permitted by the plan authority and the monopolies;

(4) A general plan for the structure of the social product is in existence.

Under these circumstances a system of priorities and quotas will guarantee the execution of the plan in its broad lines. These allocations cover reproduction of existing resources, expansion (including defense) and the total output of consumers goods, which every industry shall produce. Within each industry a quota system will provide for the distribution according to a more detailed plan or according to expressions of consumer choice. Not much room is left in this set-up for flexible prices. The partial survival of the profit motive will induce manufacturers who are offered higher prices for their products to bid up in turn the prices of their "factors". But the "office of price control" will not permit prices to go higher than is compatible with the general plan. Since all major units of production are under the control of cartels, the propensity to keep prices flexible should not be overestimated. Governmental control will be immensely facilitated by the enormous role of public works necessary to maintain full employment under all circumstances.

Full employment in the strict sense of the word can be achieved in regard to labor only. Due to technological facts, it is not possible in the case of plant and equipment. New plant and new machinery constructed according to the latest technical development require a minimum size of plant which as a rule leads to temporary overcapacity at the moment of their completion. If no ways for using this overcapacity can be found speedily, some idleness of capital will arise. This might happen with entire durable goods industries (e.g., machine tools) if the need for their product is temporarily saturated. Neither this nor other "maladjustments" can produce the cumulative effects so vicious under the free market system,[21] for the capital owner might be compensated for his loss out of pooled profits or public sources, and provision for a constant reserve in planning the labor supply will take care of the displaced workers. Technological unemployment will be handled in a similar way. It has been shown that the opposite case, periodical shortage of capital, can be avoided in a planned society.[22]

Labor under state capitalism is allocated to the different sections of production like other resources. This does not prevent the planning authorities from differentiating wages. On the contrary, premiums in the form of higher real wages can be granted wherever extra efforts are demanded. The slave driver's whip is no workable means for extracting quality products from highly skilled workers who use expensive machinery. This differentiation in wage schedules, however, is not the outcome of market conditions but of the wage administrator's decision. No entrepreneur is allowed to pay higher wages than those fixed by this agency.

With absolute control of wages, the government is in a position to handle the distribution of consumers goods with comparative ease. In cases of severe scarcity, as in wartime, direct allocation of consumers goods might be the only adequate means for their distribution. In such a case consumer choice is very limited but not entirely ruled out.[23] If, however, a somewhat more adequate supply of consumers goods is available, the consumer may be as free or, with the greater purchasing power created by full employment, even more free in his choice under state capitalism than he is now. In order to achieve this goal with the means now at hand, a pseudo-market for consumers goods will be established. The starting point for its operation is a clearly defined relation between purchasing power which will be spent for consumption and the sum of prices of all available consumers goods. Both sums must be equal. In other words, the total income paid out to consumers, minus taxes, compulsory and voluntary savings, must be the same as the price sum of all consumers goods which are for sale. If the "net" consumers income should be higher, a scramble for goods and a bidding up of prices would result (under our definition that "net" income excludes saving). If it should be lower, only part of the products could be distributed. The first step toward distributing the consumers goods is therefore to make the "net" income of all consumers in a given period equivalent to the sum of consumers goods output as decided by the general plan and the available inventory. This first step will prove insufficient for two reasons:

(1) The consumers' voluntary savings may deviate from the plan,—they may save either more or less than was expected in calculating the equilibrium. Both cases may be remedied by the use of the market laws of demand and supply, which will create inflationary or deflationary price movements to "clear the market,"—if the price controlling agencies permit it.

(2) The consumers' choices may deviate from the calculations of the planners,—they may prefer some products and reject others. Here again the old market mechanism may be allowed to come into play to enforce higher prices for goods in greater demand and to lower prices where and as long as an oversupply exists. A system of subsidies and surtaxes will eliminate serious losses as well as surplus profits which could disturb the functioning of the plan. The distributive agency may completely "overrule" the consumers' choice for all practical purposes by fixing prices either extremely high or disproportionately low. So far the price mechanism obeys the same laws as in the free market system. The difference becomes manifest in the effects which changing prices exercise on production. The price signals influence production only insofar as is compatible with the general plan and the established public policy on consumption. Price movements serve as a most valuable instrument for announcing differences between consumers' preferences and the production plan. They can not, however, compel the planning authority to follow these manifestations of consumers' will in the same way they compel every non-monopolistic producer in a free market.[24] Under private capitalism, the monopolist, in resisting the market signals, disrupts the whole market system at the expense of all non-monopolistic market parties. Under state capitalism the disconnection between price and production can do no harm

because the function of coordinating production and consumption has been transferred from the market to the plan authority. Much attention has been given to the question of how consumers' choice can be calculated in advance. No "God-like" qualities are required for the planning board. It has been shown[25] that freedom of consumers' choice actually exists only to a very limited degree. In studying large numbers of consumers, it becomes evident that size of income, tradition and propaganda are considerably levelling down all individual preference schedules. The experiences of large manufacturing and distributing concerns as well as of cartels contribute a most valuable supplement to the special literature on planning.

Economic Limitations of State Capitalism

In raising the question of economic limitations, we point to those which may restrict the arbitrariness of the decisions in state capitalism as contrasted with other social structures in which they may not appear. We are not concerned with limitations that apply to every social set-up, e.g., those which result from the necessity to reproduce the given resources and to maintain full employment and optimum efficiency. The first and most frequent objection against the economic workability of a state capitalistic system is that it is good only in a scarcity economy, especially for periods of war preparedness and war. For a scarcity economy, so runs the argument, most of the economic difficulties against which private capitalism struggles do not exist. Overproduction and overinvestment need not be feared, and all products, however inefficiently produced, and however bad their quality, find a ready demand. As soon as the temporary emergency has passed, however, and a greater supply becomes available in all fields, state capitalism will prove utterly inadequate for securing the best use of available resources, for avoiding bottlenecks in one product and overproduction in others, and for providing the consumers with what they may demand at the lowest possible cost. Even if all means of production are under governmental control, efficient planning is possible only under conditions of emergency. The argument advanced for this view can be boiled down to the following:[26] in a planned economy costs cannot be accounted for, the free choice of the consumers must be disregarded, the motives for efficient production and distribution disappear, and as a result a planned economy must under modern conditions be much less productive than a market economy.

We think that anyone who seriously studies the modern literature on planning must come to the conclusion that, whatever his objections to the social consequences of planning, these arguments against its economic efficiency no longer hold. All technical means for efficient planning, including the expansion of production in accordance with consumer wants and the most advanced technical possibilities, and taking into account the cost in public health, personal risks, unemployment (never adequately calculated in the cost sheet of private enterprise)—all these technical means are available today.

Another counter-argument holds that as soon as state capitalism turns from concentrating upon armaments to a genuine peace economy its only alternative, if it wants to avoid unemployment, is to spend a very substantial part of the national income for the construction of modern "pyramids," or to raise considerably the standard of living. No economic causes exist which could prevent a state capitalistic government from doing so. The obstacles are of a political nature and will be dealt with later.

A third argument points in the opposite direction. It objects that state capitalism necessarily leads to a standstill in technics or even a regress. Investments would slow down and technical progress cease if the market laws are put out of operation. As long as competitive armament continues, the contrary will probably be true. Besides the profit motive, the vital interests of the controlling group will stimulate both investment and technical progress. In the effort to maintain and extend its power the controlling group will come into conflict with foreign interests, and its success will depend upon its military force. This, however, will be a function of the technical efficiency. Any slackening in the speed of technical progress might lead to military inferiority and to destruction.[27] Only after all possible enemies will have disappeared because the whole world will be controlled by one totalitarian state, will the problem of technological progress and capital expansion come to the fore.

Are there, one may ask, no economic limitations at all to the existence and expansion of state capitalism? With its rise, will a utopia emerge in which all economic wants can easily be fulfilled if political factors don't interfere? Did not the liberal theory also believe it had proved that the market system will guarantee its constituents the full use of all resources if not intefered with? And did it not become apparent later that inherent forces prevented the market system from functioning and ushered in growing interference by private monopolies and the government? Forewarned as we are, we are unable to discover any inherent economic forces, "economic laws" of the old or a new type, which could prevent the functioning of state capitalism.[28] Government control of production and distribution furnishes the means for eliminating the economic causes of depressions, cumulative destructive processes and unemployment of capital and labor. We may even say that under state capitalism economics as a social science has lost its object. Economic problems in the old sense no longer exist when the coordination of all economic activities is effected by conscious plan instead of by the natural laws of the market. Where the economist formerly racked his brain to solve the puzzle of the exchange process, he meets, under state capitalism, with mere problems of administration. There are indeed limitations to state capitalism, but they derive from natural conditions as well as from the very structure of the society which state capitalism seeks to perpetuate.

Natural and Other Non-Economic Limitations[29]
(1) To be fully workable, state capitalism needs an adequate supply of raw material, plant and labor of all kinds (technicians, administrators, skilled and unskilled labor), characteristic for a highly industrialized country. Without a plentiful supply of raw materials and the outfit in machinery and skill of a modern industrial society, great waste must accompany state capitalistic intervention, possibly greater than under a market economy. For the first limitation, inadequate supply of raw materials, a typical example is offered by Nazi Germany. The enormous machinery which had to be built to compensate for the insufficiency of the raw material basis—too small to cope with the armament program—and the difficulties for the producer to obtain raw materials and, in consequence, new machinery,[30] cannot be attributed to the system itself but to the fact that one of its main prerequisites was lacking from the very beginning.

On the other hand, many of the Soviet Russian economic failures may be traced back to the lack of both raw materials and adequate development of the productive forces. Lack of trained technicians, skilled workers, and of the qualities known as work discipline, all of which are plentiful in highly industrialized countries only, go a long way in explaining the slow progress of rearming, reorganizing the transportation system and raising or even maintaining the standard of living in Soviet Russia. But even here a government controlled economic system has shown the power to survive under conditions where a system of free enterprise would have collapsed completely. Government controlled foreign trade and the development of an industry for "Ersatz" materials may overcome the limitations of a too narrow basis of raw materials. Filling the gap between a fully industrialized and a chiefly agricultural economy is a much more painful and drawn out process.

(2) Differences in vital interests will crop up in the group or groups controlling the state. They can stem from different positions within the administration, different programs for maintaining or expanding power, or the struggle for the monopoly of control. Unless adequate provisions are made for overcoming these differences, bad compromises and continuous struggle will arise.

(3) Conflicting interests within the ruling class might thwart the construction of a general plan embodying the optimum of all available resources for achieving consistent chosen ends. The choice of the ends itself represents a major problem as long as no common will has been established. In our discussion we started always from the assumption "given a general plan." This means a plan for certain ends which must be chosen from among a variety of possible ones.

Once the minimum requirements for consumption, replacement and expansion are fulfilled the planners have a great deal of leeway. If their decisions do not converge into a consistent program, no general plan for the optimum use and development of the given productive forces can be drafted.

(4) Conflicting interests, however, do not operate in the ruling group only. Since totalitarian state capitalism is the expression of an antagonistic society at its worst, the will to dominate from above and the counter-pressure from below cut deeply into the pseudo-liberty of the state capitalist planners. The planning board, while vested with all the technical means for directing the whole economic process, is itself an arena of struggle among social forces far beyond its control. It will be seen that planning in an antagonistic society is only in a technical sense the same tool as that used by a society in which harmony of interests has been established. Political considerations interfere at every step with the construction and execution of an optimum plan. The following paragraphs will offer some examples.

How will expansion of production and technical progress be motivated after fear of aggression or objects for new conquest have vanished? Will not under such conditions the dreaded technological standstill make its appearance, thus spoiling all chances of reducing the drudgery of labor while raising the standard of living?[31] A case could be made out for the view that a new set of motivations will arise under totalitarian state capitalism which will combine the drive for power over men with the will to power over nature and counteract the development toward a static economy. But this is such a distant perspective that we may leave the question open, the more so since under totalitarian capitalism there are serious reasons to keep the productive forces static.

Under a state capitalistic set-up, will the general standard of living rise beyond narrow limits if the expansion program permits? This question can be answered in the affirmative for the democratic form of state capitalism only. For its authoritarian counterpart, however, the problem is different. The ruling minority in a totalitarian state maintains its power not only by terror and atomization but by its control of the means of production and by keeping the dominated majority in complete spiritual dependence. The masses have no chance of questioning the durability and justification of the existing order; the virtues of war are developed and all "effeminacy," all longing for individual happiness, is rooted out. A rise in the standard of living might dangerously counteract such a policy. It would imply more leisure time, more professional skill, more opportunity for critical thinking, out of which a revolutionary spirit might develop. It is a widely spread error that the most dangerous revolutions are instigated by the most miserable strata of society. The revolutionary craving for liberty and justice found its most fertile breeding ground not among the paupers but among individuals and groups who were themselves in a relatively better position. The ruling group in totalitarian state capitalism might therefore decide that from the point of view of its own security a low general standard of living and long drudging working hours are desirable. An armament race and the excitement over threat of foreign "aggression" seem to be appropriate means for keeping the standard of living low and the war virtues high while maintaining full employment and promoting technical progress. Such a constellation, however, would furnish a striking example for a political limitation of productivity.

The highly speculative question might be permitted, what would happen if totalitarian state capitalism were embodied in a unified world state in which the threat of aggression had disappeared for good? Even public works of undreamed scope could not prevent the general standard of living from rising under conditions of full employment. In such a case the most clever devices of ideological mass domination and the grimmest terror are unlikely to uphold for a long period a minority dictatorship which can no longer claim itself to be necessary to maintain production and to protect the people from foreign aggression. If our assumption is correct that totalitarian state capitalism will not tolerate a high standard of living for the masses and cannot survive mass unemployment, the consequence seems to be that it cannot endure in a peace economy. As long as one national state capitalism has not conquered the whole earth, however, there will always be ample opportunities to spend most of the productive excess capacity (excess over the requirements for a minimum standard of living) for ever-increasing and technically more perfect armaments.

Why can the policy of aggression not come to a standstill before one state has conquered the entire world? Even after a totalitarian state has acquired full autarchy within its own territory, "preparedness" and foreign wars must go on at a rapid pace in order to protect against aggression from outside and revolution from within. A democratic state capitalism, while safe from within, is menaced by totalitarian aggression and must arm to the teeth and be ready to fight until all totalitarian states have been transformed into democracies. In the last century it became evident that a society based on slave labor could not exist side by side with one organized on the principle of free labor. The same holds true in our day for democratic and totalitarian societies.

Control of the State under State Capitalism

If state capitalism is a workable system, superior in terms of pro-ductivity to private capitalism under conditions of monopolistic mar-ket disruption, what are the political implications? If the state be-comes the omnipotent comptroller of all human activities, the ques-tion "who controls the comptroller" embraces the problem of whether state capitalism opens a new way to freedom or leads to the complete loss of it as far as the overwhelming majority is concerned. Between the two extreme forms of state capitalism, the totalitarian and the democratic, numerous others are thinkable. Everything depends upon which social groups in the last analysis direct the decisions of a government whose power has in all matters—"economic" as well as "non-economic"—never been surpassed in modern history. The fol-lowing is intended as a rough sketch of the social structure under totalitarian state capitalism.

(1) The government is controlled by, and composed of, a new ruling class. We have defined this new class as an amalgamation of the key bureaucrats in business, state and party allied with the remaining vested interests.[32] We have already mentioned that inherited or ac-quired wealth may still play a role in opening a way to this ruling group, but that it is not essential for participating in the group. One's position in the economic and administrative set-up, together with party affiliations and personal qualification, is decisive for one's

political power. The new ruling class, by its grip on the state, controls everything it wants to, the general economic plan, foreign policy, rights and duties, life and death of the individual. Its decisions are not restrained by any constitutional guarantees but by a set of rules only, designed for maintaining and expanding its own power. We have seen what control over the general economic plan involves: all the basic decisions on how to distribute the "factors of production" among producers and consumers goods, on the working day, labor conditions, on wages and prices. To sum up, control of the general economic plan means control over the standard of living. Antagonisms of interests among the groups within the ruling class might lead to serious difficulties. The class interest of maintaining the new status, however, will probably be strong enough for a long time to overcome these antagonisms before they can turn into a menace to the system. The persons who form the ruling class have been prepared for their task by their position in, or their cooperation with, the monopolistic institutions of private capitalism. There, a rapidly growing number of decisive functions had become invested in a comparatively small group of bureaucrats. The leader and follower principle flourished long before it was promulgated as the basic principle of society, since more and more responsibility had been centralized in the top offices of government, business, trade unions and political parties.

(2) Those owners of capital who are "capitalists" without being managers and who could exercise great political influence during the whole era of private capitalism no longer have any necessary social functions. They receive interest on their investments for as long a time and in the measure that the new ruling class may be willing to grant. From the point of view of their social utility they constitute a surplus population. Under the impact of heavy inheritance taxes, controlled stock markets and the generally hostile attitude of the new ruling class against the "*raffende Kapital*," these "capitalists" will probably disappear. The widespread hatred against them could develop only because the economic laws of capitalism had transformed their social role into that of parasites.

(3) A semi-independent group, not belonging to the ruling class but enjoying more privileges than the *Gefolgschaften*, are the free professions and the middle and small business under governmental control. Both will disappear wherever a fully developed state capitalism corresponding to our model is reached. The process of concentration which gains unprecedented momentum under state capitalism absorbs the independent small and medium enterprise. The trend

towards socialization of medicine, of journalism and other free professions transforms their members into government employees.

(4) The great majority of the people fall into the category of
salaried employees of all types. They are subject to the leader principle of command and obedience. All their political rights have been
destroyed, and carefully planned atomization has simplified the task
of keeping them under strict control. Labor's right to bargain collectively, to strike, to change jobs and residence at will (if its market
position permits) is abolished. Work becomes compulsory, wages are
fixed by government agencies, the leisure time of the worker and his
family is organized from above. In some respects, this is antithetical to
the position of labor under private capitalism and revives many traits
of feudal conditions.

(5) The new state openly appears as an institution in which all
earthly power is embodied and which serves the new ruling class as a
tool for its power politics. Seemingly independent institutions like
party, army and business form its specialized arms. A complicated
relation exists, however, between the means and those who apply
them, resulting in some genuine independence for these institutions.
Political domination is achieved by organized terror and overwhelming propaganda on the one side, on the other by full employment and
an adequate standard of living for all key groups, the promise of
security and a more abundant life for every subject who submits
voluntarily and completely. This system is far from being based upon
rude force alone. In that it provides many "real" satisfactions for its
subjects, it exists partly with the consent of the governed, but this
consent cannot change the antagonistic character of a state capitalistic
society in which the power interests of the ruling class prevent the
people from fully using the productive forces for their own welfare
and from having control over the organization and activities of
society.

We have referred here and there to what we think are particular
traits of the democratic form of state capitalism. Since no approaches
to it have so far been made in practice, and since the discussion of it is
still in a formative stage,[33] no attempt will be made here to construct a
model for it.

The trend toward state capitalism is growing, however, in the
non-totalitarian states. An increasing number of observers admit, very
often reluctantly, that private capitalism is no longer able to handle the
new tasks. "All plans for internal post-war reconstruction start with
the assumption that more or less permanent government controls will

have replaced *laissez-faire* methods both in the national and the international sphere. Thus the choice is not between totalitarian controls and return to 'free enterprise'; the choice is between totalitarian controls and controls voluntarily accepted by the people of each country for the benefit of society as a whole.''[34] It is the lesson of all large-scale measures of government interference that they will contribute to the disruption of the market mechanism if they are not coordinated into a general plan. If government is to provide for all the items recognized as mandatory in the more serious post-war reconstruction programs,[35] it must be vested with adequate powers, and these might not stop short of state capitalism.

It is of vital importance for everybody who believes in the values of democracy that an investigation be made as to whether state capitalism can be brought under democratic control. The social as well as the moral problem with which the democracies are confronted has been formulated as follows: ''. . . How can we get effective use of our resources, yet at the same time preserve the underlying values in our tradition of liberty and democracy? How can we employ our unemployed, how can we use our plant and equipment to the full, how can we take advantage of the best modern technology, yet, in all this make the individual source of value and individual fulfillment in society the basic objective? How can we obtain effective organization of resources, yet at the same time retain the maximum freedom of individual action?''[36] Totalitarian state capitalism offers the solution of economic problems at the price of totalitarian oppression. What measures are necessary to guarantee control of the state by the majority of its people instead of by a small minority? What ways and means can be devised to prevent the abuse of the enormous power vested in state, industrial and party bureaucracy under state capitalism? How can the loss of economic liberty be rendered compatible with the maintenance of political liberty? How can the disintegrative motive forces of today be replaced by integrative ones? How will the roots from which insurmountable social antagonisms develop be eliminated so that there will not arise a political alliance between dissentient partial interests and the bureaucracy aiming to dominate the majority? Can democratic state capitalism be more than a transitory phase leading either to total oppression or to doing away with the remnants of the capitalistic system?

The main obstacles to the democratic form of state capitalism are of a political nature and can be overcome by political means only. If our thesis proves to be correct, society on its present level can overcome the handicaps of the market system by economic planning. Some of the best brains of this country are studying the problem how such planning can be done in a democratic way, but a great amount of theoretical work will have to be performed before answers to every question will be forthcoming.

The Authoritarian State

By Max Horkheimer

*This article, composed in 1940 for the unpublished 1942
Gedächtnisschrift for Walter Benjamin, represents Horkheimer's
politics at its most radical juncture and indicates the place of the
Soviet Union in the complex of politically integrated social
formations. It also links traditional working-class organizations and
even orthodox Marxism to the "authoritarian state." If the article is
characterized by an exaggerated faith in the spontaneity of workers'
councils, the contrast to Pollock's stress on democratic reform is
nevertheless interesting. "The Authoritarian State" presents the
political context and meaning of "The End of Reason."*

The historical predictions about the fate of bourgeois society have
been confirmed. In the system of the free market economy, which
pushed men to labor-saving discoveries and finally subsumed them in
a global mathematical formula, its specific offspring, machines, have
become means of destruction not merely in the literal sense: they have
made not work but the workers superfluous. The bourgeoisie has been
decimated, and the majority of the middle class have lost their independence; where they have not been thrown into the ranks of the
proletariat, or more commonly into the masses of unemployed, they
have become dependents of the big concerns or the state. The El
Dorado of bourgeois existence, the sphere of circulation, is being
liquidated. Its work is being carried out in part by the trusts which,

without the help of banks, finance themselves, eliminate the commercial intermediaries and take control of the stockholders' organizations. Part of the business sphere is handled by the state. As the *caput mortuum* of the transformation process of the bourgeoisie there remain only the highest levels of the industrial and state bureaucracy. "One way or another, with or without the trusts, the official representative of capitalist society, the state, must finally take over the management of production . . . All social functions of the capitalists are now discharged by salaried civil servants . . . And the modern state is once again only the organization which bourgeois society creates for itself to maintain the general external conditions for the capitalist means of production against encroachments either by the workers or by individual capitalists . . . The more productive forces the state takes over as its own property, the more it becomes a collective capitalist, the more citizens of the state it exploits. The workers remain wage laborers, proletarians. The relationship to capital is not abolished but becomes far more acute."[1] In the transition from monopoly to state capitalism, the last stage offered by bourgeois society is "the appropriation of the large productive and commercial organisms, first by joint-stock companies, later by trusts and then by the state."[2] *State capitalism is the authoritarian state of the present.*

For the natural course of the capitalist world order, theory prescribes an unnatural end: the united proletarians will destroy the last form of exploitation, state-capitalist slavery. The rivalry of the wage-laborers among themselves had guaranteed the prosperity of the private entrepreneurs. That was the freedom of the poor. Once poverty was an estate; then it became a panic. The poor were supposed to run and shove each other aside like a crowd in a burning auditorium. The way out was the factory gate, labor for the entrepreneurs. There could never be enough of the poor; their numbers were a blessing for capital. But to the same extent that capital concentrated the workers in the large factories, it came into crisis and made its own existence a hopeless prospect. The workers cannot hire themselves out yet another time. Their interests push them inexorably to socialism. When the ruling class "must feed the workers, instead of being fed by them," revolution is at hand. This theory of the end grows out of a situation which was still ambiguous, and is itself ambiguous: either it counts on collapse through an economic crisis, thereby ruling out stabilization of an authoritarian state, as Engels in fact predicted. Or else the theory expects the triumph of the authoritarian state, thus foreclosing collapse through a crisis, which was always defined by the market economy. *But state capitalism does away with the market and hypostatizes the crisis for the duration of eternal Germany.* Its "economic inevitability" signifies a step forward, a breathing spell for the rulers. Unemployment becomes organized. Only the already well-established section of the bourgeoisie is still really interested in the market. Big industrialists today denounce liberalism only when state administration remains too liberal for them, not completely under their control. The modern planned economy can feed the masses better and be better fed by them than by the vestiges of the market. A period with its own social structure has dispensed with the free market, and demonstrates its own particular tendencies nationally and internationally.

Capitalism's ability to outlive the market economy was announced long ago in the fate of the working class organizations. The call to unite in trade unions and parties was carried out to the letter, but these organizations carried out not so much the unnatural tasks of the united proletariat, namely the resistance to class society in general, as that of submitting to the natural conditions of their own development into mass organizations. They integrated themselves into the transformations of the economy. Under liberalism they had devoted themselves to the aim of improving their lot. Because of their solvency, the influence of certain more secure strata of workers took on a greater weight. The party pressed for social legislation; the life of the workers under capitalism was to be alleviated. The union fought for advantages for skilled workers. As ideological justification there emerged phrases about factory democracy and the evolution to socialism. Work as a vocation: of the critique of work as drudgery, which was the only way the past had seen it, there scarcely remained a word. Work was transformed from the bourgeois' badge of merit into the longing of the disinherited. The large organizations spread an idea of socialization which was scarcely distinguishable from statification, nationalization or socialization in state capitalism. The revolutionary vision of emancipation continued to live only in the calumnies of the counter-revolutionaries. When fantasy had completely detached itself from any basis in fact, it substituted for the existing state apparatus the party and trade-union bureaucracies, for the principle of profit the yearly plan of the functionaries. Even utopia was structured according to directive. *Men were conceived as objects, if necessary as their own.* The bigger the organizations became, the more their leadership owed its place to a selection of the most capable. Robust health, the good fortune of being acceptable to the average member and not unacceptable to the ruling power, a dependable aversion to adventure, the gift of being able to deal with the opposition, a preparedness to proclaim the greatest incoherence as a virtue to the crowd and to oneself, nihilism and self-contempt—these are the necessary qualities.

To control and replace these leaders becomes for technical reasons more and more difficult with the growth of the apparatus. Between the real suitability of their remaining in power and their personal determination not to step down, a pre-established harmony reigns. The leading man and his clique become as independent in the working-class organization as the board of directors in an industrial monopoly is from the stockholders. The means of power, on the one hand the firm's financial reserves, on the other the funds of the party or union, are at the disposal of the leadership for use against any trouble. Those who are dissatisfied are scattered and must rely on their own pocketbooks. In an extreme case the resistance is beheaded, bought off at the stockholders' meeting or expelled from the party conference. Whatever seeks to exist under a state of domination runs the danger of reproducing it. Insofar as the proletarian opposition in the Weimar Republic did not meet its downfall as a sect, it fell victim to the spirit of administration. The institutionalization of the top ranks of capital and labor have the same basis: the change in the form of production. Monopolized industry, which makes the mass of stockholders into victims and parasites, pushes the masses of workers into supporting passivity. They have more to expect from the protection and assistance of the organizations than from their work. In the Western democracies the leaders of the big working class organizations find themselves in the same relationship to their membership as the executives of integral statism have to the society as a whole: they keep the masses, whom they take care of, under strict discipline, maintain them in hermetic seclusion from uncontrolled elements, and tolerate spontaneity only as the result of their own power. Far more than the prefascist statesmen who mediated between the monopolists of labor and industry and who could never extricate themselves from the utopia of a humanitarian version of the authoritarian state, these labor leaders strive for their own kind of national community (*Volksgemeinschaft*).

There has been no lack of rebellions against this development in the labor organizations. The protests of the splinter groups were as uniform as their fate. They attacked the conformist politics of the leadership, the development into a mass party, the rigid discipline. They discovered quite early that the original goal of the dissolution of oppression and exploitation in every form was only a propaganda phrase in the mouths of the functionaries. In the trade unions they criticized the wage settlements which limit strikes; in the party they criticized the collaboration in capitalist legislation because it is corrupting; in both organizations they criticized the realpolitik. They recognized that the thought of social revolution by legal means is more seriously compromised the more members support it. But the bureaucrats at the top, because of their position, are the better organizers, and if the party is to exist, it cannot do without experienced specialists. Everywhere the efforts of the opposition failed to take the rank-and-file with them or to develop new forms of opposition. When the opposition groups achieved greater significance after their departure, they in turn became bureaucratic institutions. *Integration is the price which individuals and groups have to pay in order to flourish under capitalism.* Even those unions whose program stood opposed to all parliamentarians found themselves, with an increase of their membership, a long way from the extravagances of the general strike and direct action. Already in World War I, by accepting a Ministry of Munitions, they made known their preparedness for peaceful cooperation. Even the Maximalists after the revolution were unable to cope with the fact that the ignominious sociology of the party apparatus still won out in the end. Whether revolutionaries pursue power as one pursues loot or criminals, is revealed in the course of action. Instead of dissolving in the end into the democracy of the councils, the group can maintain itself as a leadership. Work, discipline and order can save the republic and tidy up the revolution. Even though the abolition of the state was written on its banner, that party transfigured its industrially backward fatherland into the secret vision of those industrial powers which were growing sick on their parliamentarism and could no longer live without fascism. *The revolutionary movement negatively reflects the situation which it is attacking.* In the monopolistic period private and state control of estranged labor is expanded. In the private sector the socialist struggle is directed against the anarchy of the market economy; in the private and public sector together, resistance is directed against the last form of exploitation. The historical contradiction, of demanding at the same time both rational planning and freedom, emancipation and regulation, can be overcome; with the Maximalists nevertheless authority ultimately won out and performed miracles.

The opposition can exist as a mass party only in a market economy. The state, which became independent through the splintering of the bourgeoisie, is defined in terms of its parties. In part it pursues the general bourgeois aim of repulsing the old feudal powers, and partly represents its own social groups. The proletarian opposition has also profited from the mediation of domination through parties. The splintering of the ruling class, which was instrumental in the separation of powers and in the creation of constitutional rights of the individual, was the prerequisite for workers' associations. In Europe the freedom of assembly is one of the essential concessions of the class to the individual, as long as the individuals in the class are not directly identifiable with the state, so that it is not necessary to fear state encroachment. Even from the beginning, as is well known, respect for the individual, the sanctity of the home, and the inviolability of persons arrested, as well as other rights, were trampled upon as soon as it ceased to concern the bourgeoisie. The history of prison revolts as well as political insurrections, and especially the history of the colonies, are commentaries on the humanity of the bourgeoisie. As far as the right to organize affected the proletariat, it was from the very beginning a stepchild among human rights. "All citizens should certainly be permitted to assemble," said the advisor for Labor Problems in the Constitutional Assembly of 1791, "however, citizens of a given profession or trade should not be allowed to assemble in order to advance their own interests."[3] Under the guise of dismantling the guilds and the other corporate forms, the liberals have been able to hinder, but ultimately not prevent the development of unions. Above and beyond the tasks of bourgeois parties, the program of the socialist organizations still contained the idea of revolution. This program appeared as the quickest means of realizing the bourgeoisie's ideological goal of the general prosperity. The abolition of private ownership of the means of production, the elimination of the waste of energy and materials in the market system through planned economy, the elimination of the right of inheritance and other programs were rational demands for the time. In opposition to the bourgeoisie the socialists represented the former's most progressive phase, and pressed ultimately for a better government. The establishment of freedom was considered a mechanistic, natural consequence of the conquest of power, or was considered simply utopia.

The movement towards the authoritarian state was long foreshadowed in the radical parties of the bourgeois era. The French Revolution is a condensed version of later history. Robespierre centralized authority in the Committee of Public Safety and reduced the Parliament to a rubber stamp for legislation. He unified the function of administration and control in the Jacobin party leadership. The state regulated the economy. The rational community penetrated all aspects of life with fraternity and denunciation. Private wealth became almost illegal. Robespierre and his cohorts also planned to expropriate the internal enemy; the people's well directed anger was part of the political machinery. The French Revolution tended towards totalitarianism. Its struggle against the church arose not because of its antipathy towards religion, but from the demand that religion should also be incorporated into and serve the patriotic order. The cults of Reason and of the supreme being were spread because of the obstinacy of the Clerics. The ''Sansculottes Jesus'' announced the coming of the Nordic Christ. Under the Jacobins, state capitalism did not get beyond its bloody beginnings.[4] However, the Thermidor did not eliminate its necessity. It appeared repeatedly in the revolutions of the 19th century. In France, the successive liberal governments were always short lived. In order to control the statist tendencies rising from below, the bourgeoisie had to hastily call upon Bonapartism from above. The government of Louis Blanc fared no better than the Directory. With the crushing of the workers in June 1848, the national workshops and the right to work could only be repressed by unleashing the General. The market economy has shown itself to be increasingly reactionary. If Rousseau's insight, that the great disparities of property were in contradiction to the principle of the nation, consequently set Robespierre, the student of Rousseau, in opposition to liberalism, then the later growth of capitalist wealth could only be fused with the general interest in a national economic Commonwealth. Under the conditions set by the great industries, a battle occurred over who was to receive the heritage of competitive society. The farsighted leaders of the state felt that they were to suffer as much as the masses in the extremist parties, the workers and the ruined petty bourgeois. The murky relationship between Lassalle, the founder of the German socialist mass party, and Bismarck, the father of German state capitalism, was symbolic. Both aimed at state control. Government and opposition party bureaucrats from the left and right were pushed toward some form of authoritarian state, depending on their position in the social system. It is decisive for the individual which form it finally takes. The unemployed, rentiers, shop owners, and intellectuals await life or death, depending on whether reformism, bolshevism or fascism is victorious.

Integral statism or state socialism is the most consistent form of the authoritarian state which has freed itself from any dependence on private capital. It increases production at a rate only seen in the transition from the mercantilist period to the liberal era. The fascist countries create a mixed form. Though here too surplus value is brought under state control and distributed, it flows under the old name of profits in great amounts to the industrial magnates and landowners. Through their influence, the organization is destroyed and deflected. In integral statism, socialization is simply decreed. Private capitalists are eliminated. Henceforth, dividends are only collected from government bonds. As a result of the revolutionary past of the regime, the petty struggles between officials and departments is not, as with fascism, complicated by the differences in the social origin and connections inside the bureaucratic staff. This has led to much friction in fascist regimes. Integral statism is not a retreat but an advance of power. It can exist without racism. However, the producers, to whom capital legally belongs, "remain wage workers, proletarians," no matter how much is done for them. Factory regimentation is extended to the entire society. If the lack of modern technology and the war-like environment had not played into the hands of the bureaucracy, statism would have already outlived its usefulness. In integral statism, even apart from the militaristic encroachment, the absolutism of bureaucracy, whose authority the police enforce to the utmost in all phases of life, stands opposed to the free structuring of society. No economic or juridical measures, only the will of the ruled can lead to the democratization of the system of control. They will be trapped in the vicious circle of poverty, domination, war and poverty until they break through it themselves. Wherever else in Europe these tendencies toward integral statism are present, the prospect exists that the masses will not become enmeshed in bureaucratic control. It cannot be predicted whether or not this will succeed, and cannot therefore be worked out once and for all in praxis. Only the bad in history is irrevocable: the unrealized possibilities, missed opportunities, murder with and without legal procedures, and that which those in power inflict upon humanity. The other is always in danger.

The authoritarian state is repressive in all of its forms. The immense waste is no longer produced by economic mechanisms in the classical sense. It arises out of the exorbitant needs of the power apparatus and the destruction of any initiative on the part of those ruled: obedience is not so productive. In spite of the alleged absence of crises, there is no harmony. Even though the surplus value is no longer absorbed as profit, it is still the focal point. Circulation is eliminated and exploitation modified. The proposition widespread in the market economy, which held that the anarchy of the society corresponds to stringent factory regimentation, today has come to mean that the international state of nature, the battle for the world market, and the fascist discipline of the people are mutual conditions for one another. Even though today the elites conspire in common against their own people, they are always ready to poach even more on each other's hunting grounds. Economic and disarmament conferences postpone trade for a while. The principle of control manifests itself as a permanent mobilization. The situation remains in itself absurd. The restriction of productive forces can of course from now on be understood as a condition of power and deliberately practiced. It is the catechism of the art of authoritarian rule that the differences between the ranks, whether it be skilled or unskilled labor or between races, must be systematically furthered by all media of communication—newspapers, radio, and movies—to isolate individuals from one another. They should listen to everyone, from the Führer to the local boss, but not to each other. They should be informed about everything, from the nation's policies for peace to the use of blackout lamps, but they should not inform themselves. They should lay their hands on everything, but not on the leadership. Humanity is thoroughly educated and mutilated. If a region, for example the United States or Europe, is great and powerful enough, the machinery of oppression used against the internal enemy must find a pretext in the threats of the external enemy. While hunger and the danger of war are necessary, uncontrollable and inevitable results of a market economy, they can be constructively utilized by the authoritarian state.

Even if the end of the last phase will come at an unexpected time or place, it will hardly be brought about by the resurrected mass party, which would only replace the existing rulers. The activity of political groups and isolated persons may decisively help to prepare for freedom. The authoritarian state has to fear the opposing mass parties only as competitors. They do not threaten the principle of the authoritarian state itself. In reality the enemy is everywhere and nowhere. Only in the beginning do most of the victims come from the defeated mass party. Later the entire people sheds its blood. The selection for the concentration camps becomes more and more arbitrary. If the number of inmates increases or decreases, or even if for a period of time the empty places of those killed cannot be filled again, *in principle anyone could be there*. The crime that leads to the camps is committed every day in everyone's thoughts. Under fascism everyone dreams of assassinating the Führer, and marches in rank and file. They follow out of sober calculation: the Führer would be succeeded only by his deputy.

If the people once refuse to march anymore, they will realize their dreams. The often cited political immaturity of the masses behind which party bureaucrats like to hide is in reality nothing but skepticism toward the leadership. The workers have learned that they have nothing to expect from those who called them out from time to time, only to send them home again, but more of the same—even after a victory. In the French Revolution, it took the masses five years to become indifferent to whether Robespierre or Barras was in power. No conclusions about the future can be drawn from a lucid apathy built on a resistance to the whole political façade. With the experience that their political will can indeed change their own lives through changing society, the apathy of the masses will disappear. Such apathy is a trait of capitalism in all of its phases. A generalizing sociology suffered from the fact that it was practiced primarily by people of the middle and upper middle classes who differentiate too conscientiously. The millions below learn through their experience from childhood on that the various phases of capitalism belong to one and the same system. Authoritarian or liberal, society for them means hunger, police control and the draft. Under fascism, the masses are predominantly interested in seeing that the foreigners do not succeed, because the dependent nation will have to undergo increased exploitation. It is precisely integral statism that still offers them hope, because it hints at something better, and hope works against apathy. The concept of a transitional revolutionary dictatorship was in no way intended to mean the monopoly of the means of production by some new elite. Such dangers can be countered by the energy and alertness of the people themselves. The revolution that ends domination is as far-reaching as the will of the liberated. Any resignation is already a regression into prehistory. After the old positions of power have been dissolved, society will either govern its affairs on the basis of free agreements, or else exploitation will continue. The recurrence of political reaction and a new destruction of the beginnings of freedom cannot theoretically be ruled out, and certainly not as long as a hostile environment exists. No patented system worked out in advance can preclude regressions. The modalities of the new society are first found in the process of social transformation. The theoretical conception which, following its first trailblazers, will show the new society its way—the system of workers' councils—grows out of praxis. The roots of the council system go back to 1871, 1905, and other events. *Revolutionary transformation has a tradition that must continue.*

The future form of collective life has a chance to endure, not

thought as a political guideline: "It makes a great difference if one simply follows the course of history without reflection or with insight into its causal relations. Historical changes occur in both cases, but they announce themselves earlier, and they happen above all only after they have, depending on their nature and significance, shaken society in an appropriately foreboding way."[6] The knowledge of historical laws which govern the succession of social forms, for the Saint-Simonians, softens the impact of the revolution, while for the Marxists it strengthens it. Both ascribe to such knowledge the function of shortening a process which completes itself autonomously and almost naturally. "The revolutionary transformation," says Bebel, "that changes all social relations, and in particular the role of women, is already happening before our eyes. It is only a matter of time before society undertakes this transformation on a larger scale and accelerates and generalizes the process, thereby making everyone without exception participate in its numerous and many-faceted advantages."[7] Thus is the revolution reduced to the intensive transition to state capitalism which was then already announcing itself. Despite pious references to the Hegelian logic of leaps and reversals, transformation appeared essentially as an extension of scale: the first attempts at planning should be reinforced and distribution made more rational. The doctrine of midwifery degrades the revolution to mere progress.

Dialectic is not identical with development. Two contradictory moments, the transition to state control and liberation from it, are seized as one in the concept of social revolution. Revolution brings about what would happen without spontaneity in any case: the socialization of the means of production, planned management of production, and unlimited control of nature. And it also brings about what will not happen without resistance and constantly renewed efforts to strengthen freedom: *the end of exploitation*. Such an outcome is not a further acceleration of progress, but a qualitative leap out of the dimension of progress. The rational is never totally deducible. It is conceived everywhere in the historical dialectic as the break with class society. The theoretical arguments for the idea that state capitalism is the last stage of class society are based on the notion that the existing material conditions make possible and promote that leap. The theories from which these arguments stem indicate the objective possibilities to the conscious will. When this theory portrays the phases of bourgeois economy—bloodshed and collapse—as an immanent law of development in the transition to freedom, the notion of the self-movement of this process breaks down. One can determine today what the leaders of the masses will inflict on the masses, if both forces are not abolished. That is part of the immanent law of development. One can not determine what a free society will do or permit. The self-movement of the concept of the commodity leads to the concept of state capitalism, just as for Hegel the certainty of sense data leads to absolute knowledge. For Hegel, however, the stages of the Concept necessarily correspond to physical and social nature without any further hindrance, because the Concept and reality are not merely different but, because both in the end as well as in essence, are actually the same. Materialist thought, on the other hand, should not permit itself to consider this identity as a certainty in fact. The appearance of conditions which can be inferred from the Concept gives the idealist a feeling of contentment, and the historical materialist the feeling of rebellion. Both are disappointed when human society does in fact pass through all the phases which can be derived from their own concept as the inversion of free and equal exchange into unfreedom and injustice. The Idealist dialectic preserves the Noble, the Good, the Eternal; every historical situation is said to contain the Ideal, but not in explicit form. The identity of the ideal and the real is considered the presupposition and the goal of history. The materialist dialectic deals with the common, the bad, the transitory; every historical situation contains the ideal, but not explicitly. The identity of the ideal and reality is universal exploitation. Therefore, Marxist science constitutes the critique of bourgeois economy and not the expounding of a socialist one; Marx left that task for Bebel. Marx himself explained the reality of the ideology of bourgeois economy in the dissection of official economy. He discovered the secret of the economy itself. Smith and Ricardo are disposed of, society is indicted.

The deduction of the capitalist phases from simple commodity production through monopoly and state capitalism is of course not an experiment in thought. The principle of exchange is not only formulated in thought, but it has governed reality. The contradictions which the critique reveals in this principle have made themselves drastically obvious in history. The worker is both rewarded and cheated in the exchange of labor power as a commodity. The equality of commodity owners is an ideological illusion which breaks down in an industrial system and which yields to overt domination in an authoritarian state. The development of bourgeois society is limited in its mode of production, which is characterized by the economic principle of exchange. Despite the real validity of this principle, there has never been a congruence between its critical representation and its

historical development which could not be broken down. The difference between concept and reality—not the concept itself—is the
foundation for the possibility of revolutionary praxis. A necessary
relationship exists in class society between the changes in the mode of
production and the course of an ideology; this relationship can be
deduced conceptually. But the necessity of past events determines the
will toward freedom which is present in class society as little as does
the inevitability of future events. For every conclusion stemming from
the belief that history will follow a progressing line (regardless of
whether one considers this line to be straight, spiral, or zig-zag), there
is a counter-argument which is no less valid. Theory explains essentially the course of destiny. In all the consistency which theory can
find in economic development, in all the logic of the succession of
individual social epochs, in all the increases in productive power,
methods, and skills—the capitalist antagonisms have in fact been
growing. Through them human beings will ultimately define themselves. These antagonisms are today not only more capable of producing freedom, but also less capable. Not only freedom, but also future
forms of oppression are possible. They can be theoretically evaluated
as either regressions or as ingenious new equipment. With state
capitalism those in power can strengthen their position even more.
State capitalism is, to be sure, an antagonistic, transient phenomenon.
The law of its collapse is readily visible: it is based on the limitation of
productivity due to the existence of the bureaucracies. However, the
propagation of authoritarian forms has still much room in which to
operate; and it would not be the first time that a long period of
heightened oppression followed a period of increased independence
for the oppressed. Athenian industry and Roman landowning to a
large extent introduced slavery, since free workers became too demanding and expensive. In the last part of the Middle Ages, the
freedom which the peasants had obtained in the 14th century because
of the decrease in their numbers was taken away. The indignation at
the thought that even the limited freedom of the 19th century is being
eliminated in the long run by state capitalism, by the "socialization of
poverty," stems from the knowledge that no barriers exist any longer
for socialized wealth. But upon these conditions for social wealth rests
not only the opportunity to demolish modern slavery, but just as much
the opportunity for its continuation. The objective spirit is always the
product of the adaptation of established power to the conditions of its
existence. Despite the open conflict between church and state in the
Middle Ages, between the world-encompassing cartels of the present,

the opposing forces have neither destroyed each other, nor fully joined together. Either alternative would be the end of the ruling power which must maintain this antagonism within itself if it is to endure the antagonism between itself and those it dominates. A world cartel is impossible. It would turn at once into freedom. The few big monopolies, which maintain their competition despite identical manufacturing methods, and products, furnish a model for future international constellations. Two friendly-hostile blocs of varying composition could rule the entire world; they could offer their followers, in addition to the *fasci*, better merchandise, at the expense of colonial and semi-colonial populations. As mutual threats they could always find new reasons to continue military armament. The increase in production, which would first be accelerated and later slowed by bourgeois property relations, in itself corresponds in no way to human needs. Today this increased production serves only the ruling class. Trees should not grow up in the sky. As long as there exists in the world a scarcity of absolute necessities, in fact even a scarcity of luxury articles, the rulers will take advantage of the opportunity to isolate from one another individuals and groups, and national and social classes, and thus reproduce its own ruling position. The bureaucracy has taken control of the economic mechanism, which slipped away from the control of the bourgeoisie's pure profit principle. The specialized concept of economics, which in contrast to its critics deals with the decline of the market system, contains no further objections to the capability of the existence of state capitalism than the objections which Mises and his associates raised against socialism. These people live today only for the fight against the social reforms in democratic countries, and they have completely lost their influence. The essence of liberal criticism consists of economic-technical considerations. Without some unobstructed operation of the old mechanisms of supply and demand, productive industrial methods would not be differentiated from unproductive ones. The limited intelligence, which stuck obstinately to such arguments against historical progress, was so bound to the existing order that it did not see that the triumph of the existing order would result in fascism. Capitalism may still exist for a time, even after its liberal phase is over. The fascist phase is, of course, determined by the same economic tendencies which already have destroyed the market system. It is not the impossibility of the smooth functioning of the international market, but the international crisis which is perpetuated by the authoritarian state, which allows a humanity already demoralized by the authoritarian forms no other choice. The eternal system of the authoritarian state, as terrible as the threat may seem, is no more real than the eternal harmony of the market economy. If the exchange of equivalents was just a guise for inequality, then the fascist plan is simply robbery.

Today's possibilities are no less than the despair. State capitalism, as the most recent phase of history, contains more power to organize the economically retarded territories of the world than did the previous phase whose decisive representatives exhibit their limited power and initiative. They were moved by the fear of losing their profitable social position: they were willing to do anything which would not in the long run forfeit the help of future fascism. The regenerated form of ruling power appears in fascism and they anticipate the power they would have if victorious. The wealth accumulated over the centuries and the diplomatic experience which goes along with it is used to insure that the legitimate rulers of Europe themselves control its unification, and once again prevent integral statism. The era of the authoritarian state can be broken both by such regressions as well as by attempts to establish actual freedom. These attempts, which by their very nature tolerate no bureaucracies, can come only from the isolated. Everyone is isolated. The sullen yearnings of the atomized masses and the conscious will of the underground resistance point in the same direction. To the extent that there existed among the instigators of previous revolutions of collective resistance a sense of infallibility, the masses were only the followers. A direct line leads from the leftist opponents of Robespierre's *étatisme* to the Conspiracy of the Equals under the Directory. As long as the party is still a group not yet alienated from its anti-authoritarian goals, as long as solidarity is not replaced by obedience, as long as the party does not confuse the dictatorship of the proletariat with the rule of the most clever party tacticians—then its general line will be determined precisely by those deviations of which a ruling clique naturally knows how to quickly rid itself. As long as the avant-garde has the ability to act without periodic purges, the hope for a classless condition will continue to live on. The two phases in which, according to the prescription of tradition, a classless society is to come to fruition, have little to do with the ideology which today serves the perpetuation of integral statism. Since an unlimited amount of consumer goods and luxury items still seems like a dream, the ruling class, which should have faded away in the first phase, is said to be able to reinforce its position. Reassured by poor harvests and a housing shortage, it proclaims that the reign of the secret police will disappear when the land of milk and honey has been reached. Engels, on the contrary, is a utopian; he merges the socialization of the means of production and the end of oppression into one. "The first act in which the state really appears as a representative of the entire society, the seizure of the means of production in the name of society, is at the same time its last independent act as a state. The intervention of power of the state in social relations will become unnecessary in one area after another and then wither away naturally."[8] He did not believe that the unlimited increase in material production, the prerequisite of a human society and a classless democracy, would be attainable only when the whole world is fully populated with tractors and radios. Praxis has not disproven the theory, but rather interpreted it. The enemies of the state power have fallen asleep, but not of their own accord. With each bit of planning completed, a bit of repression was originally supposed to become unnecessary. Instead, more repression has developed in the administration of the plans. Whether the increase in production actualizes or destroys socialism cannot be decided abstractly.

Dread in the expectation of an authoritarian epoch does not hinder the resistance. The exercise of administrative functions by a class or party can be replaced after the abolition of privilege by forms of a classless democracy which can prevent the elevation of the administrative sector to positions of power. Though the bourgeoisie earlier held the government in check through its property, the administration in a new society would only be kept from becoming oppressive by the uncompromising independence of the citizenry. Even today its followers are no less a danger to the authoritarian state than the free worker was to liberalism. The belief that one is acting in the name of something greater than oneself is bankrupt. Not a few Marxists paid homage to it. Without the feeling of being a member of a large party, or having an honored leader, world history or at least infallible theory on their side, their socialism did not function. The devotion to the marching masses, the enthusiastic submission to collectivity, the whole Philistine dream which met with Nietzsche's scorn, celebrates a happy resurrection with the authoritarian youth organizations. The revolution, which was a vocation on the same level as science, led to jail or to Siberia. But since the victory, a career beckons, if nowhere else, at least in the party hierarchy. There are not only professors, but also revolutionaries of prominence. The mass media assimilate the revolution by absorbing its leaders into their list of celebrities. The isolated individual who is not appointed or protected by any power cannot expect fame. Even so, he is a power because everyone is isolated. Their only weapon is the word. The more it is bandied about by the barbarians within and the cultural sophisticates abroad, the more its power is restored. The impotent utterances in the totalitarian state are more dangerous than the most impressive party proclamations under Wilhelm II. Whenever a new jargon stands between themselves and their paying readers, it does not take the German intellectuals very long to learn to use it. Language has always been of more use to them in the struggle for existence than in the expression of truth. Their earnestness is revealed again in the betrayal of language to commerce. It is as if they feared that the German language could drive them further than seems consistent with their tolerated existence and the justified demands of their patrons. The men of the Enlightenment had much less to risk. Their opposition harmonized with the interests of the bourgeoisie, which had a good deal of power even then. Voltaire and the Encyclopedists had their protectors. Beyond that harmony, no minister of state would go along with them. Jean Meslier had to hold his tongue throughout his life; the Marquis spent his life in jails. But if the word can be a spark, it has yet to set anything on fire. It is in no sense propaganda and hardly a call to action. It seeks to say what everyone knows and at the same time forbids himself to know. It does not impose itself by the skillful uncovering of state secrets which only the powerful know. The free-floating politician of the mass party whose blustering rhetoric has faded away, today indulges in talk of statistics, the national economy and "inside stories." His manner of speaking has become prosaic and well-informed. He maintains an ostensible contact with the workers and expresses himself in export figures and synthetic materials. He knows better than the fascists and masochistically intoxicates himself with the facts, which have already passed him by. When one can no longer invoke violence, knowledge must suffice.

Whoever cares for a human arrangement of the world can look to no court of appeal, to no existing or future power. The question of what "one" should do with power once one has it, the same question which was so meaningful for the bureaucrats of the mass party, loses its meaning in a struggle against them. The question presupposes the continued existence of that which should disappear: the power to dispose of the labor of others. If society in the future really functions through free agreement rather than through direct or indirect force, the result of such an agreement cannot be theoretically anticipated. Proposals for the economy beyond those already at hand under state capitalism could eventually be useful. Contemporary reflection in the service of a transformed society should not disregard the fact that in a classless democracy plans cannot be forced on others through power or through routine, but must be arrived at through free agreement. This consciousness would keep no one who accepts the possibility of a changed world from considering how people could live without population policy and penal authority, model factories and repressed minorities. It is, of course, more questionable than the neo-humanist Germans tend to think, whether the dismantling of the authoritarian bureaucracy would be accompanied by popular orgies of revenge. If the ousting of the rulers is once again accomplished by terror, then these isolated individuals will passionately insist that it fulfill their will. Nothing on earth can any longer justify violence except the necessity of putting an end to violence itself. If the opponents are right that after the fall of the fascist machinery of terror, chaos will reign, not just for a moment but until a new form of terrorist oppression takes over, then humanity is lost. The assertion that without a new authoritarian bureaucracy the machines, the knowledge, the technical and administrative methods, the entire system for providing necessities as attained under an authoritarian state would be destroyed is a pretext. Their first concern when they think about freedom is the new penal system, not its abolition. "The masses," it says in a pamphlet of "educational material," "will free political prisoners and jail their oppressors instead." Specialists in oppression will offer their services en masse. Whether or not that happens again depends on those who are not specialists. The role of the specialists can be all the less important, since the means of production need not be developed much beyond the forms existing under integral statism. State capitalism sometimes seems almost like a parody of the classless society. There are indications that for technical reasons its centralization of production will survive. If small units take on more importance in relation to the central administration in modern industrial production and strategy, so that the elite workers have to be more and more pampered by the central leadership, then this is the visible expression of a general economic upheaval. The degradation of individuals to mere centers of reaction which respond to every stimulus, at the same time prepares their emancipation from the central command.

Thus the perfect weapons that the bureaucracy has at its disposal could not ward off change forever if it did not have something besides its immediate power. The individual has historically constituted himself in fear. There is a further stage of fear beyond the fear of death, from which point it again dissolves. The completion of centralization in society and state pushes its driving forces to decentralize. It continues the paralysis to which the age of heavy industry has already pushed the human being through his increasing dispensability, through his separation from productive labor, and through continuous worry about the wretched social welfare. The course of progress appears to the victims as though freedom or lack of freedom did not matter for their well being. Freedom suffers the same fate as did virtue in Valéry's conception. It is no longer fought over, but forgotten, and in any case embalmed like the slogan of democracy after the last war. Everyone agrees today that the word "freedom" should only be used as a phrase; to take it seriously is utopian. At one time the critique of utopia helped to maintain the thought of freedom as the thought of its realization. *Today utopia is maligned because no one really wants to see its realization.* They strangle the imagination, which Bebel already took lightly.[9] If the terror of the Gestapo at least brings into existence certain subversive tendencies, beyond the borders of Germany it also produces a disastrous respect for the lasting power of coercion. Instead of the present anti-Semitic, relentless and aggressive form of state capitalism, there are still dreams of a state capitalism which would, with the grace of the older world powers, rule the people. "There is no other socialism than that which is achieved by authoritarian means," concludes the state economist Pirou.[10] "In our era the authority of the state is exercised in the framework of the nation. Thus socialism, even when it is internationally oriented, can only carry out its program nationally." Those immediately involved in the struggle are of the same opinion as the observers. No matter how honestly they intend to build a "workers' democracy," the dictatorial measures necessary for its security, the "substitution" of a new ruling mechanism for the present one, the belief in the "vanguard role" of the party, in short, all the categories of repression which are probably necessary, conceal so well the realistic foreground that the image on the horizon always spoken of by socialist politicians looks suspiciously like a mirage. Just as liberal critics of harsh punishment who are appointed to the Ministry of Justice by a bourgeois revolution are usually worn out after a few years because their efforts are obstructed by provincial administrators, so the politicians and intellectuals seem to be exhausted by the tenacity of the existing order. The lesson to be learned from fascism, and even more from bolshevism, is that what seems like madness to a detached analysis is at times the reality, and that politics, as Hitler said, is not the art of the possible but of the impossible. Moreover, this development is not so unexpected as one might think. In order to conduct their affairs in solidarity with one another, people will have to change their natures much less than they have already been changed by fascism. The narrow-minded and cunning creatures that call themselves men will some day be seen as caricatures, evil masks behind which a better possibility decays. In order to penetrate those masks, the imagination would need powers of which fascism has already divested it. The force of imagination is absorbed in the struggle every individual must wage in order to live. But the material conditions have been satisfied. Despite the necessity of transition, dictatorship, terrorism, work and sacrifice, the alternative depends only on human will. Problems which a few decades ago were thought to be insuperable, technical or organizational barriers have been overcome for all to see. As a result the simplistic teachings of economism, which were so prosaic, were dissolved into philosophical anthropologies. When technology can produce stockings out of thin air, one then has to reach for the eternal in man, namely to declare inalterable certain psychological characteristics, in order to rationalize eternal domination.

The fact that even the enemies of the authoritarian state can no longer conceive of freedom destroys communication. A language in which one does not recognize his own desires or become impassioned is alien. Thus the bourgeoisie is no longer upset in the slightest over its own non-conformist literature; it has brought Tolstoy into the movies and Maupassant into the drugstore. Not only the categories in which the future is depicted but also those in which the present is dealt with have become ideological. The conditions for the realization of utopia are so urgently ripe that they can no longer be honestly articulated. Any thought which is difficult to use and to label rightly arouses stronger mistrust in the courts of knowledge and literature than the very professions of a Marxist doctrine. The confessions to which such thinking was seduced through friendly persuasion in the pre-fascist era, in order to be rid of it once and for all later on, were equally useless for the subjugated. Theory has no program for the electoral campaign, or even for the reconstruction of Europe which the specialists will soon see to. The readiness to obey, even when it sets out to think, is of no use to theory. Despite all the urgency with which theory attempts to illuminate the movement of the social totality even in its smallest detail, it is unable to prescribe to individuals an effective form of resistance to injustice. Thought itself is already a sign of resistance, the effort to keep oneself from being deceived any longer. Thought is not absolutely opposed to command and obedience, but sets them for the time being in relationship to the task of making freedom a reality. This relationship is in danger. Sociological and psychological concepts are too superficial to express what has happened to revolutionaries in the last few decades: their will toward freedom has been damaged, without which neither understanding nor solidarity nor a correct relation between leader and group is conceivable.

If there is no return to liberalism, the appropriate form of activity appears to be the extension of state capitalism. To work with it, expand it and extend it everywhere to advanced forms appears to offer the advantage of progress and all the security of success, which one can only desire for *politique scientifique*. Since the proletariat has nothing to expect from the old world powers, there would appear to be no choice but an alliance with the new ones. Since the planned economy which the leaders of nations are creating is closer to socialism than liberalism is, there should be an alliance between the leader and the proletariat. It would be sentimental to remain opposed to state capitalism merely because of those who have been slain. One could say that the Jews were for the most part capitalists, and that the small nations have no justification for their existence. State capitalism is said to be the only thing possible today. As long as the proletariat does not make its own revolution, there remains no choice for it and its theoreticians but to follow the *Weltgeist* on the path it has chosen. Such opinions, and there are plenty of them, are neither the most stupid nor the most dishonest. This much is true, that with the return to the old free enterprise system, the entire horror would start again from the beginning under new management. But the historical outlook of such reasoning recognizes only the dimension of the cycle of progress and regression; it ignores the active intervention of men. It values men only for what they are under capitalism: as social quantities, as things. As long as world history follows its logical course, it fails to fulfill its human destiny.

Freudian Theory and the Pattern of Fascist Propaganda[1]

By Theodor W. Adorno

Written in 1951, this essay systematizes the author's extensive work in the 1940s, informed by psychoanalysis, on the mass psychological base of fascism. It is important for us because it asks for the social-psychological conditions of the possibility (and also the limits) of modern authoritarian states. The essay further demonstrates the interrelationship of the Frankfurt critique of mass culture and the Institute's fascism theory. Adorno was to call both the culture industry and fascist propaganda "psychoanalysis in reverse."

During the past decade, the nature and content of the speeches and pamphlets of American fascist agitators have been subjected to intensive research by social scientists. Some of these studies, undertaken along the lines of content analysis, have finally led to a comprehensive presentation in the book, *Prophets of Deceit*, by L. Lowenthal and N. Guterman.[2] The overall picture obtained is characterized by two main features. First, with the exception of some bizarre and completely negative recommendations: to put aliens into concentration camps or to expatriate Zionists, fascist propaganda material in this country is little concerned with concrete and tangible political issues. The overwhelming majority of all agitators' statements are directed *ad hominem*. They are obviously based on psychological calculations rather than on the intention to gain followers through the rational statement of rational aims. The term "rabble rouser," though objectionable because of its inherent contempt of the masses as such, is adequate insofar as it expresses the atmosphere of irrational emotional aggressiveness purposely promoted by our would-be Hitlers. If it is an impudence to call people "rabble," it is precisely the aim of the agitator to transform the very same people into "rabble," i.e., crowds bent to violent action without any sensible political aim, and to create the atmosphere of the pogrom. The universal purpose of these agitators is to instigate methodically what, since Gustave Le Bon's famous book, is commonly known as "the psychology of the masses."

Second, the agitators' approach is truly systematical and follows a rigidly set pattern of clear-cut "devices." This does not merely pertain to the ultimate unity of the political purpose: the abolition of democracy through mass support against the democratic principle, but even more so to the intrinsic nature of the content and presentation of propaganda itself. The similarity of the utterances of various agitators, from much-publicized figures such as Coughlin and Gerald Smith to provincial small-time hate mongers, is so great that it suffices in principle to analyze the statements of one of them in order to know them all.[3] Moreover, the speeches themselves are so monotonous that one meets with endless repetitions as soon as one is acquainted with the very limited number of stock devices. As a matter of fact, constant reiteration and scarcity of ideas are indispensable ingredients of the entire technique.

While the mechanical rigidity of the pattern is obvious and itself the expression of certain psychological aspects of fascist mentality, one cannot help feeling that propaganda material of the fascist brand forms a structural unit with a total common conception, be it conscious or unconscious, which determines every word that is said. This structural unit seems to refer to the implicit political conception as well as to the psychological essence. So far, only the detached and in a way isolated nature of each device has been given scientific attention; the psychoanalytic connotations of the devices have been stressed and elaborated. Now that the elements have been cleared up sufficiently, the time has come to focus attention on the psychological system as such—and it may not be entirely accidental that the term summons the association of paranoia—which comprises and begets these elements. This seems to be the more appropriate since otherwise the psychoanalytic interpretation of the individual devices will remain somewhat haphazard and arbitrary. A kind of theoretical frame of reference will have to be evolved. Inasmuch as the individual devices call almost irresistibly for psychoanalytic interpretation, it is but logical to postulate that this frame of reference should consist of the application of a more comprehensive, basic psychoanalytic theory to the agitators' overall approach.

Such a frame of reference has been provided by Freud himself in his book *Group Psychology and the Analysis of the Ego*, published in English as early as 1922, and long before the danger of German fascism appeared to be acute.[4] It is not an overstatement if we say that Freud, though he was hardly interested in the political phase of the problem, clearly foresaw the rise and nature of fascist mass movements in purely psychological categories. If it is true that the analyst's unconscious perceives the unconscious of the patient, one may also presume that his theoretical intuitions are capable of anticipating tendencies still latent on a rational level but manifesting themselves on a deeper one. It may not have been perchance that after the First World War Freud turned his attention to narcissism and ego problems in the specific sense. The mechanisms and instinctual conflicts involved evidently play an increasingly important role in the present epoch, whereas, according to the testimony of practicing analysts, the "classical" neuroses such as conversion hysteria, which served as models for the method, now occur less frequently than at the time of Freud's own development when Charcot dealt with hysteria clinically and Ibsen made it the subject matter of some of his plays. According to Freud, the problem of mass psychology is closely related to the new type of psychological affliction so characteristic of the era which for socio-economic reasons witnesses the decline of the individual and his subsequent weakness. While Freud did not concern himself with the social changes, it may be said that he developed within the monadological confines of the individual the traces of its profound crisis and willingness to yield unquestioningly to powerful outside, collective agencies. Without ever devoting himself to the study of contemporary social developments, Freud has pointed to historical trends through the development of his own work, the choice of his subject matters, and the evolution of guiding concepts.

The method of Freud's book constitutes a dynamic interpretation of Le Bon's description of the mass mind and a critique of a few dogmatic concepts—magic words, as it were—which are employed by Le Bon and other pre-analytic psychologists as though they were keys for some startling phenomena. Foremost among these concepts is that of suggestion which, incidentally, still plays a large role as a stopgap in popular thinking about the spell exercised by Hitler and his like over the masses. Freud does not challenge the accuracy of Le Bon's well-known characterizations of masses as being largely de-individualized, irrational, easily influenced, prone to violent action and altogether of a regressive nature. What distinguishes him from Le Bon is rather the absence of the traditional contempt for the masses which is the *thema probandum* of most of the older psychologists. Instead of inferring from the usual descriptive findings that the masses are inferior per se and likely to remain so, he asks in the spirit of true enlightenment: what makes the masses into masses? He rejects the easy hypothesis of a social or herd instinct, which for him denotes the problem and not its solution. In addition to the purely psychological reasons he gives for this rejection, one might say that he is on safe ground also from the sociological point of view. The straightforward comparison of modern mass formations with biological phenomena can hardly be regarded as valid since the members of contemporary masses are at least *prima facie* individuals, the children of a liberal, competitive and individualistic society, and conditioned to maintain themselves as independent, self-sustaining units; they are continuously admonished to be "rugged" and warned against surrender. Even if one were to assume that archaic, pre-individual instincts survive, one could not simply point to this inheritance but would have to explain why modern men revert to patterns of behavior which flagrantly contradict their own rational level and the present stage of enlightened technological civilization. This is precisely what Freud wants to do. He tries to find out which psychological forces result in the transformation of individuals into a mass. "If the individuals in the group are combined into a unity, there must surely be something to unite them, and this bond might be precisely the thing that is characteristic of a group."[5] This quest, however, is tantamount to an exposition of the fundamental issue of fascist manipulation. For the fascist demagogue, who has to win the support of millions of people for aims largely incompatible with their own rational self-interest, can do so only by artificially creating the *bond* Freud is looking for. If the demagogues' approach is at all realistic—and their popular success leaves no doubt that it is—it might be hypothesized that the bond in question is the very same the demagogue tries to produce synthetically; in fact, that it is the unifying principle behind his various devices.

In accordance with general psychoanalytic theory, Freud believes that the bond which integrates individuals into a mass, is of a *libidinal* nature. Earlier psychologists have occasionally hit upon this aspect of mass psychology. "In McDougall's opinion, men's emotions are stirred in a group to a pitch that they seldom or never attain under other conditions; and it is a pleasurable experience for those who are concerned to surrender themselves so unreservedly to their passions and thus to become merged in the group and to lose the sense of the limits of their individuality."[6] Freud goes beyond such observations by explaining the coherence of masses altogether in terms of the pleasure principle, that is to say, the actual or vicarious gratifications individuals obtain from surrendering to a mass. Hitler, by the way, was well aware of the libidinal source of mass formation through surrender when he attributed specifically female, passive features to the participants of his meetings, and thus also hinted at the role of unconscious homosexuality in mass psychology.[7] The most important consequence of Freud's introduction of libido into group psychology is that the traits generally ascribed to masses lose the deceptively primordial and irreducible character reflected by the arbitrary construct of specific mass or herd instincts. The latter are effects rather than causes. What is peculiar to the masses is, according to Freud, not so much a new quality as the manifestation of old ones usually hidden. "From our point of view we need not attribute so much importance to the appearance of new characteristics. For us it would be enough to say that in a group the individual is brought under conditions which allow him to throw off the repressions of his unconscious instincts."[8] This does not only dispense with auxiliary hypotheses *ad hoc* but also does justice to the simple fact that those who become submerged in masses are not primitive men but display primitive attitudes contradictory to their *normal* rational behavior. Yet, even the most trivial descriptions leave no doubt about the affinity of certain peculiarities of masses to archaic traits. Particular mention should be made here of the potential short-cut from violent emotions to violent actions stressed by all authors on mass psychology, a phenomenon which in Freud's writings on primitive cultures leads to the assumption that the murder of the father of the primary horde is not imaginary but corresponds to prehistoric reality. In terms of dynamic theory, the revival of such traits has to be understood as the result of a *conflict*. It may also help to explain some of the manifestations of fascist mentality which could hardly be grasped without the assumption of an antagonism between varied psychological forces. One has to think here above all of the psychological category of destructiveness with which Freud dealt in his *Civilization and its Discontents*. As a rebellion against civilization, fascism is not simply the reoccurrence of the archaic but its reproduction in and by civilization itself. It is hardly adequate to define the forces of fascist rebellion simply as powerful id energies which throw off the pressure of the existing social order. Rather, this rebellion borrows its energies partly from other psychological agencies which are pressed into the service of the unconscious.

Since the libidinal bond between members of masses is obviously not of an uninhibited sexual nature, the problem arises as to which psychological mechanisms transform primary sexual energy into feelings which hold masses together. Freud copes with the problem by analyzing the phenomena covered by the terms suggestion and suggestibility. He recognizes suggestion as the "shelter" or "screen" concealing "love relationships." It is essential that the "love relationship" behind suggestion remains unconscious.[9] Freud dwells on the fact that in organized groups such as the Army or the Church there is either no mention of love whatsoever between the members, or it is expressed only in a sublimated and indirect way, through the mediation of some religious image in the love of whom the members unite and whose all-embracing love they are supposed to imitate in their attitude towards each other. It seems significant that in today's society with its artificially integrated fascist masses, reference to love is almost completely excluded.[10] Hitler shunned the traditional role of the loving father and replaced it entirely by the negative one of threatening authority. The concept of love was relegated to the abstract notion of *Germany* and seldom mentioned without the epithet of "fanatical" through which even this love obtained a ring of hostility and aggressiveness against those not encompassed by it. It is one of the basic tenets of fascist leadership to keep primary libidinal energy on an unconscious level so as to divert its manifestations in a way suitable to political ends. The less an objective idea such as religious salvation plays a role in mass formation, and the more mass manipulation becomes the sole aim, the more thoroughly uninhibited love has to be repressed and moulded into obedience. There is too little in the content of fascist ideology that *could* be loved.

The libidinal pattern of fascism and the entire technique of fascist demagogues are authoritarian. This is where the techniques of the demagogue and the hypnotist coincide with the psychological mechanism by which individuals are made to undergo the regressions which reduce them to mere members of a group.

By the measures that he takes, the hypnotist awakens in the subject a portion of his archaic inheritance which had also made him compliant towards his parents and which had experienced an

individual re-animation in his relation to his father: what is thus
awakened is the idea of a paramount and dangerous personality,
towards whom only a passive-masochistic attitude is possible, to
whom one's will has to be surrendered,—while to be alone with
him, 'to look him in the face', appears a hazardous enterprise. It
is only in some such way as this that we can picture the relation of
the individual member of the primal horde to the primal
father . . The uncanny and coercive characteristics of group
formations, which are shown in their suggestion phenomena,
may therefore with justice be traced back to the fact of their origin
from the primal horde. The leader of the group is still the dreaded
primal father; the group still wishes to be governed by unrestricted force; it has an extreme passion for authority; in Le Bon's
phrase, it has a thirst for obedience. The primal father is the
group ideal, which governs the ego in the place of the ego ideal.
Hypnosis has a good claim to being described as a group of two;
there remains as a definition for suggestion—a conviction which
is not based upon perception and reasoning but upon an erotic
tie.[11]

This actually defines the nature and content of fascist propaganda. It is psychological because of its irrational authoritarian aims
which cannot be attained by means of rational convictions but only
through the skillful awakening of "a portion of the subject's archaic
inheritance." Fascist agitation is centered in the idea of the leader, no
matter whether he actually leads or is only the mandatary of group
interests, because only the psychological image of the leader is apt to
reanimate the idea of the all-powerful and threatening primal father.
This is the ultimate root of the otherwise enigmatic *personalization* of
fascist propaganda, its incessant plugging of names and supposedly
great men, instead of discussing objective causes. The formation of
the imagery of an omnipotent and unbridled father figure, by far
transcending the individual father and therewith apt to be enlarged into
a "group ego," is the only way to promulgate the "passive-masochistic attitude . . . to whom one's will has to be surrendered," an
attitude required of the fascist follower the more his political behavior
becomes irreconcilable with his own rational interests as a private
person as well as those of the group or class to which he actually
belongs.[12] The follower's reawakened irrationality is, therefore, quite
rational from the leader's viewpoint: it necessarily has to be "a
conviction which is not based upon perception and reasoning but upon
an erotic tie."

The mechanism which transforms libido into the bond between

leader and followers, and between the followers themselves, is that of *identification*. A great part of Freud's book is devoted to its analysis.[13] It is impossible to discuss here the very subtle theoretical differentiation, particularly the one between identification and introjection. It should be noted, however, that the late Ernst Simmel, to whom we owe valuable contributions to the psychology of fascism, took up Freud's concept of the ambivalent nature of identification as a derivative of the oral phase of the organization of the libido,[14] and expanded it into an analytic theory of anti-Semitism.

We content ourselves with a few observations on the relevancy of the doctrine of identification to fascist propaganda and fascist mentality. It has been observed by several authors and by Erik Homburger Erikson in particular, that the specifically fascist leader type does not seem to be a father figure such as for instance the king of former times. The inconsistency of this observation with Freud's theory of the leader as the primal father, however, is only superficial. His discussion of identification may well help us to understand, in terms of subjective dynamics, certain changes which are actually due to objective historical conditions. Identification is "the *earliest* expression of an emotional tie with another person," playing "a part in the early history of the Oedipus complex."[5] It may well be that this pre-oedipal component of identification helps to bring about the separation of the leader image as that of an all-powerful primal father, from the actual father image. Since the child's identification with his father as an answer to the Oedipus complex is only a secondary phenomenon, infantile regression may go beyond this father image and through an "anaclitic" process reach a more archaic one. Moreover, the primitively narcissistic aspect of identification as an act of *devouring*, of making the beloved object part of oneself, may provide us with a clue to the fact that the modern leader image sometimes seems to be the enlargement of the subject's own personality, a collective projection of himself, rather than the image of the father whose role during the later phases of the subject's infancy may well have decreased in present-day society.[16] All these facets call for further clarification.

The essential role of narcissism in regard to the identifications which are at play in the formation of fascist groups, is recognized in Freud's theory of *idealization*. "We see that the object is being treated in the same way as our own ego, so that when we are in love a considerable amount of narcissistic libido overflows on the object. It is even obvious, in many forms of love choice, that the object serves as a substitute for some unattained ego ideal of our own. We love it on account of the perfections which we have striven to reach for our own ego, and which we should now like to procure in this roundabout way as a means of satisfying our narcissism."[17] It is precisely this idealization of himself which the fascist leader tries to promote in his followers, and which is helped by the *Führer* ideology. The people he has to reckon with generally undergo the characteristic modern conflict between a strongly developed rational, self-preserving ego agency[18] and the continuous failure to satisfy their own ego demands. This conflict results in strong narcissistic impulses which can be absorbed and satisfied only through idealization as the partial transfer of the narcissistic libido to the object. This, again, falls in line with the semblance of the leader image to an enlargement of the subject: by making the leader his ideal he loves himself, as it were, but gets rid of the stains of frustration and discontent which mar his picture of his own empirical self. This pattern of identification through idealization, the caricature of true, conscious solidarity, is, however, a collective one. It is effective in vast numbers of people with similar characterological dispositions and libidinal leanings. The fascist *community of the people* corresponds exactly to Freud's definition of a group as being "a number of individuals who have substituted one and the same object for their ego ideal and have consequently identified themselves with one another in their ego."[19] The leader image, in turn, borrows as it were its primal father-like omnipotence from collective strength.

Freud's psychological construction of the leader imagery is corroborated by its striking coincidence with the fascist leader type, at least as far as its public build-up is concerned. His descriptions fit the picture of Hitler no less than idealizations into which the American demagogues try to style themselves. In order to allow narcissistic identification, the leader has to appear himself as absolutely narcissistic, and it is from this insight that Freud derives the portrait of the "primal father of the horde" which might as well be Hitler's.

> He, at the very beginning of the history of mankind, was the *Superman*[20] whom Nietzsche only expected from the future. Even today, the members of a group stand in need of the illusion that they are equally and justly loved by their leader; but the leader himself need love no one else, he may be of a masterly nature, absolutely narcissistic, but self-confident and independent. We know that love puts a check upon narcissism, and it would be possible to show how, by operating in this way, it became a factor of civilization.[21]

group is of so deep-rooted a nature that it affects even those groups whose "ideas" apparently exclude such reactions. By 1921, he was therefore able to dispense with the liberalistic illusion that the progress of civilization would automatically bring about an increase of tolerance and a lessening of violence against out-groups.

> Even during the kingdom of Christ, those people who do not belong to the community of believers, who do not love him, and whom he does not love, stand outside this tie. Therefore, a religion, even if it calls itself the religion of love, must be hard and unloving to those who do not belong to it. Fundamentally, indeed, every religion is in this same way a religion of love for all those whom it embraces; while cruelty and intolerance towards those who do not belong to it are natural to every religion. However difficult we may find it personally, we ought not to reproach believers too severely on this account: people who are unbelieving or indifferent are so much better off psychologically in this respect. If today that intolerance no longer shows itself so violent and cruel as in former centuries, we can scarcely conclude that there has been a softening in human manners. The cause is rather to be found in the undeniable weakening of religious feelings and the libidinal ties which depend upon them. If another group tie takes the place of the religious one—and the socialistic tie seems to be succeeding in doing so—, then there will be the same intolerance towards outsiders as in the age of the Wars of Religion.[27]

Freud's error in political prognosis, his blaming, the "socialists" for what their German archenemies did, is as striking as his prophecy of fascist destructiveness, the drive to eliminate the out-group[28]. As a matter of fact, neutralization of religion seems to have led to just the opposite of what the enlightener Freud anticipated: the division between the believers and nonbelievers has been maintained and reified. However, it has become a structure in itself, independent of any ideational content, and is even more stubbornly defended since it lost its inner conviction. At the same time, the mitigating impact of the religious doctrine of love vanished. This is the essence of the "sheep and goat" device employed by all fascist demagogues. Since they do not recognize any spiritual criterion in regard to who is chosen and who is rejected, they substitute a pseudo-natural criterion such as the race,[29] which seems to be inescapable and can therefore be applied even more mercilessly than was the concept of heresy during the Middle Ages. Freud has succeeded in identifying the libidinal function of this device. It acts as a negatively integrating force. Since the positive libido is completely invested in the image of the primal father, the leader, and since few positive contents are available, a negative one has to be found. "The leader or the leading idea might also, so to speak, be negative; hatred against a particular person or institution might operate in just the same unifying way, and might call up the same kind of emotional ties as positive attachment."[30] It goes without saying that this negative integration feeds on the instinct of destructiveness to which Freud does not explicitly refer in his *Group Psychology*, the decisive role of which he has, however, recognized in his *Civilization and Its Discontents*. In the present context, Freud explains the hostility against the out-group with narcissism:

> In the undisguised antipathies and aversions which people feel towards strangers with whom they have to do, we may recognize the expression of self-love—of narcissism. This self-love works for the self-assertion of the individual, and behaves as though the occurrence of any divergence from his own particular lines of development involved a criticism of them and a demand for their alteration.[31]

The narcissistic *gain* provided by fascist propaganda is obvious. It suggests continuously and sometimes in rather devious ways, that the follower, simply through belonging to the in-group, is better, higher and purer than those who are excluded. At the same time, any kind of critique or self-awareness is resented as a narcissistic loss and elicits rage. It accounts for the violent reaction of all fascists against what they deem *zersetzend*, that which debunks their own stubbornly maintained values, and it also explains the hostility of prejudiced persons against any kind of introspection. Concomitantly, the concentration of hostility upon the out-group does away with intolerance in one's own group to which one's relation would otherwise be highly ambivalent.

> But the whole of this intolerance vanishes, temporarily or permanently, as the result of the formation of a group, and in a group. So long as a group formation persists or so far as it extends, individuals behave as though they were uniform, tolerate other people's peculiarities, put themselves on an equal level with them, and have no feeling of aversion towards them. Such a limitation of narcissism can, according to our theoretical views, only be produced by one factor, a libidinal tie with other people.[32]

This is the line pursued by the agitators' standard "unity trick." They emphasize their being different from the outsider but play down such differences within their own group and tend to level out distinctive qualities among themselves with the exception of the hierarchical one. "We are all in the same boat"; nobody should be better off; the snob, the intellectual, the pleasure seeker are always attacked. The undercurrent of malicious egalitarianism, of the brotherhood of all-comprising humiliation, is a component of fascist propaganda and fascism itself. It found its symbol in Hitler's notorious command of the *Eintopfgericht*. The less they want the inherent social structure changed, the more they prate about social justice, meaning that no member of the "community of the people" should indulge in individual pleasures. Repressive egalitarianism instead of realization of true equality through the abolition of repression is part and parcel of the fascist mentality and reflected in the agitators' "If-you-only-knew" device which promises the vindictive revelation of all sorts of forbidden pleasures enjoyed by others. Freud interprets this phenomenon in terms of the transformation of individuals into members of a psychological "brother horde." Their coherence is a reaction formation against their primary jealousy of each other, pressed into the service of group coherence.

> What appears later on in society in the shape of *Gemeingeist*, *esprit de corps*, 'group spirit', etc. does not belie its derivation from what was originally envy. No one must want to put himself forward, every one must be the same and have the same. Social justice means that we deny ourselves many things so that others may have to do without them as well, or, what is the same thing, may not be able to ask for them.[33]

It may be added that the ambivalence towards the brother has found a rather striking, ever-recurring expression in the agitators' technique. Freud and Rank have pointed out that in fairy tales, small animals such as bees and ants "would be the brothers in the primal horde, just as in the same way in dream symbolism insects or vermin signify brothers and sisters (contemptuously, considered as babies)."[34] Since the members of the in-group have supposedly "succeeded in identifying themselves with one another by means of similar love for the same object,"[35] they cannot admit this contempt for each other. Thus, it is expressed by completely negative cathexis of these low animals, fused with hatred against the out-group, and projected upon the latter. Actually it is one of the favorite devices of fascist agitators—examined in great detail by Leo Lowenthal[36]—to compare out-groups, all foreigners and particularly refugees and Jews, with low animals and vermin.

If we are entitled to assume a correspondence of fascist prop-agandist stimuli to the mechanisms elaborated in Freud's *Group Psychology*, we have to ask ourselves the almost inevitable question: how did the fascist agitators, crude and semi-educated as they were, obtain knowledge of these mechanisms? Reference to the influence exercised by Hitler's *Mein Kampf* upon the American demagogues would not lead very far, since it seems impossible that Hitler's theoretical knowledge of group psychology went beyond the most trivial observations derived from a popularized Le Bon. Neither can it be maintained that Goebbels was a mastermind of propaganda and fully aware of the most advanced findings of modern depth psycholo-gy. Perusal of his speeches and selections from his recently published diaries give the impression of a person shrewd enough to play the game of power politics but utterly naive and superficial in regard to all social or psychological issues below the surface of his own catch-words and newspaper editorials. The idea of the sophisticated and "radical" intellectual Goebbels is part of the devil's legend associated with his name and fostered by eager journalism; a legend, incidental-ly, which itself calls for psychoanalytic explanation. Goebbels him-self thought in stereotypes and was completely under the spell of personalization. Thus, we have to seek for sources other than erudi-tion for the much advertised fascist command of psychological tech-niques of mass manipulation. The foremost source seems to be the already mentioned basic identity of leader and follower which cir-cumscribes one of the aspects of identification. The leader can guess the psychological wants and needs of those susceptible to his prop-aganda because he resembles them psychologically, and is distin-guished from them by a capacity to express without inhibitions what is latent in them, rather than by any intrinsic superiority. The leaders are generally oral character types, with a compulsion to speak incessantly and to befool the others. The famous spell they exercise over their followers seems largely to depend on their orality: language itself, devoid of its rational significance, functions in a magical way and furthers those archaic regressions which reduce individuals to mem-bers of crowds. Since this very quality of uninhibited but largely associative speech presupposes at least a temporary lack of ego con-trol, it may well indicate weakness rather than strength. The fascist agitators' boasting of strength is indeed frequently accompanied by hints at such weakness, particularly when begging for monetary contributions—hints which, to be sure, are skillfully merged with the idea of strength itself. In order successfully to meet the unconscious dispositions of his audience, the agitator so to speak simply turns his own unconscious outward. His particular character syndrome makes it possible for him to do exactly this, and experience has taught him consciously to exploit this faculty, to make rational use of his irrationality, similarly to the actor, or a certain type of journalist who knows how to sell their innervations and sensitivity. Without knowing it, he is thus able to speak and act in accord with psychological theory for the simple reason that the psychological theory is true. All he has to do in order to make the psychology of his audience click, is shrewdly to exploit his own psychology.

The adequacy of the agitators' devices to the psychological basis of their aim is further enhanced by another factor. As we know, fascist agitation has by now come to be a profession, as it were, a livelihood. It had plenty of time to test the effectiveness of its various appeals and, through what might be called natural selection, only the most catchy ones have survived. Their effectiveness is itself a function of the psychology of the consumers. Through a process of "freezing," which can be observed throughout the techniques employed in modern mass culture, the surviving appeals have been standardized, similarly to the advertising slogans which proved to be most valuable in the promotion of business. This standardization, in turn, falls in line with stereotypical thinking, that is to say, with the "stereopathy" of those susceptible to this propaganda and their infantile wish for endless, unaltered repetition. It is hard to predict whether the latter psychological disposition will prevent the agitators' standard devices from becoming blunt through excessive application. In National Socialist Germany, everybody used to make fun of certain propagandistic phrases such as "blood and soil" (*Blut und Boden*), jokingly called *Blubo*, or the concept of the nordic race from which the parodistic verb *aufnorden* (to "northernize") was derived. Nevertheless, these appeals do not seem to have lost their attractiveness. Rather, their very "phoniness" may have been relished cynically and sadistically as an index for the fact that power alone decided one's fate in the Third Reich, that is, power unhampered by rational objectivity.

Furthermore, one may ask: why is the applied group psychology discussed here peculiar to fascism rather than to most other movements that seek mass support? Even the most casual comparison of fascist propaganda with that of liberal, progressive parties will show this to be so. Yet, neither Freud nor Le Bon envisaged such a distinction. They spoke of crowds "as such," similar to the conceptualizations used by formal sociology, without differentiating between the political aims of the groups involved. As a matter of fact, both thought of traditional socialistic movements rather than of their opposite, though it should be noted that the Church and the Army— the examples chosen by Freud for the demonstration of his theory— are essentially conservative and hierarchical. Le Bon, on the other hand, is mainly concerned with nonorganized, spontaneous, ephemeral crowds. Only an explicit theory of society, by far transcending the range of psychology, can fully answer the question raised here. We content ourselves with a few suggestions. First, the objective aims of fascism are largely irrational in so far as they contradict the material interests of great numbers of those whom they try to embrace, notwithstanding the prewar boom of the first years of the Hitler regime. The continuous danger of war inherent in fascism spells destruction and the masses are at least preconsciously aware of it. Thus, fascism does not altogether speak the untruth when it refers to its own irrational powers, however faked the mythology which ideologically rationalizes the irrational may be. Since it would be impossible for fascism to win the masses through rational arguments, its propaganda must necessarily be deflected from discursive thinking; it must be oriented psychologically, and has to mobilize irrational, unconscious, regressive processes. This task is facilitated by the frame of mind of all those strata of the population who suffer from senseless frustrations and therefore develop a stunted, irrational mentality. It may well be the secret of fascist propaganda that it simply takes men for what they are: the true children of today's standardized mass culture, largely robbed of autonomy and spontaneity, instead of setting goals the realization of which would transcend the psychological *status quo* no less than the social one. Fascist propaganda has only to *reproduce* the existent mentality for its own purposes;—it need not induce a change—and the compulsive repetition which is one of its foremost characteristics will be at one with the necessity for this continuous reproduction. It relies absolutely on the total structure as well as on each particular trait of the authoritarian character which is itself the product of an internalization of the irrational aspects of modern society. Under the prevailing conditions, the irrationality of fascist propaganda becomes rational in the sense of instinctual economy. For if the *status quo* is taken for granted and petrified, a much greater effort is needed to see through it than to adjust to it and to obtain at least some gratification through identification with the existent—the focal point of fascist propaganda. This may explain why ultra-reactionary mass movements use the "psychology of the masses" to a much greater extent than do movements which show more faith in the masses. However, there is no doubt that even the most progressive political movement can deteriorate to the level of the "psychology of the crowd" and its manipulation, if its own rational content is shattered through the reversion to blind power.

The so-called psychology of fascism is largely engendered by manipulation. Rationally calculated techniques bring about what is naively regarded as the "natural" irrationality of masses. This insight may help us to solve the problem of whether fascism as a mass phenomenon can be explained at all in psychological terms. While there certainly exists potential susceptibility for fascism among the masses, it is equally certain that the manipulation of the unconscious, the kind of suggestion explained by Freud in genetic terms, is indispensable for actualization of this potential. This, however, corroborates the assumption that fascism as such is *not* a psychological issue and that any attempt to understand its roots and its historical role in psychological terms still remains on the level of ideologies such as the one of "irrational forces" promoted by fascism itself. Although the fascist agitator doubtlessly takes up certain tendencies within those he addresses, he does so as the mandatory of powerful economic and political interests. Psychological dispositions do not actually cause fascism; rather, fascism defines a psychological area which can be successfully exploited by the forces which promote it for entirely nonpsychological reasons of self-interest. What happens when masses are caught by fascist propaganda is not a spontaneous primary expression of instincts and urges but a quasi-scientific revitalization of their psychology—the artificial regression described by Freud in his discussion of organized groups. The psychology of the masses has been taken over by their leaders and transformed into a means for their domination. It does not express itself directly through mass movements. This phenomenon is not entirely new but was foreshadowed throughout the counterrevolutionary movements of history. Far from being the source of fascism, psychology has become one element among others in a superimposed system the very totality of which is necessitated by the potential of mass resistance—the masses' own rationality. The content of Freud's theory, the replacement of individual narcissism by identification with leader images, points in the direction of what might be called the appropriation of mass psychology by the oppressors. To be sure, this process has a psychological dimension, but it also indicates a growing tendency towards the abolition of psychological motivation in the old, liberalistic sense. Such motivation is systematically controlled and absorbed by social mechanisms which are directed from above. When the leaders become conscious of mass psychology and take it into their own hands, it ceases to exist in a certain sense. This potentiality is contained in the basic construct of psychoanalysis inasmuch as for Freud the concept of psychology is essentially a negative one. He defines the realm of psychology by the supremacy of the unconscious and postulates that what is id should become ego. The emancipation of man from the heteronomous rule of his unconscious would be tantamount to the abolition of his "psychology." Fascism furthers this abolition in the opposite sense through the perpetuation of dependence instead of the realization of potential freedom, through expropriation of the unconscious by social control instead of making the subjects conscious of their unconscious. For, while psychology always denotes some bondage of the individual, it also presupposes freedom in the sense of a certain self-sufficiency and autonomy of the individual. It is not accidental that the nineteenth century was the great era of psychological thought. In a thoroughly reified society, in which there are virtually no direct relationships between men, and in which each person has been reduced to a social atom, to a mere function of collectivity, the psychological processes, though they still persist in each individual, have ceased to appear as the determining forces of the social process. Thus, the psychology of the individual has lost what Hegel would have called its substance. It is perhaps the greatest merit of Freud's book that though he restricted himself to the field of individual psychology and wisely abstained from introducing sociological factors from outside, he nevertheless reached the turning point where psychology abdicates. The psychological "impoverishment" of the subject that "surrendered itself to the object" which "it has substituted for its most important constituent";[37] i.e., the superego, anticipates almost with *clairvoyance* the postpsychological de-individualized social atoms which form the fascist collectivities. In these social atoms the psychological dynamics of group formation have overreached themselves and are no longer a reality. The category of "phoniness" applies to the leaders as well as to the act of identification on the part of the masses and their supposed frenzy and hysteria. Just as little as people believe in the depth of their hearts that the Jews are the devil, do they completely believe in the leader. They do not really identify themselves with him but act this identification, perform their own enthusiasm, and thus participate in their leader's performance. It is through this performance that they strike a balance between their continuously mobilized instinctual urges and the historical stage of enlightenment they have reached, and which cannot be revoked arbitrarily. It is probably the suspicion of this fictitiousness of their own "group psychology" which makes fascist crowds so merciless and unapproachable. If they would stop to reason for a second, the whole performance would go to pieces, and they would be left to panic.

Freud came upon this element of "phoniness" within an unexpected context, namely, when he discussed hypnosis as a retrogression of individuals to the relation between primal horde and primal father.

> As we know from other reactions, individuals have preserved a variable degree of personal aptitude for reviving old situations of this kind. Some knowledge that in spite of everything hypnosis is only a game, a deceptive renewal of these old impressions, may however remain behind and take care that there is a resistance against any too serious consequences of the suspension of the will in hypnosis. [38]

In the meantime, this game has been socialized, and the consequences have proved to be very serious. Freud made a distinction between hypnosis and group psychology by defining the former as taking place between two people only. However, the leaders' appropriation of mass psychology, the streamlining of their technique, has enabled them to collectivize the hypnotic spell. The Nazi battle cry of "Germany awake" hides its very opposite. The collectivization and institutionalization of the spell, on the other hand, have made the transference more and more indirect and precarious so that the aspect of performance, the "phoniness" of enthusiastic identification and of all the traditional dynamics of group psychology, have been tremendously increased. This increase may well terminate in sudden awareness of the untruth of the spell, and eventually in its collapse. Socialized hypnosis breeds within itself the forces which will do away with the spook of regression through remote control, and in the end awaken those who keep their eyes shut though they are no longer asleep.

Some Social Implications of Modern Technology

By Herbert Marcuse

First published in Studies in Philosophy and Social Sciences *Vol. IX (1941), the article is a large-scale investigation of that "fetish" of technique, or technical efficiency, which, after 1941, represented for critical theory, especially for Marcuse, the key ideological replacement of the commodity fetish under modern industralized authoritarian states. With respect to Marcuse's better-known later position, the essay incorporates two anomalous attitudes: the ultimate political neutrality of technique as such (even the existing technologies) and the possibility of progressive utilization of techniques (even bureaucratic ones) through democratic reform. Nevertheless, Marcuse, in an extremely clear fashion, specifies all those dimensions of technical reason open to repressive and ideological utilization in the hands of authoritarian regimes.*

In this article, technology is taken as a social process in which technics proper (that is, the technical apparatus of industry, transportation, communication) is but a partial factor. We do not ask for the influence or effect of technology on the human individuals. For they are themselves an integral part and factor of technology, not only as the men who invent or attend to machinery but also as the social groups which direct its application and utilization. Technology, as a mode of production, as the totality of instruments, devices and contrivances which characterize the machine age is thus at the same time a mode of organizing and perpetuating (or changing) social relationships, a manifestation of prevalent thought and behavior patterns, an instrument for control and domination.[1]

Technics by itself can promote authoritarianism as well as liberty, scarcity as well as abundance, the extension as well as the abolition of toil. National Socialism is a striking example of the ways in which a highly rationalized and mechanized economy with the utmost efficiency in production can operate in the interest of totalitarian oppression and continued scarcity. The Third Reich is indeed a form of "technocracy": the technical considerations of imperialistic efficiency and rationality supersede the traditional standards of profitability and general welfare. In National Socialist Germany, the reign of terror is sustained not only by brute force which is foreign to technology but also by the ingenious manipulation of the power inherent in technology: the intensification of labor, propaganda, the training of youths and workers, the organization of the governmental, industrial and party bureaucracy—all of which constitute the daily implements of terror—follow the lines of greatest technological efficiency. This terroristic technocracy cannot be attributed to the exceptional requirements of "war economy"; war economy is rather the normal state of the National Socialist ordering of the social and economic process, and technology is one of the chief stimuli of this ordering.[2]

In the course of the technological process a new rationality and new standards of individuality have spread over society, different from and even opposed to those which initiated the march of technology. These changes are not the (direct or derivative) effect of machinery on its users or of mass production on its consumers; they are rather themselves determining factors in the development of machinery and mass production. In order to understand their full import, it is necessary to survey briefly the traditional rationality and standards of individuality which are being dissolved by the present stage of the machine age.

The human individual whom the exponents of the middle class revolution had made the ultimate unit as well as the end of society stood for values which strikingly contradict those holding sway over society today. If we try to assemble in one guiding concept the various religious, political and economic tendencies which shaped the idea of the individual in the sixteenth and seventeenth century, we may define the individual as the subject of certain fundamental standards and values which no external authority was supposed to encroach upon. These standards and values pertained to the forms of life, social as well as personal, which were most adequate to the full development of man's faculties and abilities. By the same token, they were the "truth" of his individual and social existence. The individual, as a rational being, was deemed capable of finding these forms by his own thinking and, once he had acquired freedom of thought, of pursuing the course of action which would actualize them. Society's task was to grant him such freedom and to remove all restrictions upon his rational course of action.

The principle of individualism, the pursuit of self-interest, was conditioned upon the proposition that self-interest was rational, that is to say, that it resulted from and was constantly guided and controlled by autonomous thinking. The rational self-interest did not coincide with the individual's immediate self-interest, for the latter depended upon the standards and requirements of the prevailing social order, placed there not by his autonomous thought and conscience but by external authorities. In the context of radical Puritanism, the principle of individualism thus set the individual against his society. Men had to break through the whole system of ideas and values imposed upon them, and to find and seize the ideas and values that conformed to their rational interest. They had to live in a state of constant vigilance, apprehension, and criticism, to reject everything that was not true, not justified by free reason. This, in a society which was not yet rational, constituted a principle of permanent unrest and opposition. For false standards still governed the life of men, and the free individual was therefore he who criticised realization. The theme has nowhere been more fittingly expressed than in Milton's image of a "wicked race of deceivers, who . . . took the virgin Truth, hewd her lovely form into a thousand peeces, and scatter'd them to the four winds. From that time ever since, the sad friends of Truth, such as durst appear, imitating the careful search that Isis made for the mangl'd body of Osiris, went up and down gathering up limb by limb still as they could find them. We have not yet found them all, . . . nor ever shall do, till her Master's second coming . . . —To be still searching what we know not, by what we know, still closing up truth to truth as we find it (for all her body is homogeneal and proportionall)," this was the principle of individualistic rationality.[3]

To fulfill this rationality presupposed an adequate social and economic setting, one that would appeal to individuals whose social performance was, at least to a large extent, their own work. Liberalist society was held to be the adequate setting for individualistic rationality. In the sphere of free competition, the tangible achievements of the individual which made his products and performances a part of society's need, were the marks of his individuality. In the course of time, however, the process of commodity production undermined the economic basis on which individualistic rationality was built. Mechanization and rationalization forced the weaker competitor under the dominion of the giant enterprises of machine industry which, in establishing society's dominion over nature, abolished the free economic subject.

The principle of competitive efficiency favors the enterprises with the most highly mechanized and rationalized industrial equipment. Technological power tends to the concentration of economic power, to "large units of production, of vast corporate enterprises producing large quantities and often a striking variety of goods, of industrial empires owning and controlling materials, equipment, and processes from the extraction of raw materials to the distribution of finished products, of dominance over an entire industry by a small number of giant concerns. . . ." And technology "steadily increases the power at the command of giant concerns by creating new tools, processes and products."4 Efficiency here called for integral unification and simplification, for the removal of all "waste," the avoidance of all detours, it called for radical coordination. A contradiction exists, however, between the profit incentive that keeps the apparatus moving and the rise of the standard of living which this same apparatus has made possible. "Since control of production is in the hands of enterprisers working for profit, they will have at their disposal whatever emerges as surplus after rent, interest, labor, and other costs are met. These costs will be kept at the lowest possible minimum as a matter of course."5 Under these circumstances, profitable employment of the apparatus dictates to a great extent the quantity, form and kind of commodities to be produced, and through this mode of production and distribution, the technological power of the apparatus affects the entire rationality of those whom it serves.

Under the impact of this apparatus,6 individualistic rationality has been transformed into technological rationality. It is by no means confined to the subjects and objects of large scale enterprises but characterizes the pervasive mode of thought and even the manifold forms of protest and rebellion. This rationality establishes standards of judgment and fosters attitudes which make men ready to accept and even to introcept the dictates of the apparatus.

Lewis Mumford has characterized man in the machine age as an "objective personality," one who has learned to transfer all subjective spontaneity to the machinery which he serves, to subordinate his life to the "matter-of-factness" of a world in which the machine is the factor and he the factum.[7] Individual distinctions in the aptitude, insight and knowledge are transformed into different quanta of skill and training, to be coordinated at any time within the common framework of standardized performances.

Individuality, however, has not disappeared. The free economic subject rather has developed into the object of large-scale organization and coordination, and individual achievement has been transformed into standardized efficiency. The latter is characterized by the fact that the individual's performance is motivated, guided and measured by standards external to him, standards pertaining to predetermined tasks and functions. The efficient individual is the one whose performance is an action only insofar as it is the proper reaction to the objective requirements of the apparatus, and his liberty is confined to the selection of the most adequate means for reaching a goal which he did not set. Whereas individual achievement is independent of recognition and consummated in the work itself, efficiency is a rewarded performance and consummated only in its value for the apparatus.

With the majority of the population, the former freedom of the economic subject was gradually submerged in the efficiency with which he performed services assigned to him. The world had been rationalized to such an extent, and this rationality had become such a social power that the individual could do no better than adjust himself without reservation. Veblen was among the first to derive the new matter-of-factness from the machine process, from which it spread over the whole society: "The share of the operative workman in the machine industry is (typically) that of an attendant, an assistant, whose duty it is to keep pace with the machine process and to help out with workmanlike manipulation at points where the machine process engaged is incomplete. His work supplements the machine process rather than makes use of it. On the contrary the machine process makes use of the workman. The ideal mechanical contrivance in this technological system is the automatic machine."[8] The machine process requires a knowledge oriented to "a ready apprehension of opaque facts, in passably exact quantitative terms. This class of knowledge presumes a certain intellectual or spiritual attitude on the part of the workman, such an attitude as will readily apprehend and appreciate matter of fact and will guard against the suffusion of this knowledge with putative animistic or anthropomorphic subtleties, quasi-personal interpretations of the observed phenomena and of their relations to one another."[9]

As an attitude, matter-of-factness is not bound to the machine process. Under all forms of social production men have taken and justified their motives and goals from the facts that made up their reality, and in doing so they have arrived at the most diverging philosophies. Matter-of-factness animated ancient materialism and hedonism, it was responsible in the struggle of modern physical science against spiritual oppression, and in the revolutionary rationalism of the Enlightenment. The new attitude differs from all these in the highly rational compliance which typifies it. The facts directing man's thought and action are not those of nature which must be accepted in order to be mastered, or those of society which must be changed because they no longer correspond to human needs and potentialities. Rather are they those of the machine process, which itself appears as the embodiment of rationality and expediency.

Let us take a simple example. A man who travels by automobile to a distant place chooses his route from the highway maps. Towns, lakes and mountains appear as obstacles to be bypassed. The countryside is shaped and organized by the highway. Numerous signs and posters tell the traveler what to do and think; they even request his attention to the beauties of nature or the hallmarks of history. Others have done the thinking for him, and perhaps for the better. Convenient parking spaces have been constructed where the broadest and most surprising view is open. Giant advertisements tell him when to stop and find the pause that refreshes. And all this is indeed for his benefit, safety and comfort; he receives what he wants. Business, technics, human needs and nature are welded together into one rational and expedient mechanism. He will fare best who follows its directions, subordinating his spontaneity to the anonymous wisdom which ordered everything for him.

The decisive point is that this attitude—which dissolves all actions into a sequence of semi-spontaneous reactions to prescribed mechanical norms—is not only perfectly rational but also perfectly reasonable. All protest is senseless, and the individual who would insist on his freedom of action would become a crank. There is no personal escape from the apparatus which has mechanized and standardized the world. It is a rational apparatus, combining utmost expediency with utmost convenience, saving time and energy, removing waste, adapting all means to the end, anticipating consequences, sustaining calculability and security.

In manipulating the machine, man learns that obedience to the directions is the only way to obtain desired results. Getting along is identical with adjustment to the apparatus. There is no room for autonomy. Individualistic rationality has developed into efficient compliance with the pregiven continuum of means and ends. The latter absorbs the liberating efforts of thought, and the various functions of reason converge upon the unconditional maintenance of the apparatus. It has been frequently stressed that scientific discoveries and inventions are shelved as soon as they seem to interfere with the requirements of profitable marketing.[10] The necessity which is the mother of inventions is to a great extent the necessity of maintaining and expanding the apparatus. Inventions have "their chief use . . . in the service of business, not of industry, and their great further use is in the furtherance, or rather the acceleration, of obligatory social amenities." They are mostly of a competitive nature, and "any technological advantage gained by one competitor forthwith becomes a necessity to all the rest, on pain of defeat," so that one might as well say that, in the monopolistic system, "invention is the mother of necessity."[11]

Everything cooperates to turn human instincts, desires and thoughts into channels that feed the apparatus. Dominant economic and social organizations "do not maintain their power by force . . . They do it by identifying themselves with the faiths and loyalties of the people,"[12] and the people have been trained to identify their faiths and loyalties with them. The relationships among men are increasingly mediated by the machine process. But the mechanical contrivances which facilitate intercourse among individuals also intercept and absorb their libido, thereby diverting it from the all too dangerous realm in which the individual is free of society. The average man hardly cares for any living being with the intensity and persistence he shows for his automobile. The machine that is adored is no longer dead matter but becomes something like a human being. And it gives back to man what it possesses: the life of the social apparatus to which it belongs. Human behavior is outfitted with the rationality of the machine process, and this rationality has a definite social content. The machine process operates according to the laws of mass production. Expediency in terms of technological reason is, at the same time, expediency in terms of profitable efficiency, and rationalization is, at the same time, monopolistic standardization and concentration. The more rationally the individual behaves and the more lovingly he attends to his rationalized work, the more he succumbs to the frustrating aspects of this rationality. He is losing his ability to abstract from the special form in which rationalization is carried through and is losing his faith in its unfulfilled potentialities. His matter-of-factness, his distrust of all values which transcend the facts of observation, his resentment against all "quasi-personal" and metaphysical interpretations, his suspicion of all standards which relate the observable order of things, the rationality of the apparatus, to the rationality of freedom,—this whole attitude serves all too well those who are interested in perpetuating the prevailing form of matters of fact. The machine process requires a "consistent training in the mechanical apprehension of things," and this training, in turn, promotes "conformity to the schedule of living," a "degree of trained insight and a facile strategy in all manner of quantitative adjustments and adaptations . . ."[13] The "mechanics of conformity" spread from the technological to the social order; they govern performance not only in the factories and shops, but also in the offices, schools, assemblies and, finally, in the realm of relaxation and entertainment.

Individuals are stripped of their individuality, not by external compulsion, but by the very rationality under which they live. Industrial psychology correctly assumes that "the dispositions of men are fixed emotional habits and as such they are quite dependable reaction patterns."[14] True, the force which transforms human performance into a series of dependable reactions is an external force: the machine process imposes upon men the patterns of mechanical behavior, and the standards of competitive efficiency are the more enforced from outside the less independent the individual competitor becomes. But man does not experience this loss of his freedom as the work of some hostile and foreign force; he relinquishes his liberty to the dictum of reason itself. The point is that today the apparatus to which the individual is to adjust and adopt himself is so rational that individual protest and liberation appear not only as hopeless but as utterly irrational. The system of life created by modern industry is one of the highest expediency, convenience and efficiency. Reason, once defined in these terms, becomes equivalent to an activity which perpetuates this world. Rational behavior becomes identical with a matter-of-factness which teaches reasonable submissiveness and thus guarantees getting along in the prevailing order.

At first glance, the technological attitude rather seems to imply the opposite of resignation. Teleological and theological dogmas no longer interfere with man's struggle with matter; he develops his experimental energies without inhibition. There is no constellation of matter which he does not try to break up, to manipulate and to change according to his will and interest. This experimentalism, however, frequently serves the effort to develop a higher efficiency of hierarchical control over men. Technological rationality may easily be placed into the service of such control: in the form of "scientific management," it has become one of the most profitable means for streamlined autocracy. F. W. Taylor's exposition of scientific management shows within it the union of exact science, matter-of-factness and big industry: "Scientific management attempts to substitute, in the relation between employers and workers, the government of fact and law for the rule of force and opinion. It substitutes exact knowledge for guesswork, and seeks to establish a code of natural laws equally binding upon employers and workmen. Scientific management thus seeks to substitute in the shop discipline, natural law in place of a code of discipline based upon the caprice and arbitrary power of men. No such democracy has ever existed in industry before. Every protest of every workman must be handled by those on the management side and the right and wrong of the complaint must be settled, not by the opinion either of the management or the workman but by the great code of laws which has been developed and which must satisfy both sides."[15] The scientific effort aims at eliminating waste, intensifying production and standardizing the product. And this whole scheme to increase profitable efficiency poses as the final fulfillment of individualism, ending up with a demand to "develop the individuality of the workers."[16]

The idea of compliant efficiency perfectly illustrates the structure of technological rationality. Rationality is being transformed from a critical force into one of adjustment and compliance. Autonomy of reason loses its meaning in the same measure as the thoughts, feelings and actions of men are shaped by the technical requirements of the apparatus which they have themselves created. Reason has found its resting place in the system of standardized control, production and consumption. There it reigns through the laws and mechanisms which insure the efficiency, expediency and coherence of this system.

As the laws and mechanisms of technological rationality spread over the whole society, they develop a set of truth values of their own which hold good for the functioning of the apparatus—and for that alone. Propositions concerning competitive or collusive behavior, business methods, principles of effective organization and control, fair play, the use of science and technics are true or false in terms of this value system, that is to say, in terms of instrumentalities that dictate their own ends. These truth values are tested and perpetuated by experience and must guide the thoughts and actions of all who wish to survive. Rationality here calls for unconditional compliance and coordination, and consequently, the truth values related to this rationality imply the subordination of thought to pre-given external standards. We may call this set of truth values the technological truth, technological in the twofold sense that it is an instrument of expediency rather than an end in itself, and that it follows the pattern of technological behavior.

By virtue of its subordination to external standards, the technological truth comes into striking contradiction with the form in which individualistic society had established its supreme values. The pursuit of self-interest now appears to be conditioned upon heteronomy, and autonomy as an obstacle rather than stimulus for rational action. The originally identical and "homogenous" truth seems to be split into two different sets of truth values and two different patterns of behavior: the one assimilated to the apparatus, the other antagonistic to it; the one making up the prevailing technological rationality and governing the behavior required by it, the other pertaining to a critical rationality whose values can be fulfilled only if it has itself shaped all personal and social relationships. The critical rationality derives from the principles of autonomy which individualistic society itself had declared to be its self-evident truths. Measuring these principles against the form in which individualistic society has actualized them, critical rationality accuses social injustice in the name of individualistic society's own ideology.[17] The relationship between technological and critical truth is a difficult problem which cannot be dealt with here, but two points must be mentioned. (1) The two sets of truth values are neither wholly contradictory nor complementary to each other; many truths of technological rationality are preserved or transformed in critical rationality. (2) The distinction between the two sets is not rigid; the content of each set changes in the social process so that what were once critical truth values become technological values. For example, the proposition that every individual is equipped with certain inalienable rights is a critical proposition but it was frequently interpreted in favor of efficiency and concentration of power.[18]

The standardization of thought under the sway of technological rationality also affects the critical truth values. The latter are torn from the context to which they originally belonged and, in their new form, are given wide, even official publicity. For example, propositions which, in Europe, were the exclusive domain of the labor movement are today adopted by the very forces which these propositions denounced. In the fascist countries, they serve as ideological instruments for the attack on "Jewish capitalism" and "Western plutocracy," thereby concealing the actual front in the struggle. The materialistic analysis of present-day economy is employed to justify fascism to the German industrialists in whose interest it operates, as the regime of last resort for imperialistic expansion.[19] In other countries, the critique of political economy functions in the struggle among conflicting business groups and as governmental weapon for unmasking monopolistic practices; it is propagated by the columnists of the big press syndicates and finds its way even into the popular magazines and the addresses to manufacturers associations. As these propositions become part and parcel of the established culture, however, they seem to lose their edge and to merge with the old and the familiar. This familiarity with the truth illuminates the extent to which society has become indifferent and insusceptible to the impact of critical thought. For the categories of critical thought preserve their truth value only if they direct the full realization of the social potentialities which they envision, and they lose their vigor if they determine an attitude of fatalistic compliance or competitive assimilation.

Several influences have conspired to bring about the social impotence of critical thought. The foremost among them is the growth of the industrial apparatus and of its all-embracing control over all spheres of life. The technological rationality inculcated in those who attend to this apparatus has transformed numerous modes of external compulsion and authority into modes of self-discipline and self-control. Safety and order are, to a large extent, guaranteed by the fact that man has learned to adjust his behavior to the other fellow's down to the most minute detail. All men act equally rationally, that is to say, according to the standards which insure the functioning of the apparatus and thereby the maintenance of their own life. But this "introversion" of compulsion and authority has strengthened rather than attenuated the mechanisms of social control. Men, in following their own reason, follow those who put their reason to profitable use. In Europe, these mechanisms helped to prevent the individual from acting in accordance with the conspicuous truth, and they were efficiently supplemented by the physical control mechanisms of the apparatus. At this point, the otherwise diverging interests and their agencies are synchronized and adjusted in such a manner that they efficiently counteract any serious threat to their dominion.

functions. Even the highly differentiated professional requirements of modern industry promote standardization. Vocational training is chiefly training in various kinds of skill, psychological and physiological adaptation to a "job" which has to be done. The job, a pre-given "type of work . . . requires a particular combination of abilities,"[22] and those who create the job also shape the human material to fill it. The abilities developed by such training make the "personality" a means for attaining ends which perpetuate man's existence as an instrumentality, replaceable at short notice by other instrumentalities of the same brand. The psychological and "personal" aspects of vocational training are the more emphasized the more they are subjected to regimentation and the less they are left to free and complete development. The "human side" of the employee and the concern for his personal aptitudes and habits play an important part in the total mobilization of the private sphere for mass production and mass culture. Psychology and individualization serve to consolidate stereotyped dependability, for they give the human object the feeling that he unfolds himself by discharging functions which dissolve his self into a series of required actions and responses. Within this range, individuality is not only preserved but also fostered and rewarded, but such individuality is only the special form in which a man introcepts and discharges, within a general pattern, certain duties allocated to him. Specialization fixates the prevailing scheme of standardization. Almost everyone has become a potential member of the crowd, and the masses belong to the daily implements of the social process. As such, they can easily be handled, for the thoughts, feelings and interests of their members have been assimilated to the pattern of the apparatus. To be sure, their outbursts are terrifying and violent but these are readily directed against the weaker competitors and the conspicuous "outsiders" (Jews, foreigners, national minorities). The coordinated masses do not crave a new order but a larger share in the prevailing one. Through their action, they strive to rectify, in an anarchic way, the injustice of competition. Their uniformity is in the competitive self-interest they all manifest, in the equalized expressions of self-preservation. The members of the masses are individuals.

The individual in the crowd is certainly not the one whom the individualist principle exhorted to develop his self, nor is his self-interest the same as the rational interest urged by this principle. Where the daily social performance of the individual has become antagonistic to his "true interest," the individualist principle has changed its meaning. The protagonists of individualism were aware of the fact that "individuals can be developed only by being trusted with somewhat more than they can, at the moment, do well";[23] today, the individual is trusted with precisely what he can, at the moment, do well. The philosophy of individualism has seen the "essential freedom" of the self to be "that it stands for a fateful moment outside of all belongings, and determines for itself alone whether its primary attachments shall be with actual earthly interests or with those of an ideal and potential 'Kingdom of God.' "[24] This ideal and potential kingdom has been defined in different ways, but it has always been characterized by contents which were opposed and transcendent to the prevailing kingdom. Today, the prevailing type of individual is no longer capable of seizing the fateful moment which constitutes his freedom. He has changed his function; from a unit of resistance and autonomy, he has passed to one of ductility and adjustment. It is this function which associates individuals in masses.

The emergence of the modern masses, far from endangering the efficiency and coherence of the apparatus, has facilitated the progressing coordination of society and the growth of authoritarian bureaucracy, thus refuting the social theory of individualism at a decisive point. The technological process seemed to tend to the conquest of scarcity and thus to the slow transformation of competition into cooperation. The philosophy of individualism viewed this process as the gradual differentiation and liberation of human potentialities, as the abolition of the "crowd." Even in the Marxian conception, the masses are not the spearhead of freedom. The Marxian proletariat is not a crowd but a class, defined by its determinate position in the productive process, the maturity of its "consciousness," and the rationality of its common interest. Critical rationality, in the most accentuated form, is the prerequisite for its liberating function. In one aspect at least, this conception is in line with the philosophy of individualism: it envisions the rational form of human association as brought about and sustained by the autonomous decision and action of free men.

This is the one point at which the technological and the critical rationality seem to converge, for the technological process implies a democratization of functions. The system of production and distribution has been rationalized to such an extent that the hierarchical distinction between executive and subordinate performances is to an ever smaller degree based upon essential distinctions in aptitude and insight, and to an ever greater degree upon inherited power and a vocational training to which everyone could be subjected. Even experts and "engineers" are no exception. To be sure, the gap between the underlying population and those who design the blueprints for rationalization, who lay out production, who make the inventions and discoveries which accelerate technological progress, becomes daily more conspicuous, particularly in a period of war economy. At the same time, however, this gap is maintained more by the division of power than by the division of work. The hierarchical distinction of the experts and engineers results from the fact that their ability and knowledge is utilized in the interest of autocratic power. The "technological leader" is also a "social leader"; his "social leadership overshadows and conditions his function as a scientist, for it gives him institutional power within the group . . .," and the "captain of industry" acts in "perfect accordance with the traditional dependence of the expert's function."[25] Were it not for this fact, the task of the expert and engineer would not be an obstacle to the general democratization of functions. Technological rationalization has created a common framework of experience for the various professions and occupations. This experience excludes or restrains those elements that transcend the technical control over matters of fact and thus extends the scope of rationalization from the objective to the subjective world. Underneath the complicated web of stratified control is an array of more or less standardized techniques, tending to one general pattern, which insure the material reproduction of society. The "persons engaged in a practical occupation" seem to be convinced that "any situation which appears in the performance of their role can be fitted into some general pattern with which the best, if not all, of them are familiar."[26] Moreover, the instrumentalistic conception of technological rationality is spreading over almost the whole realm of thought and gives the various intellectual activities a common denominator. They too become a kind of technique,[27] a matter of training rather than individuality, requiring the expert rather than the complete human personality.

The standardization of production and consumption, the mechanization of labor, the improved facilities of transportation and communication, the extension of training, the general dissemination of knowledge—all these factors seem to facilitate the exchangeability of functions. It is as if the basis were shrinking on which the pervasive distinction between "specialized (technical)" and "common" knowledge[28] has been built, and as if the authoritarian control of functions would prove increasingly foreign to the technological process. The special form, however, in which the technological process is organized, counteracts this trend. The same development that created the modern masses as the standardized attendants and dependents of large-scale industry also created the hierarchical organization of private bureaucracies. Max Weber has already stressed the connection between mass-democracy and bureaucracy: "In contrast to the democratic self-administration of small homogeneous units," the bureaucracy is "the universal concomitant of modern mass democracy."[29]

The bureaucracy becomes the concomitant of the modern masses by virtue of the fact that standardization proceeds along the lines of specialization. The latter by itself, provided that it is not arrested at the point where it interferes with the domain of vested control, is quite compatible with the democratization of functions. Fixated specialization, however, tends to atomize the masses and to insulate the subordinate from the executive functions. We have mentioned that specialized vocational training implies fitting a man to a particular job or a particular line of jobs, thus directing his "personality," spontaneity and experience to the special situations he may meet in filling the job. In this manner, the various professions and occupations, notwithstanding their convergence upon one general pattern, tend to become atomic units which require coordination and management from above. The technical democratization of functions is counteracted by their atomization, and the bureaucracy appears as the agency which guarantees their rational course and order.

The bureaucracy thus emerges on an apparently objective and impersonal ground, provided by the rational specialization of functions, and this rationality in turn serves to increase the rationality of submission. For, the more the individual functions are divided, fixated and synchronized according to objective and impersonal patterns, the less reasonable is it for the individual to withdraw or withstand. "The material fate of the masses becomes increasingly dependent upon the continuous and correct functioning of the increasingly bureaucratic order of private capitalistic organizations."[30] The objective and impersonal character of technological rationality bestows upon the bureaucratic groups the universal dignity of reason. The rationality embodied in the giant enterprises makes it appear as if men, in obeying them, obey the dictum of an objective rationality. The private bureaucracy fosters a delusive harmony between the special and the common interest. Private power relationships appear not only as relationships between objective things but also as the rule of rationality itself.

In the fascist countries, this mechanism facilitated the merger

unrestricted liberty of thought and conscience and measured all social standards and relations by the individual's rational self-interest. It grew into the rationality of competition in which the rational interest was superseded by the interest of the market, and individual achievement absorbed by efficiency. It ended with standardized submission to the all-embracing apparatus which it had itself created. This apparatus is the embodiment and resting place of individualistic rationality, but the latter now requires that individuality must go. He is rational who most efficiently accepts and executes what is allocated to him, who entrusts his fate to the large-scale enterprises and organizations which administer the apparatus.

Such was the logical outcome of a social process which measured individual performance in terms of competitive efficiency. The philosophers of individualism have always had an inkling of this outcome and they expressed their anxiety in many different forms, in the skeptical conformism of Hume, in the idealistic introversion of individual freedom, in the frequent attacks of the Transcendentalists against the rule of money and power. But the social forces were stronger than the philosophic protests, and the philosophic justification of individualism took on more and more of the overtones of resignation. Toward the end of the nineteenth century, the idea of the individual became increasingly ambiguous: it combined insistence upon free social performance and competitive efficiency with glorification of smallness, privacy and self-limitation. The rights and liberties of the individual in society were interpreted as the rights and liberties of privacy and withdrawal from society. William James, faithful to the individualistic principle, asserted that, in the "rivalry between real organizable goods," the "world's trial is better than the closest solution," provided that the victorious keep "the vanquished somehow represented."[35] His doubt, however, as to whether this trial is really a fair one seems to motivate his hatred of "bigness and greatness in all their forms,"[36] his declaration that "the smaller and more intimate is the truer,—the man more than the home, the home more than the state or the church."[37] The counterposition of individual and society, originally meant to provide the ground for a militant reformation of society in the interest of the individual, comes to prepare and justify the individual's withdrawal from society. The free and self-reliant "soul," which originally nourished the individual's critique of external authority, now becomes a refuge from external authority. Tocqueville had already defined individualism in terms of acquiescence and peaceful resignation: "a mature and calm feeling,

which disposes each member of the community to sever himself from
the mass of his fellow-creatures; and to draw apart with his family and
his friends; so that, after he has thus formed a little circle of his own,
he willingly leaves society at large to itself."[38] Autonomy of the
individual came to be regarded as a private rather than a public affair,
an element of retreat rather than aggression. All these factors of
resignation are comprehended in Benjamin Constant's statement that
"our liberty should be composed of the peaceful enjoyment of private
independence."[39]

The elements of restraint and resignation which became increasingly strong in the individualist philosophy of the nineteenth century
elucidate the connection between individualism and scarcity. Individualism is the form liberty assumes in a society wherein the acquisition and utilization of wealth is dependent on competitive toil. Individuality is a distinct possession of "pioneers"; it presupposes the
open and empty spaces, the freedom of "hewing out a home" as well
as the need to do so. The individual's world is a "world of labor and
the march," as Walt Whitman says, one in which the available
intellectual and material resources must be conquered and appropriated through incessant struggle with man and nature, and in which
human forces are released to distribute and administer scarcity.

In the period of large-scale industry, however, the existential
conditions making for individuality give way to conditions which
render individuality unnecessary. In clearing the ground for the conquest of scarcity, the technological process not only levels individuality but also tends to transcend it where it is concurrent with scarcity.
Mechanized mass production is filling the empty spaces in which
individuality could assert itself. The cultural standardization points,
paradoxically enough, to potential abundance as well as actual poverty. This standardization may indicate the extent to which individual
creativeness and originality have been rendered unnecessary. With the
decline of the liberalistic era, these qualities were vanishing from the
domain of material production and becoming the ever more exclusive
property of the highest intellectual activities. Now, they seem to
disappear from this sphere too: mass culture is dissolving the traditional forms of art, literature and philosophy together with the "personality" which unfolded itself in producing and consuming them.
The striking impoverishment which characterizes the dissolution of
these forms may involve a new source of enrichment. They derived
their truth from the fact that they represented the potentialities of man
and nature which were excluded or distorted in the reality. So far were

those potentialities from their actualization in the social consciousness that much cried out for unique expression. But today, *humanitas,* wisdom, beauty, freedom and happiness can no longer be represented as the realm of the "harmonious personality" nor as the remote heaven of art nor as metaphysical systems. The "ideal" has become so concrete and so universal that it grips the life of every human being, and the whole of mankind is drawn into the struggle for its realization. Under the terror that now threatens the world the ideal constricts itself to one single and at the same time common issue. Faced with fascist barbarism, everyone knows what freedom means, and everyone is aware of the irrationality in the prevailing rationality.

Modern mass society quantifies the qualitative features of individual labor and standardizes the individualistic elements in the activities of intellectual culture. This process may bring to the fore the tendencies which make individuality a historical form of human existence, to be surpassed by further social development. This does not mean that society is bound to enter a stage of "collectivism." The collectivistic traits which characterize the development today may still belong to the phase of individualism. Masses and mass culture are manifestations of scarcity and frustration, and the authoritarian assertion of the common interest is but another form of the rule of particular interests over the whole. The fallacy of collectivism consists in that it equips the whole (society) with the traditional properties of the individual. Collectivism abolishes the free pursuit of competing individual interests but retains the idea of the common interest as a separate entity. Historically, however, the latter is but the counterpart of the former. Men experience their society as the objective embodiment of the collectivity as long as the individual interests are antagonistic to and competing with each other for a share in the social wealth. To such individuals, society appears as an objective entity, consisting of numerous things, institutions and agencies: plants and shops, business, police and law, government, schools and churches, prisons and hospitals, theaters and organizations, etc. Society is almost everything the individual is not, everything that determines his habits, thoughts and behavior patterns, that affects him from "outside." Accordingly, society is noticed chiefly as a power of restraint and control, providing the framework which integrates the goals, faculties and aspirations of men. It is this power which collectivism retains in its picture of society, thus perpetuating the rule of things and men over men.

The technological process itself furnishes no justification for such a collectivism. Technics hampers individual development only insofar as they are tied to a social apparatus which perpetuates scarcity, and this same apparatus has released forces which may shatter the special historical form in which technics is utilized. For this reason, all programs of an anti-technological character, all propaganda for an anti-industrial revolution[40] serve only those who regard human needs as a by-product of the utilization of technics. The enemies of technics readily join forces with a terroristic technocracy.[41] The philosophy of the simple life, the struggle against big cities and their culture frequently serves to teach men distrust of the potential instruments that could liberate them. We have pointed to the possible democratization of functions which technics may promote and which may facilitate complete human development in all branches of work and administration. Moreover, mechanization and standardization may one day help to shift the center of gravity from the necessities of material production to the arena of free human realization. The less individuality is required to assert itself in standardized social performances, the more it could retreat to a free "natural" ground. These tendencies, far from engendering collectivism, may lead to new forms of individualization. The machine individualizes men by following the physiological lines of individuality: it allocates the work to finger, hand, arm, foot, classifying and occupying men according to the dexterity of these organs.[42] The external mechanisms which govern standardization here meet a "natural" individuality; they lay bare the ground on which a hitherto suppressed individualization might develop. On this ground, man is an individual by virtue of the uniqueness of his body and its unique position in the space-time continuum. He is an individual insofar as this natural uniqueness molds his thoughts, instincts, emotions, passions and desires. This is the "natural" *principium individuationis*. Under the system of scarcity, men developed their senses and organs chiefly as implements of labor and competitive orientation: skill, taste, proficiency, tact, refinement and endurance were qualities molded and perpetuated by the hard struggle for life, business and power. Consequently, man's thoughts, appetites and the ways of their fulfillment were not "his," they showed the oppressive and inhibitive features which this struggle imposed upon him. His senses, organs and appetites became acquisitive, exclusive and antagonistic. The technological process has reduced the variety of individual qualities down to this natural basis of individualization, but this same basis may become the foundation for a new form of human development.

The philosophy of individualism established an intrinsic connection between individuality and property.[43] According to this philosophy, man could not develop a self without conquering and cultivating a domain of his own, to be shaped exclusively by his free will and reason. The domain thus conquered and cultivated had become part and parcel of his own "nature." Man removed the objects in this domain from the state in which he found them, and made them the tangible manifestation of his individual labor and interest. They were his property because they were fused with the very essence of his personality. This construction did not correspond to the facts and lost its meaning in the era of mechanized commodity production, but it contained the truth that individual development, far from being an inner value only, required an external sphere of manifestation and an autonomous concern for men and things. The process of production has long dissolved the link between individual labor and property and now tends to dissolve the link between the traditional form of property and social control, but the tightening of this control counteracts a tendency which may give the individualistic theory a new content. Technological progress would make it possible to decrease the time and energy spent in the production of the necessities of life, and a gradual reduction of scarcity and abolition of competitive pursuits could permit the self to develop from its natural roots. The less time and energy man has to expend in maintaining his life and that of society, the greater the possibility that he can "individualize" the sphere of his human realization. Beyond the realm of necessity, the essential differences between men could unfold themselves: everyone could think and act by himself, speak his own language, have his own emotions and follow his own passions. No longer chained to competitive efficiency, the self could grow in the realm of satisfaction. Man could come into his own in his passions. The objects of his desires would be the less exchangeable the more they were seized and shaped by his free self. They would "belong" to him more than ever before, and such ownership would not be injurious, for it would not have to defend its own against a hostile society.

Such a Utopia would not be a state of perennial happiness. The "natural" individuality of man is also the source of his natural sorrow. If the human relations are nothing but human, if they are freed from all foreign standards, they will be permeated with the sadness of their singular content. They are transitory and irreplaceable, and their transitory character will be accentuated when concern for the human being is no longer mingled with fear for his material existence and overshadowed by the threat of poverty, hunger, and ostracism.

The conflicts, however, which may arise from the natural individuality of men may not bear the violent and aggressive features which were so frequently attributed to the "state of nature." These features may be the marks of coercion and privation. "Appetite is never excessive, never furious, save when it has been starved. The frantic hunger we see it so often exhibiting under every variety of criminal form, marks only the hideous starvation to which society subjects it. It is not a normal but a morbid state of the appetite, growing exclusively out of the unnatural compression which is imposed upon it by the exigencies of our immature society. Every appetite and passion of man's nature is good and beautiful, and destined to be fully enjoyed . . . Remove, then, the existing bondage of humanity, remove those factitious restraints which keep appetite and passion on the perpetual lookout for escape, like steam from an overcharged boiler, and their force would instantly become conservative instead of destructive."[44]

Notes

Political Sociology and Critique of Politics

1. On Lenin's place in the philosophical spectrum of the Second International *vid.* A. Arato, "Between Antinomy and Myth: Marxism and Philosophy Reconsidered" in Hobsbawm, Haupt et al. eds., *A History of Socialist Thought* (Einaudi Editore, forthcoming in 1978).

2. Cf. Oscar Negt, "Marxismus als Legitimationswissenschaft" in Bukharin, Deborin et al., *Die Kontroverse über mechanischen und dialektischen Materialismus* (Frankfurt/M: Suhrkamp Verlag, 1969).

3. Trans. by R. Livingstone (Cambridge: MIT Press, 1971).

4. Trans. by F. Halliday (London: New Left Books, 1970).

5. Trans. by Q. Hoare and G.N. Smith (New York: International Publishers, 1971).

On Lukács *vid.* the special issues of *Telos* (St. Louis, Winter 1971 and Spring 1972) X and XI.

On Gramsci *vid.* C. Boggs, *Gramsci's Marxism* (London: Pluto Press, 1976); M. Vajda's review of *Prison Notebooks* in *Telos* (St. Louis, Spring 1973) XV; and special issue of *Telos* (St. Louis, Spring 1977) XXXI.

On Korsch *vid.* the special issue of *Telos* (St. Louis, Winter 1975). XXVI.

Also cf. the relevant articles in K. Klare and D. Howard eds., *The Unknown Dimension* (New York: Basic Books, 1971).

5a. For a presentation of the last two concepts, reification and mediation, see our introduction to the next part "Esthetic Theory and Cultural Criticism."

5b. On this problem cf. our introduction to the last part of the anthology "A Critique of Methodology."

6. Horkheimer, "Traditional and Critical Theory" (1937) in *Critical Theory* (New York: Seabury, 1974).

7. Cf. Horkheimer, "Authority and the Family" (1936) in *Critical Theory* and

Lukács, "The Changing Function of Historical Materialism" in *History and Class Consciousness*.

8. Horkheimer, "Postscript" (1937) in *Critical Theory*.

9. On the philosophical (not the political) aspects of this shift cf. the essay by Michael Theunissen, "Gesellschaft und Geschichte. Zur Kritik der Kritischen Theorie" (Berlin: de Gruyter, 1969).

10. Cf. "Traditional and Critical Theory."

11. Cf. "Authority and the Family."

12. In 1934 his evaluation of Soviet development seemed to be positive indeed. cf. G. Marramao, "Political Economy and Critical Theory," *Telos* (St. Louis, Summer 1975) XXIV.

13. On this cf. Horkheimer, "Die Juden und Europa" (1939) now in *Kritische Theorie* III (Frankfurt: Raubdruck; n.d.) and Marcuse, "The Struggle against Liberalism in the Totalitarian View of the State" (1934) now in *Negations* (Boston: Beacon Press, 1969).

14. Franz Neumann was the big exception. Cf. his *Democratic and Authoritarian State* (New York: Free Press, 1957).

15. Cf. Marcuse, "The Struggle against Liberalism."

16. Either the strong state is needed to rationalize the monopoly system, to carry out the last stages of monopolization (Neumann's *Behemoth*), *or* it is needed to steer a monopoly system itself much more anarchic than even liberal capitalism. (Pollock, Horkheimer before 1940) For a summary of the economic arguments cf. Marramao *op. cit.* and M. Postone and B. Brick, "F. Pollock and the Primacy of the Political," *International Journal of Politics* (Fall, 1976) Our interpretation opposes these because we do not believe that Pollock's interpretation of the Marxian crisis theory in itself led to the emergence of either the Frankfurt political sociology of the 1940s or to the "critique of instrumental reason."

17. On the cultural-historical foundations and implications of this thesis cf. our introduction to Part II below.

18. The new context had important methodological implications; it necessitated a transformation in the very meaning of critique. On this cf. introduction Part II.

19. Aside from the important complementarity between Frankfurt social philosophy and Kirchheimer's political analysis we should also notice a crucial difference. Kirchheimer was too careful an analyst to present (as did Horkheimer in 1939) the fascist state as the most consistent (and especially logically necessary) expression of *monopoly capitalism*, nor did he collapse the pluralist state and the fascist state (as did Pollock in the 1940s) as two forms of the identical *new* order, the authoritarian state. In the debate on the nature of National Socialism he avoided the implicit determinism of the more orthodox Marxist position and the convergence and totalitarianism theses of the "revisionists." Cf. M. Jay, *The Dialectical Imagination* (Boston: Little, Brown, 1973) chapter 5, for further details.

20. In particular in the 1937 *Zeitschrift* article "The Change of the Function of Law in Modern Society" now in *Democratic and Authoritarian State*.

21. The Frankfurt analysis of the crisis of modern culture and the culture industry will be key topics of Part II, below.

22. Cf. e.g. Horkheimer, "Traditional and Critical Theory," Marcuse, "The Struggle against Liberalism" and Pollock, "Bemerkungen zur Wirtschaftskrise" (1933), now in *Stadien des Kapitalismus* (Munich: Verlag C.H. Beck, 1975).

23. For a summary of the debate cf. Jay, *Dialectical Imagination,* which however restricts the implications to a single issue: monopoly or state capitalism, orthodoxy or revisionism. He does not see consequently that more was at stake than "The Institute's Interpretation of Nazism." Marramao, coming at the problem from an entirely different position, also misses many of the crucial points in his desire to measure the main line of critical theory against the orthodox critique of political economy represented by some Institute members, especially Grossmann.

24. This is true, both in the body of *Behemoth*, where a command economy is stressed as against the still-functioning monopolistic sector, and in his later writings. Cf. Neumann, *Behemoth* revised ed. (New York: Oxford University Press, 1944).

25. Now in *Stadien des Kapitalismus*.

26. The last was stressed only in the second article clearly reflecting the events of 1933.

27. Going beyond Lukács, Pollock, as we will see, understood the alternative character of economic development. Even in the 1930s he freed Lukácsian Marxism from its basic inconsistency, postulating the free self-determination of the subjective factor in the context of economic necessity.

28. And yet both were in Pollock's description very unlikely, the first because the emergence of the state as total capital would reduce the existing ruling class to a historically unprecedented rentier status, and the second because of the low level of class consciousness among the proletariat.

29. *Stadien des Kapitalismus* pp. 64-65 ff.

30. For the key differences between the German and US solution of the crisis see however M. Vajda, "The Rise of Fascism in Italy and Germany," *Telos* (St. Louis, Summer 1972) XII.

31. Cf. R. Koselleck, *Kritik und Krise* (Frankfurt/M: Suhrkamp, 1973) and J. Habermas, *Theory and Practice* (Boston: Beacon Press; 1973).

32. Pollock could not have considered the Soviet Union of the 1930s as already socialist since his own 1933 concept of socialism implied vast reduction of labor time (cf. *Stadien des Kapitalismus* p. 60). On the other hand his own *model* of any planned society involved a highly centralized economy, the homogenization of needs, "scientific management" and the extension of a factory-type control system to the whole society. This position (neither stressed nor abandoned by Pollock in his 1940s writings) was shared by Horkheimer in the 1930s but was obviously rejected in the 1940s.

33. *Stadien des Kapitalismus* pp. 60-61; p. 68.

33a. The possibility of a new social formation was raised at exactly the same time, independently but in response to the same political problem, by three breakaways from the Trotskyist movement, Rizzi, Schachtman and Burnham and by Pollock and Horkheimer. Cf. (i), (ii), (iii) amd (iv).

(i) Bruno Rizzi, *La Bureaucratisation du Monde* (Paris, 1939).

(ii) James Burnham, *The Managerial Revolution* (New York, 1941).

(iii) Max Schachtman, *The Bureaucratic Revolution: The Rise of the Stalinist State* (New York, 1962).

(iv) Leon Trotsky, *In Defense of Marxism* (New York, 1942).

34. Cf. e.g. Fromm, *Escape from Freedom* and Adorno, *Gesammelte Schriften* (Frankfurt/M: Suhrkamp, 1972, 1975) v. 8-9. We regret that in this part we can reproduce one essay only from this rich selection, the Adorno essay which is least available to an English-speaking audience. But see also the Fromm essay in Part III of this volume.

35. Cf. Bruce Brown, *Freud, Marx and the Critique of Everyday Life* (New York: Monthly Review, 1974); Russell Jacoby, *Social Amnesia* (Boston: Beacon, 1975); Michael Schneider, *Neurosis and Civilization* (New York: Seabury, 1975); Jay, *Dialectical Imagination* chapter 3. On the methodological side of this issue cf. our Part III below.

35a. Both essays are to be found in O. Kirchheimer, *Politics, Law and Social Change* (New York: Columbia U. Press, 1969). The earlier essay ''The Socialist and Bolshevik Theory of the State'' (1928) applauded Lenin's discovery of the ''primacy of politics'' and also the syndicalist theory (or myth) that he saw latent in the Bolshevik stress on councils. Even here Kirchheimer demystified the terms ''soviet democracy'' and ''soviet legality.''

36. Franz Neumann, *The Democratic and Authoritarian State*, pp. 265-66. For Neumann the ''new class'' comes into being only when definable economically. In this his analysis is similar to those of Rizzi, Burnham and Djilas among others. For a recent,far more satisfactory, political definition cf. Claude Lefort, ''What is Bureaucracy,'' *Telos* XXII (Winter 1974-1975, St. Louis).

37. For this argument cf. Part II below and especially Horkheimer's *Eclipse of Reason* and Adorno-Horkheimer, *Dialectic of Enlightenment*.

37a. Cf. Marcuse, *Soviet Marxism* (New York: Columbia U. Press, 1958) and *One-Dimensional Man* (Boston: Beacon Press, 1964).

38. Cf. Franz Neumann, *Behemoth*, pp. 221ff, and G. Marramao *op. cit.* Marramao, because of his commitment to Marxist orthodoxy as the only possibility of dynamic theorizing, suppresses the crisis theoretical aspects of Pollock's essay.

39. Jürgen Habermas, *Legitimation Crisis* (Boston: Beacon, 1975) pp. 24ff.

The End of Reason

1. *Dialogue d'Ephémère, Oeuvres complètes*, Paris 1880, Garnier, Vol. 30, p. 488.

2. Cf. *Origen against Celsus*, Book 4, ch. 25 (The Antinicene Fathers, ed. Robert and Donaldson, New York 1890, Vol. IV, p. 507).

3. Cf. Aristotle, *Politics*, I 1260a 18.

4. Kant, *Idee zu einer allgemeinen Geschichte in weltbürgerlicher Absicht*, Ninth Proposition.

5. Gottlob Ernst Schulze, *Aenesidemus oder über die Fundamente der von dem Herrn Professor Reinhold in Jena gelieferten Elementarphilosophie. Nebst einer Verteidigung des Skeptizismus gegen die Anmassung der Vernunftkritik*. 1792. In Neudrucke der Kantgesellschaft, Berlin 1911, p. 135.

6. *Essay Concerning Human Understanding*, Book IV, ch. xvii, p. 1.

7. Cf. E. Zeller, *Socrates and the Socratic Schools*, transl. by Reichel, London 1868, p. 125.

8. Cf. *Les Essais*, edited Villey, Paris 1930, Vol. II, ch. xii, p. 491 ff.

9. De Maistre, *Etude sur la Souveraineté*, Oeuvres complètes, Lyon 1891, Tome I, pp. 367-77.

10. A. Mathiez, *Contributions à l'Histoire religieuse de la Revolution Française*, Paris 1907, p. 32.

11. Letter to D'Alembert, Feb. 4, 1757, *op. cit.*, Vol. 39, p. 167.

12. Letter to D'Alembert, Sept. 2, 1768, *op. cit.*, Vol. 46, p. 112.

13. Ernst Mach, *Contributions to the Analysis of the Sensations*, transl. by C. M. Williams, Chicago 1897, p. 20.

14. I. G. Fichte, *The Science of Ethics*, transl. by A. E. Kroeger, New York 1897, p. 308.

15. I. G. Fichte, *The Science of Rights*, transl. by A. E. Kroeger, London 1889, p. 167.

15. *Anthropologie in pragmatischer Hinsicht*, § 61.

17. Voltaire, *A Philosophical Dictionary*. Article on "Good" in The Works of Voltaire, New York 1901, Vol. V, p. 264.

18. Henry Charles Lea, *A History of the Inquisition of the Middle Ages*, New York 1922, Vol. I, p. 459.

Changes In The Structure of Political Compromise

1. See, for example, H. Kelsen, *Vom Wesen und Wert der Demokratie*, 2d ed. (Berlin, 1929), and, more recently, E. P. Herring, *The Politics of Democracy* (New York, 1940).

2. E. Burke, *Collected Works*, 5th ed. (Boston, 1877), III, 485 ff.

3. Georg Simmel, *Philosophie des Geldes*, 5th ed. (Munich, 1930), p. 165.

4. Bagehot, *Collected Works*, ed. Barrington, VI, 14. "Lombard Street, 1873": "It is sometimes said that any foreign country can borrow in Lombard Street *at a price*, some countries can borrow much cheaper than others; but all, it is said, can have some money if they choose to pay enough for it. Perhaps this is an exaggeration but confined as, of course, it was meant to be to the civilized nations, it is not much of an exaggeration." As regards the conceptions of civilized and commercial, which are used synonymously, see Kunz, "Zum Begriff der *Nation Civilisée," Zeitschrift für öffent-liches Recht*, VII (1928), 86.

5. See the excellent exposition of this point in K. Loewenstein, *Volk und Parlament nach der Staatstheorie der französischen Nationalversammlung* (Munich, 1922), pp. 191 ff., especially p. 200.

6. For the best account of this see G. Leibholz, *Das Wesen der Repräsentation* (Berlin, 1929).

7. Bagehot, *op. cit.*, I, 345.

8. *Ibid.*, VI, 32.

9. Hansard, LXXIV, 720.

10. *The Economist*, March 29, 1941, p. 399.

11. Brooks Adams, *The Law of Civilization and Decay* (New York, 1895), p. 283.

12. Charles Beslay, *Mes Souvenirs* (Paris, 1873), Chapter "Ma délégation à la Banque."

13. A. Dauphin-Meunier, *La Banque de France* (Paris, 1936), pp. 220-27.

14. The resolution is quoted in Kisch-Elkan, *Central Banks* (London, 1932), p. 17.

15. Cf. the lucid exposition of the tie-up between international loans and retrogressive tendencies of governmental policies in postwar Austria and Hungary, in P. Szende, "Der Staatshaushalt und das Finanzsystem Oesterreichs und Ungarns," in *Handbuch für Finanzwissenschaft* (Tübingen, 1929), III, 206-9, 220.

16. See H. Neisser, "Die alte und die neue Reichsbank", in *Strukturwandlungen der deutschen Volkswirtschaft*, II (Berlin, 1929), 293, and *Deutschland unter dem Dawes-plan*, Bericht des Generalagenten (December 22, 1928) (Berlin, 1929), p. 116.

17. See, e.g., Otto Braun, *Von Weimar zu Hitler*, 2d ed. (New York, 1940), p. 217, whose testimony is valuable on account of his position at the time as head of the Prussian government.

18. See, e.g., Philip Snowden, *An Autobiography* (London, 1934), II, 945-47, who quite naturally, given his role at the time, tries to play down the influence of the Bank of England and of the Federal Reserve Bank, without, however, being able to deny that they asked for cuts in the social services. See also L. McWeir, *The Tragedy of Ramsay MacDonald* (London, 1938), pp. 349-57.

19. The best insight into this process is given by the memoirs of Governor Moreau: "Le relèvement financier et monétaire de la France," *Revue des deux Mondes*, March 1, March 15, April 1, and April 15, 1937. See here especially his characterization of the Herriot ministry, pp. 55 ff.: when he wants to get rid of a cabinet, he decides "de crever l'abcès" (p. 58), in the opposite case he speaks of "les intrigues de certains parlementaires" (p. 30) against the government he wants to stay in office.

See also the already cited Dauphin-Meunier and Bopp, "Government and the Bank of France," in *Public Policy*, II (1941), 3 ff.

For a general judgment by a politician who experienced some rather rough handling by these institutions, see Caillaux in *Sénat*. Session Ordinaire, July 23, 1936, p. 814: "It was always in the atmosphere of this institution to consider the notes of the Banque de France as independent of government credit and to believe that the Banque de France was not created to come to terms with the government."

20. Cf. Moreau, quoted *supra*, pp. 825-27.

21. Vincent Auriol in *Chambre*, Session Ordinaire, 1937, pp. 1964 f. He compares the manipulators of capital flight, always eager to stab their government in the back, with the French *émigré* nobility who, under the leadership of Prince Louis-Joseph Condé, tried at every turn of the French Revolution to stage a comeback.

22. See *Journal Officiel*, July 1, 1937, and especially the deliberation of the Senate on June 30, 1937, in *Sénat*, Session Ordinaire, 1937, p. 718.

23. See the remarks of Berle, *New Directions in the New World* (New York, 1940), p. 121.

24. See, e.g., the interesting discussion between governor Eccles, Federal Reserve Bank, the representative of the school of government spending as a means of upholding the existing private property relationships, which he in turn regards as the surest safeguard of democracy, and Senator Byrd of Virginia, representative of an old-fashioned "balance-the-budget" school, in the *New York Times*, December 20 and 27, 1938.

25. H. Spencer, *The Study of Sociology*, 1st ed. (New York, 1874), p. 396.

26. J. Morley, *On Compromise*, 2d ed. (London, 1877), p. 209.

27. London, 1876. See especially Chapter VI: "Of the Infirmities and Dangers to which Representative Government is Liable."

28. Otto Bauer, *Die Österreichische Revolution* (Vienna, 1923), p. 196. Cf. Gurland's critique in *Marxismus und Diktatur* (Leipzig, 1930), pp. 95 ff.

29. Schmitt, *Freiheitsrechte und institutionelle Garantien der Reichsverfassung* (Berlin, 1931), and Huber, "Bedeutungswandel der Grundrechte," *Archiv für öffentliches Recht*, XXIII (1932), 1-98.

30. *N.L.R.B. v. Chicago Apparatus Co.* (C. C. A. 7, Dec. 1940) 116 F. 2 d. 753. See also Charles Killingsworth, "Employer Freedom and the N.L.R.B.," *Wisconsin Law Review*, March, 1941, pp. 211-38.

31. W. Neuling, "Wettbewerb, Monopol und Befehl in der heutigen Wirtschaft," *Zeitschrift für die gesamten Staatswissenschaften*, XCIX (1939), 316, speaks of scanty "oases" of competition in the realm of the Food Estate.

32. According to the estimates of the Institut für Konjunkturforschung, *Weekly Reports, IX* (1936), 198, at the end of 1936 all internally produced raw materials and semifinished goods, and assuredly half of the industrial finished goods, were bound by agreements. This figure does not define the kind of agreement, whether direct monopolies or only regulatory procedures.

33. C. Russell, "Die Praxis des Zwangskartellgesetzes," *Zeitschrift für die gesamten Staatswissenschaften*, XCVII (1937), 500.

34. An acknowledgment of the thoroughgoing identity of personnel in both organizations is given by Neuling, quoted *supra*, p. 304, n. 1. For the organization in industry in general see Kuehn, "Der vorläufige Aufbau der gewerblichen Wirtschaft," *Archiv des öffentlichen Rechts*. XXVII (1936), 334-63, and the official commentary by the official of the Ministry of Economics, E. Barth, *Wesen und Aufgaben der Organisation der gewerblichen Wirtschaft* (Hamburg, 1939). As regards the relationship between cartel and official organizations see Kley, *Aufbau und Rechtscharakter der Neuorganisation der gewerblichen Wirtschaft und ihr Verhältnis zu den Kartellen*, Kölner Dissertation, 1938.

35. "Kartell im Staatsdienst," *Deutscher Volkswirt*, January 12, 1940, p. 447, and "Entlastung der Reichsstellen," *Deutscher Volkswirt*, July 12, 1940, p. 1452. For a rationalization of the impossibility of separating the functions of official groups and cartels, see Merkel, "Wirtschaftslenkung und Kartellrecht," *Kartell-Rundschau*, 1939, p. 307, and H. Drost, "Der Krieg und die Organisation der gewerblichen Wirtschaft," *Zeitschrift der Akademie für Deutsches Recht*, 1940, pp. 25-26.

36. That the persons who function as mandatories of the Reich Boards are often identical with the personnel of the cartels may be seen from the regulations for paper and wrapping material in Posse-Landfried-Syrup-Backe-Alpers, *Die Reichsverteidigungsgesetzgebung*, Vol. 2, IV, Papier, pp. 83-88.

37. An isolated but vigorous protest against this development may be found in F. Boehm, *Die Ordnung der Wirtschaft als geschichtliche Aufgabe und rechtsschöpferische Leistung* (Stuttgart a. Berlin, 1937), whose main arguments closely parallel those of the American antitrust movement.

38. Somewhat neglected so far, this role of the social honor courts, the supervision of small and medium-sized shops, is frankly acknowledged in *Soziale Praxis*, 1940, p. 1459. For the approval of those restrictions see the decision of the Cartel Tribunal of April, 26, 1939, in *Kartell-Rundschau*, 1939, p. 420, which, already employing the terminology of the combing-out legislation, stipulates that a business which cannot, without endangering its existence, withstand a decrease of RM 50 in its annual profit cannot enjoy legal protection.

39. See, e.g., the regulations for the soap industry by Posse-Landfried, quoted *supra*, Vol. 2, IV, Seife, Introductory Remarks.

40. As regards the ideology, see the wording of the decree on Gemeinschaftshilfe der Wirtschaft, February 19, 1940, *R.G.Bl.*, I, 395, which starts with the supposition that the shutdown is only of a temporary character.

41. Before the great combing-out of April 1, 1939, there were still 1,471,000 handicraft units employing less than 6 employees as compared with 1,734,000 in 1933.

42. Barth, quoted *supra*, p. 67.

43. T. Cole, "Corporative Organization of the Third Reich," *Review of Politics*, II (1940), 438-62.

44. Barth, quoted *supra*, p. 68.

45. Decrees on "Wirtschaftsverwaltung," August 27, 1939, November 28, 1939. *R.G.Bl.*, I, 1495 and 2315, with regulations of September 20, 1939, *R.G.Bl.*, I, 1872.

46. We can see the curious spectacle of the government running behind the private experts in Aryanization and trying belatedly to snatch a share of the loot, thus squeezing out the small businessman who had acquired Jewish property but did not have sufficient capital to run it, or, especially in the field of real estate, to preserve part of it for the warriors when they return from the victorious war. See the decree on the examination of Aryanization acts of June 10, 1940, *R.G.Bl.*, I, 891, where, in case of inappropriate gains through Aryanization, compensation has to be paid to the Reich.

47. Cf. L. Gebhard and H. Merkel, *Das Recht der landwirtschaftlichen Marktordnung* (1937), who present an elaborate commentary on the organization of arbitration courts as far as agricultural market regulations are concerned (statute of February 26, 1935, *R.G.Bl.*, I, 1293). They remark (III, 25) that appeals against the decisions of the committee of complaint to the arbitration court would have a chance of success only in very exceptional cases. See also W. Weber and F. Wieacker, *Eigentum und Enteignung* (Hamburg, 1935), pp. 26-33, for a list of the expropriation features in the various decrees. As regards the elimination of ordinary courts in general, see the remark of Wieacker in *Deutsches Verwaltungsrecht*, 1937, p. 466.

48. See, e.g., the decision of the Prussian Supreme Administrative Tribunal of March 29, 1935, C, 329.

49. The practice of the arbitration courts of the Food Estate has been discussed in P. Giesecke, "Entschädigungspflicht bei marktordnenden Massnahmen," in *Festgabe für Hedemann* (1938), pp. 368-81.

50. For the status of the controversy see G. Ipsen, *Politik und Justiz* (Hamburg, 1937), and S. Grundmann, "Die richterliche Nachprüfung von politischen Führungsakten," *Zeitschrift für die gesamten Staatswissenschaften*, C (1940), 512-44.

51. Cf. Under Secretary of the Treasury Reinhardt in *Deutsche Steuerzeitung*, 1935, p. 485; see also G. Schmoelders, "Die Weiterbildung des Wirtschaftsrechts," *Zeitschrift für die gesamten Staatswissenschaften*, CI (1941), 78. The organization of a Supreme Administrative Court for the whole Reich carries the new status of the judiciary to its logical conclusion when it prescribes that the judges can be removed from the Court at the end of the fiscal year. See *Frankfurter Zeitung*, April 22, 1941. As regards the small part played by the labor courts in determining the relationship between employers and employees, see Cole, "National Socialism and German Labor Courts," *Journal of Politics*, III (1941), 196.

52. As regards the civil liability of the party for offenses committed by party functionaries, see the party point of view in A. Lingg, *Die Verwaltung der NSDAP* (Munich, 1940), pp. 257 ff. The right of the courts to pass on this question is upheld by S. Grundmann, quoted *supra*, pp. 541 ff., and the decision of the *Reichsgericht* of February 17, 1939, in *Deutsches Recht*, 1939, p. 1785. The lower courts, however, more exposed to party pressure, do not seem to follow the Supreme Court. The criminal liability of party members for embezzlement is at times enforced in the courts—provided that one of the numerous amnesties does not intervene. But the secrecy of the procedure and the absolute prohibition of reports on such trials deprive them of any function of control. See E. Roper and C. Leiser, *Skeleton of Justice* (New York, 1941).

53. See O. Kirchheimer, "Criminal Law in National Socialist Germany," *Studies in Philosophy and Social Science*, VIII (1940), 444-63.

54. Reich Minister Frank speaks of "taylorism" in criminal procedure in his somewhat melancholy reflections on the fate of German criminal law under present conditions in "Die Aufgaben der Strafrechtserneuerung," *Zeitschrift der Akademie für Deutsches Recht*, 1941, p. 25. See also G. Dahm, "Richtermacht und Gerichtsverfassung im Strafrecht," *Zeitschrift für die gesamten Staatswissenschaften*, CI (1941), 287-308.

55. The remaining control organ over the bureaucracy, the Rechnungshof (Court of Accounts Control), never very effective in the observations which it issues on expenditure incurred years before, has under the Third Reich become a repository for high officials from the Weimar period who prove their right to the salary they have drawn in their former positions by checking accounts "as soldiers *in Zivil* imbued by the spirit of the leader." (H. Mueller, "Die Stellung des Rechnungshofs im 3. Reich," *Finanzarchiv*, VII [1940], 193, 205.)

56. U. Scheuner, "Deutsche Staatsführung im Krieg," *Deutsche Rechtswissenschaft*, V (1940), 26. For earlier formulations in the same direction see R. Höhn, *Wandlungen im staatsrechtlichen Denken* (Berlin, 1934), p. 39.

57. The same exempt position within the foreign and labor ministries is held by the Reich leader of the Germans abroad and by the Work Service leader of the Reich. As regards the structure of the Youth Organization, see H. Dietze, "Die verfassungsrechtliche Stellung der Hitler-Jugend," *Zeitschrift für die gesamten Staatswissenschaften*, C (1940), 113-56, who comes (p. 154) to the conclusion that the youth movement is an institution which does not belong exclusively to the party or to the government, cannot be measured by conceptions of party law or constitutional law, and thus is subject only to those of the Reich law.

58. The inherited elements in the National Socialist party are naturally effaced if the party is contrasted with the somewhat literary and artificial political styles of nineteenth-century representation instead of with the mass parties of mass democracy. Cf. Ipsen, "Vom Begriff der Partei," *Zeitschrift für die gesamten Staatswissenschaften*, C (1940), 406.

59. There are no figures available for the period since 1935, but even up to then, with the process of aggrandizement going on, the proportion of officials in the total membership of the National Socialist party increased from 6.7 per cent in 1933 to 13 in 1935. Cf. Gerth, "The Nazi Party, Its Leadership and Composition," *American Journal of Sociology*, XLV (1940), 527. Some of this increase, however, may only be apparent, as, e.g., in the case where the party acknowledges the right of a wife to transfer her low party membership number to her husband though he himself refrained from openly joining the party while he was an official. See Lingg, quoted *supra*, pp. 172-73.

60. In spite of its misleading title, which only refers to the *Landkreise* (rural districts), the statute of December 28, 1939, *R.G.Bl.*, I (1940), 45, is designed to provide general control over the relationship between the middle ranks of the bureaucracy and the corresponding party officials.

61. O. Redelberger, "Partei und Staat im Landkreis," *Reichsverwaltungsblatt*, LXI (1940), 47.

62. As regards the modified compromise, see the comment of F. Morstein Marx, "Bureaucracy and Dictatorship," *Review of Politics*, III (1941), 101.

63. This story is related in Rosenstock-Franck, *Les étapes de Léconomie fasciste italienne*, (Paris, 1939), p. 233.

64. Its wording in W. Mueller, *Das soziale Leben im neuen Deutschland* (Berlin, 1938), pp. 136-37.

65. See for the whole problem the semiofficial commentary in G. Neesse, *Führergewalt* (Tübingen, 1940).

66. Characteristic of the intimate connection between the establishment of authority placed in the German leadership and the execution of its imperialist program is a sharp refutation of the conservative writer Triepel who attempted to uphold the view that a state may be called sovereign even if it has no external independence, provided that it controls its own subjects. See H. Triepel, *Die Hegemonie* (Stuttgart, 1938), p. 143, rejected by E. Huber in his review in *Zeitschrift für die gesamten Staatswissenschaften*, C (1940), 179. In fact, the form of domination which the large-space (*Grossraum*) imperialism of Germany creates is not very amenable to the fiction of a sovereign restricted to the domestic realm. "The developing large-space order might, contrary to earlier imperialism, constitute a system of direct and open domination"—says E. Huber, "Position und Begriffe," *Zeitschrift für die gesamten Staatswissenschaften*, C (1940), 143.

State Capitalism: Its Possibilities and Limitations

1. The term "model" is used here in the sense of Max Weber's "ideal type."

2. Here understood simply as absence of technically avoidable "unemployment" of all factors of production. For the discussion of this concept see John Maynard Keynes, *The General Theory of Employment, Interest and Money*. London 1936.

3. The best short statement on the "Breakdown of the Market Mechanism" is still Appendix A to the Senate document 13 (74th Congress, 1st Session) on *"Industrial Prices and Their Relative Inflexibility"* (by Gardiner C. Means, 1935). See also the recent books on the decline of competition by Arthur Robert Burns, Edward H. Chamberlin, Joan Robinson).

4. They can be defined as those without which even the bare subsistence of society can not be reproduced. The description that follows, however, understands "necessary" functions as those achieving the best results under given historic conditions. This is what liberal theory claims for the market system.

5. In this simple scheme, luxuries are included in consumers goods and defense materials under machinery.

6. See for a discussion of the latest literature on the theory of planning: Eduard Heimann, "Literature on the Theory of a Socialist Economy," in: *Social Research*, vol. VI, pp. 87f.; Carl Landauer, "Literature on Economic Planning," in: *Social Research*, vol. VII, pp. 498f.; H. D. Dickinson, *Economics of Socialism*, London 1939.

We do not intimate that a general plan exists in Nazi Germany or has ever existed there. In its place stands the goal of arming as speedily and efficiently as possible, with full use of all resources. Some plan-elements have come into being, while the plan principle, used first as a propaganda slogan in Germany, is rapidly spreading there.

7. For an outstanding analysis of the new functions and the performance of the "pseudo-market" see A. Lowe, "Economic Analysis and Social Structure" in: *The Manchester School*, Vol. VII (1936), pp. 30f. Lowe's arguments pertain to "the pricing process under public ownership." Public control over the means of production, however, has the same economic consequences as state ownership.

8. Obviously, the first to bear the brunt of subordinating the private to the "common" interest is the "little man" in all spheres of society.

9. An example of the result is the amazing elasticity and efficiency in building up an enormous war machinery in National Socialist Germany. This, however, should not be interpreted to mean that in Germany private property interests do not endeavor to gain precedence. In motor-car standardization, for instance, the private interests of the big concerns determined all the measures taken. Since a general plan of economic policy was never published in Germany, it is impossible to decide to what extent private interests did obtain preference.

10. It appears that part of the Nazi successes may be better explained as the rational application of the best available methods in all fields (from eliminating important vitamins in the diet of conquered nations to the practical monopoly in international propaganda) than by any innate qualities of a military or organizational character. It is well to recall, in this connection, that German industry originally learned scientific management from America.

11. E.g., new investments no longer flow automatically into those economic fields where the highest profits are made but are directed by the planning board. In consequence, the mechanism known as equalization of the rate of profit no longer works.

12. Frank Munk, *The Economics of Force*, New York 1940. Lawrence Dennis, *The Dynamics of War and Revolution*, New York 1940.

13. See Rudolf Hilferding, "State Capitalism or Totalitarian State Economy" in: *Socialistichesky Vestnik*, Paris 1940 (Russian). It should be understood that "production for use" is not intended to mean "for the use of free men in a harmonious society" but simply the contrary of production for the market.

14. For an impressive discussion of this trend in Nazi Germany see Dal Hitchcock, "The German Financial Revolution" in: *Harpers Monthly*, February 1941.

15. E.F.M. Durbin, *The Politics of Democratic Socialism*, London 1940, p. 135.

16. Quoted in the *Report for the Business Executive*, November 28, 1940.

17. See Carl Dreher, "Why Hitler Wins," in: *Harpers Monthly*, October 1940.

18. So far, the nearest approach to the state capitalist model of distribution has been made in Soviet Russia. See L. E. Hubbard, *Soviet Trade and Distribution*, London 1938. The trend in Germany shows the same direction.

19. See note 6 above. The latest important publication is that of E. F. M. Durbin, *op. cit.* Most of those who advocate the superiority of a deliberately "manipulated" market confined "within the strait-jacket of planned objectives" have given little attention to the fact that planning is far from being identical with socialism. That is why their work, important as it is, appears even more as a contribution to the theory of state capitalism.

20. L. Robbins, *Economic Planning and International Order*, London 1937, p. 208.

21. See Gottfried von Haberler, *Prosperity and Depression*, Geneva 1937.

22. See Carl Landauer, *Planwirtschaft und Verkehrswirtschaft*, Munich 1931.

23. See, e.g., the "point" system for the distribution of textiles in Germany and England.

24. For this whole set of problems see Oskar Lange, *On the Economic Theory of Socialism*, edited by E. Lippincott, Minneapolis 1938.

25. See the studies of the National Resources Planning Board on *Consumer Incomes and Patterns of Resources Use*, reviewed in *Studies in Philosophy and Social Science* 1940, pp. 483-490.

26. The best survey of the history and details of the argument is *Collectivist Economic Planning*, edited by F. A. von Hayek, London 1935. For a refutation see Oskar Lange, *op. cit.*

27. The German experience shows that probably never in the history of industrialism were new inventions put into application so quickly or such an enormous percentage of the national income used for investments.

28. This also applies to the falling tendency of the rate of profit which, according to Marxian theory, plays havoc with private capitalism. If expansion of capital is subject to a general plan which is itself approved by the controlling group, the percentage of surplus value in ratio to invested capital could fall close to zero without creating any disturbances. This fall, however, is most effectively counteracted by the enforced maintenance of full employment. We shall not enter upon the discussion of whether state capitalism itself emerges under the pressure of the falling rate of profit, nor how far it makes sense to speak in terms of "value" beyond the limits of a market economy.

29. Most of the arguments that follow refer to the totalitarian form of state capitalism only.

30. See Guenter Reimann, *The Vampire Economy*. Doing business under fascism. New York 1939.

31. Julian Gumperz, *The Expansion of Production and the Totalitarian System* (unpublished), makes the point that after property "becomes a semi-sovereign function of rights, privileges, prerogatives, transactions, that is, more and more dissociated from the active and actual carrying forward of production, this latter function creates a new class and is appropriated by it . . . ." This class "represents a depository of skills, abilities, knowledges, traditions, that moves the organization of economic society from one point to another, and organizes the new level of production accomplished . . . Overproduction from which economic society has been suffering is centered to a large extent in the overproduction of this progressive class . . . and it is therefore not accidental but essential that a totalitarian economy stop, at its source, the production and reproduction of these skills . . ."

32. This holds true for Germany and Italy where semifeudal landowners and big business are still in existence and form part of the ruling clique. The situation is different in Soviet Russia where the old vested interests have been wiped out. Since in Russia property in the means of production has changed hands completely from private owners to the state and no longer exists even in its modified and reduced form discussed above, it is somewhat doubtful whether our model of state capitalism fits the Soviet Union in its present phase.

33. Charles A. Beard, *Public Policy and the General Welfare*, New York 1941, marks an important step in this discussion.

34. Vera Micheles Dean, "Toward a New World Order" in: *Foreign Policy Reports*, May 15, 1941, p. 55.

35. A British fact finding group, composed of progressive economists, businessmen, civil servants and professors, known as PEP (Political and Economic Planning), included the following items in its preliminary program prepared in 1940: maintenance after the war of full economic activity based on complete use of man power and resources, 'regardless of obsolete financial criteria'; assurance of a minimum standard of life, based on scientific standards of nutrition and proper provision for dependents; assurance of a minimum standard of housing, based on a socially planned program of housing and social amenities; provision of medical care and a reasonable measure of economic security, covering the hazards of employment, accidents, ill-health, widowhood and old age, the provision of equal opportunities for education in every country and the reestablishment of a European system of higher learning and research open to students of proved ability from all parts of the world; the provision of cultural and recreative activities and the establishment of organizations for the training and leisure of youth on a European scale." (Vera Micheles Dean, *op. cit.*, p. 55).

36. National Resources Committee, *The Structure of the American Economy*, Washington, D.C., 1939, p. 3.

The Authoritarian State

1. Friedrich Engels, *Die Entwicklung des Sozialismus von der Utopie zur Wissenschaft*, 1882 ed. (Berlin, 1924), pp. 46-47. Cf. Friedrich Engels, *Herrn Dührings Umwälzung der Wissenschaft*, 10th ed. (Stuttgart, 1919), pp. 298 ff.

2. Engels, *Die Entwicklung des Sozialismus*, p. 55.

3. Bouchez and Roux, *Histoire Parlementaire de la Révolution Française*, vol. 10 (Paris, 1834), p. 194.

4. See the works of Albert Mathiez, especially *La Réaction Thermidorienne* (Paris, 1929), and *Contributions à l'Histoire Religieuse de la Révolution Française* (Paris, 1907).

5. *Divine Comedy* (Purgatory VI, Verse 145-148).

6. Auguste Comte, "Système de politique positive," in *Oeuvres de St. Simon*, Vol. 9 (Paris, 1973), p. 115.

7. August Bebel, *Die Frau und der Sozialismus* (Stuttgart, 1919), p. 474.

8. Engels, *Die Entwicklung des Sozialismus*, p. 302.

9. See Bebel, *Die Frau und der Sozialismus*, pp. 141 ff.

10. Gaetan Pirou, *Néo-liberalisme, néo-corporatisme, néo-socialisme* (Paris, 1939), p. 173.

Freudian Theory and the Pattern of Fascist Propaganda

1. This article forms part of the author's continuing collaboration with Max Horkheimer.

2. Harper Brothers, New York, 1949. Cf. also: Leo Lowenthal and Norbert Guterman, "Portrait of the American Agitator," *Public Opinion Quart.*, (Fall) 1949, pp. 417 ff.

3. This requires some qualification. There is a certain difference between those who, speculating rightly or wrongly on large-scale economic backing, try to maintain an air of respectability and deny that they are anti-Semites before coming down to the business of Jew-baiting—and overt Nazis who want to act on their own, or at least make believe that they do, and indulge in the most violent and obscene language. Moreover, one might distinguish between agitators who play the old-fashioned, homely, Christian conservative and can easily be recognized by their hostility against the "dole," and those who, following a more streamlined modern version, appeal mostly to the youth and sometimes pretend to be revolutionary. However, such differences should not be overrated. The basic structure of their speeches as well as their supply of devices is identical in spite of carefully fostered differences in overtones. What one has to face is a division of labor rather than genuine divergencies. It may be noted that the National Socialist party shrewdly maintained differentiations of a similar kind, but that they never amounted to anything nor led to any serious clash of political ideas within the party. The belief that the victims of June 30, 1934 were revolutionaries is mythological. The blood purge was a matter of rivalries between various rackets and had no bearing on social conflicts.

4. The German title, under which the book was published in 1921, is *Massenpsychologie und Ichanalyse*. The translator, James Strachey, rightly stresses that the term group here means the equivalent of Le Bon's *foule* and the German *Masse*. It may be added that in this book the term ego does not denote the specific psychological agency as described in Freud's later writings in contrast to the id and the superego; it simply means the individual. It is one of the most important implications of Freud's *Group Psychology* that he does not recognize an independent, hypostatized "mentality of the crowd," but reduces the phenomena observed and described by writers such as Le Bon and McDougall to regressions which take place in each one of the individuals who form a crowd and fall under its spell.

5. S. Freud, *Group Psychology and the Analysis of the Ego*, London, 1922, p. 7.

6. *Ibid.*, p. 27.

7. Freud's book does not follow up this phase of the problem but a passage in the addendum indicates that he was quite aware of it. "In the same way, love for women breaks through the group ties of race, of national separation, and of the social class system, and it thus produces important effects as a factor in civilization. It seems certain

that homosexual love is far more compatible with group ties, even when it takes the shape of uninhibited sexual tendencies'' (p. 123). This was certainly borne out under German fascism where the borderline between overt and repressed homosexuality, just as that between overt and repressed sadism, was much more fluent than in liberal middle-class society.

8. *L.c.*, pp. 9 and 10.

9. ''. . . love relationships . . . also constitute the essence of the group mind. Let us remember that the authorities make no mention of any such relations.'' (*Ibid.*, p. 40.)

10. Perhaps one of the reasons for this striking phenomenon is the fact that the masses whom the fascist agitator—prior to seizing power—has to face are primarily not organized ones but the accidental crowds of the big city. The loosely knit character of such motley crowds makes it imperative that discipline and coherence be stressed at the expense of the centrifugal uncanalized urge to love. Part of the agitator's task consists in making the crowd believe that it is organized like the Army or the Church. Hence the tendency towards over-organization. A fetish is made of organization as such; it becomes an end instead of a means and this tendency prevails throughout the agitator's speeches.

11. *L.c.*, pp. 99-100. This key statement of Freud's theory of group psychology incidentally accounts for one of the most decisive observations about the fascist personality: the externalization of the superego. The term ''ego ideal'' is Freud's earlier expression for what he later called superego. Its replacement through a ''group ego'' is exactly what happens to fascist personalities. They fail to develop an independent autonomous conscience and substitute for it an identification with collective authority which is as irrational as Freud described it, heteronomous, rigidly oppressive, largely alien to the individuals' own thinking and, therefore, easily exchangeable in spite of its structural rigidity. The phenomenon is adequately expressed in the Nazi formula that what serves the German people is good. The pattern reoccurs in the speeches of American fascist demagogues who never appeal to their prospective followers' own conscience but incessantly invoke external, conventional and stereotyped values which are taken for granted and treated as authoritatively valid without ever being subject to a process of living experience or discursive examination. As pointed out in detail in the book, *The Authoritarian Personality*, by T. W. Adorno, Else Frenkel-Brunswik, Daniel J. Levinson and R. Nevitt Sanford (Harper Brothers, New York, 1950), prejudiced persons generally display belief in conventional values instead of making moral decisions of their own and regard as right ''what is being done''. Through identification, they too tend to submit to a group ego at the expense of their own ego ideal which becomes virtually merged with external values.

12. The fact that the fascist follower's masochism is inevitably accompanied by sadistic impulses is in harmony with Freud's general theory of ambivalence, originally developed in connection with the Oedipus complex. Since the fascist integration of individuals into masses satisfies them only vicariously, their resentment against the frustrations of civilization survives but is canalized to become compatible with the leader's aims; it is psychologically fused with authoritarian submissiveness. Though Freud does not pose the problem of what was later called ''sado-masochism,'' he was nevertheless well aware of it, as evidenced by his acceptance of Le Bon's idea that ''since a group is in no doubt as to what constitutes truth or error, and is conscious, moreover, of its own great strength, it is as intolerant as it is obedient to authority. It respects force and can only be slightly influenced by kindness, which it regards merely as a form of weakness. What it demands of its heroes is strength, or even violence. It wants to be ruled and oppressed and to fear its masters.'' (Freud, *op. cit.*, p. 17)

13. *Op. cit.*, pp. 58 ff.

14. *Ibid.*, p. 61.

15. *Ibid.*, p. 60.

16. Cf. Max Horkheimer, "Authoritarianism and the Family Today," *The Family: Its Function and Destiny*, ed. R. N. Anshen (Harper Brothers, New York, 1949).

17. Freud, *op. cit.*, p. 74.

18. The translation of Freud's book renders his term *"Instanz"* by "faculty," a word which, however, does not carry the hierarchical connotation of the German original. "Agency" seems to be more appropriate.

19. Freud, *l.c.*, p. 80.

20. It may not be superfluous to stress that Nietzsche's concept of the Superman has as little in common with this archaic imagery as his vision of the future with fascism. Freud's allusion is obviously valid only for the "Superman" as he became popularized in cheap slogans.

21. *L. c.*, p. 93.

22. *Ibid.*, p. 102.

23. For further details on personalization cf. Freud, *l.c.*, p. 44, footnote, where he discusses the relation between ideas and leader personalities; and p. 53, where he defines as "secondary leaders" those essentially irrational ideas which hold groups together. In technological civilization, no *immediate* transference to the leader, unknown and distant as he actually is, is possible. What happens is rather a regressive repersonalization of impersonal, detached social powers. This possibility was clearly envisaged by Freud. ". . . A common tendency, a wish in which a number of people can have a share, may . . . serve as a substitute. This abstraction, again, might be more or less completely embodied in the figure of what we might call a secondary leader."

24. *L. c.*, p. 110.

25. German folklore has a drastic symbol for this trait. It speaks of *Radfahrernaturen*, bicyclist's characters. Above they bow, they kick below.

26. Freud, *l. c.*, p. 16.

27. *L. c.*, pp. 50-51.

28. With regard to the role of "neutralized," diluted religion in the make-up of the fascist mentality, cf. *The Authoritarian Personality*. Important psychoanalytic contributions to this whole area of problems are contained in Theodor Reik's *Der eigene und der fremde Gott*, and in Paul Federn's *Die vaterlose Gesellschaft*.

29. It may be noted that the ideology of race distinctly reflects the idea of primitive brotherhood revived, according to Freud, through the specific regression involved in mass formation. The notion of race shares two properties with brotherhood: it is supposedly "natural," a bond of "blood," and it is de-sexualized. In fascism this similarity is kept unconscious. It mentions brotherhood comparatively rarely, and

usually only in regard to Germans living *outside* the borders of the Reich ("Our Sudeten brothers"). This, of course, is partly due to recollections of the ideal of *fraternité* of the French Revolution, taboo to the Nazis.

30. *L. c.*, p. 53.

31. *L. c.*, pp. 55-56.

32. *L. c.*, p. 56.

33. *L. c.*, pp. 87-88.

34. *L. c.*, p. 114.

35. *L. c.*, p. 87.

36. Cf. *Prophets of Deceit.*

37. *L. c.*, p. 76.

38. *L. c.*, p. 99.

Some Social Implications of Modern Technology

1. Cf. Lewis Mumford, *Technics and Civilization*, New York 1936, p. 364: The motive in back of "mechanical discipline and many of the primary inventions . . . was not technical efficiency but holiness, or power over other men. In the course of their development machines have extended these aims and provided a vehicle for their fulfillment."

2. Cf. A.R.L. Gurland, "Technological Trends and Economic Structure under National Socialism," in *Studies in Philosophy and Social Science*, IX (1941), No. 2, pp. 226ff.

3. Areopagitica.

4. *Temporary National Committee*, Monograph No. 22, "Technology in Our Economy," Washington, 1941, p. 195.

5. *Temporary National Economic Committee, Final Report of the Executive Secretary*, Washington 1941, p. 140.

6. The term "apparatus" denotes the institutions, devices and organizations of industry in their prevailing social setting.

7. L. Mumford, *op. cit.*, pp. 361ff.

8 *The Instinct of Workmanship*, New York, 1922, p. 306f.

9. *Ibid.*, p. 310. This training in "matter of factness" applies not only to the factory worker but also to those who direct rather than attend the machine.

10. Florian Znaniecki, *The Social Role of the Man of Knowledge*, New York 1940, p. 54f. Bernard J. Stern, *Society and Medical Progress*, Princeton 1941, Chapter IX, and the same author's contribution to *Technological Trends and National Policy*, U. S. National Resources Committee, Washington 1937.

11. Thorstein Veblen, *op. cit.*, p. 315f.

12. Thurmann Arnold, *The Folklore of Capitalism*, New York 1941, p. 193f.

13. Thorstein Veblen, *op. cit.*, p. 314.

14. Albert Walton, *Fundamentals of Industrial Psychology*, New York 1941, p. 24.

15. Robert F. Hoxie, *Scientific Management and Labor*, New York 1916, p. 140f.

16. *Ibid.*, p. 149.

17. Cf. Max Horkheimer and Herbert Marcuse, "Traditionelle und kritische Theorie," in *Zeitschrift für Socialforschung*, VI (1937), pp. 245ff.

18. Cf. the discussion on the law Le Chapelier in the National Assembly of the French Revolution.

19. Hitler's speech before the Industry Club in Düsseldorf, January 27, 1932, in *My New Order*, New York 1941, pp. 93ff.

20. *The Engineers and The Price System*, New York 1940, pp. 88ff.

21. E. Lederer, *State of the Masses*, New York 1940, p. 32f.

22. Albert Walton, *op. cit.*, p. 27.

23. W. E. Hocking, *The Lasting Elements of Individualism*, New Haven 1937, p. 5.

24. *Ibid.*, p. 23.

25. Florian Znaniecki, *op. cit.*, pp. 40, 55.

26. *Op. cit.*, p. 31—Znaniecki's description refers to a historical state of affairs in which "no demand for a scientist can arise," but it appears to refer to a basic tendency of the prevailing state of affairs.

27. Cf. Max Horkheimer, "The End of Reason," above.

28. Florian Znaniecki, *op. cit.*, p. 25.

29. *Wirtschaft und Gesellschaft*, Tübingen 1922, p. 666.

30. Max Weber, *op. cit.*, p. 669.

31. Henry A. Wallace, *Technology, Corporations, and the General Welfare*, Chapel Hill 1937, p. 56.

32. J. Burnham, *The Managerial Revolution*, New York 1941, pp. 78ff.

33. *Ibid.*, p. 83f.

34. Robert A. Brady, "Policies of National Manufacturing Spitzenverbände," in *Political Science Quarterly*, LVI, p. 537.

35. *The Thought and Character of William James*, ed. R. B. Perry, Boston 1935, II, p. 265.

36. *Ibid.*, p. 315.

37. *Ibid.*, p. 383.

38. *Democracy in America*, transl. H. Reeve, New York 1904, p. 584.

39. Quoted in E. Mims, *The Majority of the People*, New York 1941, p. 152.

40. See for example Oswald Spengler, *Man and Technics*, New York 1932, p. 96f., and Roy Helton, "The Anti-Industrial Revolution," in *Harpers*, December 1941, pp. 65ff.

41. In National Socialist Germany, the ideology of blood and soil and the glorification of the peasant is an integral part of the imperialistic mobilization of industry and labor.

42. For examples of the degree to which this physiological individualization has been utilized see *Changes in Machinery and Job Requirements in Minnesota Manufacturing 1931-36*, Works Projects Administration, National Research Project, Report No. 1-6. Philadelphia, p. 19.

43. See Max Horkheimer, "The End of Reason," above.

44. Henry James, "Democracy and Its Issues," in *Lectures and Miscellanies*, New York 1852, p. 47f.

Esthetic Theory and Cultural Criticism

The Concept of Culture*

The concept of culture is significantly ambiguous in normal usage. More often than not, "culture" is represented as the sum total of activities that possess the aura of intellectuality or spirituality, that is, the arts and the sciences. But there is also an important usage especially, but not only, in the social sciences that defines culture as the ensemble of those intersubjective traditions, meanings, values, institutions, rituals, customs and typical activities characteristic in space and time of a given social formation. The ambiguity has been noticed by the Frankfurt School even if the brunt of their critical concern focuses on culture in the first sense.[1] The two concepts of culture may in fact be related to one another. In the history of sociology and social theory, no one did more to elaborate a comprehensive and dynamic concept of culture than the turn-of-the-century German thinker Georg Simmel.[2] Drawing heavily, if implicitly, on Hegel and Marx, Simmel defined all culture as human self-creation in the context of cultivating things, or self-cultivation in the process of endowing the things of nature with use and meaning. However, for Simmel, the self-cultivation ("subjective culture") of individuals and the cultivation of things ("objective culture") by ensembles of individuals are neither parallel nor harmonious. He postulated a gradually and linearly increasing

*First four sections by Andrew Arato; last section by Eike Gebhardt.

division of labor as the red thread of history that leads not only to the powerful growth of *objective culture*, but also to the corresponding one-sidedness, deformation and overspecialization of individuals, i.e., to the crisis of *subjective culture*. True "subjective culture" was to Simmel the cultivation of the *whole* personality, and although this is ambiguous in his work, Simmel's restriction of the achievement of totalization to the great cultural "forms," art, philosophy, theology, historiography, and science, did imply the highly privileged and philosophically preferable nature of some human activities[3], i.e., what Marx more than fifty years before had called "mental work." Thus, Simmel systematically related culture in the narrow sense of intellectual self-cultivation and culture in general, the objectification and externalization of all human activities. He defined the relationship of the two in terms of an increasing split that he called the "tragedy of culture."

Marx wrote nothing on "culture" as such. Indeed, his methodological remarks on the dependence of "superstructure" on the "base" (and in particular the forms of consciousness on the contradictory structure of a mode of production) have generally been interpreted by Marxists as reason enough to disregard the "epiphenomena" of culture. However, much of Frankfurt cultural theory begins with one singularly fruitful distinction of Marx's: that between mental and manual labor. In distinction to almost all bourgeois theories of the division of labor (including Simmel's), for Marx "the division of labor proper" begins with the separation of mental and manual labor, and moreover presupposes private property and therefore the beginning of the contradiction between the interest of the separate individual (or family) and the "communal interest of all individuals," now in the alienated form of the state.[4] In this complex, mental labor, private property and the state are on the same side. From this point on, according to Marx, consciousness (i.e., mental labor) can flatter itself as being independent of the social life process, though the forms of consciousness continue to belong to the complex of the division of labor and hence possess neither independent life nor history. Aside from its illusory self-representation, consciousness or mental labor continues to represent in an illusory manner (generally on the side of real powers) the real struggle of the world. Even the post-Christian dreams of universality, liberty and equality express *both* world-historical potentialities brought about by the development of a universally interdependent and highly productive system of civil society *and* the cultural-ideological illusions that mask the particularity, unfreedom and inequality of class rule.[5] Thus, Marx located culture in the narrow sense in terms of mental labor, whose pretensions he criticized. He also had a concept corresponding to the more general concept of culture, for which he used the terms "mode of production" or "social formation" interchangeably. We will follow one of his usages and refer to "culture" in general as social formation.

The concept of mental labor marks the limits of the Frankfurt concept of culture, both in the narrow sense of "high" culture and also in its popular and mass substitutes. At times the passionate hatred of critical theory toward what Marcuse called "affirmative culture" (i.e., the mode of "high" culture that in spite of its utopian anticipations suppresses its relationship to the social life process) surpassed that of Marx:

> The products of art and science owe their existence not merely to the effort of the great geniuses that created them, but also to the unnamed drudgeries of their contemporaries. There is no document of culture which is not at the same time a document of barbarism.[6]

Thus wrote Walter Benjamin in a 1937 text reproduced below. But lest we assign the argument to his lonely and idiosyncratic position within (or without) the School, let us quote from Adorno in 1966:

> All post-Auschwitz culture, including its urgent critique, is garbage. In restoring itself after the things that happened without resistance in its own countryside, culture has turned entirely into the ideology it had been potentially—had been ever since it presumed, in opposition to material existence, to inspire that existence with the light denied it by the separation of mind from manual labor.[7]

The quotations represent what Adorno himself called *transcendent critique* of culture, an attack from an imaginary point of reference outside culture. Since for most Marxists and even for the sociology of knowledge the theoretical key to cultural or "superstructural" phenomena lies in investigating the conflicts/contradictions of the social-economic "base" that supposedly subordinates culture to the interests of a given ruling class, these modes of cultural analysis (including Marx's own in the *German Ideology*) also fall under the heading of *transcendent* or *external* critique. The danger—also present in the above quotations—is that transcendent critics, "wishing to wipe away the whole as if with a sponge . . . develop an affinity to barbarism.'' On the other hand, the opposite mode of procedure, the one Adorno usually practiced, ''immanent critique,'' faces the danger of loving immersion in the object criticized.[8] Even the above lines from *Negative Dialectics* about Auschwitz and culture end, therefore, with an ambiguous formulation:

> Whoever pleads for the maintenance of this radically culpable and shabby culture becomes its accomplice, while the man who says no to culture is directly furthering the barbarism which our culture showed itself to be.[9]

The dialectical critique of culture is forbidden either to celebrate autonomous mind or to hate it; the critique ''must both participate in culture and not participate.''[10] While the main Frankfurt theorists of culture, Adorno, Benjamin, Horkheimer, Marcuse and Lowenthal indeed moved between these poles—or better still attempted to indicate the missing *tertium* through criticizing each pole—no secure single meaning of dialectical culture critique emerges from their works.

The various answers which emerge from critical theory's confrontation with and involvement in culture had to negotiate not only between the poles of transcendent and immanent critique. Other dualities or ''antinomies'' (in Kant's sense: contrary positions which could be more or less equally defended by logical argument) quickly appeared. Is culture (in the narrow sense) to be considered as a sphere of ''autonomous ends in themselves'' or as a socially-politically-economically fungible subsphere in which even the useless becomes useful? Is there more ''truth'' latent in the ''ideologies'' of high culture or in those of ''mass'' culture? Should the critic concentrate on ''works,'' or on the production and reception of ''products''? Are politically radical works more or less critical of the existing world than autonomous works? Are the works of the past or the present the repositories of utopia? Is the reintegration of mental and manual labor, of art and life, the content of a positive utopia of liberation or of a negative administered one? The answers vary from author to author, from article to article and even at times within the same article. In 1936, Max Horkheimer concentrated on the role of culture (including high culture) in producing legitimating beliefs for political domination.[11] In 1941, he stressed instead, following Kant, the critique of instrumental reason latent in the purposelessness of genuine works.[12]

In a 1937 article, Herbert Marcuse criticized the survival of affirmative culture in the present (hoping for its revolutionary abolition). In another, he focused on the utopian contents of the affirmative culture of the past.[13] And much later, in his *Essay on Liberation* (1969), he called once again for the reintegration of culture and life through the abolition of "art" and the estheticization of daily life and work, only to claim still a few years later in *Counterrevolution and Revolt* (1972), the need to protect autonomous works even in the future. And most important, Walter Benjamin and Theodor Adorno, two close friends, engaged in a set of controversies in the 1930s about art, mass culture and politics in which Adorno used Benjamin against Benjamin and Benjamin, as we will see, could have used Adorno the sociologist against Adorno the philosopher of art.

In the context of such diversity, what is the justification for presenting the culture and the esthetic theory of the Frankfurt School under a simple heading? First, all of our theorists shared more or less the same theory of social formations [i.e., theory of culture in the general sense] inherited from Hegel, Marx, Tönnies, Weber and Lukács. Second, the esthetic alternatives [in the area of culture in the narrow sense] they developed in response to this theory of social formations matured in the context of a dialogue characterized by the mutual and complementary adequacy of their critiques of one another.

Theory of Social Formations

Under this heading, we have in mind the historical specification of the "formation" of civil society or, more narrowly, capitalism, by the epoch-making investigations of Hegel, Marx, Weber, Tönnies and Lukács. Here we can focus only on some of these theorists and such of their concepts as pertain to the Frankfurt critique of culture in the narrow sense. The system that Hegel called *bürgerliche* (civil or bourgeois) *Gesellschaft* (society) was located by Marx, especially in the 1867 *Grundrisse der Kritik der Politischen Okonomie*, in an imposing framework of historical social formations. Marx called this framework one of organic, naturally arisen *(naturwüchsig)* communities, i.e., the "precapitalist" social formations. What is common to all three great forms of organic communities (Asiatic, Classical Antiquity and Germanic) is direct personal dependence of human beings on natural (land) and quasi-natural (the community itself) presuppositions of existence.[14] Though individuality (the presupposition of which is some private property) is mentioned by Marx in the case of classical Greece and Rome, he stresses that even here individuality can operate only within restricted and "provincial" communal limits.[15] Hegel's civil society, founded on more independent individuality, is located by Marx, in spite of all earlier anticipations, only after the end of the European Middle Ages. Fully unfolded as capitalism, this system of the socialization of society [*Vergesellschaftung der Gesellschaft*] is abstractly characterized as that of "personal independence founded on objective dependence . . . in which a system of general social metabolism, of universal relations, of all-round needs and universal capacities is formed for the first time."[16] Evidently Marx's attitude to the capitalist social formation was profoundly ambiguous, and he was willing to declare it as progress only if a third great stage of history based on "free individuality" and the subordination of wealth to a new freely formed community were realized.[17] It is, however, a characteristic of capitalism that all substantial communities disintegrate under the onslaught of market, competition and large-scale, industrial division of labor, forcing the subordination of the newly freed individuals to a new system of mechanically objective dependence, e.g., economic laws of the market and production. Furthermore, the new dependence and interdependence of individuals is not only regulated by objective laws, but is also masked by the system of exchange of things, i.e., commodities. Domination and the exploitation of labor become anonymous when "the social connections of persons is transposed into a social relation between things." Here is the origin of Marx's concept of commodity fetishism. Marx stresses that the resulting objective context with its deterministic laws tendentially reduces the newly emancipated individual to an abstract individual emptied of all formally internalized communal norms, customs and habits. The "birth and decline" of the individual are thus located by Marx in the same social order which becomes the proper historical terrain of Simmel's transhistorical "tragedy of culture." For Marx in contradistinction to Simmel, the "socialization of society" represented the objective possibility of a new social individuality, a possibility that could be realized only through radical social transformation. It should be stressed that Marx did not consider the creation of "national communities" as in the French Revolution to be identical with this social transformation. The continued existence of a state, "an illusory community" separate from civil society, reveals the noncommunal nature of the realm of social reproduction.

Marx's historical theory of social formations, worked out in the *Grundrisse*, became available only after World War II. Nevertheless, theorists like Tönnies, stressing the movement from community

[*Gemeinschaft*] to society [*Gesellschaft*] as the backbone of modern history, and Lukács were able to piece much of it together from the deliberately nonhistorical volumes of *Das Kapital*, where Marx attempted to work out the systematic nature and general tendencies of capitalism. Lukács in this context was able to utilize the work of his older friend Max Weber. The Frankfurt theorists in turn projected their version of Marxian historical sociology through the conceptual spectacles of Weber and Lukács.

Max Weber's question[18] about the specificity of modernity is complementary to that of Marx—though not the Marx whose works Weber knew—even if the respective methodologies were entirely different. Weber's answers in terms of concepts like rationalization, bureaucratication and de-magicization fill in crucial aspects of what Marx only outlined as the "socialization of society" under industrial capitalism. Weber's depiction of the imprisonment of the individual in the iron cage of modernity is the point on which Marx and he were in full agreement, except that Marx also envisioned a post-capitalist liberation of the individual that would not abolish the material gains of capitalism. Weber's key concepts provide the cultural and political context of the "iron cage" that Marx largely neglected, and at the same time they challenge the plausibility of Marx's post-capitalist vision. It was to be the unsolved task of Lukács and all of critical Marxism to use Weber against Marxist orthodoxy and yet to move beyond Weber in the spirit of Marx.

Let us examine Weber's key categories of rationalization and de-magicization [*Entzauberung*, usually translated as "disenchantment"].[19] Rationalization, for Weber the key to all modernization and industrialization, represents the historical (originally under capitalism) penetration of all spheres of social life: the economy, culture (art, religion and science), technology, law and politics, and everyday life by a single logic of *formal rationality*. This "logic" is defined by the principle of orientation of human action to abstract, quantifiable and calculable, and instrumentally utilizable formal rules and norms. The key to formal rationality is the phrase "without regard for persons" which was first expressed in its purity in the battle of early modern science against anthropomorphic nature philosophy. In a more general form, the de-anthropomorphizing tendency of rationalization is expressed by Weber's concept of *Entzauberung* or de-magicization, the elimination of all that is unpredictable, "irrational," qualitative, sensuous and mysterious from both theoretical explanation and the practical conduct of life. Weber always refused to present rationalization as the self-unfolding logic of history.[20] Furthermore, he made neither the historically prior rise of science (as did 19th century positivism) nor the historically late emergence of industrial capitalism (as did the Marxists) the cause or the essence or the *telos* of rationalization. Formal rationality and/or de-magicization are first of all present in the most diverse historical settings and contexts. Roman law could rise to a higher degree of formal systematization than the English common law of the period of the Industrial Revolution. Biblical Jewish theology based on monotheism and the prohibition of images was more "disenchanted" than all forms of Christianity until at least Calvinism. Partly rational bureaucracies existed in China thousands of years before modernization in the West. Nor were the particular logics of these "rational" spheres identical except on the highest level of abstraction. The question is: Why were the somewhat heterogeneous and relatively underdeveloped spheres of formal reason combined together *only* in Western Europe? The "elective affinity" of the spheres of commercial capitalism, early nation-state, early modern science, Roman law etc., i.e., the abstract presence in all of some mode of the same formal rationality, was a necessary, but not yet sufficient condition. The formal rationality and especially the calculability of one sphere is of course directly enhanced when combined with that of another, or the others. But to Weber even this explanation smacked of unacceptable teleology. His own explanation, one that he never considered more than the best alternative hypothesis, was that a process of rationalization was blocked everywhere by the survival of traditional, quasi-magical, irrational elements within the economic ethics of world religions, everywhere except in the context of the inner-worldly ascetic ethics of Protestantism. Without the irrationally motivated[21] yet staunchly rationalistic ethics of Calvinism, and Puritanism in particular, the hallmark of Western modernity, the rational organization of free labor, based on saving and work discipline, could never have been attained.

Weber's thesis on the Protestant ethic and the spirit of capitalism rejoins the context depicted by Marx as the socialization of society, by Tönnies as the movement from community to society and by Simmel ahistorically as the general "tragedy of culture." The stress on the role of religion is no residue of an "idealist" interpretation of history, but instead locates that region of everyday consciousness which must be changed as a presupposition of wider historical transformation. In the movement from community (based on quasi-natural, irrational and traditional norms) to society (based on the emergence of individuality in a formally rational context) Weber was able to focus on those communal modes of conduct, meanings, justification and norms of Protestantism that destroyed precisely the communal foundations of life, and facilitated both the emergence of individuality and its integration in formally rational systems.[22]

Finally, one more concept of Weber's needs to be stressed, the concept of bureaucracy. For Weber the rationalization of the state, the legitimation of domination in terms of the rational rule of law always takes the hierarchical organizational form of bureaucracy.[23] But in the fully rationalized modern world, bureaucracy does not remain within those original limits. With the possible exception of the capitalist market, bureaucracy reveals itself as the most efficient mode of organization of all spheres of life from the state to the military, from religion to education, thus finally penetrating the cultural sphere itself.[24] The concept of bureaucracy also supplied Weber's key argument against Marx. Once bureaucratized, the system of modern production could be democratized only at the cost of industrial efficiency. Once bureaucratized, the modern state and its military arm can be destroyed and replaced only by enemies equally well organized. The Marxist *goals* of freedom and material wealth are therefore incompatible with one another and with the proposed *means* of the political conquest of power. Here lay the challenge to those critical Marxists who sought the synthesis of Marx and Weber.

We can focus only on the consequences of a Marx-Weber synthesis for the theory of culture. The concepts of loss of community and decline of the individual subject were expertly brought together by Georg Lukács at several points of his early career. Best known to the Frankfurt theorists were the pre-Marxist *Theory of the Novel* (1914-1916) and the key text of early critical Marxism, *History and Class Consciousness* (1920-1922). However as early as 1909-1910,[25] Lukács brought together Marx's concept of socialized, civil society and Weber's "rationalization" to indicate the simultaneous emergence and crisis of individuality. Here Lukács stressed not only the fateful integration of the individual in an objective, impersonal system, but also extended the category of de-magicization to those symbols and sensuous life-contents that had hitherto provided the materials for artistic formation. Thus he was able to discover the crisis of culture not only on the subjective side (as did Simmel) under the heading of the crisis of the individual, but also on the objective side, on the side of works and even whole genres that are becoming problematic. Lukács's history of drama thus presented the crisis of the drama form, his theory of the novel that of the ancient epic and its modern descendant, the novel. The destruction of community and the new linking of individuals through things or "thingified" (i.e., reified, *verdinglicht*) social relations leads to the crisis of all esthetics based on communication. The 1919 Marxist essay "Old and New Culture" draws the terse conclusion that Marx himself at times suspected: culture has collapsed during the capitalist epoch. But Lukács, before he came to Marx, tried to be a bit more careful. He detected in this context, for example, a decline from the beginnings of bourgeois society based on the "virtual communities," especially of early small town Protestantism, to the modern urban setting of bourgeois civilization characterized by loneliness and anomie.[26] And in *Theory of the Novel* he was able to present the modern novel as a symptomatic (and internally crisis-ridden) yet still esthetic form of the period of the crisis of the individual.

In *Theory of the Novel*, the dominating motif is the contrast between the idealized, harmonious, closed and limited organic communities of ancient Greece and the reduction of the social world of civil or bourgeois society (the site of the rise and crisis of individuality), to a *mechanical* system Lukács called "second nature." The first is expressed by the ancient epic, the second by the modern novel whose hero is the problematic individual—lonely, isolated, homeless, creative in principle but without the substantial ties that real creativity presupposes. For Lukács, a completed esthetic form implied a utopian reconciliation between creator (subject) and created (work), or harmony between intention and technique. In the case of the novel, however, a complete, harmonious, self-evident form was never attained, and the utopias internal to novels always turn out to be mere extensions of present tendencies. As a result, the possibility of moving beyond the present cannot be conceptualized within art: Lukács, foreshadowing Benjamin and Adorno, staunchly condemned all attempts to re-estheticize the bad present that led to the crisis of art and culture in the first place. The theory of reification in *History and Class Consciousness* both deepened the analysis of cultural crisis and projected a political solution to the problem the sources of which did not lie in the restricted sphere of culture.

"Reification" [*Verdinglichung*] represents an uneasy conceptual synthesis of Weber's "rationalization" and Marx's commodity fetishism.[27] Lukács took great pains to demonstrate that Marx's concept of fetish, that is, the appearance of relations of human interdependence through the market ["commodity fetish"] and those of human domination in capitalist production ["capital fetish"] as a relationship of "things" (money to money, commodity to commodity, labor power to wage), was at the very center of Marx's whole critical project.

Furthermore, he sought to show that in a developed capitalist system the fetishism of commodities penetrates all spheres of social life, the factory becoming the model of all social relations, the fate of the worker the typical human fate. In other words, he attempted to extend and expand the category of commodity fetishism beyond the merely economic—hence the new term "reification"—by translating it in terms of that rationalization which Weber discovered in all the spheres of modern capitalism. On the other hand, he tried to make Weber's category of rationalization more dynamic by identifying commodity fetishism, under a developed capitalist system, as its paradigmatic form and even more important as its hidden dynamic. He then sought to show that commodity fetishism moves toward its own self de-fetishization and self-abolition. All these intentions which attempt to give a Marxist answer to Weber's social theory are incorporated in the concept of reification.

It is important to stress that to Lukács reification was not a subjective illusion. Human relationships under capitalism are in fact "thinglike [*sachliche*] relations of persons and social relations of things [*Sache*]."[28] Lukács systematically uncovers both the objective and the subjective sides of this reduction.[29] The world of commodity exchange objectively constitutes a "second nature" of pseudothings, which from the subjective point of view appears as the estrangement of human activity and the de-activization of individuals. On the objective side, human labor is abstracted in exchange when it is reduced to labor power with a price and in production where it is made increasingly interchangeable with other abstract labors. On the subjective side, the abstraction of laboring activity appears to the worker as "de-magicization," as the "progressive elimination of the qualitative human and individual attributes of the worker."[30] Taylorism, the final step in the mechanization of the worker, separating and controlling "his psychological attributes," is the final step in de-magicization. Atomization and fragmentation characterize not only the objective subdivision of the product and the work process but also the reduction of the worker to a single, partial operation. "The laborer is mutilated into a fragment of a man."[31] He is reduced to mere spectatorship, to mere *contemplation* of his own estranged activity and that of his fellows. Atomization among workers is the consequence, as one would also expect from the broad movement described by Tönnies as that from community to society.

Lukács insists he is not merely describing the reification of the worker in capitalist production, but that the fate of the atomized, fragmented, reduced worker becomes the typical human fate in capitalist society. Having identified narrow specialization as one of the shapes of reification, he had no difficulty in extending the concept to bureaucracy and to the contemporary organization of knowledge. Having identified the passive, contemplative attitude of the specialized worker toward his own activity and toward the product (of which he produces only a small part) with the *reification of consciousness*, he was also able (though not without some distortion) to bring the narrowly specialized and anti-philosophical social and natural sciences under this heading. And even where he could identify some conscious recognition of the destructive consequences of reification, as in classical German philosophy and in art, he was able to show that the inability to imagine the conquest of commodity fetishism and reification in social practice leads to regression even in the case of the most promising attempts at "de-fetishization." It was however Lukács's belief that the social theory which is able systematically and essentially to link the phenomena of reification to the total society would be a small step toward de-fetishization if it corresponded to (or met halfway) another step, a step toward class consciousness on the part of those to whom the theory was addressed: the industrial proletariat. Lukács even attempted to work out a conception that would make the self-consciousness of workers about the reduction of the qualitative aspects in their life at least objectively possible.[32]

Lukács's answer to Weber ultimately depended on his ability to demonstrate commodity fetishism as the secret dynamic behind the rationalization of all the social spheres, and even more on his conception of the working class as ultimately the "identical subject-object" of capitalist society. The theory of reification clearly shows how workers are objects of the system. It even demonstrates that "immediately" the consciousness of workers is perhaps the most victimized by reification. Lukács's claim for their potential subjectivity depends less on the labor theory of value (which he does use) than on his belief (never really grounded) that the objectively possible self-consciousness of workers is already a practical action, an action that moreover would prepare the ground for the successful reception of revolutionary theory by its proper addressees.[33] The working class is thus only potentially the subject of the capitalist period, and is *actual-*

ly the subject only of revolutionary transformation. It is a paradox of Frankfurt theory that of its theorists, T.W. Adorno did more than anyone to interrogate contemporary culture with the concept of reification even after the main line of the School had more or less abandoned the proletariat as the subject of history.[34] On the other hand, Walter Benjamin, in his debate with Adorno, based himself on the subjectivity of the proletariat,[35] disregarding the heavy consequences of the theory of reification which at the very least showed the difficulties facing class consciousness.

The Concept of Critique

The concept of reification enabled Lukács to surpass the schematic reading of Marxism either as merely a better version of political economy and or as a theory of history based on the primacy of the economic in all social formations. In terms of his concept of the reification of consciousness, classical political economy qualifies as a more or less accurate rendition of the surface phenomena of the "second nature" of civil society. The ideological distortion of political economy becomes especially evident when its main proponents project specific characteristics of capitalism onto all social life, past and future. Marxism is first of all a *critique* of political economy because it destroys this unhistorical illusion by uncovering (as did the *Grundrisse* especially) the specificity of precapitalist social formations and by pointing out the objective possibility (for Marx generally, necessity) of a future order based on entirely new and liberated formative principles. But the best-known economic deterministic version of historical materialism does not escape the fate of political economy in the medium of critique.[36] Even if it does not project all the characteristics of capitalism into the past and the future, historical materialism does illegitimately so project the primacy of a relatively independent economic base. However, the self-critique of historical materialism, i.e., the application of the method of ideology critique to orthodox historical materialism cannot be completed, according to Lukács, until the establishment of socialist society. For the time being, the crude version of the theory remains an important weapon in the class struggle.[37] Thus, the bulk of Lukács's reification thesis is anchored in a critique of political economy, and not yet a more general concept of ideology critique that the self-critique of historical materialism (itself partly under the aegis of the reification of the economy) would have necessarily inaugurated. But as we have seen, the integration of Max Weber's work already meant that the descriptive aspects (not the dynamic) of the critique of political economy are unfolded rather as a general critique of sociology. It was through the use of the strongly Hegelian concept of "mediation" that Lukács was able to distinguish the *critique* of political economy (and sociology) from the *sciences* of political economy (and sociology).

Hegel's concept of *mediation* reformulated is a key to both Lukács's and Adorno's reconstruction of Marxism as the *critique of political economy*. For Lukács[38] a theory mediates the frozen, immediately given, "reified" surface of reality (presented by political economy and sociology) to the extent that it first recognizes [*Anerkennung*] and reduplicates, and second raises to self-consciousness [*Aufhebung*] the immanent tendencies of its object moving toward self-realization. Mediation is de-fetishization. The appearances of reality are first recognized as such, then detached from their immediate context and are finally related to the social whole, the vision of which is fragmented by reification. But this "relating" *mediates* only because the addressees of the theory—the proletariat—de-fetishize themselves in the practical recognition of themselves as commodities, as object of the capitalist system. The addressees (i.e., practical mediation when already in motion) discover the full form of their self-consciousness [*Klassenbewusstsein*] in the theory. The theory (i.e., theoretical mediation) discovers its reality (and that of its categories) in its being so recognized by its addressees. This is elegant Hegelian theorizing, but it sounds rather hollow fifty years later. Adorno's adoption of the concept of reification and mediation carries the burden of the most crucial part of these fifty years.

In spite of the tendency of *Dialectic of Enlightenment* and *Negative Dialectics* to inflate reification as the fate of civilization itself, and eventually to deny the key role of the category in an analysis with emancipators intent, Adorno's cultural critique surely accepted and worked with Lukács's exposition of the immediate forms of reification under advancing capitalism.[39] The main conceptual refinement Adorno added in this context was the already mentioned shift in emphasis to the "technological veil" spread by the logic of administration as the fullest subsumption of reality under the form of fetishism. For Adorno too the immediate, "objective" facts of fully developed civil or bourgeois society constitute a second nature. The thinglike facts of this administered second nature, facts that administrative research copies, hide not only social relations but specifically human relations of domination and control. All unreflective empirical research, by fetishizing the "false consciousness" that adheres to the frozen *immediacy* of given factuality, serves the technocratic interest of control.[40] The alternative of a critical theory of culture is therefore indicated by the category of de-fetishization, or even more generally by mediation.

The category of mediation which both Lukács and Adorno discuss extensively is the *locus classicus* of the difference between the revolutionary optimism of the former and the profound, critical pessimism of the latter. Adorno's definition of ideology and critique can best be understood in terms of this difference, one that we would like to explore. Here we will restrict ourselves, for the sake of the clearest contrast, to Lukács's 1923 position, ultimately grounded in the myth of the proletariat, and Adorno's late antinomic view, based on the dissolution of all mythology. (1) Adorno, like Lukács, always accepted the notion that mediation must be grounded in the essential nature of the object itself.[41] But where Lukács (like the early Adorno) understood this object in the sense of a unified, dynamic, social totality that comes to practical self-consciousness in revolutionary theory, in the late Adorno the unity and identity of the object itself is in doubt. On the one hand, Adorno reproduces a rather static version of the historical materialist premise that the relationship of economic base and superstructure is present in all "ideology"; on the other hand, he insists that we can have knowledge of total society only in the form of micrology—i.e., through the intensive, critical examination of single, totalized works in art and philosophy. Mediation, then, in the form of "transcendent critique," is the totalization that locates works in a social totality, economically structured but without a future-oriented dynamic. This totality, the *Gesamttotalität*, is therefore false: "the whole is untrue." Of course, the false whole does exist as the social totality totalized by the means of total, administrative-bureaucratic or even totalitarian practice.[42] Mediation, in the form of micrology, in the form of an "immanent critique" that has not forgotten its interest in a future-oriented transformation of the false whole of society, is therefore the only possible avenue for a conceptual unfolding that involves a dynamic relation of subject-object in Lukács' sense. (2) Of course, Adorno's bleak picture of the *Gesamttotalität* presupposes one crucial anti-Lukácsian premise: the nonexistence of a social *Gesamtsubjekt* of action.[43] The human beings of the administered world are fragmented subjects of damaged intersubjective knowledge that cannot constitute genuine intersubjectivity of action (collective subject) from the traces of meaning in the rubble of *objective spirit*. While in the 1930s the proletariat was for him still the potential revolutionary subject, the late Adorno only had profound fear for the emergence of a collective subject composed of the human fragments of today. The Lukácsian project of a mediation or de-fetishization in which revolutionary theory is met half-way by the self-mediation *or* self-de-fetishization of reality in the emergence of class consciousness, collapses in Adorno's work. (3) Therefore, Adorno could not admit an objectively possible identity of theoretical mediation and the practical self-mediation of the addressees of theory, and hoped only for a parallel and incomplete mediation of micrological theory and those of its objects that themselves incorporate the project of critique, i.e., autonomous works of art. Where Lukács in the manner of Hegel mediates reification toward subject-object identity, Adorno's mediation ("through the extremes") does not lead beyond antinomy, beyond unresolved contradiction. The micrological analysis of antinomic objects in a common field ("the extremes of modern music," for example) may unfold the idea behind each object until "the inherent consequence of the object is transformed into their self-criticism," but no overcoming of the initial antinomy is thereby achieved.[44] We must stress here that Adorno from the early 1930s on insisted on the cognitive function of great works of art.[45] Beethoven's achievement, for example, is often compared to Hegel's[46]: the method of each is characterized as the unfolding of a "dynamic totality." But in a period in which Hegel's theoretical object is portrayed as "untrue,"[47] Adorno was forced to re-evaluate the limits of possible cognition in both art and theory. To hold on to their essential cognitive function, both must appear as negative, as critique. In both art and theory, "the successful work . . . is not one which resolves objective contradiction in a spurious harmony, but one which expresses the idea of harmony negatively by embodying the contradictions, pure and uncompromised, in its innermost structure."[48] No lines offer a better characterization of Adorno's own self-understanding. When he moves from critique to self-critique, in the great essay "Cultural Criticism and Society,"[49] he too is able to express the harmony and unity of critical theory only negatively, by the dialectical-antinomic juxtaposition of the thoroughly criticized poles of immanent and transcendent modes of ideology critique.

The concept of ideology has a long and contradictory history.[50] Within the Marxian tradition[51] the best-known version is that in the *German Ideology*, which reduces ideology to the ideas of the ruling class—composed of falsehood or inverted truths—to be measured against the truth of science. Neither this definition nor Engels' revision in terms of reciprocal influences between superstructure and base was useful to the Frankfurt theorists.[52] What they took from Marx instead was the increasingly uneasy combination of *ideology as normatively true and empirically false consciousness (Marx in 1843 especially) and of ideology as objectively and socially necessary illusion, "fetishism" (the Marx of the mature* Critique of Political Economy). Herbert Marcuse, for example, uses both of these concepts in his 1937 essay "Affirmative Culture": the first to the extent that he juxtaposes and confronts the true, utopian and the false, legitimating, "affirmative" moments of art, and the second to the extent that he hopes to resolve the contradiction of art by the total social, revolutionary abolition of socially necessary illusion, opening the way to a new culture based on the unity of art and life. The second move especially firmly locates the critical theory of the 1930s within the realm of Lukácsian Marxism. For Lukács, too, the dialectic of true and false consciousness implied the same two notions of ideology. (1) The images of subject-object identity (reconciliation) in German classical philosophy, from Kant and Fichte to Hegel and Schiller, were truths that turned into falsehood when the philosophers, on the basis of conceptual mythologies, mistook theory for reality. (2) The empirically correct and rational presentation of social appearances (phenomena) in political economy represented "truth" in a limited, empirical sense, truth that turns out to be false when *mediation* discovers the distortion of the past, present and future dynamic-historical context of these "truths." The two notions of ideology are linked together by Lukács in that process of mediation that reveals the *objectively possible* aspiration of empirical reality to the heights of thought. For Adorno, as we have seen, it is just this process of mediation toward identity that falls apart. According to him, under late capitalism ideologies in a genuine sense collapse and give way to the antinomic alternatives of critical thought, illusionless but impotent, and mere reduplication in consciousness of the world of administered controls.[53]

Adorno locates his own difficulty in defining ideology precisely in the administered world. He gives us at least three definitions, and each fares differently in the present historical context. (1) Ideology is "objectively necessary and at the same time false" consciousness, true because it is a rational, scientific or social scientific expression of the established state of affairs, false because it is not the whole truth of that state of affairs (supressing its history, its interest structure, etc.)[54] (2) Ideologies "in the genuine sense" are ideals and norms true in themselves but false in their pretension to be already realized,[55] (e.g., the idea of justice as *more than* just equivalent exchange). (3) Ideologies that are *not* such, "in the genuine" sense, are mere reduplication of the existing reality. They appear when "purely immediate relations of power predominate." Adorno means here not so much reduplication in the sense of conceptual copy (that could still have a moment of rational representation) but irrational ideas (e.g., fascism) that are mere instruments of power in a world in which everything is instrumentalized.[56] Such a world has no "ideology," but is itself ideological, in the sense that *ideas* are merely part of the seamless web of administered reality that forces compliance (also of concepts and artistic representations) ultimately through power. But even in this context, Adorno seeks to discover through critique the hidden interest structure behind irrational "ideologies" and the "anthropological" changes in human beings that leads to the instrumental efficiency of irrational ideas. Here lies the importance for Adorno of the *critique* of fascist "ideology" and of the culture industry.

It seems to us that Adorno under the historical impact of fascism, Stalinism and the culture industry, drastically downplayed the first meaning of ideology in relation to the second and third, (absorbing it ultimately in the third).[57] He was ready often enough to utilize the results of social science, but as we will see, the relationship of empirical social science to critical philosophy was always antinomic in his work. The ultimate reason: Adorno lost hope of discovering behind present social facts dynamic objective possibilities in the manner of Marx and Lukács before him, or even Habermas after him. He responded, therefore, to the antinomy of critical thought and instrumental reason, emerging from the debris of genuine ideologies, with his own antinomic combination of immanent critique *addressing* (and mediating) the critical potentialities of genuine works and transcendent critique *denouncing* the one-dimensional world of the culture industry.

Adorno was never smugly complacent about the antinomic structure of his own critique. Turning the reflective power of critique against itself, he demonstrated in many of his writings[58] the inadequacy of either immanent or transcendent critique, and the necessity of maintaining both in uneasy opposition. To be sure, the weight of each mode of critique in their antinomic combination is for Adorno not an absolute matter. In a period (classical liberalism) when genuine ideologies play a major role in social integration, the demonstration of their interest structure (as in classical Marxist ideology critique) from the "transcendent" or "outside" point of view of total society may be the most crucial task. But in an epoch that threatens all realms of consciousness with subsumption and one-dimensional reduction, immanent criticism, immersion in the internal form and structure of cultural objects plays a redeeming, protective function. In the earlier epoch, Marxist theory had to confront liberal ideology with its moment of falsehood. In the present, critical theory must insist on the moment of truth of ideologies against technocratic reason, and even the sociology of knowledge. Adorno's own sympathies are clearly with immanent critique.[59] Both immanent and transcendent critique, however, suffer from deep internal problems. Immanent critique all too readily celebrates the autonomy of mind, postulating—as Adorno seems to do at times[60]—an almost completely independent logic of cultural forms. Measuring culture against its own normative ideal, immanent critique all too readily forgets about the ambiguous role of ideas in social conflicts and distracts from the true horrors of the social world.[61] And even if it manages to discover dynamic contradictions between idea and pretense in works—or culture as a whole—immanent critique is powerless to resolve the contradictions, to liberate mind from their explosive results, or even to discover social truth through the work.[62] But transcendent critique (which includes most socialist writers on cultural issues), by suppressing all independent logic of cultural forms, is complicitous with present and future administrations seeking to level and integrate culture. Transcendent critique is interested in the uniform whole and spares itself the conceptual effort of examining the particular "in its difference."[63] Nevertheless, only transcendent critique reproduces the image of the reified totality that all genuine critique must take into account, and only it has that total intransigence against all reification required by any future radical politics.[64] And yet, the conceptual reproduction of the reified world on its own reproduces nothing worth saving; transcendent critique cannot ultimately suppress its affinity to barbarism.

To Adorno, dialectical critique of culture or ideology is the extremely uneasy, antinomic synthesis of immanent and transcendent critique. We can take seriously his claim that dialectical critique "heightens cultural criticism until the notion of culture is itself negated, fulfilled and surmounted"[65] only if we drop the last word. Dialectical critique can, on the basis of Adorno's self-presentation, hardly be more than the successful work "which expresses the idea of harmony negatively by embodying the contradiction." Adorno's dialectic as against Hegel's "is obliged to be mindful of the duality of the moments." "The dialectical critic of culture" has no alternative but to "participate in culture and not participate."[66]

The consequences of Adorno's redefinition of cultural criticism were momentous for the development of the very form of his critical theory. The demand to liberate the critical power of the works of culture by the stringent combination of both transcendent and immanent critique is satisfied only by the analysis of those works that avoid the fetishization of culture, by taking reflection into their very structure. The culture that is possible only as culture critique exists according to Adorno only in the "post-esthetic" works of the avantgarde. On the other hand, an ideology critique that has criticized its own "transcendent" and often scientistic pretense of locating function of culture in a completely understood whole is forced to accept the self-critique of culture (especially art) on an equal footing with critical theory itself.[67] The precondition, however, is that modern art "incorporate the cracks and crevices of a world torn mercilessly apart into its representations."[68] Here lies the special importance of presenting cultural theory in terms of the critical essay form which is best suited to micrology.[69] Its critical function affirms and preserves the cognitive dimension of works of art. The parallel critique of autonomous works, however, destroys the totalizing and systematic illusion of critical theory itself, still present in Lukács's and even the early Horkheimer's and Marcuse's versions of the critical Marxist enterprise. If behind the curtain of mediation Hegelian theory discovered itself, and Lukács's version of Marxism discovered the proletariat whose proper class consciousness the theory supposedly was, then it is Adorno's view that any version of transcendent and totalizing ideology critique in the old sense will discover only the totality of the administered world. In Adorno's late pessimistic theory, only the brittle and precarious essay form of primarily immanent critique can discover the self-critique of reality which is today restricted for Adorno to critical art and philosophy. His last major works, *Negative Dialectics* and the posthumously published *Esthetic Theory*, are best understood as themselves collections of essays and, at times, even aphorisms in the manner of *Minima Moralia*.

Even though Adorno as early as 1932 began to stress the analogous tasks of art and social theory, and especially the cognitive character of an art that expresses social antinomies in its own rigorous formal language,[70] the reduction of critique of ideology to the essay form does not characterize the early self-comprehension of critical theory. Many positions of the 1930s of Marcuse and Horkheimer especially fall under what Adorno called transcendent critique.[71] The attack of course was primarily directed at orthodox historical material- ism and Mannheim's general notion of ideology. But the critical theory of Horkheimer in the 1930s, with its "hidden orthodoxy," falls under the charge to the extent that in its general vision it assigned superstructure (hence cultural phenomena) in the "last instance" the relatively insignificant role of retardation and acceleration of social change.[72] In other (though not all) respects, the self-definition of "critical theory" in the 1930s reveals the name as a code term for Marxism (or Lukácsian Marxism) and not its drastic reinterpretation as primarily negative, immanent dialectical critique. Horkheimer's list of the *differentia specifica* of critical versus traditional theory consists of the recognition of the theory's own interest structure, self- correction in terms of the up-to-date results of social science, *the point of view of totality* and a dynamic relationship to its potential addres- sees, the proletariat.[73] To be sure, Marcuse[74] and Horkheimer both argued that critical theory receives present confirmation of its interest in a future liberated society in the fantasy (read: advanced art) of the present that anticipates an entirely new utopian sensibility and the philosophy of the past. But even on this point there was some ambigui- ty. Both theorists accepted the thesis of the *German Ideology* about the abolition *(Aufhebung)* of philosophy in dialectical social theory. And Marcuse at least in his critique of "affirmative culture" used the ideology-critical confrontation of the utopian elements of high culture (with its politically conservative functions) to call for the *"Aufhebung der Kultur,"* the abolition of culture as such and the end of art in the reintegration of mental and manual labor.[75] We should recall that the second and more secret characteristic of "transcendent critique," according to Adorno, is its hidden affinity for barbarism.[76] In his last major opus, Adorno specifically locates Marcuse's critique of affir- mative culture in this dangerous neighborhood.[77]

In the context of the definition of critique, the clash between Walter Benjamin and the older critical theory is decisive. Benjamin's specific attitude toward history, even when he professed a higher degree of Marxist political commitment than the members of the "Frankfurt School," represented a more decisive break with the evolutionist theory of progress that any Marxism of his time. To Benjamin, the history of development was always that of domination. Only moments that rupture the continuity of history have anything to do with future liberation, and toward these moments, "now-times"

[*Jetztzeiten*] in which the dialectic stands still [*Dialektik im Still-stand*], he had a "conservative" attitude that has been best described as one of "*rettende Kritik*," a critique that saves or redeems.[78] For Benjamin, this attitude, which coincided with both his theological interest and his self-understanding as a collector,[79] was first combined with political resignation and melancholy, and subsequently with his defense of Brecht's political theater.[80] In neither context did he attack a culture already in dissolution in his estimation.[81] Nor did he ever propose that he had a transcendent, evolutionary scheme or even a systematic reconstruction of the totality of the present which could unambiguously guarantee a dialectical abolition-preservation of art in a society of full reconciliation. "He saw his task not in reconstructing the totality of bourgeois society but rather in examining its blinded, nature-bound and diffuse elements under a microscope."[82] Benjamin always understood the task of critique or criticism in the sense of the search for the truth of works (against mere commentary) but at the same time in terms of a strongly anti-systematic, we might[83] say essayistic impulse.[84] Many years before Adorno, Benjamin moved to recognize the critical spirit inherent in at least those works of modernity (the baroque, romanticism, Baudelaire and surrealism) which eschewed the task of symbolic reconciliation in the medium of "beautiful appearance." Benjamin hardly elevated theoretical critique higher than the immanent critique latent in works themselves. The task of his own critique was simply surgically to remove (or "to blast open"), collect and save the critical fragments of the past that could help transform "cultural heritage" from a burden to a possession, to moments of "secular illumination" which he defined in terms of the earthly promise of happiness. Thus the multitude of quotations in his *Origins of the German Trauerspiels* and the intention to compose his study of the Parisian arcades *(Passagenarbeit)* entirely of quotations. While such concepts of Lukácsian Marxism as "second nature" fetishism and praxis had already had a strong effect on him in the 1920s, Benjamin always did without the concept of *mediation*.[85] To Benjamin, even dialectic could only reveal and express antinomy and not surpass it. This is what he meant by the expression *"Dialektik im Stillstand."* On the one hand, a dialectic at standstill brings to the sharpest focus the reified, frozen "second natural" elements of bourgeois culture,[86] while on the other hand, those elements are antinomically and statically related to dreams or wishes or memories of the present ("dialectical images") concerning free collectives.[87]

The difference between the Lukácsian Marxism of early critical theory and Walter Benjamin's notion of critique was clearly noticed by Adorno in his criticism of Benjamin in the 1930s. Nevertheless, Adorno's own position eventually emerged as the uneasy synthesis of the opposing poles: critical theory and *rettende Kritik*. His critique and appropriation of Benjamin needs to be presented primarily in terms of their clashing evaluation of the relationship of art and modern technology, and of art and politics.

Modern Art and Culture Industry

Having presented some of the conceptual parameters presupposed by the Frankfurt theory of culture, we should now indicate in detail how these parameters were used. Horkheimer's "End of Reason" could equally serve as the lead article of this section. The essay, a critique of late capitalist culture and politics, gives convincing proof of its au-thor's adherence to what we outlined as the theory of social formations which emerges from the work of Marx, Weber, and Lukács, and of his ability to adopt this model to current needs and experiences. Marx, Weber and even the Lukács of *History and Class Consciousness* saw only a unified epoch of civil society as against its historical back-ground and future perspectives, while Horkheimer confronted an internal process of development from liberal to authoritarian versions of civil society. Thus in 1941 he was able to locate historically "the emergence of the individual" (as against a traditional Greek and medieval background in which a harmony existed between individual and the symbols of collectivity) in the liberal period, and the increas-ing crisis and decline of the subject in the period of the authoritarian state.[88] Furthermore, under the impact of new theories as well as experiences, he was able to specify new aspects of this decline: among them the destruction of the family, the weakening of the ego (in the psychoanalytic sense) and the emergence of false, manipulated collec-tives under the impact of mass culture and especially fascism. Hork-heimer, Marcuse and Lowenthal (in the Hamsun article below) under-stood fully that in the context of the destruction of community, of urban loneliness, industrial degradation of nature and economic crisis, the weakened egos of the present are especially exposed to the charm of demagogic movements proclaiming the fake restoration of national community, the false return to nature and the very real end of econom-ic crisis through the militarization of the economy.[89]

As in political sociology, the cultural theory of the School unanimously declared that all attempts to return to a supposed golden age were bankrupt and mortally dangerous. No one was more emphatic on this point than Walter Benjamin.

Benjamin's 1925 pre-Marxist volume *The Origin of the German Trauerspiels*[90] ["sad play" as against tragedy] was next to Lukács's *Theory of the Novel* the most important background text of Frankfurt *Kulturkritik*. Its concept of allegory has been construed by the old Lukács, by Adorno and Habermas among others, as the key to the interpretation of modern art. For the moment, we are interested in Benjamin's depiction of the historical context of the emergence of allegory as an anti-esthetic principle within art itself. This context is the "second nature" of civil society, elaborated by the art of the baroque, according to Benjamin, in terms of a "natural history" of decay, decline and disintegration. The allegories of the baroque (but also by implication those of romanticism and of the twentieth century) represent the dominant modes of expression of periods in which things lose their immediate relationship to intersubjective, evident meanings.[91] The allegories of many cultures are tightly woven, deliberately simplified schemes that unmistakably point to an external referent, usually transcendence for those members of a community who possess the key (e.g. the Bible, the Koran). The allegories of civil society are however *ruins*, and point only to the "metaphysical homelessness" (cf. Lukács's *Theory of the Novel)* of lonely creatures in despair about transcendence despite their conventional religiosity. The allegorization of art means that art has become problematic to itself, to the extent that the genuine esthetic principle of rounded, closed, *symbolic* totalities of "beautiful semblance" are accessible only to artistic epigones. The unmistakable problematic of Benjamin's study is that of the disintegration of community,[92] and the fate of the human creature in the context of a "second nature" over which he is powerless.

The theme of the decline of community accompanies Benjamin's lifework, to be later complemented by the hope for the construction of a new type of free collective. His now famous theory of the disintegration of esthetic aura[93] was connected by Benjamin himself to the destruction of the traditional, cultic fabric of natural communities and to the decline of the communal context of communicable experience. In some contexts he welcomes this decline as the condition of possibility of "a pure situation," opening up the road toward a new, collective, democratic art form. In other, less optimistic contexts that recall the *Trauerspiels* book he may be saddened about what is lost, but he is always careful not to make even the least concession to a political mobilization of lost traditions *against* modernity. In this, though certainly not in all respects, Benjamin was of one mind with Marcuse, Lowenthal, Horkheimer and Adorno.

The theory of the decline of the aura is a specific use of Weber's category of *Entzauberung* in the domain of art, a use that leads to the thematization of the "end of art." Best known in this context is Benjamin's "Work of Art in the Age of its Mechanical Reproducibility" (1936) but equally important for the sake of a many-sided picture of the concept of the aura are "The Storyteller" (1936) and "On Some Motifs in Baudelaire," (1939).[54] Two related yet distinct lines of thought emerge from these studies, and with two different cultural-political consequences. The line of thought characteristic of the "Work of Art" is determined by the struggle against the fascist utilization of tradition and by the struggle in alliance with Bertolt Brecht for a new collective-political art form. This essay defines "aura" in several, related ways. The authenticity of a nonreproducable work, unique existence in a fabric of tradition, the living relationship of a work to a religious cult and the phenomenon of distance that separates us not only from a natural landscape but from all unique, total, harmonious works of art, these are the major definitions. Works with aura produce concentration, empathy, absorption and identification on the part of the reader, or audience—modes of response that lead according to Brecht and Benjamin to political and esthetic passivity. Benjamin depicts the decline of the aura primarily in terms of technological, but also economic and social tendencies. The growth of technological methods of reproduction which Benjamin deduces from the Marxian dialectic of forces and relations of production leads to a "tremendous shattering of tradition." Modern reproduction techniques produce genres without unique, authentic works, and tear even the genres of the past from their traditional fabric which was the implicit foundation of their mystery, their uniqueness. Modern mass society (i.e. bourgeois or civil society) means the destruction of the social bases of religious cults, and the contemporary masses suspicious of cult and mystique tend to bring things closer to themselves "spatially and humanly," thereby abolishing esthetic distance. Photography, the film, radio and newspapers destroy the traditional context of auratic works and inaugurate a crisis of the traditional forms: painting, the theater and the novel in particular. The new technological means not only make the modes of response corresponding to the old, esthetic quality obsolete, but also produce new ones. The audience of a film is distracted, is bombarded by the shock inherent in *montage* and is unable to identify with actors who "play" for an objective apparatus. Benjamin, following Brecht, insists that these characteristics of film produce a distanced estrangement *(Ver-fremdungseffekt)* on the part of the audience that leads to a critical-active attitude toward what is seen. The audience as a result, acting collectively and critically has a chance to reject or to complete an intrinsically unfinished work.[95]

To the Benjamin of the "Work of Art" essay all art, all culture is necessarily functionalized. The concept of function is presented in terms of a secularization thesis rather than a Marxist class analysis. In the distant past cultic-religious functions predominated. The last form of cult value is *l'art pour l'art* which replaces religion by the "theology of art." In the age of commodification "exhibition value" replaces cult value in relationship to traditional works. But in the case of the new means of mechanical reproduction political value or political function predominates.[96] The urgency of this new situation lies in the possible alternative of a fascist politicization of art which uses the remnants or traces of older, quasi-cultic values to beautify reactionary politics. To Benjamin the only answer to the fascist challenge is that politicization of art which unites artistic production to the struggle of the worker's movement for self-consciousness.

The alternative, so sharply posed in a primarily political essay that is intrinsically related to the somewhat earlier "Author as Producer," reproduced below, and also to Brecht's *Dreigroschenprozess* is softened in Benjamin's more scholarly contemporary work. It is essential to look at this more subtle side of his argument that was worked out primarily in the 1936 "The Storyteller" and (after Adorno's criticisms to which we will later turn) the 1938 "Some Motifs in Baudelaire." Here the element of technological determinism implicit in the above argument is relativized to the extent that these essays thematize the substratum of aura that is lost: communicable experience and community. Both essays point to the destruction of genuine experience which rests on communication and to its replacement by information. There can be no communication without a shared structure of meanings in a collective memory, but the movement from *Gemeinschaft* to *Gesellschaft* that capitalism completes destroys the communal bases (ritual, ceremony, festival) of such memory. "Where there is experience in the strict sense of the word, certain contents of the individual past combine with materials of the collective past."[97] To Benjamin in the absence of community the individual is detached from a collective past. Furthermore the structure of perception in mass, industrial society is explicitly modified by the experience of shock; only the shielding of the personality as a relatively unaccessible unconscious protects against a superabundance of nonabsorbable outside stimuli. The consequences of modern technology, urbanism, and information converge with those of the dissolution of communities during the original accumulation of capital in the destruction of experience. Benjamin relocated "the decline of aura" in this context of the crisis of perception and experience. Redefined, aura is the transposition of human relations of reciprocity, "reciprocal gaze," to inanimate things—works of art (or nature). In the mechanical objective products of photography, film, the newspaper etc. we find no traces of human subjects, and unaccustomed to shared experience, modern man will not find his gaze returned in traditional works or nature itself.[98]

The 1936 and 1939 treatments of aura ("Work of Art" vs. "Some Motifs in Baudelaire") are different in three respects. (1) The 1936 essay focuses on and rejects the authoritarian implications of the traditional ("cultic") foundation of aura; whereas the 1939 essay (and even more "The Storyteller") stresses the communal, communicative, nonauthoritarian aspects of this tradition and is nostalgic (at the very least) about its decline. (2) The new means of reproduction, the new media, are evaluated in 1936 as more or less the causes of the decline of the aura, whereas in 1939 they are interpreted only as parts of an overall context that is generated by other social factors (e.g. decline of community). (3) In 1936 auratic works are unambiguously presented as the context for passive reception (the new media are the terrain of the new active and collective reception of works), whereas the "Storyteller" and "Some Motifs in Baudelaire" imply that the traditional communal context of reception was an active one and that a few works of modern art (those of Kafka, Proust, and Baudelaire) in spite of fantastic obstacles managed to combine the very experience of the loss of aura into works implying a fabric of residual communication and the anticipation of qualitatively different society or at least the reduction of the present one to ruins. We would like to focus only on the last point here. From the point of view of Benjamin's book on the baroque, the theses of which are consciously incorporated into his much later studies on Baudelaire, the attack on aura in the "Work of Art" essay is justified only by the fascist attempt to estheticize politics in the medium of symbol and beautiful illusion. From the same earlier point of view the 1936 essay can be faulted however for not recognizing that allegorical works which renounce the ideal of beauty, and present in an uncompromising and "non-affirmative" manner the present as ruin and crisis are not open to fascist mobilization but are possible contexts of critical and active reception. In fact, as Adorno was to show (and Benjamin himself noted), the new media themselves were open to a fake and manufactured aura which a capitalist culture industry might develop for a sales effort equally functional for the advertisement of movie stars, merchandise and fascist regimes.

Since Benjamin anticipated this last objection which relates to the industrial manufacture of fake, artificial aura, it becomes clear why he attributed only a negative, destructive function to the capitalist use of the new mechanical media.[99] Fake aura does not restore weakened traditions. However, not one, but two positive alternatives emerge from this thesis. The first reaches back to Benjamin's own concept of allegory. Different interpreters of Benjamin (and of allegory) stress two major characteristics of modern allegories: their built-in obsolescence and their completion only in interpretation.[100] The work, in itself fragmentary, *implies* the critical completion and reconstruction which saves its truth content even when the work itself becomes obsolete. The concept of allegory—in spite of Benjamin's historical focus—prepares the ground for three types of interpretation of modernism. First, and perhaps best known, is Lukács's claim (curiously analogous to one of the points of Adorno's *early* critique of Benjamin) that the allegories of the avant-garde fetishize the fragmented ruins of civil society and eliminate the possibility of the defetishizing totalization (in Adorno's mediation) which points beyond our world.[101] Second is Habermas's argument (derived from Adorno's *later* essayistic practice) that modernism "incorporates the cracks and crevices of a world torn apart mercilessly into its representations . . . through creating an artificial distance, it lays bare the world constructed as crisis."[102] Finally, there is the argument derived through the prism of Ernst Bloch's appropriation of Benjamin[103]—certainly justified by Benjamin's anti-authoritarian stylistic predilections—that the presentation of a world as ruin or as fragments defines modern art as experimental and in particular open to the active participation and intervention of the receivers. Benjamin's own conscious utilization of his earlier theory of allegory in his Marxist period, which presents a rather strong contrast to his two essays reproduced below, must be considered in light of these heterogeneous interpretations of the meaning of his work.

To Benjamin the collective, intersubjective moments of historical experience do not disappear without traces even in the period of civil society that is characterized by the disintegration of tradition supporting substantial experience. Paradoxically it is the experience of shock, so characteristic of industrial civilization, that involuntarily (as in Proust's "memoire involuntair") stimulates remembrance. What is remembered? Collective rituals, festivals and a different, qualitative relationship to nature.[104] Who remembers? Benjamin postulates a collective memory, repressed but not totally inaccessible, which is recalled by individuals when the "correspondence" between its symbols and events of our everyday life is attained. When is such a "remembrance" possible? Benjamin explores in this context the material texture of everyday urban life, and he lets strange and unusual correspondences emerge as unintended consequences of speech, of work, of strolling (the "flânerie" of the "flâneur"), of literary or theoretical activity. But in two instances at least the correspondences, now called "dialectical images" are consciously pursued. The poet Baudelaire, confronted with the disappearance of those experiential materials that historically supported poetry, raises the principle of this disappearance, the transformation of perception by shock, to a new poetic principle. He thus managed to fashion out of the disappearance of aura a new mode of art.[105] The result is an allegorical art that reveals once again the natural physiognomy of the present as "ruin" and juxtaposes to the ruins of the bourgeoisie elements of dream, memory and fantasy stimulated by shock but recalling or anticipating a different, collective character of experience. It is this juxtaposition that is called the "dialectical image," standing still without resolution *(Dialektik im Stillstand)* but inviting the dreamer to awake.[106] The second procedure that consciously pursues the dialectical images of the present is Benjamin's own. We believe that this was his own principle of form: to collect and reproduce in quotation the contradictions of the present without resolution. This formal principle is the outer limit of a non-authoritarian essayistic attitude to a potential audience, one that was never reached even by Adorno, who sought a more active dialectic.

It is very controversial whether the inner logic of Benjamin's esthetic theory stops with the anti-authoritarian theory of the *dialectic at a standstill*. The fact that the second major alternative within in his esthetic theory implies the discovery of the identical principle in Brecht's epic theater,[107] where the audience is ultimately never completely spared explicit political solutions and resolutions, has aroused the understandable skepticism of his friends Adorno and Scholem, recently echoed by Habermas. And yet the steps to Brecht follow from a crucial difference between Benjamin's and Adorno's esthetics. Benjamin's stress in analyzing a work is displaced (*vis-à-vis* Adorno) in the direction of the conditions of production and reception. The formal characteristics of the work itself were less important to Benjamin. It was of greater importance to him to insist on the liberating possibilities of the works of the past and the future in relationship to *collective* modes of production and reception. He was ready to surrender the aura of the creative personality even where, as in the case of Baudelaire, Kafka, Proust and himself, the works produced were open and critical. In this context he welcomed those technologies that made all individual genius obsolete, and even more the one author, Bertolt Brecht, who attempted to raise this moment of the decline of aura (along with other elements) to the formal principle of a *collective, political* art.

The 1937 essay "The Author as Producer" reproduced below is the best summary of Benjamin's defense of Brecht, but it is also remarkable for its apology for the instrumentalization of art in the Soviet Union. To be sure Benjamin attacks artistic autonomy not in the name of administration but in the name of a collective, open, experimental, technically innovative political art form. Brecht's theater is a "dramatic laboratory" which uses all of its technical sophistication to make the self-education of audiences possible. The play, "an experimental setup," fosters two dialogues: one between the producers of the play with the advanced technical means of communication, and another between actor, author, technical personnel and the "reduced men of today." The two dialogues allow the audience to become coauthor, coactor of the production. Benjamin imagined that the Soviet films of the 1920s and Soviet newspapers were already prototypes of the new active relationship between work and audience. In the 1930s this illusion could only legitimate the increasingly repressive cultural policies of the Soviet state, and Benjamin naively for a moment affirmed the right of this state to its interference with artistic autonomy.[108] This confusion of free collectivity with authority already revealed the uneasy tension of those two elements of Brecht's plays which Benjamin sought to *immediately* unify: revolutionary technique and the politics of the existing revolution. The confusion is present in the terminology. Brecht's and Benjamin's reference to "the masses" as "the matrix" of current esthetic discussion smacks of the same revolutionary instrumentalization that culture is to undergo. The full identification of industrial production (as we now know it) and artistic production points in the same direction, if we keep Marx's description of capitalist production in mind.

Even if his turn to Brecht involved some sacrifice, Benjamin was not fully inconsistent with his esthetic in turning to an author who himself had a great deal of affinity with the allegorical avant-garde. To the extent that Benjamin focused on the open, fragmentary works of the avant-garde as a terrain of critique and action, Brecht was not an unlikely object of great interest. Benjamin's interest in Brecht was facilitated above all by his interest in community, which unfortunately came to be expressed as a turn to the "masses." The problem was that both Brecht and Benjamin in the 1930s presupposed the existence of a mass revolutionary subject (if not a community, at least a political collective) whose self-recognition in the new open works somehow seemed plausible. The empirical difficulties with this self-recognition were eventually (as always) met by a preconstructed and administered political line. The discussion of the problem of community under the heading of "mass" already implies this "solution." We should note that near the end of his life Benjamin was not disposed to follow a line. Under the impact of the Moscow Trials and the Hitler-Stalin Pact, he decisively rejected Communist politics.[109] It would nonetheless be a mistake to assume his earlier acceptance of that politics was not one of the possible alternatives to a mind seeking to work out a satisfactory relationship between Marxism and modern art. It is precisely in this area that Adorno in the 1930s exposed the work of his friend to rather devastating criticism. The paradox of this debate is that Adorno himself, in spite of his greater knowledge of Marxian theory, does not emerge unscathed or unaffected.

It would be a mistake to derive Benjamin's revolutionary romanticism from the Lukács of the 1920s.[110] If Benjamin derived his stress on the subjectivity of the masses (*sic*) from Lukács, he clearly omitted the Lukácsian requirement that the reification of empirical consciousness must be "mediated." Adorno's attack proceeds exactly from this Marxist point of view. (On the other hand, Benjamin's 1940 "Theses on the Philosophy of History" will represent a break not only with Brecht's, but also with Adorno-Horkheimer's early Marxism. The authors of *Dialectic of Enlightenment* are as much Benjamin's followers as those of Lukács).

Let us list Adorno's criticisms as they emerge in his letters of 1935-1938.[111] (Some of it was incorporated in the essay reproduced below, "The Fetish Character in Music.") The criticisms fall into five groups: 1. Adorno was very critical of Benjamin's "nondialectical" reception of Marxism. He opposed Benjamin's often technologically determinist reading of the relationship of culture and economic base, as well as the assumption that culture "copies" or "reflects" the economic base directly. From almost the reverse point of view, however, Adorno felt that the concept of "dialectical image" had no relationship to the existing social totality. Who is the subject of the "dialectical image" he asked. Implicit in Adorno's argument is the position (abandoned in the 1940s) that the dialectical transition beyond bourgeois society is to be found in the point of view of the class struggle and not in isolated individuals who dream, nor in an "archaicizing" collective[112] memory. 2. Adorno was extremely critical of what he took to be the anarchist romanticism of Benjamin and Brecht, i.e., "the blind confidence in the spontaneous power of the proletariat in the historical process." In making this criticism Adorno mobilized in the name of revolutionary intellectuals the authority of Lenin's critique of "spontaneism" and the almost-literal words of the Lukács of *History and Class Consciousness*. He spoke of "the actual consciousness of actual workers, who have absolutely no advantage over the bourgeois except their interest in revolution, but otherwise bear all the marks of the typical bourgeois character."[113] 3. Adorno, inaugurating the critique of the "culture industry," denies even the negatively, destructively progressive function of the film, the radio etc. The artificial aura of films, movie stars, etc., is not a mere addendum but reveals the commodification of the forms themselves, which develops modes of response on the part of audiences and introject the commodity fetish into their psychic structure, reducing them to mere consumers of cultural commodities. Passivity or totally manipulated and controlled response is the aim, as in advertisement, and Adorno believes the aim is usually achieved. Adorno's "Fetish Character in Music," which was meant, as we have said, partly as a reply to Benjamin's thesis on mechanical reproduction, explores both the objective and subjective sides of the *culture industry* and we do not have to repeat its thesis. The essay represents a brilliant extension of Lukács's concept of reification in the direction of the study of culture,[114] and *therefore* the mobilization of almost classical Marxist arguments versus Benjamin. The culture industry indeed represents for Adorno the tendency toward the "Aufhebung" of art—but it is a false and manipulative abolition in mass culture.[115] 4. Adorno accepted, defended and eventually extended Benjamin's use of Weber's concept of de-magicization or disenchantment in the realm of culture. But anticipating his own later argument from *Dialectic of Enlightenment* he was violently afraid of a critique that de-magicizes too much, that all too willingly consents to the false abolition of art by the culture industry. In Adorno's own view autonomous art, *when it reflects on the contemporary crisis of culture and takes the reduced fragments of the present into its form principle*, severs itself of all historical connection to authoritarian magic. To Adorno the autonomous works of the avant-garde meet both of Benjamin's demands: de-magicization (but without reducing critical reason itself) and advanced technique. They thus represent *a third term* between the modern culture industry and the surpassed tradition. We should notice that Adorno refuses to apply *in this context* at least, the concept of de-magicization to individual synthesis. But for a consistent Marxist the defense of the esoteric avant-garde already implied renunciation.[116] It is revealing that in this context Adorno utilized Benjamin's allegory concept against the thesis of the decline of aura. The concept of the allegory saves some autonomous works from the charge of magical residue. The use of the concept allowed Adorno, in the footsteps of Benjamin, to construe some modernist works as critiques of the present. But he renounced Benjamin's stress on collective reception. 5. Adorno attacks finally those technical devices which Benjamin, in Brecht's footsteps, considered critical in mobilizing a mass audience *unless* those devices are integrated in the most rigorous, advanced esthetic totality, as in the case of Kafka and Schönberg. In particular, distracted, segmented, fragmented relationship to works is rejected by Adorno, especially in the "Fetish Character in Music," in the name of concentration and totalization. There is an interesting relationship of Adorno's rejection of jazz to his critique of Benjamin and Brecht: the presence of some advanced elements (shock, montage, collective production, technological reproduction) does not validate the "whole." Adorno's article against Brecht ("On Commitment," below) will extend this argument even in the case of an artist whose greatness he recognized. In the case of Brecht the linking of advanced technique with explicit social contents (the result: socialist realism) and a political line (the result: manipulation) was to Adorno disastrous. The link between jazz and Brecht was the *immediate* appeal to collectives whose *immediate* consciousness in Adorno's eyes was severely deformed by mass culture. Adorno understood the authoritarian implications of the concept of "the masses" so well that he refused to derive any clues from what is collectively or communally accessible, at least *immediately*.

Indeed all the objections of Adorno to Benjamin can be summed up in a phrase used in his third and last critical letter: "your dialectic lacks one thing: mediation."[117] Even though Adorno specifically meant Benjamin's immediate, direct and unreflective linking of "base" and "superstructure" in "correspondences," the argument penetrates deeper than just the Lukácsian claim (later slightly revised) that "materialist determination of cultural traits is only possible if it is mediated through the total social process." It was specifically Adorno's belief that Benjamin and Brecht did not relate the immediate consciousness of their supposedly revolutionary collective to the total society that reproduces reification. The result was the *antinomy* of a determinism leading to the overemphasis on the progressive nature of technology as such (for Adorno an ideological expression meaning capitalist technology), and of a voluntarism which overemphasized the present potentialities of the masses. Adorno, on the contrary not content merely to reproduce phenomena in their static opposition, took his stand for both a speculative theory and a form of art that mediate, that *totalize* the results of the objective process of rationalization, reification and de-magicization in dynamic wholes which deprive the fetishized facts of their self-evidence. He hoped for concentration and totalization also on the part of the reader, the listener, and perhaps in the 1930s the addressees of theory. But as he lost his faith in the call being answered his own theory became *antinomic.*[118]

In their exchange of the 1930s there was a noticeable desire on the part of both Benjamin and Adorno to present their positions as alternatives within a single project. Adorno quite correctly called the Benjamin of the theory of allegory his teacher, and Benjamin accepted the "Fetish Character in Music" as a necessary depiction of the "negative side" of the collapse of the aura. Adorno furthermore even incorporated several aspects of the theoretical framework he criticized into his own. The attack on "magical" aura and artifically restored aura and the affirmation of shock and dissonance are staples of his defense of the "post-auratic" art of Schönberg and Kafka. Nevertheless in the 1930s the ways have parted over the issues of collective or communal reception, the hope of which Benjamin defended, and *totalizing synthesis* and *mediation*, for the sake of which Adorno was eventually to consent even to privatization. Adorno's later sociology of music in particular systematically demonstrates the increasing confinement of *genuine* reception of *genuine* works to experts whom he hated for their specialized ignorance.[119] However Adorno understood.''[120] While the proper goal of autonomous art is the restoration of lost esthetic capacities, art paradoxically is able to resist the reality that destroys its potential audience only by even greater esotericization. This is the antinomy of modern art.

In Kantian language an antinomy is the duality between equally defensible but opposite theoretical arguments. It is the concept of antinomy that after all reunifies the projects of Adorno and Benjamin. In both of their cases the antinomy of culture blocked the way to systematic philosophy. For both of them in the end only the essay form allowed the maintenance of contradictions without spurious harmony and yet in a common field. Whether to save the posture of uncompromising critique even at the cost of privatization, or to save the relationship of art and theory to a mass audience even if critique is partly compromised—this was the bad alternative which neither could satisfactorily resolve. The opposition penetrates into the works of both Adorno and Benjamin, and yet they are ultimately at its two poles. The work of each is the only corrective for that of the other. They are the "torn halves of an integral freedom, to which however they do not add up.''[121]

Alternatives In Esthetic Theory

The subject to which art appeals, is socially anonymous at the present time. (Marcuse)

Enchantment disappears when it tries to settle down. (Adorno)

A crucial part of Adorno's esthetics, its utopian thrust, remained largely in the background in his exchange with Benjamin. Rooted in the conception of art as a mode of cognition, it was a concern he shared most with Marcuse; both paid a degree of attention, therefore, to "formal" issues in the arts that made them highly suspect to more orthodox Marxists. Not only did Adorno reject out of hand any esthetic potential of "socialist realism" or "littérature engagée" (which mandated a content regardless of its formal mediation), but like Marcuse, he gave a weight to the so-called "subjective factor" as the principle of negation (drawing violent attacks from Lukács, who frequently equated formal concerns with bad subjectivism, and with bourgeois decadence) and elevated the radical rupture with *any* status quo, the discontinuity with anything merely given, to represent the very "logic of modern art."[122]

For critical theorists, of course, the function of a theory was very much part of its content, and the reasons for the focus on subjective and formal dimensions were themselves historical. In societies thoroughly integrated by the "culture industry" (a term Adorno coined), where exchange and technological rationality have become total life forms and screens of experience, where rational alternatives were literally inconceivable, where the traditional agent of change, the proletariat, seemed to have surrendered this role, in such tendentially "one-dimensional" societies, it was difficult to maintain Hegel's (also the late Lukács's and the late Brecht's) faith that the true is the whole. Today, the empirical whole is the untrue, Adorno resignedly asserted; the historical project of "substantive reason" may no longer be vested in the "bad objectivity" of any visible agent or any status quo, but in *whatever* contained the potential for its transcendence. Even an indeterminate negation, such as Marcuse's Great Refusal, may thus be legitimate at first—to secure an arena in which alternatives become conceivable again. "In a conceptual [*geistigen*] hierarchy which relentlessly demands responsibility on *its* terms, irresponsibility alone is capable of calling the hierarchy by its proper name,"[123] Adorno charged.

The thrust of this argument derives from the later Frankfurt School's, especially Adorno's, perception of the ultimate evil: heteronomy—a kinder (and more inclusive) word for domination. Today, a quieter, more insidious bondage of consciousness has taken the place of older, more "immediate" forms of oppression (which had allowed at least for opposition in thought). Exchange rationality (reification) and administrative rationality, the prevalent contemporary forms of reason, are forms of *instrumental reason* which reduce the identity of people and things to functions of something else. Such historical shifts do not leave esthetic functions and goals unaffected. "Insofar as one can speak of a social function of works of art, it lies in their functionlessness."[124] In the face of overall instrumentalization, "the useless alone represents what at one point might become the useful, the happy use: contact with things beyond the antithesis of use and uselessness."[125] Where reason has lost the capacity for self-transcendence and even the capacity to perceive this as a loss, alternatives have to be conceived from (what looks like) the outside. Philosophically, this conclusion also entails the final dismissal of the idealist residues in Marx, such as his belief in an immanent logic of social formations to develop in a specific direction. "Esthetics" once meant theory of perception, and when the term assumed its present meaning, it became perception "disinterested" in the (pseudoobjective) "interests" structuring a given reality. "Everything esthetic is something individuated," Adorno stressed, "and is thus an exception by virtue of its own principle."[126]

It is well to keep in mind, however, that both Adorno and Marcuse relentlessly opposed "bad subjectivism", i.e. the particular in abstract, "unmediated" opposition to the (equally illusory) objective or general. "Subjectivity is the epitome [*Inbegriff*] of mediation," as Adorno formulated in "Subject and Object" (in this volume): it is the transcendental form, literally the terms in which the objective/general appears to us. As such, subjectivity coincides with the concept of technique in the arts; "technique is the very essence of mediation."[127] The "esthetic principle of individuation" that Adorno kept invoking means the directive for the artist to devise alternative forms of objects, trial objects, or counterrealities through alternative transcendental ideas which retrieve the previously invisible, ignored or suppressed, but concrete potentialities of given historical situations.

This is why an "advanced consciousness" is not something the artist may or may not have, or something which essentially does not affect his/her creativity; it is the *sine qua non* of authentic art in a situation where the content of consciousness tends increasingly to be preformed. "Problems in the theory of knowledge reemerge immediately in esthetics; how the latter can interpret its objects depends on the concepts of there objects developed in the former,"[128] Adorno concluded in his *Esthetic Theory*; similarly, Marcuse postulated that art should become "*gemälte oder modellierte Erkenntniskritik.*" In the course of this process, the artist has to work with given materials and meanings, and thus must know them thoroughly if he/she wants to avoid merely reproducing bad objectivity. *Mutatis mutandis*, the same holds for the audience: "If you do not know what you are seeing or hearing, you are not enjoying an 'immediate' relation to the work of art; you are simple incapable of perceiving it. Consciousness is not a layer in a hierarchy, superimposed on perception; but all moments of the esthetic experiences are reciprocal."[129]

Such a need to control all the determinations and mediations [*Bestimmungen*] of the material explains Adorno's preference for highly conscious and critical artists, such as Kafka, Valéry, Mann,

Schönberg, and Beckett, who do not just leave the "objective" (and heteronomous) meaning intact. For "art's innermost principle, the utopian principle, revolts against the principle of definition whose tendency is to dominate nature."[130] Defining is an arresting, ontologizing act, working at cross-purposes with the processual character of art. The moment we want to express something particular, we have to use collective, general terms, thereby eliminating the very particularity. A merely transcendent position thus can never represent esthetic individuation. Only the *act* of negating the objective or given, the act of transcending (not its result, cf. the antinomies of communicability above) embodies the principle of individuation. Not only does Adorno polemicize against the idea of timless art ("the idea of lasting works is modeled after the categories of property"[131]), but he makes it the very principle of art to seek out and "synthesize the incompatible, unidentical elements in the process of friction with one another."[132] Adorno would contend that this is not a whim of the esthetician. For, "the processual nature of art is constituted by its needs (as an artifact, as human-made, with its a priori place in the mind) for the nonidentical, the heterogenous, the not-yet-formed. Works of art need the resistance of the other against them—it induces them to articulate their own formal language. This reciprocity constitutes art's dynamism."[133] Thus, authentic art, independent of the artist's intent, continuously confronts a given reality with what it is not, but could very well be. "There is something contradictory to the idea of a conservative work of art,"[134] Adorno insisted, and Marcuse agreed: "a subversive potential is in the very nature of art."[135] In the separate realm of art, the antagonism between the real and the possible can be momentarily and partially reconciled; and although it is an illusory (*scheinhaft*) reconciliation, it is "an illusion in which another reality shows forth."[136] While unreal, the work of art may thus be true, and true to that reality with its potential than that reality itself. The opposite of truth is not illusion but reality (as is).

In a sense art is the future-oriented pursuit of truth (*vérité à faire*), just as science is the past-oriented pursuit, i.e. oriented toward the already given. Its form and its terms have yet to be created. This is what Adorno means when he insists that the artist sustain the subject-object dialectic which forces art to "articulate its own formal language," rather than collapse the dialectic into either pole (e.g. into "pure" tone or color or into mere "reflection"). "Hegel's logic taught that essence must manifest itself in appearance; that means that a presentation of an essence which ignores its relation to its appearance is false in itself [*an sich*]".[137] To be sure, the meaning of "form" is not always clear in either Adorno or Marcuse: style, idion, tone, strictly technical devices, or configuration in general all occur under the heading "form." Moreover, Adorno's correlations of formal and stylistic levels with social meanings are often highly idiosyncratic, however suggestive. The seemingly self-evident nature of some of these correlations should instead be reason for suspicion, and should itself become a topic for investigation. E.g., "Pale and faded is the light over his [Stifter's] mature prose, as if it were allergic to the happiness of color."[138] Whether these analogies hold is a matter for discussion. Yet, more often than not, they reveal striking formal and even terminological similarities between esthetic and social spheres and illustrate how form, i.e. subjective mediation, is at the same time the "locus of social content."[139]

And whereas the fetishization of art would, on the whole, fall under the general critique of fetishism, it is precisely the fact that art is exempt from immediate social function or praxis which permits it to be a trial arena for alternatives. To be sure, society protects itself from the "subversive potential" of art by creating a special sphere for it in which it is declared autonomous but also, therefore, socially irrelevant. While society can thus safely, and even justly, worship art, this fetishization is also the social protection of such a qualitative enclave. The artist must not share in the fetishization, but must avail him/herself of it. The "Social essence" of works of art, therefore, always needs dual refelction: "reflection on its *Fürsichsein*, and on its relation to soceity."[140] It must remain beyond the constraint of immediate application to the very reality it is to transcend. Marcuse fully agreed when he called for a kind of "second [voluntary] alienation" from the "established reality."[141] Given the objectivity of the latter, its transcendence is always subjective, and will thus remain a form of alienation, of productive alienation, unless the "impossible final unity of subject and object"[142] occurs.

Marcuse had once envisaged the possibility of an *Aufhebung* of art through its concrete realization. In *Eros and Civilization*, and as early as "The Affirmative of Culture" in 1937, and still in *Essay on Liberation* (1969), he projected the alternative world of harmony, nonalienation, playfulness, happiness and liberation of mind and senses which would make life itself "esthetic."[143] Since *Counterrevolution and Revolt* however, Marcuse too has reaffirmed the dialectical function of art as immanent transcendence, as the critical wedge in any body politic. "At the optimum, we can envisage a universe common to art and reality, but in this common universe, art would retain its transcendence."[144] Authentic art, i.e. qualitative transcendence of experiences homogenized by the culture industry, is not tied to a specific movement or social stratum. Proletarian art is not inherently more progressive than any other: "if such transcendence is an essential quality of all art, it follows that the goals of the revolution may find expression in bourgeois art, and in all forms of art."[145]

Much more than Adorno, Marcuse was willing to specify what the esthetic sensibility would entail in terms of attitudes and social relations. He emphasized the liberation of the senses and, at times, seemed to plead for concrete anticipations of utopian forms even in everyday spheres; analogously, he seemed (for a moment only) to see such anticipation in a number of movements of the 1960's. Via the conception of alternative forms of objects or counterrealities, art can try out new modes of relations to objects as well, including different needs, drives, sensibilities.

Although Adorno clearly put more weight on consciousness and theory as esthetic functions than did Marcuse, their views do converge on the rational status of imagination—a statis it had held since Aristotle. Imagination operates consciously as the "covetous anticipation" or creation of alternatives, not as variations or refinements, but in terms of qualitatively new values and goals. In this sense, art was a social force of production for critical theorists. The "formal principle" of art is thus "the New" per se, a category in its own right for Adorno. And whereas Benjamin too saw "the new as a quality independent of use value," he thought it "the quintessence of false consciousness whose never-tiring agent is fashion." Adorno took precisely the opposite position, trusting its transcendent nature even prior to any content: the new undercuts "false consciousness" by preventing the enshrinement (and repetition) of any particular heteronomy. Its subject (for Benjamin, the *flâneur*) does not yet exist, but is anticipated in the autonomous esthetic act. Hence the resentment against modernism by orthodox Marxism and bourgeois culture alike: they rightly experience it as a crisis ("decadence") and attack it for being "a qualitative category, not a chronological one."[146] Fond of invoking Rimbaud's dictum "*il faut être absolument moderne*, "Adorno insisted that modernism was both a moral and (thus) esthetic imperative as long as any given reality is not "reconciled" with its own possibilities.

Eduard Fuchs:
Collector and Historian

By Walter Benjamin

First published in Zeitschrift für Sozialforschung [*Vol. VI (1937)*],
*the essay documents Benjamin's particular attitude toward the past,
focusing on the special detail to be preserved for a projected future.
Our interest is not in Eduard Fuchs, a relatively insignificant Social
Democratic intellectual, but in Benjamin's penetration precisely of
those "insignificant" events, products and lives that rupture the
continuum of cultural development called "progress." Linear
progress for Benjamin could only be that of domination.
Furthermore, the presentation of Fuchs, the collector and often crude
historical materialist, must also be read as one of Benjamin's
self-presentations, and even as an* apologia pro vita sua *in the face of
criticism.*

There are many kinds of collectors and each of them is moved by a
multitude of impulses. As a collector Fuchs is primarily a pioneer. He
founded the only existing archive for the history of caricature, of
erotic art and of the genre picture *(Sittenbild)*. More important,
however, is another, complementary, circumstance: because he was a
pioneer, Fuchs became a collector. Fuchs is the pioneer of a materialist consideration of art. What made this materialist a collector, however, was the more or less clear feeling for the historical situation in
which he saw himself. This was the situation of historical materialism
itself.

This situation is expressed in a letter which Friedrich Engels sent to Mehring at the time that Fuchs, working in a socialist editorial office, won his first victories as a publicist. The letter, dated July 14, 1893, among other things elaborates on the following: "It is above all this appearance *(Schein)* of an autonomous history of constitutions, of legal systems and of ideological conceptions in each specialized field of study, which deceives most people. When Luther and Calvin 'overcome' the official Catholic religion, when Hegel 'overcomes' Fichte and Kant, and when Rousseau indirectly 'overcomes' the constitutional work of Montesquieu with his *Contrat Social*, this is a process which remains theology, philosophy and government. This process represents a stage in the history of these disciplines and in no way goes outside of these disciplines themselves. And since the bourgeois illusion of the eternity and finality of capitalist production entered the picture, the overcoming of the mercantilists by the physiocrats and Adam Smith is seen as a mere victory of thought rather than as the reflection in thought of changed economic facts. Thus, this victory becomes the finally achieved correct insight into actual relations which always and everywhere existed."[1]

Engels's argument is directed against two elements. First of all, he criticizes the convention in the history of ideas which represents new dogmas as a "development" of an earlier stage, of seeing a new poetic school as a "reaction" to a preceding one, of understanding new styles as the "overcoming" of older forms. Of course, he implicitly criticizes at the same time the practice of representing such new structures completely detached from their effect on human beings and their spiritual as well as economic processes of production. Such an argument destroys the humanities' claim to being a history of constitutions or a history of the natural sciences, of religion or of art. Yet the explosive force of this thought, which Engels carried with him for half a century, extends still deeper.[2] It places the closed unity of the disciplines and their products in question. As far as art is concerned, this thought challenges the unity of art itself, as well as that of those worlds which the concept of art claims to contain. For the person who is concerned with works of art in a historically dialectical mode, these works integrate their pre- as well as post-history; and it is their post-history which illuminates their pre-history as a continuous process of change. Works of art teach that person how their function outlives their creator and how his intentions are left behind. They demonstrate how the reception of the work by its contemporaries becomes a component of the effect which a work of art has upon us today. They further show that this effect does not rest in an encounter with the work of art alone but in an encounter with the history which has allowed the work to come down to our own age. Goethe intimated this in his habitually veiled manner when, in a conversation about Shakespeare, he said to Chancellor von Müller: "Everything which has produced a great effect can really no longer be judged." No statement is more suited to evoke that state of unrest which constitutes the beginning of any contemplation of history that has the right to call itself dialectical. This state of unrest refers to the demand on the researcher to abandon the tranquil contemplative attitude toward the object in order to become conscious of the critical constellation in which precisely this fragment of the past finds itself in precisely this present. "The truth will not run away from us"—a statement found in Gottfried Keller— indicates exactly that point in the historical image of historicism where the image is broken through by historical materialism. It is an irretrievable image of the past which threatens to disappear in any present which does not recognize its common relation with that image.

The more one considers Engels's sentences, the clearer his insight becomes that any dialectical representation of history is paid for by renouncing the contemplativeness which characterizes historicism. The historical materialist must abandon the epic element in history. For him history becomes the object of a construct *(Konstruktion)* which is not located in empty time but is constituted in a specific epoch, in a specific life, in a specific work. The historical materialist explodes the epoch out of its reified "historical continuity," and thereby lifts life out of this epoch, and the work out of the life work. Yet this construct results in simultaneous preservation and suspension *(Aufhebung)* of the life work in the work, of the epoch in the life work and of the course of history in the epoch.[3]

Historicism presents the eternal image of the past; historical materialism presents a given experience with the past, an experience which stands unique. The replacement of the epic element by the constructive element proves to be the condition for this experience. The immense forces which remain captive in historicism's "once upon a time" are freed in this experience. To bring about the consolidation of experience with history, which is original for every present, is the task of historical materialism. It is directed towards a consciousness of the present which explodes the continuum of history.

Historical materialism comprehends historical understanding as the afterlife of that which has been understood and whose pulse can be traced in the present. This understanding has its place in Fuchs's thinking, but not an undisputed one. In his thinking, an old dogmatic and naive idea of reception exists together with the new and critical one. The first could be summarized as follows: what determines our reception of a work must have been its reception by its contemporaries. This is precisely analogous to Ranke's "how it truly was" which "solely and uniquely" matters.[4] Next to this, however, we immediately find the dialectical insight which opens the widest horizons in the meaning of a history of reception. Fuchs criticizes the fact that in the history of art the question of the success of a work of art is left out of consideration. "This neglect . . . is a deficit in our whole consideration of art. And yet it strikes me that the uncovering of the real reasons for the greater or lesser success of an artist, the reasons for the duration of his success or its opposite, is one of the most important of the problems which . . . attach themselves to art."[5] Mehring understood the matter in the same way. In his *Lessing-Legende,* the reception of the poet by Heine, Gervinus, Stahr, Danzel and finally Erich Schmitt, becomes the starting point for his analyses. And it is not without good reason that Julian Hirsch's investigation into the "Genesis of Fame" appeared only shortly thereafter, though Hirsch's work has its merit less in its methodology than in its content. Hirsch envisages the same question as Fuchs. Its solution offers criteria for the standards of historical materialism. This circumstance, however, does not justify a failure to mention that such a solution does not yet exist. Rather, it must be conceded without reservations that only in isolated instances has it been possible to grasp the historical content of a work of art in such a way that it becomes more transparent to us *as a work of art.* All courting of a work of art must remain a vain endeavor as long as the work's prosaic historical content is untouched by dialectical knowledge. This, however, is only the first of the truths towards which the work of the collector Eduard Fuchs is oriented. His collections are the answers of the practical man to the irresolvable polarities of theory.

Fuchs was born in 1870. From the very beginning, he was not meant to be a scholar. Nor did he ever become a scholarly "type" despite all the scholarship which he amassed in his later life. His efforts constantly projected beyond the limits which confine the horizon of the researcher. This is true for his accomplishments as a collector as well as for his activities as a politician. Fuchs entered working life in the mid-1880s. That was during the period of the anti-socialist laws. His apprenticeship brought him together with politically interested proletarians and he was soon drawn by them into the struggle of those who were illegal at that time—a struggle which today appears to us in a rather idyllic light. These years of apprenticeship ended in 1887. A few years later, the *Münchener Post,* organ of the Bavarian Social Democrats, summoned the young bookkeeper Fuchs from a printing shop in Stuttgart. In Fuchs they believed they had found the man who would be able to relieve the administrative difficulties of the paper. Fuchs went to Munich to work side by side with Richard Calver.

The publishing house of the *Münchener Post* also published the *Süddeutsche Postillion,* a socialist magazine of political humor. By chance Fuchs had to temporarily assist with the page proofs of one issue and fill in gaps with a number of his own contributions. The success of this number was extraordinary. In the same year there appeared, brightly illustrated—colored printing was still in its infancy—the May issue of the journal, edited by Fuchs. This issue sold 60,000 copies, though the average annual distribution had been 2,500 copies. Fuchs thus became editor of a magazine devoted to political satire. Apart from the daily routine, Fuchs at once turned his attention to the history of his field. This resulted in the illustrated studies on the year 1848 in caricature and about the political affair of Lola Montez. In contrast to the history books illustrated by living artists (such as Wilhelm Blos's popular books on the revolution with pictures by Jeutsch), these were the first historical works illustrated with documentary pictures. Encouraged by Harden, Fuchs even advertised the work on Lola Montez in *Die Zukunft,* and did not forget to mention that it represented merely a part of a comprehensive work which he was going to devote to the caricature of the European peoples. The studies for this work profited from a ten-month prison sentence which he had to serve for *lèse majesté* through the press. The idea seemed obviously auspicious. A certain Hans Kraemer, who already possessed some experience in the production of illustrated almanacs, approached Fuchs with the news that he, Kraemer, had already been working on a history of caricature and suggested that they combine their studies and collaborate on the work. Kraemer's contributions, however, were awaited in vain. Soon it became evident that the whole, and quite considerable, workload rested on Fuchs. The name of the presumptive collaborator was eliminated from the title of the second edition, although it had appeared in the first. But Fuchs had given the first convincing proof of his stamina and his control of his material. The long series of his major works had begun.[6]

Fuchs's beginnings came at a time in which, as the *Neue Zeit*
once put it, the "trunk of the Social Democratic party produced ring
after ring of organic growth."[7] With this growth, new tasks in the
educational work of the party came to the fore. The greater the masses
of workers that joined the party, the less the party could afford to be
content with their merely political and scientific enlightenment, that
is, with a vulgarization of the theory of surplus value and the theory of
evolution. The party had to direct its attention to the inclusion of
historical material in both its lecture programs and in the *Feuilleton*
section of the party press. Thus, the problem of the "popularization of
science" arose in its full dimension. It was not solved. Nor was it even
possible to approach a solution as long as those to be educated were
considered a "public" rather than a class.[8] If the educational effort
had been directed toward the "class", it would not have lost its close
touch with the scientific tasks of historical materialism. The historical
material, turned by the plough of Marxist dialectics, would have
become a soil capable of giving life to the seed which the present
planted in it. That, however, did not occur. The Social Democrats
opposed their own slogan, "knowledge is power" to the slogan
"work and education," under which Schultz-Delitzsch's piously loyal unions operated their workers' education. But the Social Democrats
did not perceive the double meaning of their own slogan. They
believed that the same knowledge which secured the domination of the
proletariat by the bourgeoisie would enable the proletariat to free itself
from this domination. But in reality, a form of knowledge without
access to practice, and which could teach the proletariat nothing about
its situation, was of no danger to its oppressors. This was particularly
the case with the humanities. The humanities represented a kind of
knowledge far removed from economics, and consequently untouched by the transformation of economics. The humanities were
satisfied "to stimulate," "to offer diversion" or "to be interesting."
History is disembodied while "cultural history" is preserved. Here
Fuchs' work has its place: its greatness lies in its reaction to this state
of affairs; its problematic lies in its participation in it. From the very
beginning, Fuchs made it a principle to direct himself toward a mass
readership.[9]

Only a few recognized then how much truly depended on the
materialist educational effort. The hopes, and still more importantly,
the fears of those few were expressed in a debate whose traces can be
found in the *Neue Zeit*. The most important of these is an essay by
Korn entitled "Proletariat and Classicism." This essay deals with the

concept of heritage *(Erbe)*, a concept which has again become important today. According to Korn, Lassalle saw German idealism as a heritage to which the working class acceded. Marx and Engels understood the matter differently, however. "They did not derive the social priority of the working class as . . . a heritage, but rather from the decisive position of the working class in the production process. How can possession be spoken of, even spiritual possession, with respect to a class *parvenu* such as the modern proletariat? Every hour, every day, this proletariat demonstrated its 'right' by means of a labor process which continuously reproduces the whole cultural apparatus. Thus, for Marx and Engels the showpiece of Lassalle's educational ideal, namely speculative philosophy, was not a tabernacle. . . . and both felt more and more drawn toward natural science. Indeed, for a class whose essence is its functioning, natural science may be called science *per se*, while for the ruling and possessing class, everything that is historical comprises the given form of their ideology. In fact, history represents for consciousness the same category of possession which capital represents for economics in terms of the domination over past labor."[10]

This is a significant criticism of historicism. The reference to natural science, however—as "science *per se*"—first permits a clear view of the dangerous problematic of the educational question. Since Bebel, the prestige of natural science dominated the debate. Bebel's main work, *Woman Under Socialism,* had reached a circulation of 200,000 copies in the thirty years which passed between its first publication and Korn's essay. Bebel's high regard for natural science rests not only on the calculable accuracy of its results, but above all on its practical usefulness.[11] Somewhat later, the natural sciences occupy a similar position in Engels' thinking when he believes he has refuted Kant's phenomenalism by pointing to technology, which through its achievements shows that we do recognize "things in themselves." Natural science, which for Korn appears as science *per se*, makes this possible particularly as the foundation of technology. Technology, however, is obviously not a pure scientific fact. It is at the same time a historical fact. As such, it forces an examination of the attempted positivistic and undialectical separation between the natural sciences and the humanities. The questions which humanity brings to nature are in part conditioned by the level of production. This is the point at which positivism fails. Positivism was only able to see the progress of natural science in the development of technology, but failed to recognize the concomitant retrogression of society. Positivism overlooked the fact that this development was decisively conditioned by capitalism. By the same token, the positivists among the Social Democratic theorists failed to understand that the increasingly more urgent act which would bring the proletariat into possession of this technology was rendered more and more precarious because of this development. They misunderstood the destructive side of this development because they were alienated from the destructive side of dialectics.

A prognosis was due but failed to materialize. That failure concluded a process characteristic of the past century: the miscarried reception of technology. It consists of a series of energetic, constantly renewed efforts, all attempting to overcome the fact that technology serves this society only by producing commodities. At the beginning, there were the Saint-Simonians with their industrial poetry. They are followed by the realism of a Du Camp who sees the locomotive as the saint of the future. Finally there is a Ludwig Pfau: "It is quite unnecessary to become an angel," he wrote, "since a locomotive is worth more than the nicest pair of wings."[12] This image of technology comes from the *Gartenlaube*. This may cause one to ask whether the *Gemütlichkeit* which the nineteenth-century bourgeoisie enjoyed does not arise from the hollow comfort of never having to experience how the productive forces had to develop under their hands. This experience was really reserved for the following century. The present century experiences how the speed of traffic machines and the capacities of apparatuses for duplicating words and writing outstrip human needs. The energies which technology develops beyond this threshold are destructive. First of all, they advance the technology of war and its propagandistic preparation. One might say of this development, which was thoroughly class-conditioned, that it occurred behind the backs of the last century. That century was not yet conscious of the destructive energies of technology. This is especially true for the Social Democrats at the turn of the century. If they occasionally criticized and opposed the illusions of positivism, they remained largely trapped by them. For them, the past appeared to have been gathered up and stored forever in the sheds of the present. Although the future held the promise of work ahead, it also held the certitude of a blessed harvest.

Fuchs educated himself in this epoch and decisive aspects of his work derive from it. Expressed simply, his work participates in that problematic which is inseparable from cultural history. This problematic leads back to the quotation from Engels. One could believe this quotation to be the *locus classicus* which defines historical materialism as history of culture. Is this not the true meaning of the passage? Would it not be true that the study of individual disciplines, once the illusion *(Schein)* of unity has been removed, flows together into the study of cultural history as the inventory which humanity has preserved to the present day? In truth, to pose the question in this manner is to replace the varied and problematic unities which cultural history embraces (as history of literature and art, or history of law and religion) merely by a new and most problematic unity of all. Cultural history presents its contents by means of contrast. Yet for the historical materialist, this contrast is illusory and is conjured up by false consciousness.[13] He thus confronts it with reservations. Such reservations would be justified by the mere inspection of that which has existed: whatever the historical materialist would survey in art or science has a lineage which cannot be contemplated without dread. The products of art and science owe their existence not merely to the effort of the great geniuses that created them, but also to the unnamed drudgery of their contemporaries. There is no document of culture which is not at the same time a document of barbarism. No cultural history has yet done justice to this fundamental state of affairs, and it can hardly hope to do so.

Nevertheless, the decisive element does not lie here. If the concept of culture is problematical for historical materialism, it cannot conceive of the disintegration of culture into goods which become objects of possession for mankind. The work of the past remains uncompleted for historical materialism. It perceives no epoch in which the completed past could even in part drop conveniently, thing-like, into mankind's lap. The concept of culture, as the substantive concept of creations which are considered independent, if not from the production process in which they originate, then from a production process in which they continue to survive, carries a fetishistic trait. Culture appears in a reified form. Its history would be nothing but the sediment formed by the curiosities which have been stirred up in the consciousness of human beings without any genuine, i.e. political, experience.

Apart from that, one cannot ignore the situation that thus far no historical presentation undertaken on a cultural-historical basis has escaped this problematic. It is obvious in Lamprecht's massive *Deutsche Geschichte,* a book which for understandable reasons has more than once been criticized by the *Neue Zeit.* "As we know," Mehring writes, "Lamprecht is the one bourgeois historian who came closest to historical materialism." However, "Lamprecht stopped halfway. . . . Any concept of a historical method disappears when Lamprecht treats cultural and economic developments according to a specific method and then proceeds to compile a history of simultaneous political developments from some other historians."[14] To be sure, it makes no sense to present cultural history on the basis of pragmatic history. Yet a dialectical cultural history in itself is even more deeply devoid of sense since the continuum of history severed from the dialectic suffers in no realm so wide a dispersion as in that which is called culture.

Briefly, cultural history only seems to represent an advance of insight, but apparently not one of dialectic. For cultural history lacks the destructive element which authenticates both dialectical thought and the experience of the dialectical thinker. Cultural history, to be sure, enlarges the weight of the treasure which accumulates on the back of humanity. Yet cultural history does not provide the strength to shake off this burden in order to be able to take control of it. The same is true for the socialist educational efforts at the turn of the century which were guided by the star of cultural history.

Against this background, the historical outline of Fuchs's work becomes visible. Where his work has endurance and permanence is in those areas where it is wrested away from an intellectual constellation which has seldom appeared less favorable to it. This is the point where Fuchs the collector taught Fuchs the theoretician to comprehend much that was barred to him by his time. He was a collector who strayed into border disciplines such as caricature and pornographic representation. These border disciplines sooner or later meant the ruin of a series of clichés in traditional art history. First, it should be noted that Fuchs had broken completely with the classicist conception of art, whose traces can still be recognized in Marx. The concepts by means of which the bourgeoisie developed this notion of art no longer play a role in Fuchs's work; neither the appearance of beauty *(der schöne Schein)*, nor harmony, nor the unity of the manifold are to be found there. The same kind of collector's robust self-assertion which alienated Fuchs from the classicist theories sometimes arises, drastically and forcefully, in regard to classical antiquity itself. In 1908, drawing on the work of Slevogt and Rodin, Fuchs prophesied a new beauty "which in its final result will be indefinitely greater than antiquity. Where antiquity was only the highest animalistic form, the new beauty will be filled with a grandiose spiritual and emotional content.''[15]

In short, the order of values which determined the consideration of art for Goethe and Winckelmann has lost all influence in the work of Fuchs. Of course, it would be a mistake to assume that consequently the idealist contemplation of art itself had been entirely unhinged. That could not happen any earlier than the point at which the *disiecta membra* which idealism contains as both "historical representation" on the one hand and "appreciation" *(Würdigung)* on the other become one and are thus surpassed. This effort, however, is left to a mode of historical science which does not fashion its object out of a tangled ball of mere facticities but creates it out of the counted group of threads which represent the woof of the past fed into the warp of the present. (It would be a mistake to equate this woof with mere causal connection. Rather, it is a thoroughly dialectical mode. For centuries threads can become lost and are picked up by the actual course of history in a disjointed and inconspicuous manner.) The historical object removed from pure facticity does not need any "appreciation." It does not offer vague analogies to actuality but constitutes itself as an object in the precise dialectical problem which actuality itself is obliged to solve. That is indeed what Fuchs intends. If in nothing else, the intention can be felt in the pathos which often makes the text approach the form of a lecture. This fact, however, also indicates that much of his effort did not advance beyond its mere intention or beginnings. What is fundamentally new in the intention becomes most directly visible where the material proves favorable. This occurs in the interpretation of iconography, in the contemplation of mass art as well as in the examination of techniques of reproduction. These aspects in Fuchs's work are pioneering. They are elements of any future materialist consideration of works of art.

The three mentioned motifs have one common denominator: they contain a reference to forms of knowledge which could not prove to be anything but destructive in regard to traditional conceptions of art. The consideration of techniques of reproduction, more than any other line of research, clarifies the decisive importance of reception. Thus, it becomes to some degree possible to correct the process of reification which takes place in a work of art. The consideration of mass art leads to a revision of the concept of genius. It reminds us not to give priority to the inspiration, which participates in the becoming of the work of art, over and against the demand *(Faktur)* which alone allows inspiration to come to fruition. Finally, iconographic interpretation not only proves to be indispensable for the study and reception of mass art: it repels the excesses which any formalism immediately encourages.[16]

Fuchs had to deal with formalism. Wölfflin's doctrine achieved its popularity at the same time that Fuchs laid down the foundations of his own work. In his *Das individuelle Problem (The Individual Problem)*, Fuchs takes off on a thesis from Wölfflin's *Die klassische Kunst*. The thesis runs as follows: "Thus, Quattrocento and Cinquecento as concepts of style cannot be exhausted by their material *(stofflich)* characterization. The phenomenon . . . indicates a development of artistic vision which is essentially independent of a particular attitude of mind or of a particular idea of beauty."[17] Certainly, such a formulation can be offensive to historical materialism. Yet it also contains useful elements. For it is precisely historical materialism that is not so much interested in reducing the changes in artistic vision to a changed ideal of beauty as in tracing these changes back to more elementary processes—processes which are set in motion by economic and technological changes in production. In the above case, one would hardly fail to benefit from asking what economically conditioned changes the Renaissance brought about in housing construction. Nor would it be unprofitable to examine the role played by Renaissance painting in projecting the new architecture and in illustrating its emergence, which Renaissance painting made possible.[18] Wölfflin, of course, only very briefly touches on the question. And when Fuchs retorts that "precisely these formal elements cannot be explained any other way than by a changed mood of the times,"[19] this points directly to the dubious status of cultural-historical categories which has been discussed above.

In more than one passage, it becomes clear that polemic or discussion are not in the line of the writer Fuchs's talents. As valiant as Fuchs may appear, one cannot find in his arsenal the eristic dialectic, which, according to Hegel, "enters into the strength of the opponent in order to destroy him from within." Among scholars who followed Marx and Engels, the destructive force of thought had relaxed and no longer dared to challenge the century. The multitude of struggles had already slackened the tension in Mehring's work, although his *Lessing-Legende* remains a considerable achievement. In this book he showed what enormous political, scientific and theoretical energies were enlisted into the creation of the great works of the classic era. He thus affirmed his distaste for the lazy routine of his belletristic contemporaries. Mehring came to the noble insight that art could only expect its rebirth through the economic and political victory of the proletariat. He also arrived at the incontestable statement that "It [art] cannot deeply participate in the struggle for the emancipation of the proletariat."[20] The development of art proved him right. Such insights directed Mehring to study science with redoubled emphasis. Here he gained the solidity and severity which kept him immune from revisionism. Thus, he developed traits in his character which could be called bourgeois in the best meaning of the term. Yet these traits remained far removed from ensuring for him the title of dialectical thinker. The same traits can be found in Fuchs. In him they may be even more prominent insofar as they have been incorporated into a more expansive and sensualistic talent. Be that as it may, one can easily imagine his portrait in a gallery of bourgeois scholars. One might hang his picture next to Georg Brandes, with whom he shares the rationalistic furor, the passion to throw light onto vast historical spaces by means of the torch of the Idea (be it progress, science or reason). On the other side one could imagine the portrait of the ethnologist Adolf Bastian. Fuchs reminds one of the latter, particularly in his insatiable hunger for material. Bastian acquired legendary fame for his readiness to pack a suitcase and go on expeditions when it was necessary to clarify a question, even if it kept him away from home for months. Similarly, Fuchs obeyed his impulses whenever they drove him to search out new evidence. The works of both these men will remain inexhaustible treasures for research.

It must be a significant question for the psychologist how an enthusiast, a person who by nature embraces the positive, can have such a passion for caricature. The psychologist may answer as he likes—there can be no doubt in Fuchs's case. From the beginning, his interest in art differs from what one might call "taking pleasure in the beautiful." From the beginning, truth is mixed with play. Fuchs never tires of stressing the value of caricature as a source, as authority. "Truth lies in the extreme," he occasionally remarks. But he goes further. To him, caricature is "in a certain sense the form . . . from which all objective art takes its beginning. A single glance into ethnographic museums furnishes proof of this statement."[21] When Fuchs uses prehistoric tribes as well as children's drawings for evidence, the concept of caricature is brought into a problematic context. Yet his vehement interest in an art work's drastic aspects *(Gehalt)*, whether in its form or content,[22] manifests itself all the more primally.

This interest runs through the whole breadth of his work. In the late work *Tang Plastik (Tang Sculpture),* we can still read the following: "The grotesque is the highest escalation of what is sensually imaginable. In this sense, grotesque products become an expression of the teeming health of a time. . . . Yet one cannot dispute the fact that the motivating forces of the grotesque have a crass counterpoint. Decadent times and sick brains also incline toward grotesque representations. In such cases, the grotesque becomes the shocking reflection of the fact that for the times and individuals in question, the problems of existence have taken on an appearance of unsolvable complexity. Which of the two tendencies, however, is the creative motivating force behind a grotesque fantasy can be recognized at first glance."[23]

This passage is instructive. It makes especially apparent upon what the wide-ranging effects and popularity of Fuchs's work rest. They rest upon his gift for immediately connecting the fundamental concepts of his presentation with immediate valuations *(Wertungen)*. This often occurs in rather massive fashion.[24] Moreover, these valuations are always extreme. They occur as oppositions and in this way polarize the concept with which they are fused. That happens in his depiction of the grotesque as well as in that of erotic caricature. In times of decadence, erotic caricature becomes "tickling piquanterie" or "filth," while in times of ascendency, it "expresses super-abundant pleasure and exuberant strength."[25] Sometimes Fuchs draws on values of the heyday and decadence of a time, sometimes he draws on images of the sick and healthy. He avoids border cases in which the problematic of such images might become apparent. He prefers to stick to the "really great" which has the privilege of making room for "that which charms in the most simple manner."[26] He hardly appreciates discontinuous *(gebrochen)* periods such as the Baroque. For him, the great epoch is still the Renaissance. Here, his cult of creativity maintains the upper hand over his dislike of classicism.

Fuchs's concept of creativity has a strong biological tinge. Authors whom he dislikes, he tends to downgrade in their virility, while genius appears with attributes which occasionally take on priapic dimensions. Fuchs's argument carries the stamp of such a biologistic attitude when he sums up a judgment on Greco, Murillo and Ribera. "All three became the classic representation of baroque spirit specifically because each was a 'bungled' eroticist."[27] One must not lose sight of the fact that Fuchs developed his categories at a time in which "pathography" represented the latest standard in the psychology of art and in which Möbius and Lombroso were considered authorities.

At the same time, Burckhardt had greatly enriched the concept of genius with illustrative material in his influential *Kultur der Renaissance*. From different sources, this concept of genius fed the same widespread conviction that creativity was above all the manifestation of superabundant strength. Similar tendencies later led Fuchs to conceptions which are related to psychoanalysis. He was the first to make them fruitful for esthetics.

The eruptive and immediate elements which this conception regards as characteristic of artistic creation also dominate Fuchs's understanding of the work of art as well. Thus it is often not more than a leap that separates apperception and judgment for Fuchs. Indeed, he thinks that the "impression" is not only the obvious impetus which a spectator receives from a work, but the category of contemplation itself. This is summarized in his remarks about the Ming period whose artistic formalism he treats with critical reserve. These works "ultimately and finally no longer achieve, and sometimes do not even approach, the impression which was produced by the great lines of the Tang period."[28] This is how Fuchs the writer acquires his particular and apodictic, not to say almost rustic, style. It is a style whose characteristic quality he formulates masterfully in the *Geschichte der erotischen Kunst (History of Erotic Art)*. Here he declares: "From the correct feeling to the correct and complete deciphering of the creative forces in the work of art there is always but a single step."[29] Not everyone can achieve such a style. Fuchs had to pay his price for it. In a word, the price was that gift of creating wonder *(staunen)* which the writer failed to achieve. There is no doubt that he felt this lack. He tried to compensate for it in the most various ways. Thus, he liked nothing better than to speak of the secrets which he searches out in the psychology of creation, or of the riddles in the course of history which find their solution in materialism. Yet the impulse to immediately master matters at hand, an impulse which already had determined his conception of creativity as well as his understanding of reception, finally comes to dominate his analysis. The course of the history of art appears "necessary," the characteristics of style appear "organic" and even the most peculiar art products appear "logical". One gets the impression that in the development of his analysis these terms begin to occur less frequently than they seem to have at first. In the work on the Tang period, he still says of the fairy creatures in the painting of that time that they seem "absolutely logical" and "organic" with their horns and flaming wings. "Even the huge elephant's ears have a logical effect and their posture, too, is always logical.

Never are they merely contrived concepts, for it is always the idea which has become a life-breathing form."[30]

In these formulae, a series of conceptualizations comes to the fore which are intimately connected with the Social Democratic doctrines of the epoch. The deep effect of Darwinism on the development of the socialist understanding of history is well known. During the time of Bismarck's persecution of the socialists, the Darwinian influence served to maintain the party's faith and determination in the struggle. Later, in revisionism, the evolutionary view of history burdened the concept of "development" all the more, the less the party was willing to risk what it had gained in the struggle against capitalism. History assumed deterministic traits: "the victory of the party was inevitable." Fuchs always remained distant from revisionism. His political instincts and his martial nature led him to the left wing. As a theoretician, however, he was not able to remain free from those influences. One can feel them at work everywhere. At that time, a man like Ferri not only traced the principles of Social Democracy, but also its tactics, back to natural laws. Deficiencies in the knowledge of geology and biology were held to be responsible for anarchistic deviations. Certainly leaders like Kautsky fought against such deviations.[31] Nevertheless, many were satisfied with theses which sorted historical processes into "physiological" and "pathological" ones. Or they thought that natural scientific materialism "automatically" turned into historical materialism simply by being in the hands of the proletariat.[32] Similarly, Fuchs sees the progress of human society as a process which "cannot be held back, just as it is impossible to arrest the continuous forward motion of a glacier."[33] Consequently, deterministic understanding pairs itself with solid optimism. Yet without confidence no class could, in the long run, hope to enter the political sphere with any kind of success. But it makes a difference whether this optimism directs itself towards the active strength of the class, or whether it centers on the conditions under which the class operates. Social Democracy leaned toward the latter, questionable, kind of optimism. The epigones of the turn of the century were barred from a vision of the emerging barbarism which an Engels perceived in the *Condition of the Working Class in England,* which a Marx glimpsed in his prognosis of capitalist development, and which is today well known even to the most mediocre statesman. When Condorcet publicized the doctrine of progress, the bourgeoisie stood before the assumption of power. A century later, the proletariat found itself in a different position. For the proletariat, this doctrine could awaken illusions. Indeed, these illusions provide the background occasionally revealed in Fuchs's history of art. "Today's art," he thinks, "has brought us a hundred fulfillments which in the most diverse directions exceed the achievements of Renaissance art, and the art of the future must certainly mean something still higher."[34]

The pathos which runs through Fuchs's understanding of history is the democratic pathos of 1830. Its echo was the speaker Victor Hugo. The echo of that echo are the books in which the speaker Hugo addresses himself to posterity. Fuchs's conception of history is the same as that which Hugo celebrates in *William Shakespeare*: "Progress is the stride of God himself." And universal suffrage appears as the world chronometer which measures the speed of these strides. With the statement *"Qui vote règne"* Hugo had erected the tablets of democratic optimism. Even much later, this optimism produced strange daydreams. One of these dreams produced the illusion that "all intellectual workers, including persons of high material as well as social position, had to be considered proletarians." For it is "an undeniable fact that all persons who hire out their services for money are helpless victims of capitalism, from a *Hofrat*, strutting in his gold covered uniform, down to the most downtrodden pieceworker."[35] The tablets set up by Hugo still cast their shadow over Fuchs's work. Fuchs remains within the democratic tradition when he attaches himself to France with a particular love. He admires France as the soil of three great revolutions, as the home of the exiles, as the source of utopian socialism, as the fatherland of haters of tyranny such as Michelet and Quinet, and finally as the soil in which the Communards are buried. Thus lived the image of France in Marx and Engels, thus it descended to Mehring, and even to Fuchs it still appeared as the land of "the avant-garde of culture and freedom."[36] He compares the spirited mockery of the French with the clumsy ridicule of the Germans. He compares Heine with those who remained at home. He compares German naturalism with the satirical novels of Anatole France. In this manner, like Mehring, he was led to solid prognoses, especially in the case of Gerhart Hauptmann.[37]

France is a home for Fuchs the collector as well. The figure of the collector, more attractive the longer one observes it, has not been given its due attention so far. One would imagine no figure more tempting to the romantic storytellers. The type is motivated by dangerous though domesticated passions. Yet one searches in vain among the figures of a Hoffmann, Quincey or Nerval for that of the collector.

Romantic figures are those of the traveler, of the *flâneur,* of the gambler or of the virtuoso. That of the collector is not found here. In vain one searches through the "physiologies" which otherwise do not miss a single figure of the Paris waxworks under Louis Philippe, from the kiosk operator to the salon-lion. All the more important, therefore, is the place of the collector in the work of Balzac. Balzac erected a monument to the figure of the collector, yet he treated it quite unromantically. Balzac was always alien to romanticism anyway. There are also few pieces in his corpus in which an anti-romantic position so surprisingly claims its right as in the sketch of *Cousin Pons*. One element is particularly characteristic. As accurately as we know the inventory of the collection to which Pons dedicates his life, just as little do we learn about the history of the acquisition of this collection. No passage in *Cousin Pons* can be compared to the breathtaking suspense of the description of the uncovering of a rare find which the brothers Goncourt give in their diaries. Balzac does not represent the hunter in the hunting grounds of inventory as any collector might be considered. Every fiber of his Pons, of his Elie Magus trembles with exultation. This exultation is the pride in the incomparable treasures which they protect with never tiring care. Balzac places all his stress on the representation of the "possessor," and the term "millionaire" seems to him a synonym for the word "collector." He speaks of Paris: "There one can often meet a very shabbily dressed Pons or an Elie Magus. They seem neither to respect nor to care for anything. They pay attention neither to women nor to window displays. They walk along as in a dream, their pockets are empty, their gaze is aimless and one wonders what kind of Parisian they really are. These people are millionaires. They are collectors, the most passionate people in the world."[38]

The image of the collector sketched by Balzac comes closer to the activity and fullness of Fuchs's character than one would expect from a romantic. Indeed, pointing to the man's life nerve, one might say that as a collector, Fuchs is truly Balzacian—a Balzacian figure that outgrew the poet's conception. What could be more in accord with this conception that a collector whose pride and expansiveness lead him to bring reproductions of his collection onto the market for the sole reason of being able to appear in public with his collections? That in consequence he becomes a rich man, is again a Balzacian turn. Not only the conscientiousness of a man who sees himself as a preserver of treasures but also the exhibitionism of a great collector prompted Fuchs into publishing almost exclusively unpublished illustrative material in each of his works. This material was almost completely drawn from his own collections. For the first volume alone of his *Karikatur der europäischen Völker (Caricature of the European Peoples)*, he collated 68,000 pages and then chose only about 500. He did not permit a single page to be reproduced in more than one place. The fullness of his documentation and its wide-ranging effect go hand in hand. Both attest to his descent from the race of bourgeois giants of around 1830 as Drumont characterizes them. Drumont writes: "Almost all the leaders of the school of 1830 had the same extraordinary constitution, the same fecundity and the same tendency toward the grandiose. Delacroix paints epics on canvas, Balzac depicts a whole society and Dumas covers a four-thousand-year stretch of human history in his novels. They all have backs strong enough for any burden."[39] When the revolution came in 1848, Dumas published an appeal to the workers of Paris in which he introduced himself as one of them. In twenty years, he said, he had written 400 novels and 35 plays. He had created jobs for 8,160 people: readers, typesetters, machinists, wardrobe mistresses. Nor did he forget the claque. The feeling with which the universal historian Fuchs created for himself the economic basis for his magnificent collections is probably not quite unlike Dumas's *amour-propre*. Later, this economic base made it possible for Fuchs to deal on the Paris market almost as sovereignly as in his own collection. Around the turn of the century, the senior representative of Paris art dealers used to say of Fuchs: "C'est le monsieur qui mange tout Paris." Fuchs belongs to the type of *rammasseurs* (packrats); he takes a Rabelaisian delight in quantities, a delight which can be noted in the luxurious repetitions of his texts.

Fuchs's French family tree is that of the collector, his German one, that of the historian. The austerity of morals characteristic of Fuchs the historian marks him as a German. This austerity already characterized Gervinus, whose *Geschichte der poetischen National- literatur (History of Poetic National Literature)* could be called the first attempt at a German history of ideas. It is typical of Gervinus, just as it is later of Fuchs, to represent the great creators in quasi-martial form. This results in the dominance of the active, manly and spontane- ous elements in their nature over their contemplative, feminine and receptive characteristics. Certainly, such a representation was easier for Gervinus. When he wrote his work, the bourgeoisie was in ascen- dancy: bourgeois art was full of political energies. Fuchs writes in the time of imperialism: he presents the political energies of art polemically to an age in whose works these energies diminish from day to day. But Fuchs's standards are still those of Gervinus. In fact, they can be traced back even further into the eighteenth century. This becomes possible with reference to Gervinus himself, whose memorial speech for F.C. Schlosser lent a grandiose voice to the armed moralism of the bourgeoisie in its revolutionary epoch. Schlosser had been criticized for a "miserable moral austerity". Gervinus, however, defends him by saying that "Schlosser could and would have answered these criticisms as follows: Contrary to one's experience with novels and novellas, one does not learn a superficial enjoyment of life by looking at life on a large scale, as history, despite all the serenity of the senses and the spirit. Through the contemplation of history, one does not absorb a misanthropic scorn but a severe outlook on the world and serious principles of life. The greatest judges of the world and of humanity knew how to measure external life according to their own internal life. Thus, for Shakespeare, Dante and Machiavelli, the essence of the world made an impression which always led them to seriousness and severity.''[40] Here lies the origin of Fuchs's moralism. It is a German Jacobinism whose monument is Schlosser's world history, which Fuchs came to know in his youth.[41]

Not surprisingly, this bourgeois moralism contains elements which collide with Fuchs's materialism. If Fuchs had recognized this, he might have been able to ameliorate this conflict. He was convinced, however, that his moralistic consideration of history and his historical materialism were completely harmonious. This was illusory. Underlying this illusion is a widespread opinion badly in need of revision: that the bourgeois revolutions, as they are celebrated by the bourgeoisie, are the genealogical root of a proletarian revolution.[42] On the contrary, it is necessary to look at the spiritualism which is woven into these revolutions. The golden threads of this spiritualism were spun by morality. Bourgeois morals function under the banner of inwardness—the first signs of this were already exhibited in the reign of terror. The keystone of this morality is conscience, whether the conscience of Robespierre's *Citoyen* or that of the Kantian cosmopolitan. The attitude of the bourgeoisie proclaimed the moral authority of conscience which proved favorable to bourgeois interests but depended on a complementary attitude of the proletariat, unfavorable to the interests of the latter. Conscience carries the banner of altruism. Conscience advises the proprietor to act according to concepts which are immediately fruitful to his co-proprietors. And conscience easily advises the same for those who possess nothing. When the latter take this advice, the advantage of their behavior for the proprietors becomes all the more immediately obvious as this advice becomes more doubtful for those who follow it, as well as for their class. For this reason, the price of virtue rests on this attitude—thus a class morality becomes dominant. But the process occurs on an unconscious level. The bourgeoisie did not need consciousness to establish this class morality as much as the proletariat needs consciousness in order to overthrow that morality. Fuchs does not do justice to this state of affairs because he believes that his attack must be directed against the conscience of the bourgeoisie. He sees deceit in bourgeois ideology. "In view of the most shameless class judgments," he says, "the fulsome babble about the subjective honesty of the judges in question proves only the lack of character of those who write or speak in this way. At best, one might ascribe it to their denseness."[43] Fuchs, however, does not think of judging the concept of *bona fides* (good conscience) itself. Yet this will occur to historical materialists, not only because the historical materialist recognizes that the concept is the bearer of bourgeois class morality, but also because he will not fail to see that this concept furthers the solidarity of moral disorder with economic planlessness. Younger Marxists at least hinted at this situation. Thus the following was said about Lamartine's politics which made excessive use of *bona fides*: "bourgeois . . . democracy . . . is dependent on this value. A democrat is honest by trade. Thus, a democrat feels no need to examine the true state of affairs."[44]

Considerations which focus more on the conscious interests of individuals than the behavior which is imposed on their class, often unconsciously and as a result of its position in the production process, lead to an overestimation of the conscious elements in the formation of ideology. This is evident in Fuchs's work when he declares: "In all its essential elements, art is the idealized disguise of a given social situation. For it is an eternal law . . . that every dominant political or social situation is forced to idealize itself in order ethically to justify its existence."[45] Here we approach the crux of the misunderstanding. It rests on the conception that exploitation conditions false consciousness, at least on the part of the exploiter, because true consciousness would prove to be a moral burden. This sentence may have a limited validity for the present insofar as the class struggle has involved all of bourgeois life in the extreme. However, the "bad conscience" of the privileged is by no means self-evident for earlier forms of exploitation. Reification not only clouds the relations among human beings—the real subjects of these relations remain clouded. An apparatus of legal and administrative bureaucracies intervenes between the rulers of economic life and the exploited. The members of these bureaucracies no longer function as fully responsible moral subjects, and their "sense of duty" is nothing but the unconscious expression of this deformation.

Fuchs's moralism, traces of which can be found in his historical materialism, was not shaken by psychoanalysis either. About sexuality he makes the following statement: "All forms of sensual behavior are justified in which the creative element of this law of life becomes visible. Those forms, however, are evil in which this highest of drives becomes degraded to a mere means of refined craving for pleasure."[46] It is clear that this moralism carries the bourgeois signature. Fuchs never acquired the proper distrust for the bourgeois scorn for pure sexual pleasure and the more or less fantastic means of creating it. In principle, to be sure, he declares that one can speak of "morality and immorality only in relative terms". Yet in the same passage he states immediately an exception for "absolute immorality" which "identifies itself by transgressions against the social drives of society and are thus, so to speak, a transgression against nature." According to Fuchs, this position is characterized by the historically inevitable victory of "the masses over a degenerate individuality, for the masses are always capable of development."[47] In short, it is true of Fuchs that he "does not attack the justification for condemning allegedly corrupt drives, but beliefs about the history and extent of these drives."[48]

Because of this, the clarification of the sexual-psychological problem is hampered. Since the rule of the bourgeoisie, this clarification has become particularly important. This is where the taboo of more or less wide areas of sexual pleasure has its place. The repressions which are thus produced in the masses bring to the fore masochistic and sadistic complexes. Those in power then further these complexes by delivering up to the masses those objects which prove most favorable for their politics. Wedekind, a contemporary of Fuchs, recognized these connections. Fuchs failed to produce a social critique in this regard. Therefore, a passage where he compensates for this lack by means of a detour through natural history becomes all the more important. The passage in question is his brilliant defense of orgies. According to Fuchs ". . . the pleasure of orgiastic rites belongs to the most valuable tendencies of culture. One must understand that orgies belong to that which distinguishes us from animals. In contrast to humans, animals do not know orgies. When their hunger and thirst are satisfied, animals will turn away from the juiciest feed and the clearest spring. Further, the sexual drive of animals is generally restricted to specific and brief periods of the year. This is quite different from human beings and in particular from creative human beings. The latter do not know the concept of 'enough' at all.''[49] Fuchs's sexual-psychological statements draw their strength from thought processes in which he deals critically with traditional norms. This enables him to disperse certain petit-bourgeois illusions. That goes for nudism in which he rightly sees a ''revolution of narrow-mindedness.'' Happily, human beings are not forest animals any longer. Thus we . . . desire that fantasy, even erotic fantasy, play its part in clothing. What we do not want, however, is exactly that social organization of humanity which deprives all of this.''[50]

Fuchs's psychological and historical understanding becomes fruitful for the history of clothing in many ways. In fact, there is hardly a subject matter apart from fashion which more closely approaches the author's threefold interest, namely, his historical, social and erotic interests. This already becomes evident in his definition of fashion, which, in its language, is suggestive of Karl Kraus. Fashion, he says in his *Sittengeschichte (History of Morals)*, ''indicates how people intend to deal with the business of public morality altogether.''[51] Fuchs, by the way, did not succumb to the general mistake of examining fashion only according to esthetic and erotic viewpoints, as did, for example, Max von Boehn. He did not fail to recognize the role of fashion as a means of domination. As fashion brings out the subtler distinctions of social standing, it keeps a particularly close watch over the coarser distinctions of the classes. Fuchs dedicated a long essay to fashion in his third volume of the *Sittengeschichte*. The supplementary volume sums up the train of thought of the essay by listing the decisive elements in fashion. The first element is formed by ''the interests of class separation.'' The second is provided by ''the mode of production of private capitalism'' which tries to increase its sales volume by manifold fashion changes. Thirdly, one must not forget the ''erotically stimulating purposes of fashion.''[52]

The cult of creativity which runs through the whole of Fuchs's work drew fresh nourishment from his psychoanalytic studies. They enriched his originally biological conception of creativity, though they did not, of course, correct it. Fuchs enthusiastically adopted the doctrine of the erotic origin of the creative impulse. His notion of eroticism, however, remained tied to a drastic, biologically determined sensuality. Fuchs avoided, to the degree that it was applicable at all, the theory of complexes and sublimation, which might have modified his moralistic understanding of social and sexual relationships. Fuchs's historical materialism derives things more from the conscious economic interest of the individual than from the class interest which is unconsciously at work within the individual. Similarly, he brings the creative impulse closer to the conscious sensual intention than to the image-creating unconscious.[53] The world of erotic images which Freud made accessible as a symbolic world in his *Interpretation of Dreams* expresses itself in Fuchs's work only where his own inner involvement is most enthusiastic. In such cases, this world fills his writing even where any explicit mention of it is avoided. This can be seen in the masterful characterization of the graphics of the revolutionary era. "Everything is stiff and military. Men do not lie down since the drill square does not tolerate any 'at ease.' Even when people are sitting down they look as if they want to jump up. Their whole bodies are as full of tension as an arrow on a bow string. What goes for the lines holds true for the colors. The pictures give a cold and tinny impression over and against the paintings of the Rococo. The color had to be hard and metallic if it was to be appropriate for the content of the pictures."[54] An informative remark regarding fetishism is more explicit. Here he traces the historical equivalents of fetishism. He says that "the increase of shoe and leg fetishism points to the replacement of the priapic cult with the vulva cult." The increase in breast fetishism on the other hand points to a regressive development. "The cult of a covered foot or leg reflects the dominance of woman over man, whereas the cult of breasts indicates the role of woman as an object of pleasure for men."[55] His deepest insights into the symbolic realm Fuchs gained at the hand of Daumier. What he says about Daumier's trees must be considered one of the most auspicious finds of his whole work. In these trees, he recognizes "a totally unique symbolic form . . . which expresses Daumier's sense of social responsibility as well as his conviction that it is society's duty to protect the individual. His typical manner of depicting trees shows them always with far-reaching branches, particularly if a person stands or rests under the tree. In such trees the branches stretch like the arms of a giant, and actually seem as if they want to reach for infinity. Thus, the branches come to form an impenetrable roof which keeps danger away from all those who come under their shelter."[56] This beautiful contemplation leads Fuchs to the notion of the maternal preponderance in Daumier's work.

*   *   *

No other figure has as much life for Fuchs as Daumier, a figure that accompanied him throughout his working life. One might almost say that this made Fuchs into a dialectical thinker. At least he conceived of Daumier in all the latter's fullness and contradiction. Though Fuchs grasps the maternal elements in Daumier's art and paraphrases them rather impressively, he was just as familiar with the other side of the man and his manly and aggressive characteristics. He was right in pointing out the absence of idyllic notions in Daumier's work: not only landscapes, animals and still lifes, but also erotic motifs and self-portraits are not to be found. What impressed Fuchs most was the element of strife in Daumier's work. Or would it be too daring to look for the origin of Daumier's great caricature in a question? Daumier seems to ask himself the following: "What would the bourgeois people of my time look like if one were to imagine their struggle for existence as taking place in a *palaestra*, an arena?" Daumier translated the Parisians' public and private life into the language of the *agon*. The athletic tension of the whole body, the muscular movements capture Daumier's highest enthusiasm. That is not contradicted by the fact that there is probably no one who sketched the deepest bodily relaxation as fascinatingly as Daumier. As Fuchs remarks, Daumier's representation has a deep relationship to sculpture. And thus he carries off the types which his time has to offer, these distorted caricatures of Olympic contestants, in order to exhibit them on pedestals. His studies of judges and lawyers prove particularly favorable for this kind of consideration. The elegiac humor with which Daumier likes to surround the Greek Pantheon indicates this inspiration more immediately. Perhaps this is the solution to the riddle which Daumier, the master, represented for Baudelaire: how Daumier's caricature with all its force and impact could remain so free from resentment.

Whenever Fuchs speaks of Daumier, all his energies come to life. There is no other subject matter that could draw such divinatory flashes of insight from his knowledgeability. Here the smallest impulse becomes important. A single page, so superficially done that it would be a euphemism to call it unfinished, suffices for Fuchs to give a deep insight into Daumier's creative mania. The sheet in question represents only the upper part of a head in which the only expressive parts are the nose and eyes. Insofar as the sketch limits itself to that part, insofar as it only represents the observer, it becomes an indication for Fuchs that here the painter's central interest is at play. For, he supposes, every painter begins the execution of his paintings in precisely that place in which he is compulsively most interested.[57] In Fuchs's work on the painter we find: "Innumerable of Daumier's characters are busy with the most concentrated looking, be it a looking on the world, or a contemplating of specific things or even a concentrated look into their own interior. Daumier's people practically look with the tips of their noses."[58]

Daumier turned out to be the most auspicious subject matter for Fuchs the scholar. He was also the collector's most lucky find. With just pride, Fuchs mentions that it was his own initiative and not that of the government which prompted the first collections of Daumier (and Gavarni) in Germany. In his dislike for museums he does not stand alone among the great collectors. The brothers Goncourt preceded him in this dislike and exceeded him in their violence. Public collections may be less problematical from a social point of view, and can be scientifically more useful than private ones, yet they lack the greatest possibilities of private ones. The collector's passion is his divining rod and turns him into a finder of new sources. That holds true for Fuchs, and that is why he had to feel so opposed to the spirit which dominated the museums under Wilhelm II. These museums were intent on possessing so-called showpieces. "Certainly," says Fuchs, "today's museums tend toward such a mode of collecting simply for spatial reasons. But that does not change the fact that we thus have quite fragmentary notions of the culture of the past. We see the past in its splendid festive gown and rarely encounter it in its most shabby working clothes."[59]

The great collectors distinguish themselves mostly by the originality of their choice of subject matter. There are exceptions. The Goncourts started less with objects than with the whole that had to ensure the integrity of these objects. They undertook the transfiguration of the interior just as the latter had expired. As a rule, however, collectors have been guided by the objects themselves. The humanists on the threshold of modern history are a great example of this. Their Greek acquisitions and journeys give testimony to the purposefulness with which they collected. Guided by La Bruyère, the figure of the collector was introduced, though disadvantageously, into literature with Marolles, who served as a model for Damocède. Marolles was the first to recognize the importance of graphics. His collection of 125,000 sheets forms the nucleus of the Cabinet des Estampes. The first great effort of archaeology is Count Caylus' seven-volume catalogue of his collections in the following century. Stosch's collection of gems was catalogued by Winckelmann upon commission by the collector himself. Even where the scientific conception which wanted to materialize itself in such a collection did not last for any length of time, the collection itself sometimes endured more successfully. This is true of the collections of Wallraff and Boisserée. Arising out of the romantic Nazarene theory, which viewed the art of Cologne as the heir of the old Roman art, the founders of the collection formed the basis of Cologne's museum with their German paintings of the Middle Ages. Fuchs has to be placed in this line of great and systematic collectors who were resolutely intent on a single subject matter. It is his idea to give back to the work of art its existence within the society from which it had been cut off. The work of art had been detached from society to such a degree that the place in which the collector found it had become the art market. There the work of art endured, shrunken to a commodity, and found itself equally as removed from its creators as from those who were able to understand it. The master's name is the fetish of the art market. From a historical point of view, Fuchs's greatest achievement may be his having cleared the way for art history to be freed from the fetish of the master's signature. "That is why," according to Fuchs's essay on the Tang period, "the complete anonymity of these burial gifts means that one cannot even in a single case know the name of the individual creator. This is an important proof for the fact that in all of this it is never the question of individual artistic results, but rather of the way the totality then looked upon the world and things."[60] Fuchs was one of the first to develop the specific character of mass art and thus to germinate the impulses which he had received from historical materialism.

Any study of mass art leads necessarily to the question of the technological reproduction of the work of art. "Every time has very specific techniques of reproduction which correspond to it. The techniques of reproduction always represent the respective standard of technological development and are the result of a specific need of the time. For this reason it is not astonishing that any historical upheaval which brings into power other classes than the ruling ones, regularly goes hand in hand with changes in the techniques of pictorial reproduction. This fact needs to be pointed out with particular emphasis."[61] Insights like this proved Fuchs a pioneer. In these insights he points to objects which would represent an educational gain for historical materialism were it to study them. The technological standard of the arts is one of the most important of these insights. The continued examination of this standard makes up for many a harm which comes from the vague concept of culture in the traditional history of ideas (and occasionally even in Fuchs's own work). The fact that "thousands of simple potters were capable of creating products equally daring both in regard to their technique and to their artistry as if it were nothing,"[62] rightly appears to Fuchs as the concrete verification of old Chinese art. Occasionally his technological reflections lead him to illumined *aperçus* which run ahead of his own time. There is no other way of judging his explanation of the fact that antiquity does not know any caricature. Which idealistic representation of history would not see in this a support for the classicist image of the Greeks and their "noble simplicity and quiet greatness"? And how does Fuchs explain the matter? Caricature, he says, is mass art. There cannot be any caricature without mass distribution of its products. Mass distribution means cheap distribution. However, "except for the mining of coins, antiquity has no cheap means of reproduction."[63] The surface of the coin is too small to make room for caricature. That is why antiquity did not know caricature.

Like caricature, the genre picture was mass art. This trait attached itself to the character of caricature and defamed the already doubtful conventional historiography still more. Fuchs sees the matter differently. The fact that he considers scorned and apocryphal matters indicates his real strength. And he has cleared the way to these matters as a collector all by himself, for Marxism had but shown him the beginning. For such an endeavor a passion was needed that bordered on mania. This passion has marked Fuchs's character. Whoever goes through the long line of patrons of the arts, of dealers, of admirers of paintings and experts in sculpture in Daumier's lithographs will be able to see exactly how this passion characterized Fuchs. All these characters resemble Fuchs down to his stature. They are tall and skinny figures whose eyes project fiery glances. Not without reason has it been said that Daumier conceived in these characters the descendants of those gold-diggers, necromants and misers which can be found in the paintings of the old masters.[64] As a collector, Fuchs belongs to their race. The alchemist connects his "base" desire for making gold with a complete examination of the chemicals in which planets and elements come together in images of spiritual man. Similarly, in satisfying the "base" desire of possession, Fuchs searches through an art in whose products the productive forces and the masses come together in images of historical man. Even in his late works the passionate interest can be felt with which Fuchs turned toward these images. He writes: "It is not the least of the Chinese turrets' claims to

fame that they are the product of an anonymous popular art. There is
no heroic book which gives testimony to their creators.''[65] Such a
consideration is directed toward the anonymous artists and the objects
which preserved the trace of their hands. Would this attitude not
contribute more to the humanization of mankind than the leader cult,
which, it seems, one is once again about to impose on mankind?
Whether that is the case remains, as the past taught vainly in so many
instances, always to be taught again by the future.

The Author as Producer[1]

By Walter Benjamin

This essay, written in 1937, represents one extreme of the spectrum of Benjamin's esthetic positions. It was formulated, under the strong influence of Brecht, in the context of Soviet discussions about the function and task of literature in a socialist society or socialist movement. The reader should concentrate on Benjamin's attempt to use his conceptual apparatus, developed in the context of historical research, in defense of the possibility of an entirely new political relationship of author-work-audience. Though Lukács and especially Adorno were right to point out the questionable nature of the party-political presuppositions of essays such as this one, we must emphasize Benjamin's "democratic" corrective (the insistence on community, communication and dialogue, the attack on the "aura" of the creative personality) to the elitist implications of all Hegelianizing esthetics. The differences between the Benjamin of this essay and Adorno do not preclude some overlap; the reader will notice in this context Benjamin's stress on the critically cognitive function of art (especially Brecht's) that takes the reduced, alienated man of today as its starting point. Adorno has to reply that all political, collectivist art must inevitably compromise just this starting point. What he neglects is that to Benjamin the end point, namely speaking to and listening to the mass of the alienated, was as important as the critical dissection of the conditions responsible for alienation.

> *The task is to win over the intellectuals to the working class by making them aware of the identity of their spiritual enterprises and of their conditions as producers.*
>
> *Ramon Fernandez*

You will remember how Plato, in his model state, deals with poets. He banishes them from it in the public interest. He had a high conception of the power of poetry. But he believed it harmful, superfluous—in a *perfect* community, of course. The question of the poet's right to exist has not often, since then, been posed with the same emphasis; but today it poses itself. Probably it is only seldom posed in this *form*. But it is more or less familiar to you all as the question of the autonomy of the poet: of his freedom to write whatever he pleases. You are not disposed to grant him this autonomy. You believe that tbe present social situation compels him to decide in whose service he is to place his activity. The bourgeois writer of entertainment literature does not acknowledge this choice. You prove to him that, without admitting it, he is working in the service of certain class interests. A more advanced type of writer does recognize this choice. His decision, taken on the basis of a class struggle, is to side with the proletariat. That puts an end to his autonomy. His activity is now decided by what is useful to the proletariat in the class struggle. Such writing is commonly called *tendentious*.

There you have the catchword around which has long circled a debate familiar to you. Its familiarity tells you how unfruitful it has been. For it has not advanced beyond the monotonous reiteration of arguments for and against: *on one hand*, the correct political line is demanded of the poet; *on the other*, it is justifiable to expect his work to have quality. Such a formulation is of course unsatisfactory as long as the connection between the two factors, political line and quality, has not been *perceived*. Of course, the connection can be asserted dogmatically. You can declare: a work that shows the correct political tendency need show no other quality. You can also declare: a work that exhibits the correct tendency must of necessity have every other quality.

This second formulation is not uninteresting, and further: it is correct. I make it my own. But in doing so I abstain from asserting it dogmatically. It must be *proved*. And it is in order to attempt to prove it that I now claim your attention.—This is, you will perhaps object, a very specialized, out-of-the-way theme. And how do I intend to promote the study of fascism with such a proof?—That is indeed my intention. For I hope to be able to show you that the concept of political tendency, in the summary form in which it usually occurs in the debate just mentioned, is a perfectly useless instrument of political literary criticism. I should like to show you that the tendency of a literary work can only be politically correct if it is also literarily correct. That is to say that the politically correct tendency includes a literary tendency. And I would add straight away: this literary tendency, which is implicitly or explicitly contained in every *correct* political tendency, alone constitutes the quality of the work. The correct political tendency of a work includes its literary quality *because* it includes its literary *tendency*.

This assertion—I hope I can promise you—will soon become clearer. For the moment, I should like to interject that I might have chosen a different starting point for my reflections. I started from the unfruitful debate on the relationship between tendency and quality in literature. I could have started from an even older and no less unfruitful debate: what is the relationship between form and content, particularly in political poetry? This kind of question has a bad name: rightly so. It is the textbook case of the attempt to explain literary connections with undialectical clichés. Very well. But what, then, is the dialectical approach to the same question?

The dialectical approach to this question—and here I come to my central point—has absolutely no use for such rigid, isolated things as: work, novel, book. It has to insert them into the living social context. You rightly declare that this has been done time and again among our friends. Certainly. Only it has often been done by launching at once into large, and therefore necessarily often vague, questions. Social conditions are, as we know, determined by conditions of production. And when materialist criticism approached a work, it was accustomed to ask how this work stood in relation to the social relations of production of its time. This is an important question. But also a very difficult one. Its answer is not always unambiguous. And I should like now to propose to you a more immediate question. A question that is somewhat more modest, somewhat less far-reaching, but which has, it seems to me, more chance of receiving an answer. Instead of asking: what is the attitude of a work to the relations of production of its time? does it accept them? is it reactionary—or does it aim at overthrowing them? is it revolutionary?—Instead of this question, or at any rate before this question, I should like to propose another. Rather than asking: what is the *attitude* of a work to the relations of production of its time? I should like to ask: what is its *position* in them? This question directly concerns the function the work has within the literary relations of production of its time. It is concerned, in other words, directly with the literary *technique* of works.

In the concept of technique, I have named that concept which makes literary products directly accessible to a social and therefore a materialist analysis. At the same time, the concept of technique provides the dialectical starting point from which the unfruitful antithesis of form and content can be surpassed. And furthermore, this concept of technique contains an indication of the correct determination of the relation between tendency and quality, the question raised at the outset. If, therefore, we stated earlier that the correct political tendency of a work includes its literary quality, because it includes its literary tendency, we can now formulate this more precisely by saying that this literary tendency can consist either of progress or of regression in literary technique.

You will certainly approve if I now pass on, with only an appearance of arbitrariness, to very concrete literary conditions. Russian conditions. I should like to direct your attention to Sergei Tretiakov and to the type, defined and embodied by him, of the "operating" writer. This operating writer provides the most tangible example of the functional interdependency which always and under all conditions exists between the correct political tendency and progressive literary technique. I admit only one example: I hold others in reserve. Tretiakov distinguishes the operating from the informing writer. His mission is not to report but to struggle; not to play the spectator but to intervene actively. He defines this mission by the account he gives of his own activity. When, in 1928, at the time of the total collectivization of agriculture, the slogan "Writers to the kolkhoz!" was proclaimed, Tretiakov went to the commune "Communist Lighthouse" and there, during two lengthy says, set about the following tasks: calling mass meetings; collecting funds to pay for tractors; persuading independent peasants to enter the kolkhoz; inspecting the reading rooms; creating wall newspapers and editing the kolkhoz newspaper; reporting for Moscow newspapers; introducing radio and mobile cinemas, etc. It is not surprising that the book *Commanders of the Field*, which Tretiakov wrote following these stays, is said to have had considerable influence on the further development of collective agriculture.

You may have a high regard for Tretiakov, and yet still be of the opinion that his example does not prove a great deal in this context. The tasks he performed, you will perhaps object, are those of a journalist or a propagandist; all this has little to do with literature. However, I did intentionally quote the example of Tretiakov in order to point out to you how comprehensive is the horizon within which we have to rethink our conceptions of literary forms or *genres* in view of the technical factors affecting our present situation, if we are to identify the forms of expression that channel the literary energies of the present. There were not always novels in the past, and there will not always have to be; not always tragedies, not always great epics; not always were the forms of commentary, translation, indeed, even so-called plagiarism, playthings in the margins of literature; they had a place not only in the philosophical but also in the literary writings of Arabia and China. Rhetoric has not always been a minor form, but set its stamp in antiquity on large provinces of literature. All this is to accustom you to the thought that we are in the midst of a mighty recasting of literary forms, a melting-down in which many of the opposites in which we have been accustomed to think may lose their force. Let me give an example of the unfruitfulness of such opposites and of the process of their dialectical transcendence. And we shall remain with Tretiakov. For this example is the newspaper.

"In our writing," a left-wing author writes[2], "opposites which in happier periods fertilized one another, have become insoluble antinomies. Thus science and *belles lettres*, criticism and production, education and politics, fall apart in disorder. The theatre of this literary confusion is the newspaper, its content 'subject matter,' which denies itself any other form of organization than that imposed on it by the readers' impatience. And this impatience is not only that of the politician expecting information or of the speculator on the lookout for a tip; behind it smoulders that of the man on the sidelines who believes he has the right to see his own interests expressed. The fact that nothing binds the reader more tightly to his paper than this impatient longing for daily nourishment, the publishers have long exploited by constantly opening new columns to his questions, opinions, protests. Hand in hand, therefore, with the indiscriminate assimilation of facts goes the equally indiscriminate assimilation of readers who are instantly elevated to collaborators. In this, however, a dialectic moment is concealed: the decline of writing in the bourgeois press proves to be the formula for its revival in that of Soviet Russia. For as writing gains in breadth what it loses in depth, the conventional distinction between author and public, which is upheld by the bourgeois press, begins in the Soviet press to disappear. For the reader is at all times ready to become a writer, that is, a describer, but also a prescriber. As an expert—even if not on a subject but only on the post he occupies—he gains access to authorship. Work itself has its turn to speak. And the account it gives of itself is a part of the competence needed to perform it. Literary qualification is no longer founded on specialized but rather on polytechnic education, and is thus public property. It is, in a word, the literarization of the conditions of living that masters the otherwise insoluble antinomies, and it is in the theatre of the unbridled debasement of the word—the newspaper—that its salvation is being prepared.''

I hope to have shown by this quotation that the description of the author as a producer must extend as far as the press. For by the press, at any rate by the Soviet Russian press, one recognizes that the mighty process of recasting which I spoke of earlier not only affects the conventional distinction between *genres*, between writer and poet, between scholar and popularizer, but also revises even the distinction between author and reader. Of this process the press is the decisive example, and therefore any consideration of the author as producer must include it.

It cannot, however, stop at this point. For the newspaper in Western Europe does not constitute a serviceable instrument of production in the hands of the writer. It still belongs to capital. Since on one hand the newspaper, technically speaking, represents the most important literary position, but on the other, this position is in the hands of the opposition, it is no wonder that the insight of the writer into his social conditionality, his technical means and his political task, has to grapple with the most immense difficulties. It has been one of the decisive processes of the last ten years in Germany that a considerable proportion of its productive minds, under the pressure of economic conditions, have passed through a revolutionary development in their attitudes, without being able simultaneously to rethink their own work, their relation to the means of production, their technique, in a really revolutionary way. I am speaking, as you see, of the so-called left-wing intellectuals, and will limit myself to the bourgeois Left. In Germany, the leading politico-literary movements of the last decade have emanated from this left-wing intelligentsia. I shall mention two of them, Activism and New Matter-of-Factness, to show by these examples that a political tendency, however revolutionary it may seem, has a counterrevolutionary function as long as the writer feels his solidarity with the proletariat only in his attitudes, but not as a producer.

The catchword in which the demands of Activism are summed up is "logocracy," in plain language, rule of the mind. This is apt to be translated as rule of the intellectuals. In fact, the concept of the intellectual, with its attendant spiritual values, has established itself in the camp of the left-wing intelligentsia, and dominates its political manifestos from Heinrich Mann to Döblin. It can readily be seen that this concept has been coined without any regard for the position of the intellectuals in the process of production. Hiller, the theoretician of Activism, himself means intellectuals to be understood not as "members of certain professions" but as "representatives of a certain characterological type." This characterological type naturally stands as such between the classes. It encompasses any number of private individuals without offering the slightest basis for organizing them. When Hiller formulates his denunciation of the party leaders, he concedes them a good deal; they may be "in important matters better informed . . . , have more popular appeal . . . , fight more courageously" than he, but of one thing he is sure: that they "think more defectively." Probably so, but what does that matter, since politically it is not private thinking but, as Brecht once expressed it, the art of thinking in other people's heads, that is decisive.[3] Activism attempted to replace materialistic dialectics by the notion—in class terms unquantifiable—of common sense. Its intellectuals represent at best a social group. In other words: the principle itself on which this collective is formed is reactionary; no wonder that its effect could never be revolutionary.

However, this pernicious principle of collectivization continues to operate. This could be seen three years ago when Döblin's *Wissen und Verändern (Know and Change!)* came out. As is known, this pamphlet was written in reply to a young man—Döblin calls him Herr Hocke—who had put to the famous author the question "What is to be done?" Döblin invites him to join the cause of socialism, but with reservations. Socialism, according to Döblin, is: "freedom, a spontaneous union of men, the rejection of all compulsion, indignation at injustice and coercion, humanity, tolerance, a peaceful disposition."

However this may be, on the basis of this socialism, he sets his face against the theory and practice of the radical workers' movement. "Nothing," Döblin declares, "can come out of anything that was not already in it—and from a murderously exacerbated class war justice can come, but not socialism." "You, my dear sir," thus Döblin formulates the recommendation which, for these and other reasons, he gives Herr Hocke, "cannot put into effect your agreement in principle with the struggle (of the proletariat) by joining the proletarian front. You must be content with an agitated and bitter approval of this struggle, but you also know that if you do more, an immensely important post will remain unmanned . . . : the original communistic position of human individual freedom, of the spontaneous solidarity and union of men. . . . It is this position, my dear sir, that alone falls to you." Here it is quite palpable where the conception of the "intellectual," as a type defined by his opinions, attitudes or dispositions, but not by his position in the process of production, leads. He must, as Döblin puts it, find his place *beside* the proletariat. But what kind of place is that? That of a benefactor, of an ideological patron. An impossible place. And so we return to the thesis stated at the outset: the place of the intellectual in the class struggle can be identified, or better, chosen, only on the basis of his position in the process of production.

For the transformation of the forms and instruments of production in the way desired by a progressive intelligentsia—that is, one interested in freeing the means of production and serving the class struggle—Brecht coined the term *Umfunktionierung*. He was the first to make of intellectuals the far-reaching demand: not to supply the apparatus of production without, to the utmost extent possible, changing it in accordance with socialism. "The publication of the *Versuche*," the author writes in introducing the series of writings bearing this title, "occurred at a time when certain works ought no longer to be individual experiences (have the character of works), but should rather concern the use (transformation) of certain institutes and institutions." It is not spiritual renewal, as fascists proclaim, that is desirable: technical innovations are suggested. I shall come back to these innovations. I should like to content myself here with a reference to the decisive difference between the mere supplying of a productive apparatus and its transformation. And I should like to preface my discussion of the "New Matter-of-Factness" with the proposition that to supply a productive apparatus without—to the utmost extent possible—changing it would still be a highly censurable course even if the material with which it is supplied seemed to be of a revolutionary nature. For we are faced by the fact—of which the past decade in Germany has furnished an abundance of examples—that the bourgeois apparatus of production and publication can assimilate astonishing qualities of revolutionary themes, indeed, can propagate them without calling its own existence, and the existence of the class which owns it, seriously into question. This remains true at least as long as it is supplied by hack writers, even though they be revolutionary hacks. I define the hack writer as the man who abstains in principle from alienating the productive apparatus from the ruling class by improving it in ways serving the interests of socialism. And I further maintain that a considerable proportion of so-called left-wing literature possessed no other social function than to wring from the political situation a continuous stream of novel effects for the entertainment of the public. This brings me to the New Matter-of-Factness. Its stock-in-trade was reportage. Let us ask ourselves to whom this technique was useful.

For the sake of clarity I shall place its photographic form in the foreground. What is true of this can be applied to the literary form. Both owe the extraordinary increase in their popularity to the technology of publication: the radio and the illustrated press. Let us think back to Dadaism. The revolutionary strength of Dadaism consisted in testing art for its authenticity. Still lifes put together from tickets, spools of thread, cigarette butts, were linked with artistic elements. They put the whole thing in a frame. And they thereby show the public: Look, your picture frame ruptures the age; the tiniest authentic fragment of daily life says more than paintings. Just as the bloody finger print of a murderer on a page of a book says more than the text. Much of this revolutionary content has sought survival in photomontage. You need only think of the work of John Heartfield, whose technique made the book cover into a political instrument. But now follow the path of photography further. What do you see? It becomes ever more *nuancé*, ever more modern, and the result is that it can no longer photograph a tenement block or a refuse heap without transfiguring it. It goes without saying that it is unable to say anything of a power station or a cable factory other than this: what a beautiful world! "A Beautiful World"—that is a title of the well-known picture anthology by Renger-Patsch, in which we see New Matter-of-Fact photography at its peak. For it has succeeded in making even abject poverty, by recording it in a fashionably perfected manner, into an object of enjoyment. For if it is an economic function of photography to restore to mass consumption, by fashionable adaptation, subjects that had earlier withdrawn themselves from it—springtime, famous people, foreign countries—it is one of its political functions to renew from within—in other words: fashionably—the world as it is.

Here we have a flagrant example of what it means to supply a productive apparatus without changing it. To change it would have meant to overthrow another of the barriers, to transcend another of the antitheses, which fetter the production of intellectuals. In this case, the barrier between writing and image. What we require of the photographer is the ability to give his picture that caption which wrenches it from modish commerce and gives it revolutionary use-value. But we shall make this demand most emphatically when we—the writers—take up photography. Here, too, therefore, technical progress is for the author as producer the foundation of his political progress. In other words: only by transcending the specialization in the process of production which, in the bourgeois view, constitutes its order, is this production made politically valuable; and the limits imposed by specialization must be breached jointly by both the productive forces that they were set up to divide. The author as producer discovers—in discovering his solidarity with the proletariat—that simultaneity with certain other producers who earlier seemed scarcely to concern him. I have spoken of the photographer; I shall very briefly insert a word on the musician that we have from Eisler: "In the development of music, too, both in production and in reproduction, we must learn to perceive an ever-increasing process of rationalization. . . . The gramophone record, the sound film, jukeboxes can purvey top quality music- . . . canned as a commodity. The consequence of this process of rationalization is that musical reproduction is consigned to ever diminishing, but also ever more highly qualified, groups of specialists. The crisis of the commercial concert is the crisis of an antiquated form of production made obsolete by new technical inventions." The task therefore consisted of an *Umfunktionierung* of the form of the concert that had to fulfil two conditions: to eliminate the antithesis first between performers and listeners and second between technique and content. On this Eisler makes the following illuminating observation: "One must beware of overestimating orchestral music and considering it the only high art. Music without words gained its great importance and its full extent only under capitalism." This means that the task of changing the concert is impossible without the collaboration of the word. It alone can effect the transformation, as Eisler formulates it, of a concert into a political meeting. But that such a transformation does indeed represent a peak of musical and literary technique, Brecht and Eisler prove with the didactic play *The Measures Taken.*

If you look back from this vantage point on the recasting of literary forms that I spoke of earlier, you can see how photography and music, and whatever else occurs to you, are entering the growing molten mass from which the new forms are cast. You find it confirmed that only the literarization of all the conditions of life provides a correct understanding of the extent of this melting-down process, just as the state of the class struggle determines the temperature at which— more or less perfectly—it is accomplished.

I spoke of the procedure of a certain modish photography whereby poverty is made an object of consumption. In turning to New Matter-of-Factness as a literary movement, I must take a step further and say that it has made the *struggle against poverty* an object of consumption. The political importance of the movement was indeed exhausted in many cases by the conversion of revolutionary reflexes, insofar as they occurred in the bourgeoisie, into objects of amusement which found their way without difficulty into the big-city cabaret business. The transformation of the political struggle from a compulsion to decide into an object of contemplative enjoyment, from a means of production into a consumer article, is the defining characteristic of this literature. A perceptive critic has explained this, using the example of Erich Kästner, as follows: "With the workers' movement this left-wing radical intelligentsia has nothing in common. It is rather, as a phenomenon of bourgeois decomposition, a counterpart of the feudalistic disguise which the Second Empire admired in the reserve officer. The radical-left publicists of the stamp of Kästner, Mehring or Tucholsky are the proletarian camouflage of decayed bourgeois strata. Their function is to produce, from the political standpoint, not parties but cliques; from the literary standpoint, not schools but fashions; from the economic standpoint, not producers but agents. Agents or hacks who make a great display of their poverty, and a banquet of yawning emptiness. One could not be more totally accommodated in an uncozy situation."

This school, I said, made a great display of its poverty. It thereby shirked the most urgent task of the present-day writer: to recognize how poor he is and how poor he has to be in order to begin again from the beginning. For that is what is involved. The Soviet state will not, it is true, banish the poet like Plato, but it will—and this is why I recalled the Platonic state at the outset—assign him tasks which do not permit

him to display in new masterpieces the long-since counterfeit wealth
of creative personality. To expect a renewal in terms of such personalities and such works is a privilege of fascism, which gives rise to
such scatterbrained formulations as that with which Günter Gründel in
his *Mission of the Young Generation* rounds off the section on
literature: "We cannot better conclude this . . . survey and prognosis
than with the observation that the *Wilhelm Meister* and the *Green
Henry* of our generation have not yet been written." Nothing will be
farther from the author who has reflected deeply on the conditions of
present-day production than to expect, or desire, such works. His
work will never be merely work on products but always, at the same
time, on the means of production. In other words: his products must
have, over and above their character as works, an organizing function,
and in no way must their organizational usefulness be confined to their
value as propaganda. Their political tendency alone is not enough.
The excellent Lichtenberg has said: "A man's opinions are not what
matters, but the kind of man these opinions make of him." Now it is
true that opinions matter greatly, but the best are of no use if they make
nothing useful out of those who have them. The best political tendency
is wrong if it does not demonstrate the attitude with which it is to be
followed. And this attitude the writer can only demonstrate in his
particular activity: that is in writing. A political tendency is the
necessary, never the sufficient condition of the organizing function of
a work. This further requires a directing, instructing stance on the part
of the writer. And today this is to be demanded more than ever before.
An author who teaches writers nothing, teaches no one. What matters
therefore is the exemplary character of production, which is able first
to induce other producers to produce, and second to put an improved
apparatus at their disposal. And this apparatus is better the more
consumers it is able to turn into producers, that is, readers or spectators into collaborators. We already possess such an example, to
which, however, I can only allude here. It is the epic theater of Brecht.

Tragedies and operas are constantly being written that apparently
have a well-tried theatrical apparatus at their disposal, while in reality
they do nothing but supply one that is derelict. "The lack of clarity
about their situation that prevails among musicians, writers and critics," says Brecht, "has immense consequences that are far too little
considered. For, thinking that they are in possession of an apparatus
which in reality possesses them, they defend an apparatus over which
they no longer have any control and which is no longer, as they still
believe, a means for the producers, but has become a means against

the producers.'' This theatre, with its complicated machinery, its gigantic supporting staff, its sophisticated effects, has become a means against the producers not least in seeking to enlist the producers in the hopeless competitive struggle in which film and radio have enmeshed it. This theatre—whether in its educating or its entertaining role; both are complementary—is that of a sated class for which everything it touches becomes a stimulant. Its position is lost. Not so that of a theatre which, instead of competing with newer instruments of publication, seeks to use and learn from them, in short, to enter into debate with them. This debate the epic theatre has made its own affair. It is, measured by the present state of development of film and radio, the contemporary form.

For the sake of this debate Brecht fell back on the most primitive elements of the theatre. He contented himself, broadly, with a podium. He dispensed with wide-ranging plots. He thus succeeded in changing the functional connection between stage and public, text and performance, director and actor. Epic theatre, he declared, had to portray situations rather than to develop plots. It obtains such situations, as we shall see presently, by interrupting the plot. I remind you here of the songs, which have their chief function in interrupting the action. Here—in the principle of interruption—epic theatre, as you see, takes up a procedure that has become familiar to you in recent years from film and radio, press and photography. I am speaking of the procedure of montage: the superimposed element disrupts the context in which it is inserted. But that this procedure has here a special, perhaps indeed a perfect right, allow me briefly to indicate. The interruption of action, on account of which Brecht described his theatre as *epic*, constantly counteracts an illusion in the audience. For such illusion is a hindrance to a theatre that proposes to make use of elements of reality in experimental rearrangements. But it is at the end, not the beginning, of the experiment that the situation appears. A situation which, in this or that form, is always ours. It is not brought home to the spectator but distanced from him. He recognizes it as the real situation, not with satisfaction, as in the theatre of naturalism, but with astonishment. Epic theatre, therefore, does not reproduce situations, rather it discovers them. This discovery is accomplished by means of the interruption of sequences. Only interruption does not have here the character of a stimulant but of an organizing function. It arrests the action in its course, and thereby compels the listener to adopt an attitude vis-à-vis the process, the actor vis-à-vis his role. I should like to show you by an example how Brecht's discovery and use of the *gestus* is nothing other than the restoration of the method of montage decisive in radio and film, from an often merely modish procedure to a human event. Imagine a family scene: the wife is just about to grab a bronze sculpture to throw it at her daughter; the father is opening the window to call for help. At this moment a stranger enters. The process is interrupted; what appears in its place is the situation on which the stranger's eyes now fall: agitated faces, open window, disordered furniture. There are eyes, however, before which the more usual scenes of present-day existence do not look very different. The eyes of the epic dramatist.

To the dramatic total art work he opposes the dramatic laboratory. He makes use in a new way of the great ancient opportunity of the theatre—to expose what is present. At the center of his experiment is man. Present-day man; a reduced man, therefore, chilled in a chilly environment. Since, however, this is the only one we have, it is in our interest to know him. He is subjected to tests, examinations. What emerges is this: events are alterable not at their climaxes, not by virtue and resolution, but only in their strictly habitual course, by reason and practice. To construct from the smallest elements of behavior what in Aristotelian dramaturgy is called "action," is the purpose of epic theatre. Its means are therefore more modest than those of traditional theatre; its aims likewise. It is less concerned with filling the public with feelings, even seditious ones, than with alienating it in an enduring manner, through thinking, from the conditions in which it lives. It may be noted by the way that there is no better start for thinking than laughter. And, in particular, convulsion of the diaphragm usually provides better opportunities for thought than that of the soul. Epic theatre is lavish only in occasions for laughter.

It has perhaps struck you that the train of thought that is about to be concluded presents to the writer only one demand, the demand *to think*, to reflect on his position in the process of production. We may depend on it: this reflection leads, sooner or later, for the writers *who matter*, that is, for the best technicians in thier subject, to observations which provide the most factual foundation for their solidarity with the proletariat. I should like to conclude by adducing a topical illustration in the form of a small extract from a journal published here, *Commune*. *Commune* circulated a questionnaire: "For whom do you write?" I quote from the reply of René Maublanc and from the comment added by Aragon. "Unquestionably," says Maublanc, "I write almost exclusively for a bourgeois public. First, because I am obliged to [here Maublanc refers to his professional duties as a

grammar school teacher] and second, because I have bourgeois origins and a bourgeois education and come from a bourgeois *milieu*, and
so am naturally inclined to address myself to the class to which I
belong, that I know and understand best. This does not mean, however, that I write in order to please or support it. On one hand I am
convinced that the proletarian revolution is necessary and desirable,
on the other that it will be the more rapid, easy, successful, and the less
bloody, the weaker the opposition of the bourgeoisie . . . the proletariat today needs allies from the camp of the bourgeoisie, exactly as
in the eighteenth century the bourgeoisie needed allies from the feudal
camp. I wish to be among those allies."

On this Aragon comments: "Our comrade here touches on a state
of affairs that affects a large number of present-day writers. Not all
have the courage to look it in the face . . . those who see their own
situation as clearly as René Maublanc are few. But precisely from
them more must be required . . . it is not enough to weaken the
bourgeoisie from within, it is necessary to fight them *with* the proletariat . . . René Maublanc and many of our friends among the writers
who are still hesitating are faced by the example of the Soviet Russian
writers who came from the Russian bourgeoisie and nevertheless
became pioneers of the building of socialism."

Thus Aragon. But how did they become pioneers? Certainly not
without very bitter struggles, extremely difficult debates. The considerations I have put before you are an attempt to draw some conclusions
from these struggles. They are based on the concept to which the
debate on the attitude of the Russian intellectuals owes its decisive
clarification: the concept of the specialist. The solidarity of the
specialist with the proletariat—herein lies the beginning of this clarification—can only be a mediated one. The Activists and the representatives of New Matter-of-Factness could gesticulate as they pleased:
they could not do away with the fact that even the proletarianization of
an intellectual hardly ever makes a proletarian. Why? Because the
bourgeois class gave him, in the form of education, a means of
production which, owing to educational privilege, makes him feel
solidarity with it, and still more it with him. It was thereby entirely
correct when Aragon, in another connection, declared: "The revolutionary intellectual appears first and foremost as the betrayer of his
class of origin." This betrayal consists, in the case of the writer, in
conduct which turns him, from a supplier of the productive apparatus,
into an engineer who sees it as his task to adapt this apparatus to the
purposes of the proletarian revolution. This is a mediating activity, yet

it frees the intellectual from that purely destructive task to which Maublanc and many of his comrades believe it necessary to confine him. Does he succeed in promoting the socialization of the intellectual means of production? Does he see ways of himself organizing the intellectual workers in the production process? Has he proposals for the *Umfunktionierung* of the novel, the drama, the poem? The more completely he can orient his activity towards this task, the more correct will be the political tendency, and necessarily also the higher the technical quality, of his work. And on the other hand: the more exactly he is thus informed on his position in the process of production, the less it will occur to him to lay claim to "spiritual" qualities. The spirit that holds forth in the name of fascism *must* disappear. The spirit which, in opposing it, trusts in its own miraculous powers, *will* disappear. For the revolutionary struggle is not between capitalism and spirit but between capitalism and the proletariat.

On the Fetish-Character in Music and the Regression of Listening

By Theodor W. Adorno

Originally published in Zeitschrift für Sozialforschung *Vol. VII (1938), this essay is still one of the most impressive examples of a sociology of art. In our context, we should stress 1) Adorno's almost explicit polemic against the thesis of Benjamin's "Work of Art in the Age of its Mechanical Reproducibility"; 2) his striking utilization of Lukács's concept of reification to indicate the logic of the culture industry; and finally 3) Adorno's own theory of structural listening and the decreasing chances of "adequate" esthetic response in the age of the decline of the individual.*

Complaints about the decline of musical taste begin only a little later than mankind's twofold discovery, on the threshold of historical time, that music represents at once the immediate manifestation of impulse and the locus of its taming. It stirs up the dance of the Maenads and sounds from Pan's bewitching flute, but it also rings out from the Orphic lyre, around which the visions of violence range themselves, pacified. Whenever their peace seems to be disturbed by bacchantic agitation, there is talk of the decline of taste. But if the disciplining function of music has been handed down since Greek philosophy as a major good, then certainly the pressure to be permitted to obey musically, as elsewhere, is today more general than ever. Just as the current musical consciousness of the masses can scarcely be called Dionysian, so its latest changes have nothing to do with taste. The concept of taste is itself outmoded. Responsible art adjusts itself to criteria which approximate judgments: the harmonious and the inharmonious, the correct and the incorrect. But otherwise, no more choices are made; the question is no longer put, and no one demands the subjective justification of the conventions. The very existence of the subject who could verify such taste has become as questionable as has, at the opposite pole, the right to a freedom of choice which empirically, in any case, no one any longer exercises. If one seeks to find out who "likes" a commercial piece, one cannot avoid the suspicion that liking and disliking are inappropriate to the situation, even if the person questioned clothes his reactions in those words. The familiarity of the piece is a surrogate for the quality ascribed to it. To like it is almost the same thing as to recognize it. An approach in terms of value judgments has become a fiction for the person who finds himself hemmed in by standardized musical goods. He can neither escape impotence nor decide between the offerings where everything is so completely identical that preference in fact depends merely on biographical details or on the situation in which things are heard. The categories of autonomously oriented art have no applicability to the contemporary reception of music; not even for that of the serious music, domesticated under the barbarous name of classical so as to enable one to turn away from it again in comfort. If it is objected that specifically light music and everything intended for consumption have in any case never been experienced in terms of those categories, that must certainly be conceded. Nevertheless, such music is also affected by the change in that the entertainment, the pleasure, the enjoyment it promises, is given only to be simultaneously denied. In one of his essays, Aldous Huxley has raised the question of who, in a place of amusement, is really being amused. With the same justice, it can be asked whom music for entertainment still entertains. Rather, it seems to complement the reduction of people to silence, the dying out of speech as expression, the inability to communicate at all. It inhabits the pockets of silence that develop between people molded by anxiety, work and undemanding docility. Everywhere it takes over, unnoticed, the deadly sad role that fell to it in the time and the specific situation of the silent films. It is perceived purely as background. If nobody can any longer speak, then certainly nobody can any longer listen. An American specialist in radio advertising, who indeed prefers to make use of the musical medium, has expressed skepticism as to the value of this advertising, because people have learned to deny their attention to what they are hearing even while listening to it. His observation is questionable with respect to the advertising value of music. But it tends to be right in terms of the reception of the music itself.

In the conventional complaints about declining taste, certain motifs constantly recur. There is no lack of pouting and sentimental comments assessing the current musical condition of the masses as one of "degeneration." The most tenacious of these motifs is that of sensuality, which allegedly enfeebles and incapacitates heroic behavior. This complaint can already be found in Book III of Plato's *Republic* in which he bans "the harmonies expressive of sorrow" as well as the "soft" harmonies "suitable for drinking," without its being clear to this day why the philosopher ascribes these characteristics to the mixed Lydian, Lydian, bass Lydian and Ionian modes. In the Platonic state, the major of later Western music, which corresponds to the Ionian, would have been tabooed. The flute and the "panharmonic" stringed instruments also fall under the ban. The only modes to be left are "warlike, to sound the note or accent which a brave man utters in the hour of danger and stern resolve, or when he faces injury, defeat or death, or any other misfortune, with the same steadfast endurance." Plato's *Republic* is not the utopia it is called by the official history of philosophy. It disciplines its citizens in terms of its existence and will to exist even in music, where the distinction made between soft and strong modes was by Plato's time already little more than a residue of the mustiest superstition. The Platonic irony reveals itself mischievously in jeering at the flute-player Marsyas, flayed by the sober-sided Apollo. Plato's ethical-musical program bears the character of an Attic purge in Spartan style. Other perennial themes of musical sermonizing are on the same level. Among the most prominent of these are the charge of superficiality and that of a "cult of personality." What is attacked is chiefly progress: social, essentially the specifically esthetic. Intertwined with the forbidden allurements are sensual gaiety and differentiating consciousness. The predominance of the person over collective compulsion in music marks the moment of subjective freedom which breaks through in later phases, while the profanation which frees it from its magic circle appears as superficiality. Thus, the lamented moments have entered into the great music of the West: sensory stimulation as the gate of entry into the harmonic and eventually the coloristic dimensions; the unbridled person as the bearer of expression and of the humanization of music itself; "superficiality" as a critique of the mute objectivity of forms, in the sense of Haydn's choice of the "gallant" in preference to the learned. Haydn's choice indeed, and not the recklessness of a singer with a golden throat or an instrumentalist of lip-smacking euphony. For those moments entered into great music and were transformed in it; but great music did not dissolve into them. In the multiplicity of stimulus and expression, its greatness is shown as a force for synthesis. Not only does the musical synthesis preserve the unity of appearance and protect it from falling apart into diffuse culinary moments, but in such unity, in the relation of particular moments to an evolving whole, there is also preserved the image of a social condition in which above those particular moments of happiness would be more than mere appearance. Until the end of prehistory, the musical balance between partial stimulus and totality, between expression and synthesis, between the surface and the underlying, remains as unstable as the moments of balance between supply and demand in the capitalist economy. *The Magic Flute*, in which the utopia of the Enlightenment and the pleasure of a light opera comic song precisely coincide, is a moment by itself. After *The Magic Flute* it was never again possible to force serious and light music together.

But what are emancipated from formal law are no longer the productive impulses which rebelled against conventions. Impulse, subjectivity and profanation, the old adversaries of materialistic alienation, now succumb to it. In capitalist times, the traditional anti-mythological ferments of music conspire against freedom, as whose allies they were once proscribed. The representatives of the opposition to the authoritarian schema become witnesses to the authority of commercial success. The delight in the moment and the gay facade becomes an excuse for absolving the listener from the thought of the whole, whose claim is comprised in proper listening. The listener is converted, along his line of least resistance, into the acquiescent purchaser. No longer do the partial moments serve as a critique of that whole; instead, they suspend the critique which the successful esthetic totality exerts against the flawed one of society. The unitary synthesis is sacrificed to them; they no longer produce their own in place of the reified one, but show themselves complaisant to it. The isolated moments of enjoyment prove incompatible with the immanent constitution of the work of art, and whatever in the work goes beyond them to an essential perception is sacrificed to them. They are not bad in themselves but in their diversionary function. In the service of success they renounce that insubordinate character which was theirs. They conspire to come to terms with everything which the isolated moment can offer to an isolated individual who long ago ceased to be one. In isolation, the charms become dulled and furnish models of the familiar. Whoever devotes himself to them is as malicious as the Greek thinkers once were toward oriental sensuality. The seductive power of the charm survives only where the forces of denial are strongest: in the dissonance which rejects belief in the illusion of the existing harmony. The concept of the ascetic is itself dialectical in music. If asceticism once struck down the claims of the esthetic in a reactionary way, it has today become the sign of advanced art: not, to be sure, by an archaicizing parsimony of means in which deficiency and poverty are manifested, but by the strict exclusion of all culinary delights which seek to be consumed immediately for their own sake, as if in art the sensory were not the bearer of something intellectual which only shows itself in the whole rather than in isolated topical moments. Art records negatively just that possibility of happiness which the only partially positive anticipation of happiness ruinously confronts today. All "light" and pleasant art has become illusory and mendacious. What makes its appearance esthetically in the pleasure categories can no longer give pleasure, and the promise of happiness, once the definition of art, can no longer be found except where the mask has been torn from the countenance of false happiness. Enjoyment still retains a place only in the immediate bodily presence. Where it requires an esthetic appearance, it is illusory by esthetic standards and likewise cheats the pleasure-seeker out of itself. Only where its appearance is lacking is the faith in its possibility maintained.

The new phase of the musical consciousness of the masses is defined by displeasure in pleasure. It resembles the reaction to sport or advertising. The words "enjoyment of art" sound funny. If in nothing else, Schönberg's music resembles popular songs in refusing to be enjoyed. Whoever still delights in the beautiful passages of a Schubert quartet or even in the provocatively healthy fare of a Handel concerto grosso, ranks as a would-be guardian of culture among the butterfly collectors. What condemns him as an epicure is not perhaps "new." The power of the street ballad, the catchy tune and all the swarming forms of the banal has made itself felt since the beginning of the bourgeois era. Formerly, it attacked the cultural privilege of the ruling class. But today, when that power of the banal extends over the entire society, its function has changed. This change of function affects all music, not only light music, in whose realm it could comfortably enough be made innocuous, The diverse spheres of music must be thought of together. Their static separation, which certain caretakers of culture have ardently sought—the totalitarian radio was assigned to the task, on the one hand, of providing good entertainment and diversion, and on the other, of fostering the so-called cultural goods, as if there could still be good entertainment and as if the cultural goods were not, by their administration, transformed into evils—the neat parcelling out of music's social field of force is illusionary.

Just as the history of serious music since Mozart as a flight from the banal reflects in reverse the outlines of light music, so today, in its key representatives, it gives an account of the ominous experiences which appear even in the unsuspecting innocence of light music. It would be just as easy to go in the other direction and conceal the break between the two spheres, assuming a continuum which permits a progressive education leading safely from commercial jazz and hit songs to cultural commodities. Cynical barbarism is no better than cultural dishonesty. What it accomplishes by disillusion on the higher level, it balances by the ideologies of primitivism and return to nature, with which it glorifies the musical underworld: an underworld which has long since ceased to assist the opposition of those excluded from culture to find expression, and now only lives on what is handed down to it from above.

The illusion of a social preference for light music as against serious is based on that passivity of the masses which makes the consumption of light music contradict the objective interest of those who consume it. It is claimed that they actually like light music and listen to the higher type only for reasons of social prestige, when acquaintance with the text of a single hit song suffices to reveal the sole function this object of honest approbation can perform. The unity of the two spheres of music is thus that of an unresolved contradiction. They do not hang together in such a way that the lower could serve as a sort of popular introduction to the higher, or the the higher could renew its lost collective strength by borrowing from the lower. The whole can not be put together by adding the separated halves, but in both there appear, however distantly, the changes of the whole, which only moves in contradiction. If the flight from the banal becomes definitive, if the marketability of the serious product shrinks to nothing, in consequence of its objective demands, then on the lower level the effect of the standardization of successes means it is no longer possible to succeed in an old style, but only in imitation as such. Between incomprehensibility and inescapability, there is no third way; the situation has polarized itself into extremes which actually meet. There is no room between them for the "individual." The latter's claims, wherever they still occur, are illusory, being copied

from the standards. The liquidation of the individual is the real
signature of the new musical situation.

If the two spheres of music are stirred up in the unity of their
contradiction, the demarcation line between them varies. The advanced product has renounced consumption. The rest of serious music
is delivered over to consumption for the price of its wages. It succumbs to commodity listening. The differences in the reception of
official "classical" music and light music no longer have any real
significance. They are only still manipulated for reasons of marketability. The hit song enthusiast must be reassured that his idols are not
too elevated for him, just as the visitor to philharmonic concerts is
confirmed in his status. The more industriously the trade erects wire
fences between the musical provinces, the greater the suspicion that
without these, the inhabitants could all too easily come to an understanding. Toscanini, like a second-rate orchestra leader, is called
Maestro, if half ironically, and a hit song, "Music, maestro, please,"
had its success immediately after Toscanini was promoted to Marshal
of the Air with the aid of the radio.

The world of that musical life, the composition business which
extends peacefully from Irving Berlin and Walter Donaldson—"the
world's best composer"—by way of Gershwin, Sibelius and
Tchaikovsky to Schubert's B Minor Symphony, labeled *The Unfinished*, is one of fetishes. The star principle has become totalitarian.
The reactions of the listeners appear to have no relation to the playing
of the music. They have reference, rather, to the cumulative success
which, for its part, cannot be thought of unalienated by the past
spontaneities of listeners, but instead dates back to the command of
publishers, sound film magnates and rulers of radio. Famous people
are not the only stars. Works begin to take on the same role. A
pantheon of best-sellers builds up. The programs shrink, and the
shrinking process not only removes the moderately good, but the
accepted classics themselves undergo a selection that has nothing to
do with quality. In America, Beethoven's Fourth Symphony is among
the rarities. This selection reproduces itself in a fatal circle: the most
familiar is the most successful and is therefore played again and again
and made still more familiar. The choice of the standard works is itself
in terms of their "effectiveness" for programmatic fascination, in
terms of the categories of success as determined by light music or
permitted by the star conductors. The climaxes of Beethoven's
Seventh Symphony are placed on the same level as the unspeakable
horn melody from the slow movement of Tchaikovsky's Fifth.

Melody comes to mean eight-beat symmetrical treble melody. This is catalogued as the composer's "idea" which one thinks he can put in his pocket and take home, just as it is ascribed to the composer as his basic property. The concept of the idea is far from appropriate to established classical music. Its thematic material, mostly dissected triads, does not at all belong to the author in the same specific sense as in a romantic song. Beethoven's greatness shows itself in the complete subordination of the accidentally private melodic elements to the form as a whole. This does not prevent all music, even Bach, who borrowed one of the most important themes of *The Well-Tempered Clavier*, from being examined in terms of the category of ideas, with musical larceny being hunted down with all the zeal of the belief in property, so that finally one music commentator could pin his success to the title of tune detective.

At its most passionate, musical fetishism takes possession of the public valuation of singing voices. Their sensuous magic is traditional as is the close relation between success and the person endowed with "material." But today it is forgotten that it is material. For musical vulgar materialists, it is synonymous to have a voice and to be a singer. In earlier epochs, technical virtuosity, at least, was demanded of singing stars, the castrati and prima donnas. Today, the material as such, destitute of any function, is celebrated. One need not even ask about capacity for musical performance. Even mechanical control of the instrument is no longer really expected. To legitimate the fame of its owner, a voice need only be especially voluminous or especially high. If one dares even in conversation to question the decisive importance of the voice and to assert that it is just as possible to make beautiful music with a moderately good voice as it is on a moderately good piano, one will immediately find oneself faced with a situation of hostility and aversion whose emotional roots go far deeper than the occasion. Voices are holy properties like a national trademark. As if the voices wanted to revenge themselves for this, they begin to lose the sensuous magic in whose name they are merchandised. Most of them sound like imitations of those who have made it, even when they themselves have made it. All this reaches a climax of absurdity in the cult of the master violins. One promptly goes into raptures at the well-announced sound of a Stradivarius or Amati, which only the ear of a specialist can tell from that of a good modern violin, forgetting in the process to listen to the composition and the execution, from which there is still something to be had. The more the modern technique of the violin bow progresses, the more it seems that the old instruments are treasured. If the moments of sensual pleasure in the idea, the voice, the instrument are made into fetishes and torn away from any functions which could give them meaning, they meet a response equally isolated, equally far from the meaning of the whole, and equally determined by success in the blind and irrational emotions which form the relationship to music into which those with no relationship enter. But these are the same relations as exist between the consumers of hit songs and the hit songs. Their only relation is to the completely alien, and the alien, as if cut off from the consciousness of the masses by a dense screen, is what seeks to speak for the silent. Where they react at all, it no longer makes any difference whether it is to Beethoven's Seventh Symphony or to a bikini.

The concept of musical fetishism cannot be psychologically derived. That "values" are consumed and draw feelings to themselves, without their specific qualities being reached by the consciousness of the consumer, is a later expression of their commodity character. For all contemporary musical life is dominated by the commodity form; the last pre-capitalist residues have been eliminated. Music, with all the attributes of the ethereal and sublime which are generously accorded it, serves in America today as an advertisement for commodities which one must acquire in order to be able to hear music. If the advertising function is carefully dimmed in the case of serious music, it always breaks through in the case of light music. The whole jazz business, with its free distribution of scores to bands, has abandoned the idea that actual performance promotes the sale of piano scores and phonograph records. Countless hit song texts praise the hit songs themselves, repeating their titles in capital letters. What makes its appearance, like an idol, out of such masses of type is the exchange-value in which the quantum of possible enjoyment has disappeared. Marx defines the fetish character of the commodity as the veneration of the thing made by oneself which, as exchange-value, simultaneously alienates itself from producer to consumer—"human beings." "A commodity is therefore a mysterious thing, simply because in it the social character of men's labor appears to them as an objective character stamped upon the product of that labor; because the relation of the producers to the sum total of their own labor is presented to them as a social relation, existing not between themselves, but between the products of their labor." This is the real secret of success. It is the mere reflection of what one pays in the market for the product. The consumer is really worshipping the money that he himself has paid for the ticket to the Toscanini concert. He has literally "made" the success which he reifies and accepts as an objective criterion, without recognizing himself in it. But he has not "made" it by liking the concert, but rather by buying the ticket. To be sure, exchange-value exerts its power in a special way in the realm of cultural goods. For in the world of commodities this realm appears to be exempted from the power of exchange, to be in an immediate relationship with the goods, and it is this appearance in turn which alone gives cultural goods their exchange-value. But they nevertheless simultaneously fall completely into the world of commodities, are produced for the market, and are aimed at the market. The appearance of immediacy is as strong as the compulsion of exchange-value is inexorable. The social compact harmonizes the contradiction. The appearance of immediacy takes possession of the mediated, exchange-value itself. If the commodity in general combines exchange-value and use-value, then the pure use-value, whose illusion the cultural goods must preserve in completely capitalist society, must be replaced by pure exchange-value, which precisely in its capacity as exchange-value deceptively takes over the function of use-value. The specific fetish character of music lies in this *quid pro quo*. The feelings which go to the exchange value create the appearance of immediacy at the same time as the absence of a relation to the object belies it. It has its basis in the abstract character of exchange-value. Every "psychological" aspect, every *ersatz* satisfaction, depends on such social substitution.

The change in the function of music involves the basic conditions of the relation between art and society. The more inexorably the principle of exchange-value destroys use-values for human beings, the more deeply does exchange-value disguise itself as the object of enjoyment. It has been asked what the cement is which still holds the world of commodities together. The answer is that this transfer of the use-value of consumption goods to their exchange-value contributes to a general order in which eventually every pleasure which emancipates itself from exchange-value takes on subversive features. The appearance of exchange-value in commodities has taken on a specific cohesive function. The woman who has money with which to buy is intoxicated by the act of buying. In American conventional speech, having a good time means being present at the enjoyment of others, which in its turn has as its only content being present. The auto religion makes all men brothers in the sacramental moment with the words: "That is a Rolls Royce," and in moments of intimacy, women attach greater importance to the hairdressers and cosmeticians than to the situation for the sake of which the hairdressers and cosmeticians are employed. The relation to the irrelevant dutifully manifests its social essence. The couple out driving who spend their time identifying every passing car and being happy if they recognize the trademarks speeding by, the girl whose satisfaction consists solely in the fact that she and her boyfriend "look good," the expertise of the jazz enthusiast who legitimizes himself by having knowledge about what is in any case inescapable: all this operates according to the same command. Before the theological caprices of commodities, the consumers become temple slaves. Those who sacrifice themselves nowhere else can do so here, and here they are fully betrayed.

In the commodity fetishists of the new model, in the "sadomasochistic character," in those receptive to today's mass art, the same thing shows itself in many ways. The masochistic mass culture is the necessary manifestation of almighty production itself. When the feelings seize on exchange-value it is no mystical transubstantiation. It corresponds to the behavior of the prisoner who loves his cell because he has been left nothing else to love. The sacrifice of individuality, which accommodates itself to the regularity of the successful, the doing of what everybody does, follows from the basic fact that in broad areas the same thing is offered to everybody by the standardized production of consumption goods. But the commercial necessity of concealing this identity leads to the manipulation of taste and the official culture's pretense of individualism, which necessarily increases in proportion to the liquidation of the individual. Even in the realm of the superstructure, the appearance is not merely the concealment of the essence, but proceeds of necessity from the essence itself. The identical character of the goods which everyone must buy hides itself behind the rigor of the universally compulsory style. The fiction of the relation between supply and demand survives in the fictitiously individual nuances.

If the value of taste in the present situation is questioned, it is necessary to understand what taste is composed of in this situation. Acquiescence is rationalized as modesty, opposition to caprice and anarchy; musical analysis has today decayed as fundamentally as musical charm, and has its parody in the stubborn counting of beats. The picture is completed by accidental differentiation within the strict confines of the prescribed. But if the liquidated individual really makes the complete superficiality of the conventions passionately his own, then the golden age of taste has dawned at the very moment in which taste no longer exists. The works which are the basis of the fetishization and become cultural goods experience constitutional changes as a result. They become vulgarized. Irrelevant consumption destroys them. Not merely do the few things played again and again wear out, like the Sistine Madonna in the bedroom, but reification affects their internal structure. They are transformed into a conglomeration of irruptions which are impressed on the listeners by climax and repetition, while the organization of the whole makes no impression whatsoever.

The memorability of disconnected parts, thanks to climaxes and repetitions, has a precursor in great music itself, in the technique of late romantic compositions, especially those of Wagner. The more reified the music, the more romantic it sounds to alienated ears. Just in this way it becomes "property." A Beethoven symphony as a whole, spontaneously experienced, can never be appropriated. The man who in the subway triumphantly whistles loudly the theme of the finale of Brahms' First is already primarily involved with its debris. But since the disintegration of the fetishes puts these themselves in danger and virtually assimilates them to hit songs, it produces a counter tendency in order to preserve their fetish character. If the romanticizing of particulars eats away the body of the whole, the endangered substance is galvanically copper-plated. The climax which emphasizes the reified parts takes on the character of a magical ritual, in which all the mysteries of personality, inwardness, inspiration and spontaneity of reproduction, which have been eliminated from the work itself, are conjured up. Just because the disintegrating work renounces the moment of its spontaneity, this, just as stereotyped as the bits and pieces, is injected into it from the outside. In spite of all talk of new objectivity, the essential function of conformist performances is no longer the performance of the "pure" work but the presentation of the vulgarized one with a gesture which emphatically but impotently tries to hold the vulgarization at a distance.

Vulgarization and enchantment, hostile sisters, dwell together in the arrangements which have colonized large areas of music. The practice of arrangement extends to the most diverse dimensions. Sometimes it seizes on the time. It blatantly snatches the reified bits and pieces out of their context and sets them up as a potpourri. It destroys the multilevel unity of the whole work and brings forward only isolated popular passages. The minuet from Mozart's E-flat Major Symphony, played without the other movement, loses its symphonic cohesion and is turned by the performance into an artisan-type genre piece that has more to do with the "Stephanie Gavotte" than with the sort of classicism it is supposed to advertise.

Then there is the arrangement in coloristic terms. They arrange whatever they can get hold of, as long as the ukase of a famous interpreter does not forbid it. If in the field of light music the arrangers are the only trained musicians, they feel called on to jump around all the more unrestrainedly with cultural goods. All sorts of reasons are offered by them for instrumental arrangements. In the case of great orchestral works, it will reduce the cost, or the composers are accused of lacking technique in instrumentation. These reasons are lamentable pretexts. The argument of cheapness, which esthetically condemns itself, is disposed of by reference to the superfluity of orchestral means at the disposal of precisely those who most eagerly carry on the practice of arrangement, and by the fact that very often, as in instrumental arrangements of piano pieces, the arrangements turn out substantially dearer than performance in the original form. And finally, the belief that older music needs a coloristic freshening up presupposes an accidental character in the relation between color and line, such as could be assumed only as a result of the crudest ignorance of Vienna classicism and the so-eagerly arranged Schubert. Even if the real discovery of the coloristic dimension first took place in the era of Berlioz and Wagner, the coloristic parsimony of Haydn or Beethoven is of a piece with the predominance of the principle of construction over the melodic particular springing in brilliant colors out of the dynamic unity. Precisely in the context of such parsimony do the bassoon thirds at the beginning of the third *Leonore* overture or the oboe cadenza in the reprise of the first movement of the Fifth achieve a power which would be irretrievably lost in a multicolored sonority.

One must therefore assume that the motives for the practice of arranging are *sui generis*. Above all, arranging seeks to make the great distant sound, which always has aspects of the public and unprivate, assimilable. The tired businessman can clap arranged classics on the shoulder and fondle the progeny of their muse. It is a compulsion similar to that which requires radio favorites to insinuate themselves into the families of their listeners as uncles and aunts and pretend to a human proximity. Radical reification produces its own pretense of immediacy and intimacy. Contrarywise, the intimate is inflated and colored by arrangements precisely for being too spare. Because they were originally defined only as moments of the whole, the instants of sensory pleasure which emerge out of the decomposing unities are too weak even to produce the sensory stimulus demanded of them in fulfillment of their advertised role. The dressing up and puffing up of the individual erases the lineaments of protest, sketched out in the limitation of the individual to himself over and against the institution, just as in the reduction of the large-scale to the intimate, sight is lost of the totality in which bad individual immediacy was kept within bounds in great music. Instead of this, there develops a spurious balance which at every step betrays its falsity by its contradiction of the material. Schubert's *Serenade*, in the blown-up sound of the combination of strings and piano, with the silly excessive clarity of the imitative intermediate measures, is as nonsensical as if it had originated in a girls' school. But neither does the prize song from *Meistersinger* sound any more serious when played by a string orchestra alone. In monochrome, it objectively loses the articulation which makes it viable in Wagner's score. But at the same time, it becomes quite viable for the listener, who no longer has to put the body of the song together from different colors, but can confidently give himself over to the single and uninterrupted treble melody. Here one can put one's hands on the antagonism to the audience into which works regarded as classic fall today. But one may suspect that the darkest secret of arrangement is the compulsion not to leave anything as it is, but to lay hands on anything that crosses one's path, a compulsion that grows greater the less the fundamental characteristics of what exists lend themselves to being meddled with. The total social grasp confirms its power and mastery by the stamp which is impressed on anything that falls into its machinery. But this affirmation is likewise destructive. Contemporary listeners would always prefer to destroy what they hold in blind respect, and their pseudoactivity is already prepared and prescribed by the production.

The practice of arrangement comes from salon music. It is the practice of refined entertainment which borrows its pretensions from the *niveau* of cultural goods, but transforms these into entertainment material of the type of hit songs. Such entertainment, formerly reserved as an accompaniment to people's humming, today spreads over the whole of musical life, which is basically not taken seriously by anyone anymore and in all discussion of culture retreats further and further into the background. One has the choice of either dutifully going along with the business, if only furtively in front of the loudspeaker on Saturday afternoon, or at once stubbornly and impenitently acknowledging the trash served up for the ostensible or real needs of the masses. The uncompelling and superficial nature of the objects of refined entertainment inevitably leads to the inattentiveness of the listeners. One preserves a good conscience in the matter since one is offering the listeners first-class goods. To the objection that these are already a drug on the market, one is ready with the reply that this is what they wanted, an argument which can be finally invalidated by a diagnosis of the situation of the listeners, but only through insight into the whole process which unites producers and consumers in a diabolical harmony.

But fetishism takes hold of even the ostensibly serious practice of music, which mobilizes the pathos of distance against refined entertainment. The purity of service to the cause, with which it presents the works, often turns out to be as inimical to them as vulgarization and arrangement. The official ideal of performance, which covers the earth as a result of Toscanini's extraordinary achievement, helps to sanction a condition which, in a phrase of Eduard Steuermann, may be called the barbarism of perfection. To be sure, the names of famous works are no longer made fetishes, although the lesser ones that break into the programs almost make the limitation to the smaller repertoire seem desirable. To be sure, passages are not here inflated or climaxes overstressed for the sake of fascination. There is iron discipline. But precisely iron. The new fetish is the flawlessly functioning, metallically brilliant apparatus as such, in which all the cogwheels mesh so perfectly that not the slightest hole remains open for the meaning of the whole. Perfect, immaculate performance in the latest style preserves the work at the price of its definitive reification. It presents it as already complete from the very first note. The performance sounds like its own phonograph record. The dynamic is so predetermined that there are no longer any tensions at all. The contradictions of the musical material are so inexorably resolved in the moment of sound that it never arrives at the synthesis, the self-production of the work, which reveals the meaning of every Beethoven symphony. What is the point of the symphonic effort when the material on which that effort was to be tested has already been ground up? The protective fixation of the work leads to its destruction, for its unity is realized in precisely that spontaneity which is sacrificed to the fixation. This last fetishism, which seizes on the substance itself, smothers it; the absolute adjustment of the appearance to the work denies the latter and makes it disappear unnoticed behind the apparatus, just as certain swamp-drainings by labor detachments take place not for their own sake but for that of the work. Not for nothing does the rule of the established conductor remind one of that of the totalitarian Führer. Like the latter, he reduces aura and organization to a common denominator. He is the real modern type of the virtuoso, as bandleader as well as in the Philharmonic. He has got to the point where he no longer has to do anything himself; he is even sometimes relieved of reading the score by the staff musical advisors. At one stroke he provides norm and individualization: the norm is identified with his person, and the individual tricks which he perpetrates furnish general rules. The fetish character of the conductor is the most obvious and the most hidden. The standard works could probably be performed by the virtuosi of contemporary orchestras just as well without the conductor, and the public which cheers the conductor would be unable to tell that, in the concealment of the orchestra, the musical advisor was taking the place of the hero laid low by a cold.

The consciousness of the mass of listeners is adequate to fetishized music. It listens according to formula, and indeed debasement itself would not be possible if resistance ensued, if the listeners still had the capacity to make demands beyond the limits of what was supplied. But if someone tried to "verify" the fetish character of music by investigating the reactions of listeners with interviews and questionnaires, he might meet with unexpected puzzles. In music as elsewhere, the discrepancy between essence and appearance has grown to a point where no appearance is any longer valid, without mediation, as verification of the essence. The unconscious reactions of the listeners are so heavily veiled and their conscious assessment is so exclusively oriented to the dominant fetish categories that every answer one receives conforms in advance to the surface of that music business which is attacked by the theory being "verified." As soon as one presents the listener with the primitive question about liking or disliking, there comes into play the whole machinery which one had thought could be made transparent and eliminated by the reduction to this question. But if one tries to replace the most elementary investigative procedures with others which take account of the real dependence of the listener on the mechanism, this complication of the investigative procedure not merely makes the interpretation of the result more difficult, but it touches off the resistance of the respondents and drives them all the deeper into the conformist behavior in which they think they can remain concealed from the danger of exposure. No causal nexus at all can properly be worked out between isolated "impressions" of the hit song and its psychological effects on the listener. If indeed individuals today no longer belong to themselves, then that also means that they can no longer be "influenced." The opposing points of production and consumption are at any given time closely coordinated, but not dependent on each other in isolation. Their mediation itself does not in any case escape theoretical conjecture. It suffices to remember how many sorrows he is spared who no longer thinks too many thoughts, how much more "in accordance with reality" a person behaves when he affirms that the real is right, how much more capacity to use the machinery falls to the person who integrates himself with it uncomplainingly, so that the correspondence between the listener's consciousness and the fetishized music would still remain comprehensible even if the former did not unequivocally reduce itself to the latter.

The counterpart to the fetishism of music is a regression of listening. This does not mean a relapse of the individual listener into an earlier phase of his own development, nor a decline in the collective general level, since the millions who are reached musically for the first time by today's mass communications cannot be compared with the audience of the past. Rather, it is contemporary listening which has regressed, arrested at the infantile stage. Not only do the listening subjects lose, along with freedom of choice and responsibility, the capacity for conscious perception of music, which was from time immemorial confined to a narrow group, but they stubbornly reject the possibility of such perception. They fluctuate between comprehensive forgetting and sudden dives into recognition. They listen atomistically and dissociate what they hear, but precisely in this dissociation they develop certain capacities which accord less with the concepts of traditional esthetics than with those of football and motoring. They are not childlike, as might be expected on the basis of an interpretation of the new type of listener in terms of the introduction to musical life of groups previously unacquainted with music. But they are childish; their primitivism is not that of the undeveloped, but that of the forcibly retarded. Whenever they have a chance, they display the pinched hatred of those who really sense the other but exclude it in order to live in peace, and who therefore would like best to root out the nagging possibility. The regression is really from this existent possibility, or more concretely, from the possibility of a different and oppositional music. Regressive, too, is the role which contemporary mass music plays in the psychological household of its victims. They are not merely turned away from more important music, but they are confirmed in their neurotic stupidity, quite irrespective of how their musical capacities are related to the specific musical culture of earlier social phases. The assent to hit songs and debased cultural goods belongs to the same complex of symptoms as do those faces of which one no longer knows whether the film has alienated them from reality or reality has alienated them from the film, as they wrench open a great formless mouth with shining teeth in a voracious smile, while the tired eyes are wretched and lost above. Together with sport and film, mass music and the new listening help to make escape from the whole infantile milieu impossible. The sickness has a preservative function. Even the listening habits of the contemporary masses are certainly in no way new, and one may readily concede that the reception of the prewar hit song "Puppchen" was not so very different from that of a synthetic jazz children's song. But the context in which such a children's song appears, the masochistic mocking of one's own wish for lost happiness, or the compromising of the desire for happiness itself by the reversion to a childhood whose unattainability bears witness to the unattainability of joy—this is the specific product of the new listening, and nothing which strikes the ear remains exempt from this system of assimilation. There are indeed social differences, but the new listening extends so far that the stultification of the oppressed affects the oppressors themselves, and they become victims of the superior power of self-propelled wheels who think they are determining their direction.

Regressive listening is tied to production by the machinery of distribution, and particularly by advertising. Regressive listening appears as soon as advertising turns into terror, as soon as nothing is left for the consciousness but to capitulate before the superior power of the advertised stuff and purchase spiritual peace by making the imposed goods literally its own thing. In regressive listening, advertising takes on a compulsory character. For a while, an English brewery used for propaganda purposes a billboard that bore a deceptive likeness to one of those whitewashed brick walls which are so numerous in the slums of London and the industrial cities of the North. Properly placed, the billboard was barely distinguishable from a real wall. On it, chalk-white, was a careful imitation of awkward writing. The words said: "What we want is Watney's." The brand of the beer was presented like a political slogan. Not only does this billboard give an insight into the nature of up-to-date propaganda, which sells its slogans as well as its wares, just as here the wares masquerade as a slogan; the type of relationship suggested by the billboard, in which masses make a commodity recommended to them the object of their own action, is in fact found again as the pattern for the reception of light music. They need and demand what has been palmed off on them. They overcome the feeling of impotence that creeps over them in the face of monopolistic production by identifying themselves with the inescapable product. They thereby put an end to the strangeness of the musical brands which are at once distant from them and threateningly near, and in addition, achieve the satisfaction of feeling themselves involved in Mr. Know-Nothing's enterprises, which confront them at every turn. This explains why individual expressions of preference—or, of course, dislike—converge in an area where object and subject alike make such reactions questionable. The fetish character of music produces its own camouflage through the identification of the listener with the fetish. This identification initially gives the hit songs power over their victims. It fulfills itself in the subsequent forgetting and remembering. Just as every advertisement is composed of the inconspicuous familiar and the unfamiliar conspicuous, so the hit song remains salutarily forgotten in the half-dusk of its familiarity, suddenly to become painfully over-clear through recollection, as if in the beam of a spotlight. One can almost equate the moment of this recollection with that in which the title or the words of the initial verse of his hit song confront the victim. Perhaps he identifies himself with this because he identifies it and thereby merges with his possession. This compulsion may well drive him to recall the title of the hit song at time. But the writing under the note, which makes the identification possible, is nothing else but the trademark of the hit song.

Deconcentration is the perceptual activity which prepares the way for the forgetting and sudden recognition of mass music. If the standardized products, hopelessly like one another except for conspicuous bits such as hit lines, do not permit concentrated listening without becoming unbearable to the listeners, the latter are in any case no longer capable of concentrated listening. They cannot stand the strain of concentrated listening and surrender themselves resignedly to what befalls them, with which they can come to terms only if they do not listen to it too closely. Benjamin's reference to the apperception of the cinema in a condition of distraction is just as valid for light music. The usual commercial jazz can only carry out its function because it is not attended to except during conversation and, above all, as an accompaniment to dancing. Again and again one encounters the judgment that it is fine for dancing but dreadful for listening. But if the film as a whole seems to be apprehended in a distracted manner, deconcentrated listening makes the perception of a whole impossible. All that is realized is what the spotlight falls on—striking melodic intervals, unsettling modulations, intentional or unintentional mistakes, or whatever condenses itself into a formula by an especially intimate merging of melody and text. Here, too, listeners and products fit together; they are not even offered the structure which they cannot follow. If atomized listening means progressive decomposition for the higher music, there is nothing more to decompose in the lower music. The forms of hit songs are so strictly standardized, down to the number of beats and the exact duration, that no specific form appears in any particular piece. The emancipation of the parts from their cohesion, and from all moments which extend beyond their immediate present, introduces the diversion of musical interest to the particular sensory pleasure. Typically, the listeners show a preference not merely for particular showpieces for instrumental acrobatics, but for the individual instrumental colors as such. This preference is promoted by the practice of American popular music whereby each variation, or "chorus," is played with emphasis on a special instrumental color, with the clarinet, the piano, or the trumpet as quasi-soloist. This often goes so far that the listener seems to care more about treatment and "style" than about the otherwise indifferent material, but with the treatment validating itself only in particular enticing effects. Along with the attraction to color as such, there is of course the veneration for the tool and the drive to imitate and join in the game; possibly also something of the great delight of children in bright colors, which returns under the pressure of contemporary musical experience.

The diversion of interest from the whole, perhaps indeed from the "melody," to the charm of color and to the individual trick, could be optimistically interpreted as a new rupture of the disciplining function. But this interpretation would be erroneous. Once the perceived charms remain unopposed in a rigid format, whoever yields to them will eventually rebel against it. But then they are themselves of the most limited kind. They all center on an impressionistically softened tonality. It cannot be said that interest in the isolated color or the isolated sonority awakens a taste for new colors and new sonorities. Rather, the atomistic listeners are the first to denounce such sonorities as "intellectual" or absolutely dissonant. The charms which they enjoy must be of an approved type. To be sure, dissonances occur in jazz practice, and even techniques of intentional misplaying have developed. But an appearance of harmlessness accompanies all these customs; every extravagant sonority must be so produced that the listener can recognize it as a substitute for a "normal" one. While he rejoices in the mistreatment the dissonance gives to the consonance whose place it takes, the virtual consonance simultaneously guarantees that one remains within the circle. In tests on the reception of hit songs, people have been found who ask how they should act if a passage simultaneously pleases and displeases them. One may well suspect that they report an experience which also occurs to those who give no account of it.

The reactions to isolated charms are ambivalent. A sensory pleasure turns into disgust as soon as it is seen how it only still serves to betray the consumer. The betrayal here consists in always offering the same thing. Even the most insensitive hit song enthusiast cannot always escape the feeling that the child with a sweet tooth comes to know in the candy store. If the charms wear off and turn into their opposite—the short life of most hit songs belongs in the same range of experience—then the cultural ideology which clothes the upper-level musical business finishes things off by causing the lower to be heard with a bad conscience. Nobody believes so completely in prescribed pleasure. But the listening nevertheless remains regressive in assenting to this situation despite all distrust and all ambivalence. As a result of the displacement of feelings into exchange-value, no demands are really advanced in music anymore. Substitutes satisfy their purpose as well, because the demand to which they adjust themselves has itself already been substituted. But ears which are still only able to hear what one demands of them in what is offered, and which register the abstract charm instead of synthesizing the moments of charm, are bad ears. Even in the "isolated" phenomenon, key aspects will escape them; that is, those which transcend its own isolation. There is actually a neurotic mechanism of stupidity in listening, too; the arrogantly ignorant rejection of everything unfamiliar is its sure sign. Regressive listeners behave like children. Again and again and with stubborn malice, they demand the one dish they have once been served.

A sort of musical children's language is prepared for them; it differs from the real thing in that its vocabulary consists exclusively of fragments and distortions of the artistic language of music. In the piano scores of hit songs, there are strange diagrams. They relate to guitar, ukulele and banjo, as well as the accordion—infantile instruments in comparison with the piano—and are intended for players who cannot read the notes. They depict graphically the fingering for the chords of the plucking instruments. The rationally comprehensible notes are replaced by visual directives, to some extent by musical traffic signals. These signs, of course, confine themselves to the three tonic major chords and exclude any meaningful harmonic progression. The regulated musical traffic is worthy of them. It cannot be compared with that in the streets. It swarms with mistakes in phrasing and harmony. There are wrong pitches, incorrect doublings of thirds, fifth and octave progressions, and all sorts of illogical treatments of voices, sometimes in the bass. One would like to blame them on the amateurs with whom most of the hit songs originate, while the real musical work is first done by the arrangers. But just as a publisher does not let a misspelled word go out into the world, so it is inconceivable that, well-advised by their experts, they publish amateur versions without checking them. The mistakes are either consciously produced by the experts or intentionally permitted to stand—for the sake of the listeners. One could attribute to the publishers and experts the wish to ingratiate themselves with the listeners, composing as nonchalantly and informally as a dilettante drums out a hit song after hearing it. Such intrigues would be of the same stripe, even if considered psychologically different, as the incorrect spelling in many advertising slogans. But even if one wanted to exclude their acceptance as too farfetched, the typographical errors could be understood. On the one hand, the infantile hearing demands sensually rich and full sonority, sometimes represented by the luxuriant thirds, and it is precisely this demand in which the infantile musical language is in most brutal contradiction with the children's song. On the other hand, the infantile hearing always demands the most comfortable and fluent resolutions. The consequences of the "rich" sonority, with correct treatment of voices, would be so far from the standardized harmonic relations that the listener would have to reject them as "unnatural." The mistakes would then be the bold strokes which reconcile the antagonisms of the infantile listener's consciousness.

No less characteristic of the regressive musical language is the quotation. Its use ranges from the conscious quotation of folk and children's songs, by way of ambiguous and half accidental allusions, to completely latent similarities and associations. The tendency triumphs in the adaptation of whole pieces from the classical stock or the operatic repertoire. The practice of quotation mirrors the ambivalence of the infantile listener's consciousness. The quotations are at once authoritarian and a parody. It is thus that a child imitates the teacher.

The ambivalence of the retarded listeners has its most extreme expression in the fact that individuals, not yet fully reified, want to extricate themselves from the mechanism of musical reification to which they have been handed over, but that their revolts against fetishism only entangle them more deeply in it. Whenever they attempt to break away from the passive status of compulsory consumers and "activate" themselves, they succumb to pseudoactivity. Types rise up from the mass of the retarded who differentiate themselves by pseudoactivity and nevertheless make the regression more strikingly visible. There are, first, the enthusiasts who write fan letters to radio stations and orchestras and, at well-managed jazz festivals, produce their own enthusiasm as an advertisement for the wares they consume. They call themselves jitterbugs, as if they simultaneously wanted to affirm and mock their loss of individuality, their transformation into beetles whirring around in fascination. Their only excuse is that the term jitterbugs, like all those in the unreal edifice of films and jazz, is hammered into them by the entrepreneurs to make them think that they are on the inside. Their ecstasy is without content. That it happens, that the music is listened to, this replaces the content itself. The ecstasy takes possession of its object by its own compulsive character. It is stylized like the ecstasies savages go into in beating the war drums. It has convulsive aspects reminiscent of St. Vitus' dance or the reflexes of mutilated animals. Passion itself seems to be produced by defects. But the ecstatic ritual betrays itself as pseudoactivity by the moment of mimicry. People do not dance or listen "from sensuality" and sensuality is certainly not satisfied by listening, but the gestures of the sensual are imitated. An analogue is the representation of particular emotions in the film, where there are physiognomic patterns for anxiety, longing, the erotic look; for smiling; for the atomistic expressivo of debased music. The imitative assimilation to commodity models is intertwined with folkloristic customs of imitation. In jazz, the relation of such mimicry to the imitating individual himself is quite loose. Its medium is caricature. Dance and music copy stages of sexual excitement only to make fun of them. It is as if desire's surrogate itself simultaneously turned against it; the "realistic" behavior of the oppressed triumphs over his dream of happiness while being itself incorporated into the latter. And as if to confirm the superficiality and treachery of every form of ecstasy, the feet are unable to fulfill what the ear pretends. The same jitterbugs who behave as if they were electrified by syncopation dance almost exclusively the good rhythmic parts. The weak flesh punishes the lies of the willing spirit; the gestural ecstasy of the infantile listener misfires in the face of the ecstatic gesture. The opposite type appears to be the eager person who leaves the factory and "occupies" himself with music in the quiet of his bedroom. He is shy and inhibited, perhaps has no luck with girls, and wants in any case to preserve his own special sphere. He seeks this as a radio ham. At twenty, he is still at the stage of a boy scout working on complicated knots just to please his parents. This type is held in high esteem in radio matters. He patiently builds sets whose most important parts he must buy ready-made, and scans the air for shortwave secrets, though there are none. As a reader of Indian stories and travel books, he once discovered unknown lands and cleared his path through the forest primeval. As radio ham he becomes the discoverer of just those industrial products which are interested in being discovered by him. He brings nothing home which would not be delivered to his house. The adventurers of pseudo-activity have already organized themselves on a large scale; the radio amateurs have printed verification cards sent them by the shortwave stations they have discovered, and hold contests in which the winner is the one who can produce the most such cards. All this is carefully fostered from above. Of all fetishistic listeners, the radio ham is perhaps the most complete. It is irrelevant to him what he hears or even how he hears; he is only interested in the fact that he hears and succeeds in inserting himself, with his private equipment, into the public mechanism, without exerting even the slightest influence on it. With the same attitude, countless radio listeners play with the feedback or the sound dial without themselves becoming hams. Others are more expert, or at least more aggressive. These smart chaps can be found everywhere and are able to do everything themselves: the advanced student who in every gathering is ready to play jazz with machinelike precision for dancing and entertainment; the gas station attendant who hums his syncopation ingenuously while filling up the tank; the listening expert who can identify every band and immerses himself in the history of jazz as if it were Holy Writ. He is nearest to the sportsman: if not to the football player himself, then to the swaggering fellow who dominates the stands. He shines by a capacity for rough improvisations, even if he must practice the piano for hours in secret in order to bring the refractory rhythms together. He pictures himself as the individualist who whistles at the world. But what he whistles is its melody, and his tricks are less inventions of the moment than stored-up experiences from acquaintance with sought-after technical things. His improvisations are always gestures of nimble subordination to what the instrument demands of him. The chauffeur is the model for the listening type of the clever fellow. His agreement with everything dominant goes so far that he no longer produces any resistance, but of his own accord always does what is asked of him for the sake of the responsible functionary. He lies to himself about the completeness of his subordination to the rule of the reified mechanism. Thus, the sovereign routine of the jazz amateur is nothing but the passive capacity for adaptation to models from which to avoid straying. He is the real jazz subject: his improvisations come from the pattern, and he navigates the pattern, cigarette in mouth, as nonchalantly as if he had invented it himself.

Regressive listeners have key points in common with the man who must kill time because he has nothing else on which to vent his aggression, and with the casual laborer. To make oneself a jazz expert or hang over the radio all day, one must have much free time and little freedom. The dexterity which comes to terms with the syncopation as well as with the basic rhythm is that of the auto mechanic who can also repair the loudspeaker and the electric light. The new listeners resemble the mechanics who are simultaneously specialized and capable of applying their special skills to unexpected places outside their skilled trades. But this despecialization only seems to help them out of the system. The more easily they meet the demands of the day, the more rigidly they are subordinated to that system. The research finding, that among radio listeners the friends of light music reveal themselves to be depoliticized, is not accidental. The possibility of individual shelter and of a security which is, as always, questionable, obstructs the view of a change in the situation in which one seeks shelter. Superficial experience contradicts this. The "younger generation"—the concept itself is merely an ideological catch-all—seems to be in conflict with its elders and their plush culture precisely through the new way of listening. In America, it is just the so-called liberals and progressives whem one finds among the advocates of light popular music, most of whom want to classify their activity as democratic. But if regressive hearing is progressive as opposed to the "individualistic" sort, it is only in the dialectical sense that it is better fitted to the advancing brutality than the latter. All possible mold has been rubbed off the baseness, and it is legitimate to criticize the esthetic residue of an individuality that was long since wrested from individuals. But this criticism comes with little force from the sphere of popular music, since it is just this sphere that mummifies the vulgarized and decaying remnants of romantic individualism. Its innovations are inseparably coupled with these remnants.

Machochism in hearing is not only defined by self-surrender and pseudo-pleasure through identification with power. Underlying it is the knowledge that the security of shelter under the ruling conditions is a provisional one, that it is only a respite, and that eventually everything must collapse. Even in self-surrender one is not good in his own eyes; in his enjoyment one feels that he is simultaneously betraying the possible and being betrayed by the existent. Regressive listening is always ready to degenerate into rage. If one knows that he is basically marking time, the rage is directed primarily against everything which could disavow the modernity of being with-it and up-to-date and reveal how little has in fact changed. From photographs and movies, one knows the effect produced by the modern grown old, an effect originally used by the surrealists to shock and subsequently degraded to the cheap amusement of those whose fetishism fastens on the abstract present. For the regressive listener, this effect is fantastically foreshortened. They would like to ridicule and destroy what yesterday they were intoxicated with, as if in retrospect to revenge themselves for the fact that the ecstasy was not actually such. This effect has been given a name of its own and repeatedly been propagated in press and radio. But we should not think of the rhythmically simpler, light music of the pre-jazz era and its relics as corny; rather, the term applies to all those syncopated pieces which do not conform to the approved rhythmic formula of the present moment. A jazz expert can shake with laughter when he hears a piece which in good rhythm follows a sixteenth note with a punctuated eight, although this rhythm is more aggressive and in no way more provincial in character than the syncopated connection and renunciation of all counter-stress practiced later. The regressive listeners are in fact destructive. The old-timer's insult has its ironic justification; ironic, because the destructive tendencies of the regressive listeners are in truth directed against the same thing that the old-fashioned hate, against disobedience as such, unless it comes under the tolerated spontaneity of collective excesses. The seeming opposition of the generations is nowhere more transparent than in rage. The bigots who complain to the radio stations in pathetic-sadistic letters of the jazzing up of holy things and the youth who delight in such exhibitions are of one mind. It requires only the proper situation to bring them together in a united front.

This furnishes a criticism of the "new possibilities" in regressive listening. One might be tempted to rescue it if it were something in which the "auratic" characteristics of the work of art, its illusory elements, gave way to the playful ones. However it may be with films, today's mass music shows little of such progress in disenchantment. Nothing survives in it more steadfastly than the illusion, nothing is more illusory than its reality. The infantile play has scarcely more than the name in common with the productivity of children. Otherwise, bourgeois sport would not want to differentiate itself so strictly from play. Its bestial seriousness consists in the fact that instead of remaining faithful to the dream of freedom by getting away from purposiveness, the treatment of play as a duty puts it among useful purposes and thereby wipes out the trace of freedom in it. This is particularly valid for contemporary mass music. It is only play as a repetition of prescribed models, and the playful release from responsibility which is thereby achieved does not reduce at all the time devoted to duty except by transferring the responsibility to the models, the following of which one makes into a duty for himself. In this lies the inherent pretense of the dominant music sport. It is illusory to promote the technical-rational moments of contemporary mass music—or the special capacities of the regressive listeners which may correspond to these moments—at the expense of a decayed magic, which nevertheless prescribes the rules for the bare functioning itself. It would also be illusory because the technical innovations of mass music really don't exist. This goes without saying for harmonic and melodic construction. The real coloristic accomplishment of modern dance music, the approach of the different colors to one another to the extent that one instrument replaces another without a break or one instrument can disguise itself as another, is as familiar to Wagnerian and post-Wagnerian orchestral technique as the mute effects of the brasses. Even in the techniques of syncopation, there is nothing that was not present in rudimentary form in Brahms and outdone by Schönberg and Stravinsky. The practice of contemporary popular music has not so much developed these techniques as conformistically dulled them. The listeners who expertly view these techniques with astonishment are in no way technically educated thereby, but react with resistance and rejection as soon as the techniques are introduced to them in those contexts in which they have their meaning. Whether a technique can be considered progressive and "rational" depends on this meaning and on its place in the whole of society as well as in the organization of the particular work. Technical development as such can serve crude reaction as soon as it has established itself as a fetish and by its perfection represents the neglected social tasks as already accomplished. This is why all attempts to reform mass music and regressive listening on the basis of what exists are frustrated. Consumable art music must pay by the sacrifice of its consistency. Its faults are not "artistic"; every incorrectly composed or outmoded chord bespeaks the backwardness of those to whose demand accommodation is made.

But technically consistent, harmonious mass music purified of all the elements of bad pretense would turn into art music and at once lose its mass basis. All attempts at reconciliation, whether by market-oriented artists or collectively-oriented art educators, are fruitless. They have accomplished nothing more than handicrafts or the sort of products with which directions for use or a social text must be given, so that one may be properly informed about their deeper background.

The positive aspect for which the new mass music and regressive listening are praised—vitality and technical progress, collective breadth and relation to an undefined practice, into whose concepts there has entered the supplicant self-denunciation of the intellectuals, who can thereby finally end their social alienation from the masses in order to coordinate themselves politically with contemporary mass consciousness—this positive is negative, the irruption into music of a catastrophic phase of society. The positive lies locked up solely in its negativity. Fetishized mass music threatens the fetishized cultural goods. The tension between the two spheres of music has so grown that it becomes difficult for the official sphere to hold its ground. However little it has to do with the technical standards of mass music, if one compares the special knowledge of a jazz expert with that of a Toscanini worshipper the former is far ahead of the latter. But regressive listening represents a growing and merciless enemy not only to museum cultural goods but to the age-old sacral function of music as the locus for the taming of impulses. Not without penalty, and therefore not without restraint, are the debased products of musical culture surrendered to disrespectful play and sadistic humor.

In the face of regressive listening, music as a whole begins to take on a comic aspect. One need only listen to the uninhibited sonority of a choral rehearsal from outside. This experience was caught with great force in a film by the Marx brothers, who demolish an opera set as if to clothe in allegory the insight of the philosophy of history on the decay of the operatic form, or in a most estimable piece of refined entertainment, break up a grand piano in order to take possession of its strings in their frame as the true harp of the future, on which to play a prelude. Music has become comic in the present phase primarily because something so completely useless is carried on with all the visible signs of the strain of serious work. By being alien to solid people, music reveals their alienation from one another, and the consciousness of alienation vents itself in laughter. In music—or similarly in lyric poetry—the society which judged them comic becomes comic. But involved in this laughter is the decay of the sacral spirit of reconciliation. All music today can very easily sound as *Parsifal* did to Nietzsche's ear. It recalls incomprehensible rites and surviving masks from an earlier time, and is provocative nonsense. The radio, which both wears out music and overexposes it, makes a major contribution to this. Perhaps a better hour may at some time strike even for the clever fellows: one in which they may demand, instead of prepared material ready to be switched on, the improvisatory displacement of things, as the sort of radical beginning that can only thrive under the protection of the unshaken real world. Even discipline can take over the expression of free solidarity if freedom becomes its content. As little as regressive listening is a symptom of progress in consciousness of freedom, it could suddenly turn around if art, in unity with the society, should ever leave the road of the always-identical.

Not popular music but artistic music has furnished a model for this possibility. It is not for nothing that Mahler is the scandal of all bourgeois musical esthetics. They call him uncreative because he suspends their concept of creation itself. Everything with which he occupies himself is already there. He accepts it in its vulgarized form; his themes are expropriated ones. Nevertheless, nothing sounds as it was wont to; all things are diverted as if by a magnet. What is worn out yields pliantly to the improvising hand; the used parts win a second life as variants. Just as the chauffeur's knowledge of his old second-hand car can enable him to drive it punctually and unrecognized to its intended destination, so can the expression of a beat-up melody, straining under the pressure of clarinets and oboes in the upper register, arrive at places which the approved musical language could never safely reach. Such music really crystallizes the whole, into which it has incorporated the vulgarized fragments, into something new, yet it takes its material from regressive listening. Indeed, one can almost think that in Mahler's music this experience was seismographically recorded forty years before it permeated society. But if Mahler stood athwart the concept of musical progress, neither can the new and radical music whose most advanced practitioners give allegiance to him in a seemingly paradoxical way any longer be subsumed exclusively under the concept of progress. It proposes to consciously resist the phenomenon of regressive listening. The terror which Schönberg and Webern spread, today as in the past, comes not from their incomprehensibility but from the fact that they are all too correctly understood. Their music gives form to that anxiety, that terror, that insight into the catastrophic situation which others merely evade by regressing. They are called individualists, and yet their work is nothing but a single dialogue with the powers which destroy individuality—powers whose "formless shadows" fall gigantically on their music. In music, too, collective powers are liquidating an individuality past saving, but against them only individuals are capable of consciously representing the aims of collectivity.

Commitment

By Theodor W. Adorno

Written in 1962, this essay concludes Adorno's debate with Benjamin by criticizing all directly political art. We are presented by Adorno's frank decision to support the moment of criticism and liberation in artists such as Kafka, Beckett and Schönberg—even if his own sociology of art demonstrates the destruction of the audiences for their "autonomous works." It is one of Adorno's key theses that the artistic intentions of, say, Brecht, which he implicitly interprets in terms of Benjamin's reading, are best realized not in terms of Brecht's own political plays but in the supposedly apolitical works of the autonomous avant-garde.

Adorno also disagreed with Sartre's alternative that "human existence equals human freedom," i.e., humans are free by definition regardless of their concrete situation. According to Adorno, the problematic relation of art and society is operative within the works of art, literally in their re-vision of reality which is their material yet which it is their task to transcend. While Adorno shared Sartre's intent, he did not believe there was a shortcut to social relevance.

Since Sartre's essay *What is Literature?*, there has been less theoretical debate about committed and autonomous literature. Nevertheless, the controversy over commitment remains urgent, so far as anything that merely concerns the life of the mind can be today, as opposed to sheer human survival. Sartre was moved to issue his manifesto because he saw—and he was certainly not the first to do so—works of art displayed side by side in a pantheon of optional edification, decaying into cultural commodities. In such coexistence, they desecrate each other. If any work, without its author's necessarily intending it, aims at a supreme effect, none can thereby truly tolerate a neighbor beside it. This salutary intolerance holds not only for individual works, but also for esthetic genres or attitudes such as those once symbolized in the now half-forgotten controversy over commitment. There are two "positions on objectivity" which are constantly at war with one another, even when intellectual life falsely presents them as at peace. A work of art that is committed strips the magic from a work of art that is content to be a fetish, an idle pastime for those who would like to sleep through the deluge that threatens them, in an apoliticism that is in fact deeply political. For the committed, such works are a distraction from the battle of real interests, in which none is any longer exempt from the conflict between two great blocs. The possibility of mental life itself depends on this conflict to such an extent that only blind illusion can insist on rights that may be shattered tomorrow. For autonomous works of art, however, such considerations, and the conception of art which underlies them, are themselves the spiritual catastrophe of which the committed keep warning. Once the life of the mind renounces the duty and liberty of its own pure objectification, it has abdicated. Thereafter, works of art merely assimilate themselves sedulously to the brute existence against which they protest, in forms so ephemeral (the very charge made vice versa by committed against autonomous works) that from their first day they belong to the seminars in which they inevitably end. The menacing thrust of the antithesis is a reminder of how precarious the position of art is today. Each of the two alternatives negates itself with the other. Committed art, necessarily detached as art from reality, cancels the distance between the two. "Art for art's sake" denies by its absolute claims that ineradicable connection with reality which is the polemical *a priori* of the very attempt to make art autonomous from the real. Between these two poles, the tension in which art has lived in every age till now, is dissolved.

The Confusions of the Debate on Commitment

Contemporary literature itself suggests doubts as to the omnipotence of these alternatives. For it is not yet so completely subjugated to the course of the world as to constitute rival fronts. The Sartrean goats and the Valéryan sheep will not be separated. Even if politically motivated, commitment in itself remains politically polyvalent so long as it is not reduced to propaganda, whose pliancy mocks any commitments by the subject. On the other hand, its opposite, known in Russian catechisms as formalism, is not decried only by Soviet officials or libertarian existentialists; even "vanguard" critics themselves frequently accuse so-called abstract texts of a lack of provocation, of social aggressivity. Conversely, Sartre cannot praise Picasso's *Guernica* too highly; yet he could hardly be convicted of formalist sympathies in music or painting. He restricts his notion of commitment to literature because of its conceptual character: "The writer deals with meanings."[1] Of course, but not only with them. If no word which enters a literary work ever wholly frees itself from its meanings in ordinary speech, so no literary work, not even the traditional novel, leaves these meanings unaltered, as they were outside it. Even an ordinary "was," in a report of something that was not, acquires a new formal quality from the fact that it was not so. The same process occurs in the higher levels of meaning of a work, all the way up to what once used to be called its "Idea." The special position that Sartre accords to literature must also be suspect to anyone who does not unconditionally subsume diverse esthetic genres under a superior universal concept. The rudiments of external meanings are the irreducibly nonartistic elements in art. Its formal principle lies not in them, but in the dialectic of both moments—which accomplishes the transformation of meanings within it. The distinction between artist and *littérateur* is shallow: but it is true that the object of any esthetic philosophy, even as understood by Sartre, is not the publicistic aspect of art. Still less is it the "message" of a work. The latter oscillates untenably between the subjective intentions of the artist and the demands of an objectively explicit metaphysical meaning. In our country, this meaning generally turns out to be an uncommonly practicable Being.

The social function of the talk about commitment has meanwhile become somewhat confused. Cultural conservatives who demand that a work of art should say something, join forces with their political opponents against atelic, hermetic works of art. Eulogists of "relevance" are more likely to find Sartre's *Huis Clos* profound, than to listen patiently to a text whose language jolts signification and by its very distance from "meaning" revolts in advance against positivist subordination of meaning. For the atheist Sartre, on the other hand, the conceptual import of art is the premise of commitment. Yet works banned in the East are sometimes demagogically denounced by local guardians of the authentic message because they apparently say what they in fact do not say. The Nazis were already using the term "cultural Bolshevism" under the Weimar Republic, and hatred of what it refers to has survived the epoch of Hitler, when it was institutionalized. Today it flares up again just as it did forty years ago, at works of the same kind, including some whose origins now go a long way back and are unmistakably part of an established tradition.

Newspapers and magazines of the radical Right constantly stir up indignation against what is unnatural, over-intellectual, morbid and decadent: they know their readers. The insights of social psychology into the authoritarian personality confirm them. The basic features of this type include conformism, respect for a petrified façade of opinion and society, and resistance to impulses that disturb its order or evoke inner elements of the unconscious that cannot be admitted. This hostility to anything alien or alienating can accommodate itself much more easily to literary realism of any provenance, even if it proclaims itself critical or socialist, than to works which swear allegiance to no political slogans, but whose mere guise is enough to disrupt the whole system of rigid coordinates that governs authoritarian personalities— to which the latter cling all the more fiercely, the less capable they are of spontaneous appreciation of anything not officially approved. Campaigns to prevent the staging of Brecht's plays in Western Germany belong to a relatively superficial layer of political consciousness. They were not even particularly vigorous, or they would have taken much crasser forms after 13 August.[2] By contrast, when the social contract with reality is abandoned, and literary works no longer speak as though they were reporting fact, hairs start to bristle. Not the least of the weaknesses of the debate on commitment is that it ignores the effect produced by works whose own formal laws pay no heed to coherent effects. So long as it fails to understand what the shock of the unintelligible can communicate, the whole dispute resembles shadow-boxing. Confusions in discussion of the problem do not indeed alter it, but they do make it necessary to rethink the alternative solutions proposed for it.

Philosophy and Art in Sartre
In esthetic theory, "commitment" should be distinguished from "tendency." Committed art in the proper sense is not intended to generate ameliorative measures, legislative acts or practical institutions—like earlier propagandist (tendency) plays against syphilis, duels, abortion laws or borstals—but to work at the level of fundamen-

tal attitudes. For Sartre, its task is to awaken the free choice of the
agent, that makes authentic existence possible at all, as opposed to the
neutrality of the spectator. But what gives commitment its esthetic
advantage over tendentiousness also renders the content to which the
artist commits himself inherently ambiguous. In Sartre, the notion of
choice—originally a Kierkegaardian category—is heir to the Christian doctrine "He who is not with me is against me," but now voided
of any concrete theological content. What remains is merely the
abstract authority of a choice enjoined, with no regard for the fact that
the very possibility of choosing depends on what can be chosen. The
archetypal situation always cited by Sartre to demonstrate the irreduci-
bility of freedom merely underlines this. Within a predetermined
reality, freedom becomes a vacant claim: Herbert Marcuse has exposed the absurdity of the philosophical theorem that it is always
possible inwardly either to accept or to reject martyrdom.[3] Yet this is
precisely what Sartre's dramatic situations are designed to demonstrate. But his plays are nevertheless bad models of his own existentialism, because they display in their respect for truth the whole
administered universe which his philosophy ignores; the lesson we
learn from them is one of unfreedom. Sartre's theatre of ideas sabo-
tages the aims of his categories. This is not an individual inadequacy
of his plays. It is not the office of art to spotlight alternatives, but to
resist by its form alone the course of the world, which permanently
puts a pistol to men's heads. In fact, as soon as committed works of art
do instigate decisions at their own level, the decisions themselves
become interchangeable. Because of this ambiguity, Sartre has with
great candor confessed that he expects no real changes in the world
from literature: a skepticism which reflects both the historical muta-
tions of society and of the practical function of literature since the days
of Voltaire. The principle of commitment thus slides towards the
proclivities of the author, in keeping with the extreme subjectivism of
Sartre's philosophy, which for all its materialist undertones, still
audibly echoes German speculative idealism. In his literary theory,
the work of art becomes an appeal to subjects, because it is itself
nothing other than a declaration by a subject of his own choice or
failure to choose.

Sartre will not allow that every work of art, by its inception
alone, confronts the writer, however free he may be, with objective
demands of composition. His intention becomes simply one element
among them. Sartre's question, "Why write?", and his solution of it
in a "deeper choice," are invalid because the author's motivations are

irrelevant to the finished work, the literary product. Sartre himself is not so far from this view, when he notes that the stature of works increases, the less they remain attached to the empirical person who created them, as Hegel saw long ago. When he calls the literary work, in Durkheim's language, a social fact, he again involuntarily recalls its inherently collective objectivity, impenetrable to the mere subjective intentions of the author. Sartre therefore does not want to situate commitment at the level of the intention of the writer, but at that of his humanity itself.[4] This determination, however, is so generic that commitment ceases to be distinct from any other form of human action or attitude. The point, says Sartre, is that the writer commits himself in the present, *dans le présent*; but since he in any case cannot escape it, his commitment to it cannot indicate a program. The actual obligation a writer undertakes is much more precise: it is not one of choice, but of substance. Although Sartre talks of the dialectic, his subjectivism so little registers the particular other for which the subject must first divest itself to become a subject, that he suspects every literary objectification of petrefaction. However, since the pure immediacy and spontaneity which he hopes to save encounter no resistance in his work by which they could define themselves, they undergo a second reification. In order to develop his drama and novel beyond sheer declaration—whose recurrent model is the scream of the tortured—Sartre has to seek recourse in a flat objectivity, subtracted from any dialectic of form and expression, that is simply a communication of his own philosophy. The content of his art becomes philosophy as with no other writer except Schiller.

But however sublime, thoughts can never be much more than one of the materials for art. Sartre's plays are vehicles for the author's ideas, which have been left behind in the race of esthetic forms. They operate with traditional intrigues, exalted by an unshaken faith in meanings which can be transferred from art to reality. But the theses they illustrate, or where possible state, misuse the emotions which Sartre's own drama aims to express, by making them examples. They thereby disavow themselves. When one of his most famous plays ends with the dictum "Hell is other people," it sounds like a quotation from *Being and Nothingness*, and it might just as well have been "Hell is ourselves." The combination of solid plot and equally solid, extractable idea won Sartre great success and made him, without doubt against his honest will, acceptable to the culture industry. The high level of abstraction of such thesis-art led him into the mistake of letting some of his best works, the film *Les Jeux sont Faits* or the play *Les*

Mains Sales, be performed as political events, and not just to an audience of victims in the dark. In much the same way, the current ideology—which Sartre detests—confuses the actions and sufferings of paper leaders with the objective movement of history. Interwoven in the veil of personalization is the idea that human beings are in control and decide, not anonymous machinery, and that there is life on the commanding heights of society: Beckett's moribund grotesques suggest the truth about that. Sartre's vision prevents him from recognizing the hell he revolts against. Many of his phrases could be parroted by his mortal enemies. The idea that decision as such is what counts would even cover the Nazi slogan that "only sacrifice makes us free." In fascist Italy, Gentile's absolute dynamism made similar pronouncements in philosophy. The flaw in his conception of commitment strikes at the very cause to which Sartre wishes to commit himself.

Brecht's Didacticism

Brecht, in some of his plays, such as the dramatization of Gorky's *The Mother* or *The Measures Taken*, bluntly glorifies the Party. But at times, at least according to his theoretical writings, he too wanted to educate spectators to a new attitude, that would be distanced, thoughtful, experimental, the reverse of illusory empathy and identification. In tendency to abstraction, his plays after *Saint Joan* trump those of Sartre. The difference is that Brecht, more consistent than Sartre and a greater artist, made this abstraction into the formal principle of his art, as a didactic poetics that eliminates the traditional concept of dramatic character altogether. He realized that the surface of social life, the sphere of consumption, which includes the psychologically motivated actions of individuals, occludes the essence of society—which, as the law of exchange, is itself abstract. Brecht rejected esthetic individuation as an ideology. He therefore sought to translate the true hideousness of society into theatrical appearance, by dragging it straight out from its camouflage. The people on his stage shrink before our eyes into the agents of social processes and functions, which indirectly and unknowingly they are in empirical reality. Brecht no longer postulates, like Sartre, an identity between living individuals and the essence of society, let alone any absolute sovereignty of the subject. Nevertheless, the process of esthetic reduction that he pursues for the sake of political truth in fact gets in its way. For this truth involves innumerable mediations which Brecht disdains. What is artistically legitimate as alienating infantilism—Brecht's first plays came from the same milieu as Dada—becomes merely infantile when it starts to claim theoretical or social validity. Brecht wanted to reveal in images the inner nature of capitalism. In this sense, his aim was indeed what he disguised it as against Stalinist terror—realistic. He would have refused to deprive social essence of meaning by taking it as it appeared, imageless and blind, in a single crippled life. But this burdened him with the obligation of ensuring that what he intended to make unequivocally clear was theoretically correct. His art, however, refused to accept this *quid pro quo*: it both presents itself as didactic, and claims esthetic dispensation from responsibility for the accuracy of what it teaches.

Criticism of Brecht cannot overlook the fact that he did not—for objective reasons beyond the adequacy of his own creations—fulfill the norm he set himself as if it were a salvation. *Saint Joan* was the central work of his dialectical theatre. (*The Good Woman of Szechuan* is a variation of it in reverse: where Joan assists evil by the immediacy of her goodness, Shen Te who wills the good must become evil). The play is set in a Chicago halfway between the Wild West fables of *Mahagonny* and economic facts. But the more preoccupied Brecht becomes with information, and the less he looks for images, the more he misses the essence of capitalism which the parable is supposed to present. Mere episodes in the sphere of circulation, in which competitors maul each other, are recounted instead of appropriation of surplus-value in the sphere of production, compared with which the brawls of cattle dealers over their shares of the booty are epiphenomena incapable of provoking any great crisis. Moreover, the economic transactions presented as the machinations of rapacious traders are not merely puerile, which is how Brecht seems to have meant them; they are also unintelligible by the criteria of even the most primitive economic logic. The obverse of the latter is a political naïveté which could only make Brecht's opponents grin at the thought of such an ingenuous enemy. They could be as comfortable with Brecht as they are with the dying Joan in the impressive final scene of the play. Even with the broadest-minded allowance for poetic licence, the idea that a strike leadership backed by the Party could entrust a crucial task to a nonmember is as inconceivable as the subsequent idea that the failure of that individual could ruin the whole strike.

Brecht's Treatment of Fascism
Brecht's comedy of the resistible rise of the great dictator *Arturo Ui* exposes the subjective nullity and pretense of a fascist leader in a harsh

and accurate light. However, the deconstruction of leaders, like that of all individuals in Brecht, is extended into a reconstruction of the social and economic nexus in which the dictator acts. Instead of a conspiracy of the wealthy and powerful, we are given a trivial gangster organization, the cabbage trust. The true horror of fascism is conjured away; it is no longer a slow end-product of the concentration of social power, but mere hazard, like an accident or crime. This conclusion is dictated by the exigencies of agitation: adversaries must be diminished. The consequence is bad politics, both in literature as in practice before 1933. Against every dialectic, the ridicule to which Ui is consigned renders innocuous the fascism that was accurately predicted by Jack London decades before. The anti-ideological artist thus prepared the degradation of his own ideas into ideology. Tacit acceptance of the claim that one half of the world no longer contains antagonisms is supplemented by jests at everything that belies the official theodicy of the other half. It is not that respect for historical scale forbids laughter at house painters, although the use of that term against Hitler was itself a painful exploitation of bourgeois class consciousness. The group which engineered the seizure of power in Germany was also certainly a gang. But the problem is that such elective affinities are not extra-territorial: they are rooted within society itself. This is why the buffoonery of fascism, evoked by Chaplin as well, was at the same time also its ultimate horror. If this is suppressed, and a few sorry exploiters of greengrocers are mocked, where key positions of economic power are actually at issue, the attack misfires. *The Great Dictator* loses all satirical force, and becomes obscene, when a Jewish girl can bash a line of storm troopers on the head with a pan without being torn to pieces. For the sake of political commitment, political reality is trivialized: which then reduces the political effect.

Sartre's frank doubt whether *Guernica* "won a single supporter for the Spanish cause" certainly also applies to Brecht's didactic drama. Scarcely anyone needs to be taught the *fabula docet* to be extracted from it—that there is injustice in the world; while the moral itself shows few traces of the dialectical theory to which Brecht gave cursory allegiance. The trappings of epic drama invite the American phrase "preaching to the converted." The primacy of lesson over pure form, which Brecht intended to achieve, became in reality a formal device itself. The suspension of form turns back against its own character as appearance. Its self-criticism in drama was related to the doctrine of objectivity (*Sachlichkeit*) in the applied visual arts. The correction of form by external conditions, with the elimination of ornament in the service of function, only increases its autonomy. The substance of Brecht's artistic work was the didactic play as an artistic principle. His method, to render immediately apparent events into phenomena newly alien to the spectator, was also a medium of formal construction rather than a contribution to practical efficacy. It is true that Brecht never spoke as skeptically as Sartre about the social effects of art. But, as an astute and experienced man of the world, he can scarcely have been wholly convinced of them. He once calmly wrote that when he was not deceiving himself, the theatre was more important to him than any changes in the world it might promote. Yet the artistic principle of simplification not only purged real politics of the illusory distinctions projected by subjective reflection into social objectivity, as Brecht intended, but it also falsified the very objectivity which didactic drama labored to distil. If we take Brecht at his word and make politics the criterion by which to judge his committed theatre, by the same token it proves untrue. Hegel's *Logic* taught that essence must appear. If this is so, a representation of essence which ignores its relation to appearance must be as intrinsically false as the substitution of a lumpen proletariat for the men behind fascism. The only ground on which Brecht's technique of reduction would be legitimate is that of "art for art's sake," which his version of commitment condemns as it does Lucullus.[5]

Politics and Poetic Tone

Contemporary literary Germany is anxious to separate Brecht the artist from Brecht the politician. The major writer must be saved for the West, if possible placed on a pedestal as an all-German poet, and so neutralized *au-dessus de la mêlée*. There is truth in this to the extent that both Brecht's artistic force, and his devious and uncontrollable intelligence, went well beyond the official credos and prescribed esthetics of the People's Democracies. All the same, Brecht must be defended against this defense of him. His work, with its often patent weaknesses, would not have had such power if it were not saturated with politics. Even its most questionable creations, such as *The Measures Taken*, generate an immediate awareness that issues of the utmost seriousness are at stake. To this extent, Brecht's claim that he used his theatre to make men think was justified. It is futile to try to separate the beauties, real or imaginary, of his works from their political intentions. The task of an immanent critique, which alone is dialectical, is rather to synthesize assessment of the validity of his forms with that of his politics. Sartre's chapter "Why write?" contains the undeniable statement that: "Nobody can suppose for a moment that it is possible to write a good novel in praise of anti-Semitism."[6] Nor could one be written in praise of the Moscow Trials, even if such praise was bestowed before Stalin actually had Zinoviev and Bukharin murdered.[7] The political falsehood stains the esthetic form. Where Brecht distorts the real social problems discussed in his epic drama, in order to prove a thesis, the whole structure and foundation of the play itself crumbles. *Mother Courage* is an illustrated primer intended to reduce to absurdity Montecuccoli's dictum that war feeds on war. The camp follower who uses the Thirty Years' War to make a life for her children thereby becomes responsible for their ruin. But in the play, this responsibility follows rigorously neither from the overall situation of the war itself nor from the individual behavior of the petty profiteer; if Mother Courage had not been absent at the critical moment, the disaster would not have happened, and the fact that she has to be absent to earn some money remains completely generic in relation to the action. The picture-book technique which Brecht needs to spell out his thesis prevents him from proving it. A sociopolitical analysis, of the sort Marx and Engels sketched in their criticism of Lassalle's play *Franz von Sickingen*, would show that Brecht's simplistic equation of the Thirty Years' War with a modern war excludes precisely what is crucial for the behavior and fate of Mother Courage in Grimmelshausen's original drama. Because the society of the Thirty Years' War was not the functional capitalist society of modern times, we cannot even poetically stipulate a closed functional system in which the lives and deaths of private individuals directly reveal economic laws. But Brecht needed the old lawless days as an image of his own, precisely because he saw clearly that the society of his own age could no longer be directly comprehended in terms of people and things. His attempt to reconstruct the reality of society thus led first to a false social model and then to dramatic implausibility. Bad politics becomes bad art and vice versa. But the less works have to proclaim what they cannot completely believe themselves, the more telling they become in their own right; and the less they need a surplus of meaning beyond their being. For the rest, the real interested parties in every camp would be probably as successful in surviving wars today as they have always been.

Aporia of this sort multiply until they affect the Brechtian tone itself, the very fiber of his poetic art. Undoubted though their uniqueness may be—qualities which the mature Brecht may have thought unimportant—they were poisoned by the untruth of his politics. For what he justified was not simply, as he long sincerely believed, an incomplete socialism, but a coercive domination in which blindly irrational social forces returned to work once again. When Brecht became a panegyrist of its harmony, his lyric voice had to swallow chalk, and it started to grate. Already the exaggerated adolescent virility of the young Brecht betrayed the borrowed courage of the intellectual who, in despair at violence, suddenly hastens towards a violent practice which he has every reason to fear. The wild roar of *The Measures Taken* drowns out the noise of the disaster that has overtaken the cause, which Brecht convulsively tries to proclaim as salvation. Even Brecht's best work was infected by the deceptions of his commitment. Its language shows how far the underlying poetic subject and its message have come apart. In an attempt to overcome the gap, Brecht affected the diction of the oppressed. But the doctrine he advocated needs the language of the intellectual. The homeliness and simplicity of his tone is thus a fiction. It betrays itself both by signs of exaggeration and by stylized regression to archaic or provincial forms of expression. It can often be importunate, and ears which have not let themselves be deprived of their native sensitivity cannot help hearing that they are talked into something. It is a usurpation and almost contempt for victims to speak like this, as if the author were one of them. All roles may be played except that of the worker. The gravest charge against commitment is that even right intentions go wrong when they are noticed, and still more so when they then try to conceal themselves. Something of this remains in Brecht's later plays in the linguistic gesture of wisdom, the fiction of the old peasant sated with epic experience as the poetic subject. No one in any country of the world is any longer capable of the earthy experience of South German muzhiks: the ponderous delivery has become a propaganda device to make us believe that the good life is where the Red Army is in control. Since there is nothing to give substance to this humanity, which we have to take on trust as realized, Brecht's tone degenerates into an echo of archaic social relations, gone beyond recall. The late Brecht was not so distant from official humanism. A journalistically minded Westerner could well praise *The Caucasian Chalk Circle* as a hymn to motherhood, and who is not touched when the splendid girl is finally held up as an example to the querulous lady beset with migraine? Baudelaire, who dedicated his work to the coiner of the motto *l'art pour l'art*, would have been less suited to such catharsis. Even the grandeur and virtuosity of such poems as *The Legend of the Origin of the Book of Tao Te Ch'ing on Lao-Tzu's Journey into Exile* are marred by the theatricality of total plain-spokenness. What his classical predecessors once denounced as the idiocy of rural life, Brecht, like some existential ontologist, treats as ancient truth. His whole oeuvre is a Sisyphean labor to reconcile his highly cultivated and subtle taste with the crudely heteronomous demands which he desperately imposed on himself.

The Problem of Suffering

I have no wish to soften the saying that to write lyric poetry after Auschwitz is barbaric; it expresses in negative form the impulse which inspires committed literature. The question asked by a character in Sartre's play *Morts Sans Sépulture*, "Is there any meaning in life when men exist who beat people until the bones break in their bodies?", is also the question whether any art now has a right to exist; whether intellectual regression is not inherent in the concept of committed literature because of the regression of society. But Enzensberger's retort also remains true, that literature must resist this verdict, in other words, be such that its mere existence after Auschwitz is not a surrender to cynicism. Its own situation is one of paradox, not merely the problem of how to react to it. The abundance of real suffering tolerates no forgetting; Pascal's theological saying, *On ne doit plus dormir*, must be secularized. Yet this suffering, what Hegel called consciousness of adversity, also demands the continued existence of art while it prohibits it; it is now virtually in art alone that suffering can still find its own voice, consolation, without immediately being betrayed by it. The most important artists of the age have realized this. The uncompromising radicalism of their works, the very features defamed as formalism, give them a terrifying power, absent from helpless poems to the victims of our time. But even Schönberg's *Survivor of Warsaw* remains trapped in the aporia to which it, autonomous figuration of heteronomy raised to the intensity of hell, totally surrenders. There is something painful in Schönberg's compositions—not what arouses anger in Germany, the fact that they prevent people from repressing from memory what they at all costs want to repress. It is rather the way in which, by turning suffering into images, despite all their hard implacability, they wound our shame before the victims. For these are used to create something, works of art, that are thrown to the consumption of a world which destroyed them. The so-called artistic representation of the sheer physical pain of people beaten to the ground by rifle butts contains, however remotely, the power to elicit enjoyment out of it. The moral of this art, not to forget for a single instant, slithers into the abyss of its opposite. The esthetic principle of stylization, and even the solemn prayer of the chorus, make an unthinkable fate appear to have had some meaning; it is transfigured, something of its horror is removed. This alone does an injustice to the victims; yet no art which tried to evade them could stand upright before justice. Even the sound of despair pays its tribute to a hideous affirmation. Works of less than the highest rank are even willingly absorbed, as contributions to clearing up the past. When genocide becomes part of the cultural heritage in the themes of committed literature, it becomes easier to continue to play along with the culture which gave birth to murder. There is one nearly invariable characteristic of such literature. It is that it implies, purposely or not, that even in the so-called extreme situations, indeed in them most of all, humanity flourishes. Sometimes this develops into a dismal metaphysic which does its best to work up atrocities into "limiting situations" which it then accepts to the extent that they reveal authenticity in men. In such a homely existential atmosphere, the distinction between executioners and victims becomes blurred; both, after all, are equally suspended above the possibility of nothingness, which of course is generally not quite so uncomfortable for the executioners.

Kafka, Beckett and Contemporary Experimentalism

Today, the adherents of a philosophy which has since degenerated into a mere ideological sport, fulminate in pre-1933 fashion against artistic distortion, deformation and perversion of life, as though authors, by faithfully reflecting atrocity, were responsible for what they revolt against. The best exemplification of this attitude, still prevalent among the silent majority in Germany, is the following story about Picasso. An officer of the Nazi occupation forces visited the painter in his studio and, pointing to *Guernica*, asked: "Did you do that?". Picasso reputedly answered, "No, you did." Autonomous works of art too, like this painting, firmly negate empirical reality, destroy the destroyer, that which merely exists and by merely existing endlessly reiterates guilt. It is none other than Sartre who has seen the connection between the autonomy of a work and an intention which is not conferred upon it but is its own gesture towards reality. "The work of art," he has written, "*does not have* an end; there we agree with Kant. But the reason is that it *is* an end. The Kantian formula does not account for the appeal which resounds at the basis of each painting, each statue, each book."[8] It only remains to add there is no straightforward relationship between this appeal and the thematic commitment of a work. The uncalculating autonomy of works which avoid popularization and adaptation to the market involuntarily becomes an attack on them. The attack is not abstract, not a fixed attitude of all works of art to the world which will not forgive them for not bending totally to it. The distance these works maintain from empirical reality is in itself partly mediated by that reality. The imagination of the artist is not a creation *ex nihilo*; only dilettanti and esthetes believe it to be so. Works of art that react against empirical reality obey the forces of that reality, which reject intellectual creations and throw them back on themselves. There is no material content, no formal category of an artistic creation, however mysteriously changed and unknown to itself, which did not originate in the empirical reality from which it breaks free.

It is this which constitutes the true relation of art to reality, whose elements are regrouped by its formal laws. Even the *avant-garde* abstraction which provokes the indignation of philistines, and which has nothing in common with conceptual or logical abstraction, is a reflex response to the abstraction of the law which objectively dominates society. This could be shown in Beckett's works. These enjoy what is today the only humanly respectable fame: everyone shudders at them, and yet no one can persuade himself that these eccentric plays and novels are not about what everyone knows but no one will admit. Philosophical apologists may laud his works as sketches for an anthropology. But they deal with a highly concrete historical reality: the abdication of the subject. Beckett's *Ecce Homo* is what human beings have become. As though with eyes drained of tears, they stare silently out of his sentences. The spell they cast, which also binds them, is lifted by being reflected in them. However, the minimal promise of happiness they contain, which refuses to be traded for comfort, cannot be had for a price less than total dislocation, to the point of worldlessness. Here every commitment to the world must be abandoned to satisfy the ideal of the committed work of art—that polemical alienation which Brecht as a theorist invented, and as an artist practiced less and less as he bound himself more tightly to the role of a friend of mankind. This paradox, which might be charged with sophistry, can be supported without much philosophy by the simplest experience: Kafka's prose and Beckett's plays, or the truly monstrous novel *The Unnameable*, have an effect by comparison with which officially committed works look like pantomime. Kafka and Beckett arouse the fear which existentialism merely talks about. By dismantling appearance, they explode from within the art which committed proclamation subjugates from without, and hence only in appearance. The inescapability of their work compels the change of attitude which committed works merely demand. He over whom Kafka's wheels have passed has lost forever both any peace with the world and any chance of consoling himself with the judgment that the way of the world is bad; the element of ratification which lurks in resigned admission of the dominance of evil is burnt away.

Yet the greater the aspiration, the greater is the possibility of foundering and failure. The loss of tension evident in works of painting and music which have moved away from objective representation and intelligible or coherent meaning has in many ways spread to the literature known in a repellent jargon as "texts." Such works drift to the brink of indifference, degenerate insensibly into mere hobbies, into idle repetition of formulas now abandoned in other art forms, into trivial patterns. It is this development which often gives substance to crude calls for commitment. Formal structures which challenge the lying positivism of meaning can easily slide into a different sort of vacuity, positivistic arrangements, empty juggling with elements. They fall within the very sphere from they seek to escape. The extreme case is literature which undialectically confuses itself with science and vainly tries to fuse with cybernetics. Extremes meet; what cuts the last thread of communication becomes the prey of communication theory. No firm criterion can draw the line between a determinate negation of meaning and a bad positivism of meaninglessness, as an assiduous soldiering on just for the sake of it. Least of all can such a line be based on an appeal to the human, and a curse on mechanization. Works of art which by their existence take the side of the victims of a rationality that subjugates nature are even in their protest constitutively implicated in the process of rationalization itself. Were they to try to disown it, they would become both esthetically and socially powerless: mere clay. The organizing, unifying principle of each and every work of art is borrowed from that very rationality whose claim to totality it seeks to defy.

French and German Cultural Traditions

In the history of French and German consciousness, the problem of commitment has been posed in opposite ways. In France, esthetics have been dominated, openly or covertly, by the principle of *l'art pour l'art*, allied to academic and reactionary tendencies.[9] This explains the revolt against it. Even extreme *avant-garde* works have a touch of decorative allure in France. It is for this reason that the call to existence and commitment sounded revolutionary there. In Germany, the situation is the other way round. The liberation of art from any external end, although it was a German who first raised it purely and incorruptibly into a criterion of taste, has always been suspect to a tradition which has deep roots in German idealism. The first famous document of this tradition is that senior masters' bible of intellectual history, Schiller's *Treatise on the Theatre as a Moral Institution*. Such suspicion is not so much due to the elevation of mind to an Absolute that is coupled with it—an attitude that swaggered its way to hubris in German philosophy. It is rather provoked by the side that any work of art free of an ulterior goal shows to society. For this art is a reminder of that sensuous pleasure in which even—indeed especially—the most extreme dissonance, by sublimation and negation, partakes. German speculative philosophy granted that a work of art contains within itself the sources of its transcendence, and that its own sum is always more than it—but only therefore to demand a certificate of good behavior from it. According to this latent tradition, a work of art should have no being for itself, since otherwise it would—as Plato's embryonic state socialism classically stigmatized it—be a source of effeminacy and an obstacle to action for its own sake, the German original sin. Killjoys, ascetics, moralists of the sort who are always invoking names like Luther and Bismarck, have no time for esthetic autonomy; and there is also an undercurrent of servile heteronomy in the pathos of the categorical imperative, which is indeed on the one hand reason itself, but on the other a brute datum to be blindly obeyed. Fifty years ago Stefan George and his school were still being attacked as Frenchifying esthetes.

Today the curmudgeons whom no bombs could demolish have allied themselves with the philistines who rage against the alleged incomprehensibility of the new art. The underlying impulse of these attacks is petty bourgeois hatred of sex, the common ground of Western moralists and ideologists of socialist realism. No moral terror can prevent the side the work of art shows its beholder from giving him pleasure, even if only in the formal fact of temporary freedom from the compulsion of practical goals. Thomas Mann called this quality of art "high spirits," a notion intolerable to people with morals. Brecht himself who was not without ascetic traits—which reappear transmuted in the reserve of any great autonomous art towards consumption—rightly ridiculed culinary art; but he was much too intelligent not to know that pleasure can never be completely ignored in the total esthetic effect, no matter how relentless the work. The primacy of the esthetic object as pure refiguration does not smuggle consumption or false harmony back by a detour. Although the moment of pleasure, even when it is extirpated from the effect of a work, constantly returns to it, the principle that governs autonomous works of art is not the totality of their effects, but their own inherent structure. They are knowledge as nonconceptual objects. This is the source of their greatness. It is not something of which they have to persuade men, because it should be given to them. This is why today autonomous rather than committed works of art should be encouraged in Germany. Committed works all too readily credit themselves with every noble value, and then manipulate them at their ease. Under fascism, too, no atrocity was perpetrated without a moral veneer. Those who trumpet their ethics and humanity in Germany today are merely waiting for a chance to persecute those whom their rules condemn, and to exercise the same inhumanity in practice of which they accuse modern art in theory. In Germany, commitment often means bleating what everyone is already saying or at least secretly wants to hear. The notion of a "message" in art, even when politically radical, already contains an accommodation to the world: the stance of the lecturer conceals a clandestine entente with the listeners, who could only be truly rescued from illusions by refusal of it.

The Politics of Autonomous Art

The type of literature that, in accordance with the tenets of commitment but also with the demands of philistine moralism exists for man, betrays him by traducing that which alone could help him, if it did not strike a pose of helping him. But any literature which therefore concludes that it can be a law unto itself, and exist only for itself, degenerates into ideology no less. Art, which even in its opposition to society remains a part of it, must close its eyes and ears against it: it cannot escape the shadow of irrationality. But when it appeals to this unreason, making it a *raison d'être*, it converts its own malediction into a theodicy. Even in the most sublimated work of art there is a hidden "it should be otherwise." When a work is merely itself and no other thing, as in a pure pseudoscientific construction, it becomes bad art—literally pre-artistic. The moment of true volition, however, is mediated through nothing other than the form of the work itself, whose crystallization becomes an analogy of that other condition which should be. As eminently constructed and produced objects, works of art, even literary ones, point to a practice from which they abstain: the creation of a just life. The mediation is not a compromise between commitment and autonomy, nor a sort of mixture of advanced formal elements with an intellectual content inspired by genuinely or supposedly progressive politics. The content of works of art is never the amount of intellect pumped into them: if anything it is the opposite. Nevertheless, an emphasis on autonomous works is itself sociopolitical in nature. The feigning of a true politics here and now, the freezing of historical relations which nowhere seem ready to melt, oblige the mind to go where it need not degrade itself. Today, every phenomenon of culture, even if a model of integrity, is liable to be suffocated in the cultivation of kitsch. Yet paradoxically in the same epoch it is to works of art that has fallen the burden of wordlessly asserting what is barred to politics. Sartre himself has expressed this truth in a passage which does credit to his honesty.[10] This is not a time for political art, but politics has migrated into autonomous art, and nowhere more so than where it seems to be politically dead. An example is Kafka's allegory of toy guns, in which an idea of non-violence is fused with a dawning awareness of the approaching paralysis of politics. Paul Klee too belongs to any debate about committed and autonomous art: for his work, *écriture par excellence*, has roots in literature and would not have been what it was without them—or if it had not consumed them. During the First World War or shortly after, Klee drew cartoons of Kaiser Wilhelm as an inhuman iron eater. Later, in 1920, these became—the development can be shown quite clearly—the *Angelus Novus*, the machine angel, who, though he no longer bears any emblem of caricature or commitment, flies far beyond both. The machine angel's enigmatic eyes force the onlooker to try to decide whether he is announcing the culmination of disaster or salvation hidden within it. But, as Walter Benjamin, who owned the drawing, said, he is the angel who does not give but takes.

Translated by Francis McDonagh.

Knut Hamsun

By Leo Lowenthal

Less concerned than Adorno with formal issues of content, Lowenthal's essay, originally published in Zeitschrift für Sozialforschung *Vol. VI (1937), is a splended example of ideology critique applied to a sphere allegedly free from ideology. While the longing for and glorification of "nature" is rooted in a correct response to the experience of alienation and domination in bourgeois society, the escape to a sphere or vision abstractly opposed to it merely reinforces what it seeks to avoid. That ideology hides precisely where it is least suspected was a favorite argument of the members of the Institute.*

Lowenthal's argument embodies a typical figure of thought: an abstract, absolute opposition does not really "contradict" its opposite at all; instead, it becomes the other side of the same coin. Rejecting a life of isolation and domination, Hamsun's characters counter it with an isolated alternative whose merely reactive meaning now equally dominates them. Like their audience, they thus remain within the very mode of experience they tried to overcome.

In the periods studied so far, literary artists expressed through their characters the conviction that the activities of the individual are rooted in universally binding values and that therefore these fictional life histories could serve as a parable or a stimulus to others. By the end of the nineteenth century, however, the artist ceases to reflect this ideal of the ethical unity of men.

At his best the modern writer, like all writers, keeps alive the hopes of the individual and the ideal of his self-realization in society; even the defeats he portrays are meaningful within this context. At his worst, however, he can fall victim to an irrational escape into the arms of authoritarianism. Knut Hamsun was this kind of writer. In the twenties and thirties, his work not only enjoyed an excellent international literary reputation but also was regarded—even by liberals and socialists—as politically above reproach. However, in his act of joining Quisling's party during the Second World War, he expressed in practice the authoritarian themes and moods that had long been implicit in his novels: the pagan awe of unlimited and unintelligible forces of nature, the mystique of blood and race, hatred of the working class and of clerks, the blind submission to authority, the abrogation of individual responsibility, anti-intellectualism, and spiteful distrust of urban middle-class life in general.[1]

Nature

In Ibsen, the hymn to nature as a last gesture of hope comes at the end of his final play, *When We Dead Awaken*. Man has found, in the social realm, not true freedom but only a mirage. By contrast with its pressures and restrictions, nature appears as a realm of freedom and a source of happiness and consolation. In enjoyment of the countryside, nothing seems to remain of the perpetual toil and responsibility, competition and even hostility. Communion with nature holds out a new image of man, one that will counter the image of himself as a victim.

The meaning of nature in almost every age is inseparable from social considerations. In the Renaissance, nature meant at once a scene of man's activities, a field for conquest, and an inspiration; it formed the *mise-en-scène* of men's lives. To be sure, even then there was an element of protest—the idyls of natural life in the works of Cervantes and Shakespeare implied a rejection of the contemporary "unnatural" society. Nevertheless, the concept of nature as a counter-ideal to society strengthened the optimistic belief in progress, since it provided men with a yardstick against which shortcomings could be more clearly seen and evaluated. In the history of Western European drama from Shakespeare to Ibsen, and of poetry from Petrarch to Hölderlin, the path to nature was not a flight but a stroll toward liberation.

However, with the coming of doubt and even despair about personal fulfillment within society, the image of nature was no longer a basis for a new perspective, but became an alternative. Nature was increasingly envisaged as the ultimate surcease of social pressure. In this context, man could submit to nature and feel at peace—at least in fantasy. His soul, inviolable in ideology yet outraged in reality, could find solace in such a submission; frustrated in his attempt to participate autonomously in the societal world, he could join the world of nature. He could become a "thing," like the tree or the brook, and find more pleasure in this surrender than in a hopeless struggle against manmade forces. This is the most significant change in man's imagery of his environment to take place in the closing decades of the nineteenth century in Europe. The novels of Knut Hamsun portray this antinomy of society and nature in an extreme form.

Sentimentalism and Brutality

The image of nature in Hamsun's novels has little in common with earlier conceptions of nature as a source of directives for human conduct. It lacks the critical element that made Rousseau's naturalism, for example, a progressive political and cultural force in the eighteenth century. Since the Renaissance, man had seen himself able, at least potentially, to conquer some of nature's forces. This attitude reflected his faith in the unlimited potential of reason and, specifically, his hope for political and social reconstruction.

In Hamsun, submission to nature functions as an escape from the burden of social responsibility. This passive attitude in part explains why Hamsun's heroes are able to profess sentimental pity for the unsheltered animal, the tree in the wind or the withering foliage. In the fate of nature's children, they see a reflection of their own helplessness. To be a victim in the world of men is a threat to dignity. There is a certain solace, on the other hand, in being a victim of majestic natural forces for which man cannot be expected to be personally accountable.

Paradoxically, this new type of submission to nature is closely related to political submission. The yearning for surrender to nature as it appears in Hamsun's novels not only glorifies the awareness of individual weakness but at the same time exalts reverence for superior power in general. In our time we have seen in Europe's totalitarian movements the apotheosis of unshakable political authority—unshakable, in part, because one cannot fathom it. The timelessness and magnificence of nature reinforces the finality of the political power under which man lives. The yearning at once for stability and for glory is a trait of fascist ideologies (Hitler's "thousand years of history") that appears alongside this new type of nature worship.

The home, in the Victorian period particularly, was a refuge from the harshness of business and professional life. In Ibsen, we saw the idyl of the home devoured by the monster of competition, and nature appeared on the horizon as the utopian realm of hope. In Hamsun, flight to nature as protest becomes flight to nature as idolatry, and communion with nature is transformed from sentiment into sentimentality, and then into brutality.

Implicit in this change is an element of anti-intellectualism. The use of reason, in whatever form, is indissolubly bound up with the responsibility of the thinker. Thus, the flight to nature for the sake of abdication of human responsibility soon comes to be rationalized in thought that abhors thinking. This anti-intellectualism must be distinguished from vitalist and pragmatist philosophies earlier in this century. Bergson, Dilthey and certain American philosophers rebelled against rationalist rigidity, to be sure, but their works were nonetheless responsible theoretical enterprises oriented toward the goal of higher individual development. Vitalism (*Lebensphilosophie*) as it was taken up by the ideological spokesmen of fascism looked rather to the submergence of the individual; reason was rejected in favor of overpowering mythical forces, blood and race.

This submergence of reason accompanied a glorification of the peasant, an integral part of anti-liberal undercurrents. The peasant is seen as not alienated from his work; unlike the industrial worker, he does not seem to violate nature but follows, so to speak, its true rhythm. Since his work is hard, healthy, meaningful and in harmony with natural processes, it is set forth as the model of true manliness, dignified and silent. In the analysis that follows, an effort will be made to show that the sentimental conceptions of nature and peasant in Hamsun's novels anticipate an intrinsic part of those political ideologies that forge the concepts of leader, social coercion and soil into a tool of brutality.

Flight into Nature

At first sight, Hamsun does not seem qualified to represent the emergence of a typically modern European authoritarian ethos. (It is noteworthy, however, that it was in Germany that Hamsun obtained his greatest response from the very beginning.) Coming from a small country that, unlike the larger nations, has primary economic interests in agriculture and fishing, Hamsun might be expected to portray themes different from those of writers in highly industrialized nations. But, in fact, it is just this disparity between Norwegian conditions and the situation of the larger and industrially more advanced countries that makes Hamsun's picture of his society so reassuring at first glance and so foreboding upon closer analysis.[2]

Hamsun's first novel, *Hunger*, written in autobiographical form and published in 1890, states the themes that are almost endlessly repeated in the later novels: abandonment of any participation in public life, submission to the stream of incomprehensible and incalculable forces, distrust of the intellect, flight from the city and escape to nature.

The opening sentence of *Hunger* evokes the fate of the average city dweller:

> It was during the time I wandered about and starved in Christiania; Christiania, this singular city, from which no man departs without carrying away the traces of his sojourn there.[3]

The theme of the city is set at once. The fate of the hero is not comprehensible in terms of any conditions specific to him (he is, in this case, luckless and starving), but only in terms of the most general fact, the city. When he has finally had his fill and leaves as a newly hired sailor, the novel ends on the same note with which it began:

> Out in the fjord I dragged myself up once, wet with fever and exhaustion, and gazed landwards, and bade farewell for the present to the town—to Christiania, where the windows gleamed so brightly in all the homes.[4]

One of Hamsun's figures once replied to an apologist for the city:

> You have your home in the city, it is true, and you have decorated it with trinkets and pictures and books; but you have a wife and a maid and hundreds of expenses. In waking and sleeping you must struggle with things, and you never have peace. I have peace. Keep your spiritual goods and the books and art and newspapers, keep your coffee houses and your whiskey which always makes me sick. Here I can roam about the woods, and I feel fine. If you put intellectual problems to me and try to drive me into a corner, I merely reply that God is the source, and that men are in truth only specks and threads in the universe. Even you have gone no further.[5]

The motif of peace is rare in Hamsun's writing;[6] its use here as the key to the blessings of rustic life could perhaps be interpreted as a legitimate protest against urban conditions. When, however, a protest in the name of a seemingly higher idea becomes a wholesale condemnation of civilization, when it does not discriminate between marketplace manipulation and family life, between the newspaper and artistic creations, between anxious restlessness and emotional pleasure, between the futility of mere distraction and the earnestness of serious reading—all of which Hamsun spurns with equal rancor—then we are not dealing with alert social criticism, but with anti-intellectual resentment. Hamsun in the same breath ridicules the cheap pictures on the wall and jeers at the intellect. The final outcome of such impotent resentment is the surrender to brute power.

But first we must trace the steps of this process. What did Hamsun's heroes seek and what did they find in their flight to nature?

Solitude

When Hamsun speaks of man's solitude in nature, he seems at first glance merely to advocate liberation from the pressures of society:

> And there is another thing with which I am never finished, namely, retreating and sitting in the solitude of the woods, surrounded by beauty and darkness. That is the final joy.[7]

Nature appears to hold forth the promise of fulfilling the desire for relationships in which gratitude, joy and rest can come to fruition:

> Thanks for the lonely night, for the hills, the rush of the darkness and the sea through my heart! Thanks for my life, for my breath, for the boon of being alive tonight; thanks from my heart for these! . . . By my immortal soul, I am full of thanks that it is I who am sitting here![8]

But on closer inspection, it becomes clear that a new approach is in the making, according to which nature is more than a soothing balm:

> You must not believe that nothing happens here . . . I could send significant tales from here, but I don't do it. I have sought the woods for solitude and for the sake of my great irons. I have a few great irons within me, and they are getting red hot.[9]

These passages do not conjure up an idyllic and peaceful image of nature, but introduce a note of boastful resentment. A few pages later in the novel, the hero, thinking of the reindeer, ponders the secrets of his existence:

> I think all these things.
> And you? Have you compared your two newspapers, and do you know now what is the public opinion in Norway today about old-age insurance?[10]

Hamsun anticipates his imagined antagonist's retort, and with considerable resentment:

> Here you will certainly help yourself and make sport of me; you can say many droll things about the tree stump and me. But deep down you know that I am superior to you in this as in everything else, once I admit that I do not have as much city knowledge and that I was no student, ha ha. You can teach me nothing about wood and fields, for there I feel what no man has felt.[11]

The idea of a private kingdom to which man stubbornly clings (we have only to think of the dreams of fulfillment with which Ibsen endows his women) is transferred by Hamsun to the solitude of nature. This nature, however, is not merely an extrahuman place where one can go and from which one can return; it is a substitute for human society. Nature is the seat of magical qualities of a new kind. In the old fairy tales, men learn to speak the language of animals; in order to be lords of all creation, they seek to overcome the barriers of nature by bringing the animal world into the human through the medium of speech. Hamsun's hero, however, seeks to draw from nature the meaning which he can no longer deduce from history. What he "overhears" (the tales he could tell but does not) is not meant to increase man's knowledge of his world and himself; if the tales were told, they would report only his own resentment and contempt.

Identity

The philosophy of liberalism did not encompass the idea that the whole world had come within man's power. Subject and object were opposed in the forms of active man and conquerable nature. Nature was raw material and man the unrealized potential; man realized himself in its conquest. Social relationships were implicit in this interaction; the knowledge of nature was won through communication of man with man, and nature was transformed by organized societal enterprise. The relationship toward which Hamsun's ideas tend is of a totally different kind. Nature is no longer looked upon as an object for scientific and practical control; instead, Hamsun's hero consecrates his life in rapt surrender to nature and even in mystical identification:

> We are in the midst of an omnipresence. That is truly God. That is truly we ourselves as parts of the whole.[12]

To Hamsun, nature means peace, but a peace which has lost its spontaneity and its will to know and to control. It is a peace based on submission to every arbitrary power, a pantheism which offers an escape from the gloomy framework of history. Nature comes to mean the solace of the unchangeable and the all-pervasive:

> . . . he lost himself, was carried away and wrapt in the frenzy of sunshine . . . He was in a mysterious state, filled with psychic pleasure; every nerve in him was awake; he had music in his blood, felt akin to all nature, to the sun and the mountains and everything else, felt surrounded by a whisper of his own ego-sense from trees and tufts and blades of grass.[13]

The hero avoids asking any embarrassing questions about the rest of mankind. He shows concern only for his own fate. There is even a hint that nature is his private property and that his enjoyment of it is a kind of personal possession. Paragraph after paragraph of exalted description communicates neither observation nor knowledge, but only a desire for personal omnipotence and for pantheistic possession of the world by emotional immersion:

> The sky all open and clean; I stared into that clear sea, and it seemed as if I were lying face to face with the uttermost depth of the world; my heart beating tensely against it, and at home there.[14]

The timelessness of such pantheism gives the illusion of an immediate, complete possession of the entire world, a possession that at the same time cuts off historical progress. Gone is the optimistic dualism of liberalistic philosophy which always maintained close contact with history, considered the transitoriness of the human situation, and often gave birth to a conception of the future, utopian to be sure, in which a final stasis of perfection might be reached.

Hamsun's identification with the whole of nature can be consummated with no exertion and with no fear of disillusionment. What the utopians had envisioned as a potential unity of man and nature comes to be proclaimed as already realized: the meaning of man's life is to be found in natural factors such as blood and soil. When such a myth is consciously used in the interests of a power apparatus, as it was under fascism, men are told that their inevitable and irrevocable share of nature is their "race" and their nation.

Fury

The shift to an authoritarian concept of nature is apparent also in the changed imagery of the fury of the elements. Compare Hamsun's descriptions with similar ones in earlier literature. Hamsun writes:

> . . . lightning flashes, and soon thereafter the thunder rolls like an immense avalanche far beyond, between the mountains . . . Lightning again, and the thunder is closer at hand; it also begins to rain, a driving rain, the echo is very powerful, all nature is in an uproar, a chaos. I want to enfeeble the night by yelling at it, otherwise it will deprive me mysteriously of all my strength and will power. . . . More lightning and thunder and more driving rain, it is as if I were whipped by the echo nearby . . .[15]

Kant, too, once wrote about the power of nature:

> Bold, overhanging, and, as it were, threatening rocks, thunder-clouds piled up to the vault of heaven, borne along with flashes and peals, volcanoes in all their violence of destruction, hurricanes leaving desolation in their track, the boundless ocean rising with rebellious force, the high waterfall of some mighty river . . .[16]

At first sight, there appears to be no essential difference between the two passages. For Kant, however, the sublimity of nature and the experience of man's helplessness before it are counterbalanced by the concept of nature as subordinate in the face of humanity. It is man's own knowledge and imagination which creates the conception of the grandiosity in nature that dwarfs him. In the end, the rational faculties of man are of a higher order than the elemental force of nature, and they allow him to see it as sublime, instead of simply terrifying:

> . . . we readily call these objects sublime, because they raise the forces of the soul above the height of vulgar commonplace, and

discover within us a power of resistance of quite another kind, which gives us courage to be able to measure ourselves against the seeming omnipotence of nature.[17]

Thus, for Kant, nature is not to console man for frustrations, but to stimulate his moral and intellectual development.

In Hamsun, the relation of man to nature takes on an entirely different cast.

I stood in the shelter of an overhanging rock, thinking many things; my soul was tense. Heaven knows, I thought to myself, what it is I am watching here, and why the sea should open before my eyes. Maybe I am seeing now the inner brain of earth, how things are at work there, boiling and foaming.[18]

The locus of knowledge has become nature itself, mysterious and beyond man's capacities to know. Hamsun's questions are framed so they cannot be answered; his tired individuals seek to silence themselves as quickly as possible. They really have nothing to say, and they welcome the storm that can roar loudly enough to drown out their own silence. The relationship of man to nature as seen by Kant is reversed; for Hamsun, the storm serves as an occasion for increasing the individual's awareness of his own insignificance.

When a moment of sadness and realization of my own nothingness in the face of all the surrounding powers comes over me, I lament and think: Which man am I now, or am I perhaps lost, am I perhaps no longer existent! And I speak aloud and call my name, in order to hear whether he is still present.[19]

Anxiety enters as a component of Hamsun's pantheism. Kant's pride in human autonomy is replaced by a sentimental uneasiness that is announced in every thunderstorm and that is subsequently ramified as a jumble of mawkish sympathies for both natural objects and spiritual difficulties.[20] Hamsun's nature world foreshadows the affinity of brutality and sentimentality, a well-known phenomenon in Nazi Germany.

Rhythm

When Hamsun speaks of nature, it is generally the forest and the sea. In the world of the forest, the law of rhythm, another significant element in Hamsun's imagery of nature, emerges:

There is nothing more glorious than the soughing of the woods. It is like swinging, rocking—a madness: Uganda, Antananarivo, Honolulu, Atacama, Venezuela.[21]

The countries and cities have no concrete significance: what is essential is the sound of their names, which serves only to evoke and echo the order of natural motion. The rhythmic cycle of the seasons is also incessantly noted in the novels, where hypnotic prose again seems to imitate the phenomenon itself:

Then came the autumn, then came the winter.[22]

But the road leads on, summer follows spring in the world . . .[23]

The days passed, time passed.[24]

Innumerable sentences of this kind sometimes take the form of a linguistic leitmotif, such as the ruthlessness of life, the procession of the seasons, the march of time, the men who go over the field or walk along the road, the measured steps of life and so forth.[25] Elsewhere, we find the seasonal and the daily rhythms unified:

It is the autumn season now, a silence in the woods all round; the hills are there, the sun is there, and at evening the moon and the stars will come; all regular and certain, full of kindliness, an embrace.[26]

The rhythmic principle can also take on a normative character. What is wrong with certain people is that

they won't keep pace with life . . . but there's none should rage against life.[27]

Even man's sexual relationships are oriented to the regularity of nature. The shepherdess will walk past the hunter's cabin in the autumn just as infallibly as she comes to him in the spring:

The autumn, the winter, had laid hold of her too; her senses drowsed.[28]

Uniformity of rhythm and tempo is sought in both the natural and human spheres; the passage of time brings recurrence, and not change. Nature's timetable replaces the timetable of history. This tendency displays the same simplification that is found in Hamsun's selection of landscapes. Whoever senses and accepts these rhythmic patterns as fundamental has full knowledge immediately and without rational effort. At the same time, the endless reproduction of natural phenomena, the cyclic order of nature, as opposed to the apparent disorder and happenstance of all individual and historical facts, testifies to the powerlessness of man. It is the extreme opposite of human self-assurance before nature. In this new ideology, which seeks to transfigure helplessness and subjection, the individual in seemingly free volition lays down his arms before a mythical power. Once, nature was held to be "autonomous" only insofar as it was not yet recreated as the product of human activity. Now, however, man must expect a life without meaning unless he obediently accepts as his own what may be called the law of nature. And the social counterpart to the law of natural rhythm is blind discipline.

Hero Worship

When Hamsun speaks of the forces of nature to which man should subject himself, it is, as we have noted, mostly of the woods and the sea. But when he speaks of man himself, as he should be, he leaves these unspoiled provinces behind and speaks foremost of farming. Hamsun's emphasis is not upon the social conditions of the farm; rather, he is again involved in constructing the myth which demands the necessity of man's submission to nature. The peasant tunes himself to forces stronger than himself, and that is supposed to be the lesson he can teach us. In addition, vigorous youth and women are portrayed as truly obedient to nature's forces. Hamsun gives us, in fact, a gallery of unheroic heroes, whose qualities are primarily those of subjection and discipline.

The Peasant

Hamsun's peasants are not individuals; they are aspects of nature, and his apparent admiration of them is not a love of man, but a reverence for the domination of nature over its inhabitants.

> His [the peasant's] life was spent in this work and that, according to the season; from the fields to the woods, and back to the fields again.[29]

This sentence is typical. The peasant himself is not characterized; he is presented only as a natural phenomenon that comes and goes like the blossoming and withering of the leaves in the forest. That is precisely the identity which Hamsun seeks, an identity established by nature, not by man:

> . . . looking up at blue peaks every day of your lives; no new-fangled inventions about that, but fjeld and rocky peaks, rooted deep in the past—but you've them for companionship. There you are, living in touch with heaven and earth, one with them, one with all these wide, deep-rooted things.[30]

The course of history is reversed: "Man and nature don't bombard each other."[31] In Hamsun, nature has no place for the individual as such; his irrelevancy is not only described but glorified in the person of the peasant who is reduced to a biological speck in the rhythm of life.

> 'Tis you that maintain life. Generation to generation, breeding ever anew; and when you die, the new stock goes on. That's the meaning of eternal life.[32]

Daniel is the name of this peasant, but any other peasant could serve as well. "Daniel was the same today as yesterday . . ."[33] And the elements in nature with which the peasant deals are always the same, too.

> Wherever there was a tiny patch of fertile ground, there hay or potatoes or barley grew; in summer the cattle were out in the pasture, in winter they stood in their stalls—it was all so eternal and so changeless.[34]

In the course of the flight to nature, Hamsun's individual is stripped of his singular human qualities and subjected to "eternal" naturalness. " 'Tis the land I'm here for."[35] Service to nature is the real law of peasant life, and happiness means only that he has fulfilled his naturalistic destiny. Only submission to the laws of nature that dictate, for example, the cultivation of grain makes man an admirable figure:

> Growth of the soil was something different, a thing to be pro-cured at any cost; the only source, the origin of all.[36]

For generations back, into forgotten time, his fathers before him had sowed corn; solemnly on a still, calm evening . . . Corn was nothing less than bread; corn or no corn meant life or death.[37]

The products of cities are devaluated or totally ignored, in a kind of travesty of the theories of the physiocrats:

> "There isn't a human being anywhere in the world who can live on banks and industries. Not a single human being in the world."
> "Ho! What do they live on, then?"
> "On three things and nothing else," replies Ezra. "On the grain of the fields, the fish of the sea and the birds and beasts of the forest. On those three things. I've thought it all out."
> "There's quite a few that live on their money—"
> "No," said Ezra. "Not a single soul!"[38]

As contrasted with the emptiness of urban existence, the concreteness of the peasant's world seems to comprise the meaning of life itself:

> He did not feel poor and forlorn, as he really was; why, all the stones he had cleared looked just like a crowd of people around him, he was personally related to every stone, they were acquaintances every one, he had conquered them and got them out of the ground.[39]

The authoritarian state did not have to invent the idea of man's roots as being in blood and soil, nor devise the manipulation of this slogan as a solace for want. "We will not be any happier if we eat more bacon," says Hamsun's peasant in defending life on Norwegian soil against a life outside that might mean greater material success; the worst fate is

> . . . to be torn up by the roots from our own barren soil and transplanted into richer . . .[40]

If we accept this belief, we do not scorn the hardest labor,[41] for we know "where we really do belong."[42]

> It is a good thing to belong to one's class, otherwise one becomes an upstart and gets one's originality frittered away.[43]

A good thing if you are a peasant, that is. Hamsun's eulogy of the peasant, apparently undertaken in the spirit of social critique, ends up as a sermon on temperance, humility, privation. The message is to keep one's roots where they are, even though the soil may be very poor indeed.

As we might expect, Hamsun combines his cult of the hero and that of natural forces with praise for the vigor of youth *per se*. In comparison with this vigor, the restrained wisdom of maturity counts for little; the demand of youth for power is natural obedience to the "law of life."

> Old age should not be revered for its own sake, for it merely restricts and hinders the progress of mankind. Even primitive people despise old age,[44] and they emancipate themselves from it and its hindrances without further ado.[45]

He applies to human beings the lessons of biology—more precisely, of botany—thus:

> And what have you learned from the woods? But what did I learn in the woods? That there are young trees there.
> Now the young stand behind me, ridiculed shamelessly and barbarously by every fool, simply because they are young.[46]

This resentful yet sentimental sermon is tied to an attack on leaders who are old enough to have learned from experience.

> One should not rely too much on the leaders; the country's youth should be our hope. No; a leader is apt to prove a broken reed. It is an old law that whenever a leader reaches a certain age he pauses—yes, he even turns right about face and pushes the other way. Then it is up to the young to march on, to drive him ahead or trample him down.[47]

Hamsun's heroes do not often speak with such harsh frankness. He lends exultation to the rough tone of the young male in order to glorify manliness in general. He is happy that the peasant, reverent and serene as he is, knows how to bring his wife to her senses: "To think that a man's hard grip could work such wonders!"[48] The myth of manliness is created out of "natural" qualities of superior force.

The Vagabond

Along with the peasant, the vagabond receives affectionate treatment in every period of Hamsun's career. August, his favorite, longs "to

shoot the knife out of the hand of a man who was trying to make off
with his wallet" because that would be a thrill for the "children of the
age" in their dreary existence.[49] As a matter of fact, Hamsun seems
fascinated by such brutal mischief:

> And steal a bag of gold and silver plate from the market, and hide
> it in the mountains, so that a blue flame can float over the spot on
> autumn evenings. But don't come to me with three pairs of
> mittens and a side of bacon.[50]

In this pseudo-romantic flirting with a nuisance crime, he ridicules the
"unheroic" spirit of urban efficiency ("no thunderbolt ever falls");[51]
he cries for "gigantic demi-gods" and blunders into a political program of violence:

> The great terrorist is greatest, the dimension, the immense lever
> which can raise worlds.[52]

The peasant with his roots in the soil and the bohemian vagabond
with no ties to anything may seem mutually exclusive idols. Still,
Hamsun's ability to sympathize with such apparently opposite types
has a certain logic; their common denominator is the rejection of
organized urban culture, in favor of the application of raw, unmediated "natural" force. Incidentally, it was the socially uprooted
literati (the "armed bohemians," as they have been called) who
performed the spadework of German fascism, playing up the cult of
the hero and the maintenance of one's roots in the soil.

In Hamsun, the function of such marginal figures as the
vagabond is emphatically different from that in the literature thus far
discussed. From Cervantes through Ibsen, marginal characters have
stood outside society and criticized it in the name of freedom and self-
determination. In Hamsun, however, such figures serve as coquettish
expression of his veneration of brutality and power.

The Relation of the Sexes

The endorsement of violence and mischief seems to be a far cry from
the theme of passive surrender to nature. But the connection between
violence and passivity becomes unequivocal in Hamsun's treatment of
the relation between the sexes. In his novels, there is a conspicuous
absence of genuine yearning for love. When one of his characters is
seized by a strong passion, it is quickly transformed into sado-

masochistic torment of himself or of the partner. This is as true of the desperate ecstasy of the hero in *Hunger*, or of the literally speechless and unexpressed affair between the main characters in *Victoria*, as of the mutual hatred of the partners in *Pan*. The hero of *Mysteries* enjoys telling his beloved the most frightening and brutal stories;[53] the hero of *Pan* shoots his dog and sends the corpse as a farewell gift to the beloved from whom he has become estranged.[54]

What passes for love is closer to hostility:

> Does she then love a dead man to the point of hatred and cruelty and is she still trying to hurt him? Or is Glahn still alive and does she want to continue her torture?[55]

In general, however, sadism is much less developed than masochism. People seem to find happiness only when subjected to strength, power, and authority. On occasion, one can readily observe the shift from sadism to masochism:

> Eva answers: "It was cruel of her to laugh at you."
> "No, it was not cruel of her," I cry . . . "it was only right that she should laugh at me. Be quiet, devil take you, and leave me in peace—do you hear?"
> And Eva, terrified, leaves me in peace. I look at her, and repent my harsh words at once; I fall down before her; wringing my hands. "Go home, Eva. It is you I love most. . . . It was only a jest; it is you I love."[56]

In one of his earliest novels as well as in one of his last, a lover asks for harsh treatment:

> Only you torture me too much with your forbearance; how can you put up with my having more than one eye? You ought to take the other, you ought to take both; you shouldn't allow me to walk along the street in peace and have a roof over my head.[57]
> Hurt me in return! Do you hear! Otherwise you'll go off and believe I've been ruined by some one, but that isn't true.[58]

Satisfaction in love seems possible only in the sexual sphere, and even then it is not because sensual pleasure signifies any feelings of affection and identification, but on the contrary springs from malice and disdain, particularly for women:

> "Come and show where there's cloudberries," said Gustaf . . . And how could a woman say no? Inger ran into her little room and was both earnest and religious for several minutes; but there was Gustaf standing waiting outside, the world was at her heels, and all she did was to tidy her hair, look at herself carefully in the glass, and out again. And what if she did? Who would not have done the same? Oh, woman cannot tell one man from another; not always—not often.[59]

This spiteful eulogy of lust brings Hamsun back to his point of departure: the definition of man as mere nature. In an early novel, promiscuity seems to thrive in gaiety and freedom:

> "Iselin, I saw what you did," he says again; "I saw you."
> And then her rich, glad laughter rings through the wood, and she goes off with him, full of rejoicing from top to toe. And whither does she go? To the next mortal man; to a huntsman in the woods.[60]

But even this cavalier concession to pleasure and satisfaction describes only another form of isolation, for there is complete lack of interest in the happiness of one's partner. Sexual relations are ruled by the laws of nature which men and women instinctively obey.

> There she goes, a human being like the rest of us, a wanderer in the earth, a little girl, ah me! a life gone astray, a flying seed. She was fairly undejected in her walk . . . She had the packet of papers under her arm, she knew what awaited her at the barn, and there she went. Some call it free will.[61]
> . . . he broke through all rules of propriety and was very friendly, picked the hay from her bosom, brushed it from her knees, stroked, patted, threw his arms around her. Some call it free will . . .[62]

Whatever is distinctly human and spiritual is forgotten. Love, which for Cervantes and Shakespeare appeared as the key phenomenon in the autonomous development of modern man, becomes reduced in Hamsun to a bawdy jeer at free will.

Women

Hamsun belittles Ibsen's women, and thumbs his nose at Ibsen himself for his description of Nora (in *A Doll's House*):

> I know a sage, and he wrote of woman. Wrote of woman, in
> thirty volumes of uniform theatre poetry: I counted the volumes
> once in a big bookcase. And at last he wrote of the woman who
> left her own children to go in search of—the wonderful! But
> what, then, were the children? Oh, it was comical: a wanderer
> laughs at anything so comical.[63]

Woman attains fulfillment of her destiny when she limits her functions
to those of a housewife and a mother. This enshrinement of biological
function leads Hamsun to bitter hatred for any emancipation, intellectuality, or political reforms that women might desire[64] and finally, in
an attack on actresses, to utter comtempt for the "modern woman":

> You ladies pretend to look down on domestic life, pretend to be
> indifferent to the scanty personal respect you enjoy; you are
> either not mothers at all, or very bad ones, either incapable of
> bringing up children or pitifully imcompetent at it—every day of
> your lives you sink into deeper shame on account of this impo-
> tence. That is the truth.[65]

The ideal peasant woman, wife of the ideal peasant in *Growth of the
Soil*, unpleasant in appearance and not always faithful, has a meaningful existence as a housewife and mother: A "good nature, a clever
nature,"[66]

> . . . the Margravine . . . is indoors preparing the meal. Tall and
> stately, as she moves about her house, a Vestal tending the fire of
> a kitchen stove. Inger has made her stormy voyage, 'tis true, has
> lived in a city a while, but now she is home.[67]

This theme is constantly reiterated: woman receives her true consecra-
tion as a mother. Of the tragic ruin of a woman who sought to run away
from an unsatisfying marriage, only this is said:

> She had no occupation, but had three maidservants to her house;
> she had no children, but she had a piano. But she had no
> children.[68]

It is another woman, a paragon of mediocrity, who receives the
accolade:

> A mother many times, realizing life—it was worthy of a great
> reward.[69]

In such idealization of fertility, biology takes precedence over the conventions of middle-class morality; as in the case of Inger, sexual vicissitudes are blinked—indeed are condoned—provided the end or denouement is that of producing children. This was also a stock in trade of the Nazi ideology, which reduced womanhood to a biological function. Hamsun's language becomes almost epic when he speaks of woman as the bearer of progeny: she becomes a fertility-heroine:

> A real girl shall marry, shall become the wife of a man, shall become a mother, shall become a blessing to herself.[70]

Urban Society

The idolatry of nature is set up against "a world where cheating goes on in the dark."[71] The composition of this rejected world is quite apparent. It is, in brief, an inventory of modern urban society that Hamsun condemns—industry,[72] public officials,[73] the natural sciences,[74] the teaching profession,[75] the coffee house,[76] the corporation,[77] and countries under liberal governments—as well as the city, the intellectuals, the workers and platforms of social reform; these are all surveyed in the novels and dismissed as hateful. Significant, for example, are his contemptuous remarks on Gladstone,[78] and his rejection of "the modern type, a man of our time," who believes "all the Jew and the Yankee have taught him."[79] He has warm words of praise for Sweden because she is oriented toward Germany, not toward Switzerland,[80] and he tells the English that they "will someday be whipped to death by the healthy destiny of Germany."[81]

Numerous are his attacks on Switzerland—not just coincidentally the model of democratic experimentation. In one of his novels, a man plans to build a comfortable home for his family in the "Swiss fashion." He is taken to task by Hamsun for believing he can learn something

> . . . from a miserable little people up in the Alps, a people that throughout its history has never been or done anything worth speaking of.[82]

These attacks are typical of a romanticizing primitivism anticipating in literature the sneering propaganda of the middle-European authoritarian parties against "effeminacy" and the "morass" of the big cities. When Hamsun assumes the posture of social critic, he focuses his attention only on superficial, secondary aspects of industrial society. Everything the inquiring mind finds of interest and of crucial importance—including consideration for mutual help—is flattened out, or swept away with an imperious gesture. Not accidentally, a chief butt of his ridicule are the manufacturers of consumer goods, whom he epitomizes in those who seem most readily to lend themselves to caricature, such as producers of canned goods, candies and herring meal.[83] "Butter?" he asks:

> One did not churn butter any more—one went to the store and bought margarine. Storehouse and shed full of meat, pork and fish? One would have died of laughter at anybody who kept salt meat . . . wasn't there food to be had in tins—tinned food? It was ready cooked, it was chewed too, it was ready to put into a cloth to make a child's sucker of for all mankind . . . What did mouths want with teeth anymore? Weren't there false teeth hanging on a string in the toothmaker's shop? And as for the tinned foods . . . it dealt gently with people who had already got stomach trouble from eating it.[84]

Middle Class

For Hamsun, intellectuals and public officials exemplify middle-class triviality. The work of the journalist, the teacher and the historian find no favor in his eyes.[85] Scientists are represented as having wrought a permanent injury against man; science is an empty mechanism, an incomprehensible hodge-podge of data.[86]

The brunt of the attack is on civil servants[87] and clerks in general:

> . . . officials—believe me, they are a miserable tribe . . . Nothing but mediocre abilities and stunted energies; the triumph of the commonplace.[88]

In the midst of a hymn to nature ("I am never done with grass and stones"), Hamsun plunges into an attack on the "sons of clerks," the "official residence," and the "garden of the commonplace" where everything is decided "on account of age, length of service, and school learning."[89]

> . . . with such useless hands as theirs, which they could turn to no manual labor, they could only sit in an office writing . . . such servile work as writing the letters of the alphabet . . . The most that can befall them is to fail in an examination . . . I pity them

. . . bent over a table so long that they are round-shouldered; they are helpless with their hands; they generally wear glasses—a sign that as learning poured into their brains, it sucked the sight from their eyes . . .[90]

Now—as we see the clerk, the bureaucrat, the intellectual portrayed as sickly, decadent, impotent—there emerges by implication the counter-image of the self-assured, vigorous, tough Nordic hero. Those who do not display these virtues are summarily disqualified.

Working Class

Contempt for factory workers and for workers' movements permeates Hamsun's novels. It first appears in the disguise of his romanticizing naturalism:

What was more, I liked to be among field and forest, not with lumbermen and proletariat.[91]

But soon in the same novel, the disguise falls away and resentment comes to the fore:

These gentlemen of the proletariat think a good deal of themselves; they look down on farm workers, and will have nothing to do with them . . . Then, too, they are more popular among the girls. It is the same with men working on roads or railways, with all factory hands . . .[92]

This contemptuous sarcasm remains a key motif. In one of his last novels we read:

The moment that Alex had found himself with a job and with money in his pocket, food in his belly and clothes on his back, he had crawled to his feet and begun stalking around like a man, had even applied for membership in the trade union, to which he pointed with considerable pride.[93]

The competitive interwovenness of urban lower strata appears as a threat to the "heroic" *status quo*—life on the soil.

The others, the workingmen, businessmen, the day-laborers, go about showing their teeth at one another and fighting. That is life.

They are really fighting over the old landowner, they are fighting over his possessions.[94]

For Hamsun, the struggle for an increase in material welfare is merely vulgar. Whatever rational justifications such claims may have is no concern of his. He engages in a variety of attacks on "the proletariat's strong and blind craving for food,"[95] on "the roar of the masses," who unfortunately have learned from "mechanical reading and writing" how beautiful it is to "live by others' labor."[96] But worst of all are the destructive tendencies that are bound up with the workingman's "worldly greed."

They [the masses] want to roar and turn things upside down, and when it comes to a pinch even their own leaders can't hold them in. The whole thing's crashing, let it crash![97]

Here indeed we are face to face with the nihilistic furor of the authoritarian mentality.

Nihilism

Anti-Intellectualism
At the peak of liberalist optimism, popular manifestations of confidence in scientific progress made the coffee houses and beer halls the layman's university, with natural science, medicine, and politics the favorite subjects in the curriculum. True, these flourishing ideas were without influence, not only in the groves of Academe, but in society at large; still, the constant critical concern with the affairs of science and public life served to perpetuate a confidence in the efficacy of each member of society.

The incomprehensibility and inexorability of the social process has increasingly given rise to pseudo-philosophies and pseudo-sociologies which claim to possess superior wisdom, keys to the mystery of human relationships, recipes for the best and quickest possible solution to man's dilemmas. The attraction, in recent decades, of innumerable panaceas for curing the ills of the world through programs which promise to discover the meaning of life in nature illustrates this trend. Nudism, astrology, dietary and breathing fads are cases in point. Man seeks to draw from nature the meaning he cannot find in society.

At the same time, the results of science and education are often not experienced by broad strata of the population as aids to progress. What was actually to be gained from the work of the natural scientists, from the apparatus of schools and other cultural institutions?—so people asked. To the extent that these activities seemed unrelated to universal improvement in material welfare, an impression grew that learning was an empty program, busywork or pointless pastime. Anti-intellectualism is intimately linked with disillusionment in the credo of progress among broad social strata in Europe. To them, the intellect appeared either as an instrument of domination or as an abstract conglomeration of phrases and slogans having no reference to their own concerns.

This loss of faith by Europeans in their rationalistic daydreams, wherein their power had seemed to grow without bonds, was given respectability by the anti-liberal literati's devaluation of reason. Hamsun's anti-intellectualism soon became apparent in his attacks on earlier nineteenth-century writers. One of his heroes calls Maupassant "crude and soulless,"[98] Tolstoi "a fool in philosophy" who talks "twaddle,"[99] and Ibsen a "little writing oddity"[100] who has brought shame upon his country, a land which has engendered nothing but "peace conferences, the skiing spirit, and Ibsen so far."[101] In 1892, Hamsun already contributed to the authoritarian *Führer* cult—which jeers at the moral anxieties and compulsions of the intellectual, while arrogantly exalting the morally insensate body-beautiful ideal of the racial hero—when he joined his contempt for one of Ibsen's more remarkable sayings with an alleged physical weakness of the playwright:

> The great poet produces a pursed-lips expression, braces his chicken breast to the utmost, and delivers himself of the following words: "To make poetry is to summon oneself to the Day of Judgment."[102]

Philosophy of Life
Hamsun's heroes are querulous in posing the problem of their destiny. The hungry one asks:

> Was the hand of the Lord turned against me? But why just against me? Why, for that matter, not just as well against a man in South America?[103]

The journalist Lynge never finds an answer to his question:

Why could not everything be good, and why could not men be happy in life?[104]

A lover poses the problem:

The other he loved as a slave, as a madman and a beggar. Why? Ask the dust of the road and the leaves that fall, ask the mysterious God of life, for there is no other that knows such things.[105]

When August, the vagabond, meets with misfortune, the question is raised:

Possibly somewhere away out in the universe there was a great eye which was watching him, a power which in some way or another had learned of his labours in the desperate service of nothing at all.[106]

In the end, the answer to all these questions of suffering humanity is invariably surrender—surrender to a sphere of power existing before and beyond all individual existence. Man is not capable of changing it in any way, nor is he entitled to do so. "What is life's? All! But what is yours?"[107] And the answer demonstrates once more the worthlessness of the individual. "Life could afford to waste her, to throw her away."[108] That is true of every floundering human being— and every human being is going under. "Life is a loan . . . I know no one who has not fared as badly as myself . . ."[109] Hamsun again and again gives expression to the passivity and obedience which such inexorability of life requires. While life itself "has thrust me away into something hostile to myself," there is no court which must answer the question, "why should life do that?"[110] There is only one law here: "Life can afford to waste."[111]

Hamsun's philosophy of life has a twofold social function. On the one hand, it offers the socially less successful the consolation that their insignificant role in the economic process can be compensated for by the acceptance of the greater, metaphysical context of the omnipotence of life:

And so it is: the mere grace that we are given life at all is generous payment in advance for all the miseries of life—for every one of them. No, do you think we have the right to more sweetmeats than we get.[112]

The individual is to become reconciled to his condition in society by perceiving himself as a necessary sacrifice to a natural process, a sacrifice not merely mechanical but full of meaning.

On the other hand, this mythology offers no tangible expectations for alleviating deprivation and disillusionment. The consolation turns against those consoled. They must accept life as it is, and that means the existing relations of domination and subordination, of command and serve.

The Image of Man

Hamsun's mythology throws new light on his misanthropic contempt. His exalted picture of life stands side by side with the image of crawling and creeping man, in the same way that authoritarian propaganda later combined ostensibly lofty notions with expressions of vulgar misanthropy. A metaphysics of the miserableness of man is mobilized against the idea of human progress. Every desire for a more rational organization of society becomes incongruous.

It is significant that Hamsun uses the analogy of the anthill, so popular in liberal reformist literature as a model of constructive social order, as an image of planlessness:

> . . . but that made no difference to the town, the town remained the little crawling ant-hill it was, and this in itself must have been a proof that life itself went its way in spite of all theories . . .[113]

> Oh, that little anthill! All its inhabitants are occupied with their own affairs, they cross each other's paths, push each other aside, sometimes they trample each other underfoot. It cannot be otherwise, sometimes they trample each other underfoot.[114]

We have returned with the ants to the starting point, the myth of nature. Every recollection of historical existence has now been obliterated. We are left with an apotheosis of the merely natural—of force without reason. The exodus from social reality is complete.

Behind Hamsun's bitter responses to contemporary civilization lies the cold and nihilistic negation of the very image of man on the road to freedom. His characters are not truly individuals but irrelevant particles in an ahuman process forever beyond their control. Both as an artist and as a political partisan, he was unequal to the challenge of the great heritage of libertarian thought in the West. Cervantes and Shakespeare, Racine and Molière, Goethe and Ibsen, had this in common: all embraced the struggle of the individual with his social and natural environment; all refused to place limits on human imagination and achievement; all, with fervor and tenderness, served human liberty.

Notes

Esthetic Theory and Cultural Criticism

1. Cf. Horkheimer, "Authority and the Family" (1936) in *Critical Theory*, pp. 52ff; Marcuse, "Affirmative Culture" (1937) in *Negations*, pp. 88ff.Horkheimer's essay is perhaps the only Frankfurt treatise that ostensibly focuses on the more general concept of culture. Yet almost imperceptibly, *as* he begins to discuss the role of culture in mediating power and domination, he shifts to a conceptualization of "high culture" and an intermediate category of belief system, institutionalized and psychically introjected (pp. 59ff).

2. Cf. *Die Philosophie des Geldes* 6th ed. (Berlin: Duncker and Humblot, 1958) and the various essays collected in *On Individuality and Social Forms*, ed. D. Levine (Chicago: U. of Chicago Press, 1971) and in *The Conflict of Modern Culture*, ed. P. Etzkorn (New York: Teachers College Press, 1968). On the development of Simmel's culture concept cf. A. Arato, "The Neo-Idealist Defense of Subjectivity," *Telos* (St. Louis, Fall 1974) XXI.

3. The orthodox Hegelian side of Simmel is as we have said not expressed consistently. Because for him all cultural activity is objectification (which he identified with alienation) the individual subjects of the "great forms" are themselves alienated from their products. Only a metaphysically construed "life" in general is in dynamic harmony with its objectified forms.

4. K. Marx and F. Engels, *The German Ideology* (New York: International Publishers, 1947), pp. 20-23.

5. *Ibid.*, p. 40 and *passim*. Marx derived this particular argument from his analysis of the French Revolution and its aftermath.

6. W. Benjamin, "Eduard Fuchs: Collector and Historian" in this volume.

7. T. W. Adorno, *Negative Dialectics* trans. E.B. Ashton (New York: Seabury Press, 1973), p. 367.

8. Cf. "Cultural Criticism and Society" in *Prisms* (London: Neville Spearman,

1967), pp. 31-32 ff. Both procedures are criticized and preserved in their unresolvable opposition.

9. *Negative Dialectics*, p. 367.

10. *Prisms*, p. 33.

11. Cf. "Authority and the Family."

12. Cf. "Art and Mass Culture" in *Critical Theory*.

13. Cf. "Affirmative Culture" and "Philosophy and Critical Theory," both in *Negations*.

14. Karl Marx, *Grundrisse* trans. M. Nicolaus (London: Penguin, 1973) pp. 158ff.; pp. 471ff.

15. *Grundrisse*, p. 487.

16. *Ibid.*, p. 158.

17. For an analysis of Marx's concept of community we rely on the work of Lukacs's students, the "Budapest School," and especially on the writings of Agnes Heller, Ferenc Feher, and György Markus. Cf. for example A. Heller, "Towards a Marxian Theory of Value," *Kinesis* (Fall 1972), "The Marxian Theory of Revolution," *Telos* (Fall 1970) VI; György Markus, "Human Essence and History," *International Journal of Sociology* (Spring 1975); and Ferenc Feher, "Is the Novel Problematic?" *Telos* (St. Louis, Spring 1973) XV.

18. The most important English language studies of Max Weber are in our opinion the works of Benjamin Nelson. Cf. his latest "On Orient and Occident in Max Weber" in *Social Research* (New York, Spring 1976) XLIII and especially "Max Weber's Author's Introduction," *Sociological Inquiry* (New York, 1974) XLIV, and Wolfgang Mommsen, *The Age of Bureaucracy* (New York, Harper and Row., 1974). On the relationship of Marx and Weber see Mommsen; the still-important article by Karl Lowith, "Max Weber and Karl Marx," *Archiv Für Sozialwissenschaft und Sozial-politik* (1932) LXVII; Jean Cohen, "Max Weber and the Dynamics of Rationalized Domination," *Telos* (St. Louis, Winter 1972) XIV; and Arato, "The Neo-Idealist Defense of Subjectivity."

19. *Vid.* Cohen, *op. cit.*, pp. 65-66ff.

20. Cf. his reply to Sombart, in *The Protestant Ethic and the Spirit of Capitalism* (New York: Scribner's, 1958), where he stresses all the historical asymmetries and irregularities of the rationalization of the different spheres of life.

21. Cf. Nelson, "Orient and Occident" p. 117ff. Weber stresses furthermore that irrational inspirations of the Protestant ethic were themselves eventually sacrificed to de-magicization.

22. Weber however was never able to conceive of the new totality, i.e. capitalism as a system. His rejection of the teleological origin of the system is his advantage next to Marxism, his inability to see the system as a system onceit has been established is his disadvantage next to the Marx of *Das Kapital*.

23. Cf. Cohen, *op.cit.*, p. 71.

24. Cf. Adorno, "Kultur and Verwaltung" in *Gesammelte Schriften* VIII (Frankfurt/M: Suhrkamp Verlag, 1972).

25. *A Modern Dráma Fejlödésének Története* (The History of the Development of Modern Drama) (Budapest: Franklin, 1911) cf. Arato, "The Search for the Revolutionary Subject: The Philosophy and Social Theory of the Young Lukács, 1910-1923" unp. PhD dissertation (University of Chicago, 1975), pp. 137ff.

26. See chapter 5 of the 1911 *Soul and Form* now in English (London: Merlin Press, 1974).

27. Though many aspects of the concept of reification were present in Lukács's pre-Marxist work, here we will focus only on the 1922 essay on the topic in *History and Class Consciousness*. For further details cf. Arato, "Lukács' Theory of Reification," *Telos*, (Spring 1972) XI.

28. Cf. Marx, *Capital I* (New York: International Publishers, 1967), p. 70ff.

29. In this context he utilized Marx's analysis of manufacture and machinery in *Capital I* as well as Weber's analysis of legal, bureaucratic domination.

30. *History and Class Consciousness*, p.88.

31. Marx, *Capital*, I p.39.

32. On this cf. Arato, "Lukács' Theory of Reification," pp. 57ff.

33. On this cf. Merleau-Ponty, *The Adventures of the Dialectic* (Evanston: Northwestern University Press, 1973).

34. Cf. F. Grenz, *Adornos Philosophie in Grundbegriffen* (Frankfurt: Suhrkamp, 1974), chapter 2.

35. Cf. H. Paetzoldt, *Neo-Marxistische Aesthetik* (Dusseldorf: Schwann Verlag, 1974) v.I., p.149.

36. On this cf. the important (originally 1919) essay in *History and Class Consciousness*: "The Changing of Function of Historical Materialism."

37. The last two sentences represent the tone of Lukács's reconstructed article of 1922 and not the original of 1919. The original, written during the Hungarian Soviet Republic, far harsher against orthodoxy and even Marx himself, expresses the belief that the time of the self-critique (not "revision") of historical materialism has arrived.

38. On Lukács's concept of mediation in relation to Hegel cf. Arato, "Lukács' Theory of Reification," p.29f; p.51f.

39. Cf. Alfred Schmidt, "Die 'Zeitschrift für Sozialforschung', Geschichte und gegenwärtige Bedeutung" in *Zur Idee der Kritischen Theorie* (Hanser München, 1974), pp. 87-107.

40. T.W. Adorno, *Introduction to the Sociology of Music*, trans. by E.B. Ashton (New York: Seabury, 1976), pp. 198-200.

41. Theodor W. Adorno, *Philosophy of Modern Music*, trans. by A.G. Mitchell and W.V. Blomster (New York: Seabury, 1973), p. 26.

42. *Ibid.*

43. Quoted by Grenz, *op. cit.*, p. 53.

44. *Philosophy of Modern Music*, pp. 27-28.

45. Ferenc Feher, "Negative Philosophy of Music—Positive Results," *New German Critique* (Milwaukee, Winter 1975) IV.

46. *Negative Dialectics*, part III, chapter 2 (on Hegel).

47. *Prisms*, p. 32.

48. The first essay in *Prisms*, originally published in 1951.

49. For Adorno's own reconstruction, cf. "Ideology" in *Aspects of Sociology*, trans. by J. Viertel (Boston: Beacon, 1972), chapter 12. While Adorno is not indicated as the author, volume VIII of his *Gesammelte Schriften* (Frankfurt/M: Suhrkamp, 1972) clears up the confusion.

50. For the various meanings of critique of ideology in Marx, cf. Jean Cohen's forthcoming (New School) unpublished dissertation, "The Crisis of Class Analysis in Late Capitalism."

51. "Ideology" in *Aspects of Sociology*, pp. 188-189.

52. *Ibid*, p. 199. As we have seen at the end of the Introduction to Part I, the split in the structure of ideology need not be explained by the interpretation of Adorno himself and Marcuse (*One-Dimensional Man*), both sharing the view of a homogenization or one-dimensionalization of culture. It can be explained by the transformation of the institutional context of politically organized late capitalism (Pollock and Habermas). The latter explanation is the only one which can ground the hope of a future-oriented politics. It too, however, surrenders the Lukácsian-early-Frankfurt notion of a unified ideology critique.

53. "Ideology" in *Aspects of Sociology*, p. 189.

54. *Ibid*, p. 198. Definitions (1) and (2) are closely related, but they do begin to diverge once (3) is introduced.

55. "Ideology" in *Aspects of Sociology*, pp. 190-191. Also cf. *Prisms*, p. 34.

56. Cf. *Prisms*, p. 31, where Adorno interprets our (1) under (3).

57. The world explored by social science was seen by Adorno as fundamentally undynamic because he identified it in advance as the administered world of contemporary bureaucracy and the culture industry.

58. *Negative Dialectics*, pp. 365 ff.; *Philosophy of Modern Music*, pp. 24-28, and especially "Cultural Criticism and Society" *passim* in *Prisms*.

59. *Philosophy of Modern Music*, pp. 26-27.

60. *Introduction to the Sociology of Music*, pp. 209-210.

61. *Prisms*, pp. 27-28.

62. *Ibid.*, pp. 32-33.

63. *Ibid.*, pp. 25-29.

64. *Ibid.*, pp. 30-31.

65. *Ibid.*, p. 28.

66. *Ibid.*, p. 33

67. *Prisms*, p. 31 f. and see also Jürgen Habermas, *Theory and Practice* (Boston: Beacon Press, 1973), p. 241.

68. Habermas, *Theory and Practice*, p. 241.

69. Cf. Lukács, "On the Nature and Form of the Essay" in *Soul and Form* (London: Merlin, 1974); Adorno, "Der Essay als Form" in *Noten zur Literatur* I (Frankfurt/M: Suhrkamp, 1968).

70. Adorno, "Zur Gesellschaftliche Lage der Musik," *Zeitschrift für Sozialforschung* (Frankfurt, 1932) I, p.105.

71. Cf. Habermas, *Theory and Practice*, p. 203.

72. Cf. Horkheimer, "Authority and the Family."

73. Cf. Horkheimer, "Traditional and Critical Theory."

74. Cf. Marcuse, "Philosophy and Critical Theory" in *Negations*.

75. Cf. Marcuse, "Affirmative Culture," p. 130ff. On this point cf. the important 1972 essay by Habermas, "Bewusstmachende oder rettende Kritik—Der Aktualität Walter Benjamins" in *Kultur und Kritik* (Frankfurt/M: Suhrkamp, 1973).

76. *Prisms*, p. 32. That Adorno saw astonishingly clearly in this regard is revealed by two statements from Lukács that refer to the desirability of the destruction of bourgeois culture by barbarians, so that a new culture can be built. The first statement was repeated in the period of 1909-1910 when Lukács slowly gave up the hope that the proletariat could represent this "new barbarism." In the 1930s however in a conversation it was exactly in these terms that he defended Soviet culture. For the references cf. Arato, "Lukács' Life and Works" (forthcoming, Urizen Press).

77. Adorno, *Asthetische Theorie*, p. 374. Marcuse's most radical revision of this particular position of his *vis-à-vis* autonomous art took place after the publication of this criticism, in *Counterrevolution and Revolt* (Boston: Beacon, 1973), pp. 92-93. With respect to the "abolition" of philosophy cf. Karel Kosik's critique of Marcuse in *Die Dialektik des Konkreten* (Frankfurt/M: Suhrkamp, 1967), pp. 161-174. Also cf. the first lines of Adorno's *Negative Dialectics*, p. 3.

78. Cf. Habermas, "Bewusstmachende oder Rettende Kritik," p. 312, where on the basis of Benjamin's definition of criticism in his early book on the baroque Habermas writes: "critique exercises mortification only in order to transpose that which is worthy of knowledge from the medium of the beautiful into the medium of the true—and thereby to save it." Habermas compares Marcuse's and Benjamin's notions of critique in detail, *op. cit.*, pp. 305-311.

352 Esthetic Theory and Cultural Criticism

79. Cf. H. Arendt, "Walter Benjamin: 1892-1940," introduction to Benjamin's *Illuminations* (New York: Schocken, 1969), pp. 44-45. This introduction is useful if one divests it of Arendt's unnecessary attempt to link Benjamin to her own tradition, coming from Heidegger. Also cf. Bernd Witte, "Benjamin and Lukács," *New German Critique* (Milwaukee, Spring 1975) V.

80. Our whole discussion of Benjamin below is heavily indebted to Sandor Radnoti's unpublished Hungarian monograph "Credo and Resignation: Esthetic-Political Study on Walter Benjamin." The first chapter of this work on Bloch and Lukács is available in *Telos* (St. Louis, Fall 1975) XXV. The second chapter, on Benjamin's early esthetics, is forthcoming in 1977 in *International Journal of Sociology*.

81. Arendt, *op. cit.*, p. 45; Habermas, *op. cit.*, p. 312.

82. Adorno, *Prisms*, p. 236.

83. Arendt, *op. cit.*, pp. 4-5 and especially her translation of a short section of Benjamin's essay on Goethe's *Wahlverwandschaften*.

84. Adorno, *Prisms*, pp. 231-233.

85. As Adorno well knew, cf., e.g., *Prisms*, p. 236.

86. *Ibid.*, p. 233.

87. The antinomic nature of Benjamin's conception of "dialectic" is best worked out by Radnoti in chapter 4 of "Credo and Resignation."

88. On this point cf. two 1936 essays of Horkheimer: "Authority and Family" in *Critical Theory* and "Egoismus und Freiheitsbewegung" in *Kritische Theorie der Gesellschaft*, volume II.

89. Cf. Marcuse, "The Struggle Against Liberalism."

90. Benjamin, *Ursprung des deutschen Trauerspiels* (Frankfurt: Suhrkamp, 1972). I am relying in this context on Radnoti's "Credo and Resignation"; also cf. Paetzoldt, *Neo-Marxistische Aesthetik* I; Jameson, *Marxism and Form* (Princeton: Princeton University Press, 1971); and Lukács, "The Ideology of Modernism" in *Realism in our Time* (New York: Harper and Row, 1964). On the distinction between allegory and symbol as esthetic principles cf. Gadamer, *Truth and Method* (New York: Seabury Press, 1975), pp. 63-73.

91. Jameson, *Marxism and Form*, p. 71.

92. Cf. Radnoti, *op. cit.*, p. 71.

93. Cf. "The Work of Art in the Age of Mechanical Reproduction" (should be "its Mechanical Reproducibility") in *Illuminations*, but also the studies "The Storyteller" and "Some Motifs in Baudelaire" in the same volume.

94. All three essays in *Illuminations*. The first essay as well two other (1935 and 1938) versions of the third available in *Charles Baudelaire: A Lyric Poet in the Era of High Capitalism* (London: New Left Books, 1973), brought on the severe criticism of Adorno, now available in English: "Letters to Walter Benjamin," *New Left Review* (September-October 1973) LXXXI. Furthermore Adorno's "Fetish Character of Music and the Regression of Listening" (1938) reproduced below, was in part composed as an answer to Benjamin's "Work of Art" essay.

95. *Illuminations*, pp. 228-230; pp. 238-240.

96. *Ibid.*, pp. 223-224.

97. *Charles Baudelaire*, p. 113.

98. *Ibid.*, p. 148.

99. Cf. *Illuminations*, p. 231.

100. Cf. Radnoti, *op. cit.*, p. 50; Paetzoldt, *op. cit.*, p. 103; Gadamer, *op. cit.*, p. 66. For Benjamin's own argument cf. *Ursprung des deutschen Trauerspiels*, pp. 202-204.

101. Cf. *Az Esztétikum Sajátossága (On the Uniquenes of Esthetics)* (Budapest: Akademia, 1965) and also the cruder form of this argument in *Realism in Our Time* pp. 40-43. Adorno's first response to Benjamin's studies of Baudelaire is rather close to this much later interpretation of Lukács. The common link: the concept of mediation drawn from *History and Class Consciousness*.

102. Cf. *Theory and Practice*, p. 241. In his later essay on Benjamin, Habermas stressed not Benjamin's theoretical contributions to understanding modernism but his redemptive critical attitude toward works of the past.

103. Cf. *Paetzoldt*, p. 110.

104. Cf. *Charles Baudelaire*, p. 113.

105. *Ibid.*, p. 154.

106. *Charles Baudelaire*, p. 159; pp. 170-176.

107. Cf. "The Author as Producer" below.

108. *Ibid.*

109. On this important point that also dates the Frankfurt School's decisive rejection of the Soviet Union cf. Gershom Scholem, *Walter Benjamin—die Geschichte einer Freundschaft* (Frankfurt/M: Suhrkamp, 1975) pp. 274-275. Scholem remarks that "Theses on the Philosophy of History" (1940) was Benjamin's answer to the Pact and to orthodox Marxism. The "Theses" reproduce several lines of the Fuchs essay reprinted below, demonstrating that even earlier Benjamin's acceptance of Marxism did not extend to the theory of progress inherent in "historical materialism."

110. Cf. Paetzoldt, *op. cit.*, p. 149.

111. Cf. "Letters to Walter Benjamin."

112. Cf. Radnoti, op. cit., pp. 117-118, which provides an impressive interpretation of the present state of the Adorno-Benjamin debate of the 1930s. In this context a further key theme of Adorno from the point of view of Marxist orthodoxy is his attack on Benjamin's reduction of commodity fetishism to a metaphor.

113. Adorno, "Letters," pp. 65-67. cf. Lukács, *History and Class Consciousness* ("Reification" part III).

114. A. Schmidt, "Die Zeitschrift für Sozialforschung," p. 87ff; p. 92ff.

115. Cf. Paetzoldt, *op. cit.*, pp. 175ff; Habermas, "Bewusstmachende oder rettende Kritik," pp. 317ff.

116. Habermas, *op. cit.*, pp. 320-321.

117. Adorno, "Letters," pp. 70ff.

118. Cf. Habermas, *Legitimation Crisis*, pp. 85-86.

119. Cf. especially "The Types of Musical Conduct" in *Introduction to the Sociology of Music.*

120. Adorno, *Philosophy of Modern Music* (New York: Seabury, 1973), pp. 18-20. Cf. Horkheimer, "Art and Mass Culture" in *Critical Theory*, p. 290.

121. "Letters to Benjamin," p. 66.

122. Theodor W. Adorno, *Vorlesungen zur Aesthetik 1967-68* (Zürich: H. Mayer Nachfolger, 1973), p. 79.

123. Theodor W. Adorno, *Minima Moralia* (London: New Left Books, 1974), No. 41.

124. Theodor W. Adorno, *Aesthetische Theorie*, in *Gesammelte Schriften* (Frankfurt: Suhrkamp, 1970), Vol. VII, p. 336. Cf. also: "... the useless represents the atrophied use value." (p. 377)

125. Theodor W. Adorno, "Funktionalismus heute" in *Ohne Leitbild. Parva Aesthetica*, (Frankfurt: Suhrkamp, 1967) p. 124.

126. Theodor W. Adorno, "Erpresste Versöhnung" in *Noten zur Literatur*, Vol. II, p. 181.

127. Theodor W. Adorno, "Ohne Leitbild" in *Ohne Leitbild. Parva Aesthetica*, p. 18.

128. Theodor W. Adorno, *Aesthetische Theorie*, p. 493.

129. Ibid., p. 502.

130. Theodor W. Adorno, "Kunst und die Künste" in *Ohne Leitbild. Parva Aesthetica*, p. 180.

131. Herbert Marcuse, "Zum Begriff der Negation in der Dialektik" in *Ideen zu einer kr5itischen Theorie der Gesellschaft* (Frankfurt: Suhrkamp, 1969), p. 186.

132. Theodor W. Adorno, *Aesthetische Theorie*, p. 263.

133. Ibid.

134. Ibid., p. 264.

135. Herbert Marcuse, *Counterrevolution and Revolt* (Boston: Beacon Press, 1972), p. 103.

136. Ibid., p. 87.

137. Theodor W. Adorno, "Engagement" in *Noten zur Literatur*, Vol. III (Frankfurt: Suhrkamp, 1965), p.121. ("Commitment" in this volume.)

138. Theodor W. Adorno, *Aesthetische Theorie*, p. 346.

139. Ibid., p. 342.

140. Ibid., p. 337.

141. Herbert Marcuse, *Counterrevolution and Revolt*, p. 97.

142. Ibid., p. 108.

143. Cf. Herbert Marcuse, *Eros and Civilization* (New York: Vintage, 1962), p. 159.

144. Herbert Marcuse, *Counterrevolution and Revolt*, p. 112.

145. Ibid., p. 124.

146. Theodor W. Adorno, *Minima Moralia*, p. 140.

Eduard Fuchs: Collector and Historian

1. Quoted in Gustav Mayer, *Friedrich Engels*, Vol. 2, *Friedrich Engels und der Aufstieg der Arbeiterbewegung in Europa* (Berlin), pp. 450-451.

2. This thought appears in the earliest studies on Feuerbach and is expressed by Marx as follows: "There is no history of politics, of law, of science . . . of art, of religion, etc." *Marx-Engels Archiv*, 1, Ed. David Riazanov (Frankfurt am Main, 1928), 301.

3. It is the dialectical construct *(Konstruktion)* which distinguishes that which is our original concern in historical experience from the pieced together findings of actuality. "That which is original *(ursprünglich)* never identifies itself in the naked, obvious existence of the factual. The rhythm of the original opens itself solely to a double insight. This insight . . . concerns the pre- and post-history of the original." Walter Benjamin, *Ursprung des deutschen Trauerspiels* (Berlin, 1928), p. 32.

4. *Erotische Kunst*, 1, p. 70.

5. Gavarni, p. 13.

6. Fuchs's major works have been collected and published by Albert Langen of Munich as *Hauptwerke*. These include: *Illustrierte Sittengeschichte vom Mittelalter bis zur Gegenwart*, Vol. 1: *Renaissance*, Vol. 2: *Die galante Zeit*, Vol. 3: *Das bürgerliche Zeitalter*, also supplementary Vols. 1-3 (here cited as *Sittengeschichte*): *Geschichte der erotischen Kunst*, Vol. 1: *Das zeitgeschichtliche Problem*, Vol. 2: *Das individuelle Problem*, Part One, Vol. 3: *Das individuelle Problem*, Part Two (here cited as *Erotische Kunst*); *Die Karikatur der europäischen Völker*, Vol. 1: *Vom Altertum bis zum Jahre 1848*, Vol. 2: *Vom Jahre 1848 bis zum Vorabend des Weltkrieges* (here cited as *Karikatur*); *Honoré Daumier: Holzschnitte und Lithographien*, Vol. 1: *Holzschnitte*, Vols. 2-4; *Lithographien* (here cited as *Daumier*); *Der Maler Daumier*; *Gavarni*; *Die Grossen Meister der Erotik*; *Tang-Plastik chinesische Grab-Keramik des 7.-10. Jahrhunderts*; *Dachreiter und verwandte chinesische Keramik des 15.-18. Jahrhunderts*. Apart from these works, Fuchs dedicated special works to the caricature of woman, of the Jews and of the World War.

7. A. Max, "Zur Frage der Organisation des Proletariats der Intelligenz," *Die Neue Zeit*, 13:1 (Stuttgart, 1895), 645.

8. Nietzsche wrote as early as 1874: "Finally . . . there results the generally acclaimed 'popularization' . . . in science. This is the notorious tailoring of science's coat for the figure of a 'mixed public,' to use a tailor-like activity for a tailor-like German (sic!)." Friedrich Nietzsche, "Vom Nutzen und Nachteil der Historie für das Leben," *Unzeitgemässe Betrachtungen.* 1 (Leipzig, 1893), p. 168.

9. "A cultural historian who takes his task seriously must always write for the masses," *Erotische Kunst,* 2, Part One, Preface.

10. C. Korn, "Proletariat und Klassik," *Die Neue Zeit,* 26:2 (Stuttgart, 1908), 414-417.

11. See August Bebel, *Die Frau und der Sozialismus* (Stuttgart, 1891), pp. 177-179, and pp. 333-336, on the changes in housekeeping through technology, pp. 200-201 on woman as inventor.

12. Quoted in D. Bach, "John Ruskin," *Die Neue Zeit,* 18:1 (Stuttgart, 1900), 728.

13. This deceptive element found characteristic expression in Alfred Weber's welcoming address to the sociological convention of 1912: "Culture comes into existence only when life has become a structure which stands above its necessities and usefulness." This concept of culture contains seeds of barbarism which have, in the meantime, germinated. Culture appears as something "which is superfluous for the continued existence of life but is felt to be precisely the reason for which life is there." In short, culture exists after the fashion of an art work "which perhaps brings about the confusion of entire modes of living and life principles, and which may have dissolving and destructive effects, but which we shall feel to be higher than everything healthy and living which it destroys." Twenty-five years after this was said, "cultural states" have seen it as an honor to resemble such art works, even to be such art works. Alfred Weber, "Der soziologische Kulturbegriff," *Verhandlungen des zweiten deutschen Soziologentages: Schriften der deutschen Gesellschaft für Soziologie,* 1:1 (Tübingen, 1913), 11-12.

14. Franz Mehring, "Akademisches," *Die Neue Zeit,* 16:1 (Stuttgart, 1898), 195-196.

15. *Erotische Kunst,* 1, 125. Constant reference to contemporary art belongs to the most important impulses of Fuchs the collector. Contemporary art, too, comes to him partially through the great creations of the past. His incomparable knowledge of older caricature opens Fuchs to an early recognition of the works of a Toulouse-Lautrec, a Heartfield and a George Grosz. His passion for Daumier leads him to the work of Slevogt, whose conception of Don Quixote appears before his eyes as the only one which could hold its own beside Daumier. His studies in ceramics gives him all the authority to sponsor an Emil Pottner. All his life Fuchs had friendly relations with creative artists. Thus, it is not surprising that his manner of addressing works of art corresponds more to the ways of an artist than those of a historian.

16. The master of iconographic representation might be Émile Mâle. His research is limited to the sculpture of French cathedrals from the twelfth to the fifteenth centuries. Thus, they do not overlap with Fuchs's studies.

17. Heinrich Wölfflin, *Die klassische Kunst* (Munich, 1899), p. 275.

18. Older tablet painting *(Tafelmalerei)* granted no more than an outline of a house to men for their quarters. The painters of the early Renaissance were the first to depict interior space in which the represented figures have room to move. That is what made Uccello's invention of perspective so overpowering both for his contemporaries and himself. From then on, the creations of painting were dedicated more than before to the inhabitants (rather than to praying persons). Paintings gave examples of patterns of habitation and never tired of erecting perspectives of the villa. The high Renaissance, although much more restrained in the representation of the actual *intérieur,* continued to build on this foundation. "The Cinquecento has a particularly strong feeling for the relation between man and building, that is, for the resonance of a beautiful room. This century can hardly imagine an existence which is not architectonically framed and founded." Wölfflin, p. 227.

19. *Erotische Kunst.* 2, Part One, 20.

20. Franz Mehring, *Geschichte der deutschen Sozialdemokratie,* Part Two, *Von Lassalles offenem Antwortschreiben bis zum Erfurter Program,* Vol. 3, Part Two of *Geschichte des Sozialismus in Einzeldarstellungen* (Stuttgart, 1898), p. 546.

21. *Karikatur,* 1, 4-5.

22. Note the beautiful remark about Daumier's figures of proletarian women: "Whoever sees merely emotional themes proves that the ultimate motive forces which must be effective in order to create stirring art are a sealed book to him. Precisely because these pictures represent something altogether different from 'emotional themes' they will live eternally . . . as the moving monuments of the enslavement of maternal woman in the nineteenth century." *Der Maler Daumier,* p. 28.

23. *Tang-Plastik,* p. 44.

24. Note the thesis on the erotic effects of the work of art: "The more intensive the effect, the greater the artistic quality." *Erotische Kunst,* 1, 68.

25. *Karikatur,* p. 23.

26. *Dachreiter,* p. 39.

27. *Die grossen Meister der Erotik,* p. 115.

28. *Dachreiter,* p. 48.

29. *Erotische Kunst,* 2, Part One, 186.

30. *Tang-Plastik,* pp. 30-31. This intuitive and immediate manner of consideration becomes problematical when it attempts to fulfill the demands of the situation of a materialist analysis. It is well known that Marx did not intensively elaborate anywhere on how the relationship between superstructure and infrastructure can be thought of in individual cases. It can only be firmly established that he envisaged a series of mediations, transmissions one might say, which interpolate between the material relationships of production and the more removed domains of the superstructure, which includes art. Plekhanov says the same: "When art, which is created by the higher classes, stands in no direct relation to the process of production, then this must ultimately be explained by means of economic causes. The materialist interpretation of history . . . can be applied in this case as well. It is apparent, however, that the causal connections which doubtlessly exist between being and consciousness, between the social relations which are founded on 'labor' on the one hand, and art on the other, do not come easily to fore in this case." G. Plekhanov, "Das französische Malerei im neunzehnten Jahrhundert vom Standpunkte der materialistischen Geschichtsauffassung," *Die Neue Zeit,* 24 (Stuttgart, 1911), 544-545. So much is clear, however; Marx's classical historical dialectic considers causal contingencies as given in this relationship. In later praxis he had become more lax and was often content with analogies. It is possible that this was connected to the project of replacing bourgeois histories of literature and art by materialistic ones which are planned on an equally grand scale. This project is a characteristic mark of the epoch; it is part of the Wilhelminian spirit. This project demanded its tribute from Fuchs as well. A favorite thought of the author, which is expressed in various ways, conceived of establishing realistic art epochs for the trading nations. This goes for Holland of the seventeenth century as well as for China of the eighth and ninth centuries. Beginning with an analysis of Chinese garden economy, by means of which he explains many characteristics of the Empire, Fuchs then turns to the new sculpture which originates under the Tang rule. The monumental rigidification of the Han style becomes loosened. The interest of the anonymous masters who created the pottery is now intent upon the movements of men and animals. "Time," Fuchs elaborates, "awoke from its great slumber in those centuries in China . . . , for trade always means an intensified life—life and movement. Hence, life and movement had to come primarily into the art of the Tang period. This is the first characteristic one encounters. While, for example, the whole demeanor of the animals of the Han period is still heavy and monumental in their whole habitus, those of the Tang period exhibit everything lively, every limb is in motion." *Tang-Plastik,* p. 41. This mode of consideration rests on mere analogy: movement in trade as in sculpture. One might almost call it nominalistic. His attempts at making transparent the reception of antiquity in the Renaissance remains equally trapped in analogy. "In both epochs the economic basis was the same, only in the Renaissance this basis found itself on a higher stage of development. Both were founded on trade of commodities." *Erotische Kunst,* 1, p. 42. Finally trade itself appears as the subject of the contemplation of art and Fuchs says: "Trade has to calculate with given qualities and it can only apply concrete and verifiable quantities. That is how trade has to approach the world and things if it wants to control them economically. Consequently its aesthetic consideration of things occurs in every regard in a realistic mode." *Tang-Plastik,* p. 42. One may disregard the fact that a "realistic" representation "in every regard" cannot be found in art. In principle one would have to say that any connection appears problematical which claims equal validity for the art of ancient China and for that of ancient Holland. Indeed, a connection does not exist in this manner. A glance at the Republic of Venice suffices: Venice's art flourished because of its trade. Yet the art of a Palma Vecchio, of Titian or of Veronese could hardly be called "realistic in every regard". The only aspect of life which we encounter in this art is a festive and representative one. On the other hand, working life in all its stages demands a considerable sense of reality. From this approach the materialist cannot draw any conclusions as to the manifestation of style.

31. Karl Kautsky, "Darwinismus und Marxismus," *Die Neue Zeit,* 13:1 (Stuttgart, 1895), 710.

32. H. Laufenberg, "Dogma und Klassenkampf," *Die Neue Zeit,* 27:1 (Stuttgart, 1909), 574. Here the concept of self-activity has sunk to a sad state. The heyday of this term is the eighteenth century when the self regulation of the market was in its beginning. Then the concept celebrated its triumph in Kant in the form of "spontaneity," as well as in technology in the form of automatic machines.

33. *Karikatur,* 1, 312.

34. *Erotische Kunst,* 1, 3.

35. A. Max, "Zur Frage der Organisation," 652.

36. *Karikatur,* 2, 238.

37. Mehring commented on the trial ensuing from "The Weavers" in the *Neue Zeit.* Parts of the defense speech have regained the actuality which they had in 1893. The attorney elaborated that "he had to point out that the seemingly revolutionary passages in question are contrasted by others which are soothing and calming in character. The poet does not at all stand on the side of revolt insofar as he allows the victory of order by means of the intervention of a handful of soldiers." Franz Mehring, "Entweder Oder," *Die Neue Zeit,* 11:1 (Stuttgart, 1893), 780.

38. Honoré de Balzac, *Le Cousin Pons* (Paris, 1925), p. 162.

39. Edouard Drumont, *Les héros et les pitres* (Paris), pp. 107-108.

40. G. G. Gervinus, *Friedrich Christoph Schlosser: Ein Nekrolog* (Leipzig, 1861), pp. 30-31.

41. This direction of Fuchs's work proved useful when the imperial prosecutors began accusing him of "distributing obscene writings." An expert judgement naturally represented Fuchs' moralism with particular emphasis. This expert opinion was submitted in the course of one of the trials, all of which without exception ended in acquittal. It is the work of Fedor von Zobeltitz and its most important passage says the following: "Fuchs seriously considers himself a preacher of morals and an educator. This deeply serious understanding of life, this intimate comprehension of the fact that his work in the service of the history of humanity must be borne by the highest morality, is alone enough to protect him against the suspicion of profit-hungry speculation. Anyone who knows the man and his illumined idealism would have to smile at such a suspicion."

42. This revision has been inaugurated by Max Horkheimer in his essay "Egoismus und Freiheitsbewegung," *Zeitschrift für Sozialforschung,* 5 (1936), 161ff. The documents assembled by Horkheimer correspond to a series of interesting proofs on which the extremist Abel Bonnard bases his accusation of those bourgeois historians of the Revolution whom Châteaubriand quaintly calls "L'école admirative de la terreur." See Abel Bonnard, *Les Modérés* (Paris), pp. 179ff.

43. *Der Maler Daumier*, p. 30.

44. N. Guterman and H. Lefebvre, *La conscience mystifiée* (Paris, 1936), p. 151.

45. *Erotische Kunst*, 2, Part One, 11.

46. *Ibid.*, 1, 43. The moral-historical representation of the Directory carries traits which are just about those of a popular ballad *(Moritat)*. "The terrible book of the Marquis de Sade with its plates as bad as infamous lay open in all shop windows." And Barras expresses "the devastated fantasy of the shameless libertine." *Karikatur*, 1, 201-202.

47. *Karikatur*, 1, 188.

48. Max Horkheimer, "Egoismus und Freiheitsbewegung," p. 166.

49. *Erotische Kunst*, 2, Part One, 283. Here Fuchs is on the track of an important state of affairs. Would it be too rash to put into immediate relation the threshold between human and animal, which Fuchs sees in the orgy, with the erect posture? This allows for the unheard of occurrence of the phenomenon in natural history that the partners can look into each other's eyes during orgasm. Only thus an orgy becomes possible, but not by an increase in visual stimuli. Rather, the determining factor is that the expression of satiety and even impotence can now become an erotic stimulant itself.

50. *Sittengeschichte*, 3, 234. A few pages later, this confident judgement can no longer be found. This is evidence of the force with which it had to be wrested away from convention. Rather, he says here: "The fact that thousands of people become sexually excited when they look at a female or male nude photograph . . . proves that the eye is no longer capable of perceiving the harmonious whole but only the piquant detail." *Ibid.*, 3, 269. If there is anything sexually arousing here, it is more the exhibition of the naked body in front of the camera than the view of nakedness itself. This is probably the notion which is intended by most of these photographs.

51. *Ibid.*, 3, 189.

52. *Ibid.*, Supplementary Vol., pp. 53-54.

53. As ideology is the immediate production of interests so, for Fuchs, art is immediate sensuality. "The essence of art is: Sensuality *(Sinnlichkeit)*. Art is sensuality. Indeed it is sensuality in its most potent form. Art is sensuality become form, become visible. At the same time, it is the highest and noblest form of sensuality." *Erotische Kunst*, 1, 61.

54. *Karikatur,* 2, 223.

55. *Erotische Kunst,* 2, Part One, 390.

56. *Der Maler Daumier,* p. 30.

57. This has to be compared with the following reflection: "According . . . to my observations I think that the respective dominant elements of the artist's palette occur particularly clearly in his erotically pointed paintings. Here . . . these elements . . . experience their highest luminosity." *Die grossen Meister der Erotik,* p. 14.

58. *Der Maler Daumier,* p. 18. The famous "Art Expert," a watercolor which occurs in several versions, has to be counted among the figures in question. Fuchs one day was shown a version of the painting which so far had been unknown. He was supposed to authenticate it. Fuchs picked up the main representation of the motif in a good reproduction and then began with an extremely instructive comparison. No deviation, not even the smallest one, remained unnoticed. Each one of these deviations had to be accounted for and had to be judged as to whether it was the product of the master's hand or that of impotence. Again and again Fuchs returned to the original. Yet the way he did that seemed to indicate that he could have easily dispensed with it. He proved so familiar with its appearance, in a way that can only be the case with a painting which one carried in one's mind for years. No doubt this was the case for Fuchs. Only because of this was he able to uncover the most hidden uncertainties in the contour, to see the most insignificant color deviations of the shadows, to identify the smallest derailing of the lines. Thus he was able to put the painting in its place—not as a forgery but as a good old copy which might have been an amateur's product.

59. *Dachreiter,* pp. 5-6.

60. *Tang-Plastik,* p. 44.

61. *Honoré Daumier,* 1, 13. One should compare these thoughts with Victor Hugo's allegorical interpretation of the wedding at Cana. "The miracle of the bread loaves represents the multiplied increase of readers. The day that Christ stumbled on this symbol he had a premonition of the art of the book printer." Victor Hugo, "William Shakespeare," quoted by Georges Batault, *Le pontife de la démagogie: Victor Hugo* (Paris, 1934), p. 142.

62. *Dachreiter,* p. 46.

63. *Karikatur,* 1, 19. The exception proves the rule. A mechanical technique of reproduction served in the production of the terracotta figures. Among those many caricatures can be found.

64. See Erich Klossowski, *Honoré Daumier* (Munich, 1908), p. 113.

65. *Dachreiter,* p. 45.

The Author as Producer

1. Address at the Institute for the Study of Fascism in Paris on 27 April 1934.

2. i.e. Benjamin; cf. *Schriften*, Frankfurt, 1955, Vol. I, p. 384.

3. In place of the following sentence there was in the manuscript originally a different one that was deleted: Or, to speak with Trotsky: "If the enlightened pacifists attempt to abolish war by means of rationalistic argument, they simply make fools of themselves, but if the armed masses begin to use the arguments of reason against war, that means the end of war."

Commitment

1. Jean-Paul Sartre, *What is Literature?*, London 1967, p. 4.

2. Reference to the establishment of Berlin Wall. [editor's note]

3. Reference to Marcuse's essay "Sartre's Existentialism,", included in *Studies in Critical Philosophy*, New Left Books, London 1972, pp. 157-90. [editor's note]

4. "Because he is a man": *Situations II*, Paris 1948, p. 51.

5. Reference to Brecht's last play on the Roman general Lucullus. [editor's note]

6. *What is Literature?*, p. 46.

7. Reference to *The Measures Taken*, written in 1930, which contained an implicit justification in advance of the Moscow Trials. Zinoviev and Bukharin were condemned in 1938. [editor's note]

8. *What is Literature?*, p. 34.

9. "We know very well that pure art and empty art are the same thing and that esthetic purism was a brilliant manoeuvre of the bourgeois of the last century who preferred to see themselves denounced as philistines rather than as exploiters." *What is Literature?*, p. 17.

10. See Jean-Paul Sartre, *L'Existentialisme est un Humanisme*, Paris 1946, p. 105.

Knut Hamsun

1. In its original form the following study was written twenty years ago, some time before the political sympathies of Hamsun for the Hitler movement became public knowledge. It is presented here not only as a case of sociological prediction but as a documentation of the authoritarian character and his ideology. See, *Zeitschrift für Sozialforschung*, ed. by Max Horkheimer, vol. VI (1937), pp. 295-345.

2. We may remind the reader of our analysis of Spanish literature—another case of social marginality illuminating traits of social typicality.

3. *Hunger*, tr. by George Egerton (Knopf, New York, 1920), p. I. Whenever possible we have quoted from the American editions of Hamsun. Where these have been unavailable, German translations have been used as a basis for quotations. Quotations from American translations are reprinted by permission of Alfred A. Knopf, Inc.

4. *Ibid.*, p. 266.

5. *The Last Joy*, (*Die letzte Freude*), *Gesammelte Werke*, 12 Vols., German tr. ed. by J. Sandmeier (Albert Langen, München, n.d.), Vol. V, p. 291.

6. In connection with one of his eulogies of the natural strength of youth Hamsun criticizes the aged who "have mollycoddled it [youth] with hymns and rot about peace eternal . . . If some one smites it on one cheek it turns the other accomodatingly, and keeps its fists in its pockets with admirable self-control." (*Shallow Soil*, tr. by C. C. Hyllested, Knopf, New York, 1914, p. 120.) Brutal resentment is much more apparent here than in the sentimental dress of the quotation in the text.

7. *The Last Joy, op. cit.*, p. 376.

8. *Pan*, tr. by W. W. Worster (Knopf, New York, 1921), p. 130.

9. *The Last Joy, op. cit.*, p. 289.

10. *Ibid.*, p. 293.

11. *Ibid.*, pp. 301-302.

12. *Ibid.*, p. 376.

13. *Mysteries*, tr. by A. G. Chater (Knopf, New York, 1927), p. 67. See also, *Pan*, p. 130: "This silence murmuring in my ears is the blood of all Nature seething; it is God weaving through the world and me."

14. *Pan, op. cit.*, p. 15.

15. *The Last Joy, op. cit.*, p. 310.

16. Kant, *Critique of Aesthetic Judgment*, tr. by J. D. Meredith (Oxford, 1911), p. 110. Kantian idealism, it should be remarked, received its most winning, and perhaps most profound, application to public affairs in the teachings of Thoreau and other New England Transcendentalists, who in turn, of course, influenced Tolstoi and Gandhi.

17. Kant, pp. 110-11.

18. *Pan, op. cit.*, pp. 10-11.

19. *The Last Joy, op. cit.*, p. 311.

20. See, for example, *Pan, loc. cit.*, pp. 23-24: "I pick up a little dry twig and hold it in my hand and sit looking at it, and think my own thoughts; the twig is almost rotten, its poor bark touches me, pity fills my heart. And when I get up again, I do not throw the twig far away, but lay it down, and stand liking it; at least I look at it once more with wet eyes before I go away and leave it there.''

21. *Wanderers*, tr. by W. W. Worster (Knopf, New York, 1922), p. 320.

22. *The Road Leads On*, tr. by Eugene Gay-Tifft (Coward-McCann, New York, 1934), p. 46.

23. *The Ring is Closed*, tr. by Eugene Gay-Tifft (Coward-McCann, New York, 1937), p. 152.

24. *Vagabonds*, tr. by Eugene Gay-Tifft (Coward-McCann, New York, 1930), p. 448.

25. *Cf. Growth of the Soil*, tr. by W. W. Worster, in two volumes (Knopf, New York, 1921), Vol I, p. 7; Vol. II, p. 120; *Vagabonds*, p. 47.

26. *Growth of the Soil*, Vol. II, p. 120.

27. *Op. cit.*, Vol. II, p. 246; also *cf. Rosa*, tr. by A. G. Chater (Knopf, New York, 1926), p. 18: '' 'What are you sitting here for?' 'Ah, young man,' he said, holding up the palm of his hand. 'What am I sitting here for? I sit here keeping pace with my existence. Ay, that's what I'm doing.' ''

28. *Pan*, p. 164.

29. *Growth of the Soil, loc. cit.*, Vol. I, p 99.

30. *Ibid.*, Vol. II, pp. 243-244.

31. *Loc. cit.*

32. *Loc. cit.*

33. *Chapter the Last*, tr. by A. G. Chater (Knopf, New York, 1929), pp. 266-267.

34. *Vagabonds*, p. 47.

35. *Growth of the Soil*, Vol. I, p. 122.

36. *Ibid.*, Vol. II, p. 179.

37. *Ibid.*, Vol. I, p. 42.

38. *August*, tr. by Eugene Gay-Tifft (Coward-McCann, New York, 1931), p. 149.

39. *Chapter the Last*, p. 4.

40. *Vagabonds*, p. 540.

41. See *ibid.*, pp. 537-538.

42. *Ibid.*, p. 539.

366   *Esthetic Theory and Cultural Criticism*

43. *The Women at the Pump,* tr. by A. G. Chater (Knopf, New York, 1928), p. 316.

44. Hamsun is factually mistaken here. Primitive people often revere old age. The elders frequently enjoy the highest status in their societies.

45. *The Last Joy,* p. 351.

46. *Ibid.,* p. 318.

47. *Shallow Soil,* p. 74.

48. *Growth of the Soil,* Vol. I, p. 211.

49. *The Road Leads On,* p. 409.

50. *The Last Joy,* p. 298.

51. *Children of the Age,* tr. by J. S. Scott (Knopf, New York, 1924), p. 82.

52. *Mysteries,* p. 51.

53. See, *Mysteries,* p. 121.

54. See, *Pan,* p. 169.

55. *Rosa,* p. 55.

56. *Pan,* p. 132.

57. *Mysteries,* p. 276.

58. *The Ring is Closed,* p. 254.

59. *Growth of the Soil,* Vol. II, p. 92.

60. *Pan,* p. 34.

61. *Chapter the Last,* p. 177.

62. *Ibid.,* p. 102.

63. *Wanderers,* p. 317.

64. *Cf. Chapter the Last,* pp. 105-107.

65. *Segelfoss Town,* tr. by J. S. Scott (Knopf, New York, 1925), p. 299.

66. *Growth of the Soil, loc. cit.,* Vol. II, p. 220.

67. *Ibid.,* Vol. II, p. 253.

68. *Wanderers, loc. cit.,* p. 312.

69. *Growth of the Soil*, Vol. II, p. 9.

70. *The Last Joy*, p. 344. It is consistent with his concept of women that "the greatest thing" in which Hamsun participated was his struggle against the lenient treatment of infanticide. ("Barnemord" [Infanticide], Morgenbladet for March 6th, 1916, cited from Walter A. Berendsohn, *Knut Hamsun*, Albert Langen, München, 1929, p. 104.)

71. *Vagabonds*, p. 143.

72. See, for example, *Segelfoss Town*, p. 27; *The Women at the Pump, loc. cit.*, pp. 193-194; *August*, p. 342.

73. See, *Children of the Age*, pp. 81-82, 216; *Segelfoss Town*, pp. 166-168, 314-315; *August*, p. 231; *The Road Leads On*, p. 167.

74. *Cf.* his contempt for positivism in *Mysteries*, p. 157: "I am a fact!" See also, *The Last Joy*, p. 329; *The Women at the Pump*, p. 120.

75. See, *Chapter the Last*, pp. 80-81, 107.

76. See, for example, *The Last Joy*, p. 291.

77. See, *Mysteries*, p.66; *Chapter the Last*, p. 15.

78. See, *Mysteries*, pp. 89-90.

79. *Growth of the Soil*, Vol. II, p. 245.

80. See, *The Last Joy*, p. 337.

81. *Ibid.*, p. 328.

82. *Wanderers*, p. 207.

83. *August*, p. 351.

84. *Segelfoss Town*, p. 27.

85. See *The Last Joy*, p. 362.

86. See, *Mysteries*, p. 157; *The Last Joy*, p. 329; *The Women at the Pump, loc cit.*

87. See references enumerated in footnote 72.

88. *Children of the Age*, pp. 81-82.

89. *Ibid.*, pp 82-83.

90. *Segelfoss Town*, pp. 167-168.

91. *Wanderers*, p. 189.

92. *Ibid.*, p. 215.

93. *The Ring is Closed*, p. 191.

94. *Children of the Age*, pp. 79-80.

95. *Segelfoss Town*, p. 337.

96. *The Women at the Pump*, pp. 144-145.

97. *Ibid.*, p. 147; cf. *Segelfoss Town*, pp. 10 and 21.

98. *Mysteries*, p. 200.

99. *Ibid.*, pp. 187, 201.

100. *Ibid.*, p. 201.

101. *The Last Joy*, p. 337.

102. *Mysteries*, p. 49.

103. *Hunger*, loc. cit., p. 22.

104. *Redakteur Lynge*, German translation ed. by J. Sandmeier (Albert Langen, München, 1922), p. 31.

105. *Pan*, p. 157.

106. *August*, p. 342.

107. *Wanderers*, p. 314.

108. *Ibid.*, p. 291.

109. *The Last Joy*, p. 317.

110. *Rosa*, p. 99.

111. *Wanderers*, p. 312.

112. *Ibid.*, p. 314.

113. *The Women at the Pump*, p. 138.

114. *Ibid.*, p. 5.

A Critique of Methodology

Critical Theory and the Philosophy of Science

Science needs those who disobey it. (Theodor W. Adorno)

The idea of radically eliminating the subject not only from physics, but also from the cognitive process generally . . . is itself a research postulate in need of legitimation. (Max Horkheimer)

A theory of society has to demonstrate the relativity/contingency in the knowledge of observable facts; vice versa, empirical research has to prevent the cognitive concept of a "law" from becoming a mythological concept. (Theodor W. Adorno)

Neither reading nor experiencing are substitutes for thinking. Pure empiricism relates to thinking like eating relates to digesting and assimilating. (Arthur Schopenhauer)

Progress is leaving itself behind. (Max Horkheimer)

It is sheer nonsense to assert that critical theorists were anti-scientific. Quite to the contrary, the group relentlessly defended the sciences against neo-romantic, spiritualist and idealist attacks—as well as against their positivistic reductions.[1] They rejected the aim of certain "pseudo-sciences"[2] to bypass empirical evidence in favor of supposed "essences" beyond all appearances, and emphatically supported "the activity of science of incorporating events into more general contexts and comprising them under rules" as a "legitimate and useful business. Resistance against it in the name of freedom is a fight against windmills."[3] Horkheimer's insistence on "unconditional empirical stringency"[4] and the investigations of the Institute bear witness to their unwavering alliance with the sciences. Rather than retreat from them, critical theorists emphasized the need to keep abreast of the most advanced positions in the various disciplines—both to use and to criticize them effectively.

Yet "science and its interpretation are two different things,"[5] Horkheimer contended. In a series of seminal articles and reviews in the *Zeitschrift*, Horkheimer and Marcuse challenged certain claims of the contemporary philosophy of science (such as the programmatic universalism of a "unified science," or the tendential reduction of science and philosophy to questions of methodology), some of the self-images and supposed social functions of the scientific community, certain political claims raised in the name of scientific progress and, last but not least, the identification of scientific and technological rationality with reason in general. To the extent that certain tacit presuppositions in these concepts of science re-emerged as substantive assertions of particular social theories (and even in entire research programs), they equally criticized the practice of the established social sciences.

But Horkheimer also repeatedly stressed that critical theory was not an alternative to "traditional"[6] theory and science; these were the raw material, so to speak, of a critical science, its craftlike preliminaries. "However intense the interaction between critical theory and the special sciences—whose progress must remain the take-off point for critical theory . . . —critical theory nowhere aims at the mere increase of knowledge as such."[7] If there is any legitimacy to the claim of science being an aspect of autonomous reason, any science in their view must also be its own metascience—it must know why it is doing what it is doing. For "scientific procedure is never itself a guarantee of truth,"[8] and the progress of science, therefore, not necessarily identical with human progress. (Such, however, were precisely the assumptions put forth by much of the contemporary philosophy of science—into which philosophy in general seemed to get increasingly absorbed.) Despite assertions by Russell, Wittgenstein, Husserl et al. that science has little to offer for the solution of existential questions, the scientistic[9] claim to universal truth (or at least to the proper method to attain it) necessarily involved existential decisions; by becoming a model for "rational" living, scientism and its technological rationality tended to become a total life-form, at the expense of any other. Was there, perhaps, an ideological thrust to scientism after all? Its often merely formal concerns seemed to render that question irrelevant. Critical theorists were not convinced. They took a close look at what they summarily grouped as "positivisms"—logical positivism (especially the so-called Vienna circle of Carnap, Neurath, Schlick *et al.*), logical empiricism, realism, logical atomism, the early Wittgenstein—and found an ontology beneath their formal and methodological postulates.

To be sure, critical theorists shared the distrust of mere metaphysics with logical positivists; what made the latter suspect, however, is that they summarily dismissed as metaphysical anything transcending their own approach. "Certainly science and metaphysics cannot be considered equal branches of knowledge. To a large extent, science itself is the critique of metaphysics. Logical empiricism[10] however stigmatizes any theory as metaphysical which . . . critically examines the single disciplines themselves"[11]—the very division and organization into fields of experience which seemed to correspond to their social organization. Critical theorists turned the charge of metaphysics against the accusers: the hypostasis of a viewpoint, whether methodological, substantive, linguistic or whatever as final and valid a priori—i.e. exempt from historical modification—a viewpoint or principle from which all else is derivative, itself seemed such a metaphysical premise. Such a "transhistorical and thus overextended concept of truth seemed to derive from the idea "of a pure non-contingent infinite mind/reason, i.e. in the last analysis the idea of God."[12] "Moreover, by opposing all achievements of thought which have played crucial roles in human history with those it decrees to have been important, true and authentic, [logical empiricism] quite falls out of its [self-declared] role as a tautology and itself turns out to be . . . a subjective judgment."[13] Logical empiricists, Horkheimer charged, "posit all forms of being as constant [the same]. And yet this assertion that the correct form of all knowledge is identical with physics, and that physics is the great unified science under which all other sciences are to be subsumed—this assertion posits certain structures as unchangeable and thus represents a judgment *a priori*."[14] Such a "pro-metaphysical position absolves the given world by connecting it to a meaningful structure of being which is said to exist independent of historical changes"[15]—an ontology under the guise of a neutral methodology.

The social "relevance" of science, therefore, consisted not merely of its results; nor could it be made more progressive by simply changing its current application, as the advocates of "partisan science" and "science for the people" were demanding. By not reflecting on their paradigmatic premises, and analytic categories, scientists often take their clues from pre-rational, pre-scientific definitions of their objects. Social scientists especially tend to investigate problems without considering whom these are problems *for*. (An atrophied thought process rewarded with the label of a scholarly virtue.) In our time, Horkheimer complained, thinking is endangered not so much by the wrong paths it may pursue as by its being prematurely cut short. To the extent that an unreflexive science serves any social order, managing *its* problems and crises and thus helping to stabilize that order, it is a mere "handmaiden"[16] of the powers that be—the very powers that have a vested interest in repressing the emergence of alternative or better orders; and to that extent, science "passively participates in the common injustice."[17] Moreover, since scientific knowledge has the form of "technical," instrumental knowledge, the problems to which science addresses itself must first be translated into this manageable form—i.e. into technical problems—leaving the substance of the "problem" untouched.

With scientism and its complementary technological rationality having become the prevalent ideology of the time, Horkheimer concluded that "in as far as we can rightly speak of a crisis in science, that crisis is inseparable from the general crisis. The historical process has imposed chains on science as a force of production, and these show in the various sectors of science, in their content and form, in their subject matter and method."[18] Certain problems cannot appear as scientific problems within the scientistic paradigm—which thus awards cognitive respectability only to problems accessible to what is to be the one and only valid method—quite evidently a rather unscientific value decision. "It is not the victory of *science* that is the distinguishing mark of our nineteenth century, but the victory of the scientific *method* over science."[19] Nietzsche had indicted the arbitrary cognitive restriction. The "technical" value is built *into* the very form of scientific knowledge (and thus the very methods of attaining it). The aim of science to produce technically useable knowledge delimits desirable/permissible/prohibitive "methodical" relations to objects —an insight we express in the concept of an "approach" to them.

Comte's famous dictum about the business of science, *savoir pour prévoir*, to know in order to foresee, i.e. to bring nature under human control, almost has the ring of a tautology. Critical theorists did not challenge this aim; they just refused to exempt "control" from the status of a value.

For them, the idea of the value-freedom of the sciences was an extension of the "objectivistic illusion" that there can be perception without a perspective from which perception takes place. For scientism, values seemed added, superimposed on facts rather than being manifest in the (rarely conscious choice of) object-definitions in the first place. As Adorno was to remark later, "the [very] concept of value is already an expression of a situation in which the consciousness of the objectivity of reason is eroding."[20] "External" standards have to order what is falling apart. When we ignore the value-choice of our perspective in determining the kinds of facts we deal with, the excommunication of that perspective makes it and the facts appear independent of one another. The belief in the value-neutrality of one's approach, the assumption of a suspended perspective, simply means one has no categories with which to recognize that perspective. Without a theory to articulate and account for it, it becomes, literally, invisible. That values and decisions can be other than conscious, external or imposed, recognizable as explicit tenets one may accept or reject, that values may be built-in screens of perception and rules of association, did not commonly occur to the advocates of value-freedom.

Thus, formal logic and naive empiricism seemed to constitute a perfect working alliance: determined not to inquire into their own social/ideological genesis and function, both insisted on an ultimate basis of knowledge. Rules of inference or facts were irreducibles, were simply givens and thus *premises* (not proper objects) of investigation. For critical theorists, on the other hand, there were no such things as absolute premises of any kind: like any conception, premises were human products, usually the latest notion of an ultimate truth which thus became paradigmatic, i.e. the basis of further thought (from which it, as a fundament, remained exempt). Rules of inference then appear as functions of a reified truth. Yet, "the implicit genesis of logic" itself "lies in social behavior," Adorno asserted. "According to Durkheim, the forms of logical propositions are shaped by social experiences, such as generational and property relations."[21] This contingency is not recognized as such: for strategic reasons, particular interests always pretend to be universal ones—often persuasively, even to themselves. That the interest should be repressed is very much part of that interest, Habermas was to comment later!

Analogously, the empiricist "fetishism of facts" ignored that facts were, after all, products of collectively developed modes of perception; that we only know "mediated" facts; and that (even unconscious) theories and methods are the mediators: screens and collating rules for raw data actively shaping them into particular objects, facts or events. As Dewey knew, "to find out *what* is given is an inquiry which taxes reflection at the uttermost."[22] (Marcuse once noted that Greek skepticism had risen with doubts about sense perception. Undaunted by positivistic and "realistic" claims that the world is simply everything that is the case (in the early Wittgenstein's famous formulation), critical theorists insisted that what is the case, the supposed facts, are themselves only "something conditional."[23]

Positivists of the Vienna circle defended themselves by proclaiming that, in such criticism, "problems of appropriate description are confused with questions of fact, which leads to seemingly ontological problems."[24] Yet, this argument only shifted the actual question: where do the descriptive categories come from, and how are facts accessible without such categories? For "the origins and conditions of knowledge are not at the same time the origins and conditions of the world,"[25] and their problematic historical relation cannot be eliminated by methodological fiat. The consequence of such an attempt was pinpointed later by Adorno: "an object gets investigated by a research tool which, through its own formulation, decides what the object is: a simple circle."[26] The dubious claim, Cartesian in origin, was that facts somehow were "there," patiently waiting to be picked up, "discovered"; and that perceptual perspectives are basically distortions which had better be abandoned in favor of the neutral and universal tools—methods which simply render facts as they are, *an sich*.

Even Popper (who did not become their major target and antagonist till much later—cf. Part II of this work) occasionally conceded that facts were products of theories (or a joint product of language and reality)—which should mean that facts really have the cognitive status of hypotheses. Yet, Popper still insists on the possibility of "basic statements," evidently forgetful of his stringent criticism of Carnap's equivalent "protocol statements." Carnap had contended that simple observational statements could take the place of sense data as evidence if these could be agreed on intersubjectively. This, of course, merely shifts—and begs—the question. For no one really takes sense data as his final reference point anyway, but processed data, mediated through language and perceptual/conceptual categories. Logical positivists seemed perfectly unaware despite Wittgenstein that, "following the progress in ethnology and psychology, the constitutive function of language for sense data has been demonstrated. . . . The given is not just expressed through language, but formed as well."[27] For all their proclaimed skepticism, logical positivists doubted everything except the position from which they doubted. Rather than examine the intersubjective "protocol language" and its contingency, they simply and naively used it, and accepted as a "fortunate circumstance" (Carnap) that a shared descriptive language exists.

However, the uncritical acceptance of a widely shared form of mediation does not indicate that it is not a mediator. On the contrary, its universality only hides that very function through its monopoly. (A monistic "unified science" seemed the ultimate goal of logical positivists.) Such mediators delimit what kind of data are perceived at all. If they constitute the "facts," then other facts are literally imperceptible as long as this mediator prevails—the more universal it is, the fewer new or alternative "facts" will emerge. The shared observation language does not guarantee but may even prevent access to facts: The belief in witchcraft was fought with the same means of a strictly rationalistic philosophy. Yet in view of the great quantity of protocol statements which intersubjectively confirmed the existence/observation of witches, the empiricists should not even have been able to insist that witchcraft was unlikely,[28] Horkheimer mocked.

Traditional empiricism in this respect was not half as naive as its modern successors, Horkheimer suggested: however much Locke and Hume, through their liberalist premises, considered facts and sense evidence the final arbiter of knowledge, "their philosophy at least contains this dynamic element: it refers to a knowing subject"[29] (just as Leibniz, on the other—the rationalist—side, had insisted on a *substantia ideans*). Once this active subject was exposed as historical, it should have been obvious that the perceptual filters were historical, too. The facts given to us by the senses are socially preformed in two ways: through the historical character of the perceived object, and through the historical character of the perceiving organ.[30]

This "subject" is, of course, not an idiosyncratic individual trying to generalize. When Horkheimer speaks of a "general subjectivity on which individual cognition depends,"[31] he has in mind the collective subjectivity of an entire culture or stage of consciousness. Every culture carries its implicit "theory" which screens and packages sense stimuli, and we would not even perceive these sense stimuli as particular objects otherwise. Every "protocol" or "basic" statement contains such cultural and anthropological presuppositions.[32] They are the truly independent variables of observation; they are objective in precisely the sense that they *are* the standard of meaning.

The social construction of reality, as we would now say, is what positivists of necessity had to exclude; admitting it would have cost their method its claim to independence and universality. As Schütz was to put it somewhat later:

> All forms of naturalism and logical empiricism simply take for granted this social reality. . . . Intersubjectivity . . . and language are simply presupposed as the unclarified foundation of these theories. They assume, as it were, that the social scientist has already solved his fundamental problems, before scientific inquiry starts.[33]

Like Schütz, Horkheimer would extend the critique to the sciences in general. It makes little sense to divide the "context of genesis" from the "context of validation"; we can do so only at the price of the uncontrolled operation of the former in the "controlling categories"[34] of the latter. Hybrid concepts such as "natural law," or the obvious legal (or religious) origin of the concept of "cause" are only the most blatant examples.

Here lay one of the reasons for critical theorists to reject the notion that hypotheses—if not "deduced"—were but random serendipitous hunches of the private scientist. The paradigmatic reasons for accepting a hypothesis as valid might not be that different from those formulating it in the first place. The very expression of an "educated guess" suggests the operation of a subterranean logic of experience—a kind of pre-theoretical cultural competence—which alerts us to some features and possibilities of experience rather than to others, and provides certain modes of organizing that experience rather than others. Marcuse praised Dewey for suggesting at least "that the verifiability of a hypothesis is by far not as important as its directive power."[35] If this is true, then our present consciousness/working reason, through the hypotheses it generates, is pregnant with the future, and our "desirous anticipations"[36] may be cognitive signposts pointing to the fact that their factuality has become "conceivable" for us.

Just as our theoretical concepts are substantive hypotheses, so are the methods designed to test them. A method is simply a question, Habermas was to argue later, and surely no method will yield information which it does not ask for (through its very formulation). What we seek are explanations for whatever appears problematic to our "ideals of natural order" (Toulmin); the natural/normal does not need explanation. (By the same token, the history of scientific theories can be seen as the problem-history of humanity.) Methods/questions are thus as dependent on the cultural paradigm as are "satisfactory" explanations; for "the objects and manner of perception, the questions and the meaning of explanation testify to human activity."[37] Explanation is a pragmatic concept, and it is the varying situational ideals of a natural order, not a choice among the various nomological laws operative in an event (the classic positivist version), which decide what constitutes a "satisfactory" explanation in a given case.

Methodologies are either relative (adequate) to predefined object domains, and thus share their transcendental organization, or they must claim to be universal, in which case the question of their adequacy is undecidable and irrelevant. In either case, their validity cannot be determined regardless of their relation to their subject matter. Like explanation, validity is a pragmatic idea; its relation to the notion of currency seems no accident.

The Sociology of Knowledge and Psychoanalysis

To happiness the same applies as to truth: one does not have it, but is in it. (Theodor W. Adorno)

In the history of philosophy we repeatedly find epistemological categories turning into moral ones. (Theodor W. Adorno)

In the sphere of history, the concepts of "true" or "false" do not just apply to a consciousness, a form of thought, or a theory; they apply as well to a concrete situation—and the organization of life to which it belongs. (Herbert Marcuse)

The critic of culture must assume that he has the culture which culture itself lacks. (Theodor W. Adorno)

Critical theory's concern with mediating subjectivity was not limited to the sciences, of course (though the illusion of value-neutrality made them a particularly tempting—and fruitful—field in which to demonstrate the operation of tacit consensus and presuppositions). Concerned with the emergence or "production" of knowledge, and orientations for political reasons, Horkheimer very early gave primacy to the relations between base and superstructure, so neglected by Marx himself. The investigations were to be empirical and methodical, to detect the actual "psychic links" between "mind and reality."[38] When Horkheimer assumed the direction of the Institute, he outlined the changed focus in his inaugural speech: to put "a comprehensive empirical research apparatus into the service of problems of social philosophy," the central one being "the connection between the economic life of society, the psychic development of individuals, and the changes in cultural spheres . . . including not only the intellectual content of the sciences, art and religion, but of law, mores, fashion, public opinion, sports, entertainment, life-style etc."[39] (It went without saying that such a comprehensive project necessitated an interdisciplinary approach, simply because the nature of the "objects" in which the various spheres overlapped demanded it.)

In a sense, one could say that the historical-materialist grounding of the "constitution problem" i.e. what constituted the objects of our perception, judgment and action, was the central methodological concern of critical theory.[40] According to Habermas, the first "critical" philosopher was Kant. Rather than merely systematize the substance of knowledge, Kant focused on the *conditions* of knowing. That there were not only distortions of truth (as Bacon had suggested with his notion of "idols") but conditions of truth, i.e. regulative ideas and categorial forms through which, and only through which, we perceive sense data as particular objects or events—this discovery had been one of Kant's chief merits. In principle, we never see or know objects as they really are, but only as they are "constituted" through these filtering and ordering forms.

Traditional theories on the whole, critical theorists pointed out, tended to repeat Kant's mistake about these subjective conditions of knowledge: in its "hypostasis as form" of knowledge seemingly containing no substantive assertions, the collective subjectivity forgets "how and whereby it was constituted."[41] (Kant, though, had simply preserved a "truth" of an age prior to his own. He attributed to the "subjective" forms of knowledge the immutability traditionally ascribed the objects themselves. After Kant, however, this naiveté was no longer justifiable, and critical theorists chided the objectivistic illusion of recent positivism, which regressed to pre-Kantian certainties about a reality *per se*, or to the Kantian notion of cognitive forms valid a priori.)

This "general subjectivity upon which individual knowledge depends,"[42] described by Kant as timeless and fixed, is literally invisible in its form as "common sense"; as a condition and form of knowledge, it rarely becomes an object of knowledge. Yet these self-evident axioms of everyday practice constitute the most important dimension of an ideology: universally shared, these frameworks of our knowledge do not appear as relative or contingent. Because of this universality, they do in fact constitute the spirit, the truth of a group, no matter how historically relative and limited this spirit (and group) actually is. While these tacit and allegedly formed axioms, this framework, literally delimits what can be seen and what is conceivable, it nevertheless constitutes the logic in use of that age or group, and thus is logic per se for that age or group. In this sense, an ideology is simply the *common sense* of a given reference group.

From Bacon through d'Holbach to Daniel Bell, ideologies have been mostly seen as distortions of and barriers to an actual truth. The critical concept of ideology (and myth) emphasizes their truth as well as their concealing function (i.e. concealing their contingency). In one of his earliest works, Horkheimer had praised Vico for his insight "that the oldest legends must have contained political truths."[43] To be sure, "the limit of what we can rightfully call ideology is [itself] set by the present stage of our knowledge"[44]; i.e. the historical contingency of knowledge and ideology are two different things. That mores have the status of facts (to use Sumner's formulation) implies that facts both carry and represent the current truth and, at the same time, conceal it by concealing the active social and historical dimension behind the neutral façade of factuality. (Likewise, Marcuse had chided the academic sociology of knowledge for concerning itself only with the untruths but not with the truths of forms of consciousness.)

It would be difficult to comprehend this argument without the concomitant Hegelian concept of reason. Not a timeless human faculty hovering over the vicissitudes of history and the object world, reason, in this version, is a historical function, the dawning stage of awareness, the current comprehension/conceptualization of the way humans experience themselves. (Myths, for instance, are objectifications of reason in this sense, the first attempts of humans to deal with themselves in object form. Of course, gods are false consciousness, but their "truth" is not in their manifest content. As anthropomorphism, they allow confrontation with human attributes, which necessitates "reasons" for favoring these attributes rather than others; while they are false consciousness, they also therefore contain this emancipatory truth. (Neo-romantic ideologies are wrong and stupid in their explicit content, but have their "truth" content in their keen reaction to alienating and authoritarian forms of life.) The latest stage of such "reason" always tends to appear absolute, universal, and natural simply because it does not yet include awareness of its own limits and functions; such awareness would mean that this consciousness or reason had moved on to a higher stage of self-awareness: that it had recognized its particular form as *one*, not *the* mode of conceptualizing experience and observation.

In retrospect, we can always recognize previous forms of reason as limited—but to call them false implies they were unnecessary detours. The "working reason," or "working truth," of an age or culture cannot just have been false as long as it was a necessary stage. For all its teleological substratum, this concept of "necessary illusions" transcends the simple-minded notion of truth as existing out there, ready-made (already "coined," as Hegel used to say), patiently waiting to be discovered if we could just make up our minds to shed "false" notions and approaches. "Such Truth is more disastrous than error and ignorance because it paralyzes the forces with which one works toward enlightenment and knowledge,"[45] Nietzsche had once complained. Truth might be more usefully conceptualized as a force of production—for in this manner it includes its development and function as part of its substance. A "ready" truth would entail an ontology of the world as fixed and final, and thus entail a fatalistic ideology. (By contrast, for instance, even Fichte's "false" idealistic insistence on the *active* transcendental subject made it possible to historicize the constitution problem; consequently, at that time it was the only way to conceptualize consciousness as praxis, and praxis as the categorial constitution of the world—e.g. through labor.) That people can perceive their consciousness as contingent, i.e. that myth can turn into enlightenment, was one of the central contentions of *Dialectic of Enlightenment*. "However socially conditioned the thinking of the individuals may be. . . . it remains the thought of individuals who are not merely the products of collective processes but also make these processes the object of their thought,"[46] Horkheimer still asserted at the end of his life. That the viewpoint from which this is done is promptly mythified/fetishized in turn, was the other side of the dialectic: (the very act of) liberation reverts into heteronomy again, enlightenment into myth.

A consistently non-a priori approach must distrust any first, final or immutable principles, be they substantive, structural, formal or teleological.[47] Much to the chagrin of more orthodox Marxists, this prevented critical theorists from fetishizing even the economic base or any social objectivity, and even the critique of political economy as a theory; to them, it remained a form of historical reason. "A great truth wants to be criticized, not idolized," Nietzsche had proclaimed, and he was fondly cited by critical theorists who insisted that the "influence of social development on the structure of the theory is part of the theory's substantive content."[48] The function of a theory was very much part of the validity of its truth claim:

> Given the evolution of productive forces in antiquity, even the materialist philosophers were forced in the face of suffering to elaborate techniques of an interior life; peace of soul is the only resort in the midst of distress when all external means fail. By contrast, the materialism of the early bourgeois era aimed at developing the knowledge of nature and at attaining new powers of mastery over nature and man. The misery of the present, however, is linked to the structure of society; social theory, therefore, constitutes the content of contemporary materialism.[49]

To us, the notion of the timeliness of a theory may appear absurd; after all, we have learned that the explanatory range/power of a theory increases as it eliminates time and space indices. Yet, if the categories and concepts of a theory are the form of (historical) reason, a theory can be true only by being "self-reflexive": by making its categorial (methodological etc.) premises part of the objects it investigates. A theory is not simply true or false; a consciousness is not simply correct or false. Such judgment requires an analysis of what people *could* or *had to* think, given the terms in and under which they were experiencing the world. Likewise, the distinction between rational and irrational would require that we be in possession of a timeless reason, Adorno pointed out. Given increasingly narrow definitions of reason throughout recent history, increasingly larger areas of cognitive activities were labeled irrational. From Descartes to Kant and modern positivists, the irrational areas supposedly inaccessible to rational analysis have grown along with the refinement of the "rational method."[50] Whatever did not fit it, was exiled into the realm of irrational "decision." At the final point, Popper has called even the decision for science lacking rational grounds: it is motivated merely by "belief."

Instead of dividing the world ontologically along methodological lines, critical theorists, who distrusted any form of *prima philosophia*, tied these ontologies themselves to social conditions which necessitated and in turn were shaped by them:

> There are connections between the forms of judgment and the historical periods. . . . The classificatory judgment is typical of prebourgeois society: this is the way it is, and humans can do nothing about it. The hypothetical and disjunctive forms belong especially to the bourgeois world: under certain circumstances, this effect can take place; it is either this or that way. Critical theory maintains: it need not be so; humans can change reality, and the necessary conditions for such change already exist.[51]

In this sense forms of judgment delimit "natural" and possible forms of action as well. No matter how we hide from the formative impact of such substantive yet seemingly just formal premises by relying merely on quantitative measurement, these measurements will be no more precise and reliable (and neutral) than the concepts and categories they measure. Least visible of all are the comprehensive experiential models of which certain divisions or forms of inference are but specific examples—which may be isolated and even revised while the overall model remains intact. Critical theorists offered numerous examples of such models, each considered true and all-encompassing in its time—and thus not even considered as a model but simply as the structure of reality.

For all its questionable chronolology, Franz Borkenau's *The Transition from the Feudal to the Bourgeois World View* is an inspired study of the fundamental shifts in the "categories of natural and social science"[52] during that period. It attempts a detailed demonstration of the interrelations between the social, economic, legal, theological, psychological etc. conceptions, and of the possibilities for further conceptualizations they opened, and thus of the groundwork they laid for later developments. The interesting—and unorthodox—thesis was that a world view and images of nature depend on both the conditions of production *and* the general concepts. The "mechanical-mathematical" world view emerging during that transitional period, in the wake of changes in the spheres of production and circulation, brought with it the general trend toward leveling and isolating units, toward defining the constituents of reality (both social and natural, since both served as models for each other) in terms of status-equal monads. The reduction of qualitative differences to functional quantitative relations reduced these relations to the level of their common denominator, which is often an external criterion. People and things become "equivalents" to the precise extent that they become—formally—equals in reference to this shared principle. (The very concept of something "qualitative" has become absorbed into that of "function," Brecht once remarked, in one of Adorno's favorite formulations.) Thinking in terms of unity already contains the tendency to think in terms of equivalents, Adorno and Horkheimer were to suggest in *Dialectic of Enlightenment*, and thus provides a fertile ground for the ascent of exchange rationality. By way of the reduction of individual differences, a totalizing tendency asserts itself. And to the extent that this tendency (e.g. in terms of society as a market, in terms of growing bureaucratization etc.) becomes accepted as a form of progress and rationalization, this specific historical form of relations of exchange between social and natural "equivalents" comes to appear as more and more "natural"—the more so the more universal it becomes; and by excluding alternatives, it also becomes self-legitimating. "Rationalization," the very form of human self-definition through or for something else ("heteronomy") seems no longer a metaphysical but a *rational* demand.

This mechanistic reconceptualization of social and natural reality, of the field of human action in general, tended to explain events merely in terms of motions and forces (instead of qualities); similarly, humans tended to be conceived of as drifting in a force field of external and internal variables (e.g. their "interest").

Mannheim too had pointed to the orientational (rather than descriptive) nature of "scientific interpretations." At times, he suggested that the scientific obsession with laws and order might signal vestiges of religious and jurisdictive models or forms of consciousness—not unlike Adorno and Horkheimer who were to call causality, for instance, "the latest secularization of the creative principle." [54] Even positivists like Russell and Popper had spelled out attitudinal implications of certain theories (other than their own, of course). But they all were content to suggest correlations between social and cognitive factors (as both were "naturally" separate spheres, with independent identities), rather than to explain reasons for these groupings and correlations in the first place: for instance, what groupings *could* form given certain material conditions and forms of consciousness and psychology, or what kinds of psychology, cognition, and thus of human praxis appeared conceivable or "natural" under given conditions.

This was not just a matter of a difference of opinion about how far "back" one should trace the causes of certain forms of consciousness. Without a theory of what mediates between social and cognitive factors, i.e. of the "transcendental" constitution of consciousness and reality, their relation had to remain accidental—or exemplify a cultural truism which begs the very question it pretends to answer. Critical theorists agreed with Mannheim, for instance, that social groups will tend to pass off their interests as universal. But this hardly tempted them to reduce all ideologies and utopias to mere forms of "subjective" expression. The formal category of "elites," for example, one of Mannheim's favorites, conceals who dominates whom behind the formal statement that there is always domination; the who, how, why (and its changeability) should be the topic rather than the "mere" empirical detail of an inevitable universal experience. The alleged pluralism of social perspectives which Mannheim's "innocuous relationism" saw as adding up to a balanced whole, might turn out to be no pluralism at all but an enforced division, made—and thus changeable—by humans. Of course, carrying the analysis to this point would render the reified "principles" and "forces" of social division less compelling (or ontological), and the terms of Mannheim's explanation itself might reveal their "relationism." (It puzzled critical theorists why "the consciousness of the sociology of knowledge" should be the only one exempt from historical relativity.) All theories are not equal. Neither their transhistorical content nor any formal criterion but what, under given circumstances, "a theory includes and what it excludes, decides about its quality,"[55] Adorno commented.

And the traditional sociology of knowledge did consistently "exclude" its central problem: the nature of the *nexus*, i.e. the concrete mechanisms mediating between consciousness and society. Although recognized by some of its major representatives, this fault continues to mar the validity of otherwise sophisticated content analyses: they employ, and thus accept, the social and conceptual associations and divisions whose very existence and function should be their actual problem[56] (e.g. divisions into high and mass culture, individual and society, theory and practice, love and hate, etc.).

Insofar as orthodox Marxism and bourgeois sociology lacked a systematic theory of the necessary mediations between subjective consciousness and objective conditions, this failure was not one of imperfect research techniques but one of principle. Why certain forms of consciousness survived the changes in historical conditions which had produced them, they neither could nor cared to explain. How, on the other hand, could the working class, the subject of the revolution, come to have an "ideological" rather than "Utopian" consciousness? (This was the question informing much of the ideology critique and social philosophy of later critical theory.) But if the emancipation of concrete individuals was to remain a central concern, and if social laws acted through individuals and not just objective classes, then the consciousness of individuals was neither negligible, nor was concern with it a form of bourgeois subjectivism. As agents of history, they had been forgotten, it seemed, in favor of reified laws of which they were considered mere reflexes or exemplifications (itself a "mechanization"). The publication in 1932 of Marx's *Economic and Philosophic Manuscripts*, with their "anthropological" and humanistic emphasis, heartened those Marxists who had despaired of the official neglect of such concerns.

Responsive to Dilthey's pleas for a social psychology to substantiate historical analysis, the Frankfurtians showed early sensitivity to the possibilities of psychoanalysis. However, not until 1932, when Fromm entered the Institute, was psychoanalysis systematically incorporated into the historical materialism of the group. In a series of programmatic statements (the first of which is reproduced here), Fromm attempted a systematic merger of Marx and Freud at roughly the same time as Reich; the parameters of the attempt are too well known to require elaboration here. Fromm's early argument was as simple as it was obvious: as Freud had diagnosed pathologies as products of the individual's history, it was a short step to show that the individual's history (e.g. within the family) was itself embedded in and contingent on a larger collectivity. As an agent of socialization, the family produced the character types and behaviors typical of, and functional for, the particular socio-economic class.

Fromm explained specific kinds of drives as active and passive adaptations to specific socio-economic situations, the "primary formative factor." Without denying their biological base, Fromm could thus show the behavioral expressions of drives, and subsequently their different forms of gratification, to be dynamic responses and *necessary* forms of historical behavior. Given the psychostructure produced by different socio-economic conditions, class-specific needs, conflicts, pressures and possibilities can hardly be considered anthropological constants. Through these psychostructures, social conditions are reproduced within the individual not only in the form of explicit values and material necessities, which then tend toward congenial social forms, but of drives. As long as they remain unconscious and are perceived as "natural," these social sediments are alien forces within humans—a form of heteronomy, Adorno would have added. Changing human motivation and drives presupposes that they are recognized as products of situations, as Freud had suggested. (The early Freud had suspected, but then disregarded, the influence of the larger social framework.)

Most of the categories (and topics) of Fromm's Marx/Freud synthesis re-emerged in the various political, cultural and esthetic analyses of the group in the following decades. Most important to them, however, and surprising only at first glance, was the obstinate retention of the biological *base*, and the emphasis on the historical *forms* of drives. Thus, they challenged the universality of the Oedipal phase just as much as the specific biological interpretation of the "death drive"; like Reich, they saw the latter as the biologization of destructive tendencies in society which deflected attention from the real social pathogenesis. (In an analogous argument, Adorno derided Heidegger for enshrining as an existential "Angst" the realistic fear which social conditions instilled in individuals.)

This basic pattern of the social interpretation of supposed existential human drives and needs was to remain valid for most of the Institute except, ironically, Fromm himself. With growing disagreements, Fromm moved out of the Institute, and the other members, in often bitter attacks, chided him for surrendering the progressive thrust of his earlier approach. Not only did Fromm assume a human "nature" again, but he even surrendered what was perhaps the most critical of Freud's conceptions: the libidinal base. With it, Adorno, Horkheimer and Marcuse complained, disappeared the theoretical base for the only truly irreconcilable and incompatible dimension in humans, the deviation in principle, the always overshooting expectation, the non-identity with any status quo, the truly critical concept in Freud.

In another stroke of irony, the later Marcuse (who had shown little interest in the Marx-Freud synthesis during the thirties) attempted the merger once more, in the frame of a general theory of culture. For the most part, the Frankfurtians employed Freudian concepts to explain salient contemporary forms of consciousness and behavior (e.g. the "authoritarian personality"). Marcuse, however, sought to redeem the critical potential of psychoanalysis by turning it into a positive theory of emancipation. When he published *Eros and Civilization* in 1955, his former colleagues did not comment (except Fromm, who disapproved). In all likelihood, Marcuse's cautious attempt to spell out specifics of the future liberated personality and society (and the positive, rather than just critical, use of the biological base) may have struck them as an undue limitation of future possibilities. Yet, besides the critical potential of any positive alternative, this alternative seemed viable—a concrete possibility given the material and technological conditions of the present. In the estheticized society, critique and its instruments would be "aufgehoben"—eliminated (as critique) by being realized (in reality).

Almost two decades later, in *Counterrevolution and Revolt*, Marcuse resumed the critical focus: no conceivable historical reality could attain the unity (identity) of subject and object; the subject (as a force of production, ahead of the objective conditions) could be suspended only in a dead-end utopia. Like the libidinal base, the esthetic mode was critical in principle.

As critical theorists practiced it, both sociology of knowledge and psychoanalytic social psychology were to be critical, self-reflexive and emancipatory "tools"—without loss of their "scientificity." Systematizing the social mediations of consciousness and motivation, they were to preserve the historical "truths" as well as to expose the historical contingencies of these forms. In this sense, critical theory might be called a kind of socio-epistemology. Its underlying practical thrust is unmistakable as the basic pattern which foreshadows Habermas's later claim for psychoanalysis as a science rooted in an emancipatory cognitive interest. Fromm had argued that in contrast with survival needs, sexual drives can be satisfied without "real means"—i.e. even through fantasies—something that placed the ruling class in the position of being able to offer its choice of gratifications to the dominated classes. The primary cognitive interest (a recurrent term in Horkheimer's work) then was to keep the forms these choices took from appearing "natural" or "given," to redeem them and their specific forms of consciousness. The critique of what is excluded from these forms is not superfluous to stringent analysis, but is an inherent requirement of objectivity. If scientific interest is directed toward the "whole" truth, which, as we saw, always transcends/exceeds the given, the accurate, full and objective description of the truth is critique by definition because it exceeds the status quo.

The Concept of Reason

Reason was the only category of philosophical thought which, over the centuries, retained any relation to the empirical "fate of humanity". (Alfred Schmidt)

Because even its remotest objectifications are nourished by impulses, thought destroys in the latter the condition of its own existence. (Theodor W. Adorno)

Any contempory re-statement of liberal or socialist goals must include as central the idea of a society where men would become men of substantive reason, whose independent reasoning would have structural consequences for their societies, its history, and thus for their own life fates. (C. Wright Mills)

Fundamental to critical theory is a concept of reason as both historically objective and autonomous (i.e. capable of self-transcendence). In its current "instrumental" definition, the historical nature of reason as the dawning consciousness of an age of culture, and, consequently, its functional role in organizing the values of these historical situations, is lost. Precisely as empirical consciousness, reason simultaneously has "transcendental" status: the conceptualizations of a particular stage of insight circumscribe—literally—what is conceivable, just as these delimitations are but the crystallization of cumulative experience. Yet, as a force of production (and insights into the historical contingency of forms of reason can become such a force, critical theorists insisted), reason considers reality not reasonable per se; reality may lag behind its own possibilities, and needs to be "brought to reason."[57]

It is hardly surprising that this concept of reason has played a minimal (if any) role in contemporary philosophical discourse, whereas one of its aspects—deductive inference—has come to be practically considered identical with it. Beyond the operation of these rules of inference, cognitive acts have been exiled into psychology, i.e. into basically irrational procedures. "Reasons" and rationality seem unconnected. Defining reason in terms of operational rules quite evidently excludes such unruly behavior as asking these rules to legitimate themselves. Such a challenge would require a higher reason,[58] a court, as it were, that relates those operational rules to a purpose (which would imply that different purposes require different rules); identifying one set with reason means we consider reasonable only *its* informing purpose—an obvious, although tacit decision among alternative values. Once such a decision is enthroned, the informing values are withdrawn from rational challenge and discussion (including the one that led to this "choice"); reason proudly pronounces itself neutral and a merely formal instrument to administer and implement rules, goals and values which themselves seem neither produced, nor modifiable, by reason.

Increasingly, "thought has renounced its claim to be critical and posit goals at the same time."[59] Its reduction to "mere calculation" apart from normative decisions e.g. on goals (which thus come to appear as "irrational" decisions), bears little relation to either the intent or method of that ancestry positivists claimed; Montesquieu, Locke, the Encyclopedists *et al.* had held reason

> to be the result of free and autonomous judgment, and the rational was the activity that followed this judgment. Appeal to the facts was meant to corroborate reason, not to override it; if the facts were at variance with reason's dictates, the former were "wrong" and had to be changed in conformity with the latter's demands.
> The idea which animated positivist philosophy in the 18th century was a critical one . . .[60]

To Horkheimer, the present pervasiveness of instrumental/formal/subjective rationality (which formally enshrined certain historical/ subjective forms of reason with its characteristic forms of judgment) was a sign of historical immaturity, of a regress to heteronomy. "The calculating thought of 'Verstand'[61] belongs to a type of human being who is still relatively powerless. Despite his busyness, he is passive in decisive matters,"[62] i.e. he takes his goals from somewhere else. By contrast, critical theorists upheld a concept of reason as a "telos immanent in the historical process toward human autonomy vis-à-vis the history they have made."[63] In this version—Hegel's dialectic of limits is unmistakable—reason is neither an ontological category nor a timeless human faculty. Rather, it is a kind of historically evolving capacity for self-transcendence, inseparable from the notion that humans make their own history.

The Frankfurtians did not tire of pointing to the *active* and constitutive dimension of thought; a philosophy is not something one has, but does—a "behavior," as Adorno was fond of calling it.

Passive (non-interfering) contemplation belongs to a "naive" stage where humans confront the world as something "other": they have not recognized their share in its shaping, nor that the terms in which they relate to it are of their own making, nor that they are dealing with a conceptually or materially appropriated (inner and outer) nature whose terms they can change. "When the idea of reason was conceived, it was to do more than regulate the relation between means and ends; it was intended to determine the ends." With the same argument, critical theorists attempted to save and reformulate the once self-evident idea of individuality as the exercise of free autonomous reason (i.e. reason free of serving imposed goals, free to choose among them). The simultaneous collapse—so often invoked by them—of reason and the individual "as whose agency it [reason] has developed"[64] was clearly no coincidence for them.

The mark of individual autonomy was conscious choice,[65] which presupposed that there *were* viable alternatives and options which, in turn, presupposed their knowledge or "creation" respectively—the proper task of substantive reason. *Mutatis mutandis*, this exercise of substantive reason was predicated on the guiding interest in human autonomy: "freedom and reason are nonsense without each other."[66] In this sense, an unreasonable approach is also an amoral one. We cannot speak of a moral decision if we are coerced into it, or do not see alternate options, no matter if we make it unconsciously or voluntarily submit. Any prior guidelines relieve us of moral decisions; following one means surrendering both reason and freedom, for "binding moral directives do not exist."[67] On the one hand, the currently dominant form of reason serves as such a guideline which suspends the freedom of autonomous judgment; on the other, its particular form makes value decisions a private matter—which lets its use appear as the voluntary choice of individuals whose decision-making ability it has just suspended.

This concept of reason was not an undue mix of cognitive and irrational ingredients, but the "logical" consequence of repudiating the coercive equation: reason=rules of deductive inference; it was part of the attempt, as Adorno once put it, to "break through the coercive nature of logic by logical means," i.e. by turning logic upon itself. The exclusive ascendence of instrumental reason meant the (self-) cancellation of autonomous reason, and thus went hand in hand with (and was instrumental to) the most irrational forms of life.

Critical theorists did not abandon the belief that humans could intervene and reverse the tide; but they also saw clearly that the self-cancellation of reason was occurring not because of its corruption, but through its own immanent logic as "dialectic of enlightenment." Since part of its liberating function had been to ask any agency to legitimate its authority, reason finally had to turn that challenge against itself. It had to declare its own authority and substantive claims part of the very myths it had helped dissolve—so that it alone might reign. The dual contemporary mode of instrumental and formalized subjective rationality blocks any rational perspective from which it could be seen as a *specific* and one-sided form of reason. It indicts as irrational any perspective from which alternatives (to itself) are at all conceivable. The very capacity to both perceive this limitation and thus conceive alternatives is diminishing, and with it the autonomy to decide, which presupposes the visibility of alternatives.

Reason had once been able to claim that things could be different by pointing to its own existence as an alternative mode and order of being. Like art, like fantasy, its residual forms today, it overshoots reality. The true is the whole, Hegel had said, and that includes "real" possibilities and their realization as part of reality.[68] If reason grasps the truth of a situation, its true identity in this sense, then any concrete situation always falls short of its true identity. (When we speak of the truth *of* something, we always assume there is more than meets the eye, than can be expressed by statements corresponding to observables.)

The idea of reason in this sense, as a "project," dates back into Western antiquity, e.g. Anaxagoras, whose suggestion of a "nous"—the idea of an order in nature which replaced the older animistic world view—implied the possibility of such discrepancy. The existing order is not perfect, is not in accordance ("identical") with its idea, but has to be brought to its identity, to its "whole truth." To focus not only on what is there but on what could (and perhaps should) be is the function of substantive reason. It stands opposed to the dominance of instrumental reason, which merely serves, extends and refines what is. Since Aristotle, fantasy has been a constitutive ingredient of reason.[69] To the extent that this cognitive faculty goes beyond the status quo, it is critical of it (its limitations and the reasons for it): critique and fantasy are thus inseparable.[70]

We have come a long way from Plato's idea that it was "eros" which "enabled the sage to know the ideas. He [Plato] thus connected cognition with a moral or psychic state."[71] "Correct thinking depends on correct will, as will depends on thinking,"[72] Horkheimer declared, foreshadowing Habermas's famous dictum that *propositional truth hinges on the intention of a true society*.

The "new logic" of logical positivism, against which critical theorists were directing most of their polemic, seemed the purest manifestation of this reductive tendency, although only representative of a general trend of the time. A self-declared tautology, or "theory of deduction," it collapses the complex philosophical concept of truth into that of syntactic or methodological (formal) "correctness." "The fact that a judgment can be correct and nevertheless without truth, has been a crux of formal logic from time immemorial,"Marcuse reminded logical positivists.[73] Reducing reason to mere acumen, expertise and "trained incompetence," positivism nevertheless avails itself of the traditional prestige of science—which itself dates back, however, to the days of its critical, liberatory thrust. In earlier days, autonomous reason constructed visions of a reasonable world and demanded efforts to realize those visions. In the recent reduction of reason (still a value) to "technical" knowledge and information, the implicit directive is a technical relation to the world. Other attitudes are therefore "irrational." If critical-substantive reason once aimed at becoming a total life form, it was a liberating demand. Instrumental reason was a species of the genus: its instrumental knowledge enabled human beings to "make their own destiny." But reason, reduced to tasks of technical control, must be indifferent to *what* is to be controlled for *what* purpose. The idea of a "reasonable goal" (or of a rational choice or correction of goals) cannot be accommodated within that concept of reason.[74]

The reversal is complete, not only of ends and means, but of subject and object. The most subjective aspect, the perspective, the way of looking at things, formalized as method, something abstract and spiritual, has become the standard of objectivity; whereas "working reason," the historically grown objective logic of a given reality, is made to appear accidental. "Objective means the non-controversial aspect of things, their unquestioned impression, the façade made up of classified data; and they call subjective anything that breaches that facade . . ."[75]. In the fear of revealing their points of reference as contingent and derivative, logical positivists could not accept a changing material and social reality as the corrective of objective meaning. Be it methodological or syntactical, the positivistic criterion of meaning was a spiritual, not material one—which, in the eyes of critical theorists, identified positivism as a variant of idealism. Here lay the common denominator which, to critical theorists, made negligible all other differences between idealism, positivism and ontologies of any kind, and even certain forms of materialism: the pretense—no matter how well concealed—that we have an ultimate and unchangeable criterion for what is rational and meaningful, a first or final principle, an Archimedean fixed point from which to order empirical phenomena, not itself empirical or historical. "In order to limit itself as finite, reason must have access to the infinite on behalf of which the specific limitation is performed."[76] That anyone could claim such access, they doubted; short of it, the standards of knowledge were historical/empirical products (facts) subject to the same analysis as the object of knowledge. Standards of objectivity are as historical as the facts they constitute. For qualitative and substantive objectivity, methodologies needed to be "self-reflexive," i.e. having the premises and standards of an investigation as part of the object under investigation.

Often critical of Dewey's instrumentalism, they felt closer to him than to logical positivists because of his attempt at "a material logic in the sense . . . that the matters of logic (the objects with which logical thought deals) are drawn consistently into the arena of investigation, and the logical "forms" are discussed exclusively in their constitutive connection with this material."[77] By contrast, the "new logic" which critical theorists attacked "is called formal. Little is said in these writings of how the form is to be explained without reference to the content . . . Proudly this logic declares that nowhere does it increase substantive knowledge."[78] Nevertheless, it claimed to be the logic of inference in substantive research; it remained a puzzling issue how tautologies were to permit understanding. Form is always that of its content, Hegel had explained; but despite the admission (e.g. by Russell) that symbolic logic is little more than a shorthand, little is said about what it is a shorthand for. To critical theorists, the concepts of logical positivism are not concepts of anything; they are not substantive, and thus not a form of knowledge at all.

If methodological and syntactical standards are to be cognitive standards as well, then method and (our conceptualization of) material produce and crystallize each other. Cognitive categories are not separable from what they are categories of; if one changes, so does the other. There is no such thing as "pure" knowledge, nor a pure cognitive method. "Rather, knowledge comes to us through a network of biases, intuitions, innervations, self-corrections, anticipations and exaggerations—in short, through the tightly-woven and well grounded but by no means uniformly transparent medium of experience."[79]

The Dialectical "Method"

Dialectical thought is the attempt to break through the coercive character of logic with the means of logic itself. (Theodor W. Adorno)

Thinking does not get caught up in dialectics because it disdains the rules of formal logic, but because it obstinately sticks to these rules; it employs these rules even to think about logic itself, instead of breaking off their application at this crucial point. (Jürgen Habermas)

To "put" things is very exactly and responsibly to do them. Our expression of them, and the terms on which we understand that, belong as nearly to our conduct and our life as every other feature of our freedom. (Henry James)

Insofar as dialectics demonstrates the multiplicity, the process of growth and the limits of historical forms, it implies taking a position vis-à-vis those forms of existence. Inasfar as any such historical reality contains a claim to duration, unequivocal identity, and validity and attempts to realize that claim, this dialectical position is a critical one by definition, and it must undermine any such claim. Concrete dialectic as a positionless science is a contradiction in terms. (Herbert Marcuse)

The essence of dialectic is nothing but the systematic, methodically refined spirit of contradiction. (Hegel to Goethe)

Although considered by friend and foe as the distinguishing approach of critical theory, "dialectic" has remained a remarkably opaque concept. Dialectic, of course, is neither an ideology nor is it a method in the sense of a research technique. Its dual claim—to be both faithful to, and critical of, empirical reality—has given rise to a host of misunderstandings about its central terms. It might be useful to clarify the concept of dialectic in confrontation with the most common of these misunderstandings.

1) A trivial, but recently common misunderstanding assumes that everything that has two sides is therefore dialectical. (We will leave

aside the complex issue of whether predicates stand in a potentially dialectical relationship to an object, whether a copula is a dialectical mediator, etc.). Whether two entities stand in a dialectical relationship to each other is entirely an empirical question, particularly in the framework of such Marxian modalities as "latency" and "tendency." Juxtaposition, alliance, quantitative relation, abstract or remote opposition, static opposition, mere mental construction and division (e.g. odd and even numbers, north/south, etc.) can be modes of coexistence without dialectical negation, contradiction or mediation. Such "abstract" contradictions are undialectical by definition (e.g. that methods and material were not dialectically related in "traditional theory" was precisely what the critical theorists objected to).

"Abstract" in the Hegelian sense always implies an abstraction *from* the constitutive context of an entity, i.e. an essential incompleteness and the often concomitant assumption of a monadic "essence" apart from that content (for instance, a real self behind mere roles, games, etc.). The individual abstracted from his social context, whose terms it needs to articulate or manifest itself, no longer stands in contradiction to the general, is no longer its negation—no longer stands in any necessary relation at all. As the individual can only articulate itself in collective objective terms, ignoring or denying those terms does not eliminate them but only leaves them operative without modification by the individual. The old issue of individual spontaneity is a perfect case in point. Abstractly opposed to society, insisting on our own essential "real self" that surfaces when uninhibited by thought and other (e.g. social) mediations, we would simply reproduce whatever we have been socialized into, which remains sedimented in our consciousness without conscious correctives. *This* is what we spontaneously reproduce when we retreat from consciously handling the terms in and under which we act. The individual especially is a product of the general, Adorno insisted. Mediated consciousness is not bad, unreal consciousness but the only consciousness available. The often indiscriminate rejection by the Left of "bourgeois subjectivism" frequently fails to distinguish between abstracted, illusory, self-sufficient subjectivity, which is passive toward society, and a subjectivity which is an active form and function of determinate negation. Even a false consciousness may be a true consciousness in this sense and a harbinger of transcendence, a map of new territory. Where the distinction lies between these two kinds of subjectivity is not decided by fiat, for "how desirable and intrinsically valuable individual preliminary stages may be ... and what their historical importance is in relation to the idea [of a realistic utopia] all this will be made clear only when the idea is brought to realization."[80]

2) The most famous—and more serious—misunderstanding is Kierkegaard's misreading of Hegel's triad describing the movement of historical reality: thesis-antithesis-synthesis—a simplistic formalization with which Hegel himself was rather unhappy and which Kierkegaard misunderstood as a compromise, a kind of middle ground between thesis and antithesis. Aided probably by Hegel's use of the terms *Vermittlung* (mediation) and *Versöhnung* (reconciliation), Kierkegaard overlooked that "mediation takes place in and through the extremes"[81] (of the thesis and antithesis) and not as a simple give and take between the two. The new synthesis, therefore, is (nothing but) the new working constellation of the thesis and antithesis, a new "working reality," so to speak. This new synthesis in turn can become a thesis which engenders its own new antithesis which may again lead to a new synthesis and so on.

3) Probably the most widespread misunderstanding, commonly found among "traditional" logicians, refers to what is meant by the so-called "dialectical contradiction" itself (i.e. thesis-antithesis). The traditional objection "that two contradictory statements can never be true together"[82] overextends the applicability of the principle of the excluded third. No one ever denied the validity of this principle within formal logic. But, like Hegel, the critical theorists took seriously the postulate of traditional logic that its rules do not necessarily coincide with those of empirical reality. Dialectical logic which, according to Hegel, was to follow the movement of reality, was more comprehensive and could include traditional logic as one way of organizing reality, albeit one whose arbitrariness was not checked by any necessary relation of its inherent structure to its referents.

The dialectical contradictions within empirical reality, the antitheses which "negate" the theses, are not a matter of the absolute existence or non-existence of a predicate; the dialectical contradiction of "a" is not "non-a" but "b," "c," "d," and so on—which, in their attempt at self-assertion and self-realization, are all fighting for the same historical space. Instead of assuming a complete package of predicates as either belonging or not belonging to the object, instead of assuming pure qualities as the fixed identity of an object, critical theorists assumed multiple modalities for any historical object, different parts of which are activated, repressed or created in different and overlapping constellations. Moreover, in the process of historical realization of such objects (this process being their only reality, Marcuse proposed), their identity (i.e. their truth) was necessarily a matter of gradation, just as this truth had a necessary temporal dimension (as Aristotle had also insisted). Bloch, at one point, even spoke of "gradations of reality" in this respect. Although we experience momentary stages of this process only, there is no need, although an understandable pressure, to reify this stage. In view of these reifications, theory must strive to "dissolve the rigidity of the object fixated in the here and now, *dissolve* it into a field of the possible and the real."[83]

Repeatedly, like the great philosophical traditions they invoked, critical theorists warned against the "practice of defining" statically an illusory, isolated essence (of which operational definitions are then but mere extensions) abstracted from the ongoing historical process— though it be only the process of conceptual appropriation. To check the arbitrariness of these definitions, Horkheimer advised that we should think of *substantive* opposites to clarify our working assumptions, rather than mere formal ones: e.g. instead of the contradiction of straight vs. non-straight, the contradiction of straight vs. curved, straight vs. interrupted, straight vs. zigzag; instead of matter/non-matter, matter/ mind, matter/anti-matter, etc., which are *empirical* negations. Which is the operative negation is likewise an empirical question and thus subject to continuous shifts. No single definition does justice to these overlapping empirical and perceptual modalities; no sum of them is omnipresent in each single context. Every predicate is a hypothesis deduced from our "working reason." A mere definition reduces predicates to *one* frame of reference, i.e. one modality, and thus does not define the (multimodal) object at all, it's "truth." (An interesting example of such a dialectical opposition—where the true is the whole—is the Copenhagen quantum interpretation asserting that certain elementary particles are simultaneously matter and waves, or that it is impossible to measure the speed and location of these particles at the same time—the Heisenberg indeterminacy principle. These discoveries refer back, as Heisenberg suggested, to the constitutive function of perspective as an *integral* feature of the object.)

In the final analysis, the difference is between a formal (and thus essentially quantitative) concept of contradiction and a substantive one—a distinction philosophers of science like Hempel readily admit. How form can be discussed without reference to the content of which it is the form, remained mysterious to critical theorists. But far from rejecting formal logic, "a dialectical theory . . . true to its principles, will tend to retain the relative truths [!] of particular positions and incorporate them into its own comprehensive theory."[84]

The universalistic claims of formal logic, logical positivism and logical empiricism, and by the same token, we might add, of the "copy theory" of perception, caused some rather embarrassing problems. It proved difficult to demonstrate the connection between non-substantive, non-empirical categories and empirical reality. In order to be more than an idiosyncrasy of pure logicians and methodologists, formal logic and abstracted methodology *had* to imply, tacitly, a corresponding theory of truth; much as positivists denied it, they needed to assume that the rules operative in positive reality coincided with those of logic, and, more specifically, those of deductive inference. Otherwise it would be difficult to see why formal logic and abstracted methodology should be "more than an internal matter of working techniques of a few scholars,"[85] as Marcuse had once mused about the enterprise of the *International Encyclopedia of Unified Science* (founded by members of the Vienna circle, who most emphatically proposed these positions). For all their (justified) critique of "identity philosophy" (i.e., to simplify, the assumption of an identical structure of mind and matter), positivism's affinity to this side of Hegel, his weakest, remained hidden from their view. For, if logic was to have a cognitive dimension at all, it had to be cognition of something. If all cognitive categories are categories of reality as well, then *whatever* we know is the whole truth and nothing but the truth; on the other hand, if the categories of empirical reality are also cognitive categories, there would be nothing we could not, or even do not know.

For critical theorists, however, the experience of non-identity between these two spheres (i.e. in the final analysis, of subject and object) was the starting point, and its admission a matter of intellectual integrity. Every phenomenon we "know" is a synthesis (in the Kantian sense); but we are not commonly aware of the socio-historical "a priori" which constitutes this synthesis; that we experience an assemblage of data as a unified phenomenon at all, is *prima facie* evidence for our synthesizing activity. Unless we assume that the coordinating/synthesizing categories are timeless (as Kant and after him a certain positivism said), lags may develop, or rather are everpresent . If reality turns out not to fit the categories any more, this is not *just* an indication of the imperfection of categories, but also signals our discovery of the composite and constituted, i.e. "made" unity we had experienced.

To an extent, therefore, the experience of unity is symptomatic of "naive" consciousness, a consciousness not yet (or no longer) "self-conscious," still experiencing reality as something "out there" in its own right, yet somehow coinciding with our understanding. This naive identity of subjective cognitive forms and objective content of experience of reality is to be strictly distinguished from its "negative image"[86] the ideological pretense of such an identity: that reason and reality coincide in a given society. For all the *utopian* truth content of this ideology, it conceals that any reality is usually far from reasonable.

By contrast the dialectical/productive totality is not one of indistinguishable ingredients. The notion of unity, Plato had already argued, presupposes multiplicity and division. Non-identity is the very precondition of reality as realization: the (subjective and objective) ingredients of a synthesis move at different paces and in different directions, and the changing properties/predicates of the objects of our experience reveal the situational contingency day by day. But without such temporal syntheses (from which we tend to quickly eliminate our active contribution, converting it into a property of the object), without such self-objectifications with which, in turn, we interact as with independent "alien" entities, reality would not be realization and history would not move at all. Hegel had called the periods of non-conflict, of happiness, the "dead" periods in history. A dialectical totality "realizes itself only through its parts, through the gap, through alienation, reflection—in short, all these modes that are anathema to gestalt theory,"[87] i.e. the gestalt notion of unity. The whole is neither a mystical entity, nor are the parts self-sufficient qualitative monads, packages of static predicates ("determinations," as Hegel calls the predicates, the overlapping processual modalities we spoke of). Nor is contradiction itself the Heraclitean essence absolute idealism glorified.[88] The contradiction is not "resolved," but the abstract opposition, the isolation of thesis/antithesis is transcended, absorbed into a working synthesis, the new working reality we spoke of. The very frame of reference, (the reality, the truth) which made the poles opposites is thus transcended, while the identity of the poles is thus maintained; as in transcending a double bind, dialectical thinking is a realization that things are opposite/mutually exclusive only in specific frames of reference.

4) The dynamic "contradiction" between non-identical moments of a totality is therefore basically a "contradiction" between the subjective and objective moments of the "constitution process," of reality as realization. Their temporary unity in the experienced object retains these antithetical aspects, although it synthesizes them

into a working alliance. But the different components, in turn, develop alliances with other such packages, which changes their internal composition, makes them non-identical with their own (previous) identity and so on. A dialectical unity *is* a unity (i.e. pattern) of "opposites" and not the result of short-circuiting the tension, as contemporary, official Dialectical Materialism is wont to do. Collapsed into the concept of an all-defining matter in motion as the substratum of reality (of which consciousness is but one manifestation), dialectic in this version appears exiled into an all-defining and fetishized objectivity—and is thus effectively dissolved. No dialectic without subjectivity; as negative, as the non-identical, as transcendence by definition, subjectivity is the motor of history.

Nor is the dialectical relation a matter of mere interaction, interdependence—terms often haphazardly used to paraphrase the process. "The subject-object relation cannot be described in terms of fixed realities which are conceptually transparent and which move toward each other."[89] Rather, "dialectic is methodically the mutual negation and production of the subjective and objective moments"[90] in the formation of concepts.

As Adorno suggested, subjectivity is the *form* of the objective, the *how* (not the *what*) of reality. As distinct from the objective aspects, individual identity consists only of the *act* of transcendence of these aspects, i.e. the activity of negation. Just like reason (as its "agent"), therefore, subjectivity is neither exclusively transcendental (as Fichte would claim), nor exclusively empirical (as Dialectical Materialism would have it), nor a little of both, but it is both and both simultaneously. Our language, which distinguishes between "I" and "me" is deceptive in this respect: not only the Cartesian object, the "me" is empirical, but the "I" itself is too. The empirical knowledge, i.e. what is "conceivable," delimits what the individual (the "subject") can, or even must do. "In Hegel, the productive activity of the mind also and simultaneously appropriates its own product, just as the product appropriates [shapes] the subject."[91] "Just as, in Kant's terms, nothing is constituted without the subjective conditions of reason as the constituting agent, no such agent or mental conditions are even possible (so Hegel . . . adds) unless they be agents or conditions of real individuals—who (as parts of the general) are themselves something more than just subjective."[92] The various experiential categories (including subjectivity) are thus formed through the very object world they are to order and explain. This reciprocity of form and content—subjectivity being the categories/planes of possible experience, objectivity being what is experienced—lead Hegel to his famous dictum that form is always that of its content. Form is a synonym (*Inbegriff*) of mediation, Adorno formulated. It explains why subjectivity cannot be a substance by itself (but is the *form* in which we experience objects), and thus why the two—subjectivity and objectivity—are not separable like two substances but are "moments"/aspects of one and the same process.

Rather than try to eliminate the inevitable subjectivity operative in *any* perspective or approach, therefore, we should "bring this subjectivity back to its objectivity,"[93] Adorno demanded, i.e. be self-reflexive in our procedures. Methodologically, we should be inside and outside the object simultaneously. The open-endedness of this cognitive process (knowledge as growing consciousness) is an imperfection only if we use as a standard a closed system of informational units whose substantive irrelevance is the price paid for internal consistency.[94]

Not how systematic a theory is indicates its maturity and quality (as traditional theory would have it) but "what it includes and what it excludes." "The inconclusive dialectic does not lose the stamp of truth. . . . the critical and relativizing trait necessarily belongs to cognition."[95] In other words, only dialectical reason is capable of being its own meta-reason. "Dialectical logic does not suspend the rules of understanding [*Verstand*]. Dialectical logic, having as its object the forms of movement of the progress of knowledge, includes the collapse and restructuring of fixed systems and categories as part of its proper object domain."[96]

Finally, bound up with the dialectic of subject and object is that of theory and praxis, commonly misunderstood as the "application" of the theory. To apply a theory, however, presupposes the very gap the application pretends to bridge. If, in fact, every new insight about an object literally changes the identity of the object and thus our attitude, expectation and action toward it, theory would be adequate to reality precisely in the sense that Hegel had postulated: it would simply follow the movement of reality itself—as constituted by us— and would thus be the (our) consciousness of that reality, including our (potential) constitutive role it it. Such a theory would not need "application." This theory/consciousness *as* reality already delimits the range of possible, desirable relations that may obtain toward our creation. At the same time, such delimitation, once conscious, means that we have already transcended this stage, reaching a new perspective from which our activity appears as a delimitation—a new stage of insight, of objectifications (of our subjectivity) etc. This famous dialectic of limits cannot know the concept of an application; the idea of praxis already contains the constitutive unity of subject and object; in an applied theory, they must remain separate: an isolated subject applies an idea as it sees fit to an equally isolated object domain—their relation remains arbitrary throughout.

The Dimension of the Future

What used to be called bad utopianism—the arbitrary antithesis—has perhaps become the only utopia in a time when already the possibility of any antithesis is threatened. (T. W. Adorno)

Empiricism confuses the concept of novelty with that of an inadequate prognosis. (M. Horkheimer)

Freedom is the only "fact" that "is" only in its creation; it cannot be verified except by being exercised. (H. Marcuse)

That things remain the way they are: *that* is the catastrophe. (W. Benjamin)

Traditional theorists like Merton have conceded negligence on the part of sociologists toward the less visible and the statistically insignificant. The latter, of course, reveals the tacitly assumed correlation between quantity and significance (often mocked by Horkheimer), while the former ignores that not all relevant modalities of objects are, highly visible (in the sense of being accessible to current, restrictively questioning methodical screens). The conspicuous lack of a category of "possible cases" in contemporary sciences, about which Nelson Goodman has complained, seems no accident, therefore. It is the complement of the fatalistic and affirmative streak in contemporary scientism—"the mythic scientific respect for the given."[97]

"As concerns the future," Horkheimer charged, "not construction but induction is the characteristic mark of science. The more frequent something has been in the past, the more certain it will be in the future. . . . New forms of reality, especially those emerging from the historical activity of human beings, lie beyond empiricist theory."[98] Accordingly, "scientific prognoses rarely refer to 'significant changes', for, understandably, there is a lack of observational data."[99] What is still in process, i.e. not yet classified by definitions, not visible through a methodical screen built for past facts, is simply not "there" for them. Consequently, such central Marxian categories as latency and tendency must remain opaque: "as far as empiricism is concerned, tendency refers to probable behavior."[100] In traditional theories there is little attempt, therefore, to construct logical utopias (i.e. tentative logical extensions of existing possibilities, whose existence, critical theorists insisted, can be argued both theoretically and empirically, through perfectly stringent analysis of the given) whose "difference to an abstract utopia is that the possibility in question can be shown to be real at the present stage of the forces of production."[101] If a certain affirmative thrust is built into current methodologies, they may have to be modified, opened up: If a mode of thought reaches beyond the extension of social life in its given form, the mode of presentation is not prescribed either; rather, theory constructs empirical elements into a total image which consciously reflects reality *sub specie* of its own transcending interests.[102]

It is this interest in focusing not on what there is alone but on what there could very well be, which should make it the "goal of science . . . to cognize processes of which the dimension of the future is a necessary part."[103] Most of the time, it is true, the Frankfurtians themselves did not analyze the present under the anticipation of a concretely specified better future, but under the historical aspect of what has been, or is, preventing such a future. Nevertheless, a hermeneutic anticipation of its possibility, a cognitive interest in transcendence of all forms of heteronomy, is unmistakable. And what we want to collect data *for* decides what data we collect; if we collect them under the hypothesis that a different reality is possible, we will focus on the changeable, marginal, deviant aspects—anything not integrated which might suggest fermentation, resistance, protest, alternative—all the "facts" unfit to fit. Adorno insisted: "We do the world too much honor to think of it entirely as a system. Precisely those on whose thought and action any change—the only essential thing—depends, owe their existence to the inessential . . . to what according to the great laws of historical development, may turn out to be completely coincidental."[104]

Not accidentally, anticipatory and cognitive forms of human behavior have been shunned as difficulties by the traditional social sciences, which focus on past and *existing* variables of "influence" rather than on the "influence" of anticipation, or on forms of behavior controlled by consciousness rather than by quasi-"forces."[105] The model of humans as passive entities in a force field of variables informing most contemporary research corresponds, of course, precisely to that "prehistoric" form of socially unconscious behavior Marx (and critical theorists) wanted to change—where people behave like objects of nature, of uncomprehended forces. Given that these sciences increasingly become our only source of (supposedly reliable) knowledge, and thus supposedly our only reliable guidelines for dealing with these spheres, we may be facing increasingly self-fulfilling object domains.

But the prehistory is over; we know the way things are to be largely the way we made them. As reality ceases to appear impenetrable and thus loses its mythical authority, as the superstitious belief in the way things ("naturally") are disappears, acquiescence simply spells active approval. Reality as is now needs reasons, legitimations for being thus and not otherwise—the way it concretely *could* be. As against the current scientific fatalism, motives like dreaming, hope (cf. Bloch's category of "*docta spes*"), "covetous anticipation" etc. assume a *cognitive* function in a less zealously restrictive science. Just as we use our present perspective to look at the past, we might employ the perspective of a possible future to examine the present. After all, it is the business of the future to be dangerous, Whitehead had argued. Naturally, therefore, the established paradigm will denounce alternatives to itself as "unscientific," just as any reality as is will denounce attempts at transcending it as "unrealistic."

If critical theorists heeded Marx's and Engels's dictum that the only science is the science of history, they understood it in the sense of what the Enlightenment called "conjectural history," or *histoire raisonnée*, turned into the future. In their present form, the particular disciplines were auxiliary and preliminary stages—although their *necessity* was emphasized time and again by the Frankfurtians. But they needed to have their function defined by what Merleau-Ponty might have called a practical philosophy of history, or what Lepenies has called an experimental anthropology. The American sociologist Robert S. Lynd, a one-time member of the Institute, cited this approach as an exemplary program for the sciences: it should not be our only concern to ask whether a hypothesis is true, possible or realistic; we should, perhaps, also ask the other way around: "what sort of earth"[106] would it have to be in which this hypothesis (e.g. one describing a possible situation) *would be* realistic. Only history could verify such hypotheses—by realizing them.

On the Problem of Truth

By Max Horkheimer

Originally published in Zeitschrift für Sozialforschung, *Vol. IV (1935), Horkheimer's essay is part of a series of critical confrontations with contemporary philosophies and their social implications.*

In a sense, the article is an exemplary exercise in a critical sociology of knowledge. Beginning with the obvious co-existence of rational and irrational human pursuits, this split itself becomes the problem, rather than remaining the factual premise, as for most of Horkheimer's contemporaries. The division has grown to the same extent that rational investigation of the world has: the more the world becomes transparent, the more the secure orders disappear and the more the need for secure orders increases. Even—and in fact especially—among the most relentless rationalists, we find the readiness to bracket out and maintain certain areas allegedly inaccessible to reason.

The philosophic thought of recent decades, shot through with contradictions, has also been divided on the problem of truth. Two opposing and unreconciled views exist side by side in public life and, not infrequently, in the behavior of the same individual. According to one, cognition never has more than limited validity. This is rooted in objective fact as well as in the knower. Every thing and every relation of things changes with time, and thus every judgment as to real situations must lose its truth with time. "Every particular entity is given to us in time, occupies a definite place in time, and is perceived as lasting for a length of time and during this time developing changing activities and possibly altering its properties. Thus all our judgments on the essence, properties, activities, and relations of particular things are necessarily involved with the relationship to time, and every judgment of this sort can only be valid for a certain time."[1] Subjectively, too, truth is viewed as necessarily circumscribed. Perception is shaped not only by the object but by the individual and generic characteristics of human beings. It is particularly this subjective moment to which the modern science of mind has given its attention. Depth psychology seemed to destroy the illusion of absolutely valid truth by pointing out that the function of consciousness only made its appearance together with unconscious psychic processes, while sociology made a philosophically developed discipline out of the doctrine that every idea belongs to an intellectual pattern bound up with a social group, a "standpoint". Present-day relativism, in particular, has subjectivist characteristics, but it is by no means the sole representative of this period's intellectual attitude toward truth. Rather, it is opposed by the impulse to blind faith, to absolute submission, which has always been necessarily linked with relativism as its opposite, and is once again characteristic of the cultural situation today. In philosophy, a new dogmatism has emerged in the wake of the metaphysical reworking of the concept, at first strictly interpreted, of intuition of essences. This development in the history of ideas reflects the historical circumstance that the social totality to which the liberal, democratic and progressive tendencies of the dominant culture belonged also contained from its beginning their opposite compulsion, chance and the rule of primal nature. By the system's own dynamic, this eventually threatens to wipe out all its positive characteristics. The role of human autonomy in the preservation and renewal of social life is completely subordinated to the effort to hold together mechanically a dissolving order. The public mind is increasingly dominated by some rigid judgments and a few postulated concepts.

The appearance of this contradiction in our time repeats in distorted form a discord which has always permeated the philosophy of the bourgeois era. Its prototype in the history of philosophy is the linkage of Descartes' universal methodical doubt with his devout Catholicism. It extends to the details of his system. It reveals itself not only in the unreconciled juxtaposition of faith and contradictory knowledge, but in the theory of cognition itself. The doctrine of a solid *res cogitans*, a self-contained ego independent of the body, which serves as an absolute resolution of the attempt at doubt and is preserved immutable in the metaphysics of Descartes and his idealistic successors, reveals itself as an illusion, corresponding to the situation of the bourgeois individual and present before the inquiry rather than based on it. The independent existence of individual souls, the principle which for Descartes makes the world philosophically intelligible, is no easier to reconcile with the criteria and the whole spirit of the analytic geometry which he himself invented than is his proclamation of empty space as the sole physical substance with the theological dogma of transubstantiation. Complete doubt as to the reality of material truth, the constant emphasis on the uncertainty, conditional character and finiteness of all definite knowledge, immediately next to ostensible insights into eternal truths and the fetishization of individual categories and modes of being—this duality permeates the Cartesian philosophy.

It finds its classic expression in Kant. The critical method was supposed to perform the task of differentiating the purely conditional and empirical from "pure" knowledge and reached the conclusion that pure knowledge was possible only in regard to the conditions of the conditional. The system of the necessary subjective conditions of human knowledge is the exclusive goal of transcendental philosophy. To Hume's skepticism, Kant opposes nothing but the sensory and conceptual forms of knowledge and what can be deduced therefrom. But what comes into existence on the basis of these conditions, the theory of our actual world and not a merely possible one, knowledge of actual nature and existing human society, lacks for Kant the criteria of genuine truth and is only relative. Everything that we know of reality, of conditions in space and time, relates according to him only to appearances, and of these he claims to have shown "that they are not things (but only a form of representation), and that they are not qualities inherently belonging to the things in themselves."[2] In regard to knowledge of the world, he is no less a skeptical relativist than the "mystical" and "dreaming" idealists whom he combats. In the latest phase of transcendental philosophy, this subjective relativism is clearly formulated: "In the last analysis, all being is relative (as opposed to the false ideal of an absolute Being and its absolute truth), and is nevertheless *relative in some customary sense to the transcendental subjectivity*. But this subjectivity alone is 'in and for itself.' "[3] Along with the careful and differentiated theoretical philosophy, which did indeed keep thought rooted in the ahistorical sphere of transcendental subjectivity, there are in Kant the postulates of practical reason and—linked to them by conclusions which are in part extremely questionable—the transformation into absolute of the existing property relations under prevalent public and private law. In the *Critique of Practical Reason*, which fetishizes the concept of duty, he did not in any way overcome the need for an immovable intellectual foundation but merely met it in a way more fitting to the time than that of the rationalist ontology of the period. The theoretical philosophy itself assumes that there is absolute knowledge, independent of any sensory experience, and indeed that this alone deserves the name of truth. Even the *Critique of Pure Reason* depends on the assumption that pure concepts and judgments exist "a priori" in the consciousness, and that metaphysics not only always has been, but that it will of right exist for all eternity. Kant's work embraces in itself the contradiction between the German and English schools of philosophy. The resolution of the contradictions it produces, the mediation between critique and dogmatic system, between a mechanistic concept of science and the doctrine of intelligible freedom, between belief in an eternal order and a theory isolated from practice, increasingly and vainly occupied his own thought till the last years of his life: this is the mark of his greatness. Analysis carried through to the end and skeptical distrust of all theory on the one hand and readiness to believe naively in detached fixed principles on the other, these are characteristic of the bourgeois mind. It appears in its most highly developed form in Kant's philosophy.

This dual relationship to truth is again mirrored in the failure of the progressive methods of the scholar to influence his attitude toward the most important problems of the time, the combination of notable knowledge in the natural sciences with childlike faith in the Bible. The association of that particularly strict tendency in modern philosophy, positivism, with the crudest superstition, has already been noted in this magazine.[4] Auguste Comte not merely laid the groundwork for a whimsical cult, but prided himself on his understanding of the various theories of the beyond. William James turned to mysticism and even mediumism.[5] The brain appears to him not so much to promote as to obstruct the enlightening intuitions which exist "ready-made in the transcendental world" and come through as telepathic experiences as soon as the brain's activity is "abnormally" reduced. "The word 'influx' used in Swedenborgian circles" describes the phenomenon very well.[6] The pragmatist F.C.S.Schiller, whom James quotes, declares on this point: "Matter is not that which produces consciousness but that which limits it'' and conceives of the body as ''a mechanism for inhibiting consciousness.''[7] This inclination to spiritualism can be followed through the later history of positivism. In Germany, it seems to have reached its ultimate in the philosophy of Hans Driesch, in which a scientism carried to extremes goes together with unconcealed occultism in all questions of this world and the beyond. In this, the occultistic dilemma finds a grotesque expression in his logic and theory of knowledge through intentional formalism and rigidity and through the monomaniacal reference of all the problems of the world to some few biological experiments. On the other side, the misconception of a self-sufficient science independent of history appears through the pseudo-scientific dress of his barbarous errors in religion and practice.

Only in the decline of the contemporary epoch has it become the typical behavior of scholars for a person to develop high critical faculties in a specific branch of science while remaining on the level of backward groups in respect to questions of social life and echoing the most ignorant phrases. In the beginning of the bourgeois order, the turn to specific juristic and scientific studies without regard to social and religious demands immediately produced a moment of liberation from the theological tutelage of thought. But as a result of the alteration of the social structure, this sort of production without regard to the rational relation to the whole has become regressive and obstructive in all fields—in science just as in industry and agriculture. This abstractness and ostensible independence of the bourgeois science industry shows itself in the mass of isolated individual empirical studies, not related to any sort of theory and practice by clear terminology and subject matter. It is likewise visible in the efforts of scientists, without any significant reason, to divest their concepts of all empirical material, and especially in the inordinate mathematicization of many intellectual disciplines. The conventional attitude of the scholar to the dominant questions of the period and the confinement of his critical attention to his professional specialty were formerly factors in the improvement of the general situation. Thinkers ceased to be concerned exclusively with the welfare of their immortal souls, or to make concern for it their guide in all theoretical matters. But subsequently this attitude has taken on another meaning: instead of being a sign of necessary courage and independence, the withdrawal of intellectual energies from general cultural and social questions, the placing of actual historical interests and struggles in a parenthesis, is more a sign of anxiety and incapacity for rational activity than of an inclination to the true tasks of science. The substance underlying intellectual phenomena changes with the social totality.

It is not the intention here to go into detail in regard to the historical causes of this dual relationship to truth. The competition within the bourgeois economy, in the context of which the forces of this society unfolded, produced a critical spirit which not only was able to liberate itself from the bureaucracies of church and absolutism but, driven by the dynamic of the economic apparatus, can to a fantastic degree place nature at its service. But this power only seems to be its own. The methods for the production of social wealth are available, the conditions for the production of useful natural effects are largely known, and the human will can bring them about. But this spirit and will themselves exist in false and distorted form. The concept of having power over something includes deciding for oneself and making use of it for one's own purposes. But domination over nature is not exercised according to a unified plan and purpose, but merely serves as an instrument for individuals, groups and nations which use it in their struggle against one another and, as they develop it, at the same time reciprocally circumscribe it and bend it to destructive ends. Thus, the bearers of this spirit, with their critical capacity and their developed thinking, do not really become masters but are driven by the changing constellations of the general struggle which, even though summoned up by men themselves, face them as incalculable forces of destiny. This seemingly necessary dependence, which increasingly bears fruit in disruptive tensions and crises, general misery and decline, becomes for the greatest part of mankind an incomprehensible fate. But to the extent that the alteration of basic relationships is excluded in practice, a need arises for an interpretation based purely on faith. The conviction that a constricting and painful constellation is essentially unalterable prods the mind to give it a profound interpretation so as to be able to come to terms with it without despairing. Death as the inevitable end was always the basis of the religious and metaphysical illusion. The metaphysical need which permeates the history of this period stems from the fact that the inner mechanism of this society, which produces insecurity and continuous pressure, does not emerge into clear consciousness and is put up with as something necessary and eternal, rather than as an object of effective change. The firm faith which was part of the mortar of the medieval social structure has disappeared. The great systems of European philosophy were always intended only for an educated upper crust and fail completely in the face of the psychic needs of the impoverished and socially continually sinking sections of the citizenry and peasantry, who are nevertheless completely tied to this form of society by upbringing, work and hope, and cannot believe it to be transitory. This is why the intellectual situation has for decades been dominated by the craving to bring an eternal meaning into a life which offers no way out, by philosophical practices such as the direct intellectual or intuitive apprehension of truth and finally by blind submission to a personality, be it an anthroposophic prophet, a poet or a politician. To the extent to which individual activity is circumscribed and the capacity for it eventually stunted, there exists the readiness to find security in the protective shelter of a faith or person taken as the vessel and incarnation of the truth. In particular periods of the rise of contemporary society, the expectation of steady progress within its own framework reduced the need for an interpretation that would transfigure reality, and the rational and critical faculties achieved greater influence in private and public thought. But as this form of social organization becomes increasingly crisis-prone and insecure, all those who regard its characteristics as eternal are sacrificed to the institutions which are intended as substitutes for the lost religion.

This is, to be sure, only one aspect of the social situation out of which the shaky relationship to truth in modern times arises. A fundamental analysis of the fallacious bourgeois self-perception, which preserves the ideology of complete inner freedom in the face of the dependence and insecurity of its bearers, could show that the liberal validation of alien ideas (the mark of relativism) has a common root with the fear of making one's own decisions, which leads to belief in a rigid absolute truth: the abstract, reified concept of the individual which inescapably dominates thought in this economic system. But here the question is less one of the derivation of the phenomenon than of its practical significance. Is there really only the choice between acceptance of a final truth, as proclaimed in religions and idealistic schools of philosophy, and the view that every thesis and every theory is always merely "subjective," i.e., true and valid for a person or a group or a time or mankind as a species, but lacking objective validity? In developing the dialectical method, bourgeois thought itself has made the most ambitious attempt to transcend this antinomy. Here the goal of philosophy no longer appears, as in Kant, to be merely the system of the subjective factors of cognition; perceived truth is no longer so empty that in practice one must take refuge in the solidity of faith. While the concrete content is perceived as conditional and dependent and every "final" truth is just as decisively "negated" as in Kant, it does not for Hegel simply fall through the sieve in the sifting out of pure knowledge. Recognition of the conditional character of every isolated view and rejection of its absolute claim to truth does not destroy this conditional knowledge; rather, it is incorporated into the system of truth at any given time as a conditional, one-sided and isolated view. Through nothing but this continuous delimitation and correction of partial truths, the process itself evolves its proper content as knowledge of limited insights in their limits and connection.

To skepticism, Hegel opposes the concept of determinate negation. The progressive recognition of partial truths, the advance from one isolated definition to another, means for him not a mere lining up of attributes but a description which follows the actual subject matter in all particulars. This critique of every concept and every complex of concepts by progressive incorporation into the more complete picture of the whole does not eliminate the individual aspects, nor does it leave them undisturbed in subsequent thought, but every negated insight is preserved as a moment of truth in the progress of cognition, forms a determining factor in it, and is further defined and transformed with every new step. Precisely because of this, the methodological form of thesis, antithesis and synthesis is not to be applied as a "lifeless diagram."[8] If at any given time the antithesis expresses the critical and relativizing impetus in opposition to the assimilation and establishment of a pattern of thought, thesis and antithesis together immediately form a new insight, a synthesis, because the negation has not simply rejected the original insight but has deepened and defined it. Hegel does not end up with the bare assurance that all definite knowledge is transitory and unreal, that what we know is only appearance in contrast to an unknowable thing in itself or an intuitively perceived essence. If for Hegel the true is the whole, the whole is not something distinct from the parts in its determinate structure, but the entire pattern of thought which at a given time embraces in itself all limited conceptions in the consciousness of their limitation.

Since the dialectical method does not rest with showing that a thing is conditioned, but takes the conditioned thing seriously, it escapes the relativistic formalism of the Kantian philosophy. Hegel therefore does not need to make a fetish out of an isolated concept like that of duty. He recognizes the vain effort of all idealistic philosophy before him to make the whole content of the world disappear in some conceptual generalization and declare all specific differences unreal as opposed to such attributes as the infinite, will, experience, absolute indifference, consciousness, etc. The second-rate thought to which the world always appears as a mysterious presentation in which only the initiate knows what goes on behind the scenes, which sets philosophy to solving an ostensible riddle in order to know once and for all or even to despair that such a key is not to be found—this sort of dogmatism does not exist in Hegel. Rather, the dialectical method quickly led him to become aware of the stupidity of such philosophical work and to see in development and flux what presents itself as absolute and eternal.

Insofar as this method, in Hegel, nevertheless still belongs to an idealistic system, he has not freed his thought from the old contradiction. His philosophy too is ultimately characterized by the indifference to particular perceptions, ideas and goals which belongs to relativism, as well as by the transformation of conceptual structures into substances and the inability to take theoretical and practical account of the dogmatism and historical genesis of his own thought. Its dogmatic side has been especially often attacked in the critique of cognition since the middle of the nineteenth century. In place of those doctrines which made an abstract concept into substance, that is, which sought to raise this limited aspect over history as identical with being, and thus degenerated into naive faith, Hegel puts the hypostatization of his own system. In his polemic against skepticism and relativism[9], he himself says: "The goal is fixed for knowledge just as necessarily as the succession in the process; it is there, where knowledge no longer needs to go beyond itself, where it finds itself, and the concept fits the object, the object the concept. The progress to this end is therefore also continuous, and satisfaction is not to be found at any earlier stage." Hegel believes that he guarantees this satisfaction through the whole of his thought. For him, philosophy has the same absolute content as religion, the complete unity of subject and object, a final and eternally valid knowledge.

> What man . . . ensnared on all sides in the finite, seeks, is the region of a higher substantial truth in which all the oppositions and contradictions of the finite can find their final resolution and freedom its complete satisfaction. This is the region of the truth in itself, and not of the relatively true. The highest truth, the truth as such, is the resolution of the highest opposition and contradiction. In it the opposition of freedom and necessity, of spirit and nature, of knowledge and object, law and impulse, opposition and contradiction in general, whatever form they may take, no

longer have validity and force as opposition and contradiction. . . . Ordinary consciousness, on the other hand, does not get out of this contradiction and either despairs in it or discards it and helps itself in some other way. But philosophy steps into the middle of the mutually contradictory propositions, knows them according to their significance, i.e., as not absolute in their one-sidedness but self-resolving, and places them in the harmony and unity which is the truth. To grasp this concept of truth is the task of philosophy. . . . For philosophy also has no other subject than God and is thus rational theology, and by being in the service of truth is continuous service of God.[10]

According to Hegel himself, the doctrine of an absolute self-contained truth has the purpose of harmonizing in a higher spiritual region the "oppositions and contradictions" not resolved in the world. Especially in his later lectures and writings, he stresses that "the region of truth, freedom and satisfaction"[11] is to be found not in the mechanism of reality but in the spiritual spheres of art, religion and philosophy. He opposes this peace and satisfaction in thought not only to skeptical despair but to the active attitude which tries to overcome the incompleteness of existing conditions "in some other way."

This dogmatic narrow-mindedness is not some sort of an accidental defect of his doctrine which one can strip off without changing anything essential. Rather, it is inextricably bound up with the idealistic character of his thought and enters into all the details of his application of the dialectic. Hegel cannot be reproached for the role in his thought played by external observation, from which, as Trendelenberg points out in criticism[12], the basic concept of the dialectic, movement, comes. He himself expounded the importance of experience for philosophy. Rather, in contemplating his own system, Hegel forgets one very definite side of the empirical situation. The belief that this system is the completion of truth hides from him the significance of the temporally conditioned interest which plays a role in the details of the dialectical presentation through the direction of thought, the choice of material content, and the use of names and words, and diverts attention from the fact that his conscious and unconscious partisanship in regard to the problems of life must necessarily have its effect as a constituent element of his philosophy. Thus, his conceptions of folk and freedom, which form the backbone of many parts of his work, are not perceived in terms of their temporal presuppositions and their transitory character, but on the contrary are, as conceptual realities and forces, made the basis of the historical developments from which they are abstracted. Because Hegel does not recognize and assert the specific historical tendencies which find expression in his own work, but presents himself as absolute mind in philosophizing and accordingly preserves on ostensible distance and impartiality, many parts of his work lack clarity and, in spite of the revolutionary sharpness and flexibility of the method, take on the arbitrary and pedantic character which was so closely bound up with the political conditions of his time. In the idealistic thought to which it owes its existence, the dialectic is beset by dogmatism. Since the abstractions at which the method arrives are supposed to be moments in a system in which thought "no longer needs to go beyond itself," the relationships comprehended by it also are regarded as unalterable and eternal. If a great deal may happen in history yet to come, even if other peoples, e.g., the Slavs,[13] should take over leadership from those nations which have in the past been decisive, nevertheless no new principle of social organization will become dominant and no decisive change will take place in the organization of mankind. No historical change which brought about a new form of human association could leave the concepts of society, freedom, right, etc., unaltered. The interconnection of all categories, even the most abstract, would be affected thereby. Hence, Hegel's belief that his thought comprehended the essential characteristics of all being—the unity of which remained as it appeared in the system, a complete hierarchy and totality undisturbed by the becoming and passing of individuals —represented the conceptual eternalization of the earthly relationships on which it was based. The dialectic takes on a transfiguring function. The laws of life, in which according to Hegel domination and servitude as well as poverty and misery have their eternal place, are sanctioned by the fact that the conceptual interconnection in which they are included is regarded as something higher, divine and absolute. Just as religion and the deification of a race or state or the worship of nature offer the suffering individual an immortal and eternal essence, so Hegel believes he has revealed an eternal meaning in the contemplation of which the individual should feel sheltered from all personal misery. This is the dogmatic, metaphysical, naive aspect of his theory.

Its relativism is directly bound up with this. The dogmatic assertion that all the particular views which have ever entered the lists against one another in real historical combat, all the creeds of particular groups, all attempts at reform are now transcended and canceled out, the notion of the all-embracing thought which is to apportion its partial rightness and final limitation to every point of view without consciously taking sides with any one against the others and deciding between them—*this* is the very soul of bourgeois relativism. The attempt to afford justification to every idea and every historical person and to assign the heroes of past revolutions their place in the pantheon of history next to the victorious generals of the counterrevolution, this ostensibly free-floating objectivity conditioned by the bourgeoisie's stand on two fronts against absolutist restoration and against the proletariat, has acquired validity in the Hegelian system along with the idealistic pathos of absolute knowledge. It is self-evident that tolerance toward all views that are in the past and recognized as conditioned is no less relativist than negativist skepticism. The more the times demand unsparing outspokenness and defense of particular truths and rights, the more unequivocally it reveals the inhumanity immanent in it. If in spite of the lack of a conscious relationship between his philosophy and any particular practical principle, Hegel was guided in detail not simply by the conservative Prussian spirit but also by interests pushing him forward, his dogmatism nevertheless prevented his recognizing and defending these tendencies, which found expression in his science, as his own purposes and progressive interests. He seems to speak of himself when he describes how "the consciousness lets the idea of something good in itself, which as yet has no reality, go by like an empty cloak."[14] In Hegel, as in Goethe, the progressive impulses enter secretly into the viewpoint which ostensibly comprehends and harmonizes everything real impartially. Later relativism, in contrast, directs his demonstration of limiting conditionality mainly against the progressive ideas themselves, which it thereby seeks to flatten, that is, to equate with everything already past. In his conceptual projections, the new as well as the old easily appear as simple rationalizing and ideology. Since the recognition of the truth of particular ideas disappears behind the display of conditions, the coordination with historical unities, this impartial relativism reveals itself as the friend of what exists at any given time. The dogmatism concealed within it is the affirmation of the existing power; what is coming into being needs conscious decision in its struggle, while the limitation to mere understanding and contemplation serves what is already in existence. That impartial partisanship and indiscriminate objectivity represent a subjective viewpoint is a dialectical proposition that indeed takes relativism beyond itself.

In materialism, the dialectic is not regarded as a closed system. Understanding that the prevalent circumstances are conditioned and transitory is not here immediately equated with transcending them and canceling them out. Hegel declares: "Something is only known, indeed felt, as a limit, a defect, only when one is already beyond it. . . . It is . . . simply lack of consciousness not to see that precisely the description of something as finite or limited contains proof of the *real presence* of the infinite and unlimited, that knowledge of boundaries is only possible insofar as the unbounded is here in one's consciousness."[15] This view has as its presupposition the basic postulate of idealism that concept and being are in truth the same, and therefore all fulfillment can take place in the pure medium of the spirit. Inner renewal and exaltation, reformation and spiritual elevation, were always the solution to which he pointed. Insofar as dealing with and changing the external world was regarded as at all fundamental, it appeared as a mere consequence of this. Materialism, on the other hand, insists that objective reality is not identical with man's thought and can never be merged into it. As much as thought in its own element seeks to copy the life of the object and adapt itself to it, the thought is nevertheless never simultaneously the object thought about, unless in self-observation and reflection—and not even there. To conceptualize a defect is therefore not to transcend it; concepts and theories form an impulse to its removal, a prerequisite to the proper procedure, which as it progresses is constantly redefined, adapted and improved.

An isolated and conclusive theory of reality is completely unthinkable. If one takes seriously the formal definition of truth which runs through the whole history of logic as the correspondence of cognition with its object,[16] there follows from it the contradiction to the dogmatic interpretation of thought. This correspondence is neither a simple datum, an immediate fact, as it appears in the doctrine of intuitive, immediate certainty and in mysticism, nor does it take place in the pure sphere of spiritual immanence, as it seems to in Hegel's metaphysical legend. Rather, it is always established by real events, by human activity. In the investigation and determination of actual conditions, and even more in the verification of theories, the direction of attention, the refinement of methods, the categorical structure of subject matter, in short human activity within the framework of the given social period, play their role. (The discussion here will not deal with the question of how far all connection with such activity is avoided by Husserl's "formal ontology" which refers "to any possible world in empty generality"[17] or by formal apophantic, which likewise relates to all possible statements in empty generality, or by other parts of pure logic and mathematics, nor with how far they possess real cognitive value without regard to such a connection.)

If certain philosophical interpretations of mathematics correctly stress its a priori character, that is, the independence of mathematical constructions from all empirical observation, the mathematical models of theoretical physics in which the cognitive value of mathematics finally shows itself are, in any case, structured with reference to the events that can be brought about and verified on the basis of the current level of development of the technical apparatus. As little as mathematics needs to trouble itself about this relationship in its deductions, its form at any given time is nevertheless as much conditioned by the increase in the technical capacity of mankind as the latter is by the development of mathematics. The verification and proof of ideas relating to man and society, however, consists not merely in laboratory experiments or the examination of documents, but in historical struggles in which conviction itself plays an essential role. The false view that the present social order is essentially harmonious serves as an impetus to the renewal of disharmony and decline and becomes a factor in its own practical refutation. The correct theory of the prevalent conditions, the doctrine of the deepening of crises and the approach of catastrophes does, to be sure, find continuous confirmation in all particulars. But the picture of a better world that inheres in this theory and takes its departure from the assertion of the badness of the present, the idea of men and their capabilities immanent in it, finds its definition, correction and confirmation in the course of historical struggles. Hence, activity is not to be regarded as an appendix, as merely what comes after thought, but enters into theory at every point and is inseparable from it. Just for this reason pure thought does not here give the satisfaction of having sure and certain grasp of the question and being at one with it. It is certainly impossible to speak too highly of the conquests of the human spirit as a factor in liberation from the domination of nature and in improving the pattern of relationships. Social groups and possessors of power who fought against it, all propagandists of every sort of obscurantism, had their shady reasons and always led men into misery and servitude. But if in particular historical situations knowledge can, by its mere presence, obstruct evil and become power, the effort to make it in isolation the highest purpose and means of salvation rests on a philosophical misunderstanding. It cannot be said in general and a priori what meaning and value some particular knowledge has. That depends on social conditions as a whole at the particular time, on the concrete situation to which it belongs. Thoughts which, taken in isolation, are identical in content can at one time be unripe and fantastic and at another outdated and unimportant, yet in a particular historical moment form factors of a force that changes the world.

There is no eternal riddle of the world, no world secret the penetration of which once and for all would be the mission of thought. This narrow view—which ignores the constant alteration in knowing human beings along with the objects of their knowledge as well as the insurmountable tension between concept and objective reality—corresponds today to the narrow horizon of groups and individuals who, from their felt inability to change the world through rational work, grasp at and compulsively hold to universal recipes which they memorize and monotonously repeat. When the dialectic is freed of its connection with the exaggerated concept of isolated thought, self-determining and complete in itself, the theory defined by it necessarily loses the metaphysical character of final validity, the sanctity of a revelation, and becomes an element, itself transitory, intertwined in the fate of men.

But by ceasing to be a closed system, the dialectic does not lose the stamp of truth. In fact, the disclosures of conditional and one-sided aspects of other thought and its own forms an important impetus to the intellectual process. Hegel and his materialist followers were correct in always stressing that this critical and relativizing characteristic is a necessary part of cognition. But the certitude and verification of its own conviction does not require the assertion that concept and object are here henceforth one, and thought can rest. To the degree that the knowledge gained from perception and inference, methodical inquiry and historical events, daily work and political struggle, meets the test of the available means of cognition, it is the truth. The abstract proposition, that once a critique is justified from its own standpoint it will show itself open to correction, expresses itself for the materialists not in liberality toward opposing views or skeptical indecision, but in alertness to their own errors and flexibility of thought. They are no less "objective" than pure logic when it teaches that the relativistic "talk of a subjective truth which is this for one and the opposite for another must rate as nonsense."[18] Since that extrahistorical and hence exaggerated concept of truth which stems from the idea of a pure infinite mind and thus in the last analysis from the God concept, is impossible, it no longer makes any sense to orient the knowledge that we have to this impossibility and in this sense call it relative. The theory which we regard as correct may disappear because the practical and scientific interests which played a role in the formation of its concepts, and above all the facts and circumstances to which it referred, have disappeared. Then this truth is in fact irrecoverably gone, since there is no superhuman essence to preserve the present-day relationship between the content of ideas and their objects in its all-embracing spirit when the actual human beings have changed or even when mankind has died out. Only when measured against an extraterrestrial, unchanging existence does human truth appear to be of an inferior quality. At the same time as it nevertheless necessarily remains inconclusive and to that extent "relative," it is also absolute, since later correction does not mean that a former truth was formerly untrue. In the progress of knowledge, to be sure, much incorrectly regarded as true will prove wrong. Nevertheless, the overturn of categories stems from the fact that the relationship of concept and reality is affected and altered as a whole and in all its parts by the historical changes in forces and tasks. To a large extent the direction and outcome of the historical struggle depends on the decisiveness with which men draw the consequences of what they know, their readiness to test their theories against reality and refine them, in short, by the uncompromising application of the insight recognized as true. The correction and further definition of the truth is not taken care of by history, so that all the cognizant subject has to do is passively observe, conscious that even his particular truth, which contains the others negated in it, is not the whole. Rather, the truth is advanced because the human beings who possess it stand by it unbendingly, apply it and carry it through, act according to it, and bring it to power against the resistance of reactionary, narrow, one-sided points of view. The process of cognition includes real historical will and action just as much as it does learning from experience and intellectual comprehension. The latter cannot progress without the former.

Freed from the idealistic illusion, the dialectic transcends the contradiction between relativism and dogmatism. While it does not suppose the progress of criticism and definition at an end with its own point of view, and does not hypostatize the latter, it in no way surrenders the conviction that in the whole context to which its judgments and concepts refer, its cognitions are valid not only for particular individuals and groups but in general—that is, that the opposing theory is wrong. The dialectical logic also contains the law of contradiction; but in materialism it has completely stripped off its metaphysical character, because here a static system of propositions about reality, indeed any relation of concept and object not historically mediated, no longer appears meaningful as an idea. The dialectical logic in no way invalidates the rules of understanding. While it has as its subject the forms of movement of the advancing cognitive process, the breaking up and restructuring of fixed systems and categories also belongs in its scope along with the coordination of all intellectual forces as an impetus to human practice in general. In a time which in its lack of a way out tries to make everything into a fetish, even the abstract business of understanding, and would like thereby to replace the lost divine support, so that its philosophers rejoice in ostensibly non-temporal relations between isolated concepts and propositions as the timeless truth, the dialectical logic points out the questionable character of the interest in such "rigor" and the existence of a truth apart from it which is in no way denied by it. If it is true that a person has tuberculosis, this concept may indeed be transformed in the development of medicine or lose its meaning altogether. But whoever today with the same concept makes a contrary diagnosis, and not in terms of a higher insight which includes the determination of this man's tuberculosis, but simply denies the finding from the same medical standpoint, is wrong. The truth is also valid for him who contradicts it, ignores it, or declares it unimportant. Truth is decided not by what the individual believes and thinks of himself, not by the subject in itself, but by the relation of the propositions to reality, and when someone imagines himself the messenger of God or the rescuer of a people, the matter is not decided by him or even the majority of his fellow men, but by the relation of his assertions and acts to the objective facts of the rescue. The conditions to which those opinions point must really occur and be present in the course of events. There are at present various opposed views of society. According to one, the present wretched physical and psychological state of the masses and the critical condition of society as a whole, in the face of the developed state of the productive apparatus and technology, necessarily follows from the continued existence of an obsolete principle of social organization. According to the others, the problem is not the principle but interference with it or carrying it too far or a matter of spiritual, religious or purely biological factors. They are not all true; only that theory is true which can grasp the historical process so deeply that it is possible to develop from it the closest approximation to the structure and tendency of social life in the various spheres of culture. It too is no exception to the rule that it is conditioned like every thought and every intellectual content, but the circumstance that it corresponds to a specific social class and is tied up with the horizon and interests of certain groups does not in any way change the fact that it is also valid for the others who deny and suppress its truth and must nevertheless eventually experience it for themselves.

This is the place to define the concept of proof which dominates the logic of many otherwise opposed tendencies. Epicurus says: "Just as we do not desire the knowledge of the physician for the sake of its technical perfection itself, but consider it good for the sake of good health, and the skill of the helmsman possesses its value because it masters the methods of correct navigation but does not find recognition for its perfection, so wisdom, which must be perceived in skill in life, would not be sought after if it did not accomplish something."[19] The motif of result and proof as criteria of science and truth has never disappeared in the subsequent history of philosophy. Goethe's line "What fruitful is, alone is true" and the sentence "I have noticed that I regard as true that idea which is fruitful for me, fits in with the rest of my thought, and at the same time benefits me,"[20] appear to imply a pragmatic theory of cognition. Many phrases of Nietzsche suggest a similar interpretation. "The criterion of truth lies in the increase in the feeling of power. . . . What is truth? Inertia; the hypothesis with which satisfaction occurs; the least use of spiritual strength, etc."[21] "True means 'useful for the existence of human beings.' But since we know the conditions for the existence of human beings only very imprecisely, the decision as to true and untrue can, strictly speaking, only be based on success."[22]

With Goethe and Nietzsche, it is necessary to place such views, to which contradictions exist in their own writing, in the context of their entire thought in order to comprehend their meaning properly. But a special school of professional philosophy has grown up since the middle of the nineteenth century which places the pragmatic concept of truth in the center of its system. It has developed principally in America, where pragmatism has become the distinctive philosophical tendency through William James and subsequently John Dewey. According to this view, the truth of theories is decided by what one accomplishes with them. Their power to produce desired effects for the spiritual and physical existence of human beings is also their criterion. The furtherance of life is the meaning and measure of every science. "Our account of truth is an account of truths in the plural, of processes of leading realized *in rebus*, and having only this quality in common, that they pay."[23] If two theories are equally well fitted to produce a particular desired effect, it is at most still necessary to ask whether more intellectual energy is required with one than with the other. The proof of the idea in its working is identical with its truth, and indeed pragmatism, especially in its most recent development, places the principal emphasis not so much on the mere confirmation of a judgment by the occurrence of the predicted factual situation, as on the promotion of human activity, liberation from all sorts of internal restraints, the growth of personality and social life.

> *If* ideas, meanings, conceptions, notions, theories, systems are instrumental to an active reorganization of the given environment, to a removal of some specific trouble and perplexity, then the test of their validity and value lies in accomplishing this work. If they succeed in their office, they are reliable, sound, valid, good, true. If they fail to clear up confusion, to eliminate defects, if they increase confusion, uncertainty and evil when they are acted upon, then are they false. Confirmation, corroboration, verification lie in works, consequences. . . . That which guides us truly is true—demonstrated capacity for such guidance is precisely what is meant by truth.[24]

This view is closely related to positivism in France. If Bergson had not taken over the pragmatically restricted concept of science from Comte, it would be impossible to understand the need for a separate, supplementary, vitalistic metaphysics. The isolated intuition is the wishful dream of objective truth to which the acceptance of the pragmatic theory of cognition must give rise in a contemplative existence. The pragmatic concept of truth in its exclusive form, without any contradictory metaphysics to supplement it, corresponds to limitless trust in the existing world. If the goodness of every idea is given time and opportunity to come to light, if the success of the truth—even if after struggle and resistance—is in the long run certain, if the idea of a dangerous, explosive truth cannot come into the field of vision, then the present social structure is consecrated and—to the extent that it warns of harm—capable of unlimited development. In pragmatism there lies embedded the belief in the existence and advantages of free competition. Where in regard to the present it is shaken by a feeling of the dominant injustice, as in the far-reaching pragmatic philosophy of Ernst Mach, the problem of necessary change forms a personal commitment, a utopian supplement with a merely external connection to the other part, rather than a principle for the development of theory. It is therefore easy to separate that ideal from the empirio-critical way of thinking without doing it violence.

There are various elements contained in the concept of proof which are not always differentiated from one another in pragmatist literature. An opinion can be completely validated because the objective relationships whose existence it asserts are confirmed on the basis of experience and observation with unobjectionable instruments and logical conclusions; and it can moreover be of practical use to its holder or other people. Even with the first of these relationships, a need arises for intellectual organization and orientation. In this connection, James speaks of a "function of guidance, which repays the effort."[25]

He sees that this theoretical proof, the agreement between idea and reality, the portrayal, often means nothing more than "that nothing contradictory from the quarter of that reality comes to interfere with the way in which our ideas guide us elsewhere."[26] If the difference between this theoretical verification of truth and its practical meaning, the "furtherance of life," is nevertheless often eliminated in a given moment of history, there comes into existence that idea of a strictly parallel progress of science and mankind which was philosophically established by positivism and has become a general illusion in liberalism. But the more a given social order moves from the promotion of the creative cultural forces to their restriction, the greater the conflict between the verifiable truth and the interests bound up with this form, bringing the advocates of truth into contradiction with the existing reality. Insofar as it affects the general public rather than their own existence, individuals have reason, despite the fact that proclaiming the truth can endanger them, to sharpen it and carry it forward, because the result of their struggle and the realization of better principles of society is decisively dependent on theoretical clarity. Pragmatism overlooks the fact that the same theory can be an annihilating force for other interests in the degree to which it heightens the activity of the progressive forces and makes it more effective. The epistemological doctrine that the truth promotes life, or rather that all thought that "pays" must also be true, contains a harmonizing illusion if this theory of cognition does not belong to a whole in which the tendencies working towards a better, life-promoting situation really find expression. Separated from a particular theory of society as a whole, every theory of cognition remains formalistic and abstract. Not only expressions like life and promotion, but also terms seemingly specific to cognitive theory such as verification, confirmation, proof, etc., remain vague and indefinite despite the most scrupulous definition and transference to a language of mathematical formulae, if they do not stand in relation to real history and receive their definition by being part of a comprehensive theoretical unity. The dialectical proposition that every concept possesses real validity only as a part of the theoretical whole and arrives at its real significance only when, by its interconnection with other concepts, a theoretical unity has been reached and its role in this is known, is valid here too. What is the life promoted by the ideas to which the predicate of truth is to be attributed? In what does promotion consist in the present period? Is the idea to be considered valid when the individual who has comprehended it goes down while the society, the class, the public interest for which he fights strides forward? What does confirmation mean? Is the power of the slanderers and scoundrels to serve as confirmation of the assertions with whose help they attained it? Cannot the crudest superstition, the most miserable perversion of the truth about world, society, justice, religion, and history grip whole peoples and prove most excellent for its author and his clique? In contrast, does the defeat of the forces of freedom signify the disproof of their theory?

The concept of proof also plays a role in the materialistic way of thinking. Above all, it is a weapon against every form of mysticism because of its significance in the criticism of the acceptance of a transcendent and superhuman truth which is reserved for revelation and the insight of the elect, instead of being basically accessible to experience and practice. Yet as much as theory and practice are linked to history, there is no pre-established harmony between them. What is seen as theoretically correct is not therefore simultaneously realized. Human activity is no unambiguous function of insight, but rather a process which at every moment is likewise determined by other factors and resistances. This clearly follows from the present state of the theory of history. A number of social tendencies in their reciprocal action are described there theoretically: the agglomeration of great amounts of capital as against the declining share of the average individual in relation to the wealth of society as a whole, the increase of unemployment interrupted by ever shorter periods of a relative prosperity, the growing discrepancy between the apportionment of social labor to the various types of goods and the general needs, the diversion of productivity from constructive to destructive purposes, the sharpening of contradictions within states and among them. All these processes were shown by Marx to be necessary at a time when they could only be studied in a few advanced countries and in embryo, and the prospect of a liberalistic organization of the world still seemed excellent. But from the beginning, this view of history, now in fact confirmed, understood these developments in a particular way, that is, as tendencies which could be prevented from leading to a relapse into barbarism by the effort of people guided by this theory. This theory, confirmed by the course of history, was thought of not only as theory but as an impetus to a liberating practice, bound up with the whole impatience of threatened humanity. The testing of the unswerving faith involved in this struggle is closely connected with the confirmation of the predicted tendencies which has already taken place, but the two aspects of the verification are not identical; rather, they are mediated by the actual struggle, the solution of concrete historical problems based on the theory reinforced by experience. Continuously in this process partial views may prove incorrect, timetables be disproved, corrections become necessary; historical factors which were overlooked reveal themselves; many a vigorously defended and cherished thesis proves to be an error. Yet the connection with the theory as a whole is in no way lost in this application. Adherence to its proven teachings and to the interests and goals shaping and permeating it is the prerequisite for effective correction of errors. Unswerving loyalty to what is recognized as true is as much an impetus to theoretical progress as openness to new tasks and situations and the corresponding refocusing of ideas.

In such a process of verification the individuals and groups struggling for more rational conditions might succumb completely and human society develop retrogressively, a conceivable possibility which any view of history that has not degenerated into fatalism must formally take into account. This would refute the trust in the future which is not merely an external supplement to the theory, but belongs to it as a force shaping its concepts. But the frivolous comments of well-meaning critics who use every premature claim, every incorrect analysis of a momentary situation by the adherents of the cause of freedom as evidence against their theory as a whole, indeed against theory in general, are nevertheless unjustified. The defeats of a great cause, which run counter to the hope for its early victory, are mainly due to mistakes which do not damage the theoretical content of the conception as a whole, however far-reaching the consequences they have. The direction and content of activity, along with its success, are more closely related to their theory for the historically progressive groups than is the case with the representatives of naked power. The talk of the latter is related to their rise only as a mechanical aid, and their speech merely supplements open and secret force with craft and treachery, even when the sound of the words resembles truth. But the knowledge of the falling fighter, insofar as it reflects the structure of the present epoch and the basic possibility of a better one, is not dishonored because mankind succumbs to bombs and poison gases. The concept of verification as the criterion of truth must not be interpreted so simply. The truth is an impetus to correct practice. But whoever identifies it directly with success passes over history and makes himself an apologist for the reality dominant at any given time. Misunderstanding the irremovable difference between concept and reality, he reverts to idealism, spiritualism and mysticism.

One can find in Marxist literature formulations close to pragmatic doctrine. Max Adler[27] writes: "Theory turns directly into practice because, as Marxism has taught us to understand, nothing can be right which does not work in practice; the social theory is nevertheless only the recapitulation of the practice itself." In regard to the identity of theory and practice, however, their difference is not to be forgotten. While it is the duty of everyone who acts responsibly to learn from setbacks in practice, these can nevertheless not destroy the proven basic structure of the theory, in terms of which they are to be understood only as setbacks. According to pragmatism, the verification of ideas and their truth merge. According to materialism, verification forms the evidence that ideas and objective reality correspond, itself a historical occurrence that can be obstructed and interrupted. This viewpoint has no place for a basically closed and unknowable truth or for the subsistence of ideas not requiring any reality, but this does not mean that the concept of a conviction which, because of a given constellation of the world is cut off from verification and success, is a priori untrue. This also holds true for historical conflicts. The possibility of a more rational form of human association has been sufficiently demonstrated to be obvious. Its full demonstration requires universal success; this depends on historical developments. The fact that meanwhile misery continues and terror spreads—the terrible force which suppresses that general demonstration—has no probative force for the contrary.

The contradictions appear plainly in Max Scheler's extensive refutation of pragmatism in postwar Germany.[28] Scheler did not fail to recognize the relative truths of pragmatism: "So-called 'knowledge for knowledge's sake' . . . exists nowhere and cannot and also 'should' not exist, and has never existed anywhere in the world. When pragmatism attributes to the positive, exact sciences a primary purpose of control, it is certainly not wrong. Rather, it is vain foolishness to consider positive science too 'good' or too 'grand' to give men freedom and power, to guide and lead the world."[29] He also understood that the criteria for practical work in this doctrine were modeled exclusively on the inorganic natural sciences and then mechanically transferred unchanged to knowledge as a whole. Had he analyzed the concept of practice itself, it would have been evident that this is by no means as clear and simple as it seems in pragmatism, where it reduces and impoverishes truth. The meaning of the criterion is indeed not developed in experiments in natural science. Its essence consists in neatly isolating assertion, object and verification. The undefined and questionable aspect of the situation lies in the unarticulated relationship between the specific scientific activity and the life of the individuals involved and people in general, in the ostensible natural and self-evident character of the theoretical act. The unresolved and problematical aspect of its relationship to the concrete historical life with which it is obviously interwoven appears as soon as one more closely investigates the controlling categories and the choice of objects and methods. Practice as verification itself leads to a critique of positivist philosophy's hypostatization of natural science and its basic concepts. The help of metaphysics is not required. However much the problems of natural science are soluble within its boundaries and with its specific means, independent of anything else, technical knowledge is in itself abstract and acquires its full truth only in the theory which comprehends natural science in this particular historical situation as an aspect of society's development as a whole. If, in addition, practice is understood as the criterion not merely in the special case of physical science and the technique based on it, but in the theory of history, then it becomes clear without further ado that it embraces the whole situation of society at any given moment. It takes more than attention to isolated events or groups of events, or reference to general concepts such as that of progress, to apply the criterion of practice in deciding such questions as whether one or another judgment of the contemporary authoritarian states is correct; whether they can develop only in politically backward countries with strong remnants of a landed aristocracy or whether they should be regarded as an adequate state form for the present economic phase, hence necessarily to be expected in other areas; whether this or that theory of colonial expansion applies; whether, to come to more abstract problems, the progressive technical sealing off and mathematicization of logic and economics is more suited to their present situation than sticking to the development of concepts reflecting the historical situation. For this, one needs a definite theory of society as a whole, which is itself only to be thought of in terms of particular interests and tasks with one's own point of view and activity.

Scheler does not pursue this conceptual movement in which it becomes clear that practice as an abstract criterion of truth changes into the concrete theory of society and strips off the formalism in which it is clad in the undialectical thought of the pragmatic school. He does not push this category to the consequences which contradict the system of bourgeois thought in which it is firmly frozen. Instead, he opposes to the knowledge which can be verified and criticized through practice other forms of knowledge which according to him exist along with it and unconnected to it. He fails to recognize the elevation to a philosophical absolute of mechanical natural science as the ideological reflection of bourgeois society which was able to increase reason and thereby human "power and freedom" in a high degree in the technique of material production, and yet must block the ever more urgently necessary reorganization of human relations in production in accordance with its own principle. Thus it negates and destroys the same criteria of reason, power and freedom which in cognitive theory it recognizes in isolated areas. Nor does he relate the bourgeois reality and science which he combats to their own ideas and standards and thus show both society and ideas in their one-sidedness and abstraction and thus contribute to their supersession. Instead, like Bergson and other philosophers of this period, he goes on to proclaim his own special higher forms of cognition. In the face of the deepening contradictions between use in science and use for humanity, between use for privileged groups and for society as a whole, use for facilitating production and for easing life, the criterion of utility had become a dubious principle. Scheler does not further pursue the dialectic sketched out in his work, but rather places useful science at the very bottom in his ranking of knowledge. Turning back to earlier stages of human development, he advocates in opposition to "mastery or production knowledge" the two types of "cultural knowledge" and "redemption knowledge." He declares himself in complete agreement with the "new sub-bourgeois class" in the pragmatist interpretation of "the pretentious rationalist metaphysics of the bourgeois entrepreneurs,"[30] attacking most sharply classic German idealism and the historical materialism which issued from it. For him it is nonsense "that the human spirit and the ideal factors could ever control the real factors according to a positive plan. What J. G. Fichte, Hegel ('Age of Reason') and—following them, only postponed to a future point in time—Karl Marx, with his doctrine of the 'leap into freedom,' have dreamt will remain a mere dream for all time."[31] In contrast to this freedom, in which science would in fact have an important role to play, Scheler prophesied that the world should and could expect the rise of noble and spiritually elevated groups. If bourgeoisie and proletariat are "completely uncreative of all cultural knowledge and redemptive knowledge,"[32] this will be remedied from now on by the fact "that growing and advancing capitalism will gradually again be able to produce a whole class of purely cognitive people, and likewise of such people who have broken with the authoritative class doctrines, with bourgeois and proletarian metaphysics—that is, with the absolute mechanistic view and philosophical pragmatism. In this elite and its hands alone rests the future development of human knowledge. . . . But the future will have a new independent rise of the genuine philosophical and metaphysical spirit."[33] In connection with the passage previously cited, Epicurus defines the goal of knowledge and wisdom as the happiness and good fortune of mankind. Scheler's view and the present heralded by him are in irreconcilable opposition to this materialistic pragmatism.

In the analysis of the concept of proof and its role in open-ended, dialectical thought, it is shown that the decision on particular truths depends on still uncompleted historical processes. While progress in theory and practice is conditioned by the fact that, in contrast to relativistic neutrality, a definite theory corresponding to the highest available level of knowledge is adhered to and applied, this application reacts on the form of the theory and the meaning of its concepts. This is not merely a question of the correction of errors. Categories such as history, society, progress, science and so on experience a change of function in the course of time. They are not independent essences but aspects of the whole body of knowledge at a given time, which is developed by human beings in interaction with one another and with nature and is never identical with reality. This also applies to the dialectic itself. It is the sum total of the methods and laws which thought adheres to in order to copy reality as exactly as possible and to correspond as far as possible with the formal principles of real events.

What are the characteristics of dialectical thought? It relativizes every many-sided but isolated definition in the consciousness of the alteration of subject and object as well as their relationship. (What results in idealism from a postulated absolute, takes place in materialism on the basis of developing experience.)[34] Instead of ranging attributes alongside one another, it seeks to show, by analysis of each general characteristic in respect to the particular object, that this generalization taken by itself simultaneously contradicts the object, and that in order to be properly comprehended it must be related to the contrary property and finally to the whole system of knowledge. From this follows the principle that every insight is to be regarded as true only in connection with the whole body of theory, and hence is so to be understood conceptually that in its formulation the connection with the structural principles and practical tendencies governing the theory is preserved. Bound up with this is the rule that, while maintaining unswerving fidelity to the key ideas and goals and the historical tasks of the epoch, the style of presentation should be characterized more by "as well as" than "either-or." A basic principle is the inseparability of the regressive and progressive impulses, the preserving and decomposing, the good and bad sides of particular situations in nature and human history. Instead of accepting the legitimate analyses and abstractions of professional science but turning to metaphysics and religion for an understanding of concrete reality, it tries to place the analytically achieved concepts in relation to one another and reconstruct reality through them. These and all the other characteristics of dialectical reason correspond to the form of a complicated reality, constantly changing in all its details.

Such very general intellectual laws of motion, which are abstracted from previous history and form the content of dialectical logic in general, seem relatively constant and also extremely empty. But the special dialectical forms of description of a particular subject matter correspond to its characteristics and lose their validity as forms of the theory when their bases change. The critique of political economy comprehends the present form of society. In a purely intellectual construction, the concept of value is derived from the basic general concept of the commodity. From it, Marx develops the categories of money and capital in a closed system; all the historical tendencies of this form of economy—the concentration of capital, the falling rate of profit, unemployment and crises—are placed in relation to this concept and deduced in strict succession. At least in terms of the theoretical intention, a close intellectual relationship should exist between the first and most general concept, whose abstractness is further transcended with every theoretical step, and the unique historical event, in which every thesis necessarily follows from the first postulate, the concept of free exchange of commodities. According to the theoretical intention, whose success will not be examined here, knowledge of all social processes in the economic, political and all other cultural fields will be mediated by that initial cognition. This attempt to carry the theory through to the end in the closed form of an inherently necessary succession of ideas has an objective significance. The theoretical necessity mirrors the real compulsiveness with which the production and reproduction of human life goes on in this epoch, the autonomy which the economic forces have acquired in respect to mankind, the dependence of all social groups on the self-regulation of the economic apparatus. That men cannot shape their labor according to their common will but, under a principle which sets them against one another individually and in groups, produce with their labor not security and freedom but general insecurity and dependence; that they fall into misery, war and destruction instead of using the immeasurably increased social wealth for their happiness, and are the slaves instead of the masters of their fate—this finds expression in the form of logical necessity, proper to the true theory of contemporary society. It would therefore be wrong to think that events in a future society could be deduced according to the same principles and with the same necessity as the lines of development of the present one.

The meaning of the categories will change along with the structure of the society from which they are drawn and in whose description they play a role. The concept of historical tendency loses the compulsive character that it had in the present historical period, while preserving a relation to the category of natural necessity, which may indeed be narrowed but can never be transcended completely. The concept of the individual will lose the character of an isolated monad and simultaneously the unconditionally central place it has held in the system of thought and feeling in recent centuries at the moment when individual and general goals really coincide and are supported in the whole society, when man no longer merely imagines that he embodies absolute self-determination but is in reality a member of a freely self-determining society. With the ending of the situation in which the contradiction between particular and general purposes necessarily follows from the economic structure and the idea that the individualistic principle has been fully transcended rests partly on conscious deception and partly on impotent dreaming, the concept of the I loses its function of controlling the entire relation to the world and acquires another meaning. As long as the life of society flows not from cooperative work but from the destructive competition of individuals whose relationship is essentially conducted through the exchange of commodities, the I, possession, the mine and not-mine play a fundamental role in experience, in speech and thought, in all cultural expressions, characterizing and dominating all particulars in a decisive way. In this period, the world disintegrates into I and not-I as in Fichte's transcendental philosophy, and one's own death means absolute annihilation insofar as this relationship is not alleviated by metaphysical or religious faith. Like the categories of tendency and the individual, all other social concepts will be affected by the alteration of reality. The more formal categories such as the lawful nature of society, causality, necessity, science, etc., as well as the more material ones such as value, price, profit, class, family and nation, acquire a different look in the theoretical structures which correspond to a new situation.

In traditional logic, this alteration of concepts is interpreted in such a way that the original divisions in the system of classification of a field of knowledge are made more specific by subdivisions. The general concept of tendency then includes the historical tendencies of the present society as well as the possible tendencies of a different sort in a future society. In spite of all historical changes, Aristotle's definition of the polis—composed of individuals and groups and differing not only quantitatively but qualitatively from its elements—can be absorbed into a supreme formal category of society, valid for all forms of society, and thus preserved in its general validity. For Aristotle himself, slavery belonged to this highest category, while in later conceptual systems it is only one of the subcategories of society, contrasted to other definite types. The conceptual realism which dominates Platonic and in part medieval philosophy, and whose remnants have by no means yet been surmounted in modern logic (for instance, in modern phenomenology), has the character of discursive logic. It interprets all changes as mere additions of new subtypes under the universal types, made absolute and subsumed under the metaphysical view that all change is to be understood as the incarnation or emanation of permanent ideas and essences in ever-new particulars and exemplars. Thus, the essential would always remain in the old, there would be an eternal realm of unalterable ideas, and all change would affect only the lower levels of being. Indeed, it would not be genuinely real and would only exist for the dull senses of men. Since the Hegelian system hypostatizes the categories dealt with within its framework, it still preserves something of this realism and falls into the dualism of essence and appearance which it opposed so vigorously. The given fate of historically determined individuals and the changing circumstances of present and future history become null and void in comparison with the ideas which are supposed to underlie the past. The discursive logic of "Understanding" is only limited inside Hegel's system; in the sense of a metaphysical legend, it retains its reifying power over his philosophy as a whole. The logic of the

Understanding abstracts from the fact that in the face of the changed content of concepts, lumping them indiscriminately with those which formerly went under the same headings can become distortion, and a new definition, a new ordering and hierarchy of concepts can become necessary. Perhaps the category of tendency later becomes so restructured as to revolutionize its relation to the concept of systematic purpose on the one hand and that of the power of nature on the other. The concept of the state alters its relation to the categories of will, domination, force, society, etc. Such definite perspectives do not flow from observation of today's valid system of classification of social phenomena, but from the theory of historical development itself, of which the former is only an ordered, abstract inventory. The connection between the concrete movement of thought, as it develops in constant interrelation with the life of society, and the systems organized by the Understanding, is not examined in detail by traditional logic, which relegates it to a separate discipline as the subject of the history of science or culture. It itself deals with the relations of unchanging concepts: how one passes from one to another judiciously and conclusively and how one develops from each what it contains. Traditional logic is "a science of the necessary laws of thought, without which no use of understanding and reason takes place and which are therefore the conditions under which alone understanding can and should be congruous with itself—the necessary laws and prerequisites of its correct use."[35] Their function is "to make clear concepts intelligible."[36] This proceeds analytically, drawing out of the concept what is in it. The concept itself "remains the same; only the form is changed. . . . Just as nothing is added to a map itself when it is illuminated, so the lighting up of a concept by the analysis of its characteristics does not expand the concept itself in the least."[37] Traditional logic has nothing to do with the alteration of the "map" and the construction of new systems of classification. But if concepts are used without being strictly tied in to the existing system of reference, in which all previous discoveries of the branch concerned have been arranged, if they are used without that correct reading of the "map" which is required by the laws of logic, every intellectual outline remains blurred, or rather meaningless. The accurate description of the object results from the methodical collaboration of all cognitive forces in the theoretical construction. Aside from the table of contents for this content, which it does not itself produce, "the tabular understanding" also gives conceptual material.[38] From time to time "the empirical sciences," investigation and analysis, "have contradicted the material'' of the dialectical description ''in finding general uniformities, classifications, and laws.''[39] The real significance of this work, the cognitive value of understanding, rests on the fact that reality knows not only constant change but also relatively static structures. Because development proceeds not gradually but in leaps, there are between these junctures, leaps and revolutions periods in which the tensions and contradictions trying to break through appear as elements of a relatively closed and fixed totality, until the particular form of being turns into another. This determinate and organized state is therefore a necessary condition of truth but not its real form, movement and progress. Thus, traditional logic is inadequate for, and comprehends only individual aspects of, the historically conditioned alteration of the fundamental categories and every thought process about the subject matter. Since a concept plays a determinate role in the dialectical construction of an event, it becomes a non-autonomous aspect of a conceptual whole which has other qualities than the sum of all the concepts included in it. This whole, the construction of the particular object, can indeed only come into existence in a way appropriate to the existing knowledge if the concepts are interpreted in the sense that belongs to them in the systems of the individual sciences, in the systematic inventory of scientifically based definitions, insofar as it is a question of concepts for which special branches of science exist. In *Capital*, Marx introduces the basic concepts of classical English political economy—value, price, labor-time etc.—in accordance with their precise definitions. All the most progressive definitions drawn from scientific practice at that time are employed. Nevertheless, these categories acquire new functions in the course of the presentation. They contribute to a theoretical whole, the character of which contradicts the static views in connection with which they came into being, in particular their uncritical use in isolation. Materialist economics as a whole is placed in opposition to the classical system, yet individual concepts are taken over. The dialectical forms of the movement of thought show themselves to be the same as those of reality. A hydrogen atom observed in isolation has its specific characteristics, acquires new ones in molecular combination with other elements, and displays the old ones again as soon as it is freed from the combination. Concepts behave in the same way; considered individually, they preserve their definitions, while in combination they become aspects of new units of meaning.[40] The movement of reality is mirrored in the ''fluidity'' of concepts.

The open-ended materialistic dialectic does not regard the ''ra-

tional'' as completed at any point in history and does not expect to
bring about the resolution of contradictions and tensions, the end of
the historic dynamic, by the full development of mere ideas and their
simple consequences. It lacks the aspect of the idealistic dialectic
which Hegel described as ''speculative'' and at the same time as
''mystical,'' namely, the idea of knowing the ostensibly unconditioned and thereby being oneself unconditioned.[41] It does not hypostatize any such universal system of categories. To attain the ''positive-
ly rational,'' it does not suffice to resolve and transcend contradictions
in thought. It requires the historical struggle whose guiding ideas and
theoretical prerequisites are indeed given in the consciousness of the
combatants. But the outcome cannot be predicted on a purely theoretical basis. It will be determined, not by any firmly outlined unity such
as the ''course of history,'' the principles of which could be established indivisibly for all time, but by human beings interacting with one
another and with nature, who enter into new relationships and structures and thereby change themselves. The resolution of contradictions
in subjective thought and the overcoming of objective antagonisms
can be closely intertwined, but they are in no way identical. In a
particular historical period, a free society in the sense of the free
development of the individual and in the sense of free enterprise on the
basis of inequality will be conceptually and actually full of contradictions. The resolution in terms of ideas occurs through the concept of a
differentiated higher form of freedom. It has a decisive voice in the
real overcoming, but in no way coincides with it and predicts the
future only abstractly and inexactly. Since the logic of the open-ended
dialectic allows for the possibility that change will affect the entire
present content of the categories, without therefore considering the
theory formed from it as any less true, it corresponds exactly to the
Hegelian conception of the difference between dialectic and understanding without overlaying it with a new dogmatism. ''The intelligible exists in concepts in their fixed definition and differentiation
from others; the *dialectical* shows them in their change and disintegration.''[42] To be sure, the first is immanent in the second; without the
definition and organization of concepts, without understanding, there
is no thought and also no dialectic. But the understanding becomes
metaphysical as soon as it absolutizes its function of preserving and
expanding existing knowledge, of confirming, organizing and drawing conclusions from it, or the results of that function as the existence
and progress of truth. The revolutionizing, disintegration and restructuring of knowledge, its changing relation to reality, its changes of

function resulting from its intertwinement with history, fall outside the thought processes which traditional logic, whose theme is understanding, comprehends. Taken by itself, it leads to the erroneous concept of a detached thought with fixed, eternal and autonomous results. Nietzsche said that a great truth "wants to be criticized, not worshipped."[43] This is valid for truth in general. He might have added that criticism includes not only the negative and skeptical impulse but also the inner independence not to let the truth fall but to remain firm in its application even if it may sometime pass away. In the individual, the process of cognition includes not only intelligence but also character; for a group, not merely adaptation to changing reality but the strength to declare and put into practice its own views and ideas.

The initially discussed division in the bourgeois spirit with regard to truth, in contrast to dialectical thought, finds especially clear expression in the attitude toward religion. In the face of the primitive materialism which dominates economic life, it has become more and more internalized. The practice of general competition which characterizes contemporary reality was pitiless from the beginning, and with the exception of a few periods, has become increasingly inhuman. Its means and consequences, which at particular historical moments have led to domination by small economic groups, the abandonment of power to the most culturally backward elements of society, and the extermination of minorities, notoriously contradict the basic teachings of Christianity. In a period in which, despite great resistance, reading and writing had to become common skills for economic reasons, and the contents of the Bible could not remain a permanent secret from the masses, it had long been inevitable that the opposing principle of Christianity would be openly sacrificed to reality, and the vulgar positivism of bare facts along with the worship of success, immanent in this life-style, propagated as the exclusive and highest truth. But the gross contradiction that existed was really understood within the bourgeoisie only by religious outsiders such as Kierkegaard and Tolstoi. The monistic propaganda of Strauss and Haeckel, who proclaimed it on the basis of scientific research, saw only the difference which it implied between natural science by itself and revelation and misunderstood both the spirit of the Gospels and historical reality. These materialists on the basis of natural science had to remain sectarians, for religion was indispensable for the social groups to which they belonged. The predominant intellectual attitude in recent centuries was not that of exposing the split. Instead, religion was so robbed of any clear and definite content, formalized, adapted, spiritualized, relegated to the innermost subjectivity, that it was compatible with every activity and every public practice that existed in this atheistic reality.

Since individuals began to think more independently, that is, since the rise of the new economic order, philosophy in all fields has ever more clearly fulfilled the function of erasing the contradiction between the dominant way of life and Christian or Christian-oriented theoretical and practical doctrines and ideas. The reason for this coincides with the root of bourgeois dogmatism in general. The isolated individual, who is simultaneously regarded as free and responsible, is in the present epoch necessarily dominated by anxiety and uncertainty. In addition to this inner need, which is directly grounded in the atomistic principles of the existing order, the external concern for social peace has led to great efforts to gloss over the irreconcilability of modern science and the way people conduct their lives with the religious views on the origin and structure of the world as well as the ideas of love for one's neighbor, justice and the goodness of God. Troeltsch, a typical philosopher of religion in prewar Germany, openly states what he fears:

> To anyone even moderately acquainted with human beings, it will be inconceivable that divine authority could ever disappear without damage to the moral law, that the generally coarse-thinking average man could do without this supplement to the motivation of morality. The abstraction of a self-validating law will be forever unrealizable for him; in connection with law, he will always have to think of the lawgiver and watcher. He may think of this a bit coarsely, but not so irrationally. . . . Where atheistic morality has undone divine authority among the masses, experience shows that there is little sense of that law left. A fierce hatred of all authority and an unbounded unchaining of selfishness as the most obvious thing in the world has been, with few exceptions, the easily comprehensible logical consequence.[44]

A social situation in which there would be no "watcher," either in the form of a transcendent being or "a self-validating law," to hold the "unbounded" selfishness of the masses in check, is something he cannot conceive of. Dogmatic adherence to the inherited conceptual world seems to him a self-evident proposition, a *thema probandum*. Nevertheless, he also sees

> that the Protestant-confessional axiom must be self-revised and more freely interpreted; that its accomplishments must find a

broader, more general basis and make themselves far more independent of immediate clerical reality; that its style must leave room for detailed historical research and the definitive results of natural science, and be constantly prepared for new revisions on the basis of this work. Indeed, the possibility exists that eventually Christianity itself will cease to be axiomatic.[45]

The axioms to which earlier liberal theology could reach back have meanwhile been overturned. "Kant and Schleiermacher, Goethe and Hegel, still lived under the influence of an axiomatic validation which no longer exists."[46] He therefore recommends resorting to Kant's critical philosophy "which undertakes to discover the ultimate presuppositions in the organization of consciousness instead of metaphysics."[47] He seeks refuge in a "critique of religious consciousness"[48] and hopes

> to find a firm footing through a general theory of religion and its historical development. But this theory itself would have to be rooted in a transcendental theory of consciousness and to answer, from this ultimate basis of all scientific thinking, this ultimate and correct presupposition, two questions: the question of the justification of religion in general, and that of the difference in value between its historical forms. Theology is thereby referred to the philosophy of religion. On this basis only will it be able so to construe the essence and validity of Christianity as to satisfy the modern spirit of taking nothing for granted. The ultimate presuppositions lie in the philosophy of transcendentalism. . . .[49]

According to this, the "justification of religion in general" and even the advantages of Christianity are still the question, and the whole uncertainty, the relativistic readiness for concessions not to the selfishness of the masses but to ostensibly non-axiomatic science, becomes clear. Only one thing is preserved at any cost: "In all change there must be a permanent truth. This is a requirement of that ideal faith, to renounce which would be to renounce the meaning of the world."[50] If this so necessary faith only remains attached to an eternal meaning, one can come to terms with idealistic philosophy, Judaism, Islam, Confucianism, Brahmin and Buddhist ideas of salvation.[51]

This ambiguous relationship to religion characterizes the whole period, and only finds a particularly clear ideological expression in phenomena like Troeltsch. It is an aspect of the objective dishonesty which, despite the good conscience of the participants, dominated the

spiritual atmosphere. If one looks closely at previous history, the fact
that in many areas of public discussion the crude and obvious lie is
now treated with honor represents no incomprehensible change. The
situation of the bourgeoisie has resulted in the setting aside of intellectual development in moral and religious questions and the keeping in
twilight of central areas, as if by tacit agreement. The religious
philosophy of the middle ages outlines the spiritual horizon which
corresponded to society at the time. Its most important results therefore form historical evidence of obvious greatness. Since the irreligion
immanent in modern natural science and technology, these specifically bourgeois achievements, has found no corresponding place in the
general consciousness, and the conflicts that this involves have not
been arbitrated, official spirituality is characterized by hypocrisy and
indulgence toward particular forms of error and injustice, and this has
eventually spread over the cultural life of entire peoples. The only
great spirit who, in the face of the gross thickening of this fog which
has taken place since the middle of the last century, has achieved the
freedom from illusion and the comprehensive view which are possible
from the standpoint of the big bourgeoisie, is Nietzsche. It must
indeed have escaped him that the intellectual honesty with which he
was concerned did not fit in with this social standpoint. The reason for
the foulness against which he fought lies neither in individual nor
national character, but in the structure of society as a whole, which
includes both. Since as a true bourgeois philosopher he made psychology, even if the most profound that exists today, the fundamental
science of history, he misunderstood the origin of spiritual decay and
the way out, and the fate which befell his own work was therefore
inevitable. ("Who among my friends would have seen more in it than
an impermissible presumption, completely indifferent to happiness?")[52]

The philosophically mediated dishonesty in questions of religion
cannot be eliminated by psychological or other explanations. Whereas
Nietzsche makes the religious question and Christian morality negatively central and thereby makes an ideologue of himself, this aspect
of the existing situation also can only be eliminated by transcending it
through higher forms of society. In dialectical thought, religious
phenomena too are related to knowledge as a whole and judged at any
given time in connection with the analysis of the whole historical
situation. As important as it is to see the incompatibility of the
religious content with advanced knowledge, the present shows that
making religious questions central to the whole cultural problem can

be foolish. One can find more penetrating analysis of bourgeois society in the literature of the Catholic counterrevolution in France, in Bonald and de Maistre and the writings of the Catholic royalist Balzac, than in the critics of religion in Germany at the same period. The devout Victor Hugo and Tolstoi have more nobly depicted and more vigorously fought the horrors of existing conditions than the enlightened Gutzkow and Friedrich Theodor Vischer. In the practical questions of daily life, efforts guided by dialectical thought can lead to temporary collaboration with religiously motivated groups and tendencies and radical opposition to anti-religious ones. The complex of historical tasks which is decisive for an illusion-free and progressive attitude today does not divide people primarily on the basis of their religious preference. Groups and individuals may be characterized more quickly today on the basis of their particular interest (theoretically explicable, to be sure) or lack of interest in just conditions which promote the free development of human beings, in the abolition of conditions of oppression which are dangerous to and unworthy of mankind, than by their relation to religion. It follows from the differing cultural levels of social groups, the miserable state of education on social problems, and other factors, that religion can mean altogether different things for different classes and different ways of life. It requires not merely experience and theoretical education but a particular fate in society to avoid either inflating thought into the creation of idols or devaluing it as the sum total of mere illusions, making it an absolute lawgiver and unambiguous guide for action, or separating it from the practical goals and tasks with which it interacts. It is a utopian illusion to expect that the strength to live with the sober truth will become general until the causes of untruth are removed.

A Note on Dialectic

By Herbert Marcuse

*While Marcuse's early essays on dialectic bristle with
phenomenological categories (he had been an assistant to
Heidegger), they already embody the crucial shift from ontology to
history, from Being to concrete being-in-the-world, as Adorno
remarked with cautious praise in a contemporary review. The essay
reproduced here, written in 1960 as a new preface to his* Reason and
Revolution, *retains few traces of this heritage. Marcuse's condensed
exposé shows that dialectic, in the Hegelian sense used by the critical
theorists, is neither an abstract method nor an ideology. An important
feature of the essay is the relation Marcuse establishes to the esthetic
mode (more systematically and historically grounded in* Eros and
Civilization) *as an alternative, non-instrumental perception and thus
an aspect of autonomous reason. This essay goes a long way to
explain the interdisciplinary orientation of many of the older
Frankfurtians.*

This book was written in the hope that it would make a small contribution to the revival, not of Hegel, but of a mental faculty which is in
danger of being obliterated: the power of negative thinking. As Hegel
defines it: "Thinking is, indeed, essentially the negation of that which
is immediately before us." What does he mean by "negation," the
central category of dialectic?

Even Hegel's most abstract and metaphysical concepts are

saturated with experience—experience of a world in which the unreasonable becomes reasonable and, as such, determines the facts; in which unfreedom is the condition of freedom, and war the guarantor of peace. This world contradicts itself. Common sense and science purge themselves from this contradiction; but philosophical thought begins with the recognition that the facts do not correspond to the concepts imposed by common sense and scientific reason—in short, with the refusal to accept them. To the extent that these concepts disregard the fatal contradictions which make up reality, they abstract from the very process of reality. The negation which dialectic applies to them is not only a critique of a conformistic logic, which denies the reality of contradictions; it is also a critique of the given state of affairs on its own grounds—of the established system of life, which denies its own promises and potentialities.

Today, this dialectical mode of thought is alien to the whole established universe of discourse and action. It seems to belong to the past and to be rebutted by the achievements of technological civilization. The established reality seems promising and productive enough to repel or absorb all alternatives. Thus acceptance—and even affirmation—of this reality appears to be the only reasonable methodological principle. Moreover, it precludes neither criticism nor change; on the contrary, insistence on the dynamic character of the status quo, on its constant "revolutions," is one of the strongest props for this attitude. Yet this dynamic seems to operate endlessly within the same framework of life: streamlining rather than abolishing the domination of man, both by man and by the products of his labor. Progress becomes quantitative and tends to delay indefinitely the turn from quantity to quality—that is, the emergence of new modes of existence with new forms of reason and freedom.

The power of negative thinking is the driving power of dialectical thought, used as a tool for analyzing the world of facts in terms of its internal inadequacy. I choose this vague and unscientific formulation in order to sharpen the contrast between dialectical and undialectical thinking. "Inadequacy" implies a value judgment. Dialectical thought invalidates the a priori opposition of value and fact by understanding all facts as stages of a single process—a process in which subject and object are so joined that truth can be determined only within the subject-object totality. All facts embody the knower as well as the doer; they continuously translate the past into the present. The objects thus "contain" subjectivity in their very structure.

Now what (or who) is this subjectivity that, in a literal sense, constitutes the objective world? Hegel answers with a series of terms denoting the subject in its various manifestations: Thought, Reason, Spirit, Idea. Since we no longer have that fluent access to these concepts which the eighteenth and nineteenth centuries still had, I shall try to sketch Hegel's conception in more familiar terms:

Nothing is "real" which does not sustain itself in existence, in a life-and-death struggle with the situations and conditions of its existence. The struggle may be blind or even unconscious, as in inorganic matter; it may be conscious and concerted, such as the struggle of mankind with its own conditions and with those of nature. *Reality* is the constantly renewed result of the process of existence—the process, conscious or unconscious in which "that which is" becomes "other than itself"; and *identity* is only the continuous negation of inadequate existence, the subject maintaining itself in being other than itself. Each reality, therefore, is a *realization*—a development of "subjectivity." The latter "comes to itself" in history, where the development has a rational content; Hegel defines it as "progress in the consciousness of freedom."

Again a value judgment—and this time a value judgment imposed upon the world as a whole. But freedom is for Hegel an ontological category: it means being not a mere object, but the subject of one's existence; not succumbing to external conditions, but transforming factuality into realization. This transformation is, according to Hegel, the energy of nature and history, the inner structure of all being! One may be tempted to scoff at this idea, but one should be aware of its implications.

Dialectical thought starts with the experience that the world is unfree; that is to say, man and nature exist in conditions of alienation, exist as "other than they are." Any mode of thought which excludes this contradiction from its logic is a faulty logic. Thought "corresponds" to reality only as it transforms reality by comprehending its contradictory structure. Here the principle of dialectic drives thought beyond the limits of philosophy. For to comprehend reality means to comprehend what things really are, and this in turn means rejecting their mere factuality. Rejection is the process of thought as well as of action. While the scientific method leads from the immediate experience of *things* to their mathematical-logical structure, philosophical thought leads from the immediate experience of *existence* to its historical structure: the principle of freedom.

Freedom is the innermost dynamic of existence, and the very process of existence in an unfree world is "the continuous negation of that which threatens to deny (*aufheben*) freedom." Thus freedom is essentially negative: existence is both alienation and the process by which the subject comes to itself in comprehending and mastering alienation. For the history of mankind, this means attainment of a "state of the world" in which the individual persists in inseparable harmony with the whole, and in which the conditions and relations of his world "possess no essential objectivity independent of the individual". As to the prospect of attaining such a state, Hegel was pessimistic: the element of reconciliation with the established state of affairs, so strong in his work, seems to a great extent due to this pessimism—or, if one prefers, this realism. Freedom is relegated to the realm of pure thought, to the Absolute Idea. Idealism by default: Hegel shares this fate with the main philosophical tradition.

Dialectical thought thus becomes negative in itself. Its function is to break down the self-assurance and self-contentment of common sense, to undermine the sinister confidence in the power and language of facts, to demonstrate that unfreedom is so much at the core of things that the development of their internal contradictions leads necessarily to qualitative change: the explosion and catastrophe of the established state of affairs. Hegel sees the task of knowledge as that of recognizing the world as Reason by understanding all objects of thought as elements and aspects of a totality which becomes a conscious world in the history of mankind. Dialectical analysis ultimately tends to become historical analysis, in which nature itself appears as part and stage in its own history and in the history of man. The progress of cognition from common sense to knowledge arrives at a world which is negative in its very structure because that which is real opposes and denies the potentialities inherent in itself—potentialities which themselves strive for realization. Reason is the negation of the negative.

Interpretation of that-which-is in terms of that-which-is-not, confrontation of the given facts with that which they exclude—this has been the concern of philosophy wherever philosophy was more than a matter of ideological justification or mental exercise. The liberating function of negation in philosophical thought depends upon the recognition that the negation is a positive act: that-which-is *repels* that-which is-not and, in doing so, repels its own real possibilities. Consequently, to express and define that-which-is on its own terms is to distort and falsify reality. Reality is other and more than that codified in the logic and language of facts. Here is the inner link between dialectical thought and the effort of avant-garde literature: the effort to break the power of facts over the word, and to speak a language which is not the language of those who establish, enforce and benefit from the facts. As the power of the given facts tends to become totalitarian, to absorb all opposition and to define the entire universe of discourse, the effort to speak the language of contradiction appears increasingly irrational, obscure, artificial. The question is not that of a direct or indirect influence of Hegel on the genuine avant-garde, though this is evident in Mallarmé and Villiers de l'Isle-Adam, in surrealism, in Brecht. Dialectic and poetic language meet, rather, on common ground.

The common element is the search for an "authentic language"—the language of negation as the Great Refusal to accept the rules of a game in which the dice are loaded. The absent must be made present because the greater part of the truth is in that which is absent. This is Mallarmé's classical statement:

> Je dis: une fleur! et, hors de l'oubli où ma voix relégue aucun contour, en tant que quelque chose d'autre que les calices sus, musicalement se lève, idée même et suave, l'absente de tous bouquets.
> *I say: a flower! and, out of the oblivion where my voice banishes all contours, musically rises, different from every known blossom, the one absent from all bouquets—Idea itself and delicate.*

In the authentic language, the word

> n'est pas l'expression d'une chose, mais l'absence de cette chose. . . . Le mot fait disparaître les choses et nous impose le sentiment d'un manque universel et même de son propre manque.[1]
> *is not the expression of a thing, but rather the absence of this thing. . . . The word makes the things disappear and imposes upon us the feeling of a universal want and even of its own want.*

Poetry is thus the power "de nier les choses" (*to deny the things*)—the power which Hegel claims, paradoxically, for all authentic thought. Valéry asserts:

> La pensée est, en somme, le travail qui fait vivre en nous ce qui n'existe pas.[2]
> *In short, thought is the labor which brings to life in us that which does not exist.*

He asks the rhetorical question: "que sommes-nous donc sans le secours de ce qui n'existe pas?"[3] (*What are we without the help of that which does not exist?*)

This is not "existentialism." It is something more vital and more desperate: the effort to contradict a reality in which all logic and all speech are false to the extent that they are part of a mutilated whole. The vocabulary and grammar of the language of contradiction are still those of the game (there are no others), but the concepts codified in the language of the games are redefined by relating them to their "determinate negation". This term, which denotes the governing principle of dialectical thought, can be explained only in a textual interpretation of Hegel's *Logic*. Here it must suffice to emphasize that, by virtue of this principle, the dialectical contradiction is distinguished from all pseudo- and crackpot opposition, beatnik and hipsterism. The negation is determinate if it refers the established state of affairs to the basic factors and forces which make for its destructiveness, as well as for the possible alternatives beyond the status quo. In the human reality, they are *historical* factors and forces, and the determinate negation is ultimately a *political* negation. As such, it may well find authentic expression in nonpolitical language, and the more so as the entire dimension of politics becomes an integral part of the status quo.

Dialectical logic is critical logic: it reveals modes and contents of thought which transcend the codified pattern of use and validation. Dialectical thought does not invent these contents; they have accrued to the notions in the long tradition of thought and action. Dialectical analysis merely assembles and reactivates them; it recovers tabooed meanings and thus appears almost as a return, or rather a conscious liberation, of the repressed! Since the established universe of discourse is that of an unfree world, dialectical thought is necessarily destructive, and whatever liberation it may bring is a liberation in thought, in theory. However, the divorce of thought from action, of theory from practice, is itself part of the unfree world. No thought and no theory can undo it; but theory may help to prepare the ground for their possible reunion, and the ability of thought to develop a logic and language of contradiction is a prerequisite for this task.

In what, then, lies the power of negative thinking? Dialectical thought has not hindered Hegel from developing his philosophy into a neat and comprehensive system which, in the end, accentuates the positive emphatically. I believe it is the idea of Reason itself which is the undialectical element in Hegel's philosophy This idea of Reason comprehends everything and ultimately absolves everything, because it has its place and function in the whole, and the whole is beyond good and evil, truth and falsehood. It may even be justifiable, logically as well as historically, to define Reason in terms which include slavery, the Inquisition, child labor, concentration camps, gas chambers and nuclear preparedness. These may well have been integral parts of that rationality which has governed the recorded history of mankind. If so, the idea of Reason itself is at stake; it reveals itself as a part rather than as the whole. This does not mean that Reason abdicates its claim to confront reality with the truth about reality. On the contrary, when Marxian theory takes shape as a critique of Hegel's philosophy, it does so in the name of Reason. It is consonant with the innermost effort of Hegel's thought if his own philosophy is "cancelled," not by substituting for Reason some extrarational standards, but by driving Reason itself to recognize the extent to which it is still unreasonable, blind, the victim of unmastered forces. Reason, as the developing and applied knowledge of man—as "free thought"—was instrumental in creating the world we live in. It was also instrumental in sustaining injustice, toil, and suffering. But Reason, and Reason alone, contains its own corrective.

In the *Logic*, which forms the first part of his *System of Philosophy*, Hegel anticipates almost literally Wagner's Parsifal message: "the hand that inflicts the wound is also the hand that heals it."[4] The context is the biblical story of the Fall of Man. Knowledge may have caused the wound in the existence of man, the crime and the guilt; but the second innocence, the "second harmony," can be gained only from knowledge. Redemption can never be the work of a "guileless fool." Against the various obscurantists who insist on the right of the irrational versus Reason, on the truth of the natural versus the intellect, Hegel inseparably links progress in freedom to progress in thought, action to theory. Since he accepted the specific historical form of Reason reached at his time as *the* reality of Reason, the advance beyond this form of Reason must be an advance of Reason itself; and since the adjustment of Reason to oppressive social institutions perpetuated unfreedom, progress in freedom depends on thought becoming political, in the shape of a theory which demonstrates negation as a political alternative implicit in the historical situation. Marx's materialistic "subversion" of Hegel, therefore, was not a shift from one philosophical position to another nor from philosophy to social theory, but rather a recognition that the established forms of life were reaching the stage of their historical negation.

This historical stage has changed the situation of philosophy and of all cognitive thought. From this stage on, all thinking that does not testify to an awareness of the radical falsity of the established forms of life is faulty thinking. Abstraction from this all-pervasive condition is not merely immoral; it is false. For reality has become technological reality, and the subject is now joined with the object so closely that the notion of object necessarily includes the subject. Abstraction from their interrelation no longer leads to a more genuine reality but to deception, because even in this sphere the subject itself is apparently a constitutive part of the object as scientifically determined. The observing, measuring, calculating subject of scientific method, and the subject of the daily business of life—both are expressions of the same subjectivity: man. One did not have to wait for Hiroshima in order to have one's eyes opened to this identity. And as always before, the subject that has conquered matter suffers under the dead weight of his conquest. Those who enforce and direct this conquest have used it to create a world in which the increasing comforts of life and the ubiquitous power of the productive apparatus keep man enslaved to the prevailing state of affairs. Those social groups which dialectical theory identified as the forces of negation are either defeated or reconciled with the established system. Before the power of the given facts, the power of negative thinking stands condemned.

This power of facts is an oppressive power; it is the power of man over man, appearing as objective and rational condition. Against this appearance, thought continues to protest in the name of truth. And in the name of fact: for it is the supreme and universal fact that the status quo perpetuates itself through the constant threat of atomic destruction, through the unprecedented waste of resources, through mental impoverishment, and—last but not least—through brute force. These are the unresolved contradictions. They define every single fact and every single event; they permeate the entire universe of discourse and action. Thus they define also the logic of things: that is, the mode of thought capable of piercing the ideology and of comprehending reality whole. No method can claim a monopoly of cognition, but no method seems authentic which does not recognize that these two propositions are meaningful descriptions of our situation: "The whole is the truth," and the whole is false.

The Sociology of Knowledge and Its Consciousness

By Theodor W. Adorno

Robert Merton, C. Wright Mills et al. repeatedly complained that the sociology of knowledge failed to solve its central problem of specifying the nexus *between social and cognitive structures. Nonetheless, this field has remained limited to techniques of content analysis and correlation studies while failing to explain these categories and correlations other than by recourse to functionalist truisms. For this reason, it is important to point to some of the fundamental reasons for this failure: not imperfect research techniques but the approach itself fails to examine its own categories as problematic (e.g. divisions into popular and classical music, into high and mass culture—these should be the problem rather than the premise on which to classify responses, as Adorno used to complain when he conducted part of the Princeton Radio Research Project with Lazarsfeld). Of necessity, therefore, Mannheim (commonly taken to be the founder of the sociology of knowledge) had to arrive at a leveling pluralism where all ideological positions, all forms of consciousness were alike in that they were the natural correlative of social positions. If he had considered what concretely mediated between social being and consciousness, he might have found a different nexus in every case, depending on* what *social necessities or possibilities were at work. But such a perspective would have required a theory of the emergence of the social constellations which Mannheim, in Adorno's eyes, accepts as givens, just as he does cul-*

made sense, Adorno and Horkheimer argued, that despite his considerable acumen, Mannheim's accepting and conservative stance leads him to assume abstract principles to be the active agents of history, rather than people. Finally, if every ideological position was contingent on a social position, why should the sociology of knowledge be exempt from this postulate?

The sociology of knowledge expounded by Karl Mannheim has begun to take hold in Germany again. For this it can thank its gesture of innocuous skepticism. Like its existentialist counterparts, it calls everything into question and criticizes nothing. Intellectuals who feel repelled by "dogma," real or presumed, find relief in a climate which seems free of bias and assumptions and which offers them in addition something of the pathos of Max Weber's self-conscious and lonely yet undaunted rationality as compensation for their faltering consciousness of their own autonomy. In Mannheim as in his polar opposite, Jaspers, many impulses of Weber's school which were once deeply embedded in the polyhistoric edifice come to light. Most important of these is the tendency to suppress the theory of ideologies in its authentic form. These considerations may justify returning to one of Mannheim's older books, *Man and Society in an Age of Reconstruction.* The work addresses itself to a broader public than does the book on ideology. It cannot be held to each of its formulations. All the greater, however, is the insight it offers into the influence of the sociology of knowledge.

The mentality of the book is "positivistic"; social phenomena are taken "as such" and then classified according to general concepts. In the process, social antagonisms invariably tend to be glossed over. They survive merely as subtle modifications of a conceptual apparatus whose distilled "principles" install themselves autocratically and engage in shadow battles: "The ultimate root of all conflicts in the present age of reconstruction can be seized in a single formula. All down the line tensions arise from the uncontrolled interaction of the 'laisser-faire principle' and the new principle of regulation." As if everything did not depend on who regulates whom. Or, instead of specific groups of people or a specific structure of society, "the irrational" is made responsible for the difficulties of the age. The growth of antagonisms is elegantly described as "the disproportionate development of human capacities," as though it were a question of personalities and not of the anonymous machinery which does away with the individual. Right and wrong are glossed over in like manner;

the "average man" is abstracted from them and assigned an ontological "narrow-mindedness" which "has always been there." Of his "experimental self-observation"—the term is borrowed from more exact sciences—Mannheim frankly confesses: "All these forms of self-observation have the tendency to gloss over and neglect individual differences because they are interested in what is general in man and its variability." Not, however, in his particular situation and in the real transformations he undergoes. In its neutrality, the generalizing order of Mannheim's conceptual world is kindly disposed to the real world; it employs the terminology of social criticism while removing its sting.

The concept of society as such is rendered impotent from the outset by a language which invokes the exceedingly compromised term, "integration." Its occurrence is no accident. Mannheim's use of the concept of the social totality serves not so much to emphasize the intricate dependence of men within the totality as to glorify the social process itself as an evening-out of the contradictions in the whole. In this balance, theoretically, the contradictions disappear, although it is precisely they which comprise the life-process of "society": "Thus it is not immediately evident that an opinion which prevails in society is the result of a process of selection which integrates many similarly directed expressions of life." What disappears in this notion of selection is the fact that what keeps the mechanism creaking along is human deprivation under conditions of insane sacrifice and the continual threat of catastrophe. The precarious and irrational self-preservation of society is falsified and turned into an achievement of its immanent justice or "rationality."

Where there is integration, elites are never far away. The "cultural crisis" to which, in Mannheim, terror and horror are readily sublimated becomes for him the "problem of the formation of elites." He distills four processes in which this problem is supposed to crystallize: the growing number of elites and the resulting enfeeblement of their influence, the destruction of the exclusiveness of elite groups, the change in the process of selection of elites, and the change in their composition. In the first place, the categories employed in this analysis are highly questionable. The positivist who registers the facts *sine ira et studio* is ready to accept the phrases which conceal the facts. One such phrase is the concept of the elite itself. Its untruthfulness consists in the fact that the privileges of particular groups are presented teleologically as the result of some kind of objective process of selection, whereas in fact no one has selected these elites but themselves. In his use of the concept of the elite, Mannheim overlooks social power. He uses the notion "descriptively," in the manner of formal sociology. This allows him to shed only as much light as he wishes on each particular privileged group. At the same time, however, the concept of the elite is employed in such a way that the present emergency can be deduced from above, from some equally "neutral" malfunctioning of the elite-mechanism, without regard to the state of political economy. In the process, Mannheim comes into open conflict with the facts. When he asserts that in "mass democratic" societies, it has become increasingly easy for anyone to gain entrance into any sphere of social influence and that the elites are thereby deprived of "their exclusive character, which is necessary for the development of intellectual and psychological impulses," he is contradicted by the most humble prescientific experience. The deficient homogeneity of the elites is a fiction, one related to those of chaos in the world of values and the disintegration of all stable forms of order. Whoever does not fit in is kept out. Even the differences of conviction which reflect those of real interests serve primarily to obscure the underlying unity which prevails in all decisive matters. Nothing contributes more to this obfuscation than talk of "the cultural crisis," to which Mannheim unhesitatingly adds his voice. It transforms real suffering into spiritual guilt, denounces civilization, and generally works to the advantage of barbarism. Cultural criticism has changed its function. The cultural philistine has long ceased to be the man of progress, the figure with which Nietzsche identified David Friedrich Strauss. Instead, he has learned profundity and pessimism. In their name, he denies the humanity which has become incompatible with his present interests, and his venerable impulse to destruction turns against the products of the culture whose decline he sentimentally bemoans. To the sociologist of the cultural crisis, this matters little. His heroic *ratio* does not even refrain from turning the trite thesis of the demise of the formative power of European art since the end of the Biedermeyer period against modern art in a manner which is both romantic and reactionary.

Accepted along with elite theory is its specific coloration. Conventional notions are joined by naïve respect for that which they represent. Mannheim designates "blood, property and achievement" as the selection principles of the elites. His passion for destroying ideologies does not lead him to consider even once the legitimacy of these principles; he is actually able, during Hitler's lifetime, to speak of a "genuine blood-principle" which is supposed to have formerly

guaranteed "the purity of aristocratic minority stocks and their traditions." From this to the new aristocracy of blood and soil, it is only a
step. Mannheim's general cultural pessimism prevents him from
taking that step. As far as he is concerned, there is still too little blood.
He dreads a "mass democracy" in which blood and property would
disappear as principles of selection; the all too rapid change of elites
would threaten continuity. He is particularly concerned with the fact
that things are no longer quite right with the esoteric doctrine of the
"genuine blood-principle." "It has become democratic and quite
suddenly offers to the great masses of the population the privilege of
social ascendancy without any achievement." Just as the nobility of
the past was never any more noble than anyone else, the aristocracy of
today has neither an objective nor a subjective interest in really
relinquishing the principle of privilege. Elite theory, happy in the
invariant, unites different levels of what sociologists today call social
differentiation, such as feudalism and capitalism, under the heading
"blood-and property-principle"; with equally good humor it separates what belongs together, property and achievement. Max Weber
had shown that the spirit of early capitalism identifies the two, that in a
rationally constituted work process the capacity for achievement can
be measured in terms of material success. The equation of achievement and material success found its psychological manifestation in a
readiness to make success as such a fetish. In Mannheim, this tendency appears in sublimated form as a "status drive." In bourgeois
ideology, property and achievement were first separated when it
became obvious that "achievement" as the economic *ratio* of the
individual no longer corresponded to "property" as its potential
reward. Only then did the bourgeois truly become a *gentilhomme*.
Thus, Mannheim's "mechanisms of selection" are inventions, arbitrarily chosen coordinates distanced from the life-process of actual
society.

　　Conclusions can be drawn from them which bear a fatal resem-
blance to the lax conceptions of Werner Sombart and Ortega y Gasset.
Mannheim speaks of a "proletarianization of the intelligentsia." He is
correct in calling attention to the fact that the cultural market is
flooded; there are, he observes, more culturally qualified (from the
standpoint of formal education, that is) people available than there are
suitable positions for them. This situation, however, is supposed to
lead to a drop in the social value of culture, since it is "a sociological
law that the social value of cultural goods is a function of the social
status of those who produce them." At the same time, he continues,

the "social value" of culture necessarily declines because the recruiting of new members of the intelligentsia extends increasingly to lower social strata, especially that of the petty officialdom. Thus, the notion of the proletarian is formalized; it appears as a mere structure of consciousness, as with the upper bourgeoisie, which condemns anyone not familiar with the rules as a "prole." The genesis of this process is not considered and as a result is falsified. By calling attention to a "structural" assimilation of consciousness to that of the lowest strata of society, he implicitly shifts the blame to the members of those strata and their alleged emancipation in mass democracy. Yet stultification is caused not by the oppressed but by oppression, and it affects not only the oppressed but, in their essentials, the oppressors as well, a fact to which Mannheim paid little attention. The flooding of intellectual vocations is due to the flooding of economic occupations as such, basically, to technological unemployment. It has nothing to do with Mannheim's democratization of the elites, and the reserve army of intellectuals is the last to influence them. Moreover, the sociological law which makes the so-called status of culture dependent on that of those who produce it is a textbook example of a false generalization. One need only recall the music of the eighteenth century, the cultural relevance of which in the Germany of the time stands beyond all doubt. Musicians, except for the *maestri*, primadonnas and *castrati* attached to the courts, were held in low esteem; Bach lived as a subordinate church official and the young Hayden as a servant. Musicians attained social status only when their products were no longer suitable for immediate consumption, when the composer set himself against society as his own master—with Beethoven. The reason for Mannheim's false conclusion lies in the psychologism of his method. The individualistic façade of society concealed from him the fact that its essence consists precisely in developing forms which undergo a process of sedimentation and which reduce individuals to mere agents of objective tendencies. Its disillusioned mien notwithstanding, the standpoint of the sociology of knowledge is pre-Hegelian. Its recourse to a group of organizers, in the case of Mannheim's "law," to the bearers of culture, is based on the somewhat transcendental presupposition of a harmony between society and the individual. The absence of such harmony forms one of the most urgent objects of critical theory, which is a theory of human relations only to the extent that it is also a theory of the inhumanity of those relations.

The distortions of the sociology of knowledge arise from its

method, which translates dialectical concepts into classificatory ones.
Since in each case what is socially contradictory is absorbed into
individual logical classes, social classes as such disappear and the
picture of the whole becomes harmonious. When, for instance, in the
third section of the book, Mannheim distinguishes three levels of
consciousness: chance discovery, invention and planning, he is simply trying to interpret the dialectical scheme of epochs as that of the
fluidly changing modes of behavior of socialized man in general, in
which the determinant oppositions disappear: "It is of course clear
that the line which divides inventive thinking, which is rationally
striving to realize immediate goals, from planned thinking is not a
hard and fast one. No one can say for certain at what degree of
foresight and at what point in the widening radius of conscious
regulation the transition from inventive to planned thinking takes
place." The notion of an unbroken transition from a liberal to a
"planned" society has its correlative in the conception of that transition as one between distinct modes of "thinking." Such a conception
awakens the belief that the historical process is guided by an inherently univocal subject embodying the whole of society. The translation of
dialectical into classificatory concepts abstracts from the conditions of
real social power upon which alone those levels of thought depend.
"The novel contribution of the sociological view of the past and the
present is that it sees history as an area open to experimentation in
regulatory intervention"—as though the possibility of such intervention always corresponded to the level of insight at the time. Such a
levelling off of social struggles into modes of behavior which can be
defined formally and which are made abstract in advance allows
uplifting proclamations concerning the future: "Yet another way
remains open—it is that unified planning will come about through
understanding, agreement and compromise, i.e., that the state of mind
will triumph in the key positions of international society which hitherto has been possible only within a given national group, within whose
enclaves peace was established by such methods." Through the idea
of compromise, the very contradictions which were supposedly resolved through planning are retained; the abstract concept of planning
conceals them in advance and is itself a compromise between the
laissez-faire principle which is preserved in it and the insight into its
insufficiency.

Dialectical concepts cannot be "translated" into the categories
of formal sociology without their truths being impaired. Mannheim
flirts with positivism to the extent that he believes himself able to rely

on objectively given facts, which, however, in his rather lax manner he describes as "unarticulated." These unarticulated facts can then be put through the sociological thought-machine and thus elevated to general concepts. But such classification according to ordering concepts would be an adequate cognitive process only if the facts, which are assumed to be immediately given, could be abstracted from their concrete context as easily as it would appear to the naïve first glance. It is not adequate, however, if social reality has, prior to every theoretical ordering glance, a highly "articulated" structure upon which the scientific subject and the data of his experience depend. As analysis advances, the initial "facts" cease to be descriptive, self-contained data, and sociology is all the less at liberty to classify them to suit its needs. That "facts" must undergo this correction as the theoretical understanding of society proceeds means not so much that new subjective ordering schemes must be devised, as it would seem to naïve experience, as that the data which are presumably given embody more than mere material to be processed conceptually, namely, that they are moulded by the social whole and thus "structured" in themselves. Idealism can be overcome only when the freedom to conceptualize through abstraction is sacrificed. The thesis of the primacy of being over consciousness includes the methodological imperative to express the dynamic tendencies of reality in the formation and movement of concepts instead of forming and verifying concepts in accordance with the demand that they have pragmatic and expedient features. The sociology of knowledge has closed its eyes to this imperative. Its abstractions are arbitrary as long as they merely harmonize with an experience which proceeds by differentiating and correcting. Mannheim does not allow himself the logical conclusion that the "unbiased" registration of facts is a fiction. The social scientist's experience does not give him undifferentiated, chaotic material to be organized; rather, the material of his experience is the social order, more emphatically a "system" than any ever conceived by philosophy. What decides whether his concepts are right or wrong is neither their generality nor, on the other hand, their approximation to "pure" fact, but rather the adequacy with which they grasp the real laws of movement of society and thereby render stubborn facts transparent. In a coordinate-system defined by concepts like integration, elite and articulation, those determining laws and everything they signify for human life appear to be contingent or accidental, mere sociological "differentiations." For this reason, sociology which generalizes and differentiates seems like a mockery of reality It does not recoil before formulations like "disregarding the concentration and centralization of capital." Such abstractions are not "neutral." What a theory regards and what it disregards determines its quality. Were "disregarding" sufficient, one could, for instance, also analyze elites by observing such groups as the vegetarians or the followers of Mazdaznan and then refine this analysis conceptually until its manifest absurdity disappeared. But no corrective could compensate for the fact that the choice of basic categories was false, that the world is not organized according to these categories. All correctives notwithstanding, this falseness would shift the accents so fundamentally that reality would drop out of the concepts; the elites would be "groups of the Mazdaznan form" which happened to be characterized in addition by the possession of "social power." When at one point Mannheim says that "in the cultural sphere (properly also in the economic) there has never been an absolute liberalism, that alongside of the undirected working of the social forces there has always existed, for instance, regulation in education," he is obviously trying to establish a differentiating corrective to the belief that the principle of laissez-faire, long ago exposed as ideology, ever prevailed in an unrestricted manner. But through the choice of an initial concept which is to be differentiated only afterwards, the crucial issue is distorted: the insight that even under liberalism the principle of laissez-faire served only to mask economic control and that accordingly the establishment of "cultural goods" was essentially determined by their conformity with the ruling social interests. The insight into a basic matter of ideology evaporates into mere finesse; instead of directing itself to the concrete in the first place without hypostasizing indispensable general concepts, the method seeks to conciliate by demonstrating that it remembers the concrete too.

The inadequacies of the method become manifest in its poles, the law and the "example." The sociology of knowledge characterizes stubborn facts as mere differentiations and subsumes them under the highest general units; at the same time, it ascribes an intrinsic power over the facts to these arbitrary generalizations, which it calls social "laws," such as the one relating cultural goods to the social status of those who produce them. The "laws" are hypostasized. Sometimes they assume a truly extravagant character: "There is, however, a decisive law which rules us at the present moment. Unplanned spheres regulated by natural selection on the one hand and deliberately organized areas on the other can exist side by side without friction only *as long as the unplanned spheres predominate*"[Mannheim's italics].

Quantified propositions of this form are no more evident than those of Baaderian metaphysics, over which they have the advantage only of a lack of imagination. The falseness of Mannheim's hypostasization of general concepts can be grasped precisely at the point where he interjects the *principia media* to which he debased the laws of dialectical movement: "However much we must take the *principia media* and the corresponding concepts ('late capitalism,' 'structural unemployment,' 'lower-middle-class ideology,' etc.) as concrete expressions of a special historical setting, it should nevertheless be borne in mind that what we are doing is differentiating and individualizing abstract and general determinants (general factors). The *principia media* are in a certain sense nothing but temporary groups of general factors so closely intertwined that they operate as a single causal factor. That we are essentially dealing here with general factors in an historical and individual setting is evident from our example. Our first observation implies the general principle of the functioning of a social order with freely contracting legal personalities; the second, the psychological effect of unemployment in general, and the last, the general law that hopes of social advancement tend to affect individuals in a way which obscures their real social position." It is just as mistaken, Mannheim continues, to believe that conceptions of man in general are valid in themselves as "to neglect or ignore the general principles of the human psyche within the concrete modes of behavior of these historical types." Accordingly, the historical event seems to be determined in part by "general," in part by "particular" causes which together form some sort of "group." This, however, implies the confusion of levels of abstraction with causes. Mannheim sees the decisive weakness of dialectical thought in its misunderstanding of "general forces"—as if the commodity forms were not "general" enough for all the questions with which he deals. "General forces," however, are not independent in opposition to "particular" ones, as though a concrete event were "caused" once by a causal proposition and then again by the specific "historical situation." No event is caused by general forces, much less by laws; causality is not the "cause" of events but rather the highest conceptual generality under which concrete causal factors can be subsumed. The significance of the observation Newton made on the falling apple is not that the general law of causality "acts" within a complex which includes factors of a lower degree of abstraction. Causality operates only in the particular and not in addition to it. Only to this extent can the falling apple be called "an example of the law of gravity," the law of gravity is as much dependent on the falling of this apple as vice-versa. The concrete play of forces can be reduced to schemata of varying levels of generality, but it is not a question of a conjunction of "general" and "particular" forces. Mannheim's pluralism, of course, which conceives what is crucial as merely *one* perspective among many, is hardly eager to give up its sums of general and particular factors.

The fact, baptized in advance as a "unique situation," thereby becomes a mere example of these forces. Dialectical theory, in contrast, can no more accept the concept of the example as valid than could Kant. Examples function as convenient and interchangeable illustrations; hence they are often chosen at a comfortable distance from the true concerns of mankind today, or they are pulled, as it were, out of a hat. But they are quickly forced to pay the consequences. Mannheim writes, for instance: "An illuminating example of the disturbances which can arise from substantial irrationality may be seen where, for example, the diplomatic staff of a state has carefully thought out a series of actions and has agreed on certain steps, when suddenly one of its members falls prey to a nervous collapse and then acts contrary to the plan, thereby destroying it." It is useless to portray such private events as "factors"; not only is the "radius of action" of the individual diplomat romantically overestimated, but also unless the blunder itself served the course of political developments stronger than the diplomats' considerations, it could be corrected in five minutes over the telephone. Or, with the pictorial vividness of a children's book, Mannheim writes: "As a soldier, I must control my impulses and desires to a quite different degree than as a free hunter whose acts are only periodically purposive and who will only occasionally need to take hold of himself—for instance, at the moment when he has to fire at his prey." As is generally known, the occupation of hunter has in recent years been replaced by the sport of hunting, but even the sportsman who takes hold of himself only "at the moment when he has to fire at his prey," apparently in order not to be startled by the crack of his own rifle, will hardly bag much, probably frighten away his prey, and perhaps not even find it. The insignificance of such examples is closely related to the influence the sociology of knowledge has had. Selected for their subjective neutrality and therefore inessential in advance, the examples serve to distract. Sociology originated in the impulse to criticize the principles of the society with which it found itself confronted; the sociology of knowledge settles for reflections on hunters dressed in green and diplomats in black.

The direction in which, in terms of content, the formalism of such conceptualization tends reveals itself when programmatic demands are voiced. An "optimum" for the thorough organization of society is demanded, but no thought is given to the gap that would have to be breached to attain such an optimum. If things are only put together rationally, everything will fall into place. Mannheim's ideal of a "desired direction" between "unconscious conservatism" and "misdirected utopianism" corresponds to this: "We can see at the same time, however, the general outline of a possible solution to the present tension, namely, a sort of authoritarian democracy making use of planning and creating a stable system from the present conflict of principles." This is in accordance with the stylistic elevation of the "crisis" to a "human problem," in which Mannheim shows himself in agreement with modern German anthropologists, his declaration against them notwithstanding, and with the existentialist philosophers. Two characteristics more than all others, however, reveal the conformism of Mannheim's sociology of knowledge. First, it remains concerned with symptoms. It is thoroughly disposed to overestimate the significance of ideologies as opposed to what they represent. It placidly shares with them precisely that equivocal conception of "the irrational" to which the critical lever should be applied: "We must, moreover, realize that the irrational is not always harmful but that, on the contrary, it is among the most valuable powers in man's possession when it acts as a driving force towards rational or objective ends, creates cultural values through sublimation and cultivation, or, as pure élan, heightens the joy of living without breaking up the social order by lack of planning." There are no further hints as to the nature of this irrational, which is said to produce cultural values through cultivation, although such values are by definition the product of cultivation, or to "heighten" the joy of living, which is irrational anyway. In any case, however, the equation of the instincts with the irrational is ominous, for the concept is applied in "value-free" manner both to the libido and to the forms its repression takes. The irrational seems to endow ideologies with substantiality in Mannheim. They receive a paternal reproof but are left intact; what they conceal is never exposed. But the vulgar materialism of prevailing praxis is closely related to this positivistic tendency to accept symptoms uncritically, this perceptible respect for the claims of ideology. The façade remains intact in the glow of amenable observation, and the ultimate wisdom of this sociology is that no impulse could arise within the interior which could seriously threaten to proceed beyond its carefully marked bounds: "In actual fact, the existing body of ideas (and the same applies to vocabulary) never exceeds the horizon and the radius of activity of the society in question." Whatever "exceeds" the limits, to be sure, can easily be seen as "adjustment to the emotional evocation of spiritual values, etc.". This materialism, akin to that of the family head who considers it utterly impossible for his offspring to have a new thought, since everything has already been thought, and hence recommends that he concentrate on earning a respectable living, this seasoned and arrogant materialism is the reverse image of the idealism in Mannheim's view of history, an idealism to which he also remains true in other respects, especially in his conceptions of "rationality" and progress, an idealism according to which changes in consciousness are even capable of lifting "the structural principle of society off its hinges from the inside out, so to speak."

The real attraction of the sociology of knowledge can be sought only in the fact that those changes in consciousness, as achievements of "planning reason," are linked directly to the reasoning of today's planners: "The fact that the complex actions of a functional, thoroughly rationalized society can be thought through only in the heads of a few organizers assures the latter of a key position in society." The motif which becomes apparent here extends beyond the consciousness of the sociology of knowledge. The objective spirit, as that of those "few organizers," speaks through it. While the sociology of knowledge dreams of new academic fields to conquer, it unsuspectingly serves those who have not hesitated a moment to abolish those fields. Mannheim's reflections, nourished by liberal common sense, all amount to the same thing in the end—recommending social planning without ever penetrating to the foundations of society. The consequences of the absurdity which has now become obvious and which Mannheim sees only superficially as a "cultural crisis," are to be mollified from above, that is, by those who control the means of production. This means, however, simply that the liberal, who sees no way out, makes himself the spokesman of a dictatorial arrangement of society even while he imagines he is opposing it. Of course, the sociology of knowledge will reply that the ultimate criterion for judging planning is not power but reason and that reason includes the task of converting the powerful. Nevertheless, since the Platonic philosopher-kings it had been clear what such a conversion involves. The answer to Mannheim's reverence for the intelligentsia as "free-floating" is to be found not in the reactionary postulate of its "rootedness in Being" but rather in the reminder that the very intelligentsia that pretends to float freely is fundamentally rooted in the very being that must be changed and which it merely pretends to criticize. For it the rational is the optimal functioning of the system, which postpones the catastrophe without asking whether the system in its totality is not in fact the optimum in irrationality. In totalitarian systems of every kind, planning directed at maintaining the system leads to the barbarous suppression below the surface of the contradictions it inevitably produces. In the name of reason, the advocates of planning turn power over to those who already possess it in the name of mystification. The power of reason today is the blind reason of those who currently hold power. But as power moves towards the catastrophe it induces the mind which denies it with moderation to abdicate to it. It still calls itself liberal, to be sure, but for it freedom has already become "from the sociological point of view nothing but a disproportion between the growth of the radius of effective central control on the one hand and the size of the group unit to be influenced on the other." The sociology of knowledge sets up indoctrination camps for the homeless intelligentsia where it can learn to forget itself.

On Science and Phenomenology

By Herbert Marcuse

Written at a time when, following Thomas Kuhn's The Structure of
Scientific Revolutions, *the philosophy of science was rediscovering
the historical contingency of its paradigms, Marcuse here focuses n
the central presuppositions of the category of "reason." Reason had
not always been defined as a mere tool to devise efficient means to
implement values, which themselves remain beyond rational
discussion and challenge. Rather, it was once the distinguishing mark
of reason to formulate, examine, implement and modify the ends on
the basis of emerging historical possibilities. It was this usurpation of
substantive reason, its reduction to paradigmatic rules of deductive
inference that the critical theorists consistently fought. Intended as a
critique of a position that has recently again received attention, the
essay unfolds the historical origins and manifestations of the concept
of reason, from the days of reason as the basis for transforming the
world which gave rise to science to the point where the structuring
ends and objectives have been exiled from the self-awareness of
science.*

The Crisis of European Science and Transcendental Phenomenology
is Husserl's last work. Written in the thirties, the first part was
published in 1936, the second part only after Husserl's death.

I would like to indicate first where I see the general historical
locus of this work. It seems to me that we have to place it into the
context of the radical reexamination of the Western concept of Rea-

son, of Western rationality that begins in the last decades of the nineteenth century and to which so essentially different thinkers as Bergson, Dilthey, Max Weber, Spengler, Piaget and Bachelard belong. All of them have in common this questioning of the very idea which has guided Western thought since its Greek origins, i.e., the rationality typical of the occident. It seems to me that Husserl is the last in this group, and in a certain sense, (which may strike you as strange) the most radical of these re-examiners. In Husserl, it is modern science itself, this most sacrosanct child of Western rationality, that is questioned. In this reexamination, modern science appears as the end of a fateful development which begins with Greek thought, that is, with the origins of Western thought itself—as the "end" of this development in the twofold sense of termination and of fulfilling the *telos*, the purpose, the objective of this thought.

According to Husserl, science—modern science, Galilean as well as post-Galilean—originates in the Greek idea of knowledge and truth and comes to rest in a scientific rationality in which truth and validity contain in themselves illusion and repression. Before I try to present Husserl's radical thesis, I have to stress that it is not the result of a sociological analysis or of a sociology of knowledge. It is precisely the fascinating aspect of Husserl's work that it is a *philosophical* analysis within the academic framework of intellectual history, even within the academic division of labor. Husserl emphasizes philosophy as *Beruf*, as calling, and that philosophy is done in the *Berufszeit*, that is to say, in the time reserved, in the academic division, for such investigations. Husserl adds (and this is important: I come back to it at the end) that the calling of the philosopher is a unique calling because (and I quote him)

> this calling is linked with the "possibility of a radical transformation of humanity," and not only a radical transformation of humanity but also a "liberation," and this possibility makes the calling of the philosopher unique within the division of labor.[1]

In the course of such a philosophical undertaking (philosophical also in the sense of a discipline!), in the course of its own inner development, Husserl's analysis transcends itself, or rather it, descends from the pure theoretical to the impure pre-theoretical, practical dimension. Better—the pure theoretical analysis discovers its own internal impurity, but only to return from this impure sphere to the still pure theoretical dimension of transcendental phenomenology as constituent of the practical, pre-theoretical dimension, the *Lebenswelt*. (I use the German term *Lebenswelt*. The literal translation "life-world" is too large and too vague in this context; what Husserl means is our own empirical day-to-day world as it is given in immediate experience, practical and other—the world of life and death, in our empirical reality. So I will use either *Lebenswelt* or "empirical reality").

I will now devote some time to presenting Husserl's own thesis (the work is not fully translated; we only have Gurwitsch's excellent abstract of it), but I shall focus it in such a way that the critical problems stand out. Husserl begins with a very brief description of what he considers the Greek concept of Reason, namely the idea of human being as self-determination and determination of its world by virtue of man's intellectual faculties, the concept of Reason, according to which man's intellectual faculties are at the same time capable of determining his own life and of determining, defining and changing the universe. This conception presupposes that the universe itself which is thus rationally comprehended is in its very structure a rational system and therefore accessible to knowledge and change on the grounds of man's own rational knowledge. In other words, Reason for the Greeks is objective and subjective at one and the same time, and on this basis, Reason is the subjective as well as objective instrument for changing the world in accord with man's rational faculties and ends. But in this process, Reason itself as *theoria* is and remains the basis of the transformation of the world. Philosophy is thus established as *science*, and as the first, most excellent and general science, which must give direction and the end to all other sciences.

What are the implications of this original concept of Reason? First, it implies a supra-factual, supra-temporal validity of Reason, so that the really real as discovered and defined by Reason is rational as *against* the immediately given fact. Reason establishes an authority and reality which is in this way antagonistic to the immediately given facts. Secondly, true being is ideational being (a conclusion from the first implication), not being as we experience it immediately in the flux of our empirical, practical world. Thus "Platonism" is the basis of all scientific knowledge. Thirdly, objectivity is necessarily correlated with subjectivity, again the subjective as well as objective structure of Reason. Husserl here gives a formulation which, in an entirely different context, recaptures the very question and thesis with which Western philosophy began, namely, the final identity of Being and Reason. He says:

Can Being and Reason be separated if cognitive Reason determines (the essence of being?)[2]

So we find at the very beginning and at the late stage of western
philosophy this almost literal identity in the formulation of the basic
problem, the mysterious union and even identity of Reason and Being,
Knowing and Being. Now this concept of Reason, which is theoretical
and practical Reason in one, is understood by Husserl as a *project*. I
use the term here as it was elaborated in the philosophy of Sartre:
"project" in the sense that this idea of rationality and its application is
a specific way of experiencing, interpreting, organizing and changing
the world, a specific historical project among other possible ones, not
the only, necessary project. This project, according to Husserl, came
to fulfillment with the foundation of modern science, namely, in
Galileo's mathematization of nature. Galileo's mathematization of
nature established that purely rational, ideational system which was
the dream of all Platonism; Galileo established the ideational world
mathematically as the true reality, substituting this scientific universe
for the only given reality, namely, our empirical *Lebenswelt*. But the
very fulfillment of this project was also its collapse, according to
Husserl. For this scientific rationality, this idea of Reason and its
application, proved successful only in the positive sciences and in the
technological conquest of Nature, while the original foundation of this
entire science, that which originally was supposed to constitute the
very structure, content and end of science, namely, philosophy,
remained an impotent, abstract, meaningless metaphysical sphere of
knowledge and continued in this impotent form a hopeless academic
existence which, in addition, was more and more dissolved into
psychology. Thus separated from the basic philosophy which, according to the original ideas of Reason, was supposed to give the ends,
the objectives, the meaning of science, separated from this basic
philosophy which was supposed to provide the truly universal concepts, Reason was at the same time divorced—and this is decisive for
Husserl—from that rational *humanitas* envisaged in the original
philosophical project. Scientific, technological rationality became
reason *kath' exochen*. Divorced from the validating "ends" set by
philosophy, the rationale set by science and the rationale of its development and progress became that of the *Lebenswelt* itself, in which
and for which this science developed.[3] Instead of rationally transcending the *Lebenswelt*, science comprehended, expressed and extended
the specific rationale of the *Lebenswelt*, namely, the ever more

effective mastery of the environment (*Herrschaft über die praktische Umwelt*), including the ever more effective mastery of man.[4] But that was not the inherent *telos* of science, which was first and foremost, and not only in a chronological sense, the *telos* defined by the empirical reality in which science developed. Thus, theoretical Reason, pure Reason, without losing its scientific character as theory, becomes practical Reason. Theory, by virtue of its internal dynamic rather than on external grounds, becomes a specific, historical practice. But (and this is decisive for Husserl and the justification of his own subsequent phenomenological reduction) this entire development, this entire transformation of Reason, this essential, structural, internal commitment of pure Reason, pure theory and pure science to the empirical reality in which they originated, this entire transformation *remains hidden to science itself*, hidden and unquestioned. The new science does not elucidate the conditions and the limits of its evidence, validity and method; it does not elucidate its inherent historical denominator. It remains unaware of its own foundation, and it is therefore unable to recognize its servitude, unable to free itself from the ends set and given to science by the pre-given empirical reality. I should like to stress again, because these formulations can be easily misunderstood, that it is not a sociological relation which is here established between an empirical reality and the pure science which develops in this empirical reality. Husserl's concept goes much farther. He maintains that the empirical reality is the framework and dimension in which the pure scientific concepts develop. In other words, the empirical reality constitutes, in a specific sense, the very concepts which science believes are pure theoretical concepts.

Before I go on with Husserl's interpretation of this development, I would like to reformulate and to extend his thesis in a way which may bring out its provocative implications. What happens in the developing relation between science and the empirical reality is the abrogation of the transcendence of Reason. Reason loses its philosophical power and its scientific right to define and project ideas and modes of Being beyond and against those established by the prevailing reality. I say "beyond" the empirical reality, not in any metaphysical but in a historical sense, namely, in the sense of projecting essentially different, historical alternatives.

Now back to Husserl's interpretation.

The new science (by which he understands mainly Galilean science) establishes a rational "infinite" universe of Being (I follow his words here literally), systematically organized and defined by science itself. Within this universe, every object becomes accessible to knowledge, not incidentally, in its contingent, particular occurrence, but necessarily and in its very essence.[5] Thus, it becomes object of scientific knowledge, not as this individual object but as exemplification of general objectivity (the falling feather as *res extensa* in motion).[6] That is to say, the concrete and particular object, the Aristotelian totality is no longer the *Wesen*, the essence; Platonism supersedes Aristotelianism, not only in physics, but in the very concept of scientific rationality. And concomitant with this de-individualization, which is the pre-requisite for the quantification of the scientific universe, is the familiar reduction of secondary to primary qualities, devaluation of the inexorably individual sense experience as nonrational.[7]

As a result of this twofold process, reality is now idealized into a "mathematical manifold": everything which is mathematically demonstrated with the evidence of universal validity as a pure form (*reine Gestalt*) now belongs to the true reality of nature.[8] But (and here is the great gap which separates the new science from its classical original) in contrast to the ideational forms of Plato, the ideational forms of mathematical physics are freed from any substantive connection with other than mathematical ends. The ideational realm of Galilean science no longer includes the moral, esthetic, political Forms, the *Ideas* of Plato. And separated from this realm, science develops now as an "absolute" in the literal sense no matter how relative within its own realm it may be, absolved from its own, pre-scientific and nonscientific conditions and foundations. According to Husserl, the absolute evidence of mathematics (which as we shall see we question) was for Galileo so self-evident that he never asked for the actual foundation of its validity, for the validating ground of this evidence, and of its extension to the whole of nature. Thus, the validation of the new science remained in the dark; its own basis never became the theme of scientific inquiry; science contained an unmastered, unscientific foundation. This is of the utmost importance for *the validity of science* itself, because the relation between science and the pre-scientific empirical reality is for Husserl not an external one but one which affects the very structure and meaning of the scientific concepts themselves.

Now according to Husserl, where is this pre-scientific validating ground of mathematical science? It is originally in geometry as the art of measuring (*Messkunst*) with its specific means and possibilities.[9] This art of measuring in the empirical reality promised and indeed achieved the progressive calculability of nature, subjecting nature to the ever more exact "foresight" in mastering and using nature. (Foresight—*Voraussicht*, perhaps better translated as projection and valid, rational anticipation). Foresight and anticipation, rational anticipation can then guide the practical orientation in and the transformation of the empirical *Lebenswelt*, without however (and this is decisive) setting or defining or changing the goals and ends of this transformation. Geometry can and does furnish (and the same holds true for the extension of geometry, mathematics) the methods and ever more exact, ever more calculable approaches for the transformation and extension of the established *Lebenswelt*, but remains forever incapable of defining, anticipating or changing, by its own concepts, the ends and objectives of this transformation. In its method and concepts, the new science is essentially non-transcendent. This is what I consider as Husserl's key sentence: Science "leaves the *Lebenswelt* in its essential structure in its own concrete causality unchanged."[10]

As to the interpretation of this paradoxical and provocative thesis (so obviously paradoxical since we are used to seeing in science one of the most dynamic forces in the world): In my view, what is at stake is not the more or less external relation between science and society, but the internal conceptual structure of science itself, its pure theory and method which Husserl now reveals in their essential historicity (*Geschichtlichkeit*), in their commitment to the specific historical project in which they originated.[11] Pure science retains, *aufgehoben* (to use Hegel's term now), the practice out of which it arose, and it contains the ends and values established by this practice. The empirical reality thus performs the *sinngebende Leistung* (constituent act): It is constitutive of scientific truth and validity. Science is *Aufhebung der Lebenswelt*

(1) inasmuch as science cancels the data and truth of immediate experience,

(2) inasmuch as science preserves the data and truth of experience, but

(3) preserves them in a higher form, namely in the ideational, idealized form of universal validity.

And this threefold process takes place in the scientific abstraction. The quantified ideational forms are abstracted from the concrete qualities of the empirical reality, but the latter remains operative in the very concepts and in the direction in which the scientific abstraction moves.

In this way, the pre-scientific, pregiven empirical reality enters the scientific enterprise itself and makes it a specific project within the pre-established general project of the empirical reality. However, the abstract, ideational, mathematical form into which science transforms the empirical conceals this historical relation:

> The *Ideenkleid* (the ideational veil) of mathematics and mathematical physics represents and [at the same time] disguises the empirical reality and leads us to take for True Being that which is only a method.[12]

This is perhaps the most effective and lasting mystification in the history of Western thought! What is actually only one method appears as the true reality, but a reality with a *telos* of its own. The mathematical ideation, with all its exactness, calculability, foresight, leaves a void (*Leerstelle*) because the objectives and ends of this calculability and anticipation are not scientifically determined. This void can thus be filled by whatever specific end the empirical reality provides, the only condition being that it is within the range of scientific method. This is the famous neutrality of pure science which here reveals itself as an illusion, because the neutrality disguises, in the mathematical-ideational form, the essential relation to the pregiven empirical reality.

In Husserl's terms: The objective a priori of science itself stands under a hidden empirical a priori, the so-called *lebensweltliche* a priori.[13] Moreover, as long as this empirical a priori remains hidden and unexamined, scientific rationality itself contains its inner and own irrational core which it cannot master. According to Husserl, modern science thus operates like a machine which everyone can learn to handle without necessarily understanding the inner necessity and possibility of its operation.[14] In other words, pure science has an inherently instrumental character prior to all specific application; the Logos of pure science is technology and is thus essentially dependent on external ends. This introduces the irrational into science, and science cannot overcome its irrationality as long as it remains hidden from science. In Husserl's words: Reason is Reason only as manifest Reason (*offenbare Vernunft*), and Reason "knows itself as Reason only if it has become manifest."[15] Inasmuch as Reason remains non-manifest in science, scientific rationality is not yet the full rationality of science. How can Reason become conscious of itself?

Husserl proposes to break the mystification inherent in modern science by a phenomenological analysis which is in a literal sense a *therapeutic* method. The therapeutic in the sense that it is to get behind the mystifying concepts and methods of science and to uncover the constitutive *lebensweltliche* a priori under which all scientific a priori stands. This is to Husserl first a methodological problem. The pre-given empirical reality as a whole must become the object of the philosophical analysis, otherwise the a priori prior to the scientific a priori could never come to light. But obviously philosophy itself is part of this empirical reality and philosophy itself stands under the a priori of the empirical reality. The circle is to be broken by a dual phenomenological reduction (suspension, *epoche*): First the suspension of the objective a priori; the suspension of scientific truth and validity; secondly the suspension of the *lebensweltliche* a priori, of the *doxa* and its validity.

Now what do we retain, what remains as the residuum of this twofold suspension? In the first *epoche*, "we put in brackets" (that is to say, we do not deny but simply suspend judgment on) scientific truth and scientific validity. What remains as the residuum is (a) the entire general structure of the empirical reality, [16] the infinite manifold of things in time and space, the orta, and (b) the world itself in which all these things necessarily appear—the world as the universal, unsurpassable horizon of all particular objects. But this first *epoche* is not sufficient: it cannot do what it is supposed to do, namely, break through the mystification and uncover the ultimate foundation of scientific truth. It cannot do this because with this first "bracketing" we are still on the basis (*auf dem Boden*) of the empirical reality, within the "natural position" of our day-to-day experience. A second *epoche* is necessary which "at one stroke" leads to a total alteration of the "natural position" of experience, to the suspension of the natural validation of everything that we naturally accept as valid in our immediate experience. [17] Once we have suspended these judgments too, we reflect no longer on the pregiven world and the particular objects appearing in it, but on *how* these objects appear, on the *modes* in which this entire world is given to us. The residuum of this *epoche* is thus the world as correlate of a totality of *modes of consciousness*, as a "synthetic totality." What we have now as residuum is the *transcendental* subjectivity, [18] and to this transcendental subjectivity the world is now given as phenomenon of and for an absolute subjectivity. [19] This transcendental subjectivity is no longer any particular or individual or group subjectivity. It is "absolute" because whatever object or object-relation may appear, now appears as necessarily constituted in specific acts of synthesis which inseparably link objectivity and subjectivity. In other words, we have now what we might call the absolute original experience: the experience which is at the origin of and is constitutive of any possible objectivity that can ever become the object of scientific and of any other thought. The phenomenological reduction has now opened the dimension in which the original and most general structure of all objectivity is constituted.

I shall add only a few critical remarks. The breakthrough to the transcendental subjectivity is supposed to be the road to uncover the foundation on which all scientific validity rests. I ask the question: can the reductive phenomenological analysis ever attain its goal, namely, to go behind scientific, and pre-scientific, validity and mystification? I shall offer three suggestions.

First: The phenomenological analysis is confronted with the fact of reification (Husserl does not use this term). Reification is a form which is usually not examined. Scientific as well as pre-scientific experience are false, incomplete inasmuch as they experience as *objective* (material or ideational) what in reality is subject-object, objectivation of subjectivity. In founding the analysis on the constitutive subject-object correlation, Husserl's dual *epoche* does go behind the reification—but so does all transcendental idealism. Thus far we are, in my view, in no way beyond Kant. I know Husserl's own interpretation of the difference between phenomenology and Kant; I think that in the context of my criticism this difference is not very relevant. My point is that the phenomenological breakthrough stops short of the *actual* constituent subjectivity. Husserl transcends the objective a priori of science in the first *epoche* and the empirical a priori in the second *epoche*. He thus creates a conceptual metalanguage for the critical analysis of the empirical reality. But my question is : does this conceptual metalanguage really come to grips with the constituent subjectivity? I think not.

Second: The phenomenological reduction arrives at a subjectivity which constitutes only the most general forms of objectivity, for example, the general form of appearing as object, changing as object, being related to other objects. But does this subjectivity give us "manifest Reason" behind the disguising Reason, the validation of scientific truth? Can this transcendental subjectivity ever explain—and solve—the crisis of European science? Husserl's transcendental subjectivity is again a pure cognitive subjectivity. One does not have to be a Marxist in order to insist that the empirical reality is constituted by the subject of thought *and* of *action*, theory and practice. Husserl recognizes the historical subject in its *sinngebende Leistung*; but then, by suspending, bracketing it, the phenomenological analysis creates its own a priori, its own ideation, and its own ideological veil. Pure philosophy now replaces pure science as the ultimate cognitive law-giver, establishing objectivity. This is the *hubris* inherent in all critical transcendentalism which in turn must be cancelled. Husserl himself seems to have been aware of this *hubris*. He speaks of the philosopher as "*urquellend fungierende Subjektivität*": the philosopher functions as the primordial source of what can rationally be claimed as objective reality.

I come to the conclusion and leave it as a question. Husserl recognizes the fetishism of scientific universality and rationality by uncovering the specific historical-practical foundations of pure science. He sees that pure science is in its very structure technological— at least potentially applied science. The scientific method itself remains dependent on a specific *Lebenswelt*. This is the hidden irrational element in scientific rationality. Husserl finds the reason for this dependence in the loss of the philosophical dimension, which was originally the basic dimension of science. Classical philosophy defined the method and function of science in terms of an idea of Reason which claimed higher truth and validity than those embodied in, and established by, the given empirical reality. This validating idea of Reason was that of the *telos* of man as man, the realization of *humanitas*. According to Husserl, the humanistic structure of Reason collapses with the release of science from this philosophical foundation. This would imply that humanism becomes an ideology at the very time when modern humanism is born. In other words, the birth hour of humanism itself would be the degradation of humanism to a mere ideology. Apparently there must be something wrong with this formulation. The fact remains that humanism is still today an ideology, a higher value which little affects the inhuman character of reality. The question with which I would like to conclude is this: Is philosophy entirely innocent of this development, or does it perhaps share the *hubris* of science? Does it share the reluctance to examine its own real foundation and function and is it therefore equally guilty of failing in the task of *Theoria*, of Reason—to promote the realization of *humanitas*?

The Method and Function of an Analytic Social Psychology

Notes on Psychoanalysis and Historical Materialism

By Erich Fromm

The first in a series of manifestolike statements on the merger of Marx and Freud, Fromm's 1932 essay lifted this debate out of the ideological realm and focused it on the possible cross-fertilization of the two, regardless of their contemporary orthodox manifestations. To assess the climate in which this attempt took place, one need only recall the bitter ouster of Wilhelm Reich from both the Communist party and the International Psychoanalytic Association. The first, having declared Pavlovian psychology to be the only one compatible with dialectical materialism, rejected what they understood as the bourgeois subjectivism of psychoanalysis; the latter objected to the deterministic, mechanistic and leveling thrust of the official Communist doctrine of the day.

    For unorthodox Marxists, who could not accept the official simplistic doctrine of superstructures and consciousness being mere "reflections" of the base (whatever that meant), one central question remained open: what was the nature of the "link between economic and cultural factors"? Especially in the problematic realm of class consciousness, this question became a central issue for members of

the Institute. Fromm, who joined the Institute in 1931 when they began
to publish the Zeitschrift für Sozialforschung, began by suggesting
that drives, far from being subjective, "are active and passive
adaptations" to socioeconomic situations. And as Freud himself had
explained these adaptations through the history of the individual, this
history only needed to be extended to include the class background,
the specific pressures, needs, possibilities which that class was
experiencing as a social whole.

Ironically, Fromm who in his early stages had reflected or ignored
Freud's metapsychology, himself later joined Karen Horney, Harry
Stack Sullivan et al. in what Adorno and Marcuse were to chide as
"Freudian revisionism"—the assumption of noncontingent, basic
needs.

Psychoanalysis is a materialistic psychology which should be classed among the natural sciences. It points to instinctual drives and needs as the motive force behind human behavior, these drives being produced by physiologically based *instincts* that are not directly observable in themselves. Psychoanalysis has shown that man's conscious psychic activity is only a relatively small sector of his psychic life, that many decisive impulses behind psychic behavior are unconscious. In particular, it has unmasked individual and collective ideologies as the expression of specific wishes and needs rooted in the instincts and shows that our "moral" and idealistic motives are in some measure the disguised and rationalized expression of instinctual drives.

Quite in line with the popular division of instincts into those of hunger and love, Freud began by assuming that two groups, the instincts for self-preservation and the sexual instincts,[1] served as the real motive force behind man's psychic life. He labeled the energy inherent in the sexual instincts as libido, and the psychic processes deriving from this energy as libidinous.[2] With respect to the sexual instincts, Freud extended the ordinary use of this term and included under it all the urges which, like the genital impulses, are physically conditioned, attached to certain *erogenous zones* of the body, and seek for pleasurable tension-release.

Freud assumes that the chief principle of psychic activity is the "pleasure principle," that is, the urge to discharge instinctual tensions in a way that will bring the maximum amount of pleasure. This pleasure principle is modified by the "reality principle": taking reality into account may lead us to renounce or postpone pleasure in order to avoid a greater discomfort or to gain even greater pleasure at some future time.

Freud sees the specific instinctual structure of the individual conditioned by two factors: his inherited physical constitution and his life experiences—in particular, the experiences of early childhood. Freud proceeds on the assumption that man's inherited constitution and life experiences form a "complementary chain" and that the specific task of analysis is to explore and uncover the influence of life experiences on the inherited instinctual constitution. Thus the analytic method is exquisitely historical: *it seeks to understand the drive structure through the understanding of life history*. This method is valid for the psychic life of healthy people as well as for the sick and neurotic. What distinguishes the neurotic from the "normal" person is the fact that the latter has successfully adapted his instinctual structure to his real needs in life, while the former's instinctual structure has run up against certain obstacles that hinder him from satisfactorily adapting it to reality.

In order to make as clear as possible that sex instincts can be modified and adapted to reality, we must point out certain character-istics which clearly distinguish them from the instincts for self-preser-vation. For example, unlike the instincts for self-preservation, the sex instincts are postponable. The former are more imperative because if they are left unsatisfied too long, death will ensue; in short, prolonged postponement of their satisfaction is psychologically intolerable. This means that the instincts for self-preservation have primacy over the sex instincts—not that they play a greater role in themselves, but in case of conflict they are more urgent.

In addition, the sex-rooted drives can be repressed, while the desires emanating from the instincts for self-preservation cannot sim-ply be removed from consciousness and placed in the unconscious. Another important distinction between the two groups of instincts is the fact that the sexual instincts can be sublimated: in other words, instead of being satisfied directly, a sexual wish can be satisfied in a way that may be far removed from the original sexual goal and blended with other ego accomplishments. The instincts for self-pres-ervation are not capable of such sublimation. Furthermore, the drives toward self-preservation must be satisfied by real, concrete means, while the sex drives can often be satisfied by pure fantasies. A man's hunger can only be satisfied by food; his desire to be loved, however, can be satisfied by fantasies about a good and loving God, and his sadistic tendencies can be satisfied by sadistic spectacles and fantasies.

A final important distinction is that the sex drives, unlike the drives toward self-preservation, can find expression in ways that are highly interchangeable and replaceable. If one instinctual drive is not satisfied, it can be replaced by others whose satisfaction is possible for either internal or external reasons. The interchangeability and replaceability of the sex drives is one of the keys to understanding both neurotic and healthy psychic life, and it is a cornerstone of the psychoanalytic theory. But it is also a social fact of the highest significance. It permits the masses to be offered (and satisfied by) those precise satisfactions that are socially available and desirable from the standpoint of the ruling classes.[3]

Summing up, it can be said that the sexual instincts, which can be postponed, repressed, sublimated and interchanged, are much more elastic and flexible than the instincts for self-preservation. The former lean on the latter, and follow their lead.[4] The greater flexibility and changeability of the sex instincts does not mean, however, that they can be left unsatisfied permanently; there is not only a physical but also a psychic minimum existence, and the sex instincts must be satisfied to some minimal extent. The differences between the two groups of drives, as we have noted them here, suggests rather that the sex instincts can make great adaptations to the real possibilities for satisfaction that exist, that is, to the concrete conditions of life. They grow and develop through this adaptation, and only in neurotic individuals do we find disturbances in this capacity for adaptation. Psychoanalysis has specifically pointed to the modifiability of the sex drives. It has taught us to understand the individual's instinctual structure in terms of his life experiences, to see how the former has been influenced by the latter. *The active and passive adaptation of the biological apparatus, the instincts, to social reality* is the key conception of psychoanalysis, and every exploration into personal psychology proceeds from this conception.

In the very beginning—and even later on—Freud concerned himself with the psychology of the individual. But once the instincts were discovered to be the motive force behind human behavior, and once the unconscious was seen as the source of man's ideologies and behavior patterns, it was inevitable that analytic authors would make an attempt to move from the problem of the individual to the problem of society, from individual to social psychology. They had to try to use the techniques of psychoanalysis to discover the hidden sources of the obviously irrational behavior patterns in societal life—in religion, custom, politics and education. This obviously meant that they would encounter difficulties that were avoided so long as they restricted themselves to the realm of individual psychology.

But these difficulties do not alter the fact that the inquiry itself was a legitimate scientific consequence of the starting point of psychoanalysis. If instinctual life and the unconscious were the key to understanding human behavior, then psychoanalysis was also entitled and competent to say something about the motives underlying social behavior. For "society" too consists of living individuals who must be subject to the same psychological laws that psychoanalysis discovered in the individual.

Thus it seems erroneous if one—as Wilhelm Reich, for example—restricts psychoanalysis to the sphere of individual psychology and argues against its applicability to social phenomena (politics, class consciousness, etc.).[5] The fact that a phenomenon is studied in sociology certainly does not mean that it cannot be an object of psychoanalysis (no more than study of an object's physical characteristics rules out study of its chemical aspects). What is meant is simply that it is an object of psychoanalysis only and wholly insofar as psychic factors play a role in the phenomenon. The thesis that psychology only deals with the individual while sociology only deals with "society" is false. For just as psychology always deals with a socialized individual, so sociology always deals with a group of individuals whose psychic structure and mechanisms must be taken into account. Later we will discuss the role that psychic factors play in societal phenomena, and point to the function of *analytical social psychology*.

The theory of society with which psychoanalysis seems to have both the greatest affinity and also the greatest differences is *historical materialism*.

They seem to have the most points of contact because they both are materialistic sciences. They do not start from "ideas" but from earthly life and needs. They are particularly close in their appraisal of consciousness, which is seen by both as less the driving force behind human behavior than the reflection of other hidden forces. But when it comes to the nature of the factors that truly condition man's consciousness, there seems to be an irreconcilable opposition between the two theories. Historical materialism sees consciousness as the expression of social existence; psychoanalysis sees it as determined by instinctual drives. Certain questions are unavoidable: do the two views contradict each other? If not, how are they related? Can the use of the psychoanalytic method enrich historical materialism? If so, how?

Before we discuss these questions, however, it seems necessary to examine the presuppositions that psychoanalysis brings to a study of societal problems.[6] Freud never assumed isolated man, devoid of all social ties, to be the object of psychology.

> Individual psychology, to be sure, is concerned with the individual human being, and it examines the ways in which he tries to satisfy his instinctual drives. But only rarely and under specific exceptional circumstances is it in a position to abstract from this person's relationships with other individuals. In the individual's psychic life, other people ordinarily must be considered as either models, objects, helpers or opponents. Thus, from the beginning, individual psychology is simultaneously social psychology—in this extended but legitimate sense.[7]

On the other hand, Freud basically ruled out the illusion of a social psychology whose object is a group as such, "society," or a social complex with a "mass soul" or "societal soul." Rather, he always proceeds from the fact that every group is composed only of individuals and that only the individual as such is the subject of psychic properties. Freud likewise refused to accept the notion of a "social instinct." What people called the "social instinct," he felt, was "not a primitive, elemental instinct." He sees the "origins of its development in a narrower circle, such as the family." His views lead to the conclusion that the social attributes owe their origin, intensification, and diminution to the influence of specific living conditions and environmental relations on the instincts.

Just as, for Freud, it is always socialized man who is the object of psychology, so he sees man's environment and living conditions playing a decisive role in his psychic development and in our theoretical understanding of it. Freud recognized the biological and physiological influence of the instincts; but he specifically emphasized to what degree these instincts could be modified, and he pointed to the environment, social reality, as the modifying factor.

Thus, psychoanalysis seems to include presuppositions that make its method useful for investigations in social psychology and that rule out any conflict with sociology. It seeks to know the psychic traits common to the members of a group, and to explain these common psychic traits in terms of shared life experiences. These life experiences, however, do not lie in the realm of the personal or the accidental—the larger the group is, the more this holds true—but rather they are identical with the socio-economic situation of this particular group. *Thus analytical social psychology seeks to understand the instinctual apparatus of a group, its libidinous and largely unconscious behavior, in terms of its socio-economic structure.*

Here an objection seems to be in order. Psychoanalysis explains instinctual development in terms of the life experiences of the earliest childhood years: that is to say, in terms of a period when the human being scarcely has anything to do with "society" but lives almost exclusively in the circle of his family. How then, according to psychoanalytic theory, can socio-economic relationships acquire such significance?

There is no real problem here at all. Of course, the first critical influences on the growing child come from the family. But the family itself, all its typical internal emotional relationships and the educational ideals it embodies, are in turn conditioned by the social and class background of the family; in short, they are conditioned by the social structure in which it is rooted. (For example: the emotional relationships between father and son are quite different in the family that is part of a bourgeois, patriarchal society than they are in the family that is part of a matriarchal society.) The family is the medium through which the society or the social class stamps its specific structure on the child, and hence on the adult. *The family is the psychological agency of society.*

Up to now, the vast majority of psychoanalytic works which have tried to apply psychoanalysis to social problems have not met the requirements incumbent on any analytical social psychology.[8] Their failure begins in their assessment of the family's function. They saw clearly enough that the individual can only be understood as a socialized being. They realized that it is the child's relationships with the various family members that have a decisive influence on his instinctual development. But they have almost completely overlooked the fact that the family itself, in its whole psychological and social structure, with all its specific educational goals and emotional attitudes, is the product of a specific social and (in a narrower sense) class structure; that it is in fact simply the psychological agency of the society and class from which it comes. They had found the correct starting point for explaining the psychological influence of society on the child, but failed to take notice of it.

How was that possible? The psychoanalytic investigators were simply duped by a prejudice that they shared with every bourgeois investigator—even those who were progressive. They had turned bourgeois, capitalist society into an absolute; and they more or less consciously believed that it was the "normal" society, that its conditions and psychic factors were typical for "society" in general.

But there was another special reason why the analytical authors fell into this error. The object of their investigations were, first and foremost, sick and healthy members of modern society and largely of the middle classes; in short, they were members of the bourgeois class,[9] with the same social background. What determined and differentiated their individual lives, then, were the individual, personal and, from a social standpoint, accidental experiences above this generally shared foundation. All the persons studied shared the same psychic traits, insofar as these traits were the product of an authoritarian society organized around the facts of class structures and the methodical pursuit of maximal profit. They differed psychologically only insofar as one had an overly strict father who terrified him in childhood, another had an older sister who was the focus of all his love, and still another had such an overpossessive mother that he was never able to break his libidinal ties with her.

To be sure, these personal experiences were of the utmost importance for the development of the individual concerned. By removing the psychic problems that had arisen from these experiences, psychoanalysis did its full duty as a therapy; it transformed the patient into a human being who was now adjusted to the existing social order. The goal of therapy did not go beyond that, nor did it have to. Unfortunately, our theoretical understanding of the whole situation did not get beyond that, either. Neglect of the social structure, which conditioned the family structure, may have been a source of error; but it was irrelevant in actual practice for individual psychology. When it came to research in social psychology, however, what had once been an irrelevant mistake now became a disastrous source of error affecting the whole endeavor.[10]

Psychoanalysis had focused on the structure of bourgeois society and its patriarchal family as the normal situation. Following the approach of individual psychology, it had learned to appreciate individual differences in terms of the fortuitous traumas that befell individual men. In the beginning, psychoanalytic researchers explained the various phenomena of social psychology in a corresponding way: they viewed them in terms of traumas, of socially fortuitous events. This necessarily led to a renunciation of the authentic analytic method.

Since they did not concern themselves with the variety of life experiences, the socio-economic structure of other types of society, and therefore did not try to explain their psychic structure as determined by their social structure, they necessarily began to *analogize* instead of *analyzing*. They treated mankind or a given society as an individual, transposed the specific mechanisms found in contemporary individuals to every possible type of society, and "explained" the psychic structure of these societies by analogy with certain phenomena (usually of a neurotic sort) typical of human beings in their own society.

In doing this, they overlooked a point of view that is fundamental even to psychoanalytic individual psychology. They forgot the fact that neurosis—whether a neurotic symptom or a neurotic character trait—results from the "abnormal" individual's faulty adaptation of his instinctual drives to the reality around him; most people in a society, i.e., the "healthy" people, do possess this ability to adapt. Thus phenomena studied in social (or mass) psychology cannot be explained by analogy with neurotic phenomena. They should be understood as the result of the adaptation of the instinctual apparatus to the social reality.

The most striking example of this procedure is the absolutization of the Oedipus complex, which was made into a universal human mechanism, even though sociological and ethnological studies indicated that this particular emotional relationship was probably typical only of families in a patriarchal society. The absolutizing of the Oedipus complex led Freud to base the whole development of mankind on the mechanism of father hatred and the resultant reactions,[11] without any regard for the material living conditions of the group under study.

Even when he started from a false sociological standpoint, however, a genius like Freud was able to make worthwhile and significant discoveries.[12] But in the work of other analytical authors, this false starting point led to results which compromised psychoanalysis in the eyes of sociology, and of Marxist social theory in particular.

But the blame did not rest with psychoanalysis as such. In fact, one only had to apply the classical method of psychoanalytic individual psychology in a logical way to social psychology, in order to arrive at results that would meet with no objections. The fault was that psychoanalytic authors did not utilize this method in a correct way when they transferred it from the individual to social groups and social phenomena.

Here a further clarification is called for. We have emphasized the modifiability of the instinctual apparatus through the influence of external (and ultimately social) factors. But one should not overlook the fact that the instinctual apparatus, both quantitatively and qualitatively, has certain physiologically and biologically determined limits to its modifiability and that only within these limits is it subject to the influence of social factors. Because of the force of the energy it sends forth, moreover, the instinctual apparatus itself is an extremely active force; inherent in it is the tendency to alter living conditions so that they serve instinctual goals.

In the interplay of interacting psychic drives and economic conditions, the latter have primacy. Not in the sense that they represent the "stronger" motive; this question is spurious because we are not dealing with quantitatively comparable motives on the same plane. They have primacy in the sense that the satisfaction of the need for self-preservation is tied up with material production; and that the modifiability of the economic reality is more restricted than the modifiability of the human instinctual apparatus—in particular, the sexual instinct.

Applying the method of psychoanalytic individual psychology to social phenomena, we find that *the phenomena of social psychology are to be understood as processes involving the active and passive adaptation of the instinctual apparatus to the socio-economic situation. In certain fundamental respects, the instinctual apparatus itself is a biological given; but it is highly modifiable. The role of primary formative factors goes to the economic conditions. The family is the essential medium through which the economic situation exerts its formative influence on the individual's psyche. The task of social psychology is to explain the shared, socially relevant, psychic attitudes and ideologies—and their unconscious roots in particular—in terms of the influence of economic conditions on libido strivings.*

So far, then, the method of analytic social psychology seems to dovetail with the method of Freudian individual psychology and with the requirements of historical materialism. But new difficulties arise when this method is confused with an erroneous but widespread interpretation of the Marxist theory: the notion that historical materialism is a psychological theory or, more specifically, an economistic psychology.

If it were true, as Bertrand Russell claims,[13] that Marx saw "making money" and Freud saw "love" as the decisive motive of human conduct, then the two theories would be as irreconcilable as Russell believes. Consider his hypothetical example of the mayfly.

Assuming that such a creature could think theoretically, I do not think it would say what Russell claims it would. Instead, it would say that Russell had completely misinterpreted both psychoanalysis and Marxism; that psychoanalysis actually investigates the adaptation of biological factors (the instincts) to social reality, and that Marxism is not a psychological theory at all.

Russell is not the only one to misconstrue the two theories. He is joined by many other theoreticians, and his false view is matched by many similar ones.

The notion of historical materialism being an economistic psychology is espoused by Hendrik de Man with special emphasis.

As we know, Marx himself never formulated his theory of human motivation. As a matter of fact, he never explained what "class" meant. Death cut short his last work, when he was turning to this subject. But the basic conceptions from which he starts are not in doubt. Even undefined, the tacit presupposition underlying his work appears both in his scholarly and political activity. Every economic thesis and every political opinion of Marx rests on the presupposition that man's volitional motives, which bring about social progress, are dictated first and foremost by economic interests. Present-day social psychology would express the same thoughts in terms of the effect of the acquisitive drive on social conduct. If Marx himself regarded such formulations as superfluous, that is because he took it for granted that this was the object and aim of contemporary political economy.[14]

Now this "tacit presupposition" may well have been the self-understood conception of all contemporary (i.e., bourgeois) economists; but it certainly was not the view of Marx himself, who did not share the views of contemporary theoreticians on many points.

Though in a less explicit way, Bernstein is not far from this psychologistic interpretation when he tries to defend the honor of historical materialism with this observation:

The economic interpretation of history need not mean that only economic forces and motives are to be recognized, but simply that economics is *always the decisive factor* that serves as the cornerstone for the great movements of history.[15]

Behind these muddy formulations lies the notion that Marxism is an economic psychology, which is purified and improved by Bernstein in an idealist sense.[16]

The idea that the "acquisitive drive" is the basic or only motive of human behavior is the brainchild of bourgeois liberalism, used as a psychological argument against the possibility of the realization of socialism.[17] Marx's petit-bourgeois interpreters interpreted his theory as an economistic psychology. In reality, historical materialism is far from being a psychological theory; its psychological presuppositions are few and may be briefly listed: *men* make their own history; *needs* motivate men's actions and feelings (hunger and love)[18]; these needs increase in the course of historical development, thereby spurring increased economic activity.[19]

In connection with psychology, the economic factor plays a role in historical materialism only to the extent that human needs—primarily the need for self-preservation—are largely satisfied through the production of goods; in short, needs are the lever that stimulates production. Marx and Engels certainly stressed that the drive toward self-preservation took priority over all other needs, but they did not go into any detail about the quality of various drives and needs.[20] However, they never maintained that the "acquisitive drive," the passion for acquisition as an aim in itself, was the only or essential need. To proclaim it a universal human drive would be naively to absolutize a psychic trait that has taken on uncommon force in capitalist society.

Marx and Engels are the last people to whom one would impute the idea of transfiguring bourgeois and capitalist traits into a universal human trait. They were well aware of the place psychology had within sociology, but they neither were nor wanted to be psychologists. Moreover, apart from indications in the French Enlightenment literature (especially Helvetius), which should not, of course, be underestimated, they had no scientific materialist psychology at their disposal. Psychoanalysis was the first to provide this psychology, and showed that the "acquisitive drive," although important, did not play a predominant role in man's psychic armament by comparison with other (genital, sadistic, narcissistic) needs. Psychoanalysis, in fact, indicates that in large measure the "acquisitive drive" is not the deepest cause of the need to acquire or possess things; it is rather the expression of a narcissistic need or wish to win recognition from oneself and others. In a society that pays the highest recognition and admiration to the rich man, the narcissistic impulses will find expression as a "drive" to contribute to society in some important way. Since narcissistic needs are among the most elemental and powerful psychic strivings, it is most important to recognize that the goals (hence the concrete content) of these narcissistic aspirations depend on the specific structure of a society. The imposing role of the "acquisitive drive," then, is largely due to the especially high valuation of property in bourgeois society.

When the materialistic view of history talks about economic causes—apart from the meaning we have just explained—it is not talking about economics as a subjective psychological motive but as an objective influence on man's activity in life.[21] All man's activity, the satisfying of all his needs, depends on the specific nature of natural economic conditions around; and it is these conditions that determine how man shall live his life. For Marx, man's consciousness is to be explained in terms of his existence in society, in terms of his real, earthly life that is conditioned by the state of his productive capabilities.

> The production of ideas, conceptions and consciousness is directly interwoven with the material activity and the material activity of men; it is an expression of his real life. His thoughts and intellectual ideas are seen to be the direct outflow of his material activity. The same holds true for the intellectual productions that find expression in politics, law, morality, religion, metaphysics, etc. Men are the producers of their conceptions and ideas, but we are talking about real, concrete men who are conditioned by the specific way in which their productive capabilities and their corresponding intercourse develops. Consciousness can never be anything but conscious being, and man's being is his concrete life.[22]

Historical materialism sees history as the process of man's active and passive adaptation to the natural conditions around him. "Work is, first and foremost, a process between man and nature, a process in which man mediates, regulates and controls his interaction with nature through his own actions. Vis-à-vis the natural elements themselves, he is a natural force."[23]

Man and nature are the two poles here, interacting with each other, conditioning each other, and altering each other. The historical process is always bound up with man's own nature, and natural conditions outside man. Although Marx stressed the fact that man greatly altered both himself and nature in the historical process, he always emphasized that all such changes were tied up with the existing natural conditions. This is precisely what distinguishes his standpoint from certain idealist positions that accord unlimited power to the human will.[24] As Marx and Engels said,

The presuppositions with which we begin are not arbitrary dogmas. They are real presuppositions, from which one can abstract
only in imagination. They involve real, living individuals, their
actions, and the material living conditions which they find or
have created. Thus these presuppositions are verifiable in a
purely empirical way.

The first presupposition of human history is, of course, the
existence of living human individuals. So the first fact to be
verified is the physical organization of these individuals and the
resultant relationship between them and nature. Here we cannot
go into the physical nature of man nor the varied (geological,
climatic, etc.) natural conditions he finds around him. Every
description of history must start with these natural foundations,
and their modification in the course of history by man's activity.[25]

After the correction of the most drastic misunderstandings, what
emerges as the relation between psychoanalysis and historical
materialism?

Psychoanalysis can enrich the overall conception of historical
materialism on one specific point. *It can provide a more comprehensive knowledge of one of the factors that is operative in the social
process: the nature of man himself.* It locates man's instinctual apparatus among the natural factors that modify the social process,
although there are also limits to this modifiability. Man's instinctual
apparatus is one of the "natural" conditions that forms part of the
substructure (*Unterbau*) of the social process. But we are not talking
about the instinctual apparatus "in general," or in some pristine
biological form, since it is only manifest in some *specific* form that
has been modified through the social process. The human psyche—or
the libidinal forces at its root—are part of the substructure; but they are
not the whole substructure, as a psychologistic interpretation would
have it. The human psyche always remains a psyche that has been
modified by the social process. Historical materialism calls for a
psychology—i.e., a science of man's psychic structure; and
psychoanalysis is the first discipline to provide a psychology that
historical materialism can really use.

The contribution of psychoanalysis is particularly important for
the following reasons. Marx and Engels postulated the dependence of
all ideological processes on the economic substructure. They saw
intellectual and psychic creations as "the material basis reflected in
man's head." In many instances, to be sure, historical materialism

could provide the right answers without any psychological presuppositions. But only where ideology was the *immediate* expression of economic interests; or where one was trying to establish the correlation between economic substructure and ideological superstructure. Lacking a satisfactory psychology, Marx and Engels could not explain *how* the material basis was reflected in man's head and heart.

Psychoanalysis can show that man's ideologies are the products of certain wishes, instinctual drives, interests and needs which themselves, in large measure, unconsciously find expression as rationalizations—i.e., as ideologies. Psychoanalysis can show that while the instinctual drives do develop on the basis of biologically determined instincts, their quantity and content are greatly affected by the individual's socio-economic situation or class. Marx says that men are the producers of their ideologies; analytical social psychology can describe empirically the process of the production of ideologies, of the interaction of "natural" and social factors. *Hence psychoanalysis can show how the economic situation is transformed into ideology via man's drives.*

An important point to note is the fact that this interaction between instincts and environment results in changes within man himself, just as his work changes extra-human nature. Here we can only suggest the general direction of this change. It involves, as Freud has stressed repeatedly, the growth of man's ego organization and the corresponding growth of his capacity for sublimation.[26] Thus, psychoanalysis permits us to regard the formation of ideologies as a type of "production process," as another form of the "metabolism" between man and nature. The distinctive aspect here is that "nature" is also within man, not just outside him.

Psychoanalysis can also tell us something about the way ideologies or ideas mold society. It can show that the impact of an idea depends essentially on its unconscious content, which appeals to certain drives; that it is, as it were, the quality and intensity of the libidinal structure of a society which determines the social effect of an ideology.

If it seems clear that psychoanalytic social psychology has a valid place within historical materialism, we can now point to the way in which it can immediately resolve certain difficulties that confront the doctrine of historical materialism.

To begin with, historical materialism can now give a better answer to certain objections. Some opponents, for example, pointed to the role that ideals—e.g., love for the group, the desire for freedom—play in history. Historical materialism could, of course, spurn this type of question as a psychological problem and restrict itself to an analysis of the objective economic conditions that affect historical events. But it was not in a position to explain clearly the nature and source of these real and potent human forces, nor could it explain the role they played in the social process. Psychoanalysis can show that these seemingly ideal motives are actually the rationalized expression of instinctual, libidinous needs and that the content and scope of the dominant needs at any given moment are to be explained in terms of the influence of the socio-economic situation on the instinctual structure of the group that produces the ideology. Hence it is possible for psychoanalysis to reduce the loftiest idealistic motives to their earthly libidinal nucleus without having to consider economic needs as the only important ones.[27]

To sum up: (1) The realm of human drives is a natural force which, like other natural forces (soil fertility, natural irrigation, etc.), is an immediate part of the substructure of the social process. Knowledge of this force, then, is necessary for a complete understanding of the social process. (2) The way ideologies are produced and function can only be understood correctly if we know how the system of drives operates. (3) When economically conditioned factors hit upon the realm of drives, some modifications occur; by virtue of the influence of drives, the social process operates at a faster or slower tempo than one would expect if no theoretical consideration to the psychic factors is given.

Thus, the use of psychoanalysis within historical materialism will provide a refinement of method, a broader knowledge of the forces at work in the social process, and greater certainty in understanding the course of history and in predicting future historical events. In particular, it will provide a complete understanding of how ideologies are produced.

The fruitfulness of a psychoanalytic social psychology will depend, of course, on the significance of the libidinal forces in the social process. We could not even begin to treat this topic thoroughly in this article, so I shall content myself with a few basic suggestions and indications.

Suppose we ask which forces maintain the stability of a given society and which undermine it. We can see that economic prosperity and social conflicts determine stability or decomposition, respectively. But we can also see that the factor which, on the basis of these conditions, serves as a most important element in the social structure are the libidinal tendencies actually operative in men. Consider first a relatively stable social constellation. What holds people together? What enables them to have a certain feeling of solidarity, to adjust to the role of ruling or being ruled? To be sure, it is the external power apparatus (police, law courts, army, etc.) that keeps the society from coming apart at the seams. To be sure, it is rational and egotistic interests that contribute to structural stability. But neither the external power apparatus nor rational interests would suffice to guarantee the functioning of the society, if the libidinal strivings of the people were not involved. They serve as the "cement," as it were, without which the society would not hold together, and which contributes to the production of important social ideologies in every cultural sphere.

Let us apply this principle to an especially important social constellation: class relationships. In history as we know it, a minority rules over the majority of society. This class rule was not the result of cunning and deceit, but was a necessary result of the total economic situation of society, of its productive forces. As Necker saw it: "Through the laws of property, the proletariat were condemned to get the barest minimum for their labor." Or, as Linguet put it, they were "to a certain extent, a conspiracy against the majority of the human race, who could find no recourse against them."[28]

The Enlightenment described and criticized this dependency relationship, even though it did not realize that it was economically conditioned. Indeed, minority rule is a historical fact; but what factors allowed this dependency relationship to become stabilized?

First, of course, it was the use of physical force and the availability of these physical means to certain groups. But there was another important factor at work: the libidinal ties—anxiety, love, trust— which filled the souls of the majority in their relationships with the ruling class. Now this psychic attitude is not the product of whim or accident. It is the expression of people's libidinal adaptation to the conditions of life imposed by economic necessity. So long as these conditions necessitate minority rule over the majority, the libido adapts itself to this economic structure and serves as one of the factors that lend stability to the class relationship.

Besides recognizing the *economic conditions* of the libido structure, social psychology should not forget to investigate the *psychological basis* of this structure. It must explore, not only why this libido structure necessarily exists, but also how it is psychologically possible and through what mechanisms it operates. Exploring the roots of the majority's libidinal ties to the ruling minority, social psychology might discover that this tie is a repetition or continuation of the child's psychic attitude toward his parents, particularly toward his father, in a bourgeois family.[29] We find a mixture of admiration, fear, faith and confidence in the father's strength and wisdom, briefly, an affectively conditioned reflection of his intellectual and moral qualities, and we find the same in adults of a patriarchal class society vis-à-vis the members of the ruling class. Related to this are certain moral principles which entice the poor to suffer rather than to do wrong, and which lead them to believe that the purpose of their life is to obey their rulers and do their duty. Even these ethical conceptions, which are so important for social stability, are the products of certain affective and emotional relations to those who create and represent such norms.

To be sure, the creation of these norms is not left to chance. One whole basic part of the cultural apparatus serves to form the socially required attitude in a systematic and methodical way. It is an important task of social psychology to analyze the function of the whole educational system and other systems (such as the penal system) in this process.[30]

We have focused on the libidinal relationships between the ruling minority and the ruled majority because this factor is the social and psychic core of every class society. But other social relationships, too, bear their own distinctive libidinal stamp. The relationships between members of the same class have a different psychic coloring in the lower middle class than they do in the proletariat. Or, the relationship to the political leader is different, for example, in the case of a proletarian leader who identifies with his class and serves their interests even while he leads them, from what it is when he confronts them as a strong man, as the great father who rules as omnipotent authority.[31]

The diversity of possible libidinal relationships is matched by the wide variety of possible emotional relationships within society. Even a brief sketch is impossible here; this problem would indeed, be a major task for an analytic social psychology. Let me just point out that every society has its own distinctive *libidinal structure*, even as it has its own economic, social, political, and cultural structure. This libidinal structure is the product of the influence of socio-economic conditions on human drives; in turn, it is an important factor conditioning emotional developments within the various levels of society, and the contents of the "ideological superstructure." The libidinal structure of a society is the medium through which the economy exerts its influence on man's intellectual and mental manifestations.[32]

Of course, the libidinal structure of a society does not remain constant, no more than does its economic and social structure. But it remains relatively constant so long as the social structure retains a certain equilibrium—i.e., during the phase of relative consolidation in the society's development. With the growth of objective contradictions and conflicts within the society, and with the acceleration of the disintegration process, certain changes in the society's libidinal structure also take place. We see the disappearance of traditional ties that maintained the stability of the society; there is change in traditional emotional attitudes. Libidinal energies are freed for new uses, and thus change their social function. They no longer serve the preservation of the society, but contribute to the development of new social formations. They cease to be "cement," and turn into dynamite.

Let us return to the question we were discussing at the beginning: the relationship of the drives to life experiences—i.e., to the objective conditions of life. We have seen that analytic individual psychology views instinctual development as the result of the active and passive adaptation of the instinctual apparatus to the actual conditions of life. In principle, the same relationship holds true between a society's libidinal structure and its economic conditions: it is a process of active and passive adaptation of the society's libidinal structure to the existing economic conditions. Human beings, driven by their libidinous impulses, bring about changes in the economic conditions; the changed economic conditions cause new libidinal goals and satisfactions to arise. The decisive point is that all these changes ultimately go back to the economic conditions, that the drives and needs change and adapt themselves in accordance with economic conditions.

Clearly, analytic psychology has its place within the framework of historical materialism. It investigates one of the natural factors that is operative in the relationship between society and nature: the realm of human drives, and the active and passive role they play within the social process. Thus, it investigates a factor that plays a decisive mediating role between the economic base and the formation of ideologies. Thus, analytic social psychology enables us to understand fully the ideological superstructure in terms of the process that goes on between society and man's nature.

Now we can readily summarize the findings of our study on the method and function of a psychoanalytic social psychology. Its method is that of classical Freudian psychoanalysis as applied to social phenomena. It explains the shared, socially relevant, psychic attitudes in terms of the process of active and passive adaptation of the apparatus of drives to the socio-economic living conditions of the society.

Its task is, first of all, to analyze the socially relevant libidinal strivings: i.e., to describe the libidinal structure of a given society, and to explain the origin of this structure and its function in the social process. An important element of this work, then, will be the theory explaining how ideologies arise from the interaction of the psychic apparatus and the socio-economic conditions.

Subject and Object

By Theodor W. Adorno

A series of loosely organized but tightly argued comments on what is perhaps the central issue in epistemology, "Subject and Object" first appeared in 1969 in the collection Stichworte, *the last publication Adorno himself supervised. Difficult as these comments are on the first reading, they contain some of the most illuminating formulations of the "constitution problem", i.e., the question of through what perceptual and conceptual filters we constitute "objects" and "events" from raw stimuli. Unlike Lukács, the critical theorists did not yield to the temptation of collapsing subject and object in a particular historical agent. Adorno emphasizes the necessary gap between subject and object, so that the dynamic of the self-constitution, the dynamic of consciousness progressively liberating itself from the uncomprehended powers that guide it, would not be replaced by just another agency guiding it. An epistemological category, subjectivity is not an undesirable addition to the objective qualities of reality, best eliminated if we want reliable knowledge. There can be no knowledge without a perspective from which it is gained. The fact that this perspective may be (and usually is) collective makes it no less "subjective."*

To engage in reflections on subject and object poses the problem of stating what we are to talk about. The terms are patently equivocal. "Subject," for instance, may refer to the particular individual as well as to general attributes, to "consciousness in general" in the language of Kant's *Prolegomena*. The equivocation is not removable simply by terminological clarification, for the two meanings have reciprocal need of each other; one is scarcely to be grasped without the other. The element of individual humanity—what Schelling calls "egoity"—cannot be thought apart from any concept of the subject; without any remembrance of it, "subject" would lose all meaning. Conversely, as soon as we reflect upon the human individual as an individual at all, in the form of a general concept—as soon as we cease to mean only the present existence of some particular person—we have already turned it into a universal similar to that which came to be explicit in the idealist concept of the subject. The very term "particular person" requires a generic concept, lest it be meaningless. Even in proper names, a reference to that universal is still implied. They mean one who is called by that name, not by any other; and "one" stands elliptically for "one human being."

If on the other hand we tried to define the two terms so as to avoid this type of complication, we would land in an aporia that adds to the problematics of defining, as modern philosophy since Kant has noted time and again, for in a way, the concepts of subject and object—or rather, the things they intend—have priority before all definition. Defining means that something objective, no matter what it may be in itself, is subjectively captured by means of a fixed concept. Hence the resistance offered to defining by subject and object. To determine their meanings takes reflection on the very thing which definition cuts off for the sake of conceptual flexibility. Hence the advisability, at the outset, of taking up the words "subject" and "object" as the well-honed philosophical language hands them to us as a historical sediment—not, of course, sticking to such conventionalism but continuing with critical analysis. The starting point would be the allegedly naive, though already mediated, view that a knowing subject, whatever its kind, was confronting a known object, whatever its kind. The reflection, which in philosophical terminology goes by the name of *intentio obliqua*, is then a re-relation of that ambiguous concept of the object to a no less ambiguous concept of the subject. The second reflection reflects the first, more closely determining those vague subject and object concepts for their content's sake.

The separation of subject and object is both real and illusory. True, because in the cognitive realm it serves to express the real separation, the dichotomy of the human condition, a coercive development. False, because the resulting separation must not be hypostasized, not magically transformed into an invariant. This contradiction in the separation of subject and object is imparted to epistemology. Though they cannot be thought away, as separated, the *pseudos* of the separation is manifested in their being mutually mediated—the object by the subject, and even more, in different ways, the subject by the object. The separation is no sooner established directly, without mediation, than it becomes ideology, which is indeed its normal form. The mind will then usurp the place of something absolutely independent—which it is not; its claim of independence heralds the claim of dominance. Once radically parted from the object, the subject reduces it to its own measure; the subject swallows the object, forgetting how much it is an object itself.

The picture of a temporal or extratemporal original state of happy identity between subject and object is romantic, however—a wishful projection at times, but today no more than a lie. The undifferentiated state before the subject's formation was the dread of the blind web of nature, of myth; it was in protest against it that the great religions had their truth content. Besides, to be undifferentiated is not to be one; even in Platonic dialectics, unity requires divers items of which it is the unity. For those who live to see it, the new horror of separation will transfigure the old horror of chaos—both are the ever-same. The fear of yawning meaninglessness makes one forget a fear which once upon a time was no less dreadful: that of the vengeful gods of which Epicurean materialism and the Christian "fear not" wanted to relieve mankind. The only way to accomplish this is through the subject. If it were liquidated rather than sublated in a higher form, the effect would be regression—not just of consciousness, but a regression to real barbarism.

Fate, myth's bondage to nature, comes from total social tutelage, from an age in which no eyes had yet been opened by self-reflection, an age in which subject did not yet exist. Instead of a collective practice conjuring that age to return, the spell of the old undifferentiatedness should be obliterated. Its prolongation is the sense of identity of a mind that repressively shapes its Other in its own image. If speculation on the state of reconciliation were permitted, neither the undistinguished unity of subject and object nor their antithetical hostility would be conceivable in it; rather, the communication of what was distinguished. Not until then would the concept of communication, as an objective concept, come into its own. The present one is so infamous because the best there is, the potential of an agreement between people and things, is betrayed to an interchange between subjects according to the requirements of subjective reason. In its proper place, even epistemologically, the relationship of subject and object would lie in the realization of peace among men as well as between men and their Other. Peace is the state of distinctness without domination, with the distinct participating in each other.

In epistemology, "subject" is mostly understood to mean the "transcendental subject." According to idealist doctrine, it will either construct the objective world with raw material along Kantian lines or, since Fichte, engender that world itself. The critics of idealism were not the first to discover that this transcendental subject constituting the substance of experience was abstracted from living individuals. It is evident that the abstract concept of the transcendental subject—its thought forms, their unity, and the original productivity of consciousness—presupposes what it promises to bring about: actual, live individuals. This notion was present in the idealist philosophies. Kant, in his chapter on psychological paralogisms, did try to develop a constitutive-hierarchic difference in principle between transcendental and empirical subject; but his successors, notably Fichte and Hegel, as well as Schopenhauer, resorted to logical subtleties to cope with the immense difficulty of the circle. They frequently had recourse to the Aristotelian motif that what comes first for our consciousness—in this case, the empirical subject—is not the First in itself, that as its condition or its origin it postulates the transcendental subject. Even Husserl's polemics against psychologism, along with the distinction of genesis and validity, continues the line of that mode of argument. It is apologetic. The conditioned is to be justified as unconditional, the derived as primary. That nothing can be true except the First—or, as Nietzsche critically phrased it, what has not come into being—is a *topos* of the entire Western tradition; we find it repeated here. There is no mistaking the ideological function of the thesis. The more individuals are really degraded to functions of the social totality as it becomes more systematized, the more will man pure and simple, man as a principle with the attributes of creativity and absolute domination, be consoled by exaltation of his mind.

Yet for all that, the question of the transcendental subject's reality weighs heavier than appears in its sublimation as pure mind, fully so in the critical retraction of idealism. In a sense (although idealism would be the last to admit this) the transcendental subject is more real—that is to say, more determinant for the real conduct of men and for the resulting society—than those psychological individuals from which the transcendental one was abstracted. They have little to say in the world, having on their part turned into appendages of the social apparatus and ultimately into ideology. The living human individual, as he is forced to act in the role for which he has been marked internally as well, is the *homo oeconomicus* incarnate, closer to the transcendental subject than to the living individual for which he immediately cannot but take himself. To this extent, idealistic theory was realistic and did not need to feel embarrassed when charged with idealism by opponents. What shows up faithfully in the doctrine of the transcendental subject is the priority of the relations—abstractly rational ones, detached from the human individuals and their relationships—that have their model in exchange. If the exchange form is the standard social structure, its rationality constitutes people; what they are for themselves, what they seem to be to themselves, is secondary. They are deformed beforehand by the mechanism that has been philosophically transfigured as transcendental. The supposedly most evident of things, the empirical subject, would really have to be viewed as not yet in existence; in this perspective, the transcendental subject is "constitutive."

This alleged origin of all objects is objectified in rigid timelessness, quite in keeping with Kant's doctrine of the firm and immutable forms of transcendental consciousness. Its solidity and invariance, which according to transcendental philosophy bring forth all objects or at least prescribe their rule, are the reflective form of the reification of humans that has been objectively accomplished in the social relationship. The fetish character, a socially necessary semblance, has historically turned into the *prius* of what according to its concept would have it be the *posterius*. The philosophical problem of constitution has reversed into its mirror image; but in this very reversal, it tells the truth about the historic stage that has been reached—in a truth, of course, which a second Copernican turn might theoretically negate again. True, it has its positive aspect as well: society, as prior, keeps its members and itself alive. The particular individual has the universal to thank for the possibility of his existence—witness thought, which is a general relation, and thus a social one. It is not just as fetish that thought takes priority over the individual. Only in idealism, one side is hypostasized, the side which is incomprehensible except in relation to the other. But the datum, the irremovable *skandalon* of idealism, will demonstrate time and again the failure of the hypostasis.

It is not the old *intentio recta* that is restored by insight into the object's primacy; not the trustful bondage to the outside world as it is and as it appears this side of critique; not an anthropological state devoid of the self-consciousness that crystallizes only in the context of re-relating knowledge to the knower. The crude confrontation of subject and object in naive realism is indeed historically necessary and not removable by any act of will. At the same time it is a product of the wrong abstraction, already a piece of reification. Once we have seen through this, we would be unable without self-reflection to drag further a consciousness objectified to itself, a consciousness externalized precisely as such and virtually recoiling outward. The turn to the subject, though aiming at its primacy from the start, does not simply vanish with its revision; not the least reason why the revision occurs is the subjective interest of freedom. Rather, by primacy of the object is meant that the subject, for its part an object in a qualitatively different sense, in a sense more radical than the object, which is not known otherwise than through consciousness, is as an object also a subject.

What is known through consciousness must be something; mediation aims at the mediated. But the subject, the epitome of mediation, is the How—never the What, as opposed to the object—that is postulated by any comprehensible idea of its concept. Potentially, even if not actually, objectivity can be conceived without a subject; not so subjectivity without an object. No matter how we define the subject, some entity cannot be juggled out of it. If it is not something—and "something" indicates an irreducible objective moment—the subject is nothing at all; even as *actus purus*, it still needs to refer to something active. The object's primacy is the *intentio obliqua* of the *intentio obliqua*, not the warmed-over *intentio recta*. It is the corrective of the subjective reduction, not the denial of a subjective share. The object, too, is mediated; but according to its own concept, it is not so thoroughly dependent on the subject as the subject is on objectivity. Idealism has ignored such differences and has thus coarsened a spiritualization that serves abstraction as a disguise. Yet this occasions a revision of the stand toward the subject which prevails in traditional theory. That theory glorifies the subject in ideology and slanders it in epistemological practice. If one wants to reach the object, on the other hand, its subjective attributes or qualities are not to be eliminated, for precisely that would run counter to the primacy of the object.

If the subject does have an objective core, the object's subjective qualities are so much more an element of objectivity. For it is only as something definite that the object becomes anything at all. In the attributes that seem to be attached to it by the subject alone, the subject's own objectivity comes to the fore: all of them are borrowed from the objectivity of the *intentio recta*. Even according to idealist doctrine, the subjective attributes are not mere attachments; they are always called for by the *definiendum* as well, and it is there that the object's primacy is upheld. Conversely, the supposedly pure object lacking any admixture of thought and visuality is the literal reflection of abstract subjectivity: nothing else but abstraction makes the Other like itself. Unlike the undefined substrate of reductionism, the object of undiminished experience is more objective than that substrate. The qualities which the traditional critique of knowledge eliminates from the object and credits to the subject are due, in subjective experience, to the object's primacy; this is what we were deceived about by the ruling *intentio obliqua*. Its inheritance went to a critique of experience that realized its historical conditionality, and eventually that of society. For society is immanent in experience, not an *allo genos*. Nothing but the social self-reflection of knowledge obtains for knowledge the objectivity that will escape it as long as it obeys the social coercions that hold sway in it, and does not become aware of them. Social critique is a critique of knowledge, and vice versa.

Primacy of the object can be discussed legitimately only when that primacy—over the subject in the broadest sense of the term—is somehow definable, when it is more than the Kantian thing-in-itself as the unknown cause of the phenomenon. Despite Kant, of course, even the thing-in-itself bears a minimum of attributes merely by being distinct from the categorially predicated; one such attribute, a negative one, would be that of acausality. It suffices to set up an antithesis to the conventional view that conforms with subjectivism. The test of the object's primacy is its qualitative alteration of opinions held by the reified consciousness, opinions that go frictionlessly with subjectivism. Subjectivism does not touch the substance of naive realism; it only seeks to state formal criteria of its validity, as confirmed by the Kantian formula of empirical realism. One argument for primacy of the object is indeed incompatible with Kant's doctrine of constitution: that in modern natural science, the ratio peers over the very wall it has built, that it grabs a snippet of what differs with its well-honed categories. Such broadening of the ratio shatters subjectivism. But what defines the prior object as distinct from its subjective trappings is comprehensible in the conditionality of what conditions it, in that which in turn defines the categorial apparatus it is to be defined by, according to the subjectivist pattern. The categorial attributes without which there is no objectivity as yet, according to Kant, are posited also, and thus, if you will, they are really "merely subjective." The *reductio ad hominem* thus becomes the downfall of anthropocentrism. That even man as a *constituens* is man-made—this disenchants the creativity of the mind. But since primacy of the object requires reflection on the subject and subjective reflection, subjectivity—as distinct from primitive materialism, which really does not permit dialectics—becomes a moment that lasts.

Ever since the Copernican turn, what goes by the name of phenomenalism—that nothing is known save by a knowing subject—has joined with the cult of the mind. Insight into the primacy of the object revolutionizes both. What Hegel intended to place within subjective brackets has the critical consequence of shattering them. The general assurance that innervations, insights, cognitions are "merely subjective" ceases to convince as soon as subjectivity is grasped as the object's form. Phenomenality is the subject's magical transformation into the ground of its own definition, its positing as true being. The subject itself is to be brought to objectivity; its stirrings are not to be banished from cognition.

But the illusion of phenomenalism is a necessary one. It attests to the all but irresistibly blinding context which the subject produces as a false consciousness, and whose member it is at the same time. Such irresistibility is the foundation of the ideology of the subject. Awareness of a defect—of the limits of knowledge—becomes a virtue, so as to make the defect more bearable. A collective narcissism was at work. But it could not have prevailed with such stringency, could not have brought forth the most potent philosophies, if the fundament had not contained a kernel, albeit a distorted one, of truth. What transcendentalism praised in creative subjectivity is the subject's unconscious imprisonment in itself. Its every objective thought leaves the subject harnessed like an armored beast in the shell it tries in vain to shed; the only difference is that to such animals it did not occur to brag of their captivity as freedom.

We may well ask why human beings did so. Their mental imprisonment is exceedingly real. That as cognitive beings they depend on space, on time, on thought forms, marks their dependence on the species. Those constituents were its precipitation; they are no less valid for that reason. The a priori and society are intertwined. The universality and necessity of those forms, their Kantian glory, is none other than that which unites mankind. It needed them to survive. Captivity was internalized; the individual is no less imprisoned in himself than in the universal, in society. Hence the interest in the reinterpretation of captivity as freedom. The categorial captivity of individual consciousness repeats the real captivity of every individual.

The very glance that allows consciousness to see through that captivity is determined by the forms it has implanted in the individual. Their imprisonment in themselves might make people realize their social imprisonment; preventing this realization was and is a capital interest of the status quo. It was for the sake of the status quo, something hardly less necessary than the forms themselves, that philosophy was bound to lose its way. Idealism was that ideological even before starting to glorify the world as an absolute idea. The ~rimal compensation already includes the notion that reality, exalted ito a product of the supposedly free subject, would vindicate itself as ~ee.

Identitarian thought, the covering image of the prevailing dichotomy, has ceased in our era of subjective impotence to pose as absolutization of the subject. What is taking shape instead is the type of seemingly antisubjectivist, scientifically objective identitarian thought known as reductionism. (The early Russell used to be called a "neo-realist.") It is at present the characteristic form of the reified consciousness—false, because of its latent and thus much more fatal subjectivism. The residue is made to the measure of the ordering principles of subjective reason, and being abstract itself, it agrees with the abstractness of that reason. The reified consciousness that mistakes itself for nature is naive: having evolved, and being very much mediated in itself, it takes itself—to speak in Husserl's terms—for a "sphere of Being of absolute origins" and the Other it has equipped for the desired matter. The ideal of depersonalizing knowledge for objectivity's sake keeps nothing but the *caput mortuum* of objectivity.

Once we concede the object's dialectical primacy, the hypothesis of an unreflected practical science of the object as residual after deducting the subject will collapse. The subject is then no longer a deductible addendum to objectivity. By the elimination of one of its essential elements, objectivity is falsified, not purified. And indeed, the notion that guides objectivity's residual concept has its primal image in something posited and man-made—by no means in the idea of that in-itself for which it substitutes the cleansed object. It is the model of profit, rather, that stays on the balance sheet after all costs of production have been subtracted. Profit, however, is the subjective interest, limited and reduced to the form of calculation. What counts for the sober realism of profit thinking is anything but "the matter"; the matter is submerged in the yield. But cognition would have to be guided by what exchange has not maimed, or—for nothing is left unmaimed—by what the exchange processes are hiding. The object is no more a subjectless residuum than what the subject posits. The two contradictory definitions fit into each other: the residue, with which science can be put off as its truth, is the product of their subjectively organized manipulative procedures.

Defining what the object is would in turn be part of such arrangements. The only way to make out objectivity is to reflect, at each historic and each cognitive step, on what is then presented as subject and object, as well as on the mediations. In that sense, the object is indeed "infinitely given," as Neo-Kantianism taught. At times, the subject as unlimited experience will come closer to the object than the filtered residuum shaped to fit the requirements of subjective reason. According to its present polemical value in the philosophy of history, unreduced subjectivity can function more objectively than objectivistic reductions. Not the least respect in which all knowledge under the spell has been hexed is that traditional epistemological theses put the case upside down: Fair is foul, and foul is fair. The objective content of individual experience is not produced by the method of comparative generalization; it is produced by dissolving what keeps that experience, as being biased itself, from yielding to the object without reservations—as Hegel put it: with the freedom that would relax the cognitive subject until it truly fades into the object to which it is akin, on the strength of its own objective being.

The subject's key position in cognition is empirical, not formal; what Kant calls formation is essentially deformation. The preponderant exertion of knowledge is destruction of its usual exertion, that of using violence against the object. Approaching knowledge of the object is the act in which the subject rends the veil it is weaving around the object. It can do this only where, fearlessly passive, it entrusts itself to its own experience. In places where subjective reason scents subjective contingency, the primacy of the object is shimmering through—whatever in the object is not a subjective admixture. The subject is the object's agent, not its constituent; this fact has consequences for the relation of theory and practice.

*   *   *

Even after the second reflection of the Copernican turn, there remains some truth in Kant's most questionable theorem: in the distinction between the transcendent thing in itself and the constituted object. For then the object would be the nonidentical, free from the subjective spell and comprehensible through its self-criticism—if it is there at all, if indeed it is not what Kant outlined in his concept of the idea. Such nonidentity would come quite close to Kant's thing in itself, even though he insisted on the vanishing point of its coincidence with the subject. It would not be a relic of a disenchanted *mundus intelligibilis*; rather, it would be more real than the *mundus sensibilis* insofar as Kant's Copernican turn abstracts from that nonidentity and therein finds its barrier.

But then the object, along Kantian lines, is what has been "posited" by the subject, the web of subjective forms cast over the unqualified Something; and finally it is the law that combines the phenomena, disintegrated by their subjective re-relation, into an object. The attributes of necessity and generality that Kant attaches to the emphatic concept of the law have the solidity of things and are impenetrably equal to that social world with which the living collide. It is that law, according to Kant, which the subject prescribes to nature; in his conception, it is the highest peak of objectivity, the perfect expression of the subject as well as of its self-alienation: at the peak of its formative pretension, the subject passes itself off as an object. Paradoxically, however, this is not wrong at all: in fact, the subject is an object as well; it only forgets in its formal hypostasis how and whereby it was constituted. Kant's Copernican turn hits the exact objectification of the subject, the reality of reification. Its truth content is the by no means ontological but historically amassed block between subject and object. The subject erects that block by claiming supremacy over the object and thereby defrauding itself of the object. As truly nonidentical, the object moves the farther from the subject the more the subject "constitutes" the object.

The block on which Kantian philosophy racks its brain is at the same time a product of that philosophy. And yet, due to the *chorismos* of any material, the subject as pure spontaneity and original apperception, seemingly the absolutely dynamic principle, is no less reified than the world of things constituted after the model of natural science. For by that *chorismos* the claimed absolute spontaneity is brought to a halt—in itself, though not for Kant; it is a form supposed to be the form of something, but one which due to its own character cannot interact with any Something. Its abrupt divorcement from the activity of individual subjects, an activity that has to be devalued as contingent-psychological, destroys Kant's inmost principle, original apperception. His apriorism deprives pure action of the very temporality without which simply nothing can be understood by "dynamics." Action recoils into a second-class Being—explicitly, as everyone knows, in the late Fichte's turn away from the 1794 theory of science. Kant codifies such objective ambiguities in the concept of the object, and no theorem about the object has the right to ignore it. Strictly speaking, primacy of the object would mean that there is no object as the subject's abstract opposite, but that as such it seems necessary. The necessity of that illusion ought to be removed.

No more, to be sure, "is there" really a subject. Its hypostasis in idealism leads to absurdities. They may be summarized like this: that the definition of the subject involves what it is posited against—and by no means only because as a *constituens* it presupposes a *constitutum*. The subject itself is an object insofar as existence is implied by the idealist doctrine of constitution—there must be a subject so that it can constitute anything at all—insofar as this had been borrowed in turn, from the sphere of facticity. The concept of what "is there" means nothing but what exists, and the subject as existent comes promptly under the heading of "object." As pure apperception, however, the subject claims to be the downright Other of all existents. This, too, is the negative appearance of a slice of truth: that the reification which the sovereign subject has inflicted on everything, including itself, is mere illusion. The subject moves into the chasm of itself whatever would be exempt from reification—with the absurd result, of course, of thereby issuing a permit for all other reification.

By idealism, the idea of true life is wrongly projected inwards. The subject as productive imagination, as pure apperception, finally as free action, encodes that activity in which human life is really reproduced, and in that activity it logically anticipates freedom. This is why so little of the subject will simply vanish in the object or in anything supposed to be higher, in Being as it may be hypostasized. The self-positing subject is an illusion and at the same time historically very real. It contains the potential of sublating its own rule.

The difference between subject and object cuts through both the subject and the object. It can no more be absolutized than it can be put out of mind. Actually, everything in the subject is chargeable to the object; whatever part of it is not objective will semantically burst the "is." According to its own concept, the pure subjective form of traditional epistemology always exists only as a form of something objective, never without such objectivity; without that, it is not even thinkable. The solidity of the epistemological I, the identity of self-consciousness, is visibly modeled after the unreflected experience of the enduring identical object; even Kant essentially relates it to that experience. He could not have claimed the subjective forms as conditions of objectivity, had he not tacitly granted them an objectivity borrowed from the one to which he opposes the subject. But in the extreme into which subjectivity contracts, from the point of that extreme's synthetic unity, what is combined is always only what goes together anyway. Otherwise, synthesis would be nothing but arbitrary classification. True, without a subjectively performed synthesis, such going together is equally inconceivable. Even the subjective a priori can be called objectively valid only insofar as it has an objective side; without that side the object constituted by the a priori would be a pure tautology for the subject. Finally, due to its being insoluble, given, and extraneous to the subject, the object's content—to Kant, the material for cognition—is also something objective in the subject.

It is accordingly easy to look on the subject as nothing—as was not so very far from Hegel's mind—and on the object as absolute. Yet this is another transcendental illusion. A subject is reduced to nothing by its hypostasis, by making a thing of what is not a thing. It is discredited because it cannot meet the naively realistic innermost criterion of existence. The idealist construction of the subject founders on its confusion with something objective as inherently existent—the very thing it is not; by the standard of the existent, the subject is condemned to nothingness. The subject is the more the less it is, and it is the less the more it credits itself with objective being. As an element, however, it is ineradicable. After an elimination of the subjective moment, the object would come diffusely apart like the fleeting stirrings and instants of subjective life.

The object, though enfeebled, cannot be without a subject either. If the object lacked the moment of subjectivity, its own objectivity would become nonsensical. A flagrant instance is the weakness of Hume's epistemology. It was subjectively directed while believing it might do without a subject. To be judged, then, is the relation between individual and transcendental subject. The individual one is a component of the empirical world, as has, since Kant, been stated in countless variations. But its function, its capacity for experience—which

the transcendental subject lacks, for no purely logical construct could
have any sort of experience—is in truth far more constitutive than the
function ascribed by idealism to the transcendental subject, which is
itself a precritical and profoundly hypostasized abstraction from the
individual consciousness. Nevertheless, the concept of transcenden-
tality reminds us that thinking, by dint of its immanent moments of
universality, transcends its own inalienable individuation. The antithesis of universal and particular, too, is both necessary and deceptive. Neither one exists without the other—the particular only as
defined and thus universal; the universal only as the definition of
something particular, and thus itself particular. Both of them are and
are not. This is one of the strongest motives of nonidealist dialectics.

The subject's reflection upon its own formalism is reflection on
society, and results in a paradox: on the one hand, as the late Durkheim intended, the form-giving constitutive elements have social
sources, but on the other hand, as current epistemology can boast,
they are objectively valid; in Durkheim's argumentations, they are
already presumed in every proposition that demonstrates their contingency. The paradox is likely to be at one with the subject's objective imprisonment in itself. The cognitive function, without which
there would be neither difference nor unity on the subject's part, had
emerged from a source. It consists essentially in those form-givers; as
far as there is cognition, it has to be carried out along their lines even
where it looks beyond them. They define the concept of cognition. Yet
they are not absolute; they have come to be like the cognitive function
itself, and their disappearance is not beyond the realm of the possible.
To predicate them as absolute would absolutize the cognitive function, the subject; to relativize them would be a dogmatic retraction of
the cognitive function.

Against this, we are told that the argument involves a silly
sociologism: that God made society and society made man, followed
by God in man's image. But the priority thesis is absurd only as long as
the individual or its earlier biological form is hypostasized. In the
history of evolution, a more likely presumption would be the temporal
prius, or at least the contemporaneousness of the species. That "the"
human being antedated the species is either a Biblical reminiscence or
sheer Platonism. Nature on its lower levels teems with unindividuated
organisms. If, as more recent biologists claim, humans are actually
born so much more ill-equipped than other creatures, it probably was
only in association, by rudimentary social toil, that they could stay

alive; the *principium individuationis* would be secondary to that, a hypothetical kind of biological division of labor. That any single human should have emerged first, archetypically, is improbable. By the faith in such an emergence, the *principium individuationis*, historically fully developed already, is mythically projected backwards, or onto the firmament of eternal ideas. The species might individuate itself by mutation, in order then, by individuation, to reproduce itself in individuals along lines of biological singularity.

Man is a result, not an *eidos*; the cognitions of Hegel and Marx penetrate to the inmost core of the so-called questions of constitution. The ontology of "the" human being, the model for the construction of the transcendental subject, is oriented towards the evolved individual, as shown linguistically by the ambiguity in the article "the," which in German covers both the individual and the member of the species. Thus nominalism, the opponent of ontology, is far ahead of ontology in featuring the primacy of the species, of society. Society, to be sure, joins with nominalism in a prompt denial of the species (perhaps because it reminds them of animal life)—a denial which ontology performs by raising the individual to the form of unity and to Being-in-itself as opposed to the Many, and nominalism by unreflectingly proclaiming the individual, after the model of the human individual, as true Being. Nominalism denies society in concepts by disparaging it as an abbreviation for individuals.

Notes

Critique of Methodology

Note: In the European tradition, "methodology" refers not only to (research) techniques or to inferential procedures, but also to the epistemological reasons for their choice. Recently, the term "metascience" has tended to replace methodology in this sense. In this country, however, metascience is increasingly used for entirely separate fields of investigation, such as philosophy of science, sociology of science, and so on— as if one could do science without the "luxury" of a metascience.

The methodological concerns of critical theory, aiming ultimately at a kind of socio-epistemology, hardly signal a recent retreat in the wake of political resignation, for instance in the sense of Popper's acquiescence to social role divisions and his subsequent advice to philosophers to make their contribution to politics "with the weapons of a *critic of methods.*" *Conjectures and Refutations* (N.Y.: Harper and Row, 1968), p. 337.

On methodological matters, there was much less individual difference between the Institute members than on political or esthetic ones; the generic "critical theorists" is largely representative, therefore, of an informal consensus articulated, for the most part by Horkheimer and Marcuse. For reasons of delineating the shared concerns, we therefore cut across the lines of individuals and essays.

1. It is true that in Adorno's and Horkheimer's *Dialectic of Enlightenment*, as well as in Marcuse's *One-Dimensional Man*, there are passages which lend themselves to interpretation along anti-scientific and anti-technological lines. Always opposed to scientism as an ideology, critical theorists did, in fact, often argue that certain thought forms stipulated specific orientations toward the world. (The most elaborate form of this argument is J. Habermas's later *Knowledge and Human Interests*). Like Adorno's earlier *Metacritique of Epistemology*, the *Dialectic of Enlightenment* refers to Durkheim's analysis of logical relations as replicas of social elations, for instance. The attempt to distil the inherent orientional thrust of certain forms of thought and language, and to point to their origin in, and affinity to, certain social structures, does make the critique of knowledge a critique of society and vice versa, as Adorno once put it. The "critique of enlightenment" certainly does not occur from an antirationalist position, it should be stressed, but was "intended to prepare the way for a positive notion of enlightenment which will release it from entanglement in blind domination." (*Dialectic of Enlightenment*, p. 16)

L. Coletti's sloppy reading of these authors and his misunderstanding of their alleged fetishization of reason and supposed opposition to "facts" are exemplary of the half-informed accusation that critical theorists were anti-rational. Visibly upset by their updating of some of Marx's critical concepts, Coletti strikes out at a position critical theorists never held. They did emphasize reason as a critical and corrective force, and thus did oppose the fetishism of facts as a form of political resignation. Facts, to them, were always conceptually—and thus socially—mediated. And the emphasis on reason seemed appropriate under circumstances where the facts as given had assumed an authority that made rational critique, and thus rational alternatives, inconceivable. (Such concern with relevance seems unknown to Coletti, who is himself quite willing to fetishize some Marxian assertions as timeless truths—exactly the charge he leveled against Marcuse.)

Critical theorists did differentiate certain forms and functions of the mind however. What Coletti mistakes for a "romantic critique of the 'intellect' " is a critique of the exclusive ascendence of any one of these forms at the expense of others (for instance, the instrumental one at the expense of the critical one)—which happened to include the quiet disappearance of the very dimensions of reason in charge of conceiving and constructing concrete alternatives.

Moreover, Coletti's misreading of the rather sophisticated analyses of the collapse of the superstructure into the base in technological societies (certainly contestable in parts) reveals his critique as a piece of propaganda as much as the company into which he puts critical theorists: Bergson, Heidegger, Jaspers—not accidentally precisely the men critical theorists sharply criticized for the very points which Coletti levels against them. Even a cursory reading of Horkheimer's and Marcuse's essays of the thirties, as well as of Adorno's Husserl critique could have prevented Coletti's blunder.

2. Max Horkheimer, *Dawn and Decline*. Translated by Michael Shaw. Afterword by Eike Gebhardt. New York: The Seabury Press, 1978, p. 98.

3. Max Horkheimer, "The Latest Attack on Metaphysics," in *Critical Theory* (New York: Herder and Herder, 1972), p. 150.

4. Max Horkheimer, "Preface" to *Zeitschrift für Sozialforschung*, Vol. I, No. 1/2, p. 1.

5. Max Horkheimer, "The Latest Attack," pp. 183f.

6. "Traditional theory" was the inclusive term Horkheimer used for all "uncritical" theories, especially the variants of positivism. Cf. his programmatic essay "Traditional and Critical Theory," in *Critical Theory*.

7. Max Horkheimer, "Traditional and Critical Theory," p. 246.

8. Herbert Marcuse, "Philosophy and Critical Theory," in *Negations* (Boston: Beacon Press, 1969), p. 156.

9. Dropped.

10. Because "logical empiricism" was concerned almost exclusively with matters of formal logic and methodology, Horkheimer called the term a misnomer.

11. Max Horkheimer, "The Latest Attack," p. 185.

12. Max Horkheimer, "On the Problem of Truth," in this volume.

13. Max Horkheimer, "The Latest Attack," p. 172.

14. *Ibid.*, p. 146.

15. *Ibid.*, p. 182.

16. *Ibid.*, p. 164.

17. *Ibid.*, p. 151.

18. Max Horkheimer, "Notes on Science and the Crisis," in *Critical Theory*, p. 9. It is clear, Horkheimer wrote, "that neither the achievements of science per se, nor the improvement of industrial methods, are immediately identical with human progress. It is obvious that human beings can emotionally and mentally impoverish regardless of the progress of science and industry." "The Social Function of Philosophy," in *Critical Theory*, p. 259.

19. Friedrich Nietzsche, "Aus dem Nachlass der Achtzigerjahre," in *Werke*, Vol. III, edited by Karl Schleckta (München; Hanser, 1966), p. 814.

20. Theodor W. Adorno, "Thesen zur Kunstsoziologie," in *Kölner Zeitschrift für Soziologie und Sozialpsychologie*, March, 1967, p. 91.

21. Theodor W. Adorno, *Zur Metakritik der Erkenntnistheorie* (Stuttgart: Kohlhammer, 1956), p. 86.

22. John Dewey, *Studies in Logical Theory* (Chicago: University of Chicago Press, 1903), p. 61.

23. Theodor W. Adorno, "Soziologie und empirische Forschung," in Ernst Topitsch ed., *Logik der Sozialwissenschaften* (Köln/Berlin: Kiepenheuer und Witsch, 1967), p. 523.

24. Moritz Schlick, "Uber den Begriff der Ganzheit," in *Logik.*, p. 222.

25. Max Horkheimer, "Materialism and Metaphysics," in *Critical Theory*, p. 43.

26. Theodor W. Adorno, "Soziologie" p. 514.

27. Max Horkheimer, "The Latest Attack," p. 158 in *Critical Theory*.

28. *Ibid.*, p. 174.

29. *Ibid.*, p. 142.

30. "Traditional and Critical Theory," p. 200.

31. *Ibid.*, p. 203.

32. Horkheimer praised Husserl for instance, for exposing "the philosophical consequences of regarding the pure corporeal things of physics as abstracted from any subjective perspective ... just as if they were concrete realities in themselves." "The Latest Attack," p. 146, footnote 15.

33. Alfred Schütz, *Collected Papers* (Den Haag, 1962), Vol. I, p. 53.

34. Max Horkheimer, "On the Problem of Truth"

35. *Zeitschrift*, Vol. VIII, p. 227.

36. Theodor W. Adorno, *Minima Moralia* (London: New Left Books, 1974), p. 123.

37. Max Horkheimer, first part of "Philosophie und Kritische Theorie" (Part ¡ I by Herbert Marcuse), in *Zeitschrift*, Vol. VI, p. 625.

38. Max Horkheimer, "Die gegenwärtige Lage der Sozialphilosophie und die Aufgaben eines Instituts für Sozialforschung," in *Sozialphilosophische Studien* (Frankfurt am Main: Fischer-Athenäum, 1972), p. 42.

39. *Ibid.*, p. 43.

40. In the 1950s, Horkheimer still proposed a "Kantian sociology"—testimony to the impact the Kantian question retained as a key element of the critical approach.

41. Theodor W. Adorno, "Subject and Object," in this volume.

42. Max Horkheimer, "Traditional and Critical Theory," p. 203.

43. Max Horkheimer, *Anfänge der bürgerlichen Geschichtsphilosophie* (Frankfurt am Main: Fischer, 1971), p. 78; Horkheimer here quotes Vico himself.

44. *Ibid.*, p. 56.

45. Friedrich Nietzsche, "Aus dem Nachlass der Achtzigerjahre," p. 814.

46. Max Horkheimer, *Notizen 1950 bis 1969 und Dämmerung*, edited by Werner Brede (Frankfurt am Main: Fischer, 1974), p. 219.

47. The concomitant assumption of an ahistorical human nature—a projection of the experienced immutability and repetitiveness of the physical universe the declaration of a certain stage of consciousness as being reason per se seemed unequivocally regressive to critical theorists, as it curbed—in the self-image of humans who accepted it—the potential, and even the willingness, to transcend and remake their situation.

Vulgar Marxist teleologies which insisted on the universal applicability of the categories of the *Critique of Political Economy* were another favorite target along these lines. (Even historical materialism itself would cease to be the "correct" theory, critical theorists insisted: its categories would become—hopefully—irrelevant in the new society, obsolete because realized.)

48. Max Horkheimer, "Traditional and Critical Theory," in *Critical Theory*, p. 238. Cf. Paul Lazarsfeld's typical mistake which C. Wright Mills was to share in seeing Adorno's diatribes against certain kinds of "mindless empiricism"—as an anti-empirical attitude per se. But Adorno distinguished which critique was needed in which context: confronted with the task of content analysis which did not question, let alone explain the origin and relevance of its own categories, Adorno chided this naive brand of empiricism for simply employing these reifications instead of investigating them. In Germany, after the American exile, he defended American-style empiricism against entrenched idealist traditions. And when hard empirical research swayed Germany, he attempted again to prevent this (or any particular) approach from assuming a monopoly on research. Lazarsfeld's own admission that he may not have understood what critical theory was all about, or even what the "dialectical method" was, casts a curious light on his resentful suggestion that it may merely be the "hypnotic effect" of Adorno's language "which might . . . explain some of the attractions his publications have today for many young German students." Paul Lazarsfeld, *Qualitative Analysis* (Boston:

Allyn and Bacon, 1972), p. 169. To Lazarsfeld, of course, it could not have been substantive attractions of a comprehensive approach which Lazarsfeld would want to exclude from sociology proper: to him, Marcuse, for instance, is either merely an "historian of ideas" or a "political prophet". *Ibid.*, p. 171.

49. Max Horkheimer, "Materialism and Metaphysics", p. 24.

50. *ibid.*, pp. 39ff.

51. Max Horkheimer, "Traditional and Critical Theory," p. 227, fn. 20.

52. Franz Borkenau, "Zur Soziologie des mechanistischen Weltbildes," *Zeitschrift*, Vol. I, p. 311.

53. Cf., for instance, Theodor W. Adorno, *Minima Moralia*, p. 63: "The dissection of man into his faculties is a projection of the division of labor onto its pretended substance, inseparable from the interest in deploying and manipulating them to greater advantage."

54. Theodor W. Adorno and Max Horkheimer, *Dialectic of Enlightenment* (New York: Seabury Press, 1972), p. 5.

55. Theodor W. Adorno, "The Sociology of Knowledge and Its Consciousness," in this volume.

56. ". . . empirical research conceives the stimulus to be as devoid of content as a color stimulus in a psychological laboratory. We hold that the stimulus in popular culture is itself a historical phenomenon and that the relation between stimulus and response is preformed and prestructured by the historical and social fate of the stimulus as well as of the respondent." L. Lowenthal, "Historical Perspectives on Popular Culture," in B. Rosenberg & D.M. White, *Mass Culture* (New York: The Free Press, 1957).

57. Herbert Marcuse, "Philosophy and Critical Theory," p. 136.

58. In different terms, but without acknowledging the implications/consequences, modern positivists also recognize the necessity of assuming a transcendental framework of meta-meanings, so to speak, which explain the meanings of observed facts and events: Russell's theory, for instance, "of a hierarchy of languages . . . starts from the fact (first formulated by Tarski)that the words true or false as applied to the sentences of a given language, always require another language of higher order for their adequate definition. Herbert Marcuse, "Review of Bertrand Russell's *An Inquiry Into the Meaning of Truth*," in *Zeitschrift*, Vol. IX, p. 486.

59. Max Horkheimer, "The Latest Attack," p. 178.

60. Herbert Marcuse, "Review of John Dewey's *Theory of Valuation*," in *Zeitschrift für Sozialforschung*, Vol. IX, p. 144.

61. In the English language, where the concept of reason has seldom become thematic in philosophy (or rather, in reason itself), the common Kantian distinction between *Vernunft* and *Verstand* is rarely made; attempts to introduce it at the beginning of the 19th century, e.g. in the terms *reason* vs. *understanding*, never really caught on.

Remarks like Horkheimer's, that reason has been reduced to understanding, consequently make little sense to an English-speaking audience, and explanatory paraphrases seem unavoidable.

Reason, for Kant, is th| capacity to judge (pure reason) or act (practical reason) in accordance with principles. The concept of reason goes back to the idea of an immanent order of the world (Anaxagoras's *nous*) objective and independent of human perception. In the human mind, this order and its principles precede the use of understanding; without an empirical content of its own (according to Kant), reason contains the first principles, the regulative and orientational ideas. Understanding, on the other hand, is the capacity to order and conceptualize the empirical world. It contains the categories (which Kant thought were immutable, fixed in number and common to all humans) for empirical classification of sense data. These categories enable us to coordinate amorphous sense data into "objects."

62. Max Horkheimer, "The Latest Attack," p. 181.

63. Albrecht Wellmer, *Critical Theory of Society* (New York: Herder and Herder, 1964), p. 12.

64. Max Horkheimer, *Eclipse of Reason* (New York: Seabury Press, 1974), p. 128.

65. *Ibid.*, p. 134.

66. Theodor W. Adorno, "Aspekte," in *Drei St idien zur Hegel* (Frankfurt am Main: Suhrkamp, 1963), p. 57.

67. Max Horkheimer, "Materialismus und Moral," in *Kr'tische Theorie* (Frankfurt am Main: S. Fischer Verlag, 1968) Vol. I, p. 93.

68. Herbert Marcuse, "Review of the *International Encyclopedia of Unified Science*," in *Zeitschrift*, Vol. VIII, p. 229.

69. Herbert Marcuse, "Philosophy and Critical Theory," p. 154.

70. Theodor W. Adorno, *Minima Moralia*, p. 76.

71. Max Horkheimer, "The Social Function," p. 269.

72. Max Horkheimer, "The Latest Attack," p. 162.

73. Herbert Marcuse, "Review of the *International Encyclopedia*," p. 231.

74. Max Horkheimer, "Zum Begriff der Vernunft," in Theodor W. Adorno and Max Horkheimer, *Sociologica II* (Frankfurt am Main: Europäische Verlagsanstalt, 1962), p. 194.

75. Theodor W. Adorno, *Minima Moralia*, p. 69.

76. Theodor W. Adorno, "Blochs Spuren," in *Noten zur Literatur*, Vol II (Frankfurt am Main: Suhrkamp, 1965), p. 140.

77. Herbert Marcuse, "Review of John Dewey's *The Theory of Inquiry*," in *Zeitschrift*, Vol. VIII, p. 221.

78. Max Horkheimer, "The Latest Attack," pp. 168f.

79. Theodor W. Adorno, *Minima Moralia*, p. 80.

80. Max Horkheimer, "Traditional and Critical Theory," pp. 219f.

81. Theodor W. Adorno, "Aspekte," p. 20.

82. Karl Popper, *Conjectures and Refutations*, p. 316.

83. Theodor W. Adorno, "Soziologie und empirische Forschung," p. 512.

84. Max Horkheimer, "The Social Function of Philosophy," p. 255.

85. Herbert Marcuse, "Review of the *International Encyclopedia*," p. 228.

86. Theodor W. Adorno, "Subject and Object," in this volume.

87. Theodor W. Adorno, "Aspekte," p. 16.

88. Theodor W. Adorno, *Negative Dialectics* (New York: Seabury Press, 1973), p. 5.

89. Max Horkheimer, "Materialism and Metaphysics," p. 29.

90. Theodor W. Adorno, "Aspekte," p. 22.

91. Ernst Bloch, *Subjekt-Objekt* (Frankfurt am Main: Suhrkamp, 1962), p. 42.

92. Theodor W. Adorno, "Aspekte," p. 21.

93. Theodor W. Adorno, "Subject and Object," in this volume.

94. Cf. Stephen Toulmin, *The Uses of Argument* (Cambridge: Cambridge University Press, 1974), p. 255: "Philosophers have set up ideals of 'logical' necessity, 'logical' validity, and 'logical' possibility which can be applied to arguments outside the narrow, analytic field only at the preliminary, consistency-checking stage—or else by an illogical extension. Substantial arguments in natural science, ethics and elsewhere, have been severely handled and judged by philosophers, solely on the grounds of not being (what they never pretended to be) analytic; and their quite genuine merits have been accounted negligible as compared with that initial and inevitable sin."

95. Max Horkheimer, "On the Problem of Truth," in this volume.

96. *Ibid.*

97. Max Horkheimer, "The Latest Attack," p. 144.

98. *Ibid.*, p. 161.

99. *Ibid.*, p. 149.

100. Max Horkheimer, "Traditional and Critical Theory," p. 219.

101. Max Horkheimer, "The Latest Attack," p. 162.

102. Max Horkheimer, "Zum Problem der Voraussage in den Sozialwissenschaften," in *Kritische Theorie*, Vol. I, p. 111.

103. Theodor W. Adorno and Max Horkheimer, *Dialectic of Enlightenment*, p. 41.

104. Theodor W. Adorno, *Minima Moralia*, p. 113.

105. Cf. Charles Bolton, "Is Sociology a Behaviorial Science?" in *Pacific Sociological Review*, No. 6 (Spring, 1963), p. 6. Quoted from L. T. Reynolds and J. M. Reynolds, *The Sociology of Sociology*, (New York: McKay, 1970), p. 122: "The aim of control implies, almost by definition, an effort to restrict and, ideally, to eliminate alternatives of the subject. A social science which takes control as a major criterion for scientific success thereby has a built-in bias to focus attention upon those so-called independent variables which human subjects are least likely to be able to convert into alternatives. If evidence to date means anything, we can say that this focus leads to a concentration upon biochemical, unconscious, pre-social and non-rational influences and a studied ignoring of the processes which make human beings as cognitive, self-conscious, creative, act-constructing creatures."

106. Robert S. Lynd, *Knowledge for What?* (Princeton: Princeton University Press, 1970), p. 204.

On the Problem Of Truth

1. Ch. Sigwart, *Logic*, Freiburg im Breisgau 1889, vol. 1, p. 111.

2. Kant *Prolegomena* #13, Note III, Akademie-Ausgabe, vol. IV, p. 293.

3. Husserl, "Formale und transzendentale Logik" in *Jahrbuch für Philosophie und phänomenologische Forschung*, vol. X, Halle 1929, p. 241.

4. Cf. "Materialismus und Metaphysik," p. 61 ff.

5. J. S. Bixler, *Religion in the Philosophy of William James*, Boston 1926, p. 126 ff.

6. William James, *Human Immortality*, Boston and New York 1898, p. 27.

7. F. C. S. Schiller, *Riddles on the Sphinx*, London 1891, p. 295.

8. Hegel, preface to *Phänomenologie des Geistes*, vol. 2, p. 47.

9. *Op. cit.*, p. 73.

10. Hegel, *Vorlesungen über die Aesthetik* in vol. 12, p. 146 ff.

11. *Op. cit.*, p. 147.

12. Trendelenburg, *Logische Untersuchungen*, Leipzig 1870, vol. 1, p. 42 ff.

13. Cf. Hegel, *Vorlesungen über die Philosophie der Geschichte* in *ibid.*, vol. II, p. 447.

14. Hegel, *Phänomenologie des Geistes* in vol. 2, p. 300.

15. Hegel, *Enzyklopädie*, #60.

16. Cf. Hegel, *Wissenschaft der Logik* in vol. 5, p. 27.

17. Husserl, *Formale und Transcendentale Logik*, supra, p. 140.

18. Husserl, *Logische Untersuchungen*, Halle an der Saale 1915, vol. I, p. 115.

19. Epicurus, translated by W. Nestle in *Die Nachsokratiker*, Jena 1923, vol. I, p. 202.

20. Goethe, Letter to Zelter, Dec. 31, 1829.

21. Nietzsche, *Der Wille zur Macht* in *Gesammelte Werke*, Musarion Edition, vol. XIX, p. 45 ff., aphorisms 534 and 537.

22. Nietzsche in *ibid.*, vol. XI, p. 28.

23. William James, "*Pragmatism*," in *Writings of William James*, New York, Modern Library, p. 436.

24. John Dewey, *Reconstruction in Philosophy*, Boston, Beacon Paperback, p. 156.

25. William James, loc. cit.

26. James., *op. cit.*, p. 435.

27. Max Adler, *Marx als Denker*, Berlin 1908, p. 75.

28. Max Scheler, "Erkenntnis und Arbeit" in *Die Wissenschaften und die Gesellschaft*, Leipzig 1926.

29. *Ibid.*, p. 250 ff.

30. *Ibid.*, p. 485.

31. *Ibid.*, p. 44.

32. *Ibid.*, p. 484.

33. *Ibid.*, p. 486.

34. In the *Phänomenologie* (op. cit., p. 36), Hegel himself described the dialectic as the "science of experience, which creates consciousness." Nicolai Hartmann considers this definition as the only authoritative one (e.g. in his essay "Hegel und das Problem der Realdialektik," published in French translation in the collection *Etudes sur Hegel*, Paris 1931, cf. especially p. 17 ff). In the materialistic interpretation it acquires a more fundamental meaning than in Hegelian logic itself, since Hegel's closed metaphysics rules out, in the future course of history, decisive experience which could change currently valid conceptual structures. To be sure, Hartmann's contemplative point of view causes him to misunderstand the interaction between concept and object, so that he one-sidedly interprets the dynamic nature of thought as a "subjective law of thought" arising from the effort of the subject to follow reality and adapt itself to it. The problem of the changes occurring in praxis in the relationship between the two principles in the course of the historical process is not posed; instead, both are preserved in their isolation.

35. Kant, *Logik*, edited by Jäsche, Akademie edition, vol. IX, p. 13.

36. *Ibid.*, p. 63.

37. *Ibid.*, p. 64.

38. Hegel, *Phänomenologie des Geistes*, *op. cit.*, p. 50.

39. Hegel, *Enzyklopädie*, #12.

40. Cf. "Zum Rationalismus streit in der gegenwärtigen Philosophie," p. 141 supra.

41. Hegel, *Enzyklopädie*, #82, appendix.

42. Hegel, Philosophische Propädeutik, #12.

43. Nietzsche, *Gesammelte Werke*, Musarion edition, vol. XI, p. 15.

44. Troeltsch. "Zur Religiösen Lage, Religionsphilosophie und Ethik" in *Gesammelte Schriften*, Tübingen 1922, vol. II, p. 535.

45. *Ibid.*, p. 190 ff.

46. *Ibid.*

47. *Ibid.*, p. 191 ff.

48. *Ibid.*

49. *Ibid.*

50. *Ibid.*, p. 311.

51. Cf. *ibid.*, p. 802.

52. Nietzsche, *Ecce Homo*, in *Gesammelte Werke*, Musarion edition, vol. XXI, p. 275.

A Note on Dialectic

1. Maurice Blanchot, "Le Paradoxe d'Aytre," *Les Temps Modernes*, June 1946, p. 1580 ff.

2. *Oeuvres*, Bibliothèque de la Pleiade, vol. I, p. 1333.

3. *Ibid.*, p. 966.

4. *The Logic of Hegel*, trans. W. Wallace, Clarendon Press, Oxford, 1895, p. 55.

On Science and Phenomenology

1. Husserl, *Gesammelte Werke*, vol. VI (Den Haag 1954), ed. W. Biemel, p. 154.

2. *Ibid.*, p. 9, 12.

3. *Ibid.* p. 49 f.

4. *Ibid.* p. 67.

5. *Ibid.* p. 19.

6. *Ibid.* p. 40.

7. *Ibid.* p. 54.

8. *Ibid.* pp. 20-21.

9. *Ibid.*, pp. 27, 30.

10. *Ibid.*, p.51.

11. *Ibid.*, p. 152.

12. *Ibid.*, p. 52.

13. *Ibid.*, p. 49, 143 f.

14. *Ibid.*, p. 52.

15. *Ibid.*, p. 53.

16. *Ibid.*, p. 143 f.

17. *Ibid.*, p. 151 f.

18. *Ibid.*, p. 147f.

19. *Ibid.*, p. 155.

The Method and Function of an Analytic Social Psychology

1. Impressed by the libidinal admixtures in the instincts for self-preservation and the special significance of the destructive tendencies, Freud has modified his original position. Over against the life-maintaining (erotic) instincts, he now sets the death instinct. Significant as Freud's argument is for this modification in his original position, it is far more speculative and less empirical than his original position. To me it seems to rest upon an intermingling of biological data and psychological tendencies, an intermingling that Freud has otherwise avoided. It also stands in contrast with an original viewpoint of Freud, which saw the instincts primarily as wishing, desiring, and serving man's strivings for life. One of the consequences of Freud's overall position, it seems to me, is that man's psychic activity develops as an adaptation to life's processes and necessities, and that the instincts as such are contrary to the biological death principle. Discussion about the hypothesis of death instincts is still going on within psychoanalysis. In our presentation here, we take off from Freud's original position.

2. At the time of writing this paper I adhered to the Freudian libido theory and hence speak of "libidinal forces" (energies) or of "libidinal structure" (or drive structure) where today I would not refer to the "libido" but to passionate forces of various kinds. For the main points of this paper this difference, however, is not too relevant. (1970).

3. The stimulation and satisfaction of sadistic impulses plays a special role. These impulses grow when other instinctual satisfactions of a more positive nature are ruled out on socio-economic grounds. Sadism is the great instinctual reservoir, to which one appeals when one has no other—and usually more costly—satisfactions to offer the masses; at the same time, it is useful in annihilating the "enemy."

4. See Sigmund Freud, *Three Essays on the Theory of Sexuality.*

5. "The real object of psychoanalysis is the psychic life of socialized man. The masses come in for consideration only insofar as individual-based phenomena crop up in them (e.g., the problem of the leader), and only insofar as traits of the 'mass psyche'—anxiety, panic, obedience, etc—can be clarified from our knowledge of individuals. It would seem that the phenomenon of class consciousness is hardly accessible to psychoanalysis, and that sociological problems (mass movements, politics, etc) cannot be the object of the psychoanalytic method" (Wilhelm Reich, "Dialektischer Materialismus and Psychoanalyse," *Unter dem Banner des Marxismus* III, 5, p. 737).

Because of the theoretical importance of this methodological problem, I stress my difference with the standpoint of Reich just presented; in his latest works, Reich seems to have modified this standpoint in a very fruitful way. Later on I shall refer to my many points of agreement with his outstanding empirical investigations into social psychology.

6. On the methodological aspect, see my extensive treatment in E. Fromm, *The Dogma of Christ, op. cit.*, also S. Bernfeld, "Sozialismus und Psychoanalyse mit Diskussionsbemerkungen von E. Simmel und B. Lantos," *Der Sozialistische Arzt*, II, 2-3, 1929; Reich *op. cit.*

7. Sigmund Freud, *Group Psychology and the Analysis of the Ego.*

8. Leaving aside worthless investigations (e.g., A. Koinai's superficial studies of psychoanalysis and sociology, and such works as *Psychoanalyse der europäischen Politik*), we would apply the same criticism to authors such as Reik and Roheim who have dealt with themes in social psychology. There are exceptions, however. S.

Bernfeld has focused admirably on the social conditioning of all pedagogical efforts in *Sysiphos oder über die Grenzen der Erziehung*. Another exception is Wilhelm Reich, whose evaluation of the role of the family is in broad agreement with the view developed in this paper. In particular, Reich has done extensive research into the social conditioning and the social function of sexual morality.

9. Psychologically, we must distinguish in the individual the traits that are typical for the whole society from the traits that are typical of his class. *But since the psychic structure of the whole society is stamped on the individual classes in certain basic traits*, the specific class traits, for all their importance, are of secondary importance vis-à-vis those of the whole society. Indeed one of the characteristics of a class society, concealed by ideologies, is the opposition between the relative uniformity of the different classes' psychic structure and their conflicting economic interests. The more a society breaks down economically, socially and psychologically, the more the dominating and binding force of the overall society or ruling class disappears, the greater become the differences in the psychic structure of the various classes.

10. I no longer believe that it is only an "irrelevant error" not to understand the socially conditioned traits of the individual patient. On the contrary, without such understanding one misses essential factors in the character structure of the patient. (1970).

11. See Sigmund Freud, *Totem and Taboo*.

12. In the *Future of an Illusion* (1927), Freud softens this position that neglects social reality and its changes. Recognizing the significance of economic conditions, he moves from the standpoint of individual psychology and the question of how religion is psychologically possible for the individual (a repetition of the child's attitude toward its father) to the social psychological question why religion is socially possible and necessary. His answer is that religion was necessary so long as mankind needed religious illusions to make up for their impotence (i.e., the low degree of productive capability) vis-à-vis nature. With the growth of technology and the concomitant maturation of mankind, religion became a superfluous and pernicious illusion.

This book of Freud does not consider all the socially relevant functions of religion. In particular, it does not consider the important question of the connection between specific forms of religion and specific social constellations. But in method and content this work of Freud comes closest to a materialistic social psychology. As far as content is concerned, we need only cite this sentence from it: "It need hardly be pointed out that a culture which leaves so many members unsatisfied and discontent has little prospect of lasting long, and is doing little to achieve that goal."

Freud's book is in line with the standpoint of Marx as a young man, who could use as his motto: "The abolition of religion, the illusory happiness of the proletariat, is the demand to promote his true happiness. The demand to give up illusions about his condition is the summons to give up a condition which needs illusions. At its core, criticism of religion is critic sm of the vale of tears whose halo is religion" ("Zur Kritik der Hegelschen Rechtsphilosophie," *Lit. Nachlass*, I, [1923], 385). In his latest work dealing with problems in social psychology, *Civilization and Its Discontents*, Freud does not develop this line either in method or in content. Rather, it should be regarded as an antithesis to the *Future of an Illusion*.

13. In "Why Is Psychoanalysis Popular?" (*Forward*, 1927), Russell writes: "Of course psychoanalysis is incompatible with Marxism. For Marx stresses the economic motive which, at best, is tied up with self-preservation, while psychoanalysis stresses the biological motive which is tied up with self-preservation through reproduction. Clearly the two points of view are one-sided since both motives play a role."

Russell then talks about a hypothetical mayfly, which would have only organs for eating in the larva stage and only organs for love-making in the adult stage. What would such an insect say, if it could think? Says Russell: "In the larva stage it would be a Marxist, in the adult stage a Freudian." Russell then adds that Marx, "the bookworm of the British Museum," is the representative of the larva's philosophy. Russell himself feels closer to Freud, since the latter "is not insensitive to the joys of love-making, and does not try to explain things in terms of 'making money,' that is, in terms of the orthodox economy created by dessicated old men."

14. Hendrik de Man, *Zur Psychologie des Sozialismus*, 1927, p. 281.

15. Bernstein, *Die Voraussetzungen des Sozialismus und die Aufgaben der Sozial-demokratie*, Stuttgart, 1899, p.13.

16. At the very start of his book, *Der historische Materialismus,* Kautsky firmly rejects the psychologistic interpretation. But he then goes on to supplement historical material-ism with a purely idealist psychology, by assuming that there is a pristine "social drive."

17. Indeed, many of the objections raised against historical materialism actually apply to the specifically bourgeois admixtures smuggled into the theory by friends or oppo-nents.

18. It is clear from the whole context that by "love" I refer to Freud's early formula-tion, in which love was used in the popular sense as being identical with sexuality, including the pregenital; it would have been clearer if I had written "self-preservation and sexuality." (1970).

19. "Just as the wild beast must contend with nature to satisfy his needs, maintain his life and reproduce, so the civilized man must do the same thing in all the forms of society and with every possible means of production. As he develops, the range of his natural needs broadens, *because* his needs do; but the productive capabilities, which satisfy these needs, also expand" (Marx, *Das Kapital*, Hamburg, 1922, III, 2, p. 355, italics mine).

20. In *Marx's Contribution to the Knowledge of Man* I have corrected this view and have shown that Marx had a much more elaborate psychology than indicated in the text. (1970)

21. In his *Economic and Philosophical Manuscripts*, not yet published at the time when this paper was written, Marx makes the point very explicit. He writes ". . . the only wheels that political economy *sets in motion* are greed . . ." Even a scholar with the best intentions of being objective, R. Tucker, was influenced by the widely-held opinion that Marx assumed greed to be a *primary* motive so that he mistranslated the (difficult) German passage to mean the opposite, namely "the only wheels that *set* political economy in motion are greed." (R. Tucker, *Philosophy and Myth in Karl Marx*, Cambridge Univ. Press, 1961.) (1970)

22. Marx and Engels, Part I of *Deutscnen Ideologie*; Marx-Engels Archives, Band I, p. 239.

23. Marx, *Das Kapital*, *op. cit.*, p. 140.

24. On this point, see the work of Bukharin that underlines the natural factor in a clear way: *Die Theorie des historischen Materialismus*, 1922. This whole question is specifically dealt with in the illuminating work of K. A. Wittfogel, "Geopolitik, geographischer Materialismus und Marxismus," *Unter dem Banner des Marxismus* III, 1, 4, 5.

25. Marx and Engels. *op. cit.*, p. 237 f.

26. To me, however, there seems to be an immanent contradiction in Freud's assumption that the growth of the superego and of repressions is tied up with this also, for the growth of the ego and one's capacity for sublimation means that the person gains control over the instincts in other ways rather than through repression.

27. Lack of any adequate psychology led many proponents of historical materialism to inject a private, purely idealistic psychology in this empty place. A typical example is Kautsky, who, not as openly idealistic as Bernstein and others, assumes that man has an inborn "social instinct," and describes the relationship between this social instinct and social relationships in this way: "Depending on the strength or weakness of his social instinct, man will tend more toward good or evil. But it depends no less on his living conditions in society." (*Op. cit.*, p. 262) Clearly Kautsky's innate social instinct is nothing less than the innate moral principle; his position differs from idealist ethics only in the way he expresses it.

In his *Theorie des historischen Materialismus*, Bukharin devotes a whole chapter to the problem of psychology. He rightly points out that the psychology of a class is not identical with its "interests"—by which he means its real, economic interests, but that the psychology of a class must always be explained in terms of its socio-economic role. As an example, he cites the case where a mood of despair grips the masses or some group after a great defeat in the class struggle. "Then we can detect a connection with class interests, but this connection is of a distinctive sort: the battle was carried on by the *hidden motives* of the parties involved, and now their army lies in defeat; from this situation arises confusion and despair, and the people begin to look for miracles from heaven" (italics mine).

Bukharin then goes on to say: "In considering class psychology, then, it is evident that we are dealing with a very complicated phenomenon that cannot be explained on the basis of naked interest alone. It must be explained in terms of the concrete milieu of the class in question." Bukharin also notes that ideological processes are a particular type of social labor. But since he has no suitable psychology available to him, he cannot go on to explain the nature of this labor process.

28. Cited by Grünberg in *Verhandlungen des Vereins für Sozialpolitik*, Stuttgart, 1924, p. 31.

29. It should be remembered that this specific father-child relationship itself is socially conditioned.

30. See Fromm, ''Zur Psychologie des Verbrechers und der strafenden Gesellschaft,'' XVII *Imago*, 12. Not only does the cultural apparatus serve to direct the libido forces (especially the pregenital and the partial driǀes) in specific, socially desired directions; it also serves to weaken the libido forces to the point where they no longer are a threat to social stability. This toning down of the libido forces—i.e., turning them back into the pregenital realm—is one of the motives of the sexual morality of the given society.

31. In *Mass Psychology and Ego-Analysis*, Freud focuses on the libido factors in the relationship to the leader. But he takes both ''leader'' and ''masses'' in an abstract sense, disregarding the concrete situation surrounding them. He thus gives a universality to the psychic processes involved that does not correspond to reality. In other words, he turns one particular type of relationship to the leader into a universal type. Another critical problem of social psychology, class relationships, is replaced by a secondary problem: the ruler-mass relationship.It is noteworthy, however, that in this work Freud notes the general tendency of bourgeois social psychology to disparage the masses, and does not fall in with it.

32. What I have called here the ''libidinal structure of society,'' using Freudian terminology, I have in my later work called the ''social character''; in spite of the change in the libido theory, the concepts are the same.

Biographical Notes

Theodor W. Adorno (1903-1969) studied both philosophy and composition (the latter with Alban Berg). He eventually became co-director of the Frankfurt Institute for Social Research, which he joined in 1931 (officially in 1938). His interests ranged from empirical social research and sociology of art to the meta-theory of dialectics and philosophical esthetics. Nevertheless, the bulk of his life work, presented in essay form, is located at the fluid boundary between sociology and philosophy of culture. The major works of Adorno available in English are *Minima Moralia* (London: New Left Books, 1974), *Negative Dialectics* (New York: Seabury, 1973) *Philosophy of Modern Music* (New York: Seabury, 1973), *Prisms* (London: Neville Spearman, 1969), and *Introduction to the Sociology of Music* (New York: Seabury, 1976).

Walter Benjamin (1892-1940), a victim of European fascism, has now come into his own as one of the century's most important literary critics as well as a key neo-Marxist theorist of culture. Never an official member of the Institute, he was most important for Adorno in particular as an older friend, a theoretical predecessor and a debating partner. Three Benjamin volumes are available in English, *Illuminations* (New York: Schocken, 1969), *Understanding Brecht* (London: New Left Books, 1973) and *Charles Baudelaire* (London: New Left Books, 1973). A further volume of essays is scheduled to be published in 1978 by Harcourt Brace Jovanovich, but much of his work, including the book on the tragic plays of the baroque (coming from New Left Books), still remain unpublished in English.

Erich Fromm (born in 1900) is a psychoanalyst and philosopher. Brought up in a religious Jewish milieu, he was one of the pioneers of a Freud-Marx synthesis. He eventually associated himself with the "revisionist" wing of psychoanalysis and the "humanist" interpretation of Marx. He is still a member of the Freudian Washington Psychoanalytic Association, a member of the Frankfurt Institute from the early 1930s, and contributor to the *Zeitschrift für Socialforschung* beginning with its first issue and also to the important *Studies on Authority and the Family* (1936); his connection to the Institute lasted until 1939. Major works in English: *The Dogma of Christ* (1963), *The Crisis of Psychoanalysis* (1970), *Escape from*

Freedom (1942), *Beyond the Chains of Illusion: My Encounter with Marx and Freud* (1962), *Marx's Concept of Man* (1961), *The Anatomy of Human Destructiveness* (1973), *The Art of Loving* (1956), *The Forgotten Language* (1956), *Man for Himself* (1947), *The Revolution of Hope: Toward a Humanized Technology* (1974), *You Shall Be As Gods: A Radical Interpretation of the Old Testament & Its Tradition* (1966).

Max Horkheimer (1895-1971), a philosopher by training, became the second director of the Frankfurt Institute for Social Research in 1931. He, if anyone, was the founder of critical theory. His major works are the essays of the 1930s defining the aims, scope and method of critical theory (cf. the selection *Critical Theory*, New York: Herder and Herder, 1972) and two books published in 1947 on what he later called the critique of instrumental reason (cf. *Eclipse of Reason*, New York: Seabury, 1974; and a second work written with Theodor W. Adorno, *Dialectic of Enlightenment*, New York: Herder and Herder, 1972).

Otto Kirchheimer (1905-1965) was a co-worker of the Institute for Social Research from 1934 to 1942. However, his political background, left Social Democracy, differed from that of most critical theorists. His major interest before, during and after his collaboration with Horkheimer and others was relatively constant: the relationship of politics to constitutional and criminal law. Two major books by Kirchheimer, *Punishment and Social Structure* (1939) and *Political Justice* (1961) are available in English, as is the important essay volume, *Politics, Law and Social Change* (New York: Columbia University Press, 1969).

Leo Lowenthal (born in 19??) is a veteran of the Institute and one of its few surviving members (together with Marcuse and Fromm). He teaches in the sociology department of the University of California, Berkeley. His major works in English are: *Literature and the Image of Man* (1957), *Literature, Popular Culture, and Society* (1961), *Prophets of Deceit* (with Norbert Guterman, 1949), and *Culture and Social Behavior* (with Seymour M. Lipset).

Herbert Marcuse (born in 1898) is the best-known critical theorist outside Germany. His clear and courageous association with New Left politics made him into something of a public figure in the 1960s in West Germany, the U.S. and France. Marcuse joined Horkheimer's Institute in 1933 with a political background in extreme left Social Democracy (till 1919) after a period of study with Husserl and Heidegger. Most of Marcuse's major articles of the 1930s are available under the titles *Negations* (Boston: Beacon, 1968) and *Studies in Critical Philosophy* (Boston: Beacon, 1972). His best-known books are *Reason and Revolution* (New York: Oxford, 1941), *Eros and Civilization* (Boston: Beacon, 1951), *Soviet Marxism* (New York: Columbia, 1958) and *One-Dimensional Man* (Boston: Beacon, 1964).

Frederick Pollock (1894-1970) a political economist, was a close friend of Max Horkheimer. His major works dealt with the political, social and economic consequences of the replacement of market by planning. Among these were *Die Planwirtschaftlichen Versuche in der Sowjetunion, 1917-1922* (1929) and the essays of the 1930s and 1940s now collected under the title, *Die Stadien des Kapitalismus* (Munich: Beck Verlag, 1975). Pollock's best-known work after the war is *The Economic and Social Consequences of Automation* (Oxford: Oxford University Press, 1957).

Bibliography of the Authors' Works in English

Adorno, Theodor W. "Alienated Masterpiece: *Missa Solemnis*." *Telos* No. 28 (Summer, 1976).

Adorno, Theodor W. "Anti-Semitism and Fascist Propaganda." With Leo Lowenthal and Paul W. Massing. *Anti-Semitism: A Social Disease*. Edited by Ernst Simmel. New York: International Universities Press, 1946. Reprinted in Vol. VIII of *Gesammelte Schriften*. Frankfurt: Suhrkamp Verlag, 1975.

Adorno, Theodor W. *The Authoritarian Personality*. With Else Frenkel-Brunswik; Daniel J. Levinson; and R. Nevitt Sanford. New York: Harper & Row, 1950. Reprinted, New York: Norton Library, 1969.

Adorno, Theodor W. "Commitment." *New Left Review* No. 87/88 (December, 1974), pp. 75-89.

Adorno, Theodor W. "Contemporary German Sociology." *Transactions of the Fourth World Congress of Sociology* Vol. I (London: 1959), pp. 33-56.

Adorno, Theodor W. and Horkheimer, Max. *Dialectic of Enlightenment*. Translated by John Cumming. New York: The Seabury Press, 1972.

Adorno, Theodor W. "Freudian Theory and the Pattern of Fascist Propaganda." Vol. III of *Psychoanalysis and the Social Sciences*. Edited by Geza Roheim. New York: International Universities Press, 1951, pp. 408-433. Reprinted in Vol. VIII of *Gesammelte Schriften*. Frankfurt: Suhrkamp Verlag, 1975.

Adorno, Theodor W. "How to Look at Television." *Quarterly of Film, Radio, and Television*, Vol. III (Spring, 1954), pp. 213-235. Reprinted as "Television and the Patterns of Mass Culture." *Mass Culture*. Edited by Bernard Rosenberg and David White. Glencoe, Ill.: Free Press, 1957. pp. 474-488.

Adorno, Theodor W. "Husserl and the Problem of Idealism." *The Journal of Philosophy* Vol. XXXVII, No. 1 (January, 1940), pp. 413-429.

Adorno, Theodor W. *Introduction to the Sociology of Music*. New York: Seabury, 1976.

Adorno, Theodor W. "Is Marx Obsolete?" *Diogenes* No. 64 (Winter, 1968), pp. 1-16.

Adorno, Theodor W. *The Jargon of Authenticity*. Translated by Knut Tarnowski and Frederic Will. Evanston, Ill.: Northwestern University Press, 1973.

Adorno, Theodor W. "Lyric Poetry and Society." *Telos* No. 20 (Summer, 1974), pp. 56-71.

Adorno, Theodor W. *Negative Dialectics*. New York: The Seabury Press, 1973.

Adorno, Theodor W. "On Kierkegaard's Doctrine of Love." *Studies in Philosophy and Social Sciences* Vol. VIII (1940), pp. 413-429.

Adorno, Theodor W. "On Popular Music." *Studies in Philosophy and Social Sciences* Vol. IX (1941), pp. 17-48.

Adorno, Theodor W. *Philosophy of Modern Music*. Translated by Anne G. Mitchell and Wesley V. Blomster. New York: The Seabury Press, 1973.

Adorno, Theodor W. *Prisms*. Translated by Samuel and Shierry Weber. London: Neville Spearman Limited, 1967.

Adorno, Theodor W. "The Psychological Technique of Martin Luther Thomas' Radio Addresses." Vol. IX, Part 1 of *Gesammelte Schriften*. Frankfurt: Suhrkamp Verlag, 1975.

Adorno, Theodor W. "The Radio Symphony: An Experiment in Theory." *Radio Research 1941*. New York: Harper & Bros., 1941, pp. 110-139.

Adorno, Theodor W. "Scientific Experiences of a European Scholar in America." Vol. II of *Perspectives in American History*. Cambridge: Harvard University Press, 1968. Reprinted in *The Intellectual Migration*. Edited by Donald Fleming and Bernard Bailyn. Cambridge Belknap Press of Harvard University Press, 1969.

Adorno, Theodor W. "A Social Critique of Radio Music." *Kenyon Review* Vol. VIII, No. 2 (Spring, 1945), pp. 208-217.

Adorno, Theodor W. "Society." *Salmagundi* No. 11/12 (Fall/Winter, 1969/1970), pp. 144-153.

Adorno, Theodor W. "Sociology and Psychology." *New Left Review* No. 46/47 (Dec. 1967/Jan. 1968) pp. 67-80, pp. 79-90.

Adorno, Theodor W. "The Stars Down to Earth: The Los Angeles Times Astrology Column: A Study in Secondary Superstition." *Jahrbuch für Amerikastudien* Vol. II (1957), pp. 19-88. Reprinted in Vol. IX, Part 2 of *Gesammelte Schriften*. Frankfurt: Suhrkamp Verlag, 1975 and in *Telos* no. 19 (Spring, 1974), pp. 13-90.

Adorno, Theodor W. " 'Static' and 'Dynamic' as Sociological Categories." *Diogenes* No. 33 (Spring, 1961), pp. 28-49.

Adorno, Theodor W. "Theses Against Occultism." *Telos* No. 19 (Spring, 1974), pp. 7-12.

Adorno, Theodor W. "Theses on the Sociology of Art." *Working Papers in Cultural Studies* No. 2 (Spring, 1972), pp. 121-128.

Adorno, Theodor W. "Theses Upon Art and Religion Today." *Kenyon Review* Vol. VII, No. 4 (Autumn, 1945), pp. 677-682.

Adorno, Theodor W. "Veblen's Attack on Culture." *Studies in Philosophy and Social Science* Vol. IX, No. 3 (1941).

Adorno, Theodor W. "Wagner, Nietzsche, and Hitler." *Kenyon Review* Vol. IX, No. 1 (1974), pp. 155-162.

Adorno, Theodor W. "Why Philosophy?" *Man and Philosophy*. Edited by Walter Leifer. Munich: Max Hueber Verlag, 1964, pp. 11-24.

Benjamin, Walter. *Charles Baudelaire: A Lyric Poet in the Era of High Capitalism*. Translated by Harry Zohn. London: New Left Books, 1973.

Benjamin, Walter. *Illuminations*. Edited and with an introduction by Hannah Arendt. Translated by Harry Zohn. New York: Harcourt, Brace & World, 1968. Paperback edition, New York: Schocken Books, 1969.

Benjamin, Walter. *The Origin of the German Tragic Drama*. Translated by John Osborne. Introduction by George Steiner. London: New Left Books, 1977.

Benjamin, Walter. "Paris, Capital of the Nineteenth Century. *Dissent* Vol. XVII, No. 5 (September-October, 1970).

Benjamin, Walter. *Understanding Brecht*. Translated by Anne Bostack. Introduction by Stanley Mitchell. London: New Left Books, 1973

Fromm, Erich. *The Anatomy of Human Destructiveness*. New York: Holt, Rinehart & Winston, 1973.

Fromm, Erich. *Beyond the Chains of Illusion: My Encounter with Marx and Freud*. New York: Simon & Schuster, 1962.

Fromm, Erich. "A Counter-Rebuttal." *Dissent* Vol. III, No. 1 (Winter, 1956).

Fromm, Erich. *The Crisis of Psychoanalysis*. New York: Holt, Rinehart & Winston, 1970.

Fromm, Erich. *The Dogma of Christ, and Other Essays on Religion, Psychology, and Culture*. New York: Holt, Rinehart & Winston, 1955.

Fromm, Erich. *Escape from Freedom*. New York: Farrar & Rinehart, 1941.

Fromm, Erich. *The Heart of Man*. New York: Harper & Row, 1964.

Fromm, Erich. "The Human Implications of Instinctive 'Radicalism.'" *Dissent* Vol. II, No. 4 (Autumn, 1955).

Fromm, Erich. *Man for Himself*. New York: Rinehart, 1947.

Fromm, Erich. *May Man Prevail?* Garden City, New York: Doubleday, 1961.

Fromm, Erich. *The Revolution of Hope*. New York: Harper & Row, 1968.

Fromm, Erich. *The Sane Society*. New York: Rinehart, 1955.

Fromm, Erich. *Social Character in a Mexican Village*. With Michael Maccoby. Englewood Cliffs, New Jersey: Prentice-Hall, 1970.

Fromm, Erich. *Sigmund Freud's Mission*. New York: Harper, 1959. Reprinted by New York: Grove Press, 1963.

Horkheimer, Max. "Art and Mass Culture." *Studies in Philosophy and Social Science* Vol. IX, No. 2 (1941). Reprinted in *Critical Theory*. New York: The Seabury Press, 1972, pp. 273-290.

Horkheimer, Max. "Authoritarianism and the Family Today." *The Family: Its Function and Destiny*. Edited by R. N. Anshen. New York: Harper, 1949, pp. 359-374.

Horkheimer, Max. "The Authoritarian State." Translated by the People's Translation Service, Berkeley, mediated by Elliot Eisenberg, *Telos* No. 15 (Spring, 1973), pp. 3-20.

Horkheimer, Max. "Authority and the Family." *Critical Theory*. New York: The Seabury Press, 1972, pp. 47-128.

Horkheimer, Max. *Dawn and Decline*. Translated by Michael Shaw. Afterword by Eike Gebhardt. New York: The Seabury Press, 1978.

Horkheimer, Max and Adorno, Theodor W. *Dialectic of Enlightenment*. Translated by John Cumming. New York: The Seabury Press, 1972.

Horkheimer, Max. *Eclipse of Reason*. New York: Oxford University Press, 1947. Reprinted, New York: The Seabury Press, 1974.

Horkheimer, Max. "The End of Reason." *Studies in Philosophy and Social Sciences* Vol. IX (1941), pp. 366-388.

Horkheimer, Max. "Ernst Simmel and Freudian Philosophy." *International Journal of Psychoanalysis* Vol. XXIX, pp. 110-113.

Horkheimer, Max. "The Latest Attack on Metaphysics." *Critical Theory*. New York: The Seabury Press, 1972, pp. 132-187.

Horkheimer, Max. "The Lessons of Fascism." *Tensions that Cause Wars*. Edited by Hadley Cantril. Urbana: University of Illinois Press, 1950, pp. 209-242.

Horkheimer, Max. "Materialism and Metaphysics." *Critical Theory*. New York: The Seabury Press, 1972, pp. 10-46.

Horkheimer, Max. "Notes on Institute Activities." *Studies in Philosophy and Social Science* Vol. IX, No. 1 (1941).

Horkheimer, Max. "Notes on Science and the Crisis." *Critical Theory*. New York: The Seabury Press, 1972, pp. 3-9.

Horkheimer, Max. "On the Concept of Freedom." *Diogenes* No. 53 (Spring, 1964), pp. 73-81.

Horkheimer, Max. "Postscript." *Critical Theory*. New York: The Seabury Press, 1972, pp. 244-252.

Horkheimer, Max. "The Relation between Psychology and Sociology in the Work of Wilhelm Dilthey." *Studies in Philosophy and Social Sciences* Vol. VIII (1940), pp. 430-443.

Horkheimer, Max. "Schopenhauer Today." *The Critical Spirit: Essays in Honor of Herbert Marcuse*. Edited by Kurt H. Wolff and Barrington Moore, Jr. Boston: Beacon Press, 1967.

Horkheimer, Max. "The Social Function of Philosophy." *Studies in Philosophy and Social Science* Vol. VIII, No. 3 (1939). Reprinted in *Critical Theory*. New York: The Seabury Press, 1972, pp. 253-272.

Horkheimer, Max. "Sociological Background of the Psychoanalytic Approach." *Anti-Semitism: A Social Disease*. Edited by Ernst Simmel. New York: International Universities Press, 1946.

Horkheimer, Max. *Survey of the Social Sciences in Germany*. Washington, D.C.: 1952.

Horkheimer, Max. "Thoughts on Religion." *Critical Theory*. New York: The Seabury Press, 1972, pp. 129-131.

Horkheimer, Max. "Traditional and Critical Theory." *Critical Theory*. New York: The Seabury Press, 1972, pp. 188-243.

Kirchheimer, Otto. "Criminal Law in National Socialist Germany." *Studies in Philosophy and Social Sciences* VIII, 3 (1939).

Kirchheimer, Otto. *The Fate of Small Business in Nazi Germany*. With Arcadius R.L. Gurland and Franz Neumann (Washington, D.C. 1943).

Kirchheimer, Otto. "Franz Neumann: An Appreciation." *Dissent* Vol. IV, No. 4 (Autumn, 1957).

Kirchheimer, Otto. *Political Justice: The Use of Legal Procedure for Political Ends*. (Princeton, 1961).

Kirchheimer, Otto. *Politics, Law, and Social Change: Selected Essays of Otto Kirchheimer*. Edited by Frederic S. Burin and Kurt L. Shell (New York and London, 1969).

Kirchheimer, Otto. *Punishment and Social Structure*. With George Rusche. (New York, 1939).

Lowenthal, Leo. "German Popular Biographies: Culture's Bargain Counter." *The*

Critical Spirit: Essays in Honor of Herbert Marcuse. Edited by Kurt H. Wolff and Barrington Moore, Jr. Boston: Beacon Press, 1967.

Lowenthal, Leo. "Historical Perspectives of Popular Culture." *American Journal of Sociology* Vol. 55 (1950), pp. 323-332. Reprinted in *Mass Culture: The Popular Arts in America*. Edited by Bernard Rosenberg and David White. Glencoe, Ill.: The Free Press, 1957.

Lowenthal, Leo. *Literature and the Image of Man*. Boston: Beacon Press, 1957.

Lowenthal, Leo. *Literature, Popular Culture, and Society*. Englewood Cliffs, New Jersey: Prentice-Hall, 1961.

Lowenthal, Leo. *Prophets of Deceit*. With Norbert Guterman. New York: Harper, 1949. Second edition with a foreword by Herbert Marcuse. Palo Alto, Calif.: Pacific Books, 1970.

Lowenthal, Leo. *Culture and Social Behavior* (with Seymour M. Lipset).

Lowenthal, Leo. "Terror's Atomization of Man." *Commentary* Vol. I, No. 3 (January, 1946).

Marcuse, Herbert. *The Aesthetic Dimension: Toward a Critique of Marxist Aesthetics*. Boston: Beacon Press, 1978.

Marcuse, Herbert. "The Affirmative Character of Culture." *Negations*. Boston: Beacon Press, 1968.

Marcuse, Herbert. "Aggressiveness in Advanced Industrial Society." *Negations*. Boston: Beacon Press, 1968.

Marcuse Herbert. "Comes the Revolution." [Reply to Mr. Berman's Review of *One-Dimensional Man*] *Partisan Review* Vol. XXXII, No. 1 (Winter, 1965), pp. 159-160.

Marcuse, Herbert. "The Concept of Essence." *Negations*. Boston: Beacon Press, 1968.

Marcuse, Herbert. "The Concept of Negation in the Dialectic." *Telos* No. 8 (Summer, 1971), pp. 130-132.

Marcuse, Herbert. "Contributions to a Phenomenology of Historical Materialism." *Telos* No. 4 (Fall, 1969), pp. 3-34.

Marcuse, Herbert. *Counterrevolution and Revolt*. Boston: Beacon Press, 1972.

Marcuse, Herbert. "Dialectic and Logic Since the War." *Continuity and Change in Russian Thought*. Edited and with an introduction by Ernest J. Simons. Cambridge, Mass.: Harvard University Press, 1955, pp. 347-358. Reissued by New York: Russell & Russell, 1967.

Marcuse, Herbert. "Epilogue to the New German Edition of Marx's 18th Brumaire of Louis Napoleon." *Radical America* Vol. III, No. 4 (July/August, 1969), pp. 55-59.

Marcuse, Herbert. *Eros and Civilization*. Boston: Beacon Press, 1955. Paperbound edition with a new preface, New York: Vintage Books, 1962. Second edition with new preface, "Political Preface, 1966." Boston: Beacon Press, 1966.

Marcuse, Herbert. "Eros and Culture." *The Cambridge Review* Vol. I, No. 3 (Spring, 1955), pp. 107-123.

Marcuse, Herbert. *An Essay on Liberation*. Boston: Beacon Press, 1969.

Marcuse, Herbert "Ethics and Revolution." *Ethics and Society*. Edited by Richard T. deGeorge. New York: Anchor, 1966, pp. 130-146.

Marcuse, Herbert. "Existentialism: Remarks on Jean-Paul Sartre's *L'Etre et le Néant*." *Journal of Philosophy and Phenomenological Research* Vol. VIII, No. 3 (March, 1948), pp. 309-336.

Marcuse, Herbert. *Five Lectures*. Translated by Jeremy J. Shapiro and Shierry M. Weber. Boston: Beacon Press, 1970; paperback edition, 1970.

Marcuse, Herbert. "The Foundation of Historical Materialism." *Studies in Critical Philosophy*. London: New Left Books, 1972.

Marcuse, Herbert. "Freedom and the Historical Imperative." *Studies in Critical Philosophy*. London: New Left Books, 1972.

Marcuse, Herbert. "The Ideology of Death." *The Meaning of Death*. Edited by Hermann Feifel. New York: McGraw-Hill, 1959, pp. 66-76.

Marcuse, Herbert. "The Individual in the Great Society." Part I. *Alternatives* Vol. I, No. 1 (March/April, 1966), Part II, *Alternatives* Vol. I, No. 2 (Summer, 1966).

Marcuse, Herbert. "Industrialization and Capitalism in the Work of Max Weber." *Negations*. Boston: Beacon Press, 1968.

Marcuse, Herbert. "An Introduction to Hegel's Philosophy." *Studies in Philosophy and Social Science*. Vol. VIII (1940), pp. 394-412.

Marcuse, Herbert. "Karl Popper and the Problem of Historical Laws." *Partisan Review* (1959). Also published in *Studies in Critical Philosophy*. London: New Left Books, 1972.

Marcuse, Herbert. "Language and Technological Society." *Dissent* Vol. VIII, No. I (Winter, 1961), pp. 66-74.

Marcuse, Herbert. "Lord Action: *Essays on Freedom and Power*." *American Historical Review* Vol. LIV, No. 3 (April, 1949), pp. 557-559.

Marcuse, Herbert. *Negations: Essays in Critical Theory*. Boston: Beacon Press, 1968.

Marcuse, Herbert. "Notes on the Problem of Historical Laws." *Partisan Review* No. 26 (Winter, 1959), pp. 117-129.

Marcuse, Herbert. "Love Mystified." *Commentary* Vol. XLIII, No. 2 (February, 1967), pp. 71-76. Reprinted as "Love Mystified: A Critique of Norman O. Brown *and* A Reply to Herbert Marcuse by Norman O. Brown." *Negations*. Boston: Beacon Press, 1968.

Marcuse, Herbert. "The Obsolescence of Marxism." *Marx and the Western World*. Edited by Nicholas Lobkowicz. Notre Dame, Ind.: University of Notre Dame Press, 1967, pp. 409-418.

Marcuse, Herbert. "On Hedonism." *Negations*. Boston: Beacon Press, 1968.

Marcuse, Herbert. "On the Philosophical Foundation of the Concept of Labor in Economics." Translated by Douglas Kellner. *Telos* No. 16 (Summer, 1973), pp. 9-37.

Marcuse, Herbert. "On Science and Phenomenology." Vol. II of *Boston Studies in the Philosophy of Science*. Edited by Robert Cohen and Marx W. Wartofsky. New York: The Humanities Press, 1965, pp. 279-291.

Marcuse, Herbert. *One-Dimensional Man*. Boston: Beacon Press, 1964; paperback edition, 1966.

Marcuse, Herbert. "Philosophy and Critical Theory." *Negations*. Boston: Beacon Press, 1968.

Marcuse, Hebert. Preface to *Marxism and Freedom*, by Raya Dunayevskaya. New York: Twayne Publishers, 1958, pp. 15-20.

Marcuse, Herbert. "The Problem of Social Change in the Technological Society." Lecture presented to a UNESCO Symposium on Social Development. Printed for limited distribution under the auspices of Raymond Aron and Bert Hoselitz. Paris: April 28, 1961, pp. 139-160.

Marcuse, Herbert. "The Realm of Freedom and the Realm of Necessity: A Reconsideration." *Praxis* (Zagreb) No. 1/2 (1969), pp. 20-25.

Marcuse, Herbert. *Reason and Revolution: Hegel and the Rise of Social Theory*. New York: Oxford University Press, 1941. Second edition with "Supplementary Epilogue." New York: Humanities Press, 1954. Paperbound edition with a new preface, "A Note on Dialectic." Boston: Beacon Press, 1960.

Marcuse, Herbert. "Recent Literature on Communism." *World Politics* Vol. VI, No. 4 (July, 1954), pp. 515-525.

Marcuse, Herbert. "Re-examination of the Concept of Revolution." *New Left Review* No. 56 (July/August, 1969), pp. 27-34.

Marcuse, Herbert. "A Rejoiner to K. Loewith's Review of *Reason and Revolution*." *Journal of Philosophy and Phenomenological Research* Vol. II, No. 4 (June, 1942), pp. 564-565.

Marcuse, Herbert. "Remarks on a Redefinition of Culture." *Daedalus* Vol. XCIV, No. 1 (Winter, 1965), pp. 190-207. Reprinted in *Science and Culture*. Edited by Gerald Holton. Cambridge, Mass.: Houghton Mifflin, 1965. Second edition, Boston: Beacon Press, 1967, pp. 218-235.

Marcuse, Herbert. "A Reply to Erich Fromm." *Dissent* Vol. III, No. 1 (Winter, 1956), pp. 79-81.

Marcuse, Herbert. "A Reply to Lucien Goldmann." *Partisan Review* (1971), pp. 397-400.

Marcuse, Herbert. "Repressive Tolerance." *A Critique of Pure Tolerance*. by Herbert Marcuse; Robert P. Wolff; and Barrington Moore, Jr. Boston: Beacon Press, 1965.

Marcuse, Herbert. "Review of Georg Lukács' *Goethe und seine Zeit*." *Journal of Philosophy and Phenomenological Research* Vol. IX, No. 1 (September, 1950), pp. 142-144.

Marcuse, Herbert. "Revolutionary Subject and Self-Government." *Praxis* (Zagreb) No. 1/2 (1969), pp. 20-25.

Marcuse, Herbert. "Sartre's Existentialism." *Philosophy and Phenomenological Research*. (1948). Also published in *Studies in Critical Philosophy*. London: New Left Books, 1972.

Marcuse, Herbert. "The Social Implications of Freudian 'Revisionism.' " *Dissent* Vol. II, No. 3 (Summer, 1955), pp. 221-240. Reprinted as epilogue to *Eros and Civilization* and in *Voices of Dissent*. New York: Grove Press, 1958.

Marcuse, Herbert. "Socialism in the Developed Countries." *International Socialist Journal* Vol. II, No. 8 (April, 1965), pp. 139-152.

Marcuse, Herbert. "Socialist Humanism?" *Socialist Humanism*. Edited by Erich Fromm. New York: Doubleday, 1965, pp. 96-106. Paperback edition, New York: Anchor, 1966, pp. 107-117.

Marcuse, Herbert. "Some Social Implications of Modern Technology." *Studies in Philosophy and Social Science* Vol. IX (1941), pp. 414-439.

Marcuse, Herbert. *Soviet Marxism*. New York: Columbia University Press, 1958. Paperback edition with new preface, New York: Vintage Russian Library, 1961.

Marcuse, Herbert. "Statement on Vietnam." *Partisan Review* Vol. XXXII, No. 4 (Fall, 1965), pp. 646-649.

Marcuse, Herbert. "The Struggle Against Liberalism in the Totalitarian View of the State." *Negations*. Boston: Beacon Press, 1968.

Marcuse, Herbert. *Studies in Critical Philosophy*. Translated by Joris De Bres. London: New Left Books, 1972. Reprinted by Boston: Beacon Press, 1973.

Marcuse, Herbert. "A Study on Authority." *Studies in Critical Philosophy*. London: New Left Books, 1972.

Marcuse, Herbert. "Theory and Therapy in Freud." *The Nation* Vol. CLXXXV (September 28, 1957), pp. 200-202.

Marcuse, Herbert. "A Tribute to Paul A. Baran." *Monthly Review* Vol. XVI, No. 2 (March, 1965), pp. 114-115.

Marcuse, Herbert. "World Without Logic." *Bulletin of Atomic Scientists* Vol. XX (January, 1964), pp. 25-26.

Pollock, Friedrich. *The Economic and Social Consequences of Automation* (Oxford, 1957).

Pollock, Friedrich. "Is National Socialism a New Order?" *Studies in Philosophy and Social Sciences* IX, No. 3 (1941).

Pollock, Friedrich. "State Capitalism: Its Possibilities and Limitations." *Studies in Philosophy and Social Sciences* IX, No. 2 (1941).

Index

C

E

F

G

H

I

J

K

L

M

Q

R

S

T

U

V

W

Wagner, Richard, 38, 281-83
Wallraff (name), 251
"War economy," 139
Weber, Alfred, 357
Weber, Max, 7, 9
  basic concepts of, 191-93
  on function of law, 12
  Horkheimer's use of, 19
  Mannheim and, 453, 456
  Marx and, 191, 348
  on mass democracy and bureau-
    cracy, 154
  reason and, 467
  works on, 347
Webern, Anton, 298
Wedekind, Frank, 42
Western Marxism, *see* Critical
  Marxism

Whitehead, Alfred North, 406
Whitman, Walt, 158
Wilhelm II, Emperor of Germany,
  113, 250, 318
Winckelmann, Johann, 235, 251
Wittfogel, Karl, 527
Wittgenstein, Ludwig, 372, 373, 376
Women, 336-38
Workers' councils, 4, 104-105
Working class
  for Hamsun, 340-41
  heritage and, 231
  as "identical subject-object,"
    196, 201
  See also Labor movement; Pro-
    letariat
Writing, class struggle and, 255,
  268-69

Z

Zinoviev, G., 310, 363